THE ROLE OF WATER IN DEVELOPMENT

McGRAW-HILL SERIES IN WATER RESOURCES AND ENVIRONMENTAL ENGINEERING

Ven Te Chow, Rolf Eliassen, and Ray K. Linsley, Consulting Editors

GRAF Hydraulics of Sediment Transport

HALL AND DRACUP Water Resources Systems Engineering

JAMES AND LEE Economics of Water Resources Planning

LINSLEY AND FRANZINI Water Resources Engineering

WALTON Groundwater Resource Evaluation

WIENER The Role of Water in Development: An Analysis of Principles of Comprehensive Planning

THE ROLE OF WATER IN DEVELOPMENT

AN ANALYSIS OF PRINCIPLES OF COMPREHENSIVE PLANNING

AARON WIENER
President, TAHAL
Water Planning for Israel Ltd.

McGRAW-HILL BOOK COMPANY

New York St. Louis San Francisco Düsseldorf Johannesburg
Kuala Lumpur London Mexico Montreal New Delhi
Panama Rio de Janeiro Singapore Sydney Toronto

THE ROLE OF WATER IN DEVELOPMENT

Library of Congress Catalog Card Number
71-154240
07-070150-4

1 2 3 4 5 6 7 8 9 0 MAMM 7 9 8 7 6 5 4 3 2 1

This book was set in News Gothic by Monotype Composition Company, Inc., and printed and bound by The Maple Press Company. The designer was Edward Zytko. The editors were B. J. Clark and Claudia A. Hepburn. John A. Sabella supervised production.

CONTENTS

PREFACE

The needs of development are stupendous, and the capital and human and institutional resources available for development are inadequate. But the relative ineffectiveness of development efforts since the Second World War cannot be blamed on the scarcity of resources alone. If available resources were adequately allocated and utilized, Third World countries would today be much closer to a growth takeoff. The spectacular success of nationwide agricultural programs based on miracle rice seeds in the Far East during the late sixties strengthens the view that what is principally missing is not resources alone but "a little, a very little, clear thinking" (Lord Keynes).

Realization of the basic inadequacy of development thinking, as practiced in Third World countries, has motivated the writing of this book. The gap between what ought and could be done—according to the existing state of the art—and actual performance is wide and continues to widen. *Video meliora proboque, deteriora sequor*—I see the right path, and approve of it; I see the wrong path, and take it. The author, who has worked in Third World countries as a development planner in the fields of water supply, irrigation, and agriculture, has tried over the past ten years to determine ways to bridge this gap. The present book represents the crystallization of these efforts. It is intended for students and practitioners of development planning in the sectors of agriculture (including the irrigation subsector) and community water supplies; it aims to provide the professional executive in these development fields with the intellectual tools for doing the requisite "clear thinking."

Planning in *developed* countries has also reached a point where basic revision is needed. As single-discipline–oriented government programs gain impetus and scope and are superimposed upon activities governed by the market mechanism, single-discipline planning becomes less and less adequate. In fact, in relation to some of the recent problem complexes (e.g., environmental, transportational, educational, etc.), developed countries show some of the typical syndromes of planning deficiency usually encountered in less developed countries. Many of the approaches recommended in this book for developing countries apply equally well to the developed ones.

Development tasks are extremely complex and draw upon many disciplines, including agriculture, engineering, economics, political science, social anthropology, and management science. The information explosion has rendered it difficult to maintain the status of specialist even in a single discipline, and no one can any longer claim to be an expert in all the disciplines involved. The time of polyhistors is over.

The difficulty inherent in integrative thinking in no way negates the importance of applying interdisciplinary analysis to complex problems. From the single-discipline specialist's point of view, interdisciplinary analysis may introduce loss of rigor and an element of conjecture. However, in the author's opinion, a reasonably representative overview (with subsequent unavoidable "blur" in the disciplines involved) is both preferable to and has a higher predictive value than a collection of stricter narrow-angle analyses. At first sight the latter appears to possess better "resolution," but it evinces the distortions resulting from a single-discipline approach. The author feels that the integral approach advocated in this book will generate the quantitative data necessary for stricter analysis, improved quantification, and greater rigor.

Much lip service is presently paid to interdisciplinary thinking, but its actual application is rarely taught and even more rarely practiced. Integration of a number of disciplines calls for a higher level of abstraction than is necessary in single-discipline thinking. We were therefore often faced with the need to coin new terms and to employ a degree of abstraction beyond that usually needed in treatises on water development. This situation was unavoidable: If one wishes to gain an overview for applying a number of disciplines to a single subject, one necessarily has to adopt a higher platform of analysis than would be required for a single-discipline review.

Since the message contained in this book runs counter to development doctrines applied in most Third World countries, Part 1, "Basic Planning Approaches," attempts to remove some road blocks in thinking and to define the planner's role in the development process. Part 2, "Planning Methodology and the Planning Process," is devoted to applications of the general doctrines outlined in Part 1 to problems of developing community water supplies and irrigation, conceived in a multidimensional interdisciplinary phase space. Part 3, "Water-resources Management," focuses on the imported partial subspace of water resources and spells out the management patterns from which the planner must choose in various development contexts. Part 4 presents case histories and comments on special problems. The final chapter restates the book's main argument and stresses its implications.

ACKNOWLEDGMENT

Special thanks are due to my long-time friend and colleague Mr. Yaacov Vardi, who read the manuscript and whose advice and help were invaluable; to Mr. Shlomo Elhanani and Dr. Leonard Prager, who have greatly assisted me in improving the language and logic of the presentation; and to Miss Miriam Del Bourgo, who has most successfully acquitted herself of the monumental task of faultlessly typing the several drafts and the final version of the text.

AARON WIENER

INTRODUCTION

The scientific mind, in being totally scientific,
is being unscientific . . . .
The scientist atomizes, someone must synthesize;
the scientist withdraws, someone must draw together;
the scientist particularizes, someone must universalize;
the scientist dehumanizes, someone must humanize;
the scientist turns his back on the as yet, and
perhaps eternally, unverifiable, and someone must face it.

JOHN FOWLES: *The Aristos*

ONE
BASIC PLANNING APPROACH

When first glancing at the table of contents, the reader, expecting only subject matter directly connected with the development of water resources, may be struck by the amount of space devoted to general planning; in all probability, he will consider that this emphasis on general planning in a book devoted to a specific sphere of planning calls for explanation. In introducing this book, it will, therefore, be fitting to begin by setting out the author's conception of the relationship between general and specific planning spheres.

The main purpose of this book is to lay foundations for and expound a planning philosophy for water-resources development. This, it would seem, is a relatively narrow and specific subject. However, since the treatment is oriented both toward *production,* in its broadest context, and the achievement of *social objectives,* and since this requires investigation of almost all aspects of the socioeconomic process, it will be necessary to touch upon a number of general issues in order to lay the groundwork for the main theme.

The emphasis on the more general, more abstract issues of the planning process has another, equally important, justification. It will be shown that the procedures, strategies, and models which underlie prevailing planning practices in developing countries have serious structural weaknesses. Before approaching the more specific, more concrete part of water-resources development planning, we must, therefore, identify these weaknesses and synthesize planning procedures, strategies, and models which overcome these weaknesses and better fit the context in which we operate. The reevaluation and reconstruction of planning concepts and tools that this procedure implies will be found to be indispensable in drawing up programs for developing countries; it will be equally necessary when dealing with some of the more ramified and dynamic development complexes that we encounter in mature economies.

The broad implications of water-resources development, on the one hand, and the necessity to reexamine the explicit and implicit assumptions of the planning process, on the other hand, justify the emphasis placed on the general planning aspects.

A qualifying comment is called for at this point. The criticism of the planning processes contained in the foregoing statement refers to processes actually being applied in the emerging countries rather than to planning hypotheses, models, or strategies developed by economists, planners, university teams, or development research institutes and put forward in professional publications. Indeed, many of the points stressed here have been emphasized in such publications. Only the actual planning processes lie within the scope of this book.

The subject of this book is the role played in the development process by resources planning, in general, and by water-resources planning in particular, with special emphasis on problems encountered in underdeveloped economies. The point of view adopted is that of the senior planner of a single production sector—e.g., agriculture or potable water supply—not that of the planner of a national economy as a whole.

We will not, therefore, deal with the analysis of the major macroeconomic relationships that define the "boundary conditions" of a sectorial planning space, consisting of the allocation of resources to the sector, and the anticipated demand of the entire economy, inclusive of its export component, for the sector's products. It is assumed that these boundary conditions, which represent the interactions of the sectorial systems treated here with the rest of the economy, will have been determined, or at least estimated, within the framework of national macroeconomic planning prior to the initiation of sectorial planning.

Such a point of view, and the suboptimization it implies, may not lead to an overall national optimum solution. However, the short history of development planning has taught us that optimized national programs—being conceived under ground rules valid only in a Platonic "frictionless" utopia—are elusive affairs, firstly, because they are difficult to draw up in the context of underdevelopment and, secondly, because, being foreign to the macro- and microstructures of existing political institutions, they are not "accepted" (in the surgical sense of the word) by the body politic.

Furthermore, more often than not, it is found that the chances of initiating improvements in inadequate conceptual, decision-making, and administrative processes are better at a selected sectorial, or even subsectorial, level than at the top level of the political hierarchy, where we would assume national planning to be organizationally located.

It is this fact that highlights the responsibility of the sectorial (and possibly also of the subsectorial) planner; it puts upon the planner a dual role within the framework of sectorial planning: the one, the initiation, within prevailing resources constraints, of a sectorial development effort; the other, the conscious origination of methodological and ideological spillover into the politico-administrative machine as a whole, with a view to gradually inducing the adoption of a more relevant and more adequate problem-solving and decision-making process.

Awareness of this dual responsibility of the sectorial planner leads us to the *first basic emphasis* of this text: the desirability of applying the "metaplanning" concept at the sectorial or subsectorial level in situations in which a major success of development efforts is conditional upon general structural transformation in the sociopolitical dimension; the effective development of irrigated agriculture in developing countries certainly falls within this definition. By the concept of metaplanning, we refer to the adoption of a planning platform and point of view which encompass the planner and the sociopolitical environment relevant to the sectorial program, in addition to the sectorial or subsectorial *framework proper,* its inventory, structure, and constraints.

In psychological terms, metaplanning might be compared with the process of "Bewusstwerdung," (emerging into consciousness), i.e., a raising of the level of awareness and the expansion of the scope of consciousness. In the history of man, a continuous expansion of the scope of consciousness is necessary in order to increase the flexibility and variety of man's response patterns to an extremely variable material and psychological environment. Whenever, in our more specific context, our traditional planning approaches, models, and strategies become structurally incompatible with *unprecedented* planning problems, it similarly becomes necessary to extend the scope of consciousness to encompass the observer and the environment, in addition to the sector itself. This happens when we attempt to transfer methodology from a mature to an underdeveloped economy, or from common material and sociopsychological contexts to contexts not previously encountered in a developed country.

Expressed in logical terms, adoption of a metaplanning platform is equivalent to the introduction of a "metalanguage" when wishing to analyze the structural inadequacies of an "object language."

This leads us to the *second main emphasis,* namely, that before initiating planning in a new environment, we must first get rid of conditioned biases, models, and mental blocks carried over from a different environment. Thus, before embarking on the subsequent synthesis of new models, we must first subject our semantic and methodological stock-in-trade to a thorough *structural analysis* and then adopt tools that are structurally compatible with the phase space in which we operate.

The *third main emphasis* is a synthetic one, related to the *basic structure of the socioeconomic system* within which we operate. The *cybernetic-biological model* appears to be, structurally, the most compatible with the socioeconomic system of a developing country and with "islands of underdevelopment" within mature economies. This model certainly appears more suitable than the two classical models—the *laissez faire model* of capitalist and the *mechanistic model* of communist society—which have guided, and continue to guide, development analysis and planning.

It is to these three main aspects that the first, the general, and the second, the methodological, parts of this book are devoted.

Technological problem solving and its written deposition in technical works are almost as subjective a manifestation of the author's personality as the creation of a literary work of art. In literature, the subjective elements often prove to be the most significant aspect of the product; in technical works, they usually constitute a bias, a distortion, a "noise" which has to be "filtered out" if we are to get to the core of the "message."

One obvious way to filter out the noise that obscures the message is to explore the psychological space of the author, to probe his professional background and formation, and to trace the type of problem-solving environment in which he has been operating and which has most likely conditioned his basic professional attitudes. The following paragraphs give some indications of the author's personal bias.

By background, the author is an engineer whose professional activities have revolved around the development of water resources and irrigation; this will account for his professional limitations, his overemphasis of engineering aspects, and his disinclination to enter into theoretical controversies. Although his basic training and original problem-solving attitudes are derived from schooling received in a developed country, the professional environment in which he has been active is that of developing countries.

A realization of the ineffectiveness of development approaches evolved in mature economies for the solution of development problems of the emerging nations provided the author with the necessary jolt to surmount the mental blocks of planning orthodoxy and to look for new approaches. Since the author's turn of mind is tuned to decision making aimed at early implementation, rather than to academic investigation, his attitude to professional problem solving is problem and action oriented rather than academic.

The complexity of most of the development problems encountered in underdeveloped countries defies direct formal analysis. This induces the planner, when facing such problems, to adopt one of two basic attitudes: either he can reduce the complex reality to a simplified model responding to analytical handling, though incurring the danger of oversimplification to the point of irrelevance; or he can attempt to probe this complex reality by suitable multidimensional interventions of an exploratory kind which would supply the information required for subsequent links in a *sequential decision chain.* As a consequence of the author's basic "professional deformation," his problem-solving bias leans to the latter attitude; thus, it will be seen that the treatment in this book is *heuristic rather than analytical,* pragmatic rather than rigorous.

The subject matter of this book is complex and pertains to numerous disciplines; the ideal type of coverage would therefore be interdisciplinary. However, our sciences, methodologies, and techniques, our very language, are still single disciplinary; in John Barth's pungent language, "Our Schools and Divisions—what are they but seams in the seamless?"[1] We therefore resign ourselves, at the present state of the art, to a kind of "superimposition tech-

[1] John Barth, *Giles Goat-Boy,* Penguin Books, Inc., Baltimore, 1967, p. 480.

nique,'' using a number of single- or dual-discipline descriptions ''one on top of the other,'' like a set of complementary transparencies in a modern textbook. Use of this superimposition technique, unfortunately, involves a certain amount of unavoidable duplication and repetition.

No attempt is made to enter into specific aspects of specialized disciplines, such as water engineering, hydrology, sanitary engineering, agronomy, economics, or the behavioral and political sciences. The course adopted is that of the generalist, who focuses upon the interlocking and interaction of the various disciplines rather than upon analyses in depth of single-discipline aspects seen in isolation.

And now for a brief outline of the contents of the book:

Part 1 deals with basic planning approaches. The space in which the planner operates, the language of planning, and the points of view adopted are defined in Chapter 1, followed in Chapter 2 by a summary of the methodology expounded throughout the book. Chapters 3 to 5 deal with various aspects of the pathology of planning, such as inadequate levels of abstraction, ideologies and dogmas posing as analysis, and the gap between what we know and what we do. Chapter 6 attempts a methodological synthesis, epitomized in the concept of ''metaplanning,'' and, at the same time, stresses the resistances which such a methodological approach may be expected to meet and the diseases to which it is prone.

Part 2 (Chapters 7 to 24) is devoted to planning methodology and to the planning process, as well as to their applications in the field of water resources, community water supply, irrigation, and agricultural development. Chapters 7 to 9 are devoted to a description of the basic structural planning models, their past applications, and their role in future development planning. An attempt is made to devise a structural yardstick for development which could be applied to emergent and to mature economies, and a planning process is expounded that combines information generation, planning proper, and priming probes.

Chapters 10 to 12 are devoted to the role of heuristic approaches in underdeveloped environments, to the analyses of the role of information in planning, and to an expansion of the heuristic approach to the realms of information. Here, the concept of evaluation is extended to those dimensions of the planning space which are not usually encompassed by evaluative procedures, and the importance of applying a dynamic and multidimensional evaluative procedure in contexts of underdevelopment is stressed.

Chapters 13 to 15 are devoted to planning methodologies of water-resources development and community water supplies. The problem is first outlined in its most abstract form, the importance of a sufficiently broad definition of the planning space is then emphasized, and a methodology for national planning of community water supplies is put forward.

Chapters 16 to 19 deal with common aspects of water-resources development programs for community and irrigation water-supply projects. Here, the organizational aspects of national water-resources development are reviewed, the determination of utility rates as policy measures rather than as accounting procedures is examined, and programming procedures—as applied to comprehensive development projects—and the dynamic inventorying process are considered.

Chapters 20 to 24 are devoted to irrigated agriculture, enlarging upon a comprehensive planning methodology for national sectorial programs. Regional comprehensive development projects are juxtaposed with functional polarization of the national development effort, implying a type of program based on the strategic crop–critical input approach. Within the irrigated-agriculture framework, improving the capacity of the development authority and raising the growth capacity of the farmer are discussed. This section closes with a description of typical development sequences in the field of irrigated agriculture.

Part 3 (Chapters 25 to 29) is concerned with water-resources management in its narrower engineering-economic-organizational aspects. The phase space of water-resources management is first defined, and alternative quantitative and qualitative management policies and their respective outcomes are reviewed. This is followed by a description of typical applications of the basic management policies and by a review of special topics related to integrated management of water resources.

Part 4 (Chapters 30 to 33) is devoted to case histories, as well as to the treatment of some special problems. A case history covering the development of Israel's national water grid is followed by some composite case histories of community water-supply development. A description of the special problems encountered in the development of arid countries and of the role of desalting in a water-supply system brings Part 4 to a close.

In the final chapter (34) attempts are made to draw the basic methodological conclusions of the book.

A considerable portion of the material presented in this book was originally put forward at workshops, seminars, and professional congresses; the original texts have been revised, brought up to date, and expanded, and duplication, as far as possible, has been eliminated.

ACKNOWLEDGMENTS

Special thanks are due to Mr. Shlomo Elhanani and Dr. Leonard Prager who have greatly assisted me in improving the language and logic of presentation.

1

SPACE, LANGUAGE, AND POINT OF VIEW OF THE DEVELOPMENT PLANNER

If our poverty were due to famine or earthquake or war—
—if we lacked material things and the resources to produce them—
—we could not expect to find the Means to Prosperity except in hard work, abstinence and invention. In fact our predicament is notoriously of another kind. It comes from some failure of the mind. . . .
Nothing is required, and nothing will avail, except a little, a very little, clear thinking.

MAYNARD KEYNES

BASIC ASPECTS OF PROBLEM SOLVING IN DEVELOPMENT PLANNING

The continuum of problem solving extends all the way from the incorporation of a foreign body by a unicellular organism some two billion years ago to the complex abstract analysis of modern man. Human problem solving, geologically speaking a very recent phenomenon, has added two important features: the use of symbols and models in language and reasoning and "time binding," Korzybski's term for the accumulation and transmission of experience from generation to generation. Very recent human history has added a third important element: man's self-consciousness, his awareness of himself as a problem-solving organism acting within a social and physical environment.

This new capacity enables man to raise himself above his earlier naïve problem-solving attitude and observe himself, as it were, in the very process of problem solving, from a platform raised above his routine operation. By employing this capacity, he can bring his mind to bear not only on actual problem-solving situations but also on the embedding of this situation in its environment and on his own problem-solving attitudes and methods; to use a technical term, man adopts a *metaplanning process* and creates a *meta-*

language. Philosophy, psychology, and more recently, systems engineering and cybernetics are instances of areas in which such metalanguages have been created.

The creation of metalanguages which lend themselves to mathematical and logical notations enables us to achieve a considerable extent of rigor; however, where we have to resort to common language, we unwittingly carry over from the *object language* of the naïve problem-solving situation concepts that are not compatible with the metalanguage platform, and this may lead to paradoxes, "unsolvable" problems, and arid controversy. In such a situation, in T. S. Eliot's words,

. . . Words strain,
Crack and sometimes break, under the burden,
Under the tension, slip, slide, perish,
Decay with imprecision, will not stay in place,
Will not stay still . . . .

(*Four Quartets—Burnt Norton*)

The use of object language is, of course, perfectly adequate for "closed" problem-solving situations, in which the interconnection of the problem solver and his space with the rest of the physical and social environment is not oversignificant. However, where neglect of such interconnections would introduce a major error, we have to supplement object-language analysis by a metalanguage analysis with a view to defining the "boundary conditions" for object-language analysis. In the words of Stafford Beer,[1]

It is . . . logically impossible to use the language of the network to comment on its own structure. There are profound reasons for this which belong to metamathematics. The commentary has to be made in what is called a metalanguage, which is to say a language of higher order than that of the system itself.

A further distortion is introduced by the branching out of object language into *single-discipline languages,* each with its own professional semantics, models, and metaphors. Each discipline selects, from the protean world of multidimensional events, those dimensions which correspond to its angle of interests and creates a "phase space," i.e., a space encompassing the selected dimensions, representing its own partial view of the situation.

Inducing *development in the underdeveloped countries* is certainly *not a simple problem-solving situation.* It is now generally agreed that underdevelopment is not primarily a matter of capital formation or of natural resources; rather, it is a direct outcome of the quality, structure, and dynamics of the body politic and of its cells—individual men. To diagnose growth deficiencies and devise therapies for their correction, we must, therefore, construct a phase space that encompasses the main scope and the principal dimensions of the situation; we have to select a language that is structurally compatible with the situation; we have to adopt a platform of

[1] Stafford Beer, *Decision and Control,* John Wiley & Sons, Inc., New York, 1966, p. 208.

reasoning that allows us to evaluate the possible impact of what we propose to do upon the rest of the economy.

Even a cursory look at the development history of the Third World since the Second World War shows that, in actual fact, the methodology, semantics, and points of view adopted were mostly of the naïve, single-discipline, and static type. In every sector of the economy, at every level of the political hierarchy, some kind of planning of partial aspects of an arbitrary selection of development problems was conducted, without attempting to fuse and integrate these partial and distorted planning efforts.

The damage that can be caused by the naïve application of single-discipline semantics and methodology can be illustrated by pointing to the ubiquitous example of mismanagement in the development of irrigation: in many countries, overriding priority has been given to the hardware aspects of irrigation, while the need for the development of various agrotechnical practices and techniques, for improved production inputs, improvements in land tenure, or for the adoption of new institutional approaches has been neglected. As a result, we often find a wide gap between hardware development and the actual capacity to produce.

No wonder that these semantically misguided and therefore one-sided attempts at overcoming the basic structural weaknesses of underdevelopment have proved so abortive. In tackling problems of underdevelopment, an approach must be adopted which emphasizes the promotion of fundamental transformation processes bearing on the quality, structure, and dynamics of the body politic and of man to the same extent that the creation of new production hardware was stressed in the past.

The basic planning methodology, language, and model building for such an approach are dealt with briefly in the following.

Phase space The phase space of development will be characterized by all dimensions important for the diagnosis and therapy of underdevelopment, including the "material" dimensions of space, time, economic and natural resources and the "nonmaterial" dimensions related to the political hierarchy, the basic group, and the individuals who play the leading roles in the development process. Last, but not least, we will have to make allowance for the extent of uncertainty resulting from the inadequacies of information and measurements.

Planning space The planning space, i.e., the subspace or part of the phase space—in physical space, time, and economic activity—with which our actual planning deals, must be cut out from the national phase space in such a way that it will form a meaningful and relatively separate subsystem, whose interconnection with the rest of the system can be expressed by a relatively small number of well-defined streams.

The planner's point of view The planner's point of view should be one of self-consciousness, or understanding of the two facets of his position: the narrow angle, or object-language view, encompassing his planning space, properly speaking, and the wide angle, or metaplanning, encompassing, in addition to the planner and his planning space, his relationship with the political hierarchy and with the economy.

The planner's language and models The structure of the language we use must be compatible with the structure of our phase space. Some of the dimensions entering into the phase space of development lend themselves to measurement; others can be only partly quantified; a few lend themselves, at least in the earlier phases of our planning, only to low-order quantification. The models we use will consist therefore of subsystems, i.e., "subassemblies" of different degrees of rigor and quantification.

These basic planning requirements are reviewed in more detail in the following paragraphs, with precedence given to the structural requirements of language.

DEVELOPMENT SEMANTICS

The vital importance of the adequacy of the language for the dependability of the outcomes of our analysis has been realized for some time. Almost a hundred years ago Nietzsche wrote: "Gefahr der Sprache fuer die geistige Freiheit—jedes Wort ist ein Vorurteil." (Danger of language for the freedom of thinking—every word is a prejudice.) H. Poincaré made the same point more specifically when he wrote: "A well-made language is no indifferent thing; in order not to go beyond physics, the unknown man who invented the word 'heat' committed many generations to error. Heat has been treated as a substance simply because it was designated by a substantive, and has been considered to be indestructible."

This conception was further developed by Korzybski who devoted a great part of his work to this problem and most aptly stated the crux of the question when he wrote: "All human history shows that the correct structural formulation of a problem is usually as good as the solution of it, because sooner or later a solution always follows a formulation."

The authenticity of analysis of a set of phenomena, and the appositeness of strategies derived from such an analysis to serve as guides to action, depends on the fitness of our tool of analysis—language. Different sets of phenomena require different kinds of tools since we can hardly hope to obtain satisfactory results in the construction, say, of a miniaturized computer if plumber's tools are used. The basic terminology we use, the abstractions and constructs out of which it is construed, stems from a specific, though often unconscious, representational point of view and implies a specific model. If the structure of this model is dissimilar to that of the set of phenomena analyzed, language will, unbeknown to us, introduce a distorting bias which will prevent us from asking the right questions and obtaining the correct answers.

For this reason we have thought it fit to preface the reevaluation of doctrines of resources development and management presented here by an analysis of the semantic tools now being used in the formulation of these doctrines.

Analysis shows that orthodox semantic tools are not suited to the analysis of development phenomena in emerging economies and that use of these tools prejudices our problem solving. This is largely due to the following three main structural weaknesses:

1. Naïve use and objectivation of abstractions and of heuristic fictional constructs
2. The use of overspecialized single-discipline language
3. The use of statically oriented and linear terminology to describe and analyze dynamic and nonlinear phenomena

It is therefore proposed that this inadequate terminology be replaced by a structurally adequate, dynamic, and multidisciplined language and that this language be supported by the use of those simplified semantic crutches which we cannot do without; this is permissible so long as we bear in mind the boundaries within which these semantic crutches are adequate and the extent of falsification implied in their use.

Abuse of abstractions and constructs The first major weakness of existing development semantics is abuse of abstractions and constructs.

Abstraction is the alpha and omega, the essence and driving force of language. It is present together with the metaphor in the most primitive forms of language; it is the very basis of mathematical methodology. The principle of abstraction is even older than language and underlies the adaptive behavior of every organism to its environment. An organism subjected to the protean stream of the stimuli spawned by its environment molds them by its receptory faculties; it ordains the infinite variety of the stream of sense impressions into simplified patterns, "Gestalten" (configurations), which, imbued with biological significance, underlie its adaptive reaction patterns. These are the bottom rungs of the ladder of abstraction. At this level of abstraction, phenomena, though realized and acted upon, are still incommunicable. With the growth of the nervous system, and the increase in the complexity of its structure, additional rungs are added to the ladder of abstraction; with each rung, simplification becomes more sweeping, identification of similar phenomena becomes more comprehensive, abstractions become more general, and classification becomes more universal; on reaching the top rungs, the point of origin has, in the meantime, been lost sight of and we come upon a new device—the use of *symbols,* the use of *language.*

The invention of symbols characterizes, more than anything else, the genesis of man. Having once attached names or symbols to signify the classes into which we have constricted our world of phenomena, we are free to ply these symbols even in the absence of the originals. We can recall the past, we can plan for the future, and, further, we can exchange experience with our fellowmen, since these symbols are a social product, shared by other members of the social group. We can thus mobilize the intelligence of the whole group to bear upon a problem; furthermore, we can, by oral and later by written transmission, reach beyond the lifetime of an individual or group and become "time binders," according to the term coined by Korzybski and adopted by the general semanticists.

The development of abstraction does not end with the emergence of the first symbols, the words of our language; the tendency to classify, generalize, and unify has continued down to the present day; additional rungs of abstraction are added continuously to the ladder, until we reach the mathematical abstractions of modern science and metascience, the latest rung on the ladder.

As language and the semantic disciplines develop, level upon level of abstractions are constructed and recombined into more general abstractions. With time, these abstractions become further and further removed from their original point of departure—our sense impressions of the environment. Some of these high-level abstractions are *fictional constructs* and simplifications, intentionally devised for heuristic purposes within a certain context. (The German philosopher Vaihinger has compiled an impressive list of such fictions in his *Philosophy of the "As If."*) As generations of scientists follow one after the other, the fictitious nature of these abstractions is forgotten, the context for which they were devised sinks into oblivion, and general validity is claimed for them. Finally, by a curious but almost universal twist, these fictions are projected back into reality and we begin to believe that they constitute part of our tangible world.

We do not have to look far for living examples of such fictions. Is not "economic man" and the psychology underlying his behavior such a fiction, conceived within the socioeconomic context of eighteenth-century Europe, near the point of "takeoff"? Are not some of the difficulties in development thinking, as applied to emerging economies, due to the blind adoption of the same fiction for a completely dissimilar context?

The transfer of *metaphors,* drawn from one area of human endeavor and used to illustrate processes encountered in an entirely different area, offers similar linguistic pitfalls. Originally, the metaphor was an extremely fertile tool that was used to illustrate a yet vaguely conceived structural similarity between the problem in hand and problems pertaining to a very different universe of discourse, a creative merging, a "bisociation," to use Koestler's term, of two apparently unrelated contexts. Gradually, as it is reused, repeated, and developed, the metaphor acquires a reality of its own; its origin fades away, and it is unconsciously used in the construction of a model of the phenomenon to be analyzed. The process here encountered is a special case of the universal process of reification and objectification of words and metaphors and their projection back into the world of phenomena. The naïve transfer of Rostov's aeronautic metaphors of growth to every relevant and irrelevant development context is a current example of such transplantation and objectification of the metaphor.

Another example of the danger of establishing massive conceptual structures upon "metaphoric" foundations lies in the application of *mechanistic* terminology to complex development phenomena. Labeled by such terminology, the economy is seen as a machine with a specific "name-shield capacity" which requires specific "inputs" to produce specific "outputs." The inputs are seen as controllable variables, independent of each other and of the machine. Outputs are, as it were, the result of a simple transformation of these inputs by the machine. The economic process is considered to be additive and mechanistically determined.

This representation of the economic process will often prove to be acceptable representation in those parts of a mature economy where the human and structural dimensions do not have to be induced but can be assumed to evolve spontaneously as a consequence of the changes brought about by capital investment. In such economies, a program of public intervention can be confined to planning the development of material inputs and outputs.

The simplified model and the language used to describe it are inadequate for dealing with *emerging economies,* since any analysis making use of such tools will be completely distorted. Human and structural dimensions are critical in this development process, and it cannot be assumed that these will evolve as the direct and fully predictable output of specific material inputs combined with the appropriate edicts and "ukases" issued from the top. The emergence of these elusive human and social factors will depend on making use of existing social subsystems (or of tendencies to form such subsystems) to change the decision environment and motivation of the individual decision maker and on the interaction between decision makers. The same material inputs applied at different phases of development will result in radically different outputs. The process is nonadditive, is not wholly predictable, and cannot be fully controlled from the top; a mechanistic model will therefore have a low predictive value.

Specialized language The second principle structural weakness of orthodox semantics stems from the use of specialized single-discipline language to describe complex phenomena that can be adequately analyzed only by the use of a multidiscipline language. This inadequacy is a direct outcome of the development of science and scientific language in the last few centuries.

As we reach modern times, we find that individual sciences and disciplines have branched off from the diffuse, amorphous, and unspecialized body of ancient science and lore and that specialized abstractions and languages have developed according to their distinctive requirements.

As sciences branched out and became even more specialized, the gulf between specialized languages deepened and they became less and less compatible with each other. It thus came about that the one unique world of phenomena evoked numerous interpretations expressed in incompatible languages; this was acceptable as long as these phenomena were simple and the analytical requirement was very specific. But when complex phenomena, such as man, or society were being scrutinized, a confusing number of contradictory interpretations were obtained, no one truer than the other, and each having a certain similarity to the phenomenon under investigation, as well as to the other interpretations: each interpretation resembled a caricature seen from a special vantage point.

The available specialized languages, while adequate to represent and interpret specific aspects of a complex event as seen from specific vantage points, cannot call into being a unitary, consummate representation of such a complex event as a whole. The usually linear structure of specialized language, though similar to the microstructure of partial aspects of the event, is still incompatible with its nonlinear overall macrostructure and cannot therefore result in adequate overall representation of the whole event; a superimposition of caricatures will not yield a true portrait.

The analysis of phenomena connected with *resources development in emerging economies* involves numerous disciplines, such as engineering, economics, political science, psychology, sociology, and the science of management and organization. Since phenomena are nonadditive, a compilation of single-discipline interpretation will result in a falsified analysis of the status quo and in a wrong prediction of the future behavior of the system. Adequate interpretation can be achieved only by the adoption of a multidimensional phase space described in a multidiscipline language that tries to fashion its structure according to the structure of the actual phenomena investigated and discards the linguistic partitions created by specialized sciences. Problems of similar nature will also arise in *very developed countries* when either a *major technological process or the environment of human activity undergoes drastic change.*

The need for the multidiscipline approach has been in the air for some time: disciplines, which for ages have not been "on speaking terms," have finally realized that application of a unitary language would yield completely new insights and perspective. The most fertile application of the interdisciplinary approach is, of course, system engineering and cybernetics. Another example from a more specific field of science is psychosomatic medicine—the outcome of the semantic reform that resulted from shedding the semantic partition between psychological and physiological phenomena, a reform that may ultimately make both concepts obsolete.

Static and dynamic terminology In spite of the existence of an extensive literature on development issues, *development, as actually practiced,* is, in the majority of cases, explicitly or implicitly, based on *outdated models and semantics,* referred to in this work as the "orthodox approach." This approach assumes that the basic difference between developed and underdeveloped countries lies in the existence, or nonexistence, of a certain amount of "hardware," or to use more formal language, capital investment. Analysis of underdevelopment is therefore confined to capital investment and the potential economic impact of capital. The economy is, at least by implication, considered as being capable of "absorbing" this capital investment, in all relevant spheres of human activity, by a kind of economic "induction." The social organism is here conceived as already growth oriented, able to react integrally to the stimulus of the project, as a maternal organism to the fertilization of an egg cell.

Psychological, structural, organizational, and social problems in this process, if at all foreseen, are treated as an afterthought on *separate lanes of analysis,* on the assumption that the responses involved (material, psychological, and structural) are additive—as forces and deformations often are in mechanics—and that all such stimuli can be assumed to evoke immediate responses. Throughout the process, the use of the time dimension is confined to calculations of present worths of investment and benefit streams.

The orthodox approach thus conceives of *development* as a *linear, additive process* taking place within a *neutral and directionless time dimension;* according to this approach, the *development model* is made up of a *sequence of independent project steps* which, to facilitate analysis, can be considered separately and subsequently added to obtain the overall result. In this approach, *transients,* i.e., transition states of resources, institutions, project benefits, hardly exist; project features and their impact on resources and society are considered only for their *final state,* and *phasing,* if incorporated at all, is regarded solely as a convenience for the subdivision of investment. From this it will be obvious that in a model of this type there can be no dynamic analysis of the impact of every project step on resources and society or of the relation of every phase of change to the following one. Furthermore, since, according to this orthodox approach, the existence of an indigenous growth capacity is assumed, inducement of such growth capacity is not included among development objectives, and objectives are usually confined to the direct and indirect increase in production which it is assumed will result from the proposed capital investment.

In the *dynamic development model* as conceived in modern development thinking, the time dimension becomes all-important: at every point of the development curve, changes are brought about in all dimensions by preceding development steps; every point has a different growth potential; time has direction, and we can no longer cut up time into equivalent neutral units, treat these units individually, and then add the results. Development is treated as a process in which the point of time selected for intervention is of the utmost importance for the outcome. In the following, the term "growth capacity" will be used to describe the *potential capacity of a group or society to respond adequately to changes in its environment,* and especially to growth stimuli. Under this term, we shall include all the professional, structural, organizational, and institutional capacities of the development authorities in particular and of the economy in general that are a precondition for the creation of regional or sectorial self-sustained growth processes.

Since development is here considered to be a protean, continuously evolving process gaining momentum with time, evaluation of the increase of growth capacity, created by a development program and signifying the potential impact of the transformation brought about by a program on the very structure of society, becomes a new and most important aspect of analysis.

In such an analysis, a program will be evaluated not only for its *contribution to production* but also—and in emerging economies probably mainly—for its *contribution to the increase of this growth capacity;* here, the sequence of project steps and their timing gain new importance.

The applicability of a dynamic semantics is, of course, not confined to planning contexts in developing countries. In *developed* and even in highly developed countries, *static terminologies* are no longer adequate for dealing with *dynamic-resources contexts with major cumulative deteriorative changes* or with *fast-changing technologies.* Since such situations will become the rule rather than the exception in the highly developed countries, the application of dynamic semantics here, too, will gradually become imperative.

An example taken from hydrology will illustrate the importance of substituting a dynamic for a static terminology. Let us for instance take the term "safe yield" of a groundwater basin. By this term we refer to the constant quantity of water that can be withdrawn from a groundwater formation conceived to be at a steady state. In many cases, the *transient stages,* i.e., those stages between the initiation of exploitation and its later "mature" stage, may continue for decades and become as important as the steady-state stage. The exploitation pattern during this lengthy transition period will itself have a major influence on the time at which the steady state sets in. Furthermore, through some integrating manipulation, the locally determined steady state might, in fact, never be reached. We should, therefore, adopt an operative definition of yield equating it with the amounts of water that can be withdrawn over a period of time from a water-resources management unit (rather than from an isolated groundwater formation) under alternative exploitation patterns evolving along the time axis.

THE PHASE AND PLANNING SPACE OF DEVELOPMENT

The number of planning dimensions and the extent of their interrelationship with actual phenomena are overwhelming. Hence, it will be necessary, for representation of these phenomena in a manageable phase space, to select those dimensions which, in the judgment of the planner, have the greatest bearing on planning goals. The choice will not always be easy; in fact, inadequate planning is most commonly caused by too restrictive a selection of dimensions. The number of dimensions of a phase space will differ according to the *scope* of *public intervention* required to achieve planning objectives: the same type of project, say, a major development of irrigated agriculture, may, in a developed economy, require intervention only in the form of capital investment, relying for appropriate response in the other dimensions upon existing self-regulatory socioeconomic mechanisms. On the other hand, the success of such a project in an emerging economy may require intervention in a number of dimensions, such as the social, sociopsychological, institutional, and political. The *phase space of a developed country,* therefore, differs from that of an *emerging* one, even for the same type of operation, the latter generally calling for many more dimensions than would be necessary for the former.

A second aspect of phase space is the amount and quality of *information* available or that can be accumulated within a reasonable time about the parametric values of system variables. Information and measurement facilities may be adequate for some variables and be nonexistent for others. Thus, our phase space will consist of areas that can be satisfactorily quantified and of others where only low-order quantification or logical relationships are possible. The nonhomogeneity of information has an important influence upon our model building: the better quantified areas of our phase space lend themselves to more rigorous analysis, while the areas of low-order quantification limit us to a weaker type of analysis. It will, therefore, often be advantageous to conduct this analysis at *two levels:* a *general analysis* based on a model encompassing the *whole phase space,* including dimensions with both high- and low-order quantifications, and a *more specific, more rigorous* analysis of the subspace encompassing only *variables with high-order quantification.* The interaction between the narrower and the wider model can be allowed for by iterative procedures to be introduced at specific time intervals of the analysis. Part 3 deals with an important example of a subspace confined to variables lending themselves to high-order quantification, i.e., the resources space.

Chapter 11 will deal more fully with the influence of *uncertainty* upon our problem solving in a number of contexts, but a few general comments are required at this stage.

The very fact of scarcity of information will, in many cases, have a considerable influence upon our overall planning attitude: the *high economic value of information* in a phase space of great uncertainty makes it worthwhile to select, in the early development phases, programs for *greater information yield.* Such procedures might comprise *pilot and demonstration phases* undertaken mainly for generating information.

At this point, it would be of value to discuss the partitioning off of a *planning space* from a phase space. A *phase space,* selected for a certain purpose, constitutes a representation of those variables (or dimensions) which are expected to have a significant influence on our problem solving and of the type of relationships we assume to exist between these variables. This definition is not conceived within specific boundaries in physical space and time. In *actual problem solving,* however, we have to confine ourselves to a *certain extension* in space and time. This confinement within specific space limitations is required for administrative reasons, as also for the fact that our models would otherwise become uneconomically complex, without any corresponding gain in rigor, while the time limitation is necessary because of the increase of uncertainty with time and because of the decay of values of variables.

It would be advisable to give one instance of the use of our space-dimension terminology. By a planning space we refer to a phase subspace selected for analysis and planning and conceived with specific space boundaries and with a specific time horizon. The actual selection of boundaries in space and time for our analysis depends on numerous factors.

In some cases, specific aspects of this subsystem will be studied, such as the primary producing group and the individual producer in agricultural development contexts or the primary group in a development agency. This will be done by singling out certain controlling dimensions from the overall planning space, thus making it possible to apply a simplified single-discipline type of analysis of such a special aspect before incorporating it into the overall planning space. In such cases, we shall refer to the specific aspect or subspace according to the discipline and object selected; if, for instance, we are dealing with the object "farmer" and the dimension "psychology," we shall speak of the psychological space of the farmer.

TYPES OF MODELS USED IN DEVELOPMENT PLANNING

The type of models we select to facilitate analysis in a specific problem-solving situation depends on its main characteristics, namely, the scope and complexity of the problem, its structural properties, and the extent of quantification considered possible.

Where the controlling variables are material ones, such as demand, or natural and economic resources, the selected model is often analytical, as in the case of most water-supply problems or in the simpler cases of irrigation development. The nonmaterial and, in these cases, the less-significant variables of the phase space can then be assumed as exogenous variables related to the environment. However, where the phase space encompasses, in addition to these material variables, self-regulatory units, such as the farmer, village institutions, or the development agency, and where the prediction of the behavior of these units is decisive for the outcome of the analysis, our model should be of a more *cybernetic nature*. In this case, it will be based on biological analogies, incorporating "black boxes" and boxes of partial transparency, i.e., subunits for which we have no reliable indication of the transfer functions between inputs and outputs, or in plain language, no precise means of knowing how they operate. Major irrigation and agricultural development projects in low-income economies in most cases fall into this category.

THE PLANNER'S POINT OF VIEW—METAPLANNING

According to our definition, true development is one which induces improvements in all areas of the production and distribution process from the creation of human resources for these processes to the application of administrative and economic controls to ensure their smooth functioning. Hence, true development affects practically all aspects of economic and political life.

Development is conditional upon the creation of decision streams which, in turn, trigger off material and nonmaterial resources streams. For these resources streams, we shall make use of the military term "logistic streams." The scope and quality of development thus depends on the scope and quality of the decision streams that a society generates and on the logistic streams that can be mobilized to back them up. Although logistic streams, or rather their insufficiency, are a major constraint to the growth of most underdeveloped countries, the *controlling limitation* generally lies in the scope and the *quality of its decision streams.* The best proof of this is the poor use that some high-income underdeveloped countries, e.g., certain oil-rich countries, make of their ample economic resources.

The reason for this disability is not difficult to trace: while knowledge and know-how are, at least to a certain extent, transferable and communicable and can, therefore, be imported from more developed countries, decisions must be generated by the *national* political organization or hierarchy.

This political hierarchy can be conceived in a more abstract way, representing it by the structure generating decision streams, and in this way we arrive at the useful construct of a *decision hierarchy*. Now, political hierarchies, in their formal (i.e., officially acknowledged) and informal (i.e., unofficially operative) elements, are firmly embedded in the social and political context of nations and are, therefore, extremely difficult to uproot: like all organizational structures, the political hierarchy (and decision hierarchy representing the abstraction of the political hierarchy) has an extreme inertia and resistance to change. It is this inertia—operating at all levels of the "establishment" of developed as well as of developing countries—which is the main cause of the *gap* that can be observed at all times and in all countries between the knowledge, the awareness of what should be done for the best of our society, and what is actually being done.

If, therefore, we wish to accelerate development in a low-income country, improving the operation of the decision hierarchy must take a major place in our plan of operations. To approach this problem rationally, we have to set up some analogy and model of the political hierarchy. Recent work in a number of relevant disciplines indicates that the *biological analogy* may be the most applicable, at least for the general phase of our analysis. In this biological analogy, we conceive of the political hierarchy as a hierarchy of self-regulated subwholes or subhierarchies (and this pattern can, of course, be applied to more than one level of subdivision); each of these subhierarchies is considered to have a fair amount of self-regulation but, nevertheless, remains dependent for instructions related to strategic decisions on the next higher level. In addition to these "vertical" decision flows from the top of the hierarchy to its lower levels, the "horizontal" flows of information between subhierarchies on the same level must also be introduced. To complete the picture, there is a flow of information feedback from the lower to the higher levels, this information being subjected on its way up to a "filtering process," which passes up only the information of relevance to the higher level. This process of information flow must, of course, be conceived as subject to deterioration (in both directions).

In this model, every subwhole or subsystem is, according to Koestler,[2] both a "sub" and a "whole":

Facing downward or outward in the hierarchy, it behaves as an autonomous whole; facing upward or inward, it behaves as a dependent part which is inhibited or triggered into action by higher controls. One might call this the "Janus principle" in organic (and social) hierarchies.

The "whole" aspect of the subwhole is manifested in its autonomous and spontaneous activities . . . . The dynamic aspect of the part's autonomy is manifested in its apparently spontaneous, unprovoked rhythmic activities which are "modified but not created by the environmental input" . . . . The part's dependence on supra-ordinate controls . . . may be said to represent the interests of the whole vis-à-vis the part in question.

The top levels of the decision hierarchy, to some extent, control all the economic activity of a nation, while the planner, operating some way down the hierarchy, directly controls only a relatively small part of this activity. However, the success even of the small part of the overall program is dependent on decision streams generated by higher levels of the hierarchy. The planner should therefore set up his own limited program in a way that will contribute to an accelerated improvement of decision streams, both those directly related to his own planning space and those related to similar aspects of the economy as a whole. Improvements of the former are mandatory for the success of the planner's own project; improvement of the latter are desirable because their spillover to the overall economy may transcend the potential direct impact of the planner's own operation many times over.

The planner who takes responsibility for the development of a major project, a regional scheme, or a subsectorial or sectorial program should not, therefore, be satisfied to wait for instructions from above, executing them at the rate he receives them. If he takes this attitude, his labors will not produce the main benefit of induced development, i.e., the improvement of the decision hierarchy and the growth capacity of the nation, nor will he, within his limited area of responsibility, achieve the benefits he could obtain by adopting a more active point of view.

In short, the planner has to realize that the process of growth can and must be initiated from all possible levels of the hierarchy; if he and his peers do not initiate it at their own level, there is little hope that it will ever get off the ground, since it is rare for the requisite intellectual capacity of a nation to be placed at the apex of its political hierarchy. In essence, we stress that the planner must apply modern systems engineering and cybernetics to the analysis of development problems in ever wider contexts, at ever higher levels of abstraction; he must take up the point of view to be embraced by tomorrow's great revolution in management thinking.

The implication in this change of point of view has already been pointed

[2] Arthur Koestler, *The Act of Creation*, Pan Books Ltd., London, 1964, pp. 471–472.

out in the first section of this chapter: it requires that the planner be fully aware of his own role and his direct area of responsibility within the overall decision hierarchy and that he realizes the extent of his dependence on decision streams from higher levels; it calls for constant evaluation of the extent to which he can influence and modify these streams, and assessment of the opportune timing for such modifications.

2

OUTLINE OF A PLANNING METHODOLOGY FOR WATER-RESOURCES DEVELOPMENT IN DEVELOPING COUNTRIES

One method of delivery alone remains to us, which is simply this: we must lead men to the particulars themselves, and their series and order; while men on their side must force themselves for awhile to lay their notions by and begin to familiarize themselves with facts.

FRANCIS BACON (*Novum Organum*)

THE ROLE OF MODEL BUILDING IN HUMAN AFFAIRS

Man is the model-building animal, and model building is, from the biological aspect, an important adaptation of human responses to the requirements of an ever-changing environment. Man builds models by organizing the sensory inputs from his environment into structural entities that enable him to predict the behavior of the biologically important features around him; through such prediction he acquires the ability to manipulate these features, or to adapt himself to them where manipulation is beyond his power. Language is the basic, universal tool employed by man in his model-building activities, a tool later extended to encompass systematic reasoning, science, and technology—all model-building efforts differing only in the measure of their universality, rigor, and sophistication.

Model building is purposeful mapping. The term mapping is used to indicate that model building does not attempt to give a detailed description of the original sense context, but rather to represent selected aspects of it by the use of symbols; the term purposeful, because the features represented and their structural interrelationship are selected for their predictive value for a specific purpose. As for the model's efficiency, this is dependent on an economical selection of the features represented; hence, the efficient model contains no more than those features relevant for prediction, while its predictive value depends on the appositeness of the representation of the functional relationships between its features, as well as upon the degree of inherent predictability of the mapped phenomena. A model of high predictive value reflects all significant operational characteristics of reality, i.e., it is homomorphic.[1]

Model building is an iceberg type of activity in that most of this activity goes on beneath the surface, without our being aware of it, and hence we are conscious of only a small part of it. Satisfactory models, i.e., models which have shown themselves to have the requisite predictive value, are automatically reemployed in similar situations and gradually become part of our stock-in-trade for problem solving; poor models are, in time, discarded. A specific model, once adopted, tends to become "submerged" in the stereotyped, automatized part of our mental activities, permeating our language and generally influencing our conceptions of the subject matter of the model. Moreover, it creates a "rut" for our thinking on the subject, a rut from which we find it extremely difficult to extricate ourselves, primarily because, after a time—through projection of the model back upon reality—we are no longer aware of the model having been superimposed by us on reality or of the bias the model induces even into as "neutral" an activity as data collection.

The application of stereotyped models to everyday problem-solving situations, while it, without doubt, economizes on mental effort, carries with it the inherent weakness of all stereotypes—the loss of predictive value when applied to contexts differing from those for which they were originally conceived. The principal risk involved in their use lies, in fact, in the model user's failure even to note the existence of such differences.

THE TRANSFER OF MODELS

As understood from the above, a model is a symbolic representation, drawn up for a specific purpose, of a system of functional relationships operating in a certain environment and connected with it; models may vary in their degree of rigor from an unverbalized vague realization of relationships to precise mathematical expression. Their utility depends on how faithfully they represent the relevant aspects of internal system relationships and the interrelation between system and environment. Setting up a model for a specific purpose involves, on the one hand, selection of those functional relationships which have a major bearing upon the problem-solving situation, and which have to be represented in the model; on the other hand, it involves carving out the system represented by the model from its environment, or more explicitly, defining its boundaries. To these two aspects we must pay particular attention when we come to transfer a model from one environment to another.

[1] For a full definition and exposition of this term, see Stafford Beer, *Decision and Control*, John Wiley & Sons, Inc., New York, 1966, p. 105.

Since the purpose of representation changes from one environment to another, so the model's effectiveness changes. Models established as useful in one environment or technology, or for certain quantitative levels of the represented functions, lose their predictive value in a different environment or at different levels. This applies in the case of basic changes in the functional relationships represented by the model and in the event of changes brought about by major theoretical advances or improvements in technology or, finally, in the case of changes resulting from major cumulative qualitative changes. Eventually, such models act as mental blocks, obstructing man's or society's creative adaptation to new contexts.

Adopting a new technology or switching to a different environment requires that specialization and routine responses acquired in the old context be consciously abandoned, that we enter upon a "regression" into the "pre-model" phase of problem solving, followed by the adoption of different models fitting the new context. It would appear to be simple enough to avoid these pitfalls encountered in transferring models from one context to another. Nevertheless, time after time, man fails to realize that he is transferring models, and consequently, he runs into difficulties which stem primarily from the "submerged" part of man's model-building propensities and from his stereotyped, automatized stock-in-trade of problem-solving mechanisms.

The greater the scope of the model, the better are our chances to arrive at optimum solutions, though this, of course, entails a more complex analysis and the marshaling of additional data to support the solution. For a specific type of system, for a specific type of environment, and for specific quantitative relationships, a workable definition of boundaries between the system represented by the model and the environment will gradually evolve as a compromise between our desire, on the one hand, to make our definitions more rigorous and the necessity, on the other hand, to economize on data collection (and hence also in time) and in our expenditure on data processing and analysis. Predictions based on boundary definitions arrived at in this manner will be reliable as long as no substantial environmental or technological changes have taken place. However, where we deal with a basically different technology or environment or with major cumulative changes requiring a wider angle of view, we may find that the system contained between the old boundaries excludes a number of functional relationships which, in the new context, have become essential for predicting system behavior. Changes in technology, environment, or scale thus necessitate a *redefinition of boundaries* between the system and the environment.

REDESIGNING THE MODEL FOR A NEW CONTEXT

We may conclude from the above that redesigning our model preparatory to its transfer to the new context involves one or all of the following operations:

1. *Redefinition of the boundaries* between the system and the new environment, with a view to ensuring that all features which are likely to have a significant influence upon objective achievement within the new context are

included in the system. The features to be added in the context of underdevelopment may, for example, be related to the psychological space of the farmer or of the development project personnel, to the organizational and institutional space, to the political decision process, or to other development components.

2. Expansion of the model to accommodate such features.

3. Redesigning the model to encompass areas of thought and activity raised by new technologies or theoretical advances.

This major redesign, or retooling, of our model stock-in-trade and redefinition of boundaries cannot be carried out with the old conceptual model tools. Rather must we transcend the level of abstraction at which we have been operating and adopt a more general, all-embracing viewpoint from which we can gain a wider, fuller, and fresh understanding of the system, its environment, and of the system and environmental interconnection. In short, a *model to analyze models* is needed—a *metamodel*—a metalanguage that can be used to analyze the language we intend to use.

Our mental stock-in-trade, acquired in the past, must, therefore, be rethought and remodeled before it can be transferred to its new context. Our stereotyped and almost automatized problem solving and decision patterns must be reexamined, before these can be reused, a reexamination which has to be performed in the rarefied sphere of a higher level of abstration which we are not accustomed to operating at; it is almost as if we are trying to relearn to walk by analyzing the purpose of every movement in our body.

The process of remodeling our stock-in-trade of problem-solving tools becomes still more difficult when we consider the personnel that will have to carry out such reappraisals. They are drawn in most cases from the ranks of *experienced and successful practitioners from developed countries* (operating either on home ground or in the strange environment of one of the developing countries) or from among the relatively young, *inexperienced professional personnel* and political decision makers of the *less developed* country.

The former group is usually too firmly set in the use of their proven stock-in-trade to be amenable to "retooling," their very success in applying the old proven models within their earlier context reinforcing a natural reluctance to reconsider the relevance of these models. Their responses to a specific planning context and technology render them too specialized to be able to *reculer pour mieux sauter* (to step back in order to make a better jump forward), to use one of Koestler's favorite expressions. When dealing with a completely new context, such as that of a developing economy, which they find intractable and irresponsive to their intellectual stock-in-trade, they prefer to denounce the country, as if they had expected it to adapt itself to their model, rather than to rethink their model. Faced with major changes in technology in their own accustomed planning context, they tend to squeeze the new problems to fit their old models to the extent that appears to them necessary in order to "compensate" for changes in technology.

The young, new professional and political executive in the developing country, the proud possessor of intellectual tools only recently acquired at the universities of developed countries, or from teachers coming from or trained in these countries, is equally steadfast in his refusal to abandon his newly acquired tools and to embark on retooling, an operation for which, in all probability, he has not been trained. Faced with the low predictive value of his transferred models, he chooses, as a rule, one of the standard paths of least resistance:

1. He continues to make decisions which suit the old models and to pretend that all is well; this is easily done if he adopts irrelevant yardsticks of performance, such as the extent of financial investment rather than the increase in production or capacity to produce. This approach is referred to as the *make-believe solution.*

2. He "reconciles" the continued use of old, irrelevant models with the need for, at least, formal recognition of new, more adequate concepts which are "in the air" or in fashion by acting upon the former and talking of the latter. This elegant approach is referred to as the *magic-of-language solution.*

3. He adopts a new but, nevertheless, irrelevant stereotype, such as a political stereotype, where revelation replaces analysis and every problem is cut to size until it fits the Procrustean bed of our political choice. This approach is referred to as the *prefab solution.*

All three paths are, of course, *pseudosolutions,* escapes from the problems facing us along the reality-irreality axis into a world of make-believe. However, in the attainment of our objectives there is no substitute for true problem solving, and we cannot allow ourselves this luxury of escapism.

Nobody has expressed this more felicitously than Goethe in his *Wilhelm Meister:* "Handeln ist leicht, Denken ist schwer, nach dem Gedachten handeln unbequem." (To act is easy, to think difficult, to act upon one's thoughts inconvenient.)

It is around the redesign of models of problem solving and decision making related to the development of water resources and irrigated agriculture in developing countries, around the redefinition of system boundaries represented in such models and their environment, that our comments will turn.

In the following, an attempt has been made to epitomize the central argument of this book with a view to giving the reader a first bird's-eye view of its subject matter.

THE PRAGMATIC AND THE IDEOLOGICAL APPROACH

The structural inadequacy of semantics on which we have dwelt in Chapter 1 is not the only, and probably not even the most damaging, flaw in our analytical tools. This distinction is due to the thoughtless application of ready-made models and metaphors controlled by a priori value judgments as a substitute, "ersatz," for rational model building, or in more direct terms, the fault of substituting the *ideological* for the *pragmatic* approach.

The ideological approach is a basic attitude to problem solving in general, rooted in the systematic application of a priori type of principles to an intentionally highly simplified planning space.

The underlying a priori principles often have their roots in broader national, religious, moral, or political tenets that have been taken over uncritically from an irrelevant past. These ready-made models have a number of advantages such as economy in mental effort, as well as apparent ease of transmittal to individuals preconditioned to accepting these models. Their only disadvantage is that in most cases they do not fit the situations to which they are indiscriminately applied. However, the most disturbing aspect of this approach, as also its greatest danger, lies in its "test proofness," a term applied to that state in which "sacred-cow principles" are upheld, despite the fact that predictions based on these principles have failed to materialize (as is usually the case), and instead some less-hallowed aspect of the planning space is blamed for failure.

The pragmatic approach is conceived as the antithesis of the ideological one. When applying the pragmatic approach, the planner seeks a definition, as unbiased as he can make it, of his planning space, its problems, dimensions, structure, trends, and constraints. He then decides what type of model to select to represent the functional relationship of this space and to predict its responses.

The ideological approach, which once pervaded all human thinking, has best survived in the behavioral, institutional, political, and economic disciplines, although it can also be found in the technological sciences. It is this approach which is, in fact, one of the main mental blocks that stands in the way of truly effective conceptualization.

This basic dichotomy is illustrated by two examples from the field of water-resources development. In the first example related to *water legislation,* the ideological approach assumes that one of a limited number of doctrines (e.g., the riparian or the appropriation doctrine) has to be adopted as the basic legislative criterion. The pragmatic approach, on the other hand, views water legislation as a tool for development to be shaped purely in accordance with the requirements of the long-term program, though subject to certain politico-institutional constraints. In the second example related to *water-resources management,* the ideological approach here, too, is represented by the adoption of overriding a priori principles, e.g., the conservation approach, whereas the pragmatic approach is based on the optimization of a selected objective function, possibly also subject to certain constraints.

Wholesale breaking of Bacon's "Idols of the Tribe" and "Idols of the Market Place," therefore, constitutes an essential part of an "intellectual retooling," since, to quote from Bacon's *Novum Organum:* "words plainly force and overrule the understanding, and throw all into confusion, and lead men away into numberless empty controversies and idle fancies."

LEVELS OF ABSTRACTION

The selection of irrelevant models, structurally inappropriate semantics, and arbitrary ideologies are but various expressions of one underlying weakness of analysis: the *inadequacy of the level of abstraction.* Effective performance in every type of planning and decision-making operation requires a level of abstraction appropriate to that operation; when we operate at a lower level, we see individual trees but not the forest as a whole. On the other hand, if our level is too high, we see the context but not the actual problems.

The capacity for abstraction depends on genetic and early conditioning factors and on maturation opportunities. Genetic and early conditioning factors determine the highest level of abstraction an individual can be expected to reach, i.e., his ceiling of abstraction. Maturation opportunities, or more explicitly, man's opportunity to develop his inborn capacity in an appropriate professional environment, determine whether, in fact, he will ever reach his genetic ceiling.[2] Unfortunately, in developing countries, maturation opportunities are rare, and, hence, the prospects for full development of the potential abstractive capacities of political and professional decision makers are strictly limited. Nevertheless, professional decision makers may, within these limitations, have the opportunity to develop at least part of their potential within the framework of foreign agencies, whereas the political decision makers will not have even this limited opportunity.

No wonder, therefore, that the level of abstraction encountered in many developing, as also in some developed, countries is often found to be inadequate and the development programs formulated in these countries are found to be unbalanced and ineffective. Where the platform of vision is not sufficiently high to view the entire system under consideration, with all its interconnected and interacting subsystems, attention is unavoidably restricted to one or other of the subsystems, others are lost sight of, and what is possibly still more important, the interaction of subsystems is disregarded.

Comparison with foreign operations conducted at an adequate level of abstraction or criticism voiced by outsiders may bring with it a realization of the inadequacy of the level of abstraction. However, this is not in itself sufficient to improve matters, as long as the professional and political decision makers concerned do not possess the capacity and skill to operate at the higher level required. More often than not, this realization will lead to a *pseudoadaptation* by the professional or the politician to the higher level of abstraction, i.e., to the adoption of the external trappings, such as fashionable catchwords or formal organizational structures, while in actual fact these functionaries continue to operate unconcernedly at the old accustomed level.

Fortunately, only a small part of development planning has to be conducted at relatively high abstraction levels, i.e., with a horizon of vision extending over a whole program or over an entire sectorial plan. Once the major program has been outlined, by far the greater portion of detailed development thinking can be conducted at lower levels of abstraction. Hence, it usually suffices to catalyze the development of abstractive thinking within a relatively small selected group of planners, through the employment of a number of professionals capable of operating at the level of abstraction required by the program in hand. The group thus reinforced should be able to tackle the overall programming and planning and coordinate the working groups operating at

[2] Elliott Jaques, "Speculations Concerning Level of Capacity," *Glacier Project Papers*, William Heinemann, Ltd., London, 1965, p. 102.

lower levels of abstraction. However, major development-planning difficulties may be encountered in the political sphere which operates at a lower level of abstraction than that of the professional groups. Feedback effects from reinforced professional groups, possible parallel catalyzing approaches within the political group (where the quality of the leadership element warrants such a process), and exhortation and pressures from major funding organizations may possibly pave the way to raising the level of abstraction of the all-important political-decision process.

THE GAP BETWEEN CONCEPTION AND IMPLEMENTATION

The advancement of both the political and the professional level, by direct as well as indirect means, toward the adoption of a higher planning horizon is necessary for a more general reason, namely, to close the wide gap that exists, at every level of performance, between professional and executive problem solving and decision making. Awareness of the right path of action, imperfect though this may be, is, in general, far superior to actual performance in decision making. This problem is, in fact, age old and has been succinctly expressed in the Latin proverb: "video meliora proboque, deteriora sequor" (I perceive the right path and approve it, I observe the wrong path, and follow it).

This gap, between conceptual awareness and executive action, of course, also exists to a considerable extent in the developed countries. The gap is striking in those countries which are approaching the midpoint of development and devastating in some underdeveloped countries. Already in 1955, the Earl of Halsbury[3] wittily pointed out this gap by proposing (I trust with his tongue in his cheek) that once development objectives are agreed upon and expressed in quantified models, the strategies and tactics of economic implementation could well be left to a computer and ideological controversies between the Western and the Communist worlds could thus be resolved once and for all. The main trouble, of course, does not lie in the existing and serious imperfection of our present models for action but in the inability of the political and, to a certain extent, also of the professional level to conceive of the need for a general solution and to act accordingly.

FORMAL AND INFORMAL POWER HIERARCHIES

It should be realized that *planning is only a tool for action, and hence it is meaningful only to the extent that it leads to action.* By *action,* as understood in this context, we refer to *direct* or more often *indirect public intervention* into prevailing spontaneous processes with the ultimate objective of raising the economic and social effectiveness of the production process. The gap between conception and action—a gap which also exists in developed countries—is aggravated in the developing countries by two major handicaps: *firstly,* by the *dual organization* prevailing in many of the new nations in

[3] "From Plato to the Linear Programme," *Journal of the Operations Research Society of America,* vol. 3, no. 3, pp. 239–254, August, 1955.

which an "ideologically obsolete" informal power hierarchy permeates and, in fact, controls the formal hierarchy, which may perhaps have been borrowed from a mature economy; *secondly,* by an *inadequate conception of the development process.* The latter vitiates conceptual thinking, while the former introduces an element of conflict, in which the informal power structure (with its lower levels of abstraction), as a rule, has the upper hand. These handicaps are discussed in greater detail in the following.

Development concepts and the conceptual processes applied in emergent economies by the political and, to a certain extent, also by the professional level are characterized by extreme *fragmentation* in space and time. The development process is seen as an agglomeration of discrete single-dimension development units, termed "projects," conceived in a space of nonexistent or negligible interaction and extending over a limited period of time (at best, the time horizon of the national investment program). Interaction between projects, continuity of the development process, the potential role of the current program (i.e., the aggregate of all projects that have a major bearing upon a certain sector of the economy) in modifying the growth potential for subsequent programs are not taken into account. What is more, no real attempt is made to look into the selection of specific development objectives that fit the status quo and its inherent trends, on the one hand, or into the prevailing political philosophies and value judgments, on the other hand. Ready-made "progressive" objectives are imported from economically successful and mature economies, with the implied assumption that all roads to development are parallel.

The solution usually adopted to find a way out of the organizational dichotomy is, in fact, a pseudosolution: a theoretically adequate formal organization is instituted on top of the old informal one.

Penetration of the formal, relatively modern, and permissive organizational hierarchy by informal, older, and more authoritarian hierachies has the curious but important side effect of lessening the professional's authority. Thus, the very existence of a strong informal power hierarchy tends to widen the gap between conception and action and to suppress any attempt at innovation that does not suit the informal hierarchy, even before such an attempt has a chance to strike roots and establish itself.

The existence of the many obstacles and mental blocks that stand in the way of effective development thinking and action in the new countries is not a fortuitous phenomenon but a basic structural weakness; neither can these obstacles or blocks be bypassed or overcome by haphazard action and without sustained effort. Concerted action is therefore required in order to create the appropriate leverage for basic structural transformation in at least one of the strategic sectors of the economy; in many developing countries, the agricultural sector might be the first choice for systematic planning and tenacious implementation of an escalating multidimensional development process, which could create important spillover effects affecting the whole political hierarchy. Failure to follow this methodology will result in piecemeal, unrelated successes, which do not merge into a major development stream.

METAPLANNING

At this point, the argument moves from the analytical, the clinical, and the diagnostic approach to the *synthesis* and therapeutics of planning. The first, and possibly the most important, step toward this synthesis is the establishment of a *metaplanning model,* i.e., a *planning model of planning,* operating at a level of abstraction above our actual performance level. If, for instance, we take irrigated agriculture as our planning level, our metaplanning model should encompass, in addition to the processes originating from the sectorial planner himself, a number of decision processes originating from other sectorial decision makers at the same level, as well as from the relevant portion of the superior political and professional hierarchy.

To begin our synthesis, we must define the status quo "equation," or more explicitly, we must express in suitable form the initial decision mechanisms and patterns (the decision models) of all levels of the hierarchy. We are, furthermore, in need of an inventory of the initial resources streams and resources-outcome, or input-output, ratios, as determined from past performance in our own or other countries operating under similar conditions. These input-output ratios are, of course, only projections and hence not firm, the outcome uncertain, and this therefore makes it more difficult to arrive at dependable quantified results. Nevertheless, this should not discourage us from attempting a reasoned analysis at whatever level of quantification and ranking we can attain. This lack of rigor should not particularly bother us, since as a rule it is possible, even by a rough-and-ready type of analysis and synthesis, to set out safe *initial* lines of action.

The fact that no sustained growth has taken place in the past at a rate that would meet with our overall development aims is, by itself, sufficient to indicate that in underdeveloped countries the status quo, with its characteristic resources, structure, and capacity relationships, combined with the prevailing development-planning conception and methodology, cannot generate this growth process. Hence, methodology, decision models, resources-outcome ratios, and structure must be changed and improved upon if we wish to achieve the desired growth process.

The principal task of metaplanning is to define ways and means to create the preconditions for such a sweeping transformation. Attempts at major transformations may be expected to arouse resistance. Metaplanning will have to anticipate foci of resistance and propose an organizational location for the metaplanning group that will ensure its effectiveness in spite of resistance.

BASIC DEVELOPMENT STRATEGIES

Economic maturity is best characterized by its built-in growth tendencies and the economy's capacity to respond and adapt to a growth environment.

The primary objective in the effort to lead an emerging economy toward economic maturity must, therefore, be the creation of growth orientation and growth capacity by strengthening existing growth tendencies and capacities and inducing new ones by a development process specifically designed for that purpose.

The lack of growth orientation and capacity in emerging countries becomes obvious from the very outset of the planning process: we come up against it as soon as we attempt to define specific planning aims, objectives, and targets. The dual structure of the political hierarchy, the ambivalent semantics it uses, the discrepancy between true underlying intentions and the face value of manifest political objectives—all these require, in the early phases of development, that we graft special policies oriented toward the upgrading of the political process upon the more conventional policies oriented toward the short-term growth of the economy to the very limit of the "political feasibility" of such a graft. Originally, the share in the total program of such grafts will be relatively modest and the results of the upgrading process limited. If we assume the rather unlikely possibility that ordered development will be allowed to continue smoothly for a sufficiently long period, the effects of the graft will gradually accumulate and result in an upgrading of the political process that will make it possible to increase the percentage of desirable elements in the program, i.e., those elements which lead to the acceleration of growth rates toward rationally defined objectives.

To put it more succinctly, since the outcome of any program depends on the political decision-making process, on the one hand, and on the resources and the effectiveness of their application, on the other hand, the overriding planning target in the early phases of any major program should be the improvement of both the political decision process and the resources-outcome ratios, this improvement to be achieved concurrently with the short-term growth of the economy resulting from resources application based on the existing decision process and resources-outcome factors. Because of the lack of data on natural resources, on most resources-outcome ratios, and on trade-off ratios between objectives that we encounter, as a rule, in developing countries, it will often not be feasible to set up quantitative multidimensional models covering the complete phase space from the outset. Hence, until sufficient data have been generated by a properly planned and information-oriented development process, it will be necessary to apply heuristic strategies stemming from the common characteristic features of early development phases, rather than to use complex models. Some of these basic strategies are set forth in the following.

LONG-TERM AND SHORT-TERM STRATEGIES

The basic objective of a development program should be to maximize the present worth of the production streams generated by the development process (possibly modified by other macroeconomic objectives through trade-off relationships), due weight being given to the distribution of the additional income produced. This maximization will be secured as a result of a judicious program drawn up with the object of obtaining a mix of short-term and medium-term benefits; the former will be derived from a development process operating through the existing decision processes and resources-outcome relationships, the latter from the upgrading of these decision processes and resources-outcome relationships.

The acceptance of this basic premise leads to two of the six planning heuristics which we shall mention in this chapter. The *first heuristic* in evaluating a sectorial development program should be the extent to which the program realizes its medium-term aims of increasing the effectiveness of the application of the relevant resources streams, and also the extent to which it produces feedbacks and spills at the various levels of the decision process. These medium-term aims—and here we come to the *second principal heuristic*—must be achieved without greatly jeopardizing short-term production objectives and targets. Every such sectorial program is thus made up of a mix of medium-term capacity-oriented features and of short-term production-oriented features. The proportion in the program mix of the two main elements and of their individual subelements should be determined, on the one hand, by an optimization procedure aimed at maximizing over a medium-term planning period the overall present worth of the production streams (with certain distribution constraints); on the other hand, by metasectorial considerations, i.e., considerations which transcend the sectorial system under consideration.

The necessary scope and comprehensiveness of planning of public intervention must also be taken into consideration; this requires that we include in our model—and here we come to our *third heuristic*—all those dimensions of the planning space in which scarcities prevail and in which, it may be assumed, adequate growth will not be generated by spontaneous processes. Existing growth tendencies will have to be supplemented by induced development processes and new tendencies created, such induced development processes requiring careful planning and coordination. Processes going on in these planning dimensions should be conceived as closely interacting and interdependent. This leads us to our *fourth heuristic,* namely, that effective planning requires that the planning space be defined in a sufficiently comprehensive form so as to take in the interaction of processes in all relevant dimensions of intervention. Since in the agricultural sector of developing countries most processes will be found to be highly interdependent, the closer the model will come to embodying the sectorial conception, the better the chances will be of inducing spontaneous growth.

However, the agricultural sector cannot be completely isolated from the rest of the economy. To define the interchange between the sectorial system and its economic and political "environment" and the constraints imposed by this environment, a generalized type of intersectorial analysis will have to be undertaken, with a view to outlining the extent of intersectorial reconciliation that the proposed sectorial program will necessitate. The necessity of such an intersectorial survey, however, does not imply the dependence of a sectorial study upon a full-blown "rational" national development program at a time when the political and professional decision processes do not possess the capacity for such an ambitious undertaking.

STRATEGIES AND PLANNING APPROACHES RELATED TO INFORMATION

Introduction into our planning model of dimensions which do not lend themselves to full quantification brings with it a number of uncertainties, while even the information available on potentially quantifiable resources dimensions of our planning space is, as a rule, scarce and unreliable. Lack of information is thus the main characteristic of our comprehensive planning space. But this is not all, since part of the information we need in order to arm ourselves with reasonable predictive powers can be obtained only as feedbacks from the development process itself, while the planning and initiation of this process requires the very information which it is supposed to produce. To break this vicious circle, we must employ our fifth and sixth heuristics. The *fifth heuristic* deals with information and states that in a planning space in which insufficient information is available, programs must be modified in order to reduce the information gap by giving priority to those sections of the program which require less information, on the one hand, and by accelerating those sections of the program which will generate the much-needed information for subsequent development, on the other hand.

The *sixth heuristic* is, in effect, an extension of the fifth, requiring that in a planning space with insufficient information a new type of planning and implementation process be adopted which is based on the *dismantling in planning programs for developing countries of the partitions which in the mature economies divide the planning and implementation of programs.* Development, according to this heuristic, is conceived as an *ascending, as well as an expanding, spiral* in which every turn of the spiral achieves a certain expansion of production and growth capacity, simultaneously generating the essential information required for the next turn of the spiral. To the basic development objectives of growth capacity and current production increases already mentioned, we must, therefore, add that the program in its early development stages be aimed at *generating the basic information* required to feed subsequent development spirals. The initial turn of the spiral may be termed the *reconnaissance phase* and will include reconnaissance types of action and intervention, as well as the generation of information and preparation of plans for the next phase, the *pilot phase,* of the program. The pilot phase, in turn, will comprise, in addition to pilot-type interventions designed to improve production and growth capacity, information generation and planning for the *demonstration phase;* the expanding spiral thus continues to evolve until implementation of our sectorial program reaches self-sustained growth.

LOGISTIC IMPLICATIONS

The timing of the gradual expansion of the turns of the development spiral is, of course, also dictated by *logistic* considerations relating to the *availability and quality of material and nonmaterial resources.* As a rule, in developing countries it is impossible to mobilize from the outset human and structural resources sufficient in quantity and/or quality to tackle full-blown development programs in all economic sectors. On the other hand, development in the main sectors of the economy must, at least to some extent, be initiated concurrently because of their complementary nature. As has been amply demonstrated in most developing countries over the last twenty years, *subliminal spreading* of interventions over a large number of projects, which, as a consequence, all have "subcritical masses" of resources inputs, does not lead to the self-sustained growth processes which are the ultimate aim of planned development intervention. Hence, in order to gain some initial success within a specific sector, we must allocate our limited resources—in packages of above-critical mass and above-critical quality—to selected areas of activity (whether conceived geographically or functionally or as a combination of both) and create for such areas special organizational structures for the successive conception and execution of reconnaissance-, pilot-, or demonstration-type projects, conceived within a sectorial program. These development nuclei could be based on one or another of the development priming patterns, namely, the regional or the functional polarization patterns, and could become centers for the spillover and radiation of growth process, which, in time, would encompass the whole nation.

DEVELOPMENT NUCLEI

Under geographical or *regional polarization,* we attempt to concentrate within a closed organization sufficient human, motivational, and structural resources to make comprehensive multidimensional development possible within a limited region. The regional model thus constitutes a cutout of the sectorial one. The closed type of organization that can be effected in geographical polarization tends to facilitate catalization of changes in motivation and organization. Regional comprehensive growth nuclei, furthermore, serve as an excellent pilot operation for the generation of information on economic and sociological responses and for the elaboration of planning and implementation procedures.

In *functional polarization,* we attempt to channel the available human and structural resources on a massive scale to selected strategic production complexes by drawing up a mix of the material and nonmaterial inputs to be applied, say, to one or a number of strategic crops which promise to yield the best payoff for available inputs.

Both approaches, in addition to generating direct production responses, also bring about, to a certain extent, long-term responses related to growth orientation and growth capacity; these must be taken into account, together with the short-term responses, when evaluating projects based on these two approaches.

A combination of these two complementary approaches will often produce attractive programs.

LOGISTIC PROGRAMMING AND INVENTORYING

A number of features common to both the regional- and functional-type projects call for special emphasis; the need for careful logical and logistic programming is one such feature. Multidimensional programs require that numerous material and nonmaterial inputs be applied at specific times and in a certain sequence; these inputs can be grouped under two principal headings and each further subdivided as follows:

1. *Material Inputs:*
   a. Basic investments, i.e., the creation of new means of production
   b. Supplemental investments, i.e., investments necessary for the improvement of existing resources and for utilization of basic investments
   c. Current production inputs, e.g., seeds, fertilizers
2. *Nonmaterial Inputs:*
   a. Technological inputs, e.g., know-how, skills
   b. Motivational resources, e.g., incentives, need for achievement, indoctrination
   c. Structural resources, e.g., organizations, institutions

Programming must encompass all these inputs, and consideration must be given to their initial status and resources-outcome ratios (based on past performance), to their anticipated spontaneous changes, and to changes induced by the development process. In the event of anticipated critical scarcities in one or more inputs, programs will have to be reshuffled to reduce the need for these scarce inputs, and special supplementary programs for accelerating the generation of scarce inputs or the improvement of their resources-outcome ratios will have to be initiated, or scarce resources, both material and nonmaterial, will have to be imported from another sector or from outside the economy.

Programming is, of course, closely connected with *inventorying,* i.e., the listing of resources volumes and qualities; this, too, will have to include all the natural, capital, and human resources and inputs that enter into the development model. Here, again, we must bear in mind that it is not satisfactory to abide by *static inventory conceptions* in a context in which *dynamic* change of the resources-outcome ratios of the inventory is one of the most important of instrumental development objectives. The dynamic nature of our natural and man-made resource streams calls, therefore, for the adoption of a similarly *dynamic inventorying process* based on interacting resources streams.

TRANSFORMATION INPUTS AND THE TRANSFORMATION PROCESS

Inventorying and programming in the context of water resources and agricultural development in low-income countries invariably highlight a typical crippling *deficiency in nonmaterial resources;* a special program to overcome this deficiency by creating such resources and improving their effectiveness is indicated. By nonmaterial human resources we refer to two operational resources levels, the one acting through the development institution upon the farmer, the other acting at the production level proper, i.e., the farmer. To prime the advancement of the latter type of human resources requires that the human resources of the development institution, the *transformation inputs* as we shall call them, must first be trained, structured, and motivated toward the development objective. These transformation inputs must then be marshaled and focused with the objective of achieving, on as wide a basis as possible, a full structural *transformation of the human resources* operating at the production level.

The creation and improvement of *transformation inputs* requires careful consideration of the methods and conditions under which we can expect to obtain the desired changes within a society whose general social orientation is averse to development. It entails "unfreezing," within closed project groups, prevailing attitudes that are unfavorable to the development process; *catalyzation,* by the inclusion within the group of properly structured leadership personalities of higher levels of motivation and effectiveness; and reinforcing and "refreezing" of the new dynamic equilibria achieved.

Implementation of the *transformation process proper,* i.e., the upgrading of the responses of the farmer, should be guided by similar considerations. Its point of departure will, as a matter of course, be the existing psychological space of the producer, i.e., the farmers; specific studies should indicate how the main obstacles that obstruct the line of sight of the producer toward growth incentives can be removed, how motivation can be reinforced by risk-reduction measures and other incentives, what social structure can best sustain such new motivation, and what type of institutional framework is required to maintain the corollary material flows.

TYPICAL DEVELOPMENT SEQUENCES

An analysis and synthesis following these lines will, in many development contexts, result in development sequences in which the *first phase* will be based on the exploitation of existing means of production and investments, the main emphasis in this phase being placed on developing human resources at all levels, on improving current production inputs, and on creating an infrastructure for subsequent capital-intensive investments in new means of production and corollary supplemental investments. The *second phase* will combine approaches perfected in the first phase relating mainly to nonmaterial resources with relatively modest investment in the development of local resources and, perhaps, the supplementing of capital investments which have been made at some earlier date. The first two phases thus form the *pre-investment groundwork* for the subsequent phase, or the *major investment phase,* in new means of production, bringing about the transformation in the dimensions of know-how and skills, personality organization, and institutional structures which is a precondition for the effective absorption of the new means of production. The third and concluding phase of the overall sectorial program consists of the development of new means of production through capital-intensive investment.

The synthesis expressed in this three-phase program may sound utopian to the development practitioner, since observation of actual development programs, more often than not, shows a reverse sequence. Closer analysis indicates that this reverse sequence is, in fact, the path of least resistance in a developing economy, since it is considerably easier to spend money (with the generous help of the developed nations) than to carry through a basic structural sociopsychological change; moreover, the process of spending money displays, in addition, some built-in self-reinforcing feedback loops. Besides, the slow, uphill grass-roots process of transformation has little attraction for the typical politician with his extremely limited time horizon and his concentration on the public relations aspects of development, and it has even less charisma. Introducing the dimension of *political feasibility* to our model thus results in a watering down of the "chemically pure" utopian program with project elements which have a distinctly political flavor.

The factors mentioned above, *mutatis mutandis,* must also be considered when parceling out the rationed capital budget allocated in a national investment program for community water supplies. Here, the objective should be to provide the maximum amount of service possible with due weight given to time preference. Demand should not be considered as an independent variable, since (in addition to being income elastic) its price and facilitation-of-use[4] elasticities can, to some extent, be manipulated according to sociopolitical objectives. Units of service extended at demand levels established according to such sociopolitical criteria can be considered, for the purposes of our optimization procedure, to have basically equal social utilities. Trade-off factors may be introduced to allow for economic, social, or purely political preferences. Individual projects could thus be ranked according to their cost effectiveness in relation to the adopted utilities or the program selected which, for the given sectorial allocation, would maximize utility.

ORGANIZATION FOR NATIONAL PLANNING

Setting up the appropriate organization and institutions is a prerequisite for the successful planning and implementation of systematic and comprehensive programs. As a rule, a program is as good as the organization which puts it into effect, all flaws in organization being reflected in program conception and implementation.

To ascertain the structural requirements of a program, we must first look at the type of information, conceptions, decisions, and implemental operations required, giving special attention to the strategic or critical operations on which the success of the whole program depends. The structural requirements of these operations, on the one hand, and the organizational status quo, its inherent inertia and prevailing organizational style, on the other hand,

[4] An example of increasing facilitation of use would be decreasing spacing of street outlets in a rural water-supply scheme in a developing country.

determine the scope and structure of the organization to be adopted. Organizational synthesis resorts to complete restructuring (in the rare cases in which this proves to be politically feasible), to gradual structural modification by direct, partial intervention or feedback from the development process, or to a complete bypassing of the existing structure by setting up new organizational units.

PARTIAL SOLUTIONS: SUBSYSTEMS ANALYSIS

The numerous dimensions entering into comprehensive development models of transformation processes of irrigated agriculture in emerging economies, and the considerable uncertainty prevailing in this planning space, make it extremely difficult to put forward direct analytical solutions.

To circumvent these difficulties and to draw up workable analytical development models, we have, as a rule, to isolate the well-structured from the malstructured parts of our system.

The approach devised consists of subdividing the overall development system into a number of *subsystems,* each incorporating one or a number of the dimensions of our planning space and each conceived as interconnected with the rest by input-output streams. These subsystems may then be independently analyzed for limited time periods, this analysis giving improved estimates of the inputs absorbed and the outputs generated. The overall system can then be synthesized with the modified input-output streams. This analysis of the relevant subsystem will have to be repeated, substituting revised values of the input-output streams wherever significant inconsistencies crop up between the original assumptions and the modified values obtained for these input-output streams.

The success of such conceptual surgery depends, to a great extent, on the skill of the analyst in the selection of the subsystems; these should be selected so that each subsystem represents the main parameters of one of the controlling features of the overall model and that the more important subsystems lend themselves to quantitative analysis.

In the early phases of an agricultural development program for an arid country, several subsystems suggest themselves, each encompassing different aspects of the development program, such as water-resources management, the structural transformation of development institutions, the agricultural complex, and the transformation of the producers' psychological and institutional space.

Since the present task centers around the development of water resources and irrigated agriculture in developing countries, the general conceptual tools put forward in the above have been introduced because of their particular relevance to problems of water-resources development. For this reason, the latter part of this chapter will be devoted to elaborating the *subsystem of water resources* conceived as *part of the overall multidimensional system of water-resources and agricultural development.*

THE WATER-RESOURCES SUBSYSTEM—THE ORTHODOX APPROACH

Here, again, it will be useful to start the analysis of the methodology from a metaplanning point of view, i.e., from a level one "floor" above the operative level of planning.

The emphasis of water-resources development, according to the *orthodox planning methodology* (and when viewed from the metaplanning level), is seen as the generation of one or, sometimes, several discrete engineering interventions or steps (we might call them intervention "quanta") designed to meet the requirements of discrete demand steps; both this underlying demand and the engineering interventions planned and implemented are sharply cut off at the time horizon of the overall development program. Thus, no attempt is made in orthodox planning programs to allow for potential development requirements in the subsequent period, and, hence, the development process must be periodically reprimed. Once a time horizon is set, the time dimension ceases to exist in this type of planning space, and resources responses to engineering interventions are seen as instantaneous "Newtonian" types of reaction; at best, time is reintroduced by the backdoor, as it were, by subdividing a single intervention step into two (or possibly more) phases or substeps.

The orthodox approach is further characterized by separating the development from the management aspects of water-resources exploitation and emphasizing the former to the neglect of the latter. This is evidenced by the fact that planning engineering intervention into nature's hydrological equilibria usually concerns itself almost exclusively with the development aspects, i.e., modification of the resource in a way that will ensure a specific permanent yield at a specific point of time within the time horizon of the program. The limiting factor of the development of a specific resource is conceived to be its "safe permanent yield," i.e., the yield that can be permanently withdrawn at a predicted new steady state of the resource.

In contrast to this approach, the *management approach* attempts to achieve development objectives by the application to the resource system of a sequence of manipulative interventions that are aimed at so modifying the resource system as to make possible a specific withdrawal pattern over time. The "developed" resource system is no longer conceived as a more or less static steady-state system, but as an "upgraded" resources stream. The objective of the analysis of a resource system is not the determination of its "safe yield" at the steady state, but rather of the extent to which it can be manipulated to comply with a changing demand.

The orthodox approach has been applied for many years in the developed countries with reasonable success; however, as the scale of utilization increases, as other aspects of development impinge upon water quality, and as scarcities begin to loom larger, this approach, even in these countries, ceases to be satisfactory, while it is completely unacceptable for the developing countries.

In the development of water resources, we must consider intermediate states (transients), as well as final-resource states, i.e., final steady-state conditions. These transients, as we shall show, are especially important for meeting the requirements of the early development phases, and this again stresses the need for consideration of the management aspects.

Water-resources management should, therefore, not be relegated to a *post hoc* supplementary analysis of engineering interventions undertaken to meet a specific demand. On the contrary, water-resources management (with well-defined management objectives) should be the controlling consideration, while engineering intervention should be considered as a tool to achieve management objectives. From this we must conclude that the analysts of water-resources management should start together with (or even before) water-resources development.

THE WATER-RESOURCES SUBSYSTEM—A DYNAMIC APPROACH

The flaws and limitations in the orthodox approach noted above give some indication of the path we have to follow in order to draw up a more effective methodological approach, which we shall refer to as the "dynamic approach."

The dynamic approach conceives of water resources as *continuous resources streams* for which the planner has to design sequences of engineering intervention aimed at modifying the behavior of resources streams in compliance with the requirements of planning objectives. Under this conception, every intervention into the resources status quo creates response ripples which continue to affect the resource until these ripples decay sufficiently to be neglected. Engineering interventions have, of course, a certain inherent "lumpiness" which gives the intervention curve and the correlated supply curve their steplike form as opposed to the theoretically more desirable continuous curve. Each of these intervention steps has to be investigated for its immediate and long-term impact on the water resource, which is conceived as having been modified by previous steps as well as given to modification by interventions anticipated for the future. As stated, when weighing the potential utilization stream of a water-resource system modified by a sequence of engineering interventions, we must consider not only its final steady state but also the intermediate transients. This will be appreciated when we consider the low velocity of movement of water in porous media which results in considerable response lags in flow and quality to engineering interventions; hence, resources in their intermediate states, between the original and the final steady states, may be of sizable exploitation value, and though limited to a specific time period, use of these resources may offer considerable advantages.

The *dynamic management approach* can thus be defined as an attempt to manipulate the water-resources subsystem according to the requirements of demand (here conceived to be determined by other subsystems) in a way that will ensure the optimization of the chosen objectives (from aspects of cost, quantity, and quality and, by application of trade-off relations or constraints, combined objectives). Having selected a general management approach, we can now proceed to a definition of the management space.

DEFINITION OF THE MANAGEMENT SPACE

The management space selected for a certain set of conditions should be defined in accordance with pragmatic considerations: in certain conditions, planning can be effective only if the management space takes in the entire country; whereas in other conditions, this might be an overambitious undertaking and may, in fact, serve only to obstruct development. Boundaries of the management space will, therefore, be determined by various conditions, such as the size of the country, the degree of uniformity of resources distribution, the extent of resources scarcity, the proposed rate of growth, the adequateness of information relevant for planning, the structure of the political decision process, and the legal and institutional constraints.

When we come to define the *time horizon* in a planning space in which great uncertainty prevails, we will find that the predictive value of long-term hypotheses is limited, since the confidence intervals open up markedly with time. On the other hand, many interventions into the hydrological cycle have prolonged periods of decay which make it necessary to extend the time horizon. A pragmatic compromise satisfactory for the early phases of development may be obtained by selecting relatively short planning periods (preferably of the same duration as that of the overall national economic development plan) for the current engineering intervention, while viewing the response of the resources system to these interventions in the perspective of the extended time horizon.

Next, we shall have to determine the objective function, i.e., that function which we have selected for optimization; the appropriateness of our selection will in each case depend on a number of conditions, such as the overall socioeconomic development objectives, availability of resources, "payment capabilities" related to the various types of water use, and quality specifications. We must also bear in mind in selecting this objective function that basic determining conditions also change; we should, therefore, take into account their present status as well as attempt to predict their inherent change trends. Water may, for example, be in ample supply when considered in relation to the demand which is expected to arise within the span of the current program, but a scarcity might perhaps be anticipated to develop in the subsequent period, while the reverse may also be the case.

Both the analysis and synthesis of management patterns in such a planning space depend to a great extent on the availability and reliability of information and on the prevailing institutional, legal, and political constraints. These factors can be either treated as constraints or introduced directly into our management model as functional relationships; the feasibility of the latter approach will, of course, depend on the extent of our knowledge of their functional interrelationships with other variables of the model.

We have defined and described the space of water-resources management and, therefore, can now turn to the description of potential management patterns.

MANAGEMENT PATTERNS

The *original resources system* is made up of resources streams, located at specific points on the map plane and endowed with certain potential energies (represented by the third dimension of space), and possessing specific flow rates which change along the time dimension. Each resources stream has a specific chemical and biological quality; resources streams within a basin are usually interdependent. Similarly, the demand system also consists of streams which are defined by different map references, energy potentials, flow rates, and chemical and biological quality requirements.

Intervention sequences are made up of a number of engineering steps, designed to change the original resources system to suit the requirements of the demand streams, or to put it differently, to "upgrade" the original resources system to the requirements of the demand system.

Intervention sequences may consist of any combination of the following upgrading "tools":

1. Transfer, by "diversion" from the original hydrological system to the engineering facilities system
2. Upgrading (or its negative equivalent) potential energy (power generation, power input through pumping, power dissipation)
3. Upgrading of availability by flow regulation at the source, sometimes according to the requirements of the conveyance system, sometimes according to the requirements of ultimate demand
4. Upgrading of the overall location (i.e., map references) by the general conveyance system
5. Upgrading biological quality by treatment
6. Upgrading mineral quality by desalting processes, dilution, "kidney effects," etc.
7. Additional upgrading of flow availability by integration of individual resources into larger, more flexible, or regulated, complexes
8. Upgrading of availability according to the requirements of direct ultimate use, by deregulation of (partially or wholly) regulated conduit flows
9. Upgrading of local availability by distribution to local points of demand
10. Applicative manipulations through plumbing, irrigation installations, etc.
11. Conservation of the quality of the environment by disposal of wastes
12. Upgrading of wastes through reclamation and recycling, etc.

Many of these management variables are, of course, interconnected; some of these interconnections lend themselves to rigorous quantification, others to lower grade quantification. Management patterns for upgrading, by manipulating the controllable variables of the original resources system to the requirements of the demand system, can be listed under three basic management strategies:

1. The stable-equilibrium strategy, which aims at establishing new stable equilibria after passing through intermediate transients
2. The quasi-equilibrium strategy, which aims at maintaining an equilibrium by a series of continuously sustained interventions
3. The no-equilibrium strategy

These strategies do, of course, encompass both quantitative and qualitative variables.

The stable-equilibrium strategy, in its simplified static version, is identical with the "safe-yield" approach of orthodox planning, whereas in its more general *dynamic* form, it consists of management patterns which, after passing through *transient stages,* which may extend over many years, will converge upon ultimate steady states of flow and quality. These transient stages often harbor important exploitation opportunities which are neglected in the simplified static version, although their impact on availability, quality, and timing of supplies may prove to be decisive. From the hydrological viewpoint, these opportunities represent the *buffer stocks* (in quantity and quality) between the original and the final steady-state systems, stocks that have to be consumed or dissipated before the new steady state establishes itself. The adoption of different management patterns will result in quantitative and qualitative differences in the buffer stocks. The various possible manipulative patterns that can be applied to these stocks in space and time offer a great deal of flexibility in achieving our overall management aims during the often decisive, longish period of time until steady states are reached.

The strategy of maintaining a quasi equilibrium is based, as a rule, on the integration of an original resources system with other systems or inputs; it may, for instance, include, on the one hand, artificial recharge of groundwater formation combined with an expansion of the management space in order to maintain quantitative equilibria and, on the other hand, salt withdrawal, combined with its expulsion from the system, or dilution with imported water in order to maintain qualitative equilibria.

The no-equilibrium approach will result in the "mining" of water and ultimately the exhaustion of the resource. Justification for the adoption of this approach will depend on a number of technological and economic factors, on the one hand, and on our attitude to conservation ideologies, on the other hand. Adopting a pragmatic approach to the conservation issue will imply a dynamic interpretation of the resources inventory and of the production complexes utilizing water; the dynamic inventory interpretation will ensure that we allow, in our yield estimates of resources inventories, for anticipated changes in technologies and circumstances; dynamic interpretation of the water demand in the resources base of future production processes will consider the substitution of highly water-intensive processes by less water-intensive ones.

TYPICAL FEATURES OF INTEGRATED WATER-RESOURCES MANAGEMENT

Extent of integration The extent to which systems should be integrated depends both on technological-economic variables and on institutional-political constraints. In many cases, there may be no doubt as to the economic justification of integration, and yet institutional constraints and the political decision process often obstruct such integration in developed as well as in developing countries. In such cases, and especially where political handicaps are firmly entrenched in the body politic, conditions would have to become critical before the need to integrate resources would be conceded.

Groundwater vs. surface water Prejudices and mental blocks, rather than analysis and quantification, often determine the preference for utilizing the surface-water phase rather than the groundwater phase of a basin. Surface water for some engineers has a better "image," since it appears to be less elusive than groundwater. For some unexplained reason, engineers believe that longer periods of records are required for engineering decisions related to groundwater than for those related to surface water, whereas in fact the reverse is usually true; groundwater parameters observed at a certain point of time represent an accumulation of long-term hydrological data, while river-flow parameters represent only ephemeral responses to highly variable climatic factors. Engineers also tend to believe that the development of groundwater is more costly than that of surface water; this may be true where a major surface-water system is favorably located in relation to areas of demand and fully utilized from the outset. This is not the case in the majority of major surface-water schemes where many years, even decades, elapse before the stage of full utilization is reached.

The use of the highly subdivisible groundwater resources, where these exist, during gestation periods provides an economically attractive interim solution to meet the limited and gradually increasing demand. Groundwater development may, in fact, be considered as a stage of preinvestment before the subsequent introduction of capital-intensive major investments into surface-water schemes. This preinvestment enables the development agency to prime and initiate the major transformation of production and institutional processes—a prerequisite for bringing major investments in water resources in most developing countries to fruition.

Transformation, absorptive capacity, and payment ability evolve in roughly parallel S shape curves, with flat gradients in the priming phase and steep gradients in the build-up phase, these gradients flattening out again as we near saturation (in this context, this is, of course, only a relative term valid for a specific level of technology). The "utility" of water in its strictest sense is limited to that supply which can be absorbed, and this can be assumed to be relatively low in the priming phase. A development pattern should therefore be adopted which, in its early phases, is sufficiently subdivisible to allow prebuilding and idle-sunk investments to be minimized until the absorptive-capacity curve starts its steep incline, at which point larger steps in the supply become justified.

Similar considerations apply to information requirements for decision making. In the early phases, we may assume that information will be scanty and not too reliable, but that both its quantity and quality will increase as development proceeds. Obviously then, investments which require relatively little information and which do not unduly limit our future freedom of action will be most suitable for the early decision steps.

The use of groundwater complies with both these basic requirements, since its rate of development can be closely fitted to hug the curve of absorptive capacity, while the decisions called for early in the development process require only a limited amount of information and leave future decisions open. Judicious use of groundwater in the priming phase, where such resources are available, could thus help to overcome many of the difficulties and diseconomies encountered in water-resources development.

Regulation of an integrated system In integrated management systems, surface-water and groundwater resources, their interrelationship, as well as surface and underground storage, play specific and interrelated roles. The integrated system has considerable flexibility, allowing one type of resource to be substituted for the other according to their respective stock positions. Surface storage, with its inherent high intercepting capacity, will usually act as the primary regulator and subsurface storage as the complementary, or secondary, regulator. Such a system lends itself relatively well to quantitative evaluation and elaboration of optimized operational rules. The outflow of groundwater from the basin can, to a considerable extent, be controlled by correct siting of wells and by following a withdrawal or pumpage pattern designed to maintain the predetermined flow regime.

Integration of reclaimed water An integrated system can also be designed to incorporate reclaimed sewage and storm runoff. Use of subsurface storage, if appropriately designed and operated, for the regulation of these reclaimed resources, can assist in "upgrading" resources of low-grade quality or availability.

APPLICATIONS OF INTEGRATED WATER-RESOURCES MANAGEMENT

The theory of integrated water-resources management is now relatively well developed, and a great amount of work in this field is at present being carried out by a number of scientific institutions; nevertheless, actual applications of such management policies are still relatively rare.

The history of Israel's water development (described in Chapter 30) shows how a dramatic challenge that cannot be met by orthodox approaches can lead to new responses and solutions. A scarcity of water resources and the need for speedy development of the country to provide for a rapidly growing immigrant population led to the decision to draw up a nationwide master plan for the development of the country's water resources. This plan provided for the development of the country's water resources according to priority criteria in a way that made it possible gradually to integrate projects into increasingly larger units, which finally coalesced into one countrywide system, the Israel National Water Grid. More than 90 percent of the country's potential water resources have already been developed within the framework of the national plan, and the overwhelming portion is (directly or indirectly) interconnected and integrated in the water grid, which is operated on a national basis, and according to optimized procedures. A legal and institutional structure has also been fashioned according to the requirements of the master plan. By expansion of the system's capacity, improvement of water quality, introduction of desalted water, and optimization of operational programs, it will be possible to meet the needs anticipated in the next decade.

The need for similar nationwide, or statewide, integrated planning has now become urgent in a number of developed countries, where as a result of following the project-by-project approach, serious local resources problems have arisen. Institutions and legislation in these countries are being gradually shaped to fit the requirements of this wider approach. Similar tendencies can also be seen in the field of pollution control, where a number of notable successes have already been registered.

While the theory of integrated development is now relatively well advanced, the methodology of development planning for the agricultural sector as a whole or for major regions in developing countries is still in its infancy; successful application of such methodologies is even more rare. Attempts have been made recently in the field of regional and sectorial planning in a number of the developing countries, and the experience gained could be used to formalize a planning methodology for sectorial programs in developing countries.

COMPREHENSIVE PLANNING IN ARID ZONES

The need for comprehensive planning of water resources is of especial importance in areas in which a serious scarcity of water resources exists or is expected to develop in the foreseeable future. In conditions of scarcity, the management approaches outlined above in a general form will have to be translated into specific policies. These policies can be subdivided into four groups:

1. Reevaluation of the economics of water allocation and use, taking into consideration the prevailing scarcity. As a rule, allocation doctrines and, especially, application technologies have been developed in regions where the charge for water was held artificially at a rate lower than its actual cost. On the other hand, the high and ever-increasing cost of water in areas of scarcity requires that present conceptions be reconsidered and new ones developed which are better adapted to the availability and cost of water in such countries. These concepts should take in, among others, the possibilities of completely new water-application techniques, the substitution of alter-

native inputs and capital investment for water, and the modification or complete change of the resources base.

2. Improving the utilization of the resources system by application of a number of methods that might not be considered attractive in humid climates, such as increasing the water yield of the hydrological cycle by weather modification and evaporation reduction, increasing the water harvest by modification of soil and vegetative cover, or stepping up the yield of projects by integration and scientific operation.

3. Reducing water use or obtaining greater economic benefit from its use by application of administrative measures, e.g., rate structure, allocation, or transferability of water rights.

4. Preserving the productivity of the resources environment by eliminating wastes and avoiding mineral accumulations exceeding acceptable ceiling values or by introducing measures to counter or neutralize such accumulations.

Introduction of desalting into the water system of an arid country would constitute a further step in the same direction. The present high cost of desalted water necessitates not only analysis of the proposed uses of this water and the resultant benefits and costs, but also consideration of all forms of present water use, which it can be assumed are based on much lower water costs.

With the exploitation of all low-cost water and the introduction of water of relatively high cost, the application of desalted water to uses of low value or benefit ceases to be justifiable from the economic viewpoint and will, in fact, have to be discontinued before the introduction of the high-cost water becomes justifiable. In order to reduce the cost of desalting to be allocated to the additional produce or service directly obtained from this expansion of water-supply volume, the desalted water, by virtue of its low salt content, could be mixed with natural or reclaimed water, which may have salinities close to the tolerance limit, and thus a secondary benefit, i.e., that of creating a dilution potential, would be obtained.

An additional saving or reduction in water costs, as well as increased system effect, could be obtained by locating a desalting plant at a strategic or critical point of a water system. This integration, combined with underground storage, would also assist in maximizing the plant factors of a desalting plant and render superfluous the provision of special standby capacity for unplanned outages. Extractive processes (e.g., electrodialysis and reverse osmosis) would fulfill complementary functions in maintaining the salt balance in arid conditions.

CONCLUSION

The success of the great development efforts made in the low-income countries during the twenty postwar years has been rather limited; per capita food production in the developing world as a whole increased only by some 10 percent (as compared with 34 percent in the developed part of the world). Per capita figures are even more discouraging when we take the data for Latin America and the Far East separately.[5] This failure to maintain a growth in food production in the developing countries in keeping with population growth should be viewed against the background of a worldwide rise of expectations.

This lack of growth is, in fact, a feature of most of the developing countries and thus indicates that this is no matter of chance but rather is due to some systematic misconceptions. Analysis of the development thinking underlying major development programs shows that such misconceptions do, in fact, exist both in the developing countries that are making such great efforts to achieve sustained growth and in the developed nations that are attempting to assist them.

This misconception is rooted in the fallacious assumption that the predominantly spontaneous growth processes, which in the developed countries can be actuated by investment type of stimuli, can, by similar means, be induced in developing countries and that therefore semantics, models, and methodologies are transferable from high- to low-income countries. The experience of the postwar years shows, however, that this assumption is erroneous and that growth orientation, which impels a mature economy to respond quickly and effectively to growth stimuli, exists only to a very limited and insufficient extent in the Third World. Consequently, development in these countries must, to a large extent, be *induced,* and this not only involves the material investment dimension, but also requires that all dimensions of the society and the individual related to growth capacity must be reached; in short, the *entire psychological and institutional space* at all levels of the society and of the individual decision maker must be changed.

Such a major transformation has to be carefully planned. The plan cannot as a result of the complexity of the planning space be fully deterministic. In the final count, an overall plan can never replace current decision making, either at the institutional or at the village level. Our plan of transformation should, therefore, aim at outlining the conditions and the catalysts that make possible the necessary changes in the psychological and institutional space that are required in order to induce decision makers at all levels to arrive at decisions that are conducive to growth by their own personal motivation. To use a biological metaphor, inducing transformation is equivalent to providing a modified gene or gene group to catalyze transformation of the organism, through its own inherent mechanisms, in the direction of the desired development.

Such a development conception is very different from conceptions that have proved effective in mature economies and requires the adoption of different semantics, different models, different planning and implementation processes—in short, the application of different methodologies.

In order to develop, for each specific case, the methodology appropriate to prevailing conditions, we have to adopt a metaplanning platform which enables us to observe not only the planning space in which we have to

[5] *The State of Food and Agriculture,* 1965, F.A.O., Rome, 1965.

operate but also its relation to the physical, economic, social, and political environment; by observing the planning space from such a platform, the planner sees himself as only one of the many interacting decision processes that influence development.

In all probability, the developing nations cannot carry out this difficult job of transformation by themselves; certainly, they cannot carry it out fast enough; otherwise they would no longer fall into the category of the underdeveloped nations. Thus, the *joint effort of the developed and the underdeveloped world is required;* the role of the developed world is to provide capital and some of the trained personnel to catalyze and prime the transformation process and to transfer the necessary skills and know-how. The personnel assigned to this effort must be made to realize that the principal preconditions for the creation of a sustained growth process are the priming of preinvestment programs with a view to changing attitudes and responses and creating development information.

As for the developing nations, they have to realize the role and nature of the transformation process, to accord it the necessary priorities, and to set up the organizational structure that would make it possible, perhaps with the aid of imported reinforcements, to carry out the difficult development task.

Such basic transformations of people and institutions generally stir up highly political issues; hence, the political feasibility of such processes in most cases is dependent on the extent to which development can create reinforcing loops toward the political decision process and on the extent to which international, multilateral, and bilateral funding and aid organizations themselves will underwrite effective growth doctrines and insist upon their implementation as a condition for loans and grants.

Paradoxical though it may at first sound, inducing development in the relatively homogeneous economies of the developing world is a considerably more complex process than it is in the much more sophisticated mature economies. Realization of this basic fact, and adoption of an appropriate methodology by both the developing and the developed world, is a *sine qua non* for achieving sustained growth. In the words of Bacon in his *Novum Organum:*

> *Being convinced that the human intellect makes its own difficulties, not using the true helps which are at man's disposal soberly and judiciously; whence follows manifold ignorance of things, and by reason of that ignorance mischiefs innumerable . . . . There was but one course left, therefore,—to try the whole thing anew upon a better plan . . . raised upon better foundations . . . . For better it is to make a beginning of that which may lead to something than to engage in a . . . pursuit in courses which have no exit.*

3

PLANNING BEHAVIOR AND PATHOLOGY

Sure, he that made us with such large discourse
Looking before and after, gave us not
That capability and godlike reason
To fust in us unused.

SHAKESPEARE (*Hamlet*)

LOOKING FOR THE PERSONAL EQUATION IN PLANNING

Faced with the task of evaluating a national, a sectorial, or a subsectorial development plan, we tend, as a rule, to judge the plan as an impersonal product of objective reasoning that may just as well have been produced by a machine. Viewed thus, the plan is evaluated by applying criteria and yardsticks derived from engineering and economics, and the final product of planning is judged on its economic and technical merits without attempting to systematically trace the faults and weaknesses of the plan to flaws in the planner's conceptual tools, and without trying to devise ways and means to correct such flaws.

The *diagnostic-therapeutical approach* outlined in this chapter, as complementary to the *critical approach,* should be considered as a precondition for the improvement of the planning process and the creation of capabilities to produce better programs. Fulfillment of this condition, though essential if better planning is to be obtained, is not in itself sufficient to bring about the required improvement, since the "improved" planner still has to contend with the rest of the hierarchy, and unless the latter too is converted, the planner will himself be forced back into his old response patterns.

In this chapter, we shall concentrate on the diagnostics and therapeutics of anomalies in the planning behavior of the individual planner and his basic group. Similar aspects of the politico-administrative decision process have been dealt with in the first chapter, and will be dealt with again in different contexts in the following chapters.

Hence, the basic attitude and point of view adopted here are that a plan should be judged not only as the impersonal product of a planning methodology, but also as the very *personal* intellectual fruit of an *individual,* this fruit bearing the hallmark of the planner's "personal equation." Thus, points of view and methods that we shall employ here will not be those of engineering and economics but rather those of individual and social psychology, while the aim of our review will be to trace the connection of specific flaws in the plan to the corresponding conceptual limitations of the planner and to the framework in which he operates. We aim, therefore, in this chapter at the presentation of a psychology and psychopathology of planning.

The structure of human intellectual activities, including the intellectual products of human groups, has certain underlying interpersonal similarities. We may, therefore, expect to find certain recurring patterns of planning pathology under very different political climates and even at relatively different levels of development.

Even a cursory look at plans in emerging economies shows that repetitive symptomatic anomalies do exist and that one can classify plans according to these anomalies. However, we will find it difficult when discussing such anomalies with the planner himself to communicate to him the extent of irrationality in his plan; assuming that we do manage to get through to him, we generally set off a systematic train of rationalizations by which he attempts to show that, given the political and other constraints under which he labors, the course selected by him with its apparent irrationalities was the only possible one. In short, he tries to prove that the irrationalities in his plan do not stem from his personal inadequacies but rather from the anomalies of his politico-economic environment. Convincing though this may seem, it is not borne out by observation, for when we compare plans being implemented in countries with different politico-economical environments, we run across the same types of symptomatic anomalies, without any significant correlation between specific anomalies and specific regimes. There is, of course, no doubt that the planner is influenced in his planning by the political hierarchy, but we must also realize that the planner, when seeking to rationalize his *own* contribution to the anomalies of his plan, projects some of his own failings onto his environment in an unconscious effort to attribute irrationalities in his planning behavior to factors which are outside his own personality.

Discussing such anomalies with the planner will, by itself, have no significant effect on planning behavior, even in cases where the planner is prepared to acknowledge the irrationalities of his planning behavior. The only way to bring about a *fundamental change in planning behavior* is to *improve the level of abstraction* in the planner's basic problem-solving approach.

In the following, patterns of planning behavior common to developing economies will be studied with the object of drawing up a diagnostic definition of what we may call pathological planning behavior; this will lead us to the therapeutic and retraining approaches that it is proposed we should follow in development planning.

LEVELS OF ABSTRACTION IN PLANNING

A diagnostic analysis is outlined in the following which utilizes a conception of management behavior formulated and presented by Elliott Jaques.[1] According to this concept, management and planning capacities are classified according to the *degree of abstraction* that men are capable of applying to their professional tasks. From observations made mainly in the field of industrial management, Jaques has related scope and capacity of management with levels of abstraction, which, again, correlate to *time spans of discretion,* i.e., time spans during which the individual is capable of acting guided by his own discretion without outside guidance or scrutiny. For each one of the levels into which he subdivides the continuum of abstracting capacity, he attempts to define the extent of abstraction that can be expected to be applied at this level and the corresponding time span. According to Jaques's hypothesis, the level of the abstracting capacity of an individual depends, on the one hand, on his innate capacity and early conditioning and, on the other hand, on the maturation process, resulting from exerting abstracting capacity in his professional career under the appropriate guidance of his superiors; this maturation process, in turn, has a certain "natural" gradient. Thus, Jaques contends that an individual entering on his professional career at a certain level of abstraction is, as a rule, not able to mature beyond the level immediately above his initial one, or at most, two levels above it.

In this chapter, we shall apply Jaques's hypothesis to the planning process (with special reference to the planning of the development of natural resources in developing countries) and explore the fruitfulness of such a transposition of Jaques's general-management terms to planning semantics.

Jaques has called the bottom rung of his ladder of abstraction the "perceptual-concrete level," assigning to this rung a time span of discretion of less than three months. At this level of abstraction, the specific well-defined physical object of the "plan" is always present in the mind of the planner. The sequence of operations which he can project and plan is simple, limited in its extent, and conceived within the framework of a set model along routine lines. The structure of the universe of the planner at this stage is completely linear. Routine planning of the engineer or the seasonal agricultural plan of the agronomist may be said to lie at this level. The unit of operation at this level of planning is the simple, basic operation.

The second level of abstraction has been labeled by Jaques the "imaginal-concrete level," and to this level he has assigned a time span of discretion of about three months. At this level, the concrete object of planning is, in the mind of the planner, combined with operational abstractions, although the planner often refers back from abstractions to concrete objects. The scope of planning already comprises sequences of operations from the first level of abstraction, their coordination within a more comprehensive framework, and

[1] Elliott Jaques, "Speculations Concerning Levels of Capacity," *Glacier Project Papers,* William Heinemann, Ltd., London, 1965.

their control. Though the operations of the planner at this level need no longer be confined to routine sequences, his scope of operation remains confined to a relatively narrow segment of the phase space of development, a segment which is conceived to consist of static entities and their simple additive interrelationship. The planning of a local project, or the detailed programming of a self-sustained portion of a major project, may be considered to lie at this level; its unit of work is the first-level operation.

Level three is termed by Jaques the "conceptual-concrete level," and to this level he has assigned a time span of discretion of about one year. At this level, the planner is able to survey the whole resources complex with which he is dealing, while still expressing his problems in concrete, physical terms extended in the dimension of time. The drawing up of an annual investment program may be considered to lie at this level. The "planning space" is now much more complex than at the previous level, though it is still predominantly static and interrelationships are seen to be additive. The elements with which the planner operates are second-level sequences.

The fourth level, termed the "abstract modeling level," is considered as having a two-year time span of discretion; at this level, the shift from concrete to abstract may be considered complete. The phase space of planning is no longer made up of concrete objects or concrete sequences of operations, but of constructs representing abstract functions, their interrelationships, and their connection with the universe of concrete objects and operations. At this level, the planner begins to comprehend the relation of his specific resources functions with the other functions of the national (or regional) economy and their role in the general national metabolism. Keeping in mind this relationship, he can put forward overall goals and objectives and decide upon the strategies which will lead to these goals. His universe becomes multidimensional, i.e., it embraces numerous disciplines, although only his specific resources function is seen in structural detail against the background of the other interrelated functions. The unit of work is the complex logistic unit lifted from the third level of abstraction. The universe of abstract resources functions, in which the planner works at this level, has a well-developed time dimension, and the nonadditivity of the complex interdisciplinary phenomena begins to emerge—at least to the extent that these phenomena are significant within the time span correlated to this level. A medium-term comprehensive and interdisciplinary resources-development program can be envisaged to fall within this level of abstraction.

Jaques's fifth level, the last one[2] that we shall concern ourselves with here, is termed the "theory construction level" and is allocated a time span of discretion of five to ten years. At this level, the planning universe has become completely abstract: its building stones are the functional abstracts from level four, and it is pictured as a multidimensional dynamic field of forces in nonadditive relationships. Planning, at this level, becomes more than

[2] Jaques does not specifically define the sixth and seventh levels; these levels refer, presumably, to planning levels transcending the subject of resources planning, and hence going beyond our present area of interest.

a simple linear prediction for action; rather, it may be defined as a multilevel projection into a relatively distant future, constantly modified by a flexible steersmanship guided by feedback information from the growth process. To allow for the complexity of this multidimensional universe, the abstractions used in the construction of this model have to be more comprehensive and general and the conceptual connections bridging the gaps between the various disciplines more daring than those at previous levels.

Long-term comprehensive and interdisciplinary resources-development programs, their connection and interaction with the other physical, economical, and behavioral dimensions, the nonadditive deployment of this multidimensional stream along the dimension of time, may be considered as lying at this level of abstraction.

Having transposed Jaques's concept of levels of abstraction in management into planning semantics, we can now consider the relevance of these concepts to our subject—resources planning in developing economies—and the fruitfulness of adopting this conception.

DIAGNOSIS OF PLANNING PATHOLOGY: TRUE AND PSEUDOLEVELS OF PLANNING

Development planning for the new nations encompassing, in addition to capital investments, major transformations of the sociopolitical, economical, and institutional space requires the application of a high level of abstraction, say, level five of the Jaques classification. Unfortunately, planning at this or a similarly elevated level is, in most cases, not feasible because planners capable of thinking at this level of abstraction are not available in sufficient numbers; moreover, even if they were available, they would find it impossible to establish communication—a meeting of ideas—with the political decision-making level. This is the tragic irony of the emerging countries, for it is in these economies that high-level comprehensive planning is needed so acutely, and yet so many factors, both objective and subjective, impede its implementation. This paradoxical situation is moreover doomed to perpetuate itself, unless a way is found to break out of the vicious circles that operate against growth: the levels of abstraction required in the planners of a young nation mature only as a by-product of development, while such development in turn is dependent on a certain minimum level of planning. Basically, this is only a special case of the general dependence of growth on what we have termed growth capacity, in which the level of abstraction of planning plays a very vital part.

There appear to be two ways to break out of this vicious circle: the first is that of the agonizing trial-and-error approach with the slow shaping of a course, after many rebuffs, and the emergence, with the passage of time, of adequate "steersmen" to take the helm; the second, that of the catalyzation process—with the possible assistance of outside factors—of a growth effort in selected sectors of the economy, so designed as to develop an appropriate level of abstraction in the planner in an "artificially" accelerated manner as part of the generation of the overall growth capacity. Of these two paths, only the second seems to hold out any hope for the nonauthoritarian regimes of our present world.

The resources planner in an emergent economy, faced with the need for long-term planning, generally adopts one of two typical approaches: either he equates the level of abstraction to which he has matured with the concept of long-term resources planning and hence ends up at a planning level way below that necessary to meet the challenge, or he establishes what might be called a "pseudolevel" of planning, adopting the terminology and trappings of a high level of planning within a political organizational and conceptual environment operating at a much lower level. The dangers involved in these two approaches are described in the following, and an attempt is made to outline a practicable therapy.

Let us first consider the common case of *planning* practiced at a *level of abstraction* that is *not commensurate with development objectives*. We often come across instances of planning on a national scale practiced at the second or, at best, at the third level of abstraction. Such programs are in reality no more than catalogues of facilities proposed for construction. The sectorial or subsectorial planner, in drawing up a national development plan for his specific sector or subsector that fits into the overall national plan, is required to fill in the detail related to his resources field. However, instead of passing to the appropriate higher level of abstraction, he expands his previous approach—the approach he has up till now applied to small-scale projects—to the national scale, failing to appreciate the inadequacy of his previous tools in the new wider context. The implementation of the "facilities-catalogue" type of plan leads to results that fall short of the optimum that could be achieved with the same resources, if only the proper level of planning abstraction were applied. Basically, this type of program exhausts itself in isolated thrusts against a solid front of underdevelopment, thrusts which, because of the lack of coordination with the supporting and supplementary elements, fail to reach a stage of fruition.

The task of the outside catalyst (i.e., the leader or "shadow manager" hailing from another sector of the national economy or from outside the country) is a dual one. On the one hand, this "extraterritorial" agent has to draw up a preliminary overall program outline conceived at, say, the fifth level of abstraction, to serve for general orientation; on the other hand, he must, as a stop-gap measure, assist in the compilation of a detailed short-term or medium-term program (fitting into the above overall program outline) conceived at a level of abstraction that is one level above that practiced before by the sectorial planners, though still at least one level below the desirable one. Implementation of the planning process, catalyzed in this manner, gives to those planners who have adequate abstraction capacity the opportunity of achieving a maturation and escalation of their development thinking to a level above the previous one. The presence of the catalyzing agency—a presence that can be gradually reduced—will, within a relative short period of time, elevate the planning process to the desired level.

The case of *pseudolevels of planning* is harder to diagnose; the application of a therapy is even more difficult. The difficulty of diagnosis lies in the external similarities, at least from a distance, between a pseudoprogram and a genuine program. As for therapy, the difficulties here lie in the fact that the planner, by virtue of his adoption of a pseudolevel of planning, has provided himself with a path of escape from reality, and he therefore attempts to save face and to maintain the fiction of operating on a genuine program, even if, deep down, he is himself aware of the falsity of this claim.

Organizations conducting pseudoprograms generally endeavor to imitate and even emulate genuine foreign programs in all their more obvious external features: terminology and program format are adopted, formal organizational structure is duplicated, and nominal planning groups are set up. The capacity of abstraction of these organizations, of course, remains unchanged in spite of the formal revamping, and they are unable to initiate, guide, and control work at the higher planning levels. To a planning group operating at such an artificially elevated pseudolevel, the whole area of conceptualization lying between its nominal and its real capacity level appears to be completely unstructured, with no visible path through this uncharted territory. An organization, in which the nominal level of activity is way above the actual abstracting capacity to perform at such a level, dissipates considerable energy in futile pseudogestures mainly aimed at avoiding loss of face. Little energy therefore remains to initiate planning work at the lower levels of abstraction for which the group in question or other groups working under it have adequate training and maturity.

The outside consultant's task under these conditions is obviously very difficult, though he could possibly succeed in his task by adopting a two-pronged approach comprising both the pseudolevel and the actual capacity level, with the emphasis on the latter. At the pseudolevel, he will have to induce the group to abandon the make-believe approach and to operate, under his guidance, at, say, one level below the artificial nominal level. At actual capacity level, he will try to induce a corresponding elevation of the level of abstraction of planning. In due course, the two approaches will meet and the deadlock will be overcome.

By adopting these approaches, the outside catalyst will have a dual "therapeutic" impact:

1. He will be instrumental in establishing a more adequate overall development plan, conceived by him at an appropriate level of abstraction, while still sizing down the short-term programs to be handled by the planning group to a manageable level of abstraction.
2. He will gradually raise the level of abstraction of the planning group, inducing it to a progressive elevation of its sights.

THE ROLE OF THE CATALYZING GROUP

In the following, we shall elaborate upon these two aspects of the therapeutic impact of the outside catalyst in relation to problem situations encountered in planning in developing countries. Such planning is often carried out at abstraction levels two or three; hence the planner, operating from what might best be termed a frog's-eye view, is able to discern only specific concrete and localized problems, and consequently seeks specific localized solutions by operating with concepts that are both concrete and static. The planner, confined by his blinkers to specific and concrete realities, is thus not able to interlink his specific demand problems with the rest of the economy, nor is he able to interlink his supply problem with the overall resources field; consequently, his psychological space is restricted to the specifics of the present situation and its immediate precedents.

While laboring under this disabling lack of proficiency, the resources planner in developing economies is called upon to devise solutions for two types of problems which require an integrated approach:

1. Problems in which the main emphasis is on the economical optimization of engineering solutions
2. Problems involving major social and institutional transformation

These two problem situations are dealt with separately in the following.

In dealing with problems of the first type, the planner, operating at levels two or three, fails to see the relationship of his specific demand variable with related demand fields and the corresponding relationship of the closest and most obvious resources with other related resources fields. This results in an extremely "autarkic" type of solution which is consequently far from the optimum one, and may involve a considerable waste of scarce resources. Since the planner's concepts are concrete, nonspecific, ready-made, and conventional, he comes up with conventional ready-made solutions where custom-made solutions, resulting from a thorough analysis of a sufficiently extended planning space, may be called for. Nevertheless, he usually has little difficulty in passing off his wares to the political level, which is normally subject to the same limitations. In fact, it is simpler to launch second- and third-level programs than higher level ones.

The task of the outside catalyst in such situations is to originate and develop the long-term higher level thinking within an appropriately structured phase space that is the basis for fourth- and fifth-level planning, at least to the extent that it directly relates to imminent decisions. Concurrently, he has to break down this high-level planning sequence into lower level subsequences that are accessible from the level of capacity of abstraction at which the planner can operate or from a slightly higher level. In this manner, the planner, while carrying on actual development planning according to the conventional approach, gains an insight into the next higher level of abstraction. By adhering to this process, planners with the necessary innate capacity will mature gradually to the next higher level of abstraction, while a happy few would, in due course, rise to a still higher level. With the elevation of the level of abstraction, the time span of discretion—the planning horizon—will also grow and, in the terms of Kurt Lewin, the "psychological space" of the planner will be extended to take in a considerable stretch of the anticipated future. At this point, the outside catalyst could suggest the adoption of a formal planning organization and of planning procedures appropriate to the newly developed planning levels.

Limitations in the planner's level of abstraction, however, most seriously impair his ability to deal with the *second type* of problems, involving *major social and institutional change,* such as those encountered in programs for the development of irrigated agriculture. In such programs, as shown elsewhere, a radical transformation on interdisciplinary lines must be planned and implemented and coordination attained between the planned sector and other branches of the economy. A high level of abstraction—levels four to five—is a *sine qua non* for the successful implementation of such a complex interdisciplinary program.

The planner, operating at relatively low levels of abstraction (levels two to three), reacts to this complex situation by selecting out of the complex set of variables only those which he has learned to comprehend and quantify, pretending that these variables constitute the whole problem. Since his conceptual building stones are derived from the hardware capital investment approach of mature economies, he confines himself to hardware aspects, ending up, of course, with hardware islands encircled by a sea of underdevelopment. These islands are doomed to economic aridity unless brought to fruition by concurrent development in the relevant structural and institutional dimensions.

Under these circumstances, the task of the catalyst will be similar in nature to that performed by him in dealing with the first problem situation, though it will be much more comprehensive in scope. On the one hand, he has to create the appropriate overall generalized planning at the higher level of abstraction (close to the fifth level) in order to provide the necessary general framework for detailed lower level planning; on the other hand, he has to break down the nonadditive, multidimensional phase space representing the actual problem situation into one-dimensional, short-term tasks that lie within the planning capacity of the existing planning groups. The growth of conceptual capacity of the planning group can here too be accelerated by making use of those planning blocks which correspond to the prevailing level of abstraction, according to the more comprehensive overall program conceived at a higher level. This higher level, though initially sensed in a vague and unquantified manner, will gradually be conceived in an increasingly more specific and quantified manner. Ultimately, glimpses of a still higher level are opened up which lead to the conceptual framework actually needed for the job.

Initially, in order to institute high-level planning, the catalyst group has to supply all those elements which are missing at the outset; gradually, as individuals with high-level abstraction capacity emerge from the national group of planners, the organization can be restructured and an ever-increasing share of high-level planning assigned to the local group, until this group eventually reaches the position in which it is able to carry on planning at the appropriate level. At this stage, the outside catalyst can be "faded out."

The analysis of planning levels is complicated by the various levels of abstraction at which planning of different sectors within the same economy is carried out. Certain sectors may, for one reason or other, operate at level four, others at level three, and still others at level two. This stratification may give rise to a type of "dual economy" in which one sector will reach a relatively high level of development, while others remain stagnant or regressive. As often occurs, complementary sectors are handled by development planners operating at unequal levels of abstraction, with the result that the more effective planning groups achieve narrow thrusts of development, whose effect, however, is dissipated as a consequence of the lack of support from complementary development. As an example of such dissipated development, we may cite the construction of resource headworks, dams, and other major facilities sufficient to meet the needs of the country for the next thirty years, without significant complementary progress in the subsidiary facilities to distribute the water and to irrigate and drain the land, or in the entire dependent system of facilities, services and transformations connected with the use of water or with other aspects of the agricultural production process.

The discouraging side to such "dual" or "plural" planning level economies is that the divergence of levels tends to widen with time, unless systematic remedial action is taken at the prompting of an appropriately higher level of planning, a level that could conceive and control all relevant sectors of the economy, as well as their interconnection with the rest of the economy. The mechanism apparently at work in perpetuating these sectorial divergences in development appears to be similar to that operating at maintaining the dual-economy type phenomena within two regions of the same country or at preserving the economic differences between different countries: success attracts resources and high-quality manpower and gives birth to the appropriate political ideology.

All these factors tend to push the successful sector still farther forward, sometimes even beyond the needs of the foreseeable future, leaving the ailing supporting sectors devoid of resources and political interest, and thus increasing the disequilibrium between basic and supporting sectors. Sometimes the "progressive" sector acquires power, resources, and planning insight to such an extent that it is likely to engulf the organizations of the supporting ailing sectors, incorporating them into one overall organization, for which the progressive sector provides the appropriate high-level long-term planning and control, which has developed over the years. However, such "conquests" are not always the consequence of actual planning superiority; sometimes centralized types of organization are set up, at the recommendation of expatriate advisers, on the naïve assumption that conceptual inadequacy can be cured by adopting an organizational structure patterned for an adequate conceptual level. This pseudotherapy leads only to the creation of pseudolevels of abstraction and the appurtenant pseudogestures, to which we have referred earlier.

PREVENTIVE MEASURES

We have so far touched only upon the diagnosis and therapy of the pathology of planning, and it is now necessary to outline a "preventive medicine" to minimize the effects of such maladjustments in emergent economies.

An effective way of avoiding in the developing countries the consequences of planning conducted at inadequate levels and, at the same time, contributing to a systematic improvement of the planner's capacity of abstraction would be to scale down program complexity during the maturation period of the abstracting capacity of the planner to an extent that could be reconciled with achieving basic program objectives. In such program sequences, the requirements for high-level planning are relatively small in the earlier programs, and increase only to the extent that the necessary high-level planning capacity can be developed as a by-product of the development process. Even such scaled-down programs, it is true, require, from the outset, a certain amount of metaplanning in order to make the necessary overall choices and establish the necessary strategies; however, this metaplanning can usually be achieved with the assistance of foreign advisers or consultants. Thus, metaplanning and intermediate-level capacities gradually evolve as program sequences are implemented. As these higher level planning capacities grow, more comprehensive and more ambitious programs can be adopted, provided they are justified economically and otherwise.

It is, of course, impossible to give generally valid rules for the drawing up of development programs guided by such principles, since every situation requires its own individual solution, though the kind of considerations that should be applied when drawing up such program sequences can be indicated. In the earlier programs, emphasis should be placed upon increasing the efficiency of resources actually in use and on the creation of the sociopsychological, institutional, and organizational infrastructure for agricultural production. Subsequent programs should concentrate on the development of locally available resources and continue the preinvestment type of infrastructural development of the earlier programs. Only after reaching the requisite planning capacity will major development and resettlement programs be initiated.

The adoption of these or similar approaches complies with the basic pragmatic rule (or heuristic) that increasing the growth capacity of a nation—and raising planning levels is certainly an important part of this growth capacity—should be considered as one of the more important instrumental objectives of development. A deeper understanding of the quantitative relationship of this capacity to the economic outcomes of programs would put us in a position to incorporate these functional relationships in our planning model.

4

THE ANALYTICAL VS. THE IDEOLOGICAL APPROACH

There is, it seems to us,
At best only a limited value
In the knowledge derived from experience
The knowledge imposes a pattern and falsifies
For the pattern is new in every moment
And every moment is a new and shocking
Valuation of all we have been

T. S. ELIOT (*Four Quartets—East Coker*)

POLARITY OF PROBLEM-SOLVING ATTITUDES

In the previous chapter, we dealt, in the main, with the psychology of the individual problem solver; in this chapter we shall deal with the *sociopsychological aspects of problem solving*. These sociopsychological aspects are no less important than those related to the psychology of the individual, since problem solving in modern society is conducted mostly within social groups, and, consequently, the individual decision maker is greatly influenced by his social conditioning.

The problem solving dealt with in this chapter is actually encountered in project and program planning and is not, of course, the theoretical problem solving carried on by university or other research teams.

Even the most naïve idealist would find it difficult to classify problem solving and decision making as a purely rational activity. Indeed, a close look at problem solving and decision patterns shows these to consist of a complex and shaggy tangle of idiosyncrasies, bias, and warp which is put forward as making up a purely rational analysis. In order to deal with these deviations from the path of "ideal" rational problem solving, we must first set up a classification which will enable us to rate problem solving and decision making according to their true relevance to the problem we face.

To this end, three continuous scales or axes are proposed; these, like most scales adopted for the rating of complex social phenomena, are interrelated, and though their disjuncture may seem arbitrary, they, nevertheless, assist us in classifying decision anomalies and, through such classification, bring us closer to determining the cause or origin of these phenomena and to their diagnosis. The low ratings on these scales, i.e., those ratings which are inadequate for attaining effective development, are conceived to lie at the left end of the scales, and the high or desirable ratings at the right end. The three scales are:

1. The *level-of-insight scale,* indicating the amount of insight involved in a problem-solving operation. Stereotype and generic routines would be at the left end of this scale; skills in the center; and true rational analysis, tailored according to the requirements of each specific situation, at the right end.
2. The *level-of-abstraction scale,* indicating the extent of generalization and abstraction applied. The immediate concrete objectives in our direct line of sight would lie at the left end of this scale; intermediate objectives, involving a "halfway" level of abstraction, in the center; and universal and long-term aims at the right extreme.
3. The *level-of-authenticity scale,* indicating the extent to which the manifest objectives differ from latent extant objectives. Adherence to senseless "pseudo-objectives,"[1] i.e., tools tentatively adopted in the past with the view to achieving specific ideological objectives and which have been transformed over time into independent objectives, would lie at the left end of this scale; oscillation between "pseudo" and "extant" objectives at the center; and clearly conceived extant objectives at the right extreme.

Since these scales attempt to measure deviations from ideal analytical problem solving, they will tend to converge at the right or "desirable" end, which represents "true" analytical problem solving.

The basic dichotomies inherent in problem solving, when treated from the analytical as against the ideological approach, can be traced back to the habitual adoption by the *analytical problem solver* of points at the *right end* of our three scales, as apposed to the selection by the *ideological problem solver* of points at the *left end* of the scales.

The analytical problem solver is accustomed to looking at every situation without bias or "set"; he attempts to diagnose situations, to define objectives, and to devise the appropriate means and tools to achieve these objectives. Expressed in cybernetic terms, he provides himself with the *requisite response variety* demanded by the situation.

The *ideological problem solver,* on the other hand, introduces his bias early in the diagnostic and data-collection phase; his objectives are prefabricated, a priori type of goals, dictated by his ideological indoctrination; by cutting down his conceptual operations to a limited number of preset response patterns, he *reduces his response variety* to a level which, for most situations, is below the required minimum. On the other hand, his attitude, as a rule, gains in forcefulness and pungency what it loses in rigor and authenticity. We shall return to this important aspect of ideological problem solving

[1] Aurel David, *La Cybernétique et l'Homme,* Collection Idées, Éditions Gallimard, Paris, 1965.

in the following section in which ideological problem solving is described in greater depth.

THE IDEOLOGICAL PROBLEM-SOLVING ATTITUDE

Etiology Ideological problem-solving attitudes are socially conditioned response patterns in which preset, a priori type of problem-solving stereotypes are combined with and grafted upon self-transcending emotions, i.e., emotional sets which transcend the narrow boundaries of the self, reflecting man's dependence upon family, tribe, church, and society.[2] These self-transcending emotional sets may, in turn, have their origins in one of the following:

1. Political, religious, or combined doctrines, relying for their justification on revelation or on "sacred" axioms treated as if they were revelations
2. Social traditions representing fossils of originally pragmatic decision patterns which have outlived their usefulness
3. Professional "guild" doctrines which lay down basic professional codes of problem solving

Ideological attitudes, being rooted in emotionally highly energized parts of the personality of man, are highly change resistant. This is both their strength and their weakness: their strength because the psychological energy provided by the major ideological systems contributes motivation and drive, where other energy sources are lacking; their weakness because this very energy charge causes the problem solver to overrate the adequacy of his intellectual tools and induces him to distort his interpretation of the situation rather than to change his decision tools and patterns.

However, the energy charge of ideological problem-solving patterns is not the only obstacle to their modification. The "test proofness" of ideological systems is the second important obstacle to change since no observational or theoretical evidence is ever accepted as disproof of an ideological set, and whoever attempts to disprove such a set is branded as a revisionist, a deviationist, a paid agent of the opposite ideology, or an amateur.

At this stage, we can conclude only that it is indeed difficult to determine for each specific case how much economic utility and intellectual honesty it is worth surrendering in order to make use of the energy charge of existing ideological systems.

Pathology Drawing a "red herring" across the field of judgment is the basic pathological mechanism underlying ideological problem-solving attitudes. The role of the red herring is here played by artificial constraints which are implanted into our reasoning by ideologies, thus distracting our attention from the straightforward path of reasoning. These constraints of reasoning can be defined as extremely unbalanced selections of reference points on the

[2] This concept is admirably presented by Arthur Koestler in his recent book *The Ghost in the Machine,* Hutchinson, London, 1967, p. 190.

scales of problem solving described above, which incline to the left—geometrically, of course, and not politically—rather than to the right end of these scales. These selections lead to three types of (again overlapping) fallacies which can be considered to constitute the intellectual stock-in-trade of ideological problem solving:

1. Substituting dogmas, arbitrary ideological axioms, and professional routines for objectives
2. Substituting intermediate objectives for overriding system objectives
3. Substituting pseudoobjectives for true system objectives

The first type of fallacy is closely related to that expressed in Bacon's "Idols of the Theatre," idols which have "immigrated into men's minds from the various dogmas of philosophies" and from "many principles and axioms of science, which by tradition, credulity, and negligence have come to be received."

A typical example of ideological problem solving incorporating this fallacy is the construction of a legislative system upon a priori types of doctrine, instead of upon the actual requirements of the society or of the program; other examples are the establishment of constraints to resources-development programs on the basis of conservation doctrines and the overemphasis on capital-intensive projects through neglect, for political reasons, of a proper evaluation of the opportunity cost of capital.

The organizational subdivision of science and education into separate professional schools, faculties, and departments and the resultant "unionization" of science have probably played a decisive role in the setting up of professional single-discipline dogmas of problem solving.

Any phenomenon that could not be described or explained by such dogmas or could not be observed and measured by conventional yardsticks was not considered as a fitting subject for study. Until recently, study of these phenomena was held to be "out of bounds" for academic science, and any effort in the direction of integration was labeled as amateurish and lacking in rigor. Whatever could not be fitted into the Procrustean bed of scientific dogma, and, in fact, anything not given to quantification, was just swept under the carpet.

The second fallacy, the substitution of partial or intermediate objectives for overall system objectives, is also frequently supported. This fallacy expresses itself in selecting one single dimension from among the numerous development dimensions and then raising it to the status of the controlling system dimension. The choice is usually made by following the path of least resistance, i.e., in accordance with a development philosophy that is carried on at a relatively low level of abstraction. The chosen level will usually be that of material concrete targets. As an instance of this approach, a country deciding to increase agricultural production by making available a vital production input, e.g., fertilizers, would emphasize fertilizer manufacturing proper, while neglecting the complex infrastructural aspects, such as distribution, intermediate storage, mixing, sales outlets, farmer credits, applied research, and extension activities. This fallacy can be logically expressed by the following relationship: if a, b, and c are necessary and sufficient preconditions for d, we draw the unwarranted conclusion that solely by providing a, will d come about.

The third fallacy, that of substituting the means for the end, the tool for the target, the pseudoobjective for the true objective, is perhaps the most dangerous one, especially as it rarely occurs in its "chemically pure" form, but generally contains elements of the first and second fallacies (substituting dogma for objectives and intermediate for system objectives). Both variants are often grafted upon political or religious dogma and upon deeply conditioned self-transcending emotional sets. Policies stemming from this type of fallacy usually have a characteristic history: in their formative period (coinciding with the formative period of the political movement creating these policies), the pseudoobjective is recognized as a tool to achieve overall guiding objectives defined by ("concealed" might be a more apposite term) vaguely delineated portmanteau concepts. When the policy—and usually also the political movement responsible for it—reaches its operative phase, the guiding objectives are conveniently left in the ideological cloakroom (which by that time will already house the discarded conceptual luggage of other policies); the pseudoobjective is then officially raised to the status of the true objective.

This third fallacy occurs in two variants: the pseudoobjective can be either an appropriate, i.e., a necessary, but not a sufficient tool or an inappropriate, i.e., an irrelevant, tool to achieve the forgotten original system ojective.

Lenin's policy slogan that socialism equals electrification plus soviets is an example of the first category of pseudoobjectives. Since soviets are outside the scope of this discourse, our comments will be confined to electrification. Electrification is without doubt an important tool in economic progress (and we may assume that such progress is a contributing factor to socialism). However, it must be realized that it is no more than a tool and that overemphasis on one tool will result in the neglect of other requisite tools and will lead to complete disequilibrium of the overall system. The absurdity of the pseudoobjective is shown if we take it to its extreme; if electrification is one of the more important yardsticks of socialism (since the soviets have, in any case, been left long ago in the ideological cloakroom, this is all that remains from Lenin's original formula), then the U.S.A. is obviously the most socialist country in the world.

An example of the second variant of the pseudoobjective is massive collectivization in agriculture. In the original reasoning, collectivization was presumably considered, for ideological reasons, to constitute a necessary, and also a sufficient, tool for increasing agricultural productivity and achieving the desired distribution of the agricultural product. In actual fact, collectivization (at least in its Russian and East-European version) proved to be a very ineffective tool in achieving these objectives. However, in the course of time, the original objectives were lost sight of and collectivization was raised to the status of an objective. Planning efforts were therefore focused on attempts to improve the effectiveness of collectivization by exerting (what proved to be futile) pressures upon participants and by bastardizing the solution with doctrines foreign to the context of the pseudoobjective. In such a chain of development, the obvious way out—that of adopting a more adequate tool—becomes politically the least feasible. In spite of these political difficulties, the latter solution was adopted by some of the East-European countries with considerably better success than that obtained by the application of purely dogmatic solutions. Parallel examples taken from industrial development could, of course, be cited, but these would add nothing new to the argument.

THE ANALYTICAL PROBLEM-SOLVING ATTITUDE

The analytical problem-solving attitude will not be described in detail in this chapter since the remaining chapters of Part 1 are devoted solely to defining this attitude and the other parts describe it, as well as its applications, in more specific terms.

We shall confine ourselves at this point to a short outline of the most characteristic features of the analytical problem-solving attitude juxtaposed with the respective factors of the ideological one.

If the analytical attitude had to be defined in a nutshell, it would best be expressed in E. M. Forster's famous two key words "only connect." A short cookbook type of guide on how to go about it is attempted in the following.

1. The first response of the planner to a problem-solving situation should be not to look for a professional stereotype, or a pseudoobjective, but rather to look out for them and, once identified and diagnosed, to treat them as mental blocks and get rid of them.
2. The objectives included in the planner's terms of reference should then be subjected to a searching analysis, with a view to identifying and exposing objectives stemming from the three types of fallacies of the ideological attitude.
3. The phase space and the planning space of the terms of reference should undergo a similar analysis, with a view to adjusting them to the requirements of the adopted objectives.
4. The solutions conceived in the adopted phase space should be subjected to an analysis of constraints related to those dimensions not included in the phase space proper owing to the lack of quantitative information, and it should be established how these constraints can modify our solutions.
5. Throughout this analysis, it should be borne in mind that all development is carried out by human beings operating on other human beings and that man is a complex animal. Limiting planning to a narrow factual track, exclusively oriented toward a material objective, may be a necessary condition for creating development; it is rarely a sufficient condition.

A wise planner will realize that the incorporation of psychological sideshows may be as important as, or possibly even more important than, the emphasis on the principal one: it is not sufficient to tell people what they ought to do, one must concurrently also create the atmosphere, sets, and motivation to make them want to do it.

The planner is not the only, nor possibly the most important, link in the development chain that is affected by the dichotomy of ideological versus analytical problem solving and decision making. This distinction probably belongs to the executive and political decision hierarchy to which the next chapter will be devoted.

5
THE GAP

L'administration n'est pas le gouvernement . . . .
L'administrateur administre la maladie; il ne la guérit point.[1]

ALAIN (*Propos*)

THE MECHANISM CAUSING THE GAP

We shall attempt in this chapter to determine the causes for the ever-widening *gap between problem solving and political action.* It is an old commonplace that man's capacity as an individual to observe, hypothesize, analyze, diagnose, predict, and synthesize ways and means to manipulate and control his environment has, over historic time, far exceeded the growth of his capacity, when conceived as part of a social organism, to respond, decide, and act according to the findings of his problem solving. If in his knowledge of the physical world, man has traveled vast distances since the period of classical Greece, he has progressed little, if at all, in his political behavior. This will be realized by considering how lost Aristotle would be if, by some feat of science-fiction magic, he were to awaken to find himself in the physics laboratory of a modern university; it would doubtless take him several years to catch up. If, on the other hand, Pericles were to perform the same feat of "time traveling," he would feel absolutely at home in the Presidential Office and would, except, of course, for the language barrier, be in a position to make a successful political appearance on television within a fortnight.

The universal prevalence, in the time and space dimensions, of this gap points to the existence of some *general underlying mechanism,* a mechanism possibly stemming from the very structure of human organization. Its existence may possibly be explained by the different parts of the human personality involved in problem solving and action. Problem solving is predominantly a "rational" activity, i.e., an activity conducted on the verbal-logical level of our mind and taking place mainly in the phylogenetically recent part of the brain; to the extent that older parts participate, their contribution is subjected to the "filtering action" of the new brain structure.

[1] Administration is not government . . . . The administrator administers to the disease; he does not cure it.

Political activity, although conducted at a lower "logical" plane than problem solving, is, nevertheless, a much more complex operation and calls for the maintenance of continuous influence and control over people and groups. For its successful performance, it requires (in addition to the activation of the new brain) the mobilization of those energies accompanying the activities of the old brain structures, paradoxically both those connected with the self-assertive tendencies of man, and those connected with man's self-transcending, outgoing tendencies.

The postulation that the personality profile of the politician must have a minimum ration of intelligence and of the self-assertive complex (ambition, aggressiveness, etc.) is self-evident. Postulation of the self- transcending complex (equivalent here to self-identification with wider social issues and groups) may, however, be doubted. A closer observation of the phenomenon of political leadership will, however, show that it is, in fact, this self-transcending complex (creating the mechanism of political man's identification with a cause or a party, though this need, of course, not be a catholic marriage) which lends the ring of authenticity and charisma to the public appearances of a leader and, finally, provides that admixture of paranoic traits which apparently is part and parcel of great leadership. The need for "a touch of paranoia" has been well put by C. P. Snow in his novel *The Corridors of Power,*[2] "a touch of paranoia (being) a very useful part of one's equipment. On far more people than not, it had a hypnotic effect."

It should be clear from the above that rating criteria for man the problem solver and for man the politician must, therefore, differ: whereas the problem solver must be judged mainly on the basis of his intelligence and creativity, the politician will be judged on a much wider spectrum of personality traits. In brief, this rating must also refer to the extent of dynamic equilibrium that he succeeds in striking between the almost irreconcilable coexisting categories that enter into his "professional personality," i.e., logic-verbal thinking, and the energy-laden emotional universe of self-assertive and self-transcending tendencies.

Man in his problem-solving capacity, operating mainly with the logical and technological tools developed in recent historic times, is predominantly modern, rational man, whereas in his political capacity, laboring under the "schizophysiology"[3] of the human brain, he has to devise an uneasy balance between modern man and his phylogenetic past.

The extent to which the top executive of a hierarchy should be both problem solver and politician is dependent on the type of hierarchy. The more a leader is dependent on the consensus of his own and other hierarchies and on public opinion, the more "political-personality" traits he will require for the attainment of high political office. Politicians who have periodically to put themselves up for public election need a good measure of these political-personality traits. On the other hand, the more the leader's success depends

[2] C. P. Snow, *The Corridors of Power,* Charles Scribners Sons, New York.

[3] Arthur Koestler, *The Ghost in the Machine,* Hutchinson, London, 1967, chap. XVI.

on measurable criteria of performance, the greater his need for the problem-solving complex in his personality mix.

This basic mechanism, assumed in the above as the cause for the ever-growing gap between problem solving and political action, explains why this gap is wider in the underdeveloped than in the more developed economies. The set of problem-solving tools which the technocrat from an underdeveloped country is able to acquire differs little from the set available to his counterpart in the high-income countries. True, the personality of the former may still be deeply rooted in the traditional culture of his society, but it is his set of intellectual tools rather than his personality which determines the quality of his analysis. The politician, on the other hand, in addition to being subjected to the same type of "regression" as his counterpart from the high-income countries, operates within a much cruder and more primitive political framework than that of his counterpart—a framework in which old traditional elements interact with imitated and still undigested new elements to produce an extremely unstable state of coexistence. Hence, the personality admixture required for success in such a political framework must include a much greater share of those traits rooted in the older brain centers; in this lies the explanation for the wider gap between problem solving and political action in the underdeveloped countries.

The mechanism causing the gap is structural and, therefore, completely impersonal, a fact that the problem solver in developed, as well as in underdeveloped, countries is rarely willing to concede. In general, he, the problem solver, ascribes the responses of the politician—responses which appear to him to be irrational and damaging—to the latter's personal wickedness or immorality; living in an ivory tower of technology, he has neither the experience nor the insight to trace the wholly structural nature of the mechanism underlying the politician's behavior. This has perhaps been best expressed by Anatole France in the concluding chapter of his *Revolt of the Angels,* where he claims that, even if pure intellect (personified in the novel by Satan) were to acquire world rule from the political principle (personified by God), he would, within a short time, acquire all the—from the intellectual's point of view—repelling traits and attributes of the political principle.

However, *volens, nolens,* the problem solver must operate in political space, and has to sell his ware to political man; he must, therefore, attempt to understand the workings of the mechanism that makes political man tick. We shall elaborate on this in the following.

PROMOTION IN POLITICAL BUREAUCRACIES

To understand the behavior of political man, we must first investigate the makeup of men who enter the political race, or to put it differently, we must look into the process by which the politician and political executive are selected and promoted.

To explain this process, we propose to draw from the analysis developed by Gordon Tullock[4] who illustrates the *principle of promotion* underlying his model of the political process by analogy with the working principle of a gaseous diffusion plant. The mechanism of this plant consists of a series of chambers, separated by porous membrane barriers, through which a mixture of two gases of different specific weights is diffused, the lighter gases passing through these membranes faster than the heavier gas. Thus, as we move through the series of chambers in the direction of the diffusion process, the concentration of the lighter gas increases.[5]

If we substitute political candidates up for promotion for gases, two (or more) sets of personality traits for the two specific weights, and officials weighing the candidates for promotion for the membranes, we arrive at our promotion model. Tullock's basic thesis is that the overruling "merit" criterion for successful promotion in such a model is the individual's ambition to rise, or his careerism, this trait operating at times under some form of disguise. As promotional "diffusion" proceeds, only those candidates with a high concentration of ambition are promoted. If we assume that the selection also takes into account a second trait, such as intelligence, as a subsidiary merit criterion, this would also be concentrated by the diffusion process. However, if of two candidates A and B up for rating, candidate A has a slightly higher ambition and a slightly lower intelligence than candidate B, then candidate A will be the one to gain promotion. Thus, as we move along the series of diffusion chambers, the intelligence content of candidates will increase at a slower rate than that of ambition.

With this basic promotional mechanism in mind, we can now examine the various patterns of personality traits obtained as a result of such promotional procedures in organizations whose main interest lies in problem solving or in political action.

The performance of every planning and political function requires a certain range of traits in the personality profile that includes intellectual faculties mixed with similar self-assertive and self-transcending tendencies.

To the extent that the function is mainly of the problem-solving type, the personality-profile requirements will, in the main, stress intellectual faculties without, however, foregoing the need for the other two sets. Higher level technological posts, for instance, will require a greater admixture of the self-assertive and self-transcending personality traits.

For political posts in the lower echelons, selection will be based mainly on the self-assertive and, to a minor extent, the self-transcending sets, with intellectual faculty as a "secondary" trait; as we move to the higher ranking political echelons, selection will depend on a balanced combination of intelligence, self-assertion, and self-transcendence.

To put the same thing in differently slanted terminology, selection according to "merit," as usually practiced, consists of a reasonably rational process of selecting according to job requirements, though these requirements vary greatly from technological to political posts, as also from the lower to the

[4] Gordon Tullock, *The Politics of Bureaucracy*, Public Affairs Press, Washington, 1965.
[5] *Ibid.*, pp. 16, 17.

higher echelons of each category. This, of course, does not mean that in a bureaucracy every man is in the right position—no selection mechanism operated by man will ever achieve this—however, it does mean that in a reasonably effective organizational structure, selection is on the average reasonably competent. The average problem solver selected for the various technological echelons constitutes, therefore, a reasonable selection from available resources for the duties he is required to perform, which range from purely problem-solving ones at the lower levels, to a mix of management, motivational, and leadership duties combined with technological problem solving at the higher levels. Similarly, politicians selected at their respective levels also constitute a reasonable selection, from the available position, ensuring that the lower levels have the capacity to influence and manage people and groups, while the higher levels have the capacity to motivate and provide leadership for the lower ones—all, of course, combined with a reasonable capacity for problem solving.

CONSEQUENCES OF THE POLITICAL-PROMOTION PROCESS

It is with the latter activity that our trouble starts, for good problem solving presupposes an adequate level of abstraction—a capacity which, at least in the past, has not ranked highest in the selective "diffusion" process for high political office. It is this dichotomy that causes the "gap," since to be able to make good decisions on major issues, a level of abstraction and insight is required that is rarely found in the holders of high political office. Furthermore, the gap caused by this dichotomy, unless reduced by specific countermeasures, may increase with time, because the requisite level of abstraction and insight has a tendency to rise as the economy develops.

A selection process such as outlined above has a high built-in inertia: the "filters" through which officeholders "diffuse" are the higher echelon officeholders who have themselves been selected by the same rating principles and, consequently, tend to uphold and perpetuate these principles. To this we must account the extreme difficulty of changing the style of a long-established bureau, even when a new minister, with a different management style, takes over. A further contributing factor to the inertia of a bureau style is the "self-prefiltering" process applied by candidates for office, in order to improve their chances of promotion. This prefiltering consists, as a rule, in mimicking bureau style and in filtering out behavior elements that clash with this style.

So far we have dealt with the distortion introduced into the political decision process by the apparently unavoidable limitations in the politicians' conceptual range in relation to problem solving. However, this limitation is not the only, and possibly not the most important, distorting element. By selecting persons for political office on the basis of ambition and other self-assertive tendencies, we place at the top of the political and administrative hierarchy (the destination of the final product of the diffusion process) a concentration of officeholders characterized by the supremacy of personal self-interest; such an unbalanced mix of personality traits is certain to distort decision making on public issues. To reduce the effect of this distortive factor, organizational structure and objectives and performance ratings within organizations should be set up in a way that will minimize the discrepancy between public and personal objectives.

Patterns of personality traits within the top echelons of organizations vary widely; nevertheless, there would appear to be some uniformity resulting from the "age" of organization, on the one hand, and its rate of growth, on the other hand. This theme is pursued by Anthony Downs[6] who has pointed out that as bureaus age, or to the extent that their growth decelerates, the number and influence of officeholders of the more aggressive type in which the self-assertive tendencies predominate, i.e., the "climbers," tend to decline. Vice versa, young or rapidly growing bureaus, as a rule, attract climbers, and the concentration of climbers at the top of the hierarchy is certain to influence the management style of a bureau decisively. Similar tendencies also operate in relation to the problem-solving parts of the organization.

COMMUNICATION BETWEEN THE PROBLEM-SOLVING AND THE POLITICAL SECTORS OF BUREAUCRACIES

We can now turn to the communication aspects between the "two cultures" of our model, the problem solvers and the politicians.

The problem of communication in the underdeveloped countries is an extremely difficult one: professionals, only recently converted to modern technological and economic approaches, find themselves faced by a political decision-making machine which, while it may choose to pay lip service to development dogmas in fashion, especially if they happen to fit in with the professed political philosophy, is, nevertheless, governed by an obsolete power structure and hamstrung by its limited understanding of the complex issues of development. To this we must add that problem solvers in such countries, especially in the early formative period, have a low achievement, a limited perseverance, and an inadequate decision capacity; hence, their contact with the political machine leads to one of the following three outcomes:

1. The problem solvers, by virtue of the intellectual capacity of a leader or by some chance factor, eventually succeed in breaking through the vicious circle of noncommunication between the two cultures and thus in starting a process of circular causation of improving communication. This, however, rarely occurs.
2. The problem solvers yield to despair, become frustrated, and retire into an ivory tower of pseudoplanning activity.
3. The problem solvers despair of coverting the political machine and attempt to adopt the basic attitudes of political man.

It is true that these patterns, in part, are also found in the developed

[6] Anthony Downs, *Bureaucratic Structure and Decision Making*, The Rand Corporation, Santa Monica, Calif., 1966.

countries; however, the tensions between the two cultures in such countries is lessened by the relative narrowness of the gap, by the higher status and access to public opinion of the professional sector, and by their greater achievement orientation, perseverance, and decision capacity. Furthermore, we have to keep in mind the "development paradox," i.e., that development issues in underdeveloped countries are much more complex than similar issues in mature countries, and that demands made upon the political level in connection with development in the latter countries may, therefore, be less exacting than those made upon politicians in the former countries.

Difficulties of communication between the problem solver and the politician can be grouped in three categories:

1. Difficulties arising from those *personality traits* which have brought the politician to his present position. Following these traits, he is likely to give preference to vested interests or, in the extreme case, to act in self-interest rather than along lines of action prescribed by the national interest.
2. Difficulties stemming from political man's *intellectual limitations* in grasping the more abstract and complex aspects of major development issues (limitations which are often shared by the problem solvers), and which bear on the dynamic, multidimensional, nonadditive nature of the phase space of development. Political man (and often to a certain extent also the problem solver) prefers to simplify phase space, to overlook its "nontangible" dimensions, and to concentrate on its "tangible" ones.
3. Difficulties relating to the *time preference* and the related time horizon of planning. The politician, for a number of reasons, has a higher time preference, and therefore a higher "discount" rate to allow for his time preference, than the planner. Uncertainty as to what the future will bring and the relatively short time span allocated to an administration are perhaps the most important of these reasons.

A major effort must, therefore, be made on both sides to bring about a significant improvement in communications. The planner must be made to understand that his yardsticks, his coins, are not those of the politician; vice versa, the politician must realize at least the basic fact that programs as he himself envisages them cannot, for inherent structural reasons, lead to the kind of growth rate that he would like to see achieved. For obvious reasons, the major burden falls upon the planner since to make his program politically feasible he has to transpose it into terms that make sense to the politician. On the one hand, this may require that the program mix be "downgraded" until it becomes acceptable to the politician; on the other hand, that expected benefits be recoded into the politician's success coin. Hence, the planner may have to downgrade by increasing time preference (i.e., by emphasizing immediate production aspects), giving priority to projects with low initial investments, giving preference to politically sensitive regions, and incorporating, where possible, pet political ideas or projects. As for the recoding of political benefits, this may call for the translation of project analysis and alternative action into the prevailing political semantics.

ORGANIZATIONAL DISTORTION AND ITS CONSEQUENCES

The direct downgrading of planning caused by the intervention of the political level into the planning process is not the only, and possibly not even the most damaging effect. This distinction is probably due to the indirect long-term effect of the *inadequate and ineffective organizational* structure imposed by the political level upon government, science, and technology. The political level tends to transfer its static, single-discipline, additive concepts of the development process into the organizational structure set up to plan and implement development into the institutes of science and technology, and into government departments; in these latter departments, considerations of political arithmetic will also support the tendency for compartmentalization and dismemberment of organization. The warp thus introduced pervades the entire planning process until a vicious circle is formed: inadequate thinking is mirrored in inadequate organization; inadequate organization causes further planning distortions.

Once such an organizational structure of development planning and implementation has struck roots, it becomes fossilized and canonized by vested interest groups and by senior officials' interest in its perpetuation; its further propagation becomes then the paramount issue for such officials. Thus, the political level creates a reinforcing feedback for the attitudes that it represents, attitudes which are much more effective since they originate from the most respected social groups in the community, i.e., the scientific and technological establishment.

6

THE AGE OF METAPLANNING: A SYNTHESIS

The piano tuner has been in the house for a long time now, and the hour has come for a sonata to be played or even a concerto.

PHILIP TOYNBEE

COMMON CAUSES OF DISTORTION IN PLANNING

In the preceding chapters, an attempt has been made to analyze the range and capacity of the individual instruments which, together, constitute the orchestra of planning. This analysis indicated that most of our instruments are out of tune, while even those in tune, when played solo, do not possess sufficient variety of expression to reproduce the complexity and momentum of the actual phase space. We must, therefore, ensure that all the available instruments are harmonized in one orchestra if we are to obtain the required range of expression. In this chapter, concluding Part 1, some tentative comments will be offered on the "theory of orchestration"; Part 2 represents an attempt to compose a "sonata" based on this theory.

Semantics, levels of abstraction, models and their transfer, the dichotomies of ideology versus analysis and of analysis versus politico-executive decision making—all these are partial aspects, each reflecting the general inadequacy of conception and representation of the development process. These aspects were examined separately in the previous chapters. An integrative theory of representation must expose the underlying common etiology and the distortion introduced into analysis by such partial representation and point out ways to an integrated representation.

The distortion of representation encountered in development thinking as actually practiced in the developing world stems from the following two sources:

1. Inadequate structure of the phase space under investigation; in other words, the type and number of dimensions selected for the mapping of the development process are deficient.

2. Inadequate system definition; here, the definition, in space and time, of the boundaries that separate the system under investigation from "environmental" systems is too restrictive, and insufficient allowance is made for interconnection across the interface with environmental systems.

By use of the vague qualification "inadequate," we acknowledge our inability to give a more rigorous and generally applicable rule of what can be considered an "adequate" determination. The numerous factors involved in the representation of development processes make it extremely difficult, if not impossible, to devise such a rule. Nevertheless, a few heuristically conceived comments on this complex subject are given in the following.

Let us first turn to the adequacy of the structure of the phase space; here, our first consideration should be to achieve a structural similarity between the essential processes to be represented and our representational grid. The adoption of a homomorphic relationship, i.e., a relationship which, while simplifying and abstracting to the necessary extent, still maintains the principal operational similarity, would satisfy this requirement. The most frequent distortion that creeps in here is due to the adoption of a mechanistic kind of *model,* i.e., a model that bases explanation of the development process on predetermined overall strategies which, it is assumed, fully explain the behavior of all subassemblies. In its place, a biological or cybernetic model is required representing a system of self-regulating subassemblies, interacting in accordance with instructions issued by a controlling center, and itself governed by feedbacks from the subassemblies. Indeed, Stafford Beer has already advocated the introduction of such models into management science, and similar approaches have also been adopted in recent development literature.[1]

The second consideration associated with the definition of the phase space is related to the selection of the *representational dimensions.* The most frequent error here is that of omission, a neglect of the more complex and possibly even the controlling dimensions.

Regarding the adequacy of the definition of the *boundaries of our actual planning space,* we must bear in mind that too restrictive a definition may obscure important medium-term and long-term trends, while awareness of such trends may be essential for effective decision making, as also required for immediate action.

The root of both types of distortion lies in an insufficient level of abstraction and in too restricted an angle of vision: our point of view, from within the subsystem, is too narrow and prevents us from seeing enough of the overall system in order to properly grasp the mutual interrelationship of the subsystems and main systems. The proper perspective can be obtained only by taking up a higher level of abstraction, by adopting a metalanguage.

THE NECESSITY OF METAPLANNING AND ITS LIMITATIONS

The basic thesis of the first part of this book is that a wider application of metaplanning, both in the developed and in the developing parts of the world, has now become a necessity. Application of metaplanning is essential if we

[1] Stafford Beer, mainly in his *Decision and Control,* John Wiley & Sons, Inc., New York, 1966.

are to achieve a satisfactory development rate in the Third World and to halt, in the developed countries, the serious trends toward imbalance that can already be observed in some aspects of urban growth.

Delay in the adoption of metaplanning in the *Third World* will lower productivity of investments and slow down the rise of growth capacity—the necessary preconditions for the emergence of a sustained growth process.

As for the *developed countries,* delay in the introduction of metaplanning will favor a hypertrophy of tendencies to pollute, corrupt, dull, coarsen, equalize, and generally devalue our physical and mental environment beyond our capacity to control, correct, improve, and integrate. From this we may conclude that lack of metaplanning will lead, in the course of time, to runaway conditions in both the low-income and the high-income economies.

The concept of "metaplanning" implies a juxtaposition of the elevated point of view of the metaplanner and of the "frog's-eye" point of view of the planner of a subsystem; the existence of metaplanning presupposes:

1. That there is "somebody" who can set "desirable" aims and goals toward which the overall system should move
2. That this personality is endowed with sufficient intelligence to command the whole system
3. That his reasoning can cope with the numerous interrelated dimensions of our phase space
4. That, last but not least, he is "benevolent," truly imbued with the desire to lead society toward the "desirable" goals

In short, this *homo planificans* must combine the qualities of prophet and philosopher king and, at the same time, be a well-integrated human being.

To describe the axiomatic presuppositions of metaplanning, we have used loose descriptive terms drawn from everyday language, since if we attempted at this stage to use more rigorous definitions, we would be faced with the difficulty of infinite regressions: every term would point toward a more general one, and this one toward a still more general one, and so on ad infinitum.

We would come up against infinite regression in the definition of aims, of phase space dimensions, of boundaries in space and time, in fact, in practically every basic aspect of our metaplanning activity. Ultimately, everything is connected with everything else, operations in one point of space influence operations at all other points of space, and we must assume that all past interventions will influence all operations planned for the future. Thus, truly comprehensive planning requires a Laplacian Godlike intelligence possessing the "differential equation" and the "boundary conditions" of (at least) the globe, and being able from there to predict the future behavior of humanity and its environment.

Many years ago, Leon Trotsky, one of the cleverest of dogmatists, derided the self-identification of the planning bureaucracy with such an all-knowing Godlike intelligence. In his words,[2]

[2] Quoted by A. Waterston, *Development Planning,* The Johns Hopkins Press, Baltimore, 1965.

If there existed a universal mind that projected itself into the scientific fancy of Laplace, a mind that could register simultaneously all the processes of nature and society, that could measure the dynamics of their motion, that could forecast the results of their interaction, such a mind, of course, could a priori draw up a faultless and an exhaustive economic plan, beginning with the number of hectares of wheat and down to the last button for a vest. In truth, the bureaucracy often conceives that just such a mind is at its disposal.

Although modern science fiction may claim that the science of systems, automation, and the use of giant computers have brought us much closer to such utopian planning,[3] one thing is certain, namely, that an all-inclusive interdisciplinary analysis cannot be undertaken in the initial and early phases of development when it is most needed.

The model of society decried in the above quotation is but a caricature of the historic-materialistic tradition of representing society as a complex machine that blindly executes operations imposed upon it by a controlling program drawn up by the ruling bureaucracy. It is upon such a mechanistic model of society that the communistic state planning lampooned by Trotsky is based.

Suffering from the professional deformation of lifelong conditioning by the dogma of historic materialism, he notices the exaggerations but not the structural incompatibility of the mechanistic type model of society. He, nevertheless, points to the absurdity of expecting that such a science-fiction social machine can reach its target and, at least by implication, recognizes the necessity of adopting a different approach to planning, whereas the planning bureaucracies he describes would, of course, when faced with failure, resort to futile "modifications" and "remakings" of society in order to make it behave according to their prediction.

True metaplanning, however, in contrast to Trotsky's caricature of mechanistic planning, confines its attempts at control to the principal coordinative aspects of subsystems; furthermore, metaplanning is not rigid or static but flexible and adaptive, and is constantly modified by information feedbacks from lower levels. Thus, the metaplanner does not pretend, and is not required, to know everything; it is sufficient if the decision "system" as a whole "knows" and reacts, at its several levels, to the stimuli of the environment.

Such a cybernetic conception, although it reduces some of our structural perplexities, nevertheless does not provide the answers to the most vexing questions: Who should define our paramount welfare function and how? *Quis custodiet ipsos custodes?* (How should we guard the guards themselves?) How are we to avoid the corruption of power? But should we, in fact, be looking for perfect models or for "ultimate" answers? Are we not deluding ourselves by assuming that such universally valid answers exist?

But let us come back to the present. The requisite and feasible level of metaplanning to be adopted depends on the complexity of the operation, the

[3] John Barth's farcical utopia of a computer-controlled society, *Giles Goat-Boy,* illustrates that such a society may not be more attractive than the present-day world.

structural maturity of the organization, the quality and amount of information, and the intelligence of the planners. As a rule, the level of metaplanning should rise with time and with the increase in maturity of society; this will involve a gradual increase in the scope and time horizon of planning to the extent necessary for securing the required overall control. What is needed, in fact, is not an increase in the depth of control from the top, reaching, in time, to the lowest levels of the decision hierarchy, but rather the building up of a gradually growing superstructure of controls, encompassing and coordinating partly self-regulating subsystems, until this controlling superstructure encompasses the national economy as a whole and, from there, spreads to a regional supranational grouping.

This concept may sound rather utopian in a world reverberating with the strife of political, religious, and racial dogma. The paranoia of dogma, so aptly described in Koestler's *The Ghost in the Machine,*[4] should not, however, blind us to the fact that a considerable measure of high-level metaplanning is, in fact, already practiced under various guises. As instances of this metaplanning, we may quote regulative anticyclical planning, national integrative planning, supranational regional economic planning, regulation of the world monetary systems, aid to the underdeveloped countries, and international commodity agreements. All these are at least partially successful, fragmentary attempts at metaplanning at various levels; such attempts are, in fact, on the increase, and nothing, in the long run, can reverse this process.

AIMS, OBJECTIVES, AND TARGETS OF METAPLANNING

The selection of planning objectives is the most important, but, at the same time, the most vexing and problematic part of metaplanning.

At the outset, let us define our terms: by aims, we refer to the desirable overall, long-term states of society, expressed in interdisciplinary, multidimensional style; by objectives, to the still unquantified long-term states of society, expressed in a single planning dimension, usually an economic or social one; and by targets, the quantified objectives of short-term to medium-term programs.

The term "goal setting" will be used to refer to these three terms. However, whatever time horizon we use in our goal setting, we shall still be faced with major structural difficulties; if we choose the narrower short-term targets to guide our programs, we shall miss the main point of metaplanning—that of commanding a wider view of our decision options and of time. If, on the other hand, we are guided by long-term interdisciplinary aims, we are again up against infinite regression, since any aim we choose will point toward a more comprehensive one. However difficult a task, selection of planning aims, objectives, and targets still remains the most essential part of planning. Although it is true that the success of programs depends as much on our capacity to implement as on the appositeness of our selection of objectives, if our selection of objectives is wrong it will be of little consolation to know

[4] Arthur Koestler, *The Ghost in the Machine,* Hutchinson, London, 1967.

that all our efforts have brought us to a point where we really did not want to go.

The first question that poses itself here is, At which end should we start our analysis? The logical choice would be to start with aims. However, the difficulty with selecting aims, as defined today by the current value-imposing dogmas, is that their definition may be so vague and general as to be almost meaningless from the operative point of view.

Objectives may, therefore, be a better point of departure, especially if we attempt gradually to broaden our angle of view to encompass wider aims. The first difficulty in taking objectives as the point of departure lies in the selection of the yardstick with which to express our objectives. The yardstick used will usually be determined by the professional background of the planner. In most cases, a lower level planning and what true metaplanning there exists are usually carried out by economists; the yardstick adopted is therefore an economic one, such as the per capita GNP of a nation. Some schools of thought also allow for distribution of the product and introduce welfare type of objectives. However, man is not only a consuming mechanism, and there is no reason to believe that optimizing consumption will also always optimize man's operational level related to other aspects of his personality. If metaplanning were conducted by psychologists, and there might be a number of valid reasons for such a choice, they would certainly propose different objectives, and programs based on such objectives might prove to be more meaningful than those stemming from economic optimization—assuming, of course, that our models of human behavior and responses would be better than they are today. After all, physical survival is certainly one of the overriding aims of a society, and psychological considerations are as relevant as economic ones to the "survival capacity" of nations—at least in the jungle of paranoic responses in which man has lived since the dawn of history.

Our real trouble starts, of course, when we begin to realize the multidimensional structure of every aim and the interrelation of these dimensions: to remain with our economics-psychology dichotomy, economic performance is, to a great extent, dependent on psychological factors, and psychological factors are, vice versa, modified by economic ones. The obvious solution, of course, consists in setting up a new dimension combining the partial utility functions of the two composite objectives into one aggregate function; but what yardstick would we use for such an aggregate function and what algebraic laws of operation would we postulate? As long as we have no answer to these and similar questions, we shall have to put up with the present basic limitation of optimizing, that is, choosing objectives for which valid yardsticks and algebras exist, and introduce other objectives as constraints.

GOAL SETTING AND THE POLITICAL HIERARCHY

Another major difficulty related to the selection of aims and objectives stems from the fact that, while it is obvious that such selections are made at the top of the political hierarchy, it cannot be assumed that the highest intelligence, the highest capacity of abstraction, the greatest freedom from mental blocks, and the greatest personal integrity are to be found at the top—except in a utopian society. Gordon Tullock in *The Politics of Bureaucracy*[5] and Anthony Downs in *Bureaucratic Structure and Decision-Making*[6] have both demonstrated that the criteria for moving to the top of the bureaucratic and political hierarchies are very different from those which would be required for "good" objective selection, if such a demonstration were still needed.

What is more, the top level of the political hierarchy will often find it difficult, if not impossible, to define a truly compatible and meaningful set of aims and objectives that fits its own society. Here, one of the first duties of the metaplanner will be to explore the underlying social and psychological mechanisms of political goal setting, to *lire pour autrui* (read for, or on behalf of, others) to use Aurel David's apt term,[7] to analyze their applications in terms accessible to the political decision maker, to point out their internal incompatibilities and discrepancies, and to evaluate the consequences of the alternative lines of action actually open for choice. Such an exercise would amount to tracing—in the tangled network of political dogma and rhetoric—the actual choices open to a specific society. It may be asked whether this roundabout way is the best method for obtaining "good" choices; but this question is academic, because the top of the political hierarchy happens to be the place where actual decisions are made.

Furthermore, the improvement of the political decision mechanism that will result from such a *lire pour autrui* operation may be more important for society than the direct benefits reaped by an improved specific decision itself. To achieve such an improvement, the metaplanner must define his alternative choices and outcomes in terms and metrics that are meaningful to the decision maker. It would, for example, be meaningless to ask the decision maker what probabilities he felt should be attached to a number of possible outcomes. On the other hand, it would be most meaningful to ask him whether he felt that a certain additional capital outlay was justified in order to provide a specific solution with the requisite flexibility.

Although we have pointed out some of the pragmatic bypasses around some of the intrinsic structural difficulties of goal setting, the basic problem still remains: that of selection of aims. Obviously, this most important part of planning does not lend itself to full scientific analysis, and it is (has been, and most probably will be) vested in the hands of a caste that has intrinsically little chance of hitting unaided upon the "right path." Nietzsche[8] described the former limitation almost a hundred years ago.

[5] Gordon Tullock, *The Politics of Bureaucracy,* Public Affairs Press, Washington, 1965.

[6] Anthony Downs, *Bureaucratic Structure and Decision-Making,* The Rand Corporation, Santa Monica, Calif., 1966.

[7] Aurel David, *La Cybernétique et l'Humain,* Collection des Idées, Éditions Gallimard, Paris, 1965, p. 77.

[8] Friedrich Nietzsche, *Die Unschuld des Werdens* (*der Nachlass*), vol. II, p. 3, Aphorism 3, Alf. Kröner Verlag, Stuttgart, 1956. (Science has brought us many benefits; now we are about to submit to it wholly, out of mistrust toward religion and related disciplines. What fallacy! *Science cannot be normative,* it cannot point a direction, it can be of use only when one knows one's course. Generally speaking, it is mythology to assume that science will always find out what is most useful and vital to mankind—it may, in fact, be as harmful as beneficial. The highest form of morality might possibly be impossible to attain in broad daylight.)

Die Wissenschaft hat viel Nutzen gebracht, jetzt moechte man, in Misstrauen gegen die Religion und Verwandtes, sich ihr *ganz unterwerfen. Aber* Irrtum! *Sie kann* nicht befehlen, *wegweisen; sondern erst wenn man weiss wohin? kann sie nuetzen. Im allgemeinen ist es Mythologie, zu glauben dass die Erkenntnis immer das, was der Menschheit am nuetzlichsten und unentbehrlichsten sei, erkennen werde—sie wird eben so schaden koennen als nuetzen—die hoechsten Formen der Moralitaet sind vielleicht unmoeglich bei voller Helle.*

Can our ultimate aims (which may, for want of something better, be defined from a heuristic, intuitional point of view as ensuring survival as a race at the highest possible operational level) be reconciled with our present propensity to confine planning to maximizing the GNP, while neglecting sociopsychological dimensions and the quality of our environment? Are we, in the more developed countries, as Galbraith so forcefully claims, not buying a high GNP at too high a price, involving, possibly fateful, deterioration of sociopsychological space and environment? Are we, in the absence of self-corrective mechanisms, not leading man on a suicidal course? Are we not set upon a course of optimizing mankind out of existence?

DEVELOPMENT OBJECTIVES OF LOW-INCOME COUNTRIES

Low-income countries have at least one advantage: they do not have to worry too much about existential long-term aims. Here, at least, one thing is clear, namely, that short-term and medium-term targets must be substantially achieved before it will be meaningful to introduce long-term goal setting. Achievement of reasonable nutritional, educational, housing, clothing, and leisure levels must precede attempts to set comprehensive and more sophisticated aims. However, even in the developing countries, the planner has to face a number of important alternatives. The most important of these alternatives, related to the development of primary resources, lies between the expansion of the "classical" means of production (land, water, capital, and labor) and the improvement of the nontangible means of production, the growth capacity.[9] Choice of the former emphasizes maximization at short range of the product generated by society, without paying overmuch attention to the continuity of the development process. On the other hand, choice of the latter stresses the permanent and cumulative improvement of response patterns of individuals, groups, and institutional decision hierarchies to growth stimuli with a view to creating a growth-oriented society. In actual fact, no program belongs completely to one or the other type; every program comprises a certain mix of production and capacity goal setting. Determination in the program mix of the right proportion of the two goal-setting attitudes is one of the most vexing problems of planning in developing countries; this problem will be treated in more detail in Part 2.

[9] Alexander and Adler have pointed out the importance in developing countries of improving the "absorptive capacity," a term similar to that used here, but slightly narrower in its implications. Japanese national planning has also put heavy emphasis on long-term structural features.

METAMORPHOSIS OF OBJECTIVES

Life must be lived forwards, but can only be understood backwards.

KIERKEGAARD

Selection of goals has so far been treated as a static once-for-all type of activity, whereas in reality aims and objectives, of course, also change, this change introducing a new dimension of complexity.

Aims and objectives are selected in accordance with the goal-setting tendencies of societies, based on sets of values which may be conceived partly in rigorous quantitative metrics, partly in specific nonquantified terms, and partly in nonspecific dogmatic sets intertwined with emotional complexes. This mixed bag of values will be referred to as the *goal-setting complex.*

Societies are subject to continuous changes, these changes possibly arising from one or more of the following reasons:

1. They may be the outcome of a gradual or sudden (revolutionary) shift in the sociopolitical structure, with the result that different strata of society move to the top of the decision hierarchy, bringing with them their own goal-setting complexes.
2. They may be the outcome of the spillover effect upon the political-decision hierarchy of large-scale development.
3. They may be due to mimicry which often plays a major role, political systems often preferring to identify themselves with a prevailing political dogma and adopting the appropriate goal-setting complexes, lock, stock, and barrel.

Thus, metaplanning must allow for the fact that aims and objectives are themselves not stationary, partly for reasons not directly connected with the development process planned, partly as a consequence of the development process. Conceptually, a development process may be represented by the transformation or transfer functions, representing the changes required to turn an existing socioeconomic system from its status quo into the desired goal system.

In countries where development requires major structural transformations, the definition of goal-setting complexes and of the transfer functions will, in turn, have to be broken down into viable intermediate targets and intermediate transfer functions (leading from one intermediate viable target to another). Since goal systems (and transfer functions connected with them) are conceived as continuously changing, the development process forms a sequence of transformations which, when looked at from any intermediate or from what we have defined as the goal (ex post) point of view, looks very different from what it looked like from the original (ex ante) point of view. In other words, the actual trajectory of development will differ considerably from the line originally conceived.

This qualification still leaves us one last fallacy to dispose of: that of the existence of a final goal position at the time horizon. Nowadays, we conceive development as a continuous process, assuming that the existence of a goal system is a matter of planning convenience. If the time horizon is sufficiently distant, little distortion is introduced into planning by introducing a time boundary (and its corresponding goal position), especially if we make appropriate allowance for continuity of the process by selection of appropriate "boundary conditions." However, as we approach the goal point, the distortion caused by the introduction of the time horizon may become significant; to avoid this distortion, the time horizon must be reset and a new, more distant goal system adopted, thus demoting the original goal to an intermediate goal.

The distortion introduced into planning by confining analysis to a specific program strictly limited in time, rather than undertaking analysis of the continuous development process, has more serious consequences in developing than in developed countries. This is because the generation of cumulative growth processes in the developing countries is dependent on the materialization of gradual cumulative transformation processes extending over considerable periods of time—hence, the importance of the conception of a continuous development process. In mature economies, on the other hand, growth depends less on the gradual transformation of socioeconomic structure than on prompt responses from the existing structure; hence, the lesser importance of allowing for the continuity of the development process.

THE SIGNIFICANCE OF METAPLANNING IN DEVELOPED AND DEVELOPING COUNTRIES

In an idealized interpretation, the operation of a *developed economy* could be represented by a hierarchy, or rather a hierarchy of hierarchies, of highly self-regulating subsystems. Under normal conditions, these subsystems tend toward the attainment of an internal dynamic equilibrium by their direct interaction, supplemented to a limited extent by top-level government interventions which are aimed at enclosing the self-regulatory processes within certain constraints, at performing those services which do not lend themselves to self-regulatory mechanisms, and at providing long-term planning and guidance. For short-term and medium-term processes, the task of the government is regulative rather than normative: it will intervene in the self-regulatory mechanisms, active within and between the subsystems of the economy, only if these mechanisms do not gravitate toward an equilibrium, this intervention being aimed solely at inducing self-regulation.

To judge by past performance, self-regulatory mechanisms (supplemented by limited government control) operate satisfactorily as long as all major subsystems of the economy change concurrently and adapt their own regulatory mechanisms to such changes. In highly developed economies, freely exposed to the powerful winds of rapidly changing technology, one subsystem may change at a rate far exceeding that of remaining subsystems. Such acromegalic growth of individual subsystems may create imbalances that can no longer be corrected by the existing regulatory mechanisms; it may even become "cancerous" and create metabolic by-products that cumulatively pollute and poison the physical, social, and psychological environment. If unchecked and uncontrolled, such local "overexcitation" of individual subsystems will cause either a lag in adjustment or dangerous vibrations in the remaining subsystems; in cybernetic language, existing regulatory mechanisms no longer possess the requisite variety of response to adapt to major changes in their environment created by local overexcitation.

Under these conditions, *metaplanning* becomes necessary to supplement existing regulatory mechanisms and to generate the requisite response variety by improving existing mechanisms, adding *parallel* ones, or in more serious cases of imbalance, creating new regulatory mechanisms to be superimposed in *series* upon the existing ones; such metaplanning initiates interventions into the existing system which result in an expansion of the range of regulative processes. Thus, metaplanning, in mature economies, does not aim at replacing existing self-regulatory mechanisms by dictates from the top of the hierarchy; rather, it attempts to restore the "requisite response variety" by bringing into being complementary mechanisms which, when operating in series with existing ones, are able to adapt to local overexcitation and lead to a new, higher level of dynamic equilibrium.

Some types of *totalitarian planning,* for reasons of dogma, consider self-regulation in itself at any level of the economy to be unorthodox and attempt, if faced with local overexcitation, to adapt to the new situation by adding additional top-level controls and by completely "eliminating" self-regulation. Such "treatment" of pathological symptoms of regulation, however, only adds fuel to the fire and necessitates setting up still more control levels, themselves engendering further problems—in short, again, infinite regression. A cybernetic (biological) mechanism which is no longer adequate should, therefore, be replaced not by a mechanistic one, but by a more complex cybernetic one.

Metaplanning in *developing economies,* as contrasted with its role in the mature economies, is of far greater importance. Mature economies are characterized by a built-in tendency to gravitate toward dynamic equilibria; though operating in an ever-changing "overexcited" environment, induction is sufficient to conduct excitation quickly and effectively from one subsystem to another, each subsystem having the requisite response variety to adapt itself to stimuli from other parts of the system. The environment of the developing economies, on the other hand, is only slowly changing and economically "underexcited"; as a consequence of its poor conductivity and lack of requisitive response variety, its capacity to respond to changes artificially introduced into any of its subsystems is seriously impeded.

To attain self-sustained growth, the whole tone of society and the economy must be raised; however, this cannot be achieved spontaneously by a preexisting self-regulatory mechanism since neither an organism nor a society can pull itself up by its own bootstraps. On the other hand, the system is too complex to be transformed mechanistically, i.e., by predetermined rigid strategies imposed from the top or from the outside. The type of corrective intervention which is, in fact, required in developing economies is in principle, though not in scope and complexity, similar to that described above for overexcited subsystems of a mature economy; it is one of gradual "enrichment'' of the existing subsystems until a response variety is achieved that is adequate to the new and quickly changing environment, supplemented by the establishment of new subsystems and regulatory mechanisms.

However, the ''quantitative'' difference in scope and complexity between the interventions required in underdeveloped and mature economies also carries with it a major ''qualitative'' difference. Only minor adaptation, but no basic change, is required in the overall system of *mature* economies to ensure an adequate response to any discrete development step. The entire operation involved in such a step can, therefore, be represented by a status quo system, a single transfer function designed to transform the status quo system into the goal system, and by the target system.

In developing economies, however, the whole system, as well as its individual subsystems, is not change oriented, and the achievement of any major discrete development step is dependent on inducing major transformation in all subsystems. Consequently, after a major development step has been brought to a successful conclusion, the system will differ considerably from its original form. Furthermore, since development is a protracted process, changes have to be planned in a way that will enable the system to continue to operate adequately throughout the transformation process, all transition phases, or transients of transformation, constituting viable states of the system in which the self-regulatory processes continue to function. Furthermore, as already pointed out, each of the intermediate states of a society in transformation has a different goal-setting complex; aims and objectives of planning will therefore change during the transformation process. Development in low-income economies therefore requires a complex representational system model, comprising the original system and a series of gradually evolving intermediate transfer functions leading to intermediate target systems. Therefore, in these economies there will be a big difference between targets and transfer functions leading to these targets, when viewed from ex post and ex ante vantage points.

So far, metaplanning has been dealt with in the abstract, as a function exercised by a benevolent fatherlike image; in the following, metaplanning will be viewed as part of the actual political decision process.

METAPLANNING AND THE POLITICAL DECISION PROCESS

Planning and metaplanning can be conceived as related to streams of resources (sources) and requirements (sinks), in which the resources streams are ''upgraded'' (by transfer functions) in accordance with the needs of the requirement streams.

This conception of the phase space of development is, however, not yet complete, since, as a result of confining it to the physical phase of the space, it still lacks its informational phase and control phase, which are reviewed in this section.

In every body politic, the physical phase space of development is controlled by decision streams issuing from the political hierarchy. These decision streams constitute orders to act in a certain way, backed by the authority that makes such orders mandatory. Since it is these decision streams (downgraded by "noise") that trigger off the physical development process, their content and authority will be a decisive dimension of our phase space. A closer study of this aspect of development is, therefore, warranted.

Such a study can best be made by conceiving of a development phase space from which all "physical" features have been abstracted and which consists solely of decision streams. We shall refer to this phase space as the "decision space," in analogy to the psychological space which we touched upon earlier.

This abstract and arbitrary representational system does not, of course, claim to be an adequate tool for an exhaustive analysis of the various aspects of our universe of discourse. However, it does serve to highlight the extremely important and usually neglected influence of the political decision process on the scope and quality of development.

The decision space should be conceived of as a universe of political structure through which information streams flow from the top of the political hierarchy to the bottom (decision streams) and from the bottom to the top (information feedback). *Decision streams* in their flow downward are continuously amplified and recoded in more specific and specialized terms and are to a certain extent distorted by "noise" accruing at the various levels passed by the streams. *Information feedback,* on the other hand, undergoes on its way upward an abstracting process through "variety absorbers"; it is also subject to a parallel process of deterioration through accumulating "noise." This distortion in both directions of flow may be caused partly by bias and angle of view, partly by self-interest, and partly by sheer ignorance and lack of understanding.

Since decision making is one of the most important aspects of metaplanning, measures for its improvement should be one of the metaplanner's top priorities.

A specific decision space is characterized by:

1. The specific content of decision streams. This is determined by the economic sector we are dealing with.
2. The amount of authority behind the decision streams. If we view the decision hierarchy as a geometrical structure, authority will, like potential energy, increase with the "elevation" of the decision maker.
3. The distribution of the decision streams. Again, using the same analogy, the higher the decision maker is located, the wider the potential angle of distribution.
4. The decision maker's basic problem-solving strategy. The basic problem-solving attitude of the decision maker is assumed to vary, on a highly simplified linear scale, between self-centered and self-transcending motivation; the position of the average political decision maker is assumed to be very close to the "self-centered" end on this scale.[10]

[10] The bureaucratic models presented in Anthony Downs's *Bureaucratic Structure and Decision-Making* and Gordon Tullock's *The Politics of Bureaucracy* are based on such a simplifying assumption.

5. The *angle of view* of the decision maker. The decision maker has a certain angle of vision dependent on his elevation, but the higher his position, the more prone to distortion will the information be that is passed on to him.

The requirements for establishing criteria for the improvement of the political decision process are discussed in the following.

The first theoretical requirement will be the establishment of a *yardstick of quality* of the process. Fundamentally, the decision processes are a tool for the attainment of selected development objectives, and the process selected should therefore be the process that optimizes the objective function. However, what is needed here is not an algorithmic type of approach, but a heuristic one. From the latter point of view, the extent of success that can be expected from a decision stream (expressed in terms of the selected objective) depends on the adequacy of its content, on its authority, and on its distribution; without aspiring to rigor, we might say that what we want to maximize, when aiming at improving the political-decision process, is some type of "product" of content, authority, and distribution.

Abstracting from the content, we should, therefore, in our metaplanning, aspire to reach with streams of improvement measures the highest possible level of the decision hierarchy, since the higher we get, the greater will be the "potential energy" of the decision stream (as expressed in the authority behind these decisions and their spreading). If, on the other hand, we intend to concentrate upon improving the content of the decision streams, we should analyze how the point of view and problem-solving strategies of the decision maker can be improved. The adequacy of these attitudes will depend on intelligence and creativity, on the one hand, and on the position of the problem solver on the "self-centered, self-transcending scale," on the other hand; a good problem solver has to be both intelligent and, to a great extent, self-transcending.

If we adopt Tullock's and Downs's models of promotional selection of bureaucratic and political executives, we may assume that intelligence at the top of the pyramid, though considerable, does not reach the desirable level; furthermore, as we move toward the top, people tend to move toward the self-centered end of the scale. In order to improve the content of decision streams, it may, therefore, be good strategy to start primary action somewhere halfway up the pyramid and leave the top level to a secondary campaign, in which the "converted halfway-up executives" would play the part of apostles.

The level of the hierarchy we aspire to reach should, however, be sufficiently high to ensure the success of the specific development operation which constitutes our leverage of attack, since success of the development operation is the precondition of its impact on the decision hierarchy, and this success, or vice versa, is dependent on an adequate controlling decision process.

To be effective, the "improving message" aimed at the higher levels of the hierarchy should be couched in terms of the fundamental decision-making strategy of the political executive; in other words, it has to be minted *in his success coin,* e.g., we may have to prove that the proposed plan of action will increase the authority of the executive. Since problem-solving attitudes of individual political decision makers are mostly mixed and since, in every specific case, the mix may differ, the content of the program may have to be modified in a way that ensures the political decision maker that the payoff in his individual strategic coin will be adequate.

The last-mentioned policies will lead to an improvement of the whole decision process through an expansion of authority and distribution of the decision streams of the "improved" decision makers, who, according to our earlier assumptions, are also the "best" decision makers.

The term "improvement" has been used here so often that it would be advisable to define the good planning attitude; an attempt at such a definition is made in the following section.

THE "ADEQUATE" METAPLANNING ATTITUDE

Planning aims will first have to be defined before putting forward criteria for determining the adequacy of planning attitudes. Planning, as understood in the context of metaplanning, is the analysis and synthesis of those control functions which have to be superimposed upon spontaneous, mostly self-regulatory, socioeconomic processes in order to accelerate and rechannel these processes in a way that will, within prevailing logistic limitations, maximize objective achievement.

The most important requirements for an adequate metaplanning attitude are as follows:

Structural Homomorphy The structure of language and of models used for representation should be homomorphic with the structure of our universe of discourse.

Requisite Variety The variety of our problem-solving models should match the variety of relevant aspects of our universe of discourse.

Awareness of the "Openness" of Our System Theoretically, every system is an open one. Definite boundaries in space and time are set up purely for heuristic and economic reasons; however, if in the analysis we approach the boundaries (in space and time) of our system, certain distortions will occur which can be minimized only if we then allow for the fact that the system is actually partially open.

Awareness of Dimensions Omitted from Analysis The awareness of the fundamental openness of the system should extend not only to its boundaries in space and time, but also to the essential dimensions that had to be omitted from the analysis of phase space because of the limitations in our information or methodology. Whenever analysis comes close to the sphere of influence of the omitted dimensions, we should allow for their influence upon the system. Thus, the metaplanner should, at a certain phase of the analysis, become aware of his position vis-à-vis the system and of his relation and that of the system to the overall political decision process.

Compatibility of Objectives Overall aims have to be transposed into several levels of objectives, each appropriate to the respective level of the decision hierarchy and to the respective sector within a specific level. The metaplanner must, therefore, ensure internal compatibility of these several objectives, at least for the sector which he commands by his analysis.

Allowance for Logistic Contraints The planner should realize that logistic constraints (especially those related to institutional and human resources) may, in the short run, constitute controlling handicaps. To reduce the braking action of these constraints, part of the available material, human, and institutional resources should be allocated to the improvement of growth capacity. Similar considerations apply to the availability and strength of the support of the political decision process.

Avoidance of Routine Responses Wherever the metaplanner in his analysis stumbles upon or suspects a mental block or a conditioned dogma, he should, in W. H. Auden's words, "prohibit sharply the rehearsed response."

Balancing of Heuristic and Analytical Thinking The metaplanner should strike a correct balance between algorithmic-analytical and heuristic thinking, i.e., between rigorously quantified and partly quantified homomorphic representation. Every planning operation contains a mix of both; the proportion in the mix depends on the complexity of the phase space, the amount of information available, and the extent of our knowledge of structural relationships existing in the phase space. In the earlier phases, the mix is based, in the main, on heuristic thinking; as information and hypotheses accumulate, analytical thinking starts nibbling at heuristic thinking and increases in scope. Whatever phase we are in, limitations in analytical knowledge do not justify postponing analysis and action. On the contrary, in most complex situations, early analysis and action, based on a predominantly heuristic approach, and containing a great deal of trial-and-error type operations, generate the information and hypotheses which create the preconditions for a more analytical approach.

RESISTANCE MECHANISMS AGAINST METAPLANNING

Despite the existence of situations calling for the adoption of metaplanning, it is rarely or at best sporadically applied. This indicates the existence of mechanisms and counterforces within the body politic which militate against its use; some of these mechanisms are discussed in this section.

Historically, metaplanning has been adopted only when lower level planning has broken down or in instances of national emergency; in other words, institutions and people delay introducing or even thinking about metaplanning as long as they can get along somehow with lower level planning. Rationally, the right time to introduce metaplanning is when lower level planning shows signs of strain, while still continuing to perform in a relatively satisfactory manner. Its application at such a time is the only way of giving breathing space for the analysis and synthesis in depth required for adequate metaplanning. In actual fact, metaplanning, in general, emerges only when two events occur at the same time, namely:

1. A breakdown in at least one major sectorial dimension
2. The traumatic realization that such a breakdown is directly attributable to lack of coordination within the relevant sector or between sectors

The occurrence of only the first of these two events is, by itself, not sufficient to lead to metaplanning.

Professor Abel Wolman[11] has pointed out this fact in relation to the metaplanning of water-resources development on a national level in the U.S.A. He has shown that the failure to draw up a national water-resources policy was certainly not due to the lack of data; in fact, sufficient data had been accumulated over the years by a number of high-level national committees. Rather, in Professor Wolman's opinion, a grave resource situation of traumatic implications was necessary to bring out the need for metaplanning of this resource on a national scale.

This failure to adapt to the requirements of a situation is but a special case of a more general bureaucratic behavioral set, which can be expressed by the three Gresham laws of policy making:

1. Short-term policy drives out long-term policy.
2. Problem solving at lower levels of abstraction drives out problem solving at higher levels of abstraction.
3. Concerns of one's own department drive out those of other people's departments.

There is no easy and effective way to shorten the often damaging time lag between the necessity for metaplanning and its actual acceptance. Action aimed at reducing this time lag is limited to preparing the ground for acceptance of new policies and for a smoother switchover, by tracing interdimensional and intersectorial connections, by tracing incipient symptoms of degeneration of prevailing low-level policies, and by pointing out the imminence of the persuading crisis. These palliatives and preparatory tactics in the absence of a dramatic or traumatic situation will, in most cases, not be strong enough to bring about a basic change in the bureaucratic decision process because of the countermechanisms that operate in the hierarchy against metaplanning.

ANALYSIS OF MECHANISMS OPERATING AGAINST METAPLANNING

Approaches to explaining the resistance mechanisms operating in government bureaucracies against metaplanning can be conceived as differing along a

[11] Abel Wolman, "The Metabolism of Cities," *Scientific American*, vol. 213, no. 3, September, 1965, pp. 179–190.

scale the extreme ends of which might be characterized as normative and analytic.

The point of departure for the normative approach is a Platonic idea or ideal of a perfect bureaucracy; its analytic procedure consists in comparing the bureaucracy under study with the ideal one, with a view to pointing out where, and to what extent, the former deviates from the latter. This school of thought was described some 300 years ago by Spinoza: "For they conceive of men, not as they are, but as they themselves would like to be. Whence it has come to pass that, instead of ethics, they have generally written satire and that they have never conceived a theory of politics, which could be turned to use."[12]

The basic assumption of the analytic approach is that our only chance of modifying social structures lies in analyzing their actual nature and dynamics, with a view to modifying them to the greatest possible extent. Again, in Spinoza's words, "I have looked upon passions . . . and the other perturbations of the mind, not in the light of vices of human nature, but as properties just as pertinent to it (i.e., to the study of politics), as are heat, cold, storm, thunder and the like, to the nature of the atmosphere."[13]

Only such a realistic attitude can lead to effective tactics that would have a chance of bringing about a basic change, for "A dominion, then, whose well-being depends on any man's good faith, and whose affairs cannot be properly administered, unless those who are engaged in them will act honestly, will be very unstable."[14]

It will therefore be the *analytic approach* which will be used in the following review of resistance mechanisms that are active in most societies against metaplanning.

Study of the emergence of metaplanning, within a national framework, shows us that in some cases it is initiated and induced from the very top level of the decision hierarchy; in others it is first conceived at the departmental or agency level just below the "top." The counterforces or countermechanisms aroused differ for these two cases and, hence, are dealt with separately in the following.

Let us first consider a typical case of metaplanning initiated from the *top level* of the hierarchy. Here, the chief executive of a nation may hold that, owing to a dramatic maladjustment within a particular sector, to an intersectorial maladjustment, or simply through the desire to "mimic," metaplanning has become necessary. He therefore decides on the establishment of a national planning authority formally located somewhere near the top of the hierarchy. To simplify our analysis, let us, furthermore, make the rather improbable assumption that the Planning Authority from the outset is capable of performing its job. The authority, in the course of its work, arrives at deci-

[12] *Introduction to a Political Treatise, the Chief Works of Spinoza,* Dover Publications, Inc., New York, 1951, p. 287.
[13] *Ibid.*, p. 288.
[14] *Ibid.*, p. 289.

sions which it submits for approval to the chief executive and ministries concerned. However, these ministries will realize immediately that action in accordance with the decision submitted for approval will have the effect of limiting their own freedom to make decisions, as well as involving loss of status. Generally, the activities of the metaplanning group cut across the sphere of operations of a number of ministries, hence, possibly for the first time, the ministries rally together to form a united front to take concerted action against the common enemy, the Planning Authority.

At the same time, the chief executive—the originator of the new Planning Authority—will also not take too kindly to the setting up of this intermediate decision level, since it obstructs his direct approach to his ministers and cramps his decision style, which usually consists of case-by-case decisions by "hunches." Irritation with the planning "eggheads" leads eventually to bypassing of the planning group and to an "unholy alliance" of the chief executive and his ministers against it. In certain cases, the chief executive may, at the outset, have identified himself to too great an extent with the Planning Authority to permit him such an overt bypassing, and in such cases, to neutralize planning, he may himself make the authority's major decisions. However, since his level of abstraction is, as a rule, inadequate for true metaplanning, his decisions will be equally inadequate; under such a leadership, the planning group quickly degenerates into a staff group devising rationalizations for the hunches of the chief executive. If we now put aside our original assumption that a newly fledged planning group is capable from the outset of performing its task of drawing up satisfactory plans, and if, furthermore, we keep in mind that such a group has little chance of mobilizing major vested interest groups to its defense, it will be understood that the hopes for the pursuit of metaplanning in such hierarchies are indeed slender. The demoted planning group is, as a rule, not dispersed, but its influence gradually wanes. This, nevertheless, does not prevent it from producing national economic plans, destined to be swept under the carpet.

In the second case, metaplanning, or rather partial metaplanning, is initiated by one of the government's economic departments, usually the strongest. This department may be attracted to the idea of metaplanning because of the anticipated increase it would bring in its own power and prestige. Here, the operative countermechanisms are generally limited to the interdepartmental level since the top level of the hierarchy considers that such partial metaplanning efforts—channeled through the top—do not constitute an intermediate decision level and thus do not limit its decision scope.

Government ministries, except in cases of temporary alliance against third parties, generally "coexist" in a state of permanent cold war in which every department attempts to curb the activities of its rivals. As a rule, one department, or a number of departments, for one reason or another, emerges victoriously from this strife, continues to draw strength, personnel, and budgets, and, in time, achieves a certain degree of success. There are few self-regulative mechanisms to correct this form of power accumulation; hence, the process is cumulative and receives the blessing of the chief executive, since such departments tend to improve his image without necessarily infringing on his status.

In this case, partial metaplanning, initiated by a "strong" ministry may thus, from the outset, be supported from the top of the hierarchy; this support, coupled with the ministry's initial position of strength vis-à-vis other ministries, may improve its chances of survival and assure its ultimate success. Partial metaplanning, having once proved its usefulness, will start to catch on, and this effect, combined with the cumulative change gradually brought about at the top of the hierarchy, may, in time, lead to a more general application of metaplanning.

Departmental attitudes toward metaplanning can be best understood if we analyze the problem-solving attitudes and decision processes of a bureaucracy in the low- and high-level planning context. The space of low-level planning is confined to the area of operation and the disciplines which are the department's direct concern. Problem solving, in the ideal case, aims at optimizing an objective function within this departmental planning space; the planner does not attempt to see beyond departmental boundaries, since he assumes that departmental suboptimization is the shortest way to increasing the power and prestige of the department and of the minister. Solutions thus become extremely autarkic; this is not particularly important as long as the problem concerned is not organizationally located too close to the departmental boundaries. However, as we approach these boundaries, the distortion introduced by neglecting boundary conditions, or, more specifically, the effect the solution has on other departments and the effect of the latter departments' operation on the former departments, becomes more important.

Metaplanning, on a national scale, presupposes that every ministry sets the collective objectives of the state above its own; in other words, it assumes the presence of problem solving and decision attitudes diametrically opposed to those which are known to operate.

The adoption of metaplanning is therefore contingent on its imposition from above or on a modification of the organizational structure in a way which ensures that metaplanning becomes desirable from the departmental point of view.

The first alternative—imposition of metaplanning from above—requires the combined existence of the following:

1. A powerful and enlightened top executive "sold" on the idea
2. An authoritative planning group possessing the necessary tact and insight
3. A collective of ministers in which no one minister is strong enough to sabotage planning procedures imposed from above

To achieve successful metaplanning through modification of the organizational structure entails the setting up of a steering group of the metaplanning department in a way that ensures a sufficient degree of identification of the ministries concerned with metaplanning; this could be obtained through the setting up of a government body in which the ministers or departmental heads participate. However, interdepartmental clashes will still occur within such a steering group, whenever the interest of two or more ministries cannot be easily reconciled. To arrive at a binding decision, the head of the steering group would have to have a higher level of authority than its members, i.e., he would have to be the chief executive, his deputy, or, say, the head of the Budget Bureau, or the Minister of Finance. This, however, brings us back to where we started from, since we would then be faced by a cabinet (at ministerial or deputy ministerial level) exposed to plans prepared by planning specialists. There is, however, a marginal difference since the participation of ministers or departmental heads in the metaplanning steering committee imposes an obligation to show at least partial results from metaplanning. Whether this obligation will be sufficient to give to metaplanning the necessary initial momentum depends on the internal balance of power of the steering group, the insight of its members, and especially, the attitude and authority of the chairman of this group and his relations to the chief executive.

The fact that the fate of metaplanning is, as a rule, governed by proper distribution and self-interest within the bureaucratic subsystem, rather than by the need for planning, is well illustrated by the ups and downs in the recent history of planning in France. In his survey on the French economy, Norman Macrae describes the status of the Commissariat du Plan, France's national metaplanning agency:[15]

... in the days of the unstable Fourth Republic, when French Governments were liable to be changed every other Tuesday, the educated civil service began to exhibit a remarkable contempt for politicians .... But now, there are several ministers who seem plausible stars .... In these conditions, the Commissariat du Plan now loses ground.

Numerous other examples could be quoted both from the underdeveloped as well as from the developed countries. The autarkically oriented, "self-centered" tendencies which mark the interdepartmental struggles against national planning can also be seen at the international level; here, too, metaplanning is restricted since it meets with similar resistance, originating from similar mechanisms which operate between the "participating" governments. Notable exceptions are those organizations which have specific "nonpolitical" objectives and which draw their decision-making authority from an independent executive body that is, to a great extent, governed by the high-ranking technocrats of the organization.

With the course of time, the metaplanning group will itself constitute a bureaucratic subsystem, becoming subject to the mechanism of promotional selection and decision making, a fact which will tend to depress the quality of its work. Metaplanning groups in the developing countries will also suffer from lack of experience and orientation; where expatriates are commissioned to provide the necessary orientation, planning will suffer from the uncritical transfer of models and methodology from mature countries and from the neglect of the specific sociopolitical dimension.

[15] Norman Macrae, *The Economist*, May 18, 1968, p. xxiv.

The above analysis demonstrates that the "political feasibility" of metaplanning depends not so much on its economic feasibility and rationality as on its integration within the political-decision process. Neglect of this fact has been the principal reason for the widespread failure of metaplanning. The "right" kind of metaplanning is not the type of planning that evolves from a purely economic analysis undertaken in a sociopolitical vacuum; rather, it can be defined as the highest degree of planning coordination acceptable to the controlling political decision process and, at the same time, capable of assisting in the development of a higher "absorptive capacity" to metaplanning within the political process. This, incidentally, raises the interesting question of whether this absorptive capacity could not be developed by adapting the structural organization of the governmental decision process to the organizational requirements of metaplanning (where metaplanning happens to be a vital necessity, or critical activity, as we shall call it). The answer to this question (which, in our opinion, should with qualifications be in the affirmative) will be of interest to chief executives who find themselves in the rare situation in which they can restructure government organization according to national development requirements, rather than according to the dictates of crude political arithmetics.

As long as the planning process is left to its own devices and the chief executive does not take the initiative, the chances of the emergence of metaplanning will depend on one or a combination of the following circumstances:

1. Shock in one or more dimensions that can be clearly traced to the breakdown of lower level planning. Failure of a major water-supply system during a drought period (here metaplanning, initiated during the drought, may itself "dry up" during an ensuing humid period) is one example of such a shock or breakdown. The dropping out of the bottom of the world market in a specific commodity (such as coffee) is a similar example; in this case, the market upheaval could lead to international metaplanning in the form of an international commodity agreement, indirectly affecting an entire economic sector in all the countries concerned, i.e., the agricultural sector in this case.
2. An overall national emergency, such as war or its imminent danger, may subdue (at least temporarily) departmental resistances and procrastination.
3. Economic maturation, such as has occurred apparently in France and Japan. This problematic eventuality requires a complementary supporting political power balance and a rarely encountered distribution of insight.
4. The coming into power of a party which has adopted metaplanning as its political dogma. Here, the success of metaplanning depends on the reconciliation of dogma with the politico-bureaucratic reality and on the adequacy and relevance of its metaplanning ideas.

As stated above, the formidable resistance which the political bureaucracy mobilizes against metaplanning, even before the seed has had a chance to germinate, is the main reason for the rare emergence and the still rarer consummation of metaplanning, even in situations where it is obviously the only effective antidote. Considered as a whole, the political bureaucracy, as we know it today, just does not have the requisite variety to respond to disturbances of the environment which affect more than one of its organizational subsystems. Inadequate response leads to intensification of the disturbance, until eventually a crisis of sufficient proportions occurs which results in the unseating of vested bureaucratic and other interests and creates, through shock, the necessary politico-psychological preconditions for higher level planning possessing the requisite response variety. *Planning by crisis* is, in fact, a fitting description of the response behavior of an organizational structure whose response threshold is a crisis.

THE PATHOLOGY OF METAPLANNING

Metaplanning, at various levels of abstraction, has been conducted on a considerable scale throughout the last two decades. While some of this metaplanning has been tolerably successful, most such attempts, and especially those undertaken in, or on behalf of, the developing world, have proved abortive. It would, therefore, be worthwhile, in concluding this chapter, to indicate some of the propensities of metaplanning to turn sour.

The "One-Dimensional" Planning Fallacy Phase space is conceived mainly in one dimension, and since the metaplanner by training is, usually, an economist, his planning dimension is fundamentally economic. However, as the creation of a growth process is dependent on major changes in the psychological, social, political, and institutional dimensions—which are not represented in the "one-dimensional" world—programs exclusively based on such representation do not bring about the desired rate of growth.

The "Ivory-Tower" Fallacy This is a special case of the one-dimensional planning fallacy; a rational plan is believed to be a good plan because it is rational. The "irrational" psychological, psychosociological, and political dimensions are conveniently left out of the representation; it is then claimed that the plan is good, while politicians and the government are generally held to be wicked. The impotent planning authority, safely tucked away in a corner and at a "safe" distance from real authority, is the most common symptom of this planning disease.

The Fallacy of the Preconceived Therapy This is a direct outcome of ideological problem solving; under this fallacy, the type of "therapy" to be applied and the "therapist's" exclusive task are preconceived, requiring manipulation and manhandling of the patient until he fits the therapy. A. I. MacBean has neatly summarized the dangers of this attitude: "Before attempting to prescribe a cure, one should in general be sure (a) that the patient really is sick; (b) that the causes are understood; (c) that the prescribed cure is not going to be worse than the disease."[16]

The Structural Procrustean Bed Fallacy This is founded on the concept of stretching or squeezing a situation until it fits into an incompatible struc-

[16] A. I. MacBean, *The Economist*, May 13, 1967, p. 690.

tural grid. The adoption of a deterministic, mechanistic model structure, where a flexible, probabilistic, and cybernetic one is indicated, is the most common example of this fallacy. Authoritative national planning has lately shown many symptoms of ailing from the two last-mentioned fallacies.

The Practice of Mimicry This is the pseudoadaptation of planning fashions by would-be planners—an attempt to apply other people's therapies and tools to one's own diseases. Unfortunately, the other people usually suffer from a very different disease. Of course, the underlying logic is unassailable: other economies have been cured in this manner; so why not ours? The introduction of highly sophisticated industrial and agricultural production complexes into underdeveloped countries is the most common example of this planning attitude.

The above clinical digression demonstrates that metaplanning, in addition to being exposed to attack or neglect by the political process, is liable to attack by a number of diseases stemming from the human limitations of the planner; if attacked by such diseases—as it might be, especially in its earlier phases when it is most prone to such attack—metaplanning will either produce sickly fruit or quietly degenerate and continue to vegetate in a forgotten corner. The greatest damage resulting from such degeneration is that it discredits planning when planning is most vitally needed, i.e., in the phase of underdevelopment. The political decision process is only too apt to apply to metaplanning the attitude common in the Ottoman Empire to its road system: that there were good indications where one ought not to drive.

TWO
PLANNING METHODOLOGY AND THE PLANNING PROCESS

7

DEVELOPMENT PLANNING

No vested interest is so powerful as the vested interest in an idea.
BURKE

THE TWO ASPECTS OF DEVELOPMENT PLANNING

The term planning in this context refers to development planning with special emphasis on the planning of resources development. The essence of this planning is to allocate scarce resources in a manner which will maximize the achievement of selected objectives.

Development planning has both a static and a dynamic aspect. When considering the *static* aspect, we postulate the immutability of the politico-administrative structure and the transfer functions effected by it and focus attention upon the alternative allocation of scarce resources. When considering the *dynamic* aspect, we focus attention, primarily, upon ways and means for improving transfer functions, with special emphasis on those which are operative in the politico-administrative structure of development. Thus, according to the static viewpoint, inputs selected to be fed into the politico-administrative process should be aimed at achieving short-term "optimized" direct outputs (measured in terms of the objective function); whereas, according to the dynamic viewpoint, these inputs would be aimed at improving the process itself, thereby increasing the efficiency of use of scarce resources in subsequent operations.

On closer analysis, it will be seen that these two opposite aspects of development planning stem from a very real development dichotomy which can be expressed as follows: Should we use our resources primarily in order to maximize immediate production, through appropriate use of the existing politico-administrative process? Or should the major part of these resources be diverted to improving the politico-administrative dimension with the object of improving growth capacity and, ultimately, of priming a process of cumulative growth?

As with most dichotomies, the present one also labors under the semantic distortions inherent in the two-valued logic of opposites. In actual fact, no planning act is completely static, since every resources flow changes the structure through which it flows; neither is any planning exclusively dynamic, since every flow applied with a view to improving the structure leads—as a "by-product"—to increased production. Every program thus consists of a mix of both aspects. Our quandary arises, therefore, from the need to select a *mix of static and dynamic aspects* that is appropriate for the particular set of conditions and objectives.

Both aspects of development planning in underdeveloped countries require *public intervention,* as is evidenced by the fact that satisfactory growth rates have nowhere—in such countries—been achieved spontaneously, i.e., by the operation of existing socioeconomic mechanisms. Intervention is needed, therefore, both for the "static" aspect—that of creating an adequate production environment, or the means of production—as well as for the "dynamic" one—that of improving the structural features, or the response capacity of the economy to the new production environment.

These interventions are not intended to replace self-regulating socioeconomic mechanisms, but rather to "prime" the emergence of the requisite mechanisms, where these do not exist, or to improve existing ones, where their effectiveness no longer suffices to meet the needs of a new production environment. According to this planning concept, public intervention, although necessary in the early "priming" phases of development, will decrease in importance with the emergence of spontaneous self-regulative mechanisms of requisite variety, and will eventually be confined to overall control functions. Hence, in order to accommodate both aspects of the planning process, we must expand our earlier definition of development planning to read thus: *development planning* deals with the allocation of scarce resources with a view to initiating interventions into existing socioeconomic mechanisms that will simultaneously *upgrade the response environment and the response capacity* of these mechanisms. By response environment, in this context, we refer mainly to land, water, production inputs, production tools, and to modes of use (tenure, credits, techniques); by response capacity, we refer to the ability of the individual producer and of producer groups to develop the requisite variety to respond to the improved environment.

THE THREE BASIC PLANNING MODELS

The aim of science is to seek the simplest explanation of complex facts . . . . Seek simplicity and distrust it.
A. N. WHITEHEAD (*The Conquest of Nature*)

This definition, like any other that could be devised, implies, of couse, a specific basic model of society and economy. The model we have chosen is neither the mechanistic model on which communistic planning is based nor the atomistic-rationalistic one of classical economy on which most laissez faire economic doctrines are based. Instead, we have selected the cybernetic-biological model as the basis for our planning ideology. Since most of the differences in planning ideology may be traced to the structural properties of these underlying models, we shall study them in greater detail.

On a scale of conceptual models of the economy, the mechanistic model will lie at one extreme, the cybernetic model at the midpoint, and the atomistic-rationalistic, or laissez faire, model at the opposite extreme.

From the cybernetic point of view, the essential dysfunction of the *mechanistic model* is its noncompliance with Ross Ashby's law of "requisite variety." The production environment, on the one hand, and the "grass-root" levels of the production process, on the other hand, generate a tremendous amount of variety, which is not compensated for by a generation of the requisite amount of variety at intermediate control levels, the only levels which, because of their organizational proximity to the source of variety proliferation, could do so. As a substitute, ukase-type rulings of little relevance to the actual variety of the environment are issued by the system brain fulfilling the function of a "variety sponge"; however, only "variety can absorb variety," and hence these rulings serve only to "kill" variety and lead to solutions that are grossly ineffective from the point of view of the system objectives.

In countries adhering to the Marxist-mechanistic model, the situation is further aggravated, to an extent that makes the emergence of a compensatory process extremely unlikely, by the action ideology of the decision makers at the top level. This action ideology is largely determined by the following two mechanisms:

1. The criteria of promotion. Criteria applied to the political hierarchy in regimes of this type, more than in any other, emphasize political rather than intellectual capabilities.

2. The dogmatic turn of mind and basic conditioning in these regimes—characteristics which, without doubt, lie at the opposite pole to variety generation. Since the prevailing political dogma is conditioned and indoctrinated to an extent that it becomes completely internalized and acts as the paramount criterion of choice, there appears to be no way of converting producers of ready-made responses, tailored according to mid-nineteen-century dogmas, into late twentieth-century variety proliferators. In this connection, the British historian Hugh Trevor Roper has noted[1] that, "This contrast between the death of the mind, where real problems are concerned, and its continued activity, even subtlety, in trivial peripheral areas, often leads to bizarre results."

The laissez faire model envisages "brain" activity and regulation to be dispersed throughout the "atoms" of society, the individual producers and consumers; it assumes that through their perfectly rational choices, arrived at within a fully "transparent" economic environment, optimum allocation of resources is automatically achieved from the point of view both of the "atom," i.e., the individual decision maker, and of the overall system. In such a universe, consisting of perfectly rational, independently acting decision makers, equipped with perfect information and operating in a "frictionless"

[1] Hugh Trevor Roper, *Encounter,* April, 1968, p. 8.

environment, intervention from above is thought to be superfluous, since perfect "atomic" responses, it is claimed, tend to create perfect response environments, and vice versa.

The laissez faire model, considered from the cybernetic point of view, is also the opposite of the mechanistic one, since it assumes that homeostasis, a relatively stable state of equilibrium between all elements, is operative at all levels of the socioeconomic system. This state is achieved as a result of a postulated all-pervasive, self-regulatory mechanism which is assumed automatically to reconcile objectives of the individual economic decision maker with those of the system as a whole. In other words, it assumes that the "socioeconomic" orchestra does not need a "conductor," since every member, just by playing according to his personal idiosyncrasy, is bound to make a harmonic contribution to the whole. Cybernetically, this model implies that streams of adequate information are universally available and furthermore that channels exist for the dissemination of this information to all nodes of interaction down to the "atomic decision points" of the individual decision maker, and vice versa. It also assumes the existence of the requisite response variety to such information at all levels.

In the cybernetic-biological model, the economy is represented as a *hierarchic system,* made up of partially self-regulated subsystems, sub-subsystems, etc. The overall controlling functions are conceived to be located at the "top" of the hierarchy in the "system brain"; it is here that new environments for the subsystems are initiated and appropriate new response variety is incited. The subsystems, in turn, have their own subsystem "brains" which process instructions received from the system "brain," as well as the stimuli absorbed from their environment, into self-regulated operations at their own level, and into instructions recoded for lower levels.

An underdeveloped society is conceived as operating predominantly in response to impulses generated at subsystem and sub-subsystem levels, while control impulses from the system brain remain, most of the time, below threshold. However, operation at the lower system levels cannot generate the impulses necessary to create a new environment and to raise the overall system to a higher level of operation; such a major change can be primed only by the overall system brain, i.e., by *public intervention,* originating at the top level of the hierarchy, and operating upon the existing partially self-regulated socioeconomic mechanisms. Such intervention from the top should, however, be aimed not at the "grass-root" levels of the system, but primarily at the subsystem "brains" at the next lower level of the hierarchy, with a view to priming, at that level, the spontaneous socioeconomic mechanisms which this level is capable of inciting. In other words, intervention from the top should not replace autonomous processes, but rather should raise them to new functional levels at which these processes would be capable of adapting to an improved environment through improved response variety.

The mechanistic model has its roots in the materialistic-rationalistic philosophy of enlightenment of the second half of the eighteenth century. Marx's prime contribution to this model was the emphasis on the predominance of the production process which he considered to be the controlling factor in society; on this ideological foundation, modern communistic planning has grafted twentieth-century programming techniques.

The mechanistic model conceives of society as a fully predictable and deterministic structure best represented by a complex machine. This machine is viewed as being made up of subassemblies and sub-subassemblies; however, these subassemblies are not assumed to have any autonomous or self-regulative functions, and they have, therefore, to be fully programmed from above. The operation of the whole system is thus seen as being fully initiated and controlled by the system brain; this brain maintains all activity in the system by generating a continuous stream of detailed instructions and information which is transmitted to the subsystems, sub-subsystems, and so on down to the final component of the economy, i.e., consumer choices and preferences. This mechanism also provides for countermeasures to quell any tendency to self-regulation or independent spontaneous responses on the part of any of the intermediate subsystems or elements, and even the most dogmatic defenders of mechanistic models recognize that such tendencies exist; in this manner, provision is made to press the existing socioeconomic structure back into the Procrustean bed of the model.

Each of the models described above is considered in the following in the context of development.

THE RELEVANCE OF THE STATE OF DEVELOPMENT TO THE SELECTION OF THE MODEL

Welche Regierung die beste sei? Diejenige, die uns lehrt uns selbst zu regieren.[2]

GOETHE (*Maximen und Reflexionen*)

All three models are, of course, biased, and oversimplified, idealized representations of socioeconomic structures. No past or existing society has ever operated according to any one of these three basic models. Each society has, however, had its own specific "principal distortion," stemming, in part, from the underlying model conception. This conscious or unconscious use of a specific bias in a specific society can be ultimately traced to rationalizations rooted in political ideologies.

All three models disregard the existence of socioeconomic "friction," the "noise" emanating from various sources that causes instructions and information feedback to deteriorate, and which strictly limits the control capacity of a social structure; in short, all neglect the basic fact that human responses tend to be "human, all too human."

Nevertheless, both the classical (atomistic) and the mechanistic models are known to have served their purpose, at least within a specific range of conditions in the mature economies: the atomistic for all branches of the production process in these economies; the mechanistic, at least, for most branches

[2] What type of government is the best? the one that teaches us to govern ourselves.

of industrial production in the East European countries. The reason for this relatively satisfactory performance of the two orthodox models in mature economies lies apparently in the existence of some limited structural compatibility between the warp and woof of their socioeconomic structure and the structure of the models; models, as we have noted in an earlier chapter, retain their predictive value as long as the model and the represented process retain their structural similarity. However, if we attempt to apply the orthodox model beyond the boundaries of structural compatibility, e.g., to the context of an underdeveloped country, we cannot any more be sure of its effectiveness.

Reviewing the performance of the two orthodox models from the point of view of cybernetics, we find that planning according to the Marxist-mechanistic model was successful in those areas of economic activity in which lack of variety proliferation was least damaging, i.e., those areas which lend themselves best to programming from the top, such as heavy industry. The laissez faire model, on the other hand, was applied satisfactorily in those societies and areas of economic activity in which both variety proliferation at the grass-root level and economic "induction" were adequate, and hence could be successfully applied to most economic activities in mature economies.

Despite their suitability in these contexts, both models have been found lacking in predictive value in the mature economies in those areas in which gross structural incompatibility has arisen between the model and reality. The Marxistic-mechanistic model experienced its worst setback in the field of agriculture, a field of economic activity that is characterized by extreme variety proliferation at the production level, proliferation which can be effectively absorbed only by appropriate variety proliferation at the lowest decision levels. Countering it by fixed ready-made controls from the top will, it is true, "kill" variety; however, in the process, it will also kill most of the economic outcomes.

Similarly, the laissez faire model has, for instance, failed mainly in those socioeconomic fields where vicious circles continued to exist in an environment abounding in "positive, circular causation" (to use Myrdal's expressive term), for example, in depressed areas which remained depressed even when the national economy was in a state of ebullient growth. These vicious circles can be broken only by public intervention planned and implemented on lines similar to those advocated here for underdeveloped countries. More recently, the laissez faire model has failed in those areas in which new problems have arisen as a result of the headlong acceleration of growth.

Mature economies, through the forces of the market and the growth orientation of individuals, behave, within a certain all-important range, as if they had an atomistic-rationalistic structure. Any public intervention that may still be necessary to accelerate spontaneous growth can, therefore, to a great extent, rely on the adaptive responses of existing structures; thus, growth in this context involves no major structural change. So much for the mature economies.

When we come to the *underdeveloped economies,* we find that both models lose their applicability, since these economies are structurally very different from the mature economies, whether they conform to the laissez faire or to the mechanistic ideology.

In these economies, subsystems are much more autarkic, the interlinking induction of the market is much less effective, and individuals are much less growth oriented. Growth must, therefore, be preceded or, at least, be accompanied by major structural changes, and, hence, the model must comprise and map those structural features which have to be transformed in order to achieve growth. Since the organic analogy best represents the dynamics of the responses of society, a cybernetic-biological type of model appears to fulfill these representational requirements. It is this type of model which we propose, therefore, to adopt as the basic structural grid for planning in underdeveloped countries.

The usefulness of the cybernetic-biological model (hereafter referred to as the cybernetic model) is, however, not limited to the study of underdeveloped economies. As already noted, even in developed countries, existing socioeconomic structures cannot always be relied upon to respond adequately to radical changes in the environment. Wherever unprecedented scale, technology, and sociopsychological forces make their appearance in these countries, the laissez faire type of policy based on the atomistic model breaks down, because the existing socioeconomic structure can no longer respond adequately to the unprecedented range of change of the environment. Under such conditions, a mature society, in fact, develops behavioral patterns which are similar to those of underdeveloped countries. In such situations it may be assumed that the cybernetic model will operate with greater success.

THE ROLE OF PLANNING IN UNDERDEVELOPED COUNTRIES

We may conclude from the above that planning is of much greater importance in underdeveloped than in developed economies: developed countries are, to a great extent, able to generate growth stimuli spontaneously, whereas in underdeveloped countries both the basic growth conditions, namely, a growth environment and the required socioeconomic structure, have to be remodeled, a remodeling which is conditional upon public intervention.

Furthermore, only by planning can the stream of "positive, circular causation"—a condition for the cumulative growth process—be generated in the developing economies. To be fully effective, planning in underdeveloped countries must make its impact on the political decision makers, as well as on its technocrats and administrators. Among technocrats and administrators, development calls for energy, motivation, need for achievement, and perseverance linked to the aims and targets of society, all personality traits which are in short supply; among the political decision makers, development calls for insight and motivation. Planning can have an energy-focusing and structuralizing effect; with proper leadership, it can mobilize the self-transcending tendencies of man to serve as a motivational undercarriage; if handled imaginatively, it can create the vital charismatic elements which may make all the difference between rapid progress and slow plodding. This revitalizing influence of a psychologically conceived planning process will, in time, pervade all sectors of the development establishment and eventually reach the ultimate destination of development, the final producer and consumer.

NATIONAL VS. SECTORIAL PLANNING

The difficulties encountered in implementing metaplanning on a national scale have been pointed out in Chapter 6. In the light of these difficulties, the question arises whether planning on a national, or even on a sectorial, scale should be attempted at all. Would it not be more realistic, therefore, to confine ourselves to a project-by-project planning approach and postpone planning on a wider scope and at greater depth until the mythical future, when governmental bureaucracy might be ready to endorse national planning?

In the underdeveloped countries, the necessity for national development planning is now almost universally recognized, and, hence, the "principle of planning" in these countries does not require any special sales effort. The problem remains, however, that planning, as actually practiced, is ineffective and limited and does not serve as a guide to action; planning and implementation, in fact, appear to be "parallel" operational lines never intended to meet. As practiced in underdeveloped countries, planning often seems to be in the nature of a pseudogesture.

However, even such ineffective planning provides a general definition of objectives and aggregate resources allocation. Once this information becomes available, we need not necessarily approach national planning in the logical rational order, i.e., from the whole to the part, from the general to the specific. Instead, we can single out for an intensive planning effort on a national scale that economic sector which is most essential for national growth—we shall call this the "strategic sector"—and apply to it a comprehensive planning approach using a phase space with an adequate number of dimensions. Although more complex than orthodox project-by-project planning, comprehensive sectorial planning requires fewer dimensions and, what is more important, much less coordination than full-blown national planning. In addition to determining resource allocations, in the narrower sense of the word, comprehensive sectorial planning will assist in defining the program requirements related to the political decision-making process and to the implementation and the transformation process, as well as in specifying the logistic constraints stemming from scarcities in material, human, and institutional resources. Often, the strategic sector will also be the sector the growth of which is most dependent on planning, and, hence, allocation of the limited skilled human resources to this sector will constitute an economical resources use from the point of view of the nation.

A reasonably effective comprehensive sectorial plan (as described in Chapter 20) will, also often, serve as a good primer for wider planning efforts. The main handicap resulting from confining comprehensive planning to one sector lies in the difficulty in obtaining the necessary complementary support from the nonplanned sectors of the economy. However, the very demonstration of the need for such support already constitutes a first step toward the expansion of comprehensive planning to other complementary sectors. Where the mobilization of complementary support is not feasible at the outset, it may be necessary to resort to organizing such support within the framework of the planned sector, at least as a "temporary" measure. The disadvantage of such *ad hoc* procedures is, of course, that instead of gradually raising the organizational efficiency of the administrative machine, it encourages the multiplication of organizational units with greatly overlapping terms of reference; we shall come back to this vexing question in Chapters 16, 20, and 34.

As we have already repeatedly pointed out, one of the principal side effects of planning is its "positive, circular causation" in relation to the improvement of the planning process itself. Every comprehensive sectorial plan, in addition to its direct downward effects (or *downward loop,* as we shall call it) upon the relevant sector, has secondary sideway effects (or a *sideway loop*) upon the other sectors and their directors and an upward effect (or *upward loop*) upon the higher and highest levels of the hierarchy. Although these secondary "spills" are substantially reduced in strength and adulterated by "noise," they still have an important and widely dispersed priming effect; what they lose in punch, they gain in range.

LIMITATIONS OF PLANNING

In the final count, planning is but one of the inputs of the development process. It thus constitutes only an instrumental objective, and as such it has no absolute value, its value depending on the kind of political decision, implementation, and transformation responses which it elicits in conjunction with (or in opposition to) the other factors that enter into the development process. Among the negative factors, the most important are the self-centered motivational complex of the political decision maker (especially if "mounted" upon an undercarriage of self-transcending and dogmatic sets), limitations in insight, and the distortions due to "noise" in the narrower meaning of communication theory. Thus, the "best" plan is not the plan with the most convincing reasoning, but the one which, everything considered, will result in actual development achievement combined with a transformation of the organizational structure.

Now that we have analyzed the underlying models of planning, their value and limitations, the time has come to take a look at planning as actually practiced; after all, the proof of the pudding is in the eating.

HISTORIC FLASHBACK

The origins of planning date far back, long before the emergence of man, the planning animal.

Considered in its widest context, planning is delayed reaction, with the object of incorporating, into the delayed-response patterns, forecasts, which are based on the remembered or transposed experience of the past and on anticipated conditions and requirements.

Instinctive chains of action in the animal kingdom may be considered to constitute the oldest "planning" activity: they are but prefabricated programmed "plans of the race," which are transmitted, genetically or by early conditioning, from generation to generation. Although adequate for the set of conditions in which they have developed, such fixed planning chains are extremely inflexible.

The type of planning developed by man, by trial and error, in the early phases of recorded history, although still completely programmed, is, nevertheless, incomparably more adaptive. Such planning processes, comprising true cumulative learning, and transmitted within the social group from generation to generation, are, therefore, adequate and operative for a much wider range of conditions. Alternation of cultivation and fallow cycles in agriculture are important examples of such traditional lore to which each new generation has brought only minor improvements. The remarkable feature of this type of planning is the interconnection between the purely economic and transcendental aspects of the "plans"; this interconnection is not a result of comprehensive analysis and synthesis, but rather a direct consequence of the "integrative" character of prelogical thinking.

Such "plans of the tribe" remain satisfactory guides of action as long as changes in overall conditions do not exceed a specific range, and as long as an expanding scale does not set quantitative limitations. However, when faced with a completely new material and psychological environment, "prefabricated" programs no longer have the "requisite variety" for adequate response; yet, since respond one must, man continues to react persistently in the orthodox way—in spite of unsatisfactory outcomes.

Planning, in the modern sense of the word, aspires to a much more ambitious aim than the planning processes of the past: it represents an attempt to design a consistent and optimized line of action toward predetermined objectives through the use of ways and means selected specifically to fit conditions encountered in the past and conditions anticipated to develop in the future. Planning in the modern sense of the word has, throughout recorded history, been practiced rarely and only in response to critical conditions. Planning, on a national scale, has been confined in the Western World, with a few notable exceptions, to traumatic situations that occurred during certain periods in certain countries.

The most instructive examples of national planning are those of the "hydraulic societies" and wartime planning. The *hydraulic societies*[3] arose out of the necessity in ancient times to control and manage major rivers on which the subsistence and survival of entire nations depended. As a result of this necessity, elaborate plans were drawn up and highly organized nationwide engineering, administrative, and political operations executed. In these societies the attempt was made, perhaps for the first time in human history, to

[3] This term was coined, and the relevant phenomena were described, by Professor Wittfogel in *Oriental Despotism,* Yale University Press, New Haven, Conn., 1957.

undertake comprehensive planning on a national scale which covered the most vital aspects of human economic activity. This planning exercise was sufficiently successful to enable major engineering projects to be constructed and successfully operated for many centuries. Hydraulic societies were, however, based on an extremely autocratic political philosophy, which could certainly not be applied in modern times. Hence, the lesson of the hydraulic societies for today's underdeveloped countries is extremely limited.

The other example of planning relates to war. The rapid induction of "artificial" scarcity conditions has led, in modern wartime conditions, to widely accepted comprehensive planning on a national scale. In fact, success in the prosecution of war has been shown to depend, in no small measure, on planning the deployment of maximum forces against the enemy and stepping up the production of war material in the hinterland, without denuding the country of the elements required for physical survival. In order to mobilize, in a short time, the necessary resources, massive government intervention, based on comprehensive dynamic multidimensional planning, was shown to be a necessity in such conditions. Wartime planning, aiming at the lightning conversion of the economy from a peacetime to a wartime basis, and, subsequently, maintaining and stepping up the operation of the wartime economy, contains most of the essentials of the type of planning required for major socioeconomic transformations such as those involved in converting a subsistence economy to a modern one. The main manifest difference lies in the disparity of the time scale and time horizons, in that planning for war is devoid of long-term goals, and in the difference in the quality of human resources and in the institutional framework.

Many of the processes connected with planning in emerging economies are in essence present in wartime planning; among these we can cite dynamic inventorying of resources, definition of overall objectives and strategies, optimization of the allocation of resources with a view to achieving these objectives, employment of every means known to psychology to increase motivation in relation to planning objectives, all-embracing reorganization of the economy tailored to the requirements of the plan, intensive analysis of all these processes along the time axis. All these activities are seen as interconnected and are planned according to the multidimensional approach.

The necessity for comprehensive national planning in wartime has never seriously been contended, largely owing to the effective concentration of decision-taking processes at the political level and the willingness of the individual temporarily to surrender freedom and to make sacrifices in the face of the peril to the national existence, and in face of the dramatic circumstances under which a number of serious scarcities develop overnight, even in economies of affluence. With the passing of the emergency, the importance of central management and control of scarce resources—so fundamental to the conduct of the war—is eclipsed, and planning is promptly discarded.

From the point of view of the outsider, many underdeveloped countries appear to be in a state of "economic siege" and a major national "overall" effort of the nature of wartime planning seems to be warranted in order to raise this siege; unfortunately, the existence of an economic siege is usually not sufficient to motivate the political decision process to undertake such an effort.

Systematic *national peacetime planning*, in the modern sense of the word, was first introduced in the twenties by the Soviet Union. The very fact that planning was a communistic "invention" has not endeared it to the conservative stalwarts in the noncommunistic world, and this is probably one of the reasons why planning came so late to the Western countries, and especially to the Third World countries which are in dire need of effective planning. The communistic type of planning is comprehensive, mandatory, and spelled out to the last detail; its advantages are inherent in its comprehensiveness and its power of enforcement; its basic disadvantage stems from the mechanistic nature of the planning model, namely, lack of self-regulation mechanisms at the base of the decision hierarchy. The "reform" movements that have recently been espoused by a number of communistic countries, recognizing this basic weakness of mechanistic planning, attempt to reintroduce some of the self-regulatory mechanisms, such as a partial market mechanism, with the object of getting the best of both worlds, the communistic as well as the capitalistic. This reform movement has so far focused upon the industrial-production process, where the gradual adoption of Western type self-regulative mechanisms appears to involve fewer difficulties and lesser changes; it has not yet been applied, on a large scale, to the sector that needs it most, i.e., the agricultural sector—except in those communistic countries which decided, at one time or another, to discontinue the process of "socialization" of agricultural production.

In the noncommunistic developed world, planning came into the limelight mainly as a consequence of two traumatic experiences:

1. The economic crisis of the thirties and Keynes's analysis of the feasibility of preventive and corrective action

2. The Second World War and its aftermath, requiring the rapid reconstruction of Europe

These experiences, concurrently with the realization of the successes of early Soviet planning, have made planning fashionable at least in Europe, so much so that the countries that did not then introduce national planning (like the U.K.) developed a "bad conscience." However, to paraphrase the Latin saying that books have their fates, plans, too, have their particular fates: some remain satisfied with purely regulatory interventions; some start off on a more ambitious basis but revert to a regulative character; some finally start off on a mandatory basis but gradually become more and more permissive.

What most Western planners have in common is their exclusive emphasis on the economic aspects of development. Myrdal[4] traces this overemphasis to the influence of Marxian ideology:

The majority of contemporary Western economists, with a few notable

[4] Gunnar Myrdal, *Asian Drama*, Pantheon Books, a division of Random House, Inc., New York, 1968, vol. III, p. 1905.

exceptions, are planners, at least with regard to the underdeveloped countries. But influenced by Marx to a degree they are rarely aware of, they usually make the first assumption that economic advance will have strong and rapid repercussions on attitudes and institutions, especially on those important for development.

Andrew Shonfield, of the Royal Institute of International Studies of the U.K., has described early attempts at planning in the West as "concerned mainly with the improvement in control over the business cycle. Indeed, in several countries it was the search for better methods of short-term control over the economic system which led to long-term planning . . . it is in most countries an activity of very recent origins belonging to the 1960's rather than to the fifties."[5]

In the Western forms of planning as practiced in the developed countries, the implementation of the material aspects of development is rarely fully spelled out and made mandatory. In the French approach to planning, bottlenecks in the development front are pointed out and economic incentives created (for example, through planned channeling of government funds) to establish facilities to overcome them. In the U.S.A., the main emphasis is on corrective short-term measures to control the business cycle, without, however, completely losing sight of indicative long-term planning.

The very antithesis of the communistic approach to planning can probably best be seen in some oligarchic societies which completely repudiate the need for planning or draw up spurious plans without any intention of implementing even a part of these plans.

In the underdeveloped economies, the national planning approach has now been generally accepted as a prerequisite for sustained growth. It is also generally recognized that planning and implementation processes in emerging economies require a far more comprehensive scope and a greater depth than those in the developed countries. Although these facts are fully appreciated in most developing countries, the know-how and political motivation required for adequate planning and implementation are, unfortunately, still lacking.

PRESENT PLANNING PRACTICES

Waterston[6] has enumerated three principal basic planning practices that are at present in use:

1. The project-by-project approach
2. The integrated investment planning approach
3. The comprehensive national planning approach

Although most of the underdeveloped countries claim that their development is guided by a comprehensive national plan, in reality such plans are often only disguised integrated investment plans or project catalogues; adop-

[5] Andrew Shonfield, "The Progress (and Perils) of Planning," *Encounter*, August, 1965.

[6] A. Waterston, *Development Planning; Lessons of Experience*, The Johns Hopkins Press, Baltimore, 1965, p. 706.

tion of comprehensive development semantics does not necessarily make a plan comprehensive. As a rule, both the first and the second approaches, possibly tempered by a touch of the third, are applied concurrently in different sectors of the same economy. Moreover, we should keep in mind that the sharp distinction implied in the above definitions is artificial and that, in actual analysis, it will often be difficult to classify planning approaches according to one or another of these definitions.

The project-by-project approach takes as its point of departure a very generally conceived and unquantified development objective. The planner then shops around for projects which fit the objective. Every individual project that is thus picked out is evaluated according to quantifiable criteria (if international or bilateral financing is required, criteria of the specific funding institution are adopted); if the project meets the requirements of such criteria, and if funds can be made available, budgetary appropriations are then made. The objective might, for example, be expressed in the form of a general requirement such as "agricultural production has to be raised," possibly supplemented by an instrumental objective, e.g., "the provision of irrigation water and the settlement of new areas." Most projects that are not absolutely futile fit such a wide and permissive range of objectives, and a number of those included in the list may comply with the adopted investment criteria. However, no attempt is made to draw up an exhaustive list of all alternative lines of action and to compare their efficiency in the use of scarce resources for the attainment of objectives. Both the advantages and disadvantages of such an arbitrary limitation in the project list are obvious; where the controlling scarce commodity is planning insight, the project-by-project approach (which incidentally meets the requirements of many funding agencies) might be the path of least resistance for priming the development process.

The integrated investment plan approach represents the next highest degree of planning sophistication; under this approach, objectives for each sector of the economy become both more specific and more quantified, and alternative projects are drawn aimed at achieving such objectives. These alternative projects are then compared within each sector and (in the better type of programs) ranked according to their efficiency in the use of scarce resources (usually capital) to reach sectorial objectives and according to, what is euphemistically termed, extra-economic considerations (which might be anything from constituency politics to an *idée fixe* of a political executive). Allocation of resources between the various sectors of the economy is, as a rule, made according to "pragmatic" considerations. Some of the more common allocation principles are: allocation according to the "as-had" approach and sharing out resources according to party representation in coalitions or according to political dogma or economic "intuition" (such as every penny for industrialization).

Since the sectorial list usually requires resources in excess of those available to the sector, the ranked sectorial project list has to be cut off at the point at which the sectorial allocation is reached. Officially, it will be claimed that projects included in the sectorial program are selected in accordance with ranking procedures based on one of the generally accepted economic criteria such as benefit-cost ratios, net present worth, or the internal rate of return. In actual fact, the selection, in the majority of cases, is limited from the outset by the number of engineering plans that are available—generally, only a small number of such plans have been prepared, and the selection in such cases is often a foregone conclusion.

THE DIFFICULTIES OF NATIONAL COMPREHENSIVE PLANNING

The integrated investment list meets the most obvious requirement of a rational program: to select, between alternative lines of action required to reach an objective, those lines which will result in the highest economical, political, or psychological utility. This requirement is a necessary, though not in itself sufficient, condition of rational planning; in order to show that it is conclusive, our analysis will have to include three additional tests, namely, the exhaustiveness of the project list, the adequacy of the phase space, and the rationality of intersectorial allocation; these three tests are described briefly in the following.

The Test of Exhaustiveness A complete project catalogue representing all reasonable lines of action will have to be drawn up before the integrated investment list is selected. Otherwise, there is no guarantee that we will, in fact, be using scarce resources in a specific sector in the best possible way to attain our objectives. Making a selection from an incomplete list may condemn us to choosing the best of the available alternatives, without giving consideration to possibly more attractive alternatives not listed in the catalogue.

The Test of Adequacy of the Phase Space The planning process must encompass all relevant dimensions of scarcity, if we are to be sure that all bottlenecks in our material, human, and politico-institutional planning space have been taken into account.

The Test of Intersectorial Allocation The aggregate of resources is scarce, and we must therefore ensure, after determining or selecting the relevant intersectorial trade-offs, that the overall benefit achieved by allocating the aggregate of resources to the various sectors will, in fact, create the maximum "welfare."

Comprehensive national planning, as practiced at present, attempts to comply with only the last of these requirements, i.e., intersectorial allocation, and rarely meets the other two requirements. Moreover, the introduction of some measure of rationality into intersectorial trade-off relationships often makes the development plan extremely controversial from the point of view of party, personality, and departmental politics.

The subject of intersectorial allocation and trade-offs is also difficult to deal with from the theoretical point of view, and conclusive results can be obtained only by investigating the long-term economic effects of alternative intersectorial allocation patterns. In actual fact, such alternative analyses are rarely made, and even if they were carried out, the trade-off relationship between objectives (such as sectorial products and product distributions) would probably at the present stage of the art of planning still have to be based on value decisions. The significance of the outcome of such an analysis would be questionable, even if a rigorous intersectorial approach were feasible, since it still leaves open the question of whether aggregate economic efficiency should, in fact, be used as the paramount scale or, more specifically, whether the marginal utility of newly created income should be considered as identical for all income ranges.

In actual planning practice, the point of departure for sectorial allocation will be the estimate of internal demand for sectorial commodities based on an assumed increase in per capita income that is derived from rough national macroeconomic arithmetic and estimates of export demand.

However, forecasts of sectorial demand increases, calculated from average aggregate income growth, often prove to be unreliable: intersectorial allocation, on the one hand, and intrasectorial allocation between the subsectors of a specific sector operating at different production efficiencies, on the other hand, can significantly modify aggregate demand. For example, confining allocation to the industrial sector will not result in any direct increase in the purchasing power of the population within the agricultural sector and may thus limit marketing opportunities for industrial products; neither will it bring about any significant compensatory demand increase for agricultural products in the higher income population of the towns (because of the urban population's relatively lower income elasticity of demand for food). Similarly, overemphasis in the allocation of resources to enclaves of commercial agriculture still leaves the bulk of the population untouched and sets severe limits to its potential purchasing power. From the above, the importance of evaluating the impact of alternative allocative patterns on potential purchasing power and demand can be seen.

The conceptual origins of comprehensive national planning in developing countries have been transferred from similar planning efforts in the communistic countries and from planning in some Western economies. This applies not only to the methodology but also to the types of public interventions listed in the plan. However, since the list of required interventions in underdeveloped economies obviously differs from lists drawn up for developed economies, any list of interventions considered by underdeveloped countries—on the analogy of planning mature economies—cannot be exhaustive.

Although our analytical methods improve as we move from project-to-project planning to integrated investment plans and thence to comprehensive national programs, all three planning approaches still have two common deficiencies:

1. A number of the most vital planning dimensions are excluded from the planning space.

2. None of the three types of planning stands up to the test of exhaustiveness.

The analytical gains made as planning becomes more comprehensive are often purchased at high cost: planning necessarily becomes more abstract and inclusive, contact with political decision makers is lost, and resistance mechanisms against planning build up (Chapter 6); in other words, as the economic viability of planning increases, its political viability decreases. This relationship is amply illustrated by the numerous abortive comprehensive plans drawn up in the fifties and early sixties in Latin America and elsewhere.

COMPREHENSIVE SECTORIAL PLANNING

The fact that planning as now practiced has met with only limited success does not prove that effective planning is either impossible or unnecessary; on the contrary, if fragmentary planning of scarce resources has led to unsatisfactory allocation of the capital ration, how can we expect that unplanned allocation of these resources, handled by the same bureaucratic hierarchy, would give a higher efficiency. As long as an economy, or its principal sector, retains a predominantly nonmarket character, as long as capital is rationed and allocated by government, the emergence of cumulative growth is conditional upon planned government intervention; moreover, the more comprehensive, the more exhaustive, and the more integrated planning becomes (within the confines of political feasibility), the better are the chances of success. Myrdal has arrived at a similar conclusion in his *Asian Drama*[7]: "The need for a set of policies on a broad front, in which all state intervention is coordinated, is very much greater in underdeveloped than in developed countries."

However, if underdevelopment does not "accept" comprehensive planning, in spite of it being a condition for the emergence from underdevelopment, how can we hope to short-circuit this vicious circle? Before we attempt a synthetic approach, we shall have to elaborate on this analysis.

The underlying cause for the failure of comprehensive planning lies in the basic incompatibility between planning and the political process: true comprehensive planning is organically hierarchic, i.e., it is conceived at a number of hierarchically controlled, partly self-regulative levels, in which comprehensiveness increases systematically from bottom to top and horizontal and vertical coordination is enforced from top to bottom. The political process is, however, often pluralistic, and even where it is authoritative, the controlling executive—because of limitations in his capability—does not function as the top-level coordinating hierarchical control, but rather as a substitute for the second-level decision makers. Such deficiencies in high-level coordination necessarily reduce the degree of comprehensiveness of planning.

To prime positive causation, it is proposed to bypass the structural incompatibility between planning and the political process by confining comprehensive planning to the area of control of one senior political decision maker (usually one sector) and thus significantly reducing the necessity to determine intersectorial trade-offs and coordinations. On the other hand, to compensate for the loss of scope, the depth of planning within the selected sector should

[7] Myrdal, *op. cit.*, vol. III, p. 1902.

be increased so that the program analysis comprises all relevant potential interventions and thus becomes a truly exhaustive study of development potentialities. This type of planning will be called comprehensive sectorial planning.

It would be overoptimistic to assume that by confining comprehensive planning to one sector, the structural and conceptual incompatibility between planning and the political process can be avoided; however, this intentional limitation will certainly reduce the chances of foundering, especially during the sensitive maturation period, before full operative momentum has been achieved. Should such comprehensive sectorial planning still be too ambitious, a planning bridgehead could be secured by confining the comprehensive approach to one of the several subsectors controlled by a "tertiary" political executive; this bridgehead, once secured, could be used as a basis for "horizontal" expansion to the other subsectors of the same sector.

The spillover effects of comprehensive planning, practiced within one sector, will, in time, make it possible to expand such planning to other sectors and, at an appropriate moment, to raise it to a level where it would cover the entire national economy, if at such time national comprehensive planning might prove to be necessary.

Confining the approach to one or two sectors will not seriously cramp the growth of the national economy, provided a strategic sector is selected, and provided its growth can be assumed to create, in addition to direct benefits, important spillover effects. The strategic sector in most underdeveloped countries is the agricultural one, and, in fact, most development planners agree today that agricultural development is a necessary, though not in itself a sufficient, condition for the emergence of balanced economic growth.

Operationally, comprehensive sectorial planning should proceed on the following lines:

1. A sketchy macroanalysis of aggregate functions of the whole economy would be drawn up to give a rough definition of boundary conditions of the selected sector, i.e., the demand made by the rest of the economy (and by the export market) upon the sectorial production process and the resources the economy chooses to allocate to the latter.

2. Planning from the top would be undertaken to define program objectives and targets and to draw up an exhaustive list of relevant potential interventions (or inputs, or input mixes, in logistic language) that may be applied to the existing sectorial production process, with a view to upgrading the production environment and to improving the response variety of individuals and groups to the upgraded environment; to evaluation of input-output ratios of alternative input mixes; and to ranking of such alternative input mixes according to "cost effectiveness" in terms of the selected objectives.

3. This would be followed by planning from the bottom, i.e., translation of input mixes selected under 2 into specific projects; ranking of these projects and determination of the best project combination that can be obtained for the sectorial capital allocation.

4. Finally, the informational, logistic, and politico-institutional feasibility of the selected project list would be evaluated and reshuffled (including the addition of input and information generating projects) to the extent found necessary.

A detailed description of the sectorial planning process is given in Chapter 20.

PSEUDOPLANNING

The necessity of planning, at least for the developing countries, is today fully recognized both by planners from the developed economies and by those originating from the underdeveloped countries. However, in many such countries, neither the planning organization nor the political decision process is capable, or willing, to cope with the complexities of a comprehensive plan.

However, since planning has become a kind of status symbol, a "plan-or-perish" attitude now seems to prevail, and planners occasionally feel that even if, for no fault of their own, they cannot come up with the real article, they should at least produce and present to the political level the trappings of a plan. Real planning is an uphill job, not only because it involves considerable technological and organizational efforts, but mainly because, from the chronically short-term point of view of the politician, intrinsically long-term measures are unattractive. Furthermore, before one can embark on planning proper, the main sociopolitical objectives and strategies have to be clearly stated, and this, in a true development plan, will include "a pervasive social transformation . . . a wholesale metamorphosis of habits, a wrenching reorientation of values . . . an unweaving and reweaving of the fabric of daily existence itself . . . in any society such a transformation is a profoundly dislocating experience."[8]

The politician therefore usually prefers to remain closeted in his world of double-think and triple-talk, instead of committing himself unequivocally to a specific internally compatible set of values, objectives, and strategies.

True planning, i.e., planning bent on implementation, then must use genuine coin, while in politics counterfeit currency does equally well, and in time succeeds in driving the genuine article out of circulation by the operation of a political Gresham's law. This tactical approach of the political level is not necessarily due to any "innate viciousness" of politicians, but rather to their pragmatic understanding of the politico-psychological situation in the initial phases of development. For development implies the sacrifice of possible benefits of today for the sake of the benefits of tomorrow and is hence a policy of a long time span. Lifting an underdeveloped economy from its stagnancy, changing vicious circles to "positive, circular causation," involves a painful transformation, a "scandal" according to Austruy's definition[9]; it comprehends the birth of a new society, often preceded by acute birth pangs. Notwithstanding their ultimate moral justification, it is difficult to sell long-term policies to the public, while subjecting them to initial and painful phases of development.

[8] Robert L. Heilbroner, *The Great Ascent*, Harper Torchbooks, New York, 1963, pp. 53–54.
[9] J. Austruy, *Le Scandal du Développement*, Éditions Marcel Rivière et Cie, Paris, 1965.

It is, therefore, not surprising that in emerging economies easily marketable surrogates often substitute for planning. From the point of view of political expediency, a glamorous list of superlative hardware, well-adorned with economic padding, does nicely for a plan. In its political aspects, this has often been extremely successful, but in a new economy it has seldom effected true development to a degree commensurate with the outlay. The growth bulge created by such a program on an isolated sector of the general front of stagnation cannot carry the rest of the front with it, due to the lack of "economic induction" so characteristic of developing economies.

"Development enclaves" in a sea of underdevelopment are, and have been for some time, very much in vogue; they have the advantage of easily diverting the longings and yearnings of a poor nation into easily accessible channels; dams and large basic industries are examples of such diversion. These enclaves become status symbols, appealing to that section of public opinion for which the existence of a true plan has little appeal; they become the chthonic symbol of national aspirations for development and, as such, have considerable psychological importance, as is instinctively realized at the political level. While exhibiting all these major political advantages, development enclaves still demand no change in the traditional structure of the society or the economy; they cause no major upheaval of vested interest; in short, they involve none of the "scandals" of the development proper. Such pseudodevelopment may result in psychological and political enchantment, but it cannot lead, and in actual experience has not led, to self-sustained growth.[10]

[10] Heilbroner, *op. cit.*, p. 53.

8

THE DEVELOPMENT-UNDERDEVELOPMENT SCALE: A STRUCTURAL INTERPRETATION

The movement of the whole social system upwards is what all of us in fact mean by development.
GUNNAR MYRDAL (*Asian Drama*)

EXISTING YARDSTICKS OF DEVELOPMENT

In his book *Asian Drama*,[1] Gunnar Myrdal ridicules attempts to placate the sensibilities of the underdeveloped nations by the use of circumscriptions and euphemisms in place of the epithet "underdeveloped." He contends—and rightly so—that the use of terms such as "developing," "emerging," "newly emerging" in place of underdeveloped is purely "diplomacy by terminology," since these terms fail to stress what is most conspicuous by its absence and what is most needed in these countries, namely, growth orientation. Myrdal advocates that the term "underdeveloped," which for "diplomatic" reasons has fallen into disrepute, should, therefore, be restored to its original place. Professor Myrdal's critique notwithstanding, we have chosen to use a number of these spurned coinages interchangeably, if only to relieve the monotony of constantly repeating the negatively charged term underdeveloped.

Myrdal has set up *six broad categories* to characterize a country's position on the development scale, three of the six categories representing economic parameters, two noneconomic ones, and the last category, that of "policies," a combined integrative category. After touching upon definitions of development trends and indices, he concludes that "development cannot be defined in terms of growth of national income per head, but has to be defined as the upward movement of the entire social system . . . . A change in the national income per head can thus never be used as more than a rough and ready indicator of that more complex change in the whole social system that we really want to record."

[1] Gunnar Myrdal, *Asian Drama*, Pantheon Books, a division of Random House, Inc., New York, 1968, vol. III, p. 1830, Appendix I.

It is to the elaboration of this incisive critique of current terminology and metrics of development that the present chapter will be devoted, beginning with a review of some of the specific major deficiencies of prevailing development metrics, as listed in the following:

1. The terms developed and underdeveloped, or any of the more diplomatic coinages used interchangeably, suffer blatantly—as will most definitions stemming from a *two-valued logic*—from the distortions involved in dividing the universe of discourse into two classes: those which have a certain property and those which lack this property (in our case, those which are and those which are not developed). If we set aside all other difficulties of classification, "development" has to be conceived as varying along a continuous scale, rather than as being classifiable under two mutually exclusive categories, each representing the extreme values of such a development scale.

2. Difficulties in classification also arise from the fact that there is *no single quality* that can be successfully used as a *yardstick* of development. As stated above, Myrdal has recognized six broad categories, while other investigators have suggested different categories. All these existing descriptive classifications that are used to express a country's state of development suffer from the lack of a "common denominator" (or trade-off ratio) by which readings representing such categories can be translated into a single metric for comparative purposes. To overcome this difficulty, it has been suggested that we compare "profiles" of measurements of a number of categories; such profiles, it is true, would indicate the "underlying" similarities between countries of similar profiles, but would still leave open the question of how these profiles are to be compared and how to establish the cause of these profile similarities, i.e., how the common structural features correlated with these similarities are to be accounted for.

3. The existence of "dual" and even "plural" economies within one nation, and often also within one economic sector, robs aggregate national figures of the little comparative value they might otherwise have had. Such multiplicity of development levels within one economy or sector is far from being a transitory phenomenon since it is often the consequence of deep underlying structural differences.

4. Existing development yardsticks and profiles are capable of expressing the development differentials that prevailed between various countries only around the middle of the twentieth century and are consequently very much *dated*. We are therefore much in need of a yardstick of development that could be applied to the past and future, as well as to the present, and which, perhaps, could periodically be submitted to recalibration. In the absence of such a yardstick, the relativity and "datedness" of our measurement require that we introduce a yardstick of yardsticks to enable us to compare past and present development measurements—and also to facilitate future comparisons. Failure to allow for this "relativity" of measurement could lead us to draw absurd conclusions, such as that Greece of classical times was exceedingly underdeveloped, while, on the other hand, a number of oil-rich ministates of our times would be thought of as considerably more developed.

Again, we would arrive at curious results if we undertook to evaluate the state of development of the U.S.A. of today as seen from the point of view of an observer of, say, the first or second decade of the twenty-first century.

In attempting to draw up a development metrics, we must ask ourselves what our aim is in measuring the degree of development. Do we aim at ranking development levels of various countries, or do we seek to determine where exactly on an idealized "trajectory" of development we should place nation X at time T? If we assume that a pragmatic motivation underlies such measurements, the latter objective appears to be the more valuable.

To conclude the above criticisms of prevailing measurement approaches on a constructive note, we propose that the usual per capita GNP figures be supplemented by a limited number of indicators capable of expressing some of the internal structural features of an economy. Among these, the following are proposed:

1. That ratios be given to express the production and employment volumes of the primary, secondary, and tertiary sectors
2. That median, in addition to average, figures be cited
3. That upper and lower quartiles be given to supplement median sectorial figures in cases where the existence of regional or sectorial "dual" or "plural" economic levels is particularly marked

The difficulties encountered in drawing up a "descriptive" type of measurement all point to one basic fact, namely, that we are measuring symptoms, i.e., we are attempting to compare economies by comparing symptoms rather than by tracing their underlying common "structural" similarities or dissimilarities.

In the following, we shall trace such structural causative elements of underdevelopment, without, at this state, arriving at a measurement approach; we shall then examine the direction which future measurement attempts may have to follow.

THE SYMPTOMATIC VS. THE DIAGNOSTIC RANKING APPROACH

The prevailing measurement approach to development is based on two main parameters:

1. The absolute level of a per capita production function, selected to represent overall development
2. The current growth rate (or gradient) of this function

No consistent attempt is made to reduce these two scales to one ranking scale. By following this approach, we confine ourselves to measuring the level and gradient of a selected indicative function, without attempting to identify and measure the causative functions that characterize a certain degree of development. In other words, we resign ourselves to a descriptive approach based on the measurement of symptoms, instead of diagnosing and measuring the underlying factors.

To identify the factors that "explain" development, we must first draw up a general representational model of society. Here, again, as in the case of other socioeconomic phenomena, we must choose between the three basic models: the Marxist-mechanistic, the laissez faire–atomistic, and the cybernetic-biological.

Explanation of the development mechanisms by the Marxist-mechanistic model is simplistic fundamentalistic; since the "superstructure" of society is assumed to be fully "determined" by the production process, changes in the production process "inevitably" lead to an appropriate adaptation of the superstructure. Thus, according to this hypothesis, we can quietly concentrate on upgrading the production process, without having to worry about institutional adaptation; the parameters which characterize the production process will, therefore, constitute an adequate representation of the degree of development.[2]

The laissez faire model, although diametrically opposed to the Marxistic one, will lead to the same conclusions, since it assumes that every decision maker responds rationally to a change in the production process and that by rationally selecting a line of action intended to maximize his own benefit he inevitably also maximizes society's benefit. Hence, here too, all we need to do is to change the production process, i.e., the response environment of the individual decision maker.

Unfortunately, actual experience does not bear out the conclusions of either model—at least as far as *agricultural growth* in the underdeveloped countries is concerned. This is partially explained by the fact that when faced by a new agricultural production environment, the individual producer responds in one of two ways:

1. He ignores the new environment, and continues in his old path.
2. He responds to the new environment, according to response patterns transferred from his old production environment.

The producer thus, as a rule, shows none of the responses attributed to him by the Marxist-mechanistic or the laissez faire model.

The reason for this "paradoxical" behavior of the producer and his institutions lies in the distortion inherent in his evaluative process and action ideology, a distortion which can be explained by the limitations of his psychological space. This rigidity of response pattern on the part of the agricultural producer will be dealt with in Chapter 23.

As in the earlier context, the cybernetic model appears to be the most fruitful. This model does not presuppose the universal existence of "inevitable" mechanisms operating between the producer, the new production environment, and the relevant control levels: rather, it postulates a heterogeneity of regulatory mechanisms which in certain states of the socioeconomic system (i.e., those of "development maturity") will lead to its full adaptation by a positive causation process, while in different states (i.e., those of underdevelopment), it will not be sufficiently strong, nor possess sufficient variety, and will, therefore, fail to lead to adaptation.

[2] This is elaborated in Myrdal's work, *op. cit.*, vol. III, Appendix 2.

In the final analysis, *development maturity* is directly related to adaptive capacity at all levels of the socioeconomic system; more specifically, this capacity has two major aspects, namely, the capacity of the executive levels of the socioeconomic hierarchy to create *new production environments* for the producer and the capacity of the producer to respond adequately and *adapt* to the new production *environment.*

These two capacities have one common denominator, that of "requisite variety," or, expressed otherwise, the capacity to transcend the limitations inherent in traditional problem solving (with its extremely limited variety of alternative lines of action) and to "proliferate variety" in producing environments and response patterns. It is this capacity that we propose to call "growth capacity." The thesis of the present chapter is that this growth capacity is the most important single factor in determining the place of a socioeconomic system on the underdevelopment-development scale; this capacity is described more fully in the following section.

GROWTH CAPACITY

Consideration of growth capacity starts best from an inspection of a socioeconomic system in which growth capacity is still "dormant," as is the case in an underdeveloped sector of an underdeveloped country, e.g., a subsistence agricultural sector. Even in such a "traditional" socioeconomic system, we shall still find a hierarchic structure; however, in contrast to the multilevel pattern of a modern economy, a traditional hierarchy is extremely flat, i.e., it comprises a great number of subsystems (in parallel) and a limited number of levels (in series). Furthermore, there is less integration between the different levels than that found in modern economies. The extent of self-regulation within subsystems is considerable, while the amount of control and imposed change originating from the next higher integrative level is relatively small. Since the change in the production environment imposed by the higher levels is, as a rule, limited, the response range developed within such a relatively stable environment is extremely narrow, and response patterns tend to be repetitive and traditional. Neither the coordinating level nor the production level possesses the requisite variety to initiate a change or to respond to it. Thus, a socioeconomic system with these characteristics suffers from political, psychological, social, and institutional built-in resistance mechanisms operating against change and progress, mechanisms which can be overcome only by an outside intervention of sufficient impact.

The aim of such an *intervention* should be the "creation" of new variety of all relevant levels: at the higher levels, new variety has to be "created" for the initiation of changes in the production environment; at the production levels, new response variety to the modified production environment has to be initiated. According to this conception, intervention aimed at "developing" part of a socioeconomic system cannot lay down the fixed response patterns postulated by the mechanistic school, nor can it rely on the spontaneous emergence of new responses, as held by the laissez faire school. It should rather aim at *improving the cybernetic structure of the coordinating level and of the production level,* in order to elicit from the structurally modified system a new variety which would be expressed in advancing and upgrading the production environment, in improving response patterns, in strengthening coordinative control, and in vertical integration.

Proliferating variety at the production subsystem level involves the following:

> Increasing the response variety of the ultimate individual decision maker, the farmer, by structuring his psychological space in a way that will bring new production complexes within his conceptual reach and will enable him to make an economically meaningful selection.
>
> Increasing the response variety of the institutional network to complement the response variety of the farmer's decision process. Increasing the response variety at these two interacting levels of the production process will upgrade the first basic loop of self-regulation—that lying between the producer and his "grass-root" institutions—and push them out of their static equilibrium.
>
> Increasing the response variety of the whole subsystem by enriching the institutional infrastructure through the creation of new institutional units which can interact either in parallel or in series with existing ones.

At the next higher coordinative levels, increasing response variety will imply:

> Generating response variety for the productive level by initiating improved or new production environments offering greater opportunities for new response variety at the subsystem level.
>
> Initiating selection mechanisms which will assist the production level in selecting, from among the various possible responses, those which are economically preferable; this may, for instance, be achieved by the creation of incentives which would tend to channel selection in the desirable direction, until such selection mechanisms could be relied upon to operate spontaneously.

Seen from a different angle, the ultimate effect of variety proliferation can be expressed as the creation of a new, higher level, *harmony* between the objectives of the production level and those of the coordinative level and the initiation, through such a new harmony, of self-perpetuating and self-reinforcing loops between the two levels that will lead to cumulative growth of the whole sector.

Relations between the coordinative and the production level in developing countries are often found to differ considerably from those described in this idealized picture. The professed objective of the coordinative level is the creation of an improved production environment, aimed at enabling the production level to extricate itself from its present state of stagnation. On the other hand, the controlling objectives of the production level turn on the conservation of homeostasis at the prevailing level of activity and on minimizing risk, since every deviation from this state appears to involve risks that are not in proportion to the possible benefits to be obtained.

Owing, on the one hand, to the coordinative level's lack of proficiency and to the low specific intensity of its coordinative operations and, on the other hand, to the production level's lack of response variety, the resistance mechanism at this production level tends to be stronger than the diffuse and maloriented forces exerted by the coordinative level; consequently, the production level falls back, after some vacillation, to its old homeostatic level. Chronic disharmony of objectives between the coordinative and the production level is thus created.

Harmonizing the objectives of the two levels and increasing their sensitivity toward stimuli and influences from the outside world are therefore conditional on the requisite proliferation variety at the producer level. In fact, once a self-reinforcing loop is set up between the production and the coordinative level, the process of self-regulation at the production level becomes more and more spontaneous and also more responsive to impulses from the rest of the system; in other words, its "resonance" increases, and it becomes market oriented.

Because of the existence of strong inertial forces resisting movement from a low ultrastable to a higher dynamic equilibrium, a great initial "momentum" must be mobilized in order to effect the initial displacement. Limitations in available "displacement momentum" often dictate a strategy of concentrating all available forces on a limited front. Reducing new environmental and response variety to such a limited front does not automatically ensure that the new approach will penetrate to other important sections of the sector; it will, nevertheless, ensure a breakthrough in the strongly entrenched positions of traditional responses and soften up other sections of the sectorial front for subsequent further penetration. The rapid development of West African export agriculture during and after the Second World War, as well as the ensuing growth in other branches of the economy, is a good example of the operation of this mechanism.

At this point, we may attempt to expand our definition of growth capacity to allow for the existence of ultrastability in the homeostatic loops at the production level. Growth capacity could then be defined as follows: the capacity of a socioeconomic system to modify its structure in a way that will increase both variety and conductivity to the extent relevant to the role of that level with a view to initiating the following processes for the next lower level:

1. An improved production environment
2. Movement from traditional ultrastable homeostasis to dynamic equilibria
3. Proliferation of response variety to the improved environment
4. The setting up of selection mechanisms for the individual decision makers which would assist in harmonizing their several objectives with those of society
5. Greater coordination and control

THE PURPOSE OF DEVELOPMENT YARDSTICKS

The mechanism proposed in the preceding sections for determining the position of a socioeconomic system on the development-underdevelopment scale has one important disadvantage, namely, it does not yet lend itself to quantification. If the purpose of a yardstick is to supply readings for comparative purposes, the cybernetic yardstick does not appear to be a satisfactory choice. However, in this context, we must ask ourselves whether the ultimate purpose of a development yardstick is comparison, or whether we consider comparison only as an intermediate step to predict the "trajectory" of the behavior of a socioeconomic system. From the planner's point of view, only the second approach is meaningful.

The use of orthodox development yardsticks for predictive purposes, such as per capita GNP, implies two assumptions:

1. That the trajectories of various economies are sufficiently similar to be comparable
2. That the reading of the selected parameter for a specific country truly characterizes its "development stage" and defines its position on the "typical" trajectory and, thereby, gives the anticipated tread of this trajectory for the near future

However, per capita GNP or the respective sectorial figures are aggregate averages, masking the basic differences that exist between the compared socioeconomic systems, between the various sectors of one system, and between the subsectors of one sector. Comparisons based solely on such aggregate averages will therefore have low predictive value.

If we aim at predictive value, we should better attempt to compare the causative structural mechanisms, their flaws, dysfunctions, vicious circles, and lack of adaptation. This comparison is advocated since only by understanding these structural elements will we be able to trace the reasons for the inadequate behavior of the socioeconomic system or subsystem, to outline methods for its improvement, and to predict the modification of its behavior in response to alternative interventions.

Moreover, we should select the state of these mechanisms as an indication of the grade of development, even if such a comparison does not lend itself to quantification, since unquantified comparison of the relevant differences might be more fruitful than a quantified comparison of the less relevant or masked features.

A study and comparison of the mechanism and structural features of development along the lines proposed will have the following outcome:

1. It will indicate the course, or trajectories, of past developments of sectors and subsectors of the national economy and their response to interventions.
2. It will define the point on typical sectorial or subsectorial development trajectories of similar socioeconomic systems (for which good records are available) at which we ought to place the system under investigation.
3. It will point out the type of interventions necessary to improve the trend of the trajectory.

The development forecast of a sector or subsector will depend on its present location on the structural development trajectory, i.e., the level of development so far achieved, and on the "gradient" of the curve at this point; this gradient depends, in turn, on the adequateness of growth capacity.

It may thus be concluded that a comparative analysis of the status of an economy should employ these two structural indicators, as well as the recognized orthodox development and growth indicators.

MATURITY

The importance of research into control increases yearly as the magnitude of uncontrolled forces continues to rise.
STAFFORD BEER (*Cybernetics and Management*)

A mature society is a society possessing a requisite growth capacity, a society in which each of the several levels of the decision hierarchy has the capacity to generate adequate response environments for the next lower level, and in which that lower level, in turn, possesses a requisite response variety to adequately adapt itself to such a dynamically changing environment—in harmony with the control functions exercised by the higher level.

Tracing this pattern of mutual response enrichment from level to level, we finally arrive at the top level of the hierarchy only to ask ourselves the vexing question: *Who provides the enrichment of the response environment for this top level? Quis custodiet ipsos custodes?* This is certainly no idle question, as creativity does not, as a rule, constitute the decisive criterion for the selection of top decision makers.

It is difficult to give a straightforward and explicit answer to this question, since in modern society no institutionalized process fulfills this function. Starry-eyed adherents of traditional democracy may think that the function of proliferation of variety for the top executive level is the sacred right and duty of institutions composed of the people's representatives. However, actual observation of the parliamentary process shows that this process, more often than not, has a variety annihilation function, rather than that of variety generation. This is not surprising if we bear in mind that members of parliaments are promoted in accordance with political criteria and that similar criteria operate in selecting the hierarchy's highest functionaries.

Nevertheless, it appears that mature societies do have the capacity to generate a considerable amount of variety at the top hierarchic level. However, the processes through which this top-level variety is generated are neither generalized nor fully institutionalized; on the contrary, they have their origin in the very pluralistic nature and in the lack of homogeneity and consistency of the hierarchic structure of modern society. Modern society consists of a number of relatively independent, though interacting, hierarchies, each controlling a specific aspect and sector of activities. These include, to quote only some of the more important ones, the political, economic, military, and trade-union hierarchies and the scientific, technological, artistic, youth-transient, and mass-media hierarchies. Each of these partial and specialized hierarchies possesses its own promotion criteria, its own ethical values and yardsticks. These criteria are excellent sounding boards for the variety generated anywhere in society—instruments of "amplification" for innovations that have "passed" the test.

It is this plurality and openness of the hierarchic structure of modern society that provide a fertile environment for variety generation and amplification in all spheres of life and that exert an ever-growing influence at all levels of the decision hierarchy. If left to proliferate without plan and control, the plurality of the hierarchic structure could seriously jeopardize the democratic decision process; if properly trimmed and channeled, it could compensate and correct distortion introduced by the political hierarchy into problem solving and action ideology. Its very existence, as well as its growing impact, exerts a "softening" influence on the building up and fossilization of inertial resistances to change.

The vital importance of variety generation at the top may, occasionally, become so conspicuous that—temporarily or permanently—the prevailing criteria of promotion are disregarded and candidates are actually selected for their creativity.

MATURITY AND IMMATURITY IN DEVELOPED ECONOMIES

Maturity is the extreme "positive" point on the underdevelopment-development scale. No country is ever fully mature, none completely immature. Maturity levels within the same nation will vary from region to region, sector to sector, subsector to subsector, and—what might possibly be the most significant variation—they will change with time within the same society, sector, and region.

Maturity depends on the operation of certain cybernetic mechanisms, which remain operative only within a certain range of conditions, and which will cease to respond adaptively in the case of movement of the environment outside this range.

A certain sector, faced by such an extreme change of conditions, reacts in one of two ways:

1. By adaptation through structural accretion, i.e., by development of new integrative mechanisms, thus creating a higher level of coordination. This solution is, as it were, couched in the "cybernetic metalanguage." The new control mechanism will be superimposed upon existing control mechanisms to form the newly integrated control system which will lead the sector to new adaptive levels.
2. By adaptation through crisis. In this case, no new integrative mechanism is developed and, consequently, the socioeconomic system ceases to be mature in the relevant dimension. Cumulative deterioration will then set in and lead to a localized crisis situation.

   At this point, external and, possibly, internal forces which had until then been neutralized by inertial counterforces will come to the fore, tending to create the higher integrative mechanism described under 1. This form of adjustment will be referred to as "adaptation by crisis." However, there is some danger of overshooting inherent in this path of adaptation, both in relation to the structural rigidity of the newly added control mechanisms and in relation to the range of counteraction.

The cybernetic mechanism—from which the *mature behavior* of systems will stem—is connected with the *criterion of integrative compatibility* of viable systems. A system complies with this criterion, and exhibits a purposeful overall adaptation, if the regulative stimuli originating from the $(n + 1)$th level of the system can keep the responses of the (n)th level within a range that is acceptable from the point of view of the objectives of the $(n + 1)$th level. In such a system, the regulative loops between the various levels, combined with the self-regulative loops at these several levels, make the system as a whole move in the direction of the system objectives.

When this mechanism breaks down, objectives of the (n)th level and metaobjectives of the $(n + 1)$th level start to grow apart; in other words, integration breaks down, and the system or subsystem no longer functions as a whole. To the outside observer, such a system will appear to have lost the capacity of purposeful behavior; it will have ceased to comply with the criterion of integrative compatibility.

It is the very rate of growth and change in all spheres of life and activity of modern mature societies that creates the risk that change will "outgrow" the adaptive capacity of the socioeconomic mechanism, i.e., that the mechanism will lose the requisite variety required by the new situation and cease to comply with the criterion of integrative compatibility. Hypotheses on the best way to restore the integrative capacity of the system can again be based on one of the three fundamental models of society. In this case, application of the laissez faire model will, for reasons outlined above, lead to gradual deterioration of our physical, mental, and political environments and call for an extreme brinksmanship of adaptation, in which ruin is narrowly avoided only through a process of adaptation by crisis. Application of the mechanistic model will lead to rigid totalitarian planning and control, with all its inefficiency and dogmatism further aggravated by the extreme intellectual dearth of variety at the top of the decision hierarchy which has been selected according to "Realpolitik" promotional criteria. The cybernetic model, imitating nature's evolutionary patterns of grafting new integrative mechanisms upon existing ones, has the best chance of developing an adequate planning base for public intervention in those sectors of a mature economy which have ceased to be mature.

Thus, the increase in the rate of change that spreads over more and more areas of the socioeconomic process reintroduces into mature society the question of structural underdevelopment, a question that creates new challenges to the democratic process. In nontotalitarian regimes, this new challenge must be met by a new type of response, by the introduction of a new dimension of integration quickened by a *pluralistic structure* consisting of a number of relatively independent hierarchies. As structural underdevelopment spreads, these new dimensions of a *pluralistic democracy* will have to be channeled and at least partly institutionalized and new control processes established that will lead to a new higher type of integration. Such an institutionalization would, however, have to avoid jeopardizing the tasks and aims of development by adopting promotional criteria that would bring to the top of these nonpolitical hierarchies personalities with profiles similar to those promoted within the political hierarchy. The new processes will require analytical capability, intellectual honesty, courage, and perseverance; in other words, a wide-angle mind, capable of transcending its own egocentric space and of facing the true problems of the nation. The 64,000-dollar question is, of course, whether such a selection procedure in the "nonpolitical" dimensions of society is "politically feasible."

Another different kind of danger the pluralistic democratic decision process has to avoid is the loss of coherence. If every one of the numerous nonpolitical hierarchies is to have its say, how will the political or administrative decision-maker's prerogative to decide be preserved? What guarantee is there that this jungle of proliferating opinions, criticisms, advice, and warnings implied in the pluralistic democracy will not paralyze the decision maker? Will it not, indeed, lead to the worst decision, i.e., the decision to make no decision? Certainly, if this is the case, then the cure will be worse than the disease. A theoretical way out of this impasse might be by partial institutionalization of the pluralistic process, in a manner that would ensure that the more "intellectual" hierarchies would deal with long-term trends, basic strategies, major conservation policies, etc., while the politico-administrative process would finalize short-term planning and tactics of implementation. These are vague and possibly not very helpful generalizations; however, the problem is so new, the data are so scarce, that nothing better can be offered at this stage.

9
THE PLANNING PROCESS

Il y a l'avenir qui se fait et l'avenir qu'on fait.
L'avenir réel se compose des deux . . . .
Mais la parole de l'homme est plutôt: "Je fais";
car c'est l'action qui est grosse d'avenir.[1]

ALAIN (*Propos*)

In the preceding chapters, the main emphasis has been placed on the differences between the requirements of development plans in developed and underdeveloped countries, as well as on the paradox of development inherent in the fact that the complex economies of the developed countries need less elaborate plans than the much simpler economies of the underdeveloped countries.

This chapter stresses a different, though related, aspect, namely, the existence of *parallel differences in the planning process,* that is, in the ways and means of arriving at a plan. The differences in the planning process between developed and underdeveloped countries stem from differences in the *purpose* of the planning process, rather than from differences in the content of planning. In a developed country, the sole aim of the planning process is to produce a satisfactory plan; in an underdeveloped country, on the other hand, the purpose of planning will also be related to the improvement, through the planning process, of the *capacity of the planner* and the planning organization and of planning information. In the developed countries we consider the planning process adequate and therefore aim only at achieving a good end product. In the underdeveloped countries, the process, i.e., personnel, organization, and information, is inadequate, and we therefore have to divide our attention between improving the capacity aspect of the planning process and improving its end product. To achieve the former aspect, we have to build into the planning process such selected features of the implementation process as are necessary to generate the requisite information, to prove out the relevant organizational patterns and methodology, and to provide adequate training opportunities; by improving the capacity aspect of the planning process, we shall, of course, also improve its end product, the plan.

[1] There is the future that evolves and the future that one can make. The real future is composed of both . . . .
But man's motto is rather "I make"; for action is pregnant with the future.

These structural differences which distinguish the developed from the underdeveloped economies, and the greater uncertainty prevailing in the latter countries, make it necessary in the early phases of development to *integrate planning and implementation processes into a single combined operation.* Only gradually, and only after having passed through a number of well-defined phases, will it be possible to relax the link (bond) between planning and implementation, to reduce the comprehensiveness of planning, and to resolve the combined processes into their orthodox components, as known to us from the developed environment.

TRANSIENTS AND TARGETS

A plan, as conceived in the developed world, is the juxtaposition of a definition of an initial status quo and a desired target state. In this type of planning process, the logistics required to "upgrade" the status quo to target state requirements are usually analyzed and listed only for inputs coming under the investment category.

In the *developed world,* transients, i.e., the transition stages that set in when the status quo (or any intermediate state) is disturbed by the application of the "development inputs," until the "final" target[2] steady state is reached, are usually not explicitly defined. Where defined, the analysis of transients—in the developed countries—is confined to elaborating the phasing of the investment aspects of the program.

Omission in the mature economies of this spelling out of transients does not reduce the value of planning, since public intervention in these economies consists mainly of capital investment, and since such an investment program is adequately defined by specification of the target state.

In *underdeveloped countries,* however, where public intervention must encompass all areas of economic activity, as well as the institutional framework of society, and where the very fate of a program is conditional upon the complete transformation of this framework, *transients* take on an all-important role; in other words, development in these countries is equivalent to living permanently in a universe of transients. Furthermore, since it is beyond our power to "shut down" the economy until this transformation process is completed, we have to design our transients in a way that, while incorporating a certain volume of "upgrading" in the essential planning dimensions, they, nevertheless, will maintain their "operational viability."

The very fact that planning in underdeveloped countries embraces the social and psychological, as well as the physical, space has a decisive influence on planning approach and methodology. Firstly, much less reliable information is available for the sociopsychological dimensions than for the physical ones. Moreover, information is much more specific and, therefore, less transferable from one context to another. Secondly, the phase space of develop-

[2] "Final" in this context is, of course, only final from the relative ex ante point of view of the planner concentrating upon a specific planning period and, consciously or unconsciously, neglecting the continuity of development.

ment has to be envisaged as being made up of a multidimensional stream of interacting operations, while both our professional thinking and our institutional hierarchy are single dimensional and take into account very little interdisciplinary interaction. Conventional, single-discipline, informational, analytical, and institutional grids will therefore not structurally fit the phase space for which they are intended. In spite of this structural discrepancy between grid and phase space, we can, nevertheless, achieve a relatively adequate "fit" by subdividing programs into relatively short subphases (each representing a transient toward the program objectives); for each of these short subphases, substitution of a group of parallel single-discipline analyses and interventions for the multidimensional counterpart will not introduce too great an error. At the beginning of each new transient, or transition stage, the influence of recent interaction between the dimensions of phase space should be ascertained and allowed for, before we proceed to analysis.

RESOURCES AND TRANSFER FUNCTIONS

Stated in more rigorous terms, the development process and the planning process related to it can be represented by two groups of variables and the functional relationships between them:

The Development Resources Inputs These comprise the logistic resources—material and nonmaterial—that we have to apply to the status quo complex in order to "upgrade" it, i.e., to modify it, in its various dimensions, according to the requirements of our objectives.[3]

The Transfer Functions These are the functions brought into play by the application of resources inputs and which result in the desired outcomes.

The Outcomes or Outputs These constitute the levels of upgrading of the status quo complex in the various dimensions of the phase space effected by the resources inputs.

The status quo complex is characterized by a certain status quo in the three basic resources groups: the physical resources, constituting the natural means of production such as land, water, and climate and their improvements by past investments; the human resources, consisting of the individuals employing these means of production and their response patterns, motivation, know-how, and skills; and the institutional resources that are instrumental in supporting the activities of the individual producers and in discharging functions related to production and distribution that cannot be performed by the individual alone.

The development resources input package mobilized by the program for upgrading the status quo complex comprises resources that can be subdivided into the same three basic resources groups: physical resources, represented

[3] The concepts development resources inputs and status quo complex are spelled out in more detail in Chapter 20; there the more specific terms development resources vector and natural resources vector are substituted for the above general terms.

here by investments; human resources, represented by training and motivating inputs; and institutional resources, represented by human resources trained in the establishment, upgrading, and running of institutions.

The transfer functions, operating between development resources inputs and outcomes, can be subdivided according to the resources inputs with which they are associated: transfer functions associated with investments relate to the upgrading of the preexisting production environment; those associated with human resources relate to the improvement of know-how, motivation, and response patterns of the human resources employed in the development and production processes; while the transfer functions associated with institutional resources relate to the upgrading of existing and the establishment of supplementary institutions.

Every major change, both in the developed and the underdeveloped countries, is dependent on the deployment of a "package" or mix comprising these three types of resources inputs in various proportions. The difference between planning for developed and underdeveloped countries is to be sought, on the one hand, in the relative share of the three types of resources inputs in the package and, on the other hand, in the extent to which preexisting structure is expected to spontaneously "generate" the nonmaterial types of resources, or in the extent to which existing resources may be "attracted" to the program. In *developed* countries, existing human and institutional resources suffice, as a rule, to meet the requirements of the development programs, "upgrading," where needed, evolving as a spontaneous adaptation of preexisting resources to the investment stimulus created by the program. Thus, public intervention in the developed economies is required to make available only physical resources, i.e., investments; furthermore, even these resources need not be covered in toto by public intervention, since private initiative will often be willing to take up the complementary type of investments.

In *underdeveloped* countries, however, little, if any, spontaneous adaptation of the human and institutional resources base to development stimuli can be expected, nor will private investment play a significant role. Public intervention, therefore, has to make up for these deficiencies in spontaneous adaptation by subscribing to the entire "package" of resources inputs required for implementation of the program.

This difference in the makeup of the resources input package between development programs in developed and underdeveloped countries usually goes hand in hand with a difference in the transfer functions relating these inputs to outputs. The transfer function is much more effective in the developed countries. In the early phases of development the ratios are so unfavorable, i.e., the resources input per unit of output are so high, that an "upgrading" of the transfer function presents itself as one of the paramount intermediate targets on the way to a self-accelerating growth process. Upgrading of transfer functions requires diversion to the development of capacity aspects of part of the resources that would otherwise be available for the improvement of the basic production environment. Thus, the development process in underdeveloped countries must allow for the allocation of packages of resources inputs for direct upgrading of the production environment, as well as for allocation of input packages for improvement of the transfer function.

UNCERTAINTY IN DEVELOPED AND UNDERDEVELOPED COUNTRIES

The developed world differs from the underdeveloped in one other important aspect, namely, in the extent and type of uncertainty within which the planning process has to operate. The planning process in the developed world has, it is true, also to cope with the considerable extent of uncertainty connected with the future development of technology and human motivation, and with the requirements and responses of the outside world, i.e., the environment beyond system boundaries. This uncertainty is of a type that cannot be reduced by experiments or pilot operations. It is, therefore, from the planner's point of view, an uncontrollable variable. To put it differently, we cannot expect in developed countries to generate significant additional information of this type as a by-product of a development program extending over a relatively limited period of, say, five to six years; fortunately, we are also not dependent in our development efforts upon such additional information.

The underdeveloped countries labor under the same kind of uncertainty and, moreover, are plagued by an additional and a more damaging type of uncertainty that is related to resources-outcome ratios. This latter type of uncertainty is a double one: firstly, parametric data are lacking on the transfer functions in their present state and, hence, on resources-outcome ratios related to direct resources inputs into the existing status quo complex; secondly, no data are available as to the effectiveness of applying "transformation inputs" with a view to *improving transfer functions* and through them also to establishing, ultimately, better resources-outcome ratios.

The uncertainty related to resources-outcome ratios differs from the uncertainty described above (which underdeveloped countries share with the developed ones) by the fact that the former lends itself to reduction by specific operations: information related to resources-outcome ratios can be generated as a by-product of development operations and its accumulation speeded up by the early initiation of pilot-type projects that are especially designed for high *information yield.* The uncertainty related to transfer functions should, therefore, be viewed, at least partially, as a *controllable* variable. This *information-oriented pilot project,* which in underdeveloped countries may be indispensable for the creation of an adequate investment environment, is required in the developed countries only in connection with the introduction of a new technology for which some of the resources-outcome ratios are not yet known; in this case, it will usually be the economic aspects, rather than the human and institutional ones, that we will be interested in quantifying. Only rarely—and probably only under extreme conditions of innovation, transformation, or deterioration—have mature economies been faced in the past with the necessity of initiating special pilot projects comprising a balanced makeup of the three types of resources inputs and aimed mainly at generating information.

PLANNING AND IMPLEMENTATION

Summarizing our analysis of the structural differences between the planning processes in developed and underdeveloped countries, we may say that planning in developed countries is conducted within a structural framework which can be assumed to remain unchanged during the planning period and which possesses adequate information on resources-outcome ratios. A program under such conditions can be fully defined from the ex ante point of view, and its substance will not be greatly affected by the process of implementation, unless major technological changes or major changes of the "boundary conditions" of the system occur. The planning and the implementation processes in mature countries can, therefore, be separated and will often be located in different parts of the sectorial decision hierarchy.

In underdeveloped countries, on the other hand, the final planning objective, the final status of the structural framework, the exact resources volumes, and the detailed development path cannot be fully determined from the ex ante point of view. The earlier phases of the implementation process will, through continuous information feedback and conditioning effects, have a major influence on subsequent phases of planning, and where such feedbacks prove to be still insufficient, implementation may have to be modified in order to speed up information generation and conditioning. In fact, the planning process here will have to be based on an almost continuous process of reevaluation of accumulated information and redirection of operations in the light of such reevaluation.

Because of their intimate interconnection, the implementation and planning processes in underdeveloped countries cannot, therefore, be separated, at least not in the early development phases; they have, in fact, to be conceived as one combined planning-implementation process, which it is proposed to call the priming spiral.

The priming spiral will consist of a number of logically and logistically interconnected phases, each characterized by specific planning and implementation aspects. In this spiral, every phase constitutes a preinvestment basis for the subsequent phase, generating the necessary minimum information required for decision making related to subsequent phases and effecting the necessary "upgrading" of planning and implementation institutions and the necessary improvement of transfer functions. With the accumulation of information and the upgrading of institutions, the base of the priming spiral, i.e., the scope of planning and implementation, can be expanded; the process thus has a potential built-in self-amplifying and self-accelerating mechanism.

The exact course the priming spiral will take in every specific case will, of course, depend on the context, though all development spirals have a number of common characteristics; these are outlined in the following section.

THE PRIMING SPIRAL

Common features of priming spiral phases Under the conception of the priming spiral, each "turn," or phase, of the spiral is a logical outcome of the preceding turn and leads on to the subsequent turn, each turn having a considerably larger "radius" than the preceding one. The following features are common to every turn, or phase.

1. Each phase defines in detail the resources inputs it requires for the current phase and identifies the bottlenecks anticipated for subsequent phases.
2. Each phase reviews transfer functions and assesses the upgrading that may become necessary at subsequent stages.
3. Each phase implements operations aimed at transforming the human and institutional matrix.
4. In each phase, a plan of operations and detailed plans for the subsequent phase are prepared.

Thus, each turn of the priming spiral constitutes an integrated combination of mutually supporting inventorying, planning, and implementation operations. As spontaneous growth processes are set up, mainly in the human and institutional dimensions, information feedback becomes less important for later planning phases, and the priming spiral gradually turns itself into a conventional planning and implementation process.

The reconnaissance phase The reconnaissance phase, the initial phase of the priming spiral, consists of a preliminary stocktaking of available natural and investment resources and of "negative resources," or scarcities and bottlenecks, to be anticipated in the subsequent sectorial development process. At this stage, inventorying has to rely upon existing information. Lacunae of information are identified and, where and when required, programs elaborated for the generation of additional information. To assess scarcities and bottlenecks accurately, resources inventories are compared with resources requirements, which again presupposes the existence of, at least preliminary, plans based on explicit objectives. Since neither planning objectives nor comprehensive planning is available, analysis in the reconnaissance phase is confined to the identification, by analogy with similar cases, of the more obvious bottlenecks and inadequacies which it can be assumed will stand in the way of sectorial development and to the drawing up of plans for initial pilot projects to overcome these bottlenecks. At this phase, most of our planning efforts must be based on the heuristic approach to be outlined elsewhere. The reconnaissance phase will thus make available for the subsequent turns of the priming spiral the following important information:

1. A very preliminary inventory of the status quo of sectorial, physical, human, and institutional resources
2. A similar estimate of development resources, physical, human, and institutional, that it is anticipated will become available for the development of the sector
3. A tentative evaluation of the most immediate direct and instrumental development targets
4. The areas of major resources bottlenecks and plans for the operations necessary to eliminate these bottlenecks
5. An outline of information lacunae.

The pilot phase The purpose of the pilot program phase is a triple one:

1. To provide controlled experimental environments to test out development approaches under field conditions and to obtain relevant response parameters.

2. To implement special projects aimed at overcoming crippling inadequacies and scarcities in human resources and institutional patterns anticipated to develop in relation to the planning and implementation operations in subsequent phases.

Special programs will, furthermore, have to be initiated for increasing the number of "second-degree" human resources, i.e., professionals for such training operations.

3. To identify and plan operations proposed for the following phase.

At this stage, it may also be necessary to introduce "third-degree" inputs, i.e., professional leadership resources from outside the sector or the country, with the object of providing the catalyzing effect necessary for the motivational upgrading of development personnel.

In order to be fully effective, pilot programs, though limited in size, should, nevertheless, be comprehensive in their coverage of planning dimensions and should attempt to stimulate, in miniature, all the problems likely to be encountered in subsequent larger projects. To put it differently, the purpose of the pilot phase is to generate information and second-degree human and institutional inputs.

Although information obtained at this stage will be of vital importance for the subsequent development phases, we still have to allow for the fact that because of the relatively small scale of operations, some distortion as a consequence of the "ubiquity" of boundaries is unavoidable.

The priming and demonstration phase The priming phase has the following main objectives:

1. To develop and expand, on a significant scale, but with minimum capital investment outlay, the human and institutional infrastructure for later major, highly indivisible investments connected with the upgrading of the physical production matrix.

2. To continue to accumulate information by response measurements in projects defined above.

3. To accelerate and expand the special projects aimed at the creation of first- and second-degree human and institutional resources, according to requirements anticipated to develop in the first stages of the subsequent investment phase.

4. To draw up plans of operation and detailed plans for these first stages.

5. To systematically disseminate information and development patterns proved in operations detailed under 1, 2, and 3 to adjoining areas not yet directly involved in the development effort. Such initial spillover effects might prove to be extremely useful priming operations for later full-scale projects in these adjacent areas.

The investment phase The investment phase is the crowning phase of the priming spiral; in this phase we hope to reap the benefits of having created a human and institutional matrix in the preceding phases. Production responses to judiciously located and planned investments may be expected to be both rapid and satisfactory in volume, and capital-return ratios, therefore, favorable.

The rate of development in the investment phase will depend (in addition to constraints created by the sectorial demand function) on the following factors:

1. The availability of investment resources
2. The extent and grade of transformation of the human and institutional matrix and the continued existence of human and institutional bottlenecks in the development agencies, and of inadequacies in the political decision process
3. The rate of expansion and upgrading of development resources inputs, due consideration being given to the response lag corresponding to every group of resources

CONCLUSIONS

The differences between the planning processes of underdeveloped and of developed countries cited in this chapter stem from major structural differences between the two types of economies. These structural differences indicate the need for the following:

1. To plan and organize public intervention for viable transients in all planning dimensions in the underdeveloped world, instead of planning only for a final target in the physical investment dimension, as in the developed world
2. To plan and implement upgrading of transfer functions in the underdeveloped countries instead of operating with practically unchanging transfer functions, as in the developed countries
3. To rapidly overcome the lack of parametric information in the underdeveloped countries through the implementation of pilot projects, as against the situation in the developed economies where such information can usually be assumed to be available
4. Finally, to allow for the fact that response lags in a number of vital nonphysical dimensions are of far greater importance in the underdeveloped countries, whereas in the developed countries, responses are, as a rule, adequate

From this analysis of the basic structural differences between the underdeveloped and the developed worlds, it can be concluded that a different planning approach and methodology are required, as also a different relation between the planning, information gathering, and implementation aspects of the development process. Since the development process in underdeveloped environments is highly dynamic and intended to effect deep structural changes in all dimensions of the phase space, the planning, information gathering, implementation processes must continuously adapt themselves to such changes. The concept of the priming spiral has been introduced to allow for this necessity.

10
DEVELOPMENT HEURISTICS

Submit action to the test of thought,
and thought to the test of action.
GOETHE

THE PLANNER'S CONCEPTION OF HIS ROLE IN THE DEVELOPMENT PROCESS

The planner's conception of his role in the development process may be considered as varying along a continuous conceptual scale, the two opposite and extreme points of this scale being the "unidirectional" conception and the "radial" conception.

According to the unidirectional conception, the planner considers himself as a link in a hierarchical decision chain in which each link is entrusted with implementation of instructions received from the next higher level, or link, including the recoding of some instructions in expanded form for implementation at lower levels. As long as he performs his tasks of conducting or amplifying these instructions, the planner considers that he has fully discharged his responsibilities both to the organization he serves and to his country. He does not consider himself responsible for initiating action to prime improvements in parts of the system which lie within his sphere of activity or influence; he thus conceives development to be a unidirectional process flowing from the top to the bottom of the hierarchy. Furthermore, if faced with inadequate information, his response is one of suspension of action. The bias underlying this conception is a mechanistic interpretation of organization which excludes self-regulation or the initiation of action at intermediate levels.

The planner, operating under the radial conception, representing the opposite end of the scale, is guided by a cybernetic interpretation of the decision process, conceiving the system as made up of a number of subsystems which, though governed, controlled, and regulated from top levels, still generate considerable self-regulation and corrective action at intermediate and lower levels. Under this conception, the planner feels that his responsibility extends over the whole "potential radius" of his influence, i.e., sideways, downward, and upward.

The unidirectional role conception is suitable for public intervention in a "mature" system, a system which is adequately structured and in which its role occupants have satisfactory qualifications. In a mature system, operations consist of public interventions which are mainly of a "physical" nature, this system relying on existing spontaneous processes and self-regulative loops for the creation of the complementary "nonphysical" processes. There is, therefore, no need in this type of system to allocate significant portions of resources for upgrading the nonphysical dimensions such as the internal structure of the system and its human-institutional resources. Information in such contexts is usually adequate for decision making.

The radial role conception seems to be more suited to immature systems which still require major internal transformations and basic upgrading of transfer functions. The need for development intervention in these systems is, of course, more urgent than in mature systems, because of the low level of productivity prevailing in the former and their greater dependence on structural improvements and, finally, because of the information generation aspects of development action, since in these contexts, information is either inadequate or nonexistent. Here, procrastination is equivalent to delaying the priming of the development process in all its aspects.

PERFECTIONISM VS. PRAGMATIC ACTIVISM

Closely interrelated with the unidirectional-radial scale is the scale expressing the planner's attitude to development action, the extreme points on this scale being the attitudes of perfectionism and pragmatic activism.

The basic bias underlying perfectionism is a "Platonic" one. According to this attitude, the planner considers his planning space to be potentially deterministic and fully predictable (only time, patience, and money are required to actually reach the Platonic ideal planning space). Since his basic conditioning is professional, and professional responsibility occupies a very high place in his code of ethics, the planner can satisfy his sense of responsibility only if he is armed with good information and good "tools." He cannot allow himself to accept a compromise in any aspect connected with his professional integrity, even in the event that the generation of information or of tools requires excessive periods of time or entails high cost. According to this attitude, action must be delayed until the planning space has become so well determined that its behavior is fully predictable.

In reality, no such perfectly predictable planning space exists owing to the following:

1. Every planning space constitutes a pragmatic "cut" from a phase space extending infinitely in time and space and a selective omission of the less relevant dimensions.

2. The planning space may change significantly during the time required to collect the relevant information.

3. Information must be considered as only one of the inputs; it should, therefore, be subjected to the same kind of analysis of marginal economic return to which we subject other inputs, since the return on information, beyond a certain point, will be lower than its incremental cost.

If taken to its extreme, the perfectionist attitude will divert the planner from his basic purpose, namely, to provide a guide for action.

The planner adopting an attitude of pragmatic activism recognizes the basically stochastic nature of many of the variables of our planning space and hence does not attempt to behave as if it were deterministic and fully predictable; he tries, instead, to adapt the planning process to the planning space as it is. Thus, the activistic planner, in an underdeveloped economy, acknowledges the basic fact that information on the most vital variables can be generated only by development action and that, therefore, perfectionist attitudes only perpetuate stagnation as a consequence of the operation of a number of vicious circles, such as scarcity of information—lack of action—continued scarcity of information; inadequate planning organization—no planning activity—no improvement of planning organization; and an inadequate institutional space—no development activity—continuation of inadequate institutional space.

THE ROLE OF THE HEURISTIC APPROACH

Since in the planning space of underdevelopment most of our purely analytical tools are of only limited value because of limitations in insight and information, and since action in this space is most vital to prime cumulative positive causation, we must devise a pragmatic heuristic approach that can serve us through the initial stages, when information and hypotheses are at their lowest level. As the development process unfolds and information feedbacks are created, as our understanding of our planning space and planning methodology improves, we shall gradually be able to introduce more and more analytical tools.

The design of heuristic strategies to guide us in the early phases of development is facilitated by the basic structural similarities of various manifestations of underdevelopment. These similarities under conditions of underdevelopment can be summarized under the following five headings:

Complementary nature of inputs In order to obtain a desired change in a specific planning space, a specific mix of inputs (ranging all the way from straightforward investments in facilities to inputs intended to modify institutional structure and people's behavior) is required. The proportion, within this package, of the various inputs may, of course, vary somewhat from case to case. However, we cannot assume linearity of input-output ratios, since the reduction, below the optimum proportion, of a specific input may result in a reduction of output that is out of proportion to the input reduction. The total absence of some inputs might lead to complete, or almost complete, loss of effectiveness of the whole mix.

Critical mass Inputs if present in an input package in proportions below a specific threshold cannot be effective; similarily, an input package below a critical mass ceases to be effective.

Differences in lead time and response lag Lead time is the minimum period that must elapse between conception and commissioning of a project, i.e., the time required for the completion of reconnaissance and feasibility studies, design, tendering, and construction.

Response lag is that period of time which elapses before a significant response to a specific input within an input package is obtained. The duration of the response lag depends on the types of input and the maturity of the socioeconomic system.

Lead time of investment types of inputs is relatively short—except for very large and indivisible projects. Lead time is also less dependent on the volume and quality of local, human, and institutional resources, since foreign resources can be mobilized to keep lead times within reasonable limits.

On the other hand, response lags will be long especially for inputs required for the upgrading of human and institutional resources, and, moreover, these response lags cannot be significantly reduced by the import of human resources. They will be longest in inputs related to the political hierarchy and its decision process; often, in this field, a program must show that it is actually succeeding before a positive response is obtained, though this success is not in itself sufficient to guarantee this response.

Because of the complementary nature of inputs in the input package, planning must allow for differences in response lag of the constituent inputs by appropriate selective timing and programming of the various inputs.

The controlling input scarcity The scarcity that, at a certain state of the planning space, controls the possible scope of the program is here referred to as the *controlling input scarcity*. Often, in an underdeveloped economy, there may be an ample supply of unutilized or underutilized "natural" resources, such as land, water, labor, and in some exceptional cases, e.g., the oil-rich mini-nations, of extensive capital resources. At the same time, we may be faced in these countries with a scarcity of other resources (usually in the human or institutional dimensions), which will constitute the controlling input scarcity.

The interconnection between structure and outcome The behavior, response, and operation of an organization or institution mirror its underlying structure: every flaw in its operation can be traced back to a flaw in its structure. Structure, in turn, is, of course, modified by operation. Therefore, including in the design of operations features that have the power to accelerate modification of structure constitutes an effective way to establish positive cumulative causation.

THE ROLE OF THE OBJECTIVE FUNCTION

Similarities in objectives are the second major area of similarities that make it possible to set up heuristically rooted development strategies.

Basically, programs are undertaken in order to maximize—subject to sectorial allocations and other prevailing constraints—a specific objective function, expressing a single objective or a mix of objectives.

Objectives set up in this context can be subdivided into two major groups: *direct or final objectives* concerned with the production of certain commodities or services and *indirect objectives* referred to here as *instrumental objectives,* these being the means and tools that have to be created and employed to reach a direct objective. In spite of the relative simplicity of this classification principle, it is often difficult to decide whether a specific objective is a member of the first or of the second group. In fact, every apparently direct objective may be interpreted as an instrumental one, if viewed from a "higher" point of view; in other words, we have here another case of infinite regression.

The main objectives of the group of *direct objectives*—within the context dealt with here—are as follows: increasing the aggregate sectorial production; improving the balance of payments; reducing unemployment; "improving" the distribution of added production between regions, or between producer groups within the sector; and increasing the propensity to save. In most underdeveloped countries, all these objectives will play some role in setting up the "objective package" of a program.

Since analysis and ranking have to be carried out on the basis of a single objective function, one of the objectives, usually the aggregate product, may be chosen as the principal one and trade-offs decided upon to express the utility of the remaining objectives in terms of the principal one.[1]

Instrumental objectives in conditions of underdevelopment turn, in the main, on the "growth capacity" of a nation, i.e., they aim at strengthening all the human and structural dimensions that influence resources-outcome ratios. Typical instrumental objectives in underdeveloped countries might include: expansion and improvement of planning capacity, of the volume of transformation inputs (i.e., human resources trained and motivated to transform responses of the basic producer and his institutions), and of the institutional space at all levels.

Theoretically, the value of instrumental objectives could be quantitatively expressed in terms of achievement of the principal objective function; however, resources-outcome ratios are usually not sufficiently known to enable such an analysis to be undertaken. At the same time, the crippling deficiency in underdeveloped countries of these instrumental resources is so obvious that it seems justified, in the early development phases, to put this group up as a special set of objectives and to treat them as if they were direct "final" objectives. Nevertheless, we shall have to make an allocation decision between the two groups of objectives, if we wish to prime development. This, of course, again raises the question of trade-offs between the first and the second group of objectives, a question that is even more difficult to answer than that related to internal trade-offs within the first group of objectives. Making an allocation decision does, of course, imply selecting a trade-off, because when we decide upon a line of action and the abandonment of others, we anticipate a specific

[1] An alternative procedure that does not require advance decisions on trade-offs is described in Chapter 20.

level of achievement in terms of the relevant direct and indirect objectives. The selection of these specific levels of achievement, rather than some other levels, of course, argues an implicit trade-off between the direct and instrumental objectives.

A further difficulty arises from the fact that most of the objectives are not truly independent. In the following and concluding part of this section, some of the arguments commonly encountered in connection with these objectives and the interrelationship of these objectives will be reviewed.

Aggregate product vs. distribution of added income The choice of trade-offs between these two related objectives depends on structural economic considerations and on political value judgments. Regarding economic considerations: in underdeveloped countries which still import certain commodities that could be produced by the sector in question, the aggregate product objective usually outweighs that of the improvement of income distribution, unless the underdeveloped country is in the rare and enviable position of not having a balance-of-payments problem. This also applies to countries in which sectorial exports are an important source of foreign currency, at least as far as these export commodities are concerned; the rapid increase of internal demand for sectorial products, following from accelerated growth in other economic sectors, has a similar effect.

On the other hand, stagnation of internal sectorial demand for its own sectorial products leads to emphasis or priority being given to improving the distribution of additional income over the expansion of the aggregate volume. As a rule, income elasticity of demand for agricultural products is highest in the low-income population of the least developed rural regions. Development of production in these regions, rather than in higher income regions, will lead, therefore, through the rise in local income levels, to a parallel rise in the demand for locally produced agricultural products, combined with a more modest growth of demand for the simpler, and probably less import-dependent, commodities and services generated within other sectors.

The relevance of political values and considerations depends, to a great extent, on the prevailing actual "Realpolitik," rather than upon manifest political doctrines: the wider the gap between these two, the more political decision makers incline toward token and pseudosolutions of the distributive problem, and the heavier their actual decisions lean upon maximizing aggregate volumes. The greater the emphasis upon distributive problems in actual Realpolitik, the higher the priority given to distribution objectives; in extreme cases, overemphasis on improving income distribution can even lead to a serious slowing down of the aggregate production volume.

When selecting a position in the aggregate volume–income distribution dichotomy, we should bear in mind the interrelation between aggregate product volumes of the agricultural sector and demand increases for agricultural products resulting from income rises in other sectors: slowing down the agricultural aggregate volume may, in some situations, lead to increased imports and/or price inflation. Hence, the compromise to be sought would consist of putting higher emphasis upon the aggregate volume in the early phase until both local and export demand can be met in full from production derived from areas and producer groups possessing high productive capacity. Concurrently, major efforts (requiring human more than capital inputs) aimed at the transformation of the human and institutional infrastructure should be undertaken for the retarded areas and producer groups. This approach would ensure relative economic stability, while still creating the necessary preinvestment basis for a later switch in basic policies. In the subsequent stage, emphasis could be shifted to the retarded areas and producers, to the extent at least that the political process will accept this, bearing in mind that the political process might in the meantime have become much more biased toward the high productivity areas.

Employment Since almost all underdeveloped countries have unemployment or underemployment problems of one kind or other, the employment of labor or intensification of its employment has a high economic and political priority, even if the return on additional labor is modest in the initial period; because of the low opportunity cost of labor, even a modest return on labor will result in an increase in the aggregate product. Professor Georgescu-Roegen has elaborated on this in his paper "Economic Theory and Agrarian Economics";[2] he concludes his comments on the subject thus: "where the geo-historical conditions of an economy are such that all available resources must be used in production as long as they increase output, the argument regarding the superiority of large-scale production is poor economics . . . the 'equilibrium' price of labour is at least equal to the minimum of biological subsistence."

Balance-of-payments objectives These objectives loom large in all underdeveloped economies, with but few exceptions. After management and entrepreneurial talent, foreign currency is probably the resource that is generally in shortest supply and, at the same time, has the highest opportunity cost in the economy. Improving the balance of payments by reducing imports and increasing exports therefore ranks high among development objectives, especially where this improvement can be obtained mainly by marshaling local resources that are in ample supply; labor and, in some cases, land or water resources are examples of local resources which can be mobilized to this end.

Propensity to save Evaluation of the influence of various types of projects and various intersectorial allocations on the propensity to save is not easy, for even if, as a rule, propensity to save increases with the rise in income levels, it is not clear whether, for a specific income level, the propensity to save of urban and rural populations is comparable. In this connection, we must bear in mind that the unrecorded part of savings and investments is often larger in rural than in urban areas. Propensity to save could possibly be strengthened in the agricultural sector by fashioning projects in a way that would create for

[2] *Oxford Economic Papers*, vol. 12, pp. 1–43, February, 1960, Clarendon Press, Oxford.

the small holder easily accessible and rewarding investment opportunities within his own production complex.

THE ANALYTICAL VS. THE HEURISTIC APPROACH

The above analysis points to the great difficulty in adopting a *purely analytical approach* for the complex multidimensional phase space of underdevelopment. We are, first, faced with the problem of selecting trade-offs between the various potential objectives that harmonize with our political value judgment; we must then estimate for resources-outcome ratios for the various inputs and input packages in spite of the scarcity of relevant measurements; we have finally to devise means of overcoming constraints arising from the limitation in the "capacity" of the planning, the executive, and the political decision processes and of the production level. On the other hand, the importance of initiating, as early as possible, a "priming spiral," i.e., operations aimed at structural transformation and information accumulation, has been pointed out in Chapter 9.

The fact that most contexts of underdevelopment have *structural similarities,* as outlined in Chapter 8, simplifies the planning of priming operations. The difficulty in applying the analytical approach, the vital necessity of early action, and the structural similarities inherent in contexts of underdevelopment—all lead to the conclusion that a heuristic approach should be adopted in the early phases of development. However, there is a complex of biases and attitudes in existence—this complex might be called the "guild bias"—which militates against conscious adoption of the heuristic approach.

The guild bias can, within certain limits, be considered as a useful adaptation of our limited registering and reasoning powers to the proliferating variety of the outside world. In order to be able to form those hypotheses on which our welfare, and sometimes even our survival, depends, (1) we abstract the inessential from the essential by making a selection relevant to our purpose, and (2) we introduce division of labor, by imposing different selective principles upon different specialists, such as asking one to work out a biological interpretation, another a physical one.

Over the last 300 years, the "exact" sciences have, with prodigious success, developed two basic *guild attitudes: division of labor* (specialization) and *quantification of analysis.* As a result of this success, the prestige of specialization and quantification has risen to a point where it has become professionally discreditable to introduce different scientific attitudes even into ill-structured and complex areas of investigation for which the classical approach could be predicted to prove barren.

The prestige connected with the guild attitude of the exact sciences has resulted in a lack of interest in attempting to combine analytical and heuristic tools into a flexible and pragmatic problem-solving attitude that would be suitable for the complex phase space of development. Instead of undertaking such a retooling process, development thinking has concentrated upon degrading the complexity of the phase space of development until it becomes accessible to the classical tools of analysis. The proliferating variety of the universe of discourse was pruned and pared down until the resulting "representational" map was simple enough to be tackled by quantitative analysis, even if in these pruning operations it became necessary to discard the structural features that were most relevant to the predictive value of the hypothesis.

Discrepancies will be observed between actual and predicted responses, when submitting predictions based on such oversimplified hypotheses to the test of reality in a specific environment. Such discrepancies will point toward the weak points of the hypothesis and indicate the kind of corrections that have to be introduced into the original hypothesis in order to improve its predictive value. "Corrected" hypotheses, adapted by feedback information to a specific context, will have a surprisingly good predictive value for the context for which they have been corrected and will make it possible to introduce a considerable extent of quantification. However, it is when we come to transfer these hypotheses to structurally different societies that we court trouble. In a different context, these corrected hypotheses will lose most of their predictive value, since most of the corrections and adaptations developed in a specific society will lose their validity in a structurally different society.

Technologists and scientists, nevertheless, still will cling to their original hypotheses and quantified analyses; their minds, trained at a simplified conceptual space developed in their own society, will be baffled by the proliferating variety of unaccustomed phenomena in the new context and the absence of an ordering principle which would make "pruning" possible. They, therefore, as a rule, apply the summary procedure of pruning everything that cannot be handled by quantitative analysis. In cybernetic terms, they have sinned against Ross Ashby's law of requisite variety that "only variety can destroy variety."[3] Feeling that their capacity to absorb, order, pattern, and resolve cannot cope with the variety of the system, they adopt the expedient of looking at the system with partly opaque glasses, i.e., with an irrelevant variety absorber that makes arbitrary abstractions or, at best, abstractions that have led to satisfactory working hypotheses only in other structural contexts.

The heuristic approach expounded in this chapter aims at avoiding the distortion stemming from the pruning of reality undertaken in order to make it amenable to quantitative analysis; it proposes instead that we resign ourselves to "professionally" less "rigorous" but in fact more appropriate tools. This would apply especially to the initial phases of development when, on the one hand, an integrated (but not necessarily fully quantified) systems approach is all-important and, on the other hand, data are still too scarce for a quantitative analysis. The tool built into the heuristic approach is what one might call "pattern recognition" applied to the different varieties of development situations: identification of structural similarities, drawing up of conclusion patterns resulting from such similarities, and selecting operational strategies or heuristics complying with such conclusion patterns. Since we cannot represent the relevant detail of our universe of discourse by the rigid but—owing to unavoid-

[3] As quoted in Stafford Beer, *Decision and Control*, John Wiley & Sons, Inc., New York, 1966, p. 279.

able simplifications—wide-meshed grid of quantitative analysis, we propose to select for the planning of the priming and early development operations the more flexible, but at the same time narrower meshed, grid of a comprehensive system analysis. Some of the more obvious heuristics applying to the early phases of resources development are outlined in the following section.

COMMON HEURISTICS FOR THE EARLY PHASES OF DEVELOPMENT

Heuristic one: continuous development front The complementary nature of most development inputs and the great dependence of satisfactory resources-outcome ratios upon the correct proportioning and timing of the various essential inputs within the input package call for the creation of a continuous development front that extends over all the essential inputs necessary to achieve the objective. We must make allowance for the following in planning this development front:

1. Differences in the response lag for the different inputs. Our plan should therefore provide for such timing of the allocation of inputs as will ensure a coordinated timing of responses according to the requirements of the plan.
2. The possibility of a gradual reduction of response lags as a consequence of "learning" and of the structural transformation resulting from the development process.
3. The emergence, in time, of spontaneous processes within the society. These processes will reduce society's dependence upon planned allocation of certain inputs by public intervention.

Thus, paradoxically, the continuous development front of public intervention is most required at a time when it is still most difficult to create; furthermore, when conditions become more favorable for its emergence, it ceases to be a necessity.

Heuristic two: the threshold test Development in its early phases implies the disturbance of traditional ultrastable equilibria; this disturbance can be achieved only through the application of an input package of a certain "critical mass" in which the essential inputs are represented in specific proportions and applied with a specific timing. Input packages of "subcritical mass" will not reach the threshold of response and will, therefore, not dislodge the system from its status quo equilibrium. Since the development task in underdeveloped countries is immense and the resources inventory sparse, the critical-mass requirement leads to the focusing on limited fronts of those scarce resources which are available, in packages of above-threshold mass.

This focusing can be on either one or a number of limited areas–this will lead to the formation of regional development foci, or on one or a number of limited production complexes, the latter leading to operations emphasizing functional foci. Both these approaches are described in greater detail in Chapter 22.

Heuristic three: adaptation to controlling scarcity Since every type of program requires input packages containing specific minimum and optimum amounts and timing of the various inputs, and since availability of these inputs varies from country to country, and, within the same country, from time to time, every specific development complex has its own specific controlling input, that is, the input that will constitute the *controlling scarcity* factor of the program and determine its feasible scope.

Once this controlling scarcity is determined, either by analogy with similar cases or by a preliminary program analysis, we should reevaluate program priorities in two directions:

1. Reshuffle priorities of potential projects to increase the return on the controlling scarce input, without excessive loss in economic efficiency
2. Reshuffle priorities of potential projects and, where necessary, revise the project catalogue, so as to ensure the inclusion of projects that will speed up the generation of the scarce input

Heuristics three and four represent strategies aimed at accelerating the emergence of essential instrumental objectives rather than of direct ultimate objectives.

Heuristic four: emphasis upon growth capacity To accelerate the creation of growth capacity, special projects, aimed specifically at generating the relevant inputs, may become necessary. As a complementary orientation, the organization of the more orthodox type of projects could be set up in a way that would ensure a more rapid emergence of scarce inputs as a by-product of development.

Use of material resources for the rapid development of growth capacity may somewhat reduce the resources available for development of the physical means of production; however, this reduction is rarely significant, since, as a rule, the development of human and institutional resources is controlled by the availability of training resources, rather than capital resources.

Heuristic five: postponement of indivisible investment Capital allocations should be planned and programmed to ensure the greatest possible stream of benefits for the available investment stream. The strategies which can be derived from this obvious normative statement deserve special study. Every economically justifiable effort should be made to minimize the cost sunk in unutilized installations or portions of installations, since the aggregate volume of investment funds available is extremely limited, development needs are pressing, and investment opportunities for these limited funds are numerous. Time preference and opportunity costs of capital are therefore high. This will apply especially to the early development phases, when response lags are longest and returns on investments therefore at their lowest ebb. This important strategy can be spelled out in a number of substrategies, including, among others, the following:

Phasing of Investment The lead time of capital investment in the sector of irrigated agriculture is, as a rule, shorter than the response lag of other complementary inputs. Investments should, therefore, be phased so that lead time of investment coincides to the greatest possible extent with response times of the complementary inputs, allowing of course for the inherent indivisibility of some types of investment and for justifiable economy of scale. Phasing of investments will thus reduce the loss incurred in idle sunk capital and thereby increase the aggregate benefit stream that can be derived from a specific allocation to the sector.

Spreading of Investments Spreading investments over a relatively larger receiving population tends to reduce the braking effect of the response lag that is characteristic of the noncapital input dimensions. This substrategy again tends to reduce the losses incurred from unutilized capacity.

Expanding the Boundary of the Planning Space This is a specific form of phasing. The boundaries of the planning space for investments contemplated for the near future are given an intentionally narrow definition, if it can be shown that a later expansion of the boundaries of the planning space can provide the potential solutions to meet the demand which it is anticipated will develop at that later date. The term expansion of boundaries should not be taken solely in its geographical sense (e.g., the inclusion of additional basin areas or of adjoining basins) but should be taken also to refer to alternative types of water resources (e.g., surface water to supplement groundwater, storage to supplement a run-of-the-river type of diversion). As one project generation follows another, so later generations are integrated with earlier ones into larger supply units. This substrategy makes it possible to increase both financial and decision liquidity at a time when money and information are at their lowest ebb.

Heuristic six: priority to highly divisible investments Giving priority to projects of high divisibility is indicated in the underdeveloped economies, mainly because of the difference in lead times of investments and response lag of the noninvestment type of inputs. This heuristic favors the development of local low-cost resources and application of the more subdivisible types of inputs, especially of those which have short response lags, at least as long as response lags in noninvestment dimensions remain the controlling factors in project fruition.

Heuristic seven: selection of appropriate scale Often in economic comparisons of alternative scales of installations, the mistake is made of neglecting the differences in response lag of the various types of inputs and the consequent lagging of demand growth. The fact that capacity for which no demand can be developed has nil utility is also not always fully allowed for. These two basic facts should be taken into account in comparing the economy of scale of alternative capacities of facilities.

Heuristic eight: information yield Information is an important aspect related to all inputs in the input package and to resources-outcome ratios, as well as to our understanding of the status quo. Hence, quantity and quality of information have an important influence on project economics. The economics of information accumulation is treated in a separate chapter (Chapter 11), and we shall, therefore, confine ourselves here to the general statement that accumulation of information should be considered as one of the important economic issues of program planning.

Heuristic nine: increase extra-program spills Dissemination of information related to technologies, methodologies, and approaches and induction of transformation processes from a development focus to surrounding areas (sideways loop) and to higher decision levels (upward loop) are important external economies and spillover effects of development programs. Since a program oriented toward increasing spillover effects may accelerate the creation of adequate development orientation in a considerable section of the relevant sector, spillover effects may take on an importance that approaches the direct effects of the project (downward loop). What such spillover effects lose in intensity, they gain in extension of coverage.

Program organization, its communication in all directions, and its public relation aspects should therefore all be governed by the aspiration to increase desirable spillover effects, especially to such areas of the economy or the political decision hierarchy where they can be expected to do most good.

CONCLUSIONS

Basically, heuristics are simplified and standardized solutions stemming from specific contexts, which, however, can be assumed to remain valid for broad spectra of conditions. Their application, beyond the range of conditions for which they have been originally designed, implies of course approximations that lead to increasing distortion as we move from the areas of legitimate applicability to the limits of applicability. Hence, some of the heuristics will "at their limits" lead to conflicting recommendations. In the early development phases, the deviation of results arrived at by these heuristics from the analytical line of analysis (assuming such an approach to be within our reach) will, as a rule, not be very great, except for the boundary cases.

The heuristics outlined in this chapter have been derived from major structural similarities found in typical contexts of underdevelopment. They are intended not to replace analytical thinking, but only to substitute for it and supplement it in cases where analysis is not possible owing to the scarcity of data and the lack of an appropriate methodology.

If combined with and tempered by sound judgment, the proposed heuristics can serve as useful tools in the absence of better tools, especially at a time when we are in dire need of some kind of comprehensive tool to carry out the most vital task in the development sequence, the priming of the development process.

These tools will assist us in avoiding the two most characteristic aberrations of development thinking, namely, the postponement of action, until "adequate" information becomes available, and Procrustean surgery, i.e., pruning and mutilating the diversity of reality until a representation is obtained which fits the capacity of available analytical tools.

11
THE ROLE OF INFORMATION

If a man will begin with certainties, he shall end in doubts; but if he will be content with doubts, he shall end in certainties.

FRANCIS BACON (*The Advancement of Learning*)

The management requirement is . . . to obtain very few and highly digested data at the moments alone when the system calls for a decision.

STAFFORD BEER (*Decision and Control*)

Information is an all-important resource of the planning process and thus also a basic input in development programs. Availability and dependability of information on present and future conditions exercise a decisive modifying influence on analysis and planning, an influence which should be expressed in the actual structure of the planning process. This chapter, therefore, outlines the modifications required in the orthodox planning process in order to adapt it to conditions of uncertainty.

A phase space, in which the principal parameters are well defined, can, without significant distortion, be treated as deterministic. We may continue to treat this phase space as deterministic even in conditions of moderate uncertainty; such a simplification will introduce a noticeable distortion, but this does not necessarily invalidate results or forecasts. Finally, we come to the phase space of marked uncertainties; in such conditions the phase space, from the operational point of view, no longer bears any resemblance to a deterministic phase space and can, therefore, no longer be treated as deterministic, since such treatment would introduce severe errors and seriously detract from the reliability of our forecasts. Applying a deterministic planning process to such a phase space cannot be considered as a realistic adaptation to prevailing conditions and would be more in the nature of a pseudosolution. Only the adoption of a planning process specifically designed for conditions of uncertainty can meet the needs of this phase space.

THE TWO TYPES OF UNCERTAINTY

Uncertainty and information (representing, as it were, the opposite ends of a continuous scale) will be treated here purely from the operational point of view of the resources planner, without attempting to enter into the mathematical and philosophical meaning of probability. From this point of view, two types, or categories, of uncertainty can be distinguished:

1. Uncertainties due to the stochastic nature of the parametric values of variables. This type of uncertainty is only to a limited extent accessible to resolution through the setting up of "causative" type theories and their firming up by experimental observation; quantification of such uncertainties will, therefore, be mostly of a statistical nature.

2. Uncertainties stemming from our ignorance of causative mechanisms and which can be resolved by setting up causative type theories, by experimental observation, and by quantification based on a "causative" type of explanation.

The boundaries between these two types of uncertainty are neither clearly defined nor impregnable. As we extend our scientific knowledge, it becomes possible to move some phenomena from the first category to the second. However, for the time being, and especially when dealing with underdevelopment, the above classification will be found to have considerable operational value.

It has been repeatedly pointed out that uncertainty degrades the phase space of underdevelopment much more than it degrades the phase space of development. The difference, however, is not limited to the quantity, availability, and dependability of information, but also extends to the type of uncertainty that prevails. Developed countries, to the extent that they suffer from uncertainty, do so mainly from uncertainty of the first, the stochastic, type. Underdeveloped countries, on the other hand, are blessed equally with both types. There is little we can do about the first type of uncertainty, except to be patient, to collect statistical data on probability distribution, and, perhaps, to exercise some mathematical ingenuity to "stretch" the value of existing data. In contrast to this, the prevalence of uncertainty of the second type in underdeveloped countries (combined with lack of data related to uncertainty of the first type) calls for a rather far-reaching adaptation of the planning process, with a view to minimizing risk, in spite of uncertainty, and accelerating, in a planned way, the generation of data, with special emphasis on data related to the second category of uncertainty. The prevalence of the two types of uncertainty in the underdeveloped countries requires, therefore, that we remodel the planning and implementation process and incorporate into this process special experimental types of operations for speeding up the generation of information.

INFORMATION AS A DEVELOPMENT INPUT

Information is only one of many development inputs; development, in turn, is but a transformation process adopted in order to reach certain objectives. Information is, thus, purely an instrumental objective and not a final purpose in itself, a basic fact we sometimes tend to forget.

Consequently, information has to compete with other inputs for capital and, still more so, for human resources. Theoretically, the allocation of inputs and human resources would be at its optimum when the marginal returns on all inputs are equal; however this theory, despite its rigor, is not very useful, since it is extremely difficult, if not impossible, to calculate and compare these marginal returns. This difficulty in quantification should, however, not bring us to despair of the value of analysis, since even the setting up of an ordinal scale will greatly assist in allocating human resources between the various development operations, including that of information generation. In fact, adoption of the modified planning process advocated here removes the sharp division between data generation, planning, and implementation and "diffuses" the former between the two latter occupations. This, it is true, makes quantification of the "return-on-data" collection programs still more difficult, but, on the other hand, it greatly accelerates the overall growth process.

The value of information in decision making also depends on the stage of development at which a decision must be taken. The incremental value of data is greatest in the initial stages when information is still at its lowest level, since even a limited addition to our information assists greatly in underpinning (or overturning) our hypotheses; on the other hand, as a corpus of data on a specific subject accumulates, returns diminish. However, we often come across an opposite trend, since if we adopt a strategy at a time when information is at its lowest ebb, our initial decisions need be partial and short term only, thus leaving a lot of "decision liquidity" (discussed elsewhere in this chapter) for later decision points. As the decision sequence unrolls, "decision liquidity" diminishes and the risk of misinvestment (because of the gradual reduction of feasibility of later corrective action) due to insufficient data becomes more disturbing; in other words, information becomes more valuable, since the dependence of the later decisions of a decision sequence upon adequateness of data is much greater than before.

However, the value of information is, above all, dependent on the relative scope of the total resource inventory and the resources share which it is proposed to incorporate into the planned intervention; the closer these two scopes are to each other (i.e., the more pronounced the scarcity of the resource in relation to requirements), the greater is the value of information.

The above comments have all been made from the point of view of an "information specialist" observing, from the outside, the impact of his subject on a system. The next logical step is to put information back into the system where it belongs. This reintegration leads to the important conclusion that it may be desirable to modify our action ideology with a view to decreasing our dependence on information, as long as the latter is in short supply. If, for example, we choose a phased program, in lieu of immediate full-scale implementation, the sensitivity of our first phase action to uncertainty, and with it dependence on relevant information, will decrease markedly. There are numerous other heuristics that can be used to obtain similar effects. Viewed from inside the system, information (and here both basic types of information are included) thus becomes one of the variables that enter into an overall optimization analysis.

However, this is easier said than done, and in most cases an ordinal type of scale is all we can aim at. It is because of the almost insurmountable difficulties of this overall optimization process of a system, which has more unquantifiable than quantifiable dimensions, that we shall have again to lean heavily upon pragmatic rather than analytical action ideology, upon heuristics rather than upon quantification. In the remaining sections of this chapter, an attempt will be made to describe some of the more important heuristics that have been found useful in connection with the planning of water resources and irrigated agriculture. Although these heuristics are derived from this rather specific context, their applicability need not be limited to the original context.

Before turning to heuristics proper, and for the sake of clarity and brevity, some of the terms used will be defined.

DEFINITION OF BASIC TERMS

1. Minimum information threshold: the minimum amount of information required to make a planning decision. Information thresholds vary, according to the kind of decisions involved and their interrelationship with possible relevant future decisions, from yes-no type of answers to full quantification.

2. Information gain: the relevant information accumulated between two consecutive decision points on the step function representing a proposed sequence of action.

3. Information or confidence range: the area between envelopes of anticipated values for a specific estimate of a parameter.

4. Design value: the parametric estimate, within the confidence range, selected for an indicative, deterministic type of analysis, i.e., one neglecting uncertainty.

5. Sensitivity of solution to data variation: the difference in economic and extra-economic efficiency between a deterministic type of solution based on "design values" and a solution worked out for envelopes of the confidence range. In such a sensitivity analysis, extreme values of one variable might be combined with average values of other variables, or, alternatively, with their extremes. The weight that we assign to each such combination will depend on the probability that we attribute to its occurrence.

6. Optimal information range: The amount of information whose collection and analysis is economically justifiable for a specific decision; this information package is, of course, larger than that of the information threshold.

7. Information yield: the information that we anticipate to accrue from following a specific line of action, either as its main result, i.e., from experiments, or as its by-product, e.g., the information yield from the development process.

8. Action or decision liquidity: the measure, within a specific context, of the freedom that a present decision leaves for future relevant and complementary action, or the measure of the extent that present decision does not commit future action. This could, for example, be expressed as a ratio of present to aggregate investment, or as a ratio of the amount of water at present developed to the overall estimated yield of resources.

TYPES OF INFORMATION IN THE WATER-LAND-MAN PLANNING SPACE

In general, we have to accumulate a considerable body of specific information before we can extend the value of this information by correlating it with information collected elsewhere under comparable conditions and by this correlation add synthetic data to recorded data.

Further, before we can legitimately claim to recognize a similarity in patterns, we must first identify a pattern in our specific context. "Pattern recognition" in a new environment in which we are called upon to act, and for which practically no data are available, rests on only very general considerations, and hence we are liable to arrive at serious misleading conclusions.

The above is true for the present state of the art. However, it is hoped that as more and more parametric data accumulate and are compared, our capacity to identify an increasing number of patterns will grow and we shall better be able to define their range of validity; the greater the body of such comparative studies, the greater is the transferability of data.

In all, six main types of information entering into the water-land-man planning space are listed in the following; the most important characteristic of these types of information is their high specificity and the corollary limitation in their transferability.

1. Water resources, their spontaneous fluctuations and responses to human manipulation: the relevant parameters are: location in plane, potential energy (third dimension of space); rate of flow function; biological quality; and mineral quality.
2. Soil resources: properties in the natural state such as their extent, depth, texture, and structure; the direct response of soil to human intervention, such as the application and removal of water, the application of agricultural inputs and agrotechnical practice; and the indirect effects of human intervention, such as erosion.
3. Human resources: those controlling the development process; their present psychological space and their responses to change in psychological space; the same type of information on human resources at the production level, i.e., the farmers.
4. Institutional resources: at all relevant levels from village institutions to the political hierarchy; the present status of these resources; inertial forces acting against change; the "critical mass" of intervention required to effect change; and anticipated responses to intervention.
5. Economic information: volumes and costs of intervention and inputs, and volumes and prices of outputs and demand.
6. Technological resources: know-how and techniques related to all types of resources and their possible upgrading.

INFORMATION LOGISTICS

Information constitutes one of the most important inputs of development planning, and hence the availability of adequate information should not be taken for granted; rather, the creation and gathering of information must be considered logistically and be planned and programmed like that of any other essential development program input. As for the information requirements at every decision point of a development sequence, these can be represented (for each of the essential variables entering into our development equation) by two families of curves: the curves of minimum threshold and the curves of optimal information range, i.e., the economically justified amounts of information.

From the above definition of terms, it follows that actual information inputs at every decision point should be above the respective minimum information threshold curves (otherwise a decision would not be warranted) and should approach, as closely as possible, the optimal information range curve. Approaching the latter curve means that, for every decision involved, we have as much information as we ought to have; surpassing this ceiling signifies that we have overinvested in information generation.

Viewed from a specific decision point of a specific decision sequence, our basic rule of information logistics should be to strive to set up a program in a way that will ensure that the information gain between two decision points on a decision sequence is at least equal to the incremental information requirement between these points.

Every line of action generates a certain amount of information: its information *yield*. In some cases, this information yield may be relatively small, as, for example, in repetitive action sequences of the investment types; in other cases, it may be the most significant output, as in data collection and pilot operations. Similarly, every action requires a certain information input; even "pure" information-gathering operations require a certain primary information input, such as a basic hypothesis for the programming and selection of the information-gathering operation.

Most of the relevant information required in projects in which the human-institutional dimensions play an important role can be generated only as a by-product of the development process. Where subsequent decisions are conditional on such information gain, it will be necessary to organize the development process in a way that will ensure that its information yield will meet anticipated requirements. Thus, the planning of information logistics for complex transformation projects is in itself a complex operation intimately bound up with the planning of the essence of the project.

To rectify the situation in those cases where the curve of expected information availability at a certain decision point falls below the minimum information threshold curve, we will have to choose one of the following three approaches:

1. Speeding up information generation by modifying the sequence so as to generate greater information yields or by setting up special programs to generate information
2. Choosing a decision sequence with a lower minimum information threshold at the critical decision point
3. A combination of these two approaches

From the point of view of information, an ideal sequence of action is the one for which expected information availability approaches the optimal information range. However, the actual information situation in developing countries is, as a rule, close to the lower limit of information feasibility and requires that we operate on the basis of an information-availability curve which hugs minimum threshold values. As a matter of course, decisions made under conditions of information scarcity will be somewhat more costly than those made under conditions of adequate information availability, since they entail overdesign and the acceptance of a greater range of risks; this is the penalty we have to pay for operating in a planning space of high uncertainty. However, we can, to a certain extent, reduce this penalty by modifying our decision models to the requirements of a planning space of high uncertainty and adopting corresponding decision strategies. The next section of this chapter will be devoted to some of these strategies.

In drawing up these strategies, the decision maker's subjective judgment should be focused upon (usually semiquantifiable) decisions which, it is assumed, lie within a reasonable discrimination range for the typical decision maker, being similar to the type of decisions he is accustomed to make. On the other hand, one should steer clear of decision dichotomies in which the decision maker would be faced by alternatives, which, in an abstract presentation, would be practically meaningless to him. For instance, asking a decision maker to assign probability values to the occurrence of unpredictable and, for him, uncontrollable alternative events would be pointless. However, taking a decision which would involve an additional cost of, say, 10 percent for phased implementation of a project, in order to minimize the risks inherent in the immediate decision and thus purchase freedom for future decisions, might be considered by the average decision maker to constitute a truly meaningful selection, though it would still indirectly imply the assignment of probabilities.

INFORMATION HEURISTICS

The principal objective of heuristic decision strategies in a planning space characterized by great uncertainty in most basic information parameters is to reduce the gap between information availabilities and information thresholds and requirements, and to adopt lines of action of low sensitivity to variation of those parameters for which information is inadequate, at a time when uncertainty is highest. These heuristic strategies are briefly described in the following.

Heuristic one—the reconnaissance probe The purpose of this probe is to establish the basic body of information necessary to prime a new sequence of action and to determine the extent to which information from other similar contexts could be used to amplify available information. Establishing a reconnaissance probe will involve the identification of available information, the tentative definition of alternative potential project objectives, the definition of the type of pilot operations required to generate the relevant information for a feasibility type of planning, and, finally, the drawing up of a detailed plan of operation for such pilot operations.

Heuristic two—pilot operations These operations have a triple purpose:

1. They must generate information by tentative implementation probes at a rate that should, to the extent possible, be compatible with the rate of information requirements of feasibility type of planning.
2. They must bring about a transformation and demonstration effect on those who have to plan and implement the project proper.
3. They must define information-generation programs for the subsequent phase of operations in order to preserve the continuity of the information-generation process.

Heuristic three This strategy consists of the following:

Reshuffling the Decision Sequence to Lower Minimum Information Thresholds A typical development sequence contains alternative self-contained units of action (action steps on the curve representing the sequence of action), some of which can be substituted for each other. If the expected information availability of the sequence, as it stands, is at certain points below threshold, an attempt can be made to reshuffle these interchangeable steps with a view to closing the information gap. This could be done by giving priority to steps involving a lower information threshold, even if such a shift entails increased costs, provided these additional costs are preferable to the risks incurred in the original sequences. A good example of this strategy is the change in the sequence of development in a project originally based on the utilization of surface water before groundwater. Under this strategy, priority would be given to groundwater development, which, owing mainly to its extreme subdivisibility, has low minimum information thresholds.

Reshuffling the Sequence to Raise Information Yields Every action step results in a certain feedback yield of information, and some steps might even be taken with the primary objective of generating information. By giving precedence to action steps with high information yields, we could accelerate the accumulation of information and thus again assist in closing the information gap. Here, too, a typical example of this strategy would be to give precedence to groundwater development, which has a higher information yield than surface water.

Subdividing Decision Steps in Order to Lower the Minimum Information Threshold Information availability for a certain decision step characterized by certain supply capacities may be below the threshold for such capacities, while the decision step itself may be subdivisible; subdivision in such a case may result in a sufficient lowering of the minimum information threshold. Since each such partial-capacity decision step may have a lower threshold than a single full-capacity step, this strategy may again contribute toward closing the information gap. This subdivision of capacity will at some later date require the connection of the partial-capacity installations in parallel (as with the two barrels of a phased conduit) or in series (as with the addition of a booster pumping station into a gravity conduit).

Project "Generations" Project generations represent a more general form of the subdivision strategy. This concept involves the construction of a major supply capacity in consecutive project generations, where the earliest, relatively low-capacity generation with low information threshold values can subsequently be reinforced by supplies that will become available by the construction of later generations. The feed-in point of such supplementary supplies could be different from that of the first-generation project, and thus an additional potential dimension of flexibility can be created by functional reshuffles of the project layout of the first-generation project, resulting from integration with the second-generation layout. Since decisions on the sizes and feed points of second- and third-generation projects, and on the amount of the supplementary supply to be made available through them to the first-generation project, need not be made when deciding upon the first-generation project, both the information threshold and the optimal range of such a first-generation project will be found to be exceptionally and attractively low.

Modifying the Ratio of Capital to Operation and Maintenance Costs In a deterministic planning space, the size and type of installations to be selected for a specific supply capacity will be the outcome of a simple optimizing calculation of the present worth of loan servicing and of operation and maintenance cost streams. In a probabilistically defined planning space, expected values of costs might be adopted; however, in the ubiquitous "ill-structured" decision situations prevailing in the early phases of development, probabilities seldom lend themselves to quantification, and decisions often have to be made with unquantifiable probabilities. Generally, it will be found that the more uncertainty we anticipate at a certain decision point, the lower the ratio of capital to operation and maintenance costs that should be selected, since projects with low ratios of capital to operation and maintenance costs tend to require a lower information threshold. How far we should go in this direction will be determined by comparing the loss of economic efficiency involved in such a selection with the expected value of the lowering of the risk thus achieved.

Expanding Planning Space Provision for inclusion, in the later phases of a long-term program, of an expanding planning space (comprising, for example, an adjoining hydrological basin) may assist in lowering the information threshold of immediate decision steps. Planned expansion of the planning space may be economically feasible even where it involves a considerable future rise in unit costs of water originating from the proposed expanded part of the planning space, since the impact on current decisions of the present worth of such a cost increase anticipated for the distant future will not be very weighty.

Giving Preference to Projects with Short Lives Adopting designs with a short useful life also tends to lower information thresholds through reducing risks in capital investment. Here, again, we purchase a lowering of risks at the expense of economic efficiency.

Giving Preference to Projects with Built-in Safety Margins Some sources have considerable inherent safety margins, since they may be connected to some buffer stock or storage which exercises an inertial type of slowing-down effect upon the responses of the source to engineering intervention; groundwater formations often have this property. Selection of projects with sources having such buffer stocks exercises a cushioning effect—should the original estimates on which our decisions are based prove to be incorrect.

Threshold Reduction of a Sequence of Action A waterworks usually consists of a group of installations connected in series, each having its specific information threshold. The controlling threshold of the sequence will be that of the installation with the highest threshold of the group. Thus, we may be faced with a situation where we have sufficient data for making decisions relating to all but, say, one installation. Under these circumstances it may prove possible to circumvent such a decision handicap either by temporary "bypassing" the high-threshold installation or by replacing it with a temporary makeshift. However, both lines of action involve the acceptance of a reduced supply (and possibly also of temporarily reduced economic efficiency) for the period of postponement of the high-threshold installation. Temporary feeding of a river-based supply from a run-of-the-river type diversion, possibly backed up by a groundwater supply drawing upon a small stock utilized only during periods of low flow, is an example of this approach.

Information on the Political Decision-making Process By far the most important heuristic strategy is to draw up projects or programs in a way that ensures their *political feasibility*. All projects or programs, after passing the most refined analysis, have ultimately to pass the rough-and-ready test of political feasibility. Rough as this may be, the behavior of the political decision maker is difficult to predict. However, similarities in basic situations tend to produce similar political reaction patterns. In principle, the political decision-maker's tolerance for sectorial requests for funds will depend on competing pressures from other sectors of the economy. Thus, if capital funds are thought to be reasonably adequate, resistance to investment projects will be relatively low, and vice versa. To overcome resistance to initial approval and appropriation, a certain "momentum" is needed: the higher the resistance, the higher the momentum required. Where immoderate claims are made upon an inadequate capital budget, a wise sectorial programmer will propose projects which require a relatively small "starting momentum" or, if necessary, he will modify original investment patterns in a way which reduces the initial investment (and thereby also the resistance and the corollary momentum), at the cost of later compensating investments. Fair judgment of the acceptable momentum often proves to be the most strategic information of all. In making predictions of the behavior of the political decision maker, we should also bear in mind that his responses are apt to change through a process of feedback from development, the politician, like everybody else, being influenced by the outcome of decision strategies applied in the past.

PLANNING IN CONDITIONS OF UNCERTAINTY

Two basic approaches exist to planning in conditions of uncertainty.

1. Where we can define probability distribution of outcomes in a reasonably rigorous way, we can calculate the expected values of outcomes and determine, after making a selection of the appropriate decision criterion, the line of action to adopt.

2. Where probability distribution of outcomes cannot be quantified, we can decide which parameter ranges we propose to take into account and then determine the sensitivity of outcomes to parametric variations within the selected ranges and their combinations. Some alternative sequences of action will show relatively low sensitivity (within the chosen combinations of ranges), coupled with a relatively low loss of efficiency (as compared with the deterministic solution based on "design values"). Such a sequence should be selected.

The first approach is indicated, as a rule, in action sequences involving mainly physical and economic variables. This does not, of course, imply that sequences in which social and psychological variables loom large do not lend themselves to quantification as to their probability distribution. Such quantification, however, presupposes the existence of a body of relevant observational data; rarely, if ever, does this exist at the time when we have to make our most vital decisions, i.e., in the initial stages of development. Even in cases for which probabilistic quantification is feasible, the question still remains as to which decision criterion is the appropriate one to select. The sensitivity analysis approach has the obvious advantage of wider applicability; it suffers from the disadvantage of masking the option of probability distribution that the selection of a certain alternative, in fact, implies. The sensitivity approach is, therefore, indicated for the complex early development phases under conditions of underdevelopment.

Finally, attention is drawn to a type of "optical illusion" to which most of us are prone, namely, *underestimating the extent of uncertainty*. When reviewing possible outcomes, we are not usually in a position to list all factors that may modify our assumptions or to identify all unpredictable future developments; furthermore, we also tend to neglect influence from outside the system that may bear upon outcomes within the system. As a consequence, we tend to underestimate the importance of low sensitivity of outcomes and the value of decision or action liquidity. In arriving at our final conclusion, we should compensate for this built-in bias and grant to decision liquidity and low sensitivity a higher utility and value than we can directly prove.

CONCLUSIONS

A planning space characterized by great uncertainty requires that far-reaching changes be introduced into the decision, planning, and implementation models transferred from spaces having more adequate information. Under conditions of uncertainty, the value of time is higher than in a planning space with better information; in the former case, the value of time is represented not only by "time preference" but also by the information that can be generated over time, either by information-oriented operations or as a by-product of development. Better information is a precondition for an economically more efficient decision process. Conditions of uncertainty also necessitate greater integration and a more extensive adoption of the "system approach." Integration should be applied to various types of uses, to various planning spaces, or to their combination. Such integration, on the one hand, tends to decrease uncertainty (because of the better chance of compensating undesirable responses of the system for deviations from design data); on the other hand, it increases flexibility of response under unforeseen circumstances through "mutual aid" between the integrated resources.

In the final account, we look in conditions of uncertainty to what one might call "liquidity of future action"; as long as we are unsure of the behavior of our planning environment, we should commit ourselves as little as possible and leave open as many lines of future action as we can.

12
PROGRAM EVALUATION

The reasonable man adapts himself to the world; the unreasonable man persists in trying to adapt the world to himself. Therefore, all progress depends on the unreasonable man.

G. B. SHAW (*Maxims for Revolutionists*)

ORTHODOX VS. DYNAMIC EVALUATION

Before proceeding to a comparison of evaluative procedures, a few of the key terms to be used in this chapter will be defined.

1. Project: a set of interconnected operations relating to the application of specific resources or input packages to a specific system aimed at obtaining (through the transfer functions that characterize the system) the desired specific outcomes or outputs.
2. Program: a set of related projects associated with a sector or subsector of the economy.
3. Systems: in this context, subsystems, or sub-subsystems, of the national socioeconomic system. Although they have been cut from the overall system for pragmatic reasons, they have to be conceived as closely interconnected with the overall system, through ties which are represented by the boundary conditions.
4. Statically oriented evaluation: the comparison of outcomes of specific input packages operating on a system by relating them to a standard, or by comparing them to alternative lines of action capable of leading to the same or to similar results, the system structure (and resources-outcome ratios connected with it) being assumed to remain unchanged.
5. Dynamically oriented evaluation: a comparison encompassing, within the category of planned outcomes, the change in resources-outcome ratios which results from the upgrading or transformation inputs applied to the system structure, in addition to the evaluation of direct outputs as related to inputs. "Upgrading" in this context refers to modifications of the system structure that will result in an improved resources-outcome ratio.

The statically oriented evaluative approach does not attempt to compare the extent of upgrading induced in the system structure—and in the resources-outcome ratio related to system structure—by the action of input packages, although it seems evident that rapid cumulative growth is conditional upon such upgrading. Neglect of these structural aspects is, of course, a direct result of the planner's bias. In orthodox evaluation, the planner operates according to either the mechanistic or the atomistic socioeconomic model. If he subscribes to the mechanistic model, he may feel that upgrading of the system structure within the project is not essential, since he proposes anyhow to rely completely upon absolute control from the top; if he subscribes to the atomistic model, he will feel that no basic structural change is feasible or necessary, since his diffuse decision space is practically unstructured.

When we switch to the dynamically oriented evaluation procedure, we also, by inference, adopt a cybernetic model of the socioeconomic complex and with it the following basic implications:

1. Recognition of the pragmatic nature of the "cut" of the subsystem. This cut isolates the project planning space from the national phase space by introducing, at the boundaries of the project planning space, boundary conditions which represent the influence of the national phase space on the project, and vice versa. This approach leads us to the realization that every operation within the project system, in addition to leaving some permanent imprint on the project system (and its structure), also makes a possibly highly diluted impact on the external world.
2. Realization that the output of a system depends, on the one hand, on the volume and quality of the input package and, on the other hand, on the system structure and the resources-outcome ratios that are characteristic of this structure; hence, the evaluation should stress both aspects of the system output. Special emphasis should be placed in the underdeveloped countries upon the system structure, since without transformation of this structure there is no hope of initiating a rapid cumulative growth process.
3. Recognition of the nature of the basic dysfunctions of the system that have to be corrected before one can hope to achieve satisfactory resources-outcome ratios.

The question that arises here is what influence the adoption of a specific evaluation approach will have on the effectiveness of the selection process. The difference is not so much one of principle as one of degree, since, whether we allow for it or not, every input package effects a certain change upon the structure through which it flows, and every project effect, to some extent, "radiates" outside the project boundaries. However, these random changes and influences are marginal and have little, if any, cumulative effect in the short run. If, on the other hand, we desire to emphasize the necessity of rapid structural change as our most important instrumental project objective, we must also systematically evaluate programs according to their *transformation effects;* major progress can be achieved only if such structural changes are significant in volume, as well as cumulative and focused on the areas of the most crippling dysfunctions.

IMPACT LOOPS OF PROGRAMS

The above analysis of alternative evaluative approaches demonstrates the importance in underdeveloped economies of structural features and changes.

This section will be devoted to elaborating an evaluative approach of program effectiveness in which the *transformation aspect* of the program constitutes an essential part of the evaluation.

Our description of the evaluative process will start with a review of the socioeconomic hierarchy as a whole. Structural profiles of hierarchies in different societies show extreme variations, and to simplify our description we shall abstract from this variety and assume the existence of only four basic levels in our idealized hierarchy: the top executive, the minister (at the sectorial or program level), the project manager (at the project level), and the "grass-roots" production level within the project area proper.

Every major operation, e.g., a sectorial or subsectorial program or a large-scale project, creates ripples of influence originating from the operation and directed toward three levels: vertically downward toward the grass-roots level of the project area proper (the project or *downward loop*); horizontally, as it were, toward the parallel sectorial or subsectorial level (the *sideward loop*); and, finally, vertically upward toward the higher levels of the hierarchy (the *upward loop*). As the "organizational distance" of travel of such impulses increases, their intensity, of course, decreases. The three types of impulse destinations respond by issuing "reflected" impulses (feedbacks) toward the operation. In the case of downward loops, the original impulses received take the form of specific instructions, and the feedback consists of information on performance and obstacles; in the case of sideward loops, information is for coordinative purposes and reports on the coordination achieved; in the case of upward loops, the information obtained relates to performance and the instructions received relate to acceleration and deceleration, respectively.

The flow of such information originating from one subsystem, through channels that reach far into other subsystems of the economy, is bound gradually and cumulatively to change the development concepts of decision makers in parallel subsystems, e.g., other ministers and project managers, and of decision makers organizationally located "above" the program, such as the responsible minister or the chief executive. Admittedly, information streams reach them in an extremely garbled and diluted form, and their relevance to their own areas of responsibility is not immediately obvious, though in due time the bearing of such information spills upon their own problem solving and decision making will become abundantly clear. Since the areas of responsibility of the numerous decision makers reached by the horizontal and upward streams are many times larger than that of the program manager originating the spills, "dilution" of these information streams is often compensated for by the "multiplier effect" of the dissemination process. In certain cases, these "external economies" of a program may become as important as the internal ones.

It should furthermore be borne in mind that modification of the attitudes of officials in the top echelons and, to a certain extent, also of those on the sideward loop likewise directly benefits the program itself, since the success of a program largely depends on the quality of the decision streams issuing from these levels.

The question of allocation of resources between the downward loop and the upward and sideward loops does not pose any real decision problems, at least not as far as capital resources are concerned, since effective secondary loops require only negligible amounts of capital resources; their effectiveness depends rather on minor modifications of project operations and procedures, in accordance with certain tactical heuristics, some of which are outlined in the following.

To influence a political decision maker, we must first attempt to understand his "personal equation" and adopt a tactical approach that harmonizes with it. His time span of expectation is relatively short; hence, we should fashion a program in a way that will produce at least some results within this time span. His resistance to committing large sums to individual projects is considerable since he is not in a position to judge project benefits; hence, the curve representing capital investment over time should be skewed to the right (i.e., to the future). His resistance to initiating institutional changes and to acting against the interest of major vested interests is equally great, and, hence, in the early phases, we should minimize such operations. In short, to reach the high-level political decision maker, we must attempt to make program objectives, and especially those of the early phases, blend, as closely as we can, with the political and career objectives of the decision maker, and see to it that the information stream that reaches this top-level official makes this consonance abundantly clear. For greater effectiveness of these "spillover" streams, the program manager should mobilize, in addition to the direct channel available to him, alternative channels for the dissemination of information, in the hope that part of this diffuse stream will reach the top by roundabout ways and "reinforce" the direct stream of communication.

From this we see that evaluation procedures should, therefore, include an analysis of the anticipated program impact upon parallel and higher levels of the decision hierarchy; where such impact is deemed to be insufficient, appropriate measures should be taken to upgrade relevant procedures and tactics. Such upgrading measures aimed at harmonizing a project with political objectives involve, of course, a sacrifice in project utility; on the other hand, neglecting the political aspect may well jeopardize the very existence of the project.

INTRASYSTEM EFFECTS: THE DOWNWARD LOOP

The emphasis in the preceding section has been placed on the extra-system effects. The main effort of evaluation will, however, be focused upon the intrasystem or downward loop. Let us, therefore, return from the wider phase space of the overall socioeconomic system and cross the boundaries into our program subsystem.

Here, two extreme basic allocation patterns are open to us:

1. Focusing on *short-term* production aspects by allocating material and human resources inputs in a way that will maximize (through the prevailing structure which is assumed to remain practically unchanged during the planning period) the sectorial product or some combined production-type objective function combining, for example, aggregate production with income distribution

2. Focusing on medium and *long-term* production aspects by allocating inputs in a way that will maximize the upgrading of the structural features of the subsystem and, through such upgrading, will subsequently maximize cumulative growth

Every actual program will, in fact, incorporate a mixed strategy, adopting the two basic allocative patterns in various proportions.

If the time extension of our analysis were sufficiently long, and if information on resources-outcome ratios and their rate of improvement were adequate, there would be no theoretical difficulty in arriving at an analytical determination of the optimized mix (for a selected objective function) of the two allocation categories; this would be effected by comparing outcomes for a number of alternative allocative patterns (measured in terms of the selected objective) resulting from a different emphasis upon short-term and long-term objectives, respectively. The selected alternative would be the one which maximizes the objective function. At the present stage, it would probably be difficult to perform such a long-term analysis because of insufficient information; there is, however, every reason to assume that such an analysis will become feasible, once transformation-oriented programs are established and procedures adopted to measure the relevant resources-outcome ratios in various socioeconomic structural contexts. Parametric measurements from a different development context could be used to carry out preliminary analysis in similar socioeconomic environments until more refined analyses, based on specific data, become feasible.

But even at the present stage, in which rigorous quantitative evaluation is not yet possible, we should not be deterred by the difficulties in quantifying evaluative procedures, nor should we allow ourselves to arrive at the erroneous and completely unwarranted conclusion that what cannot be quantified had better be left alone. This, in fact, would be just another example of the well-known "strategy" of looking for a lost coin, at nighttime, on the well-lit but wrong side of the street. In this specific case, action without quantified analysis is made possible by the existence of some built-in features in underdeveloped agriculture which enable us to arrive at conclusions on the basis of a nonquantified analysis. These features are described in the following.

There are usually a number of projects in which the major investment has already been made, or, at least, already decided upon, but in which project fruition lags behind or has not even begun owing to the inadequate growth capacity of the producer group and of lower level institutions. The obvious solution in such situations consists in the application of *complementary input packages* designed to speed up the development of these growth capacities. Initially, it will be necessary to make a guess as to the types and volumes of the required inputs, but deployment of these inputs will, in any case, be limited by logistic constraints. Only after these inputs have been applied in the field will we be in a position to collect information on resources-outcome ratios; these ratios can then be used to quantify input packages in the more extensive later phases of the project.

The fact that inadequate growth capacity has a crippling effect on productivity in existing projects provides, of course, a kind of negative proof that similar handicaps may also be expected in future projects. We are, therefore, justified in accepting as a foregone conclusion that the development of growth capacity should precede, or at least be simultaneous with, the investment-intensive development of natural resources.

In actual fact, projects, or project portions, aiming mainly at the upgrading of growth capacity hardly compete with investment-oriented projects for capital funds, since, in the typical case, we are bound to reach logistic and organizational limits with capacity-type projects (mostly related to human resources) long before we reach capital constraints. The crippling effects of the lack or inadequacy of the complementary aspects of projects related to growth capacity are often so glaringly conspicuous, and the human resources available to upgrade such capacity so limited, that quantification appears as a rather irrelevant sophistication. Hence, in such situations we must insist on the earliest possible deployment of the available human resources on the growth-capacity front, combined with subsequent collection of field data on resources-outcome ratios. If input proportions are appropriately varied in the initial experimental phase, such exploratory intervention will yield an important body of measurements, and these measurements can be used to quantify the later more extensive phases of the program for which quantification is truly relevant.

As long as our parametric information is insufficient for rigorous quantification, difficulties will be experienced in comparing and ranking projects of similar nature or orientation. Since outcomes will be controlled by the critically scarce resource, the pragmatic approach, i.e., that of attempting to maximize the outcome per unit of critically scarce input, will probably be the best available approximation.

PRAGMATIC EVALUATION APPROACH

Underdevelopment is certainly not caused by lack of sophistication in orthodox evaluative procedures. Small errors of plus or minus in calculating the efficiency of a project do not constitute a decisive factor in forecasting the contribution of a project or program to the country's development. What really matters in the final count are the answers we give to the following two questions:

1. How does a program contribute to the improvement of the structural framework of the socioeconomic system and the related growth capacity?
2. What type of evaluative procedure, what yardsticks used to measure objective achievement of alternative choices, will elicit the most meaningful decisions from the political hierarchy?

To answer the first question, we must analyze the sector as a whole, at least on general lines (the methodology for such an analysis is described in Chapter 20), and determine from this analysis the most crippling structural inadequacies. Orthodox evaluation of project economics should be supplemented by an evaluation of the contribution of every individual project toward overcoming these inadequacies and creating transformation inputs.

However, before such ranking is attempted, we must submit the project list of the program to what we may call the test of exhaustiveness, i.e., we have to check whether all reasonably promising projects capable of achieving our direct and selected instrumental objectives have, in fact, been included in the program; ranking a program that has not been submitted to this test often implies that we are resigned to achieving the less important objectives in the most efficient way.

This subject is treated in greater detail in Chapter 20, and we therefore turn in the following section to the second question, i.e., to the ways and means of optimizing the response of the political decision maker.

THE DECISION-MAKER'S RESPONSE

The quality of decisions and the fate of development depend, to a great extent, on the effectiveness of communication between the technocrat and the bureaucrat, between the professional and the political decision makers. Development is so complex a process that the politician is compelled to lean heavily on the professional; however, the existence of this dialogue does not by itself guarantee the emergence of communication. In fact, the reverse is closer to the truth, for political and professional personnel are, as likely as not, to be so far apart that communication between them has to be expressly planned. The need for this planning of communication between the bureaucrat and the technocrat arises mainly out of the great difficulty encountered in establishing a single and universally accepted yardstick and metric of evaluation.

Rarely, if ever, are we in a position to reduce all the objective functions we wish to include in a complex development program to a common denominator and to quantify all dimensions of phase space. As a rule, the question of tradeoffs between objectives remains wide open until a decision is taken at the political level, and the anticipated results of programs will have to be expressed partly in quantified terms, partly in ordinal terms, and partly in purely descriptive terms.

The ultimate selection of the most desirable program, therefore, largely depends on what is usually referred to as judgment, i.e., a rather erratic evaluation process which does not appear to be based on a definable set of rules of operation. Nevertheless, this process responds better to certain principles of ordering and evaluation than to others. Here, in this context, a better response signifies closer compliance with the prevailing set of value judgments and with internal consistency.

Since this judgment process is performed by the decision makers at the top of the political hierarchy, we should ask ourselves what principles of ordering and evaluation have the best chance of eliciting a "good" decision from the decision makers, for it is the quality of these decisions, rather than the quality and sophistication of the evaluative process, that determines the success of the program.

The effectiveness of this decisive dialogue between the bureaucrat and the technocrat will largely depend on the latter's ability to *lire pour autrui* (to read with other peoples' eyes).[1] More specifically, this ability consists of the following:

1. The technocrat's insight into the mechanism of the bureaucrat's judgment
2. His capacity to transpose his grading and evaluative procedures and his alternative choices into terms that elicit "good" judgments from the bureaucrat
3. His talent of presentation of such a transposed analysis

In spite of the fact that innumerable decisions of bureaucrats have been and are being made and that many of them are reasonably well recorded, little practical information exists on the psychology of bureaucratic decision making; anything said here on this problem will be rather thin stuff and, at that, mostly of a conjectural nature. Until better systematic guidance is available, the technocrat will have to maintain an empirical study of the decision-making strategies of the bureaucrats who control his operations and develop a knack of predicting their responses.

The chapter headings for a future psychology of the decision mechanism might read as follows:

The Personality Profile of the Political Decision Maker This study would occupy itself with the types and proportions of psychological traits selected by the promotional process and their influence on judgment and decision (this aspect has been covered in some detail in Chapter 5). Study of this personality profile may indicate the bureaucrat's preference for the concrete over the abstract, for the simple (or simplified) over the complex, etc. Though this may be obvious, as well as common knowledge, it is, nevertheless, rarely allowed for by the technocrat.

The Manifest and Latent Decision Criteria of the Bureaucrat The *manifest* criteria concern themselves with the image the bureaucrat wishes to create, the *latent* with his actual personality traits and the requirements of the hierarchy to which he belongs.

The manifest criteria can best be studied in the public acts of the hierarchy and their records; their importance is, however, limited, for whatever the nature of the manifest decision taken, and whatever the underlying decision criteria, the bureaucrat will always find a way to perform the "Alice in Wonderland" trick of making the words mean what one wants them to mean. Though the methods of "semantic transposition" exercised by political bureaucrats in a democracy are much less crude than those of the masters of a totalitarian

[1] Aurel David, *La Cybernetique et l'Humain,* Collection Idées, Éditions Gallimard, Paris, 1965.

hierarchy (the unsurpassed champions in this art), they will in essence be no different.

It is the latent, the unavowed, criteria that most repay study. Although it may be extremely difficult to trace the complete set of criteria which underlie a specific decision, the "teasing out" of the controlling criterion may prove to be a rewarding job, as Anthony Downs[2] proved when he employed a single criterion, i.e., that of the contribution of a decision to the chances of political reelection, to construct a set of decision strategies of political decision makers. There is a fair chance that a detailed study of the decision criteria followed by the political bureaucrats who control the development issues would come up with a similar type of criterion. Assuming this to be the case, the criterion of political reelection, if pursued in our context, will result in a number of specific strategies which could serve as excellent guides for the technocrat on how to evaluate the "political feasibility" of a program.

The Politician's Decision Strategies This topic leads naturally to the next area of study, that of tracing the kinds of strategies and heuristics which the political bureaucrat uses.

The Political Decision-maker's Generic and Mental Blocks The political decision maker has his "generic" and individual mental blocks. Generic blocks are direct outcomes of his dogmatic indoctrination, whether religious, political, national, or professional; they will be strongest in totalitarian regimes and "closed-shop" guilds. His individual mental blocks may be related to his personal experience and personality traits.

Political feasibility is the last and most decisive test that a program has to undergo; it is its moment of truth, and if it fails in this political test, no amount of elaboration or sophistication in the other dimensions of evaluation will be of any value. Hence, no effort should be spared in evaluating political feasibility and in transposing objectives and choice criteria into terms that are meaningful to the political decision maker. It would, for example, be pointless, in most cases, to consult the political decision maker on the relative utility that he attributes to additional unit income in the lower income bracket as compared with the higher income bracket; however, the same question when transposed into production aggregates, income distribution, and employment patterns of concrete alternative programs becomes politically meaningful to the decision makers. Thus, while we may assume that his judgment mechanism does not respond suitably to the first type of abstract questioning, there is a good chance that he will be able to meaningfully process the transposed type of questioning.

THE CHECKLIST OF FEASIBILITY TESTS

The kind of tests to which development programs in underdeveloped economies should be submitted are listed briefly in the following.

[2] Anthony Downs, *An Economic Theory of Democracy*, Harper & Brothers, New York, 1957.

Orthodox evaluation of feasibility centers around two major feasibility tests:

1. The postulate of engineering feasibility, namely, proof that a specific set of installations can be safely built and dependably utilized over the specified lifetime at a specified cost
2. The postulate of economic feasibility, namely, proof that the relation of the benefits created by a project to the costs involved comply with certain standard rules and is more favorable than that of the alternative programs

Whereas the test of engineering feasibility can be conducted in a phase space containing only physical and quantifiable dimensions, the test of economic feasibility involves estimates of production generated by a project and should be conducted in a multidimensional and only partly quantifiable phase space. The conduct of such a multidimensional analysis will often prove to be extremely difficult, and an approximative procedure may have to be introduced to simplify analysis. Supplementing the conventional economic feasibility test by a number of complementary tests related to the nonphysical dimension omitted in the orthodox tests constitutes an appropriate substitute for a multidimensional analysis that does not involve too much loss of rigor. These complementary tests are the following:

1. Exhaustiveness: proof that the program list subjected to evaluation does, in fact, include all important alternative projects and project features that can be assumed to lead to the achievement of the objectives of the development program (Chapter 20).
2. Continuity of the development process: proof that the present program complies reasonably well with the preinvestment requirements of the subsequent program. In other words, proof that the present program contains a sufficient resources allocation for capacity development, so as to ensure optimal results also from the long-term point of view. Where analytical evaluation is not possible, the check as to whether or not this program complies with this postulate may have to be a rough and ready one.
3. Compliance of boundary conditions: proof that the boundary conditions resulting from the program, in fact, comply with those originally assumed when defining the planning space. These boundary conditions are drawn up according to original assumptions of project outcomes (such as aggregate production, production distribution, prices of products). However, the program analysis may give somewhat different values. The program analysis may have to be reiterated with the revised values should these discrepancies reach a significant level.
4. Adequate information and flexibility: proof that planning ideology has been adapted to operating in a multidimensional space plagued with great uncertainty. The test of adequate flexibility is carried out to give proof that the program has, in fact, been evaluated from this point of view and that "liquidity of action" has been given its proper place in such an evaluation (see Chapter 11).
5. Logistic feasibility: proof that the human and material resources inventory in all its subdivisions is sufficient to implement the operations in all relevant dimensions of the phase space included in the program (see Chapter 18).

6. Institutional feasibility: proof of the existence of a structural homology of the decision and implementation patterns assumed in programs with those of the actual political and administrative hierarchy. Lack of such homology will lead to serious breakdowns in coordination and will endanger project effectiveness (see Chapter 20, Political and Institutional Aspects of Sectorial Programs).

7. Political feasibility: proof that the proposed fulfillment of program objectives, if transposed into metrics used by the political hierarchy, will be acceptable to the relevant political decision maker (see the preceding section).

We have traveled a long distance from the orthodox evaluation procedure of resources projects in underdeveloped countries, a procedure which has been transferred from the developed countries. The structural complexities involved in the transformation process of underdeveloped socioeconomic systems require similar complexities of evaluation procedures. This book, in fact, attempts to elaborate upon the principles of such an expanded evaluative procedure.

13
THE DECISION SPACE

... toute la doctrine de l'action en deux chapîtres dont chacun n'a qu'un mot. Premier chapître, continuer. Deuxième chapître, commencer. L'ordre, qui étonne, fait presque toute l'idée ... Continuer c'est le seul moyen de changer.[1]

ALAIN (*Propos*)

Planning, in the usual sense of the word, consists of scheduling the disposition of logistic streams, material as well as nonmaterial, with a view to upgrading the status quo geometry of phase space according to the requirements of a target geometry. Since the purpose of a plan is to serve as a guide to action, the tacit assumption inherent in the planning process is that planning a specific disposition of logistic streams will, in fact, release the relevant decisions; this assumption will often prove to be unwarranted. Planning can be compared to the loading of a gun, which is a necessary but not a sufficient condition for shooting at a target; to shoot purposefully we have to perform two additional discrete acts, i.e., to point the gun and to press the trigger. Transposed into the development context, this implies that development action involves, in addition to the development plan, the ability to channel logistic streams purposefully and the authority to decide to do so.

As a rule, major decisions related to development are made by the political hierarchy and its administrative branches rather than by the planner. The *chances of success* of a plan will, therefore, be controlled by the *quality of decision streams* which the plan will trigger off, rather than by the quality of the plan as such.

To optimize outcomes we, therefore, ought to draw up plans in a way that will result in the best possible decision sequences. To simplify the exposition of such an optimization process, we propose, in this chapter, to *isolate the decision sequences from the phase space in which they are embedded, thus obtaining a new abstract construct: decision space.* The purpose of this chapter is to study lines of action and strategies necessary for optimizing outcomes in such a decision space. We need to keep in mind that since deci-

[1] ... the entire ideology of action in two chapters, each of which consists of but one word. Chapter One: continue. Chapter Two: begin. The surprising order contains practically the whole idea ... Continuing is the only way of changing.

sion space is only a *heuristic construct* that has been abstracted from a multidimensional phase space, optimization in a decision space will constitute only a suboptimization. However, as the decision process is mostly neglected in the planning process, the suboptimization of our specific development problems in abstract decision space will constitute a most useful indication of the kind of *correctives* that ought to be applied to lines of action which have been arrived at without taking into account the "decision dimension." Analysis of abstract decision space as related to resources development is the subject of this chapter.

DECISION SPACE AND POLITICAL SPACE

If we observe a series of decisions that are related to a specific development field or sector, we shall find that they are not discrete and independent "events" but interconnected and interdependent parts of an organizational pattern of decisions. This organizational pattern, and the underlying politico-administrative organization, will vary from society to society and within the same society from sector to sector. We shall, however, always be able to observe some common overall structural features which can be resolved into a combination of *vertical decision sequences* (i.e., a decision pattern exclusively controlled from the top), of *branching patterns* (a decision pattern where few higher level decisions trigger off numerous lower level decisions and this pattern repeats itself at still lower levels), and finally of a *random* type of *networks* where we are unable to trace any regular pattern. Since decision space is an abstraction of political space, organizational patterns of decision sequences are but simplified representations of political patterns of organization.

The three organizational patterns of decision sequences correspond to the familiar *three organizational models of society:* the vertical sequences to the mechanistic, the branching pattern to the cybernetic, and the random pattern to the laissez faire. Since every actual society will contain elements of all three organizational principles, we shall find in every specific decision sequence a mixture of all three decision patterns. However, one of these patterns, that corresponding to the prevailing basic political philosophy, will be the controlling one.

In a society subscribing to the *Marxist-mechanistic model,* decision making will be almost completely centralized, and the fully spelled-out top-level decisions will be conducted to lower organizational levels for implementation. Feedbacks on performance will again be channeled to the top-level decision-making center. In such an overcentralized system, "noises" accruing in the protracted dissemination and feedback processes will cause great distortions. The general atmosphere will be highly authoritative and will discourage individuals at each level from reviewing and evaluating their present and potential roles within the overall process. In other words, the mechanistic decision philosophy will tend to confine each level to its own object language and discourage the development of metalanguage attitudes. In such a society, the study of the decision process will focus on the decision behavior of the top level; sources of noise at intermediate and lower levels and the kind of bias introduced by them will constitute a complementary subject of study.

Behavior structure in a society that advocates the *laissez faire* philosophy could, from an ex post point of view, be studied only statistically; an ex ante type of study would attempt to analyze the sociopsychological mechanisms that are involved in such diffuse decision processes.

Finally, a society that would be governed according to a *cybernetic model* would tend to create, at each level of the hierarchy, such decision streams as are necessary to release at the next lower level complementary decision streams elaborating on the higher level theme, the range of elaboration being confined by constraints laid down by the higher level. These constraints need not be rigid, but ought to be constantly modified by mutual gradual adaptation between the relevant levels. In such a society, the study of the decision process would be a more complex task extending through all the levels of the decision-making hierarchy.

In real societies, we shall never find a "pure" case: the dominant political doctrine, with its correlated model, will be diluted by admixtures from opposing doctrines and models. Programs undertaken with a view to improving decision processes ought to allow for this fact. However, before attempting to describe such programs, we ought to view the politico-administrative hierarchies within which decision processes originate, their performance, the mechanisms causing variations of performance, and the criterion for evaluating and ranking performance.

PERFORMANCE CRITERION: THE IDEAL HIERARCHY

We shall begin our study of politico-administrative hierarchies by first defining the performance criterion. There exists, of course, no single generally valid performance criterion: each one of the three basic models of the socioeconomic process (mechanistic, cybernetic, and laissez faire) will lead to a different criterion; as always, criteria will here too depend on the kind of bias which we, consciously or unconsciously, introduce into our analysis. Since our central thesis is that a cybernetic model best fits the development context, we shall confine ourselves here to performance criteria that evolve from adoption of this model.

In such a socioeconomic model, performance would be judged adequate if the nth level of the hierarchy generates decision streams and causes information feedbacks that comply with the following conditions:

1. nth level decision streams will trigger off requisite complementary decision streams at the next lower $(n+1)$th level, the latter being conceived in the object language of the $(n+1)$th level.
2. nth level decision streams, conceived at the metalanguage level in relation to the $(n+1)$th level, will constitute fully defined terms of reference and dynamic boundaries and constraints for the latter level.

3. Information streams will be initiated from the $(n + 1)$th level to serve as corrective feedbacks for the nth level.

Such performance criteria imply that every level analyzes and makes decisions at a level of abstraction that is above the next lower level, or, in other words, that the object language at the nth level constitutes a true metalanguage in relation to the $(n + 1)$th level. This would again presuppose the existence of two basic capacities at the nth level of the hierarchy:

1. Capacity to synthesize and integrate the discrete units of the next lower level into one whole

2. A "wide-angle" mind with requisite "depth of field" (to continue the photographic metaphor) to survey the branching out of decisions at the $(n + 1)$th level

To perform according to this criterion, a society would have to fill all roles of the politico-administrative hierarchy with occupants who comply with these requirements; to achieve this, society would have to use these requirements to set up promotional criteria, which would, in turn, presuppose the existence of a "perfect" hierarchy, in which similar criteria had been used in the past to promote decision makers. We are faced once more by the hen-egg paradox: adequate promotion procedures presuppose an "adequate" socioeconomic hierarchy which has been applying adequate promotional procedures in the past.

In real-life societies, as we have pointed out repeatedly, the politico-administrative hierarchy does not select for the capacities that would be needed for our ideal process. On the other hand, some upcoming professional hierarchies in mature pluralistic societies do apply, albeit in diluted form, promotional procedures that emphasize those capacities which we have found necessary for adequate decision processes. Reference is here made to the hierarchies of science, professional management, etc. However, these specialized hierarchies do not yet have a decisive vote in any society, and their influence in developing societies is negligible. Therefore, when studying decision space in the context of development, we shall still have to focus on the politico-administrative hierarchy rather than on the specialized ones.

REAL-LIFE POLITICO-ADMINISTRATIVE HIERARCHIES

The underlying assumption of the democratic process is the existence of a self-regulative mechanism whereby the individual politician (or group of politicians controlling a party machine), motivated by personal and career considerations, and through the operations of these very same considerations, acts for the benefit of the public at large; if he acted otherwise, the public would cut short his political career by rejecting him at the next election. The similarity of this basic assumption with that of the corollary principle of classic economics is obvious. The existence and operation of this self-regulating political mechanism can be demonstrated in almost every type of democratic regime; however, its effectiveness will often be extremely imperfect. The reasons for the ineffectiveness of the process are numerous; we shall enumerate the five most conspicuous ones:

1. The public has a very limited understanding of what is beneficial for itself. In a modern economy, the benefits to the individual or to a specific group will greatly depend on those accruing to the commonwealth, which can be expressed only in the metalanguage of the commonwealth; no public speaks this type of metalanguage—at best they dispose of an imperfect object language of a limited particular vested interest group.

2. The metalanguage defining the benefits to the commonwealth presupposes a longer time span of analysis than is applied by the public.

3. To exercise a true regulative feedback effect upon the political machine, analysis of the situation and opinion formation by the public would have to be independent of the political machine, which as a rule is not the case. The mass media are at the disposal of the political machine and are unscrupulously used for the manipulation of public opinion. Thus, the "public at large," even if it had a valid opinion of its own, would not have at its disposal the media and channels to disseminate it and thus make it effective.

4. To act consistently, the public would have to have a good memory, which it conspicuously lacks.

5. The politician, realizing his dependence on some kind of response from at least part of the public, will select a strong group of vested interests (making up in power what they lack in numbers) to represent his "public" and will buy their political support by pandering to their interests.

Although detail and nuance will vary from culture to culture, the actual political process will be based on such "unholy alliances" between the organized element of the public, i.e., vested interest groups and party politicians. Such alliances are based upon pledges of mutual support to achieve the mutually acceptable narrow aims which, although devised in the object language of the respective interest groups, are broadcast in the permissive political jargon in which flabby clichés pose as metalanguage objectives of society.

THE PLURALISTIC NATURE OF THE POLITICO-ADMINISTRATIVE SYSTEM

The national political process, though the most powerful, is certainly not the only one that influences resources development. There exists a number of independent or semidependent systems which all generate their own more or less independent decision streams; the decision space that we have to consider is therefore a pluralistic one. In addition to the national political process, we might have to consider church, state, regional, municipal, and local authorities, the unions, the army, private national capital, and international capital.

Each of these secondary systems will have its own criteria for promotion, its own organizational patterns, its own regulative feedback mechanisms. Each of these secondary systems will, furthermore, exercise a certain force or power within the overall "field" of the national socioeconomic system, and it will be this relative power rather than its capacity to analyze and plan which will determine the actual role played by each secondary system. Since no common integrating factor exists to control and coordinate their activities, these independent and semidependent systems will sometimes be found to be operating at cross purposes.

The variety of promotional criteria in the various secondary systems of a pluralistic society will tend to temper power structure and decision patterns of the national political system which is often controlled by limited groups representing vested interests. The degree of influence of secondary systems will vary from society to society and will change with time. Certain structural features common to most societies can be defined as follows:

1. As the socioeconomic system matures, the extent and power of the pluralistic aspects increase.
2. The more democratic the political feedback process is, the more pluralistic the system; the more authoritarian, the less pluralistic.

Coordinating decision streams generated by a pluralistic system of hierarchies will be much more complex than the integration decision streams originating from a simple hierarchy.

Integration at the nth level will in this context be equivalent to defining the metalanguage resolution of discrepancies and encroachments at the next lower, the $(n + 1)$th, level. Cybernetically speaking, the system is sound to the extent that such metalanguage resolution is achieved; to the extent that efforts at resolution break down, or can be effected only very imperfectly, hypo- and hyperfunctions of partial aspects will become rampant. Once such dysfunctions are institutionalized, the body politic will become diseased.

The politico-administrative system, as we find in real-life investigations, appears to be prone to such disease formation for what might be called structural reasons: the type of people who have risen to the top levels of the political machine by prevailing political promotional criteria often do not possess the integrating capacity required at their respective levels to resolve clashes between decision streams originating at lower levels. This structural deficiency will be especially pronounced in underdeveloped socioeconomic systems.

The fundamental task of the development planner is to operate within a specific political space—not to reshape it basically (this might be a political aim). His most ambitious aim could be to exert upon political space a gradual modifying and improving influence through feedback from development operations. The analysis of decision space on the following pages is an attempt to devise ways, means, procedures, and strategies to supplement and influence an existing decision generation with a view to achieving a more effective development process.

MANIPULATING A PLURALISTIC DECISION SPACE

Definition of decision space Decision space has to be conceived as composed of a number of partly interconnected decision hierarchies (DH_n), each consisting of more or less interrelated and interconnected individual or institutional decision makers (X_n) which constitute the "nodes" of the decision systems. Decision space thus represents a network of networks with a limited amount of interconnection between them.

Due to the operation of political, social, and economic processes, the decision systems as well as their interconnections change with time; this necessitates the introduction of the time dimension (t). In the context of resources development, decision streams generated by decision makers (X_n) at the nodes of decision systems will, as a rule, refer to the upgrading of a preexisting resources geometry (R) according to the requirements of a target geometry (T).

At the time (t), decision maker (X_n), constituting a node of the decision hierarchy (DH_n), will generate decision streams that are the result of his analysis conducted in his object language, which is appropriate to his level and place within the hierarchy. These decision streams will tend to achieve the upgrading of that part of the preexisting resources geometry (R) that is within his angle of view to the requirements of the corresponding part of the target geometry (T)—allowing for the constraints imposed upon decision maker (X_n) by the decision hierarchy (DH_n) of which he forms a part and the constraints imposed, through decision hierarchy (DH_n), by other decision hierarchies of the socioeconomic system.

Other decision makers acting within their respective decision hierarchies, will in turn generate their respective individual decision streams, each couched in the object language appropriate to the level and position of their nodes. Such individual decision makers will influence each other directly (i.e., not through the intermediary of the upper levels of the decision hierarchy of which they are part) to the extent that their decision streams overlap; when faced by such overlaps, the decision maker will tend to resist those parts of encroaching decision streams which cannot be reconciled with his own.

The constraints imposed on individual decision nodes (X_n) by his decision hierarchy (DH_n) ought to represent the resolution of the discrepancies between the individual decision streams originating from decision nodes (X_n), as understood by the higher levels of the decision hierarchy (DH), according to the requirements of the system as a whole; in actual fact, these higher level decision streams will rarely be sufficiently comprehensive, nor will they be invested with the necessary authority, to act as true integrating streams.

Planning interventions in the decision space The purpose of planned intervention in a decision space is to modify the decision environment at all levels of decision making so as to generate decision streams that will comply with the requirements of a solution couched in the metalanguage of the system as a whole, or at least of those parts of the system significantly related to development objectives. To achieve this purpose, the planner of such interventions would have to perform the following operations:

1. Establish the *metalanguage* for the relevant decision hierarchies.
2. Establish, in this metalanguage of the system, an *optimum overall solution* for upgrading existing resources geometry according to the requirements

of target geometry—still neglecting the constraints imposed by the existing decision process.

3. Devise, for all levels of the decision hierarchies involved, interventions, which we propose to call "reconciliation streams" (R C), which ought to have the power to modify and constrain the decision environment at all nodes (X_n) of a specific decision hierarchy (DH_n) in a way that will lead every decision maker (X_n) to generate decision streams that, while couched in his own specific object language, will nevertheless approximate decision streams that the decision maker would have generated were he guided by the "ideal" solution (see 2 above).

4. Establish an *organizational structure* to continuously generate and disseminate such reconciliation streams and invest it with the necessary authority to enforce compliance.

5. To the extent that the metalanguage solution (see 2) necessitates reconciliation streams of great volume and scope, *review the organizational structure* of decision space and propose restructuring that would bring the decision process closer to the requirements of the ideal metalanguage solution. Here the establishment of new authorities, legislation, etc., might be indicated.

When planning reconciliation streams, the planner has to allow not only for the existing decision space and its modification requirements, but also for anticipated spontaneous changes and anticipated requirements for modification that *future* programs might impose. He therefore will have to add to the interventions related to short-term programs a judicious admixture of medium- and long-term interventions which, by their very nature, require longer application periods.

The modification of decision space The essence of decision-space modification as here envisaged is the superimposition upon an existing decision structure of a new control center or the upgrading of existing ones. The new center can provide the necessary metalanguage analysis of the resources development problems of the overall system; it can derive from such analysis the definition of the reconciliation streams that have to flow from the center toward all relevant decision nodes of the system. Such reconciliation streams are necessary in order to modify object language decision streams that are generated by the original decision environments at these nodes in accordance with the requirements of the metalanguage solution devised by the center.

The proposed procedure does not attempt to impose upon decision nodes the use of metalanguage which is not germane to decision makers at such nodes; it operates within the existing decision structure and assumes the continued employment at all nodes of the relevant object languages. Its effect is achieved by superimposing upon preexisting decision processes, conducted in the relevant object language, incentives, constraints, and controls (constituted by the reconciliation streams) capable of modifying the decision environments in all relevant nodes so that the resulting decision streams—though still conducted in the object languages of the nodes—will be in line with the requirements of the metalanguage solution. Performance feedback returning to the control center will indicate the necessity and scope of second-degree reconciliation streams to correct for unsatisfactory performance of the first-degree streams.

Dependent on the "power field" of each decision node, reconciliation streams issuing from the control center toward such nodes will vary in their nature (anywhere on the "carrot-stick" scale) and strength. Powerful decision nodes might have to be manipulated by incentive-type reconciliation streams of generous dimensions, while weaker nodes might be brought in line by direct control from the control center. Generally, the total volume of reconciliation streams that will have to be applied to a specific system will depend, on the one hand, on the extent of discrepancy between object-language decisions of the individual decision makers and their metalanguage counterparts and, on the other hand, on the power relationship between individual decision nodes and their control center. If such discrepancies are wide and the power relation between nodes and center favors the former, the volume of reconciliation streams that would have to be applied to correct the situation would become too cumbersome and the necessity of a basic structural change would then arise. Such a change could be achieved by modifying the power balance between nodes and the center through the creation of, say, a new basin-wide development authority invested with sufficient powers to impose the metalanguage solution through direct ruling and through reconciliation streams.

The planner of reconciliation streams ought further to keep in mind the *dynamic nature of the decision field* in which he operates: every reconciliation stream successfully applied and every specific group of decision streams issuing from decision nodes not only will generate change within the specific area of the field related to such streams, but will also affect the overall resources geometry and the general outlook of the individual decision maker. Therefore, when planning reconciliation streams, we need not attempt from the outset to modify fundamentally the decision attitudes of individual decision makers according to the long-term requirements of the program as a whole, but we can confine ourselves to generate such reconciliation streams as are required for imminent decisions. Such short-term reconciliation streams ought to be supplemented by some "preinvestment" in reconciliation streams related to such aspects of future decisions that have a long response lag. As the next decision sequence comes into view, the decision space, as modified by prior decisions and reconciliation streams, would have to be reconsidered and the type of new reconciliation streams, necessitated by the new decision sequence in the modified decision space, determined.

The above comments on modification of the decision space imply the awareness, somewhere near the top of the relevant decision hierarchy, of the necessity of a control function, in other words, of a metalanguage approach, and the readiness and authority to impose such an approach on the lower-level decision makers. In developing countries, more often than not, decision hierarchies will be found lacking in both awareness and authority. Under such conditions, one of two approaches might be adopted:

1. An intelligent decision maker near the top of the hierarchy, or an international funding agency interested in the program, might commission an outside group to undertake a metalanguage analysis.

2. One might resign oneself to regulation by crisis, i.e., let matters drift until the program approaches the point where it becomes obvious to the top of the hierarchy that integration is necessary.

If the first approach is adopted, the metalanguage planning group will, after defining the metalanguage solution, compare the existing decision space with that which is indicated by the metalanguage solution and then define the type of control center needed and the reconciliation streams to be generated by it, the aim being to reconcile actual structure of decision space with the structural requirements of the metalanguage solution.

The ideal decision space, the frame of reference for such a metalanguage analysis, is cybernetically structured. In such a space, all subsystems (and sub-subsystems), while acting according to their own lower level criteria and object-language solutions, will still be subjected to such an amount of guidance and control from higher levels of the hierarchy as will ensure continuous modification, coordination, and integration of the individual object-language decision streams issuing from lower level nodes into one purposeful overall effort defined by the objectives of the whole system, i.e., its metalanguage solution.

For reasons discussed in earlier chapters, such a self-regulative system will almost never be operative or feasible in actual political space. What our approach of manipulating actual decision space can, nevertheless, attempt to achieve is to substitute for the self-regulative pattern of the ideal decision space the "artifically" imposed modifications represented by the reconciliation streams, with a view to bringing actual decision space closer to the requirements of the ideal case.

THE NATURE OF RECONCILIATION STREAMS

The nature of reconciliation streams will vary according to the type of problem and the power balance encountered between individual decision makers (nodes) and the decision hierarchy control center. The type and volume of reconciliation streams will range all the way from basic reorganization, undertaken with a view to tightening top-level control, to the creation of incentives and disincentives introduced in order to induce individual decision makers to select decision streams that are reconciliable with metalanguage solutions.

In the following, an attempt is made to describe a few typical points on the continuous scale of potential reconciliation streams.

Incentives In decision spaces in which the integrative power of the center of the decision hierarchy is weak as compared with the power of individual decision makers, the only way to make the latter act according to the requirements of a metalanguage program is to modify the decision space at its individual nodes through the creation of appropriate incentives, thus making it worthwhile for each specific node to generate decision streams that are reconcilable with the metalanguage solution. Since the discrepancies between the "pure" object-language solutions at the individual nodes and the metalanguage approach will vary from node to node, the type and scope of incentive to be comprised in the reconciliation streams will vary accordingly. The incentive approach does not attempt to impose a solution, but relies on existing decision nodes operating in a modified decision environment.

Constraints The use of constraints as reconciliation streams will ensure that the potential range of object language decision streams generated by individual nodes will be limited to such streams as are reconcilable with the metalanguage point of view; within these constraints, the freedom of action of the individual decision maker is preserved. Constraints can consist of basic ground rules which have to be followed, criteria which have to be complied with, and, finally, specific direct restrictions to the freedom of selecting solutions.

Other modifications The decision space at individual nodes can also be modified in additional ways: object-language decisions might be made less attractive through the introduction of appropriate fiscal measures: participation of public financing in the funding of development might be made conditional upon the adoption of the metalanguage approach; subsidiary regional control centers might be created to strengthen metalanguage influence on object-language thinking at individual nodes.

Creating mandatory metalanguage solutions In this approach, decision making at nodes is limited to the object-language elaboration of the local features of an overall metalanguage solution that is developed in the decision hierarchy's control center. This approach results in imposing upon decision nodes specific custom-made constraints that evolve from the metalanguage solution.

Organizational integration Organizational integration constitutes a continuation and institutionalization of the preceding approach. Here, theoretically, we approach the ideal cybernetic organization of the decision process.

In the light of the numerous nuances of permissiveness and institutionalization open to us for modification of the decision space, the question arises as to which approach to select in each specific case. Our selection ought to be guided by an awareness that the objective of the process of suboptimization analyzed in the present chapter is to improve decision space in order to achieve better decision streams.

If this objective can be materialized only by the adoption of a permissive approach, such an approach ought to be adopted even at the cost of failing to comply with some of our metalanguage ambitions; here, as elsewere, the better is the enemy of the good.

On the other hand, where a more institutionalized approach will appear both desirable and feasible, institutionalization ought to be adopted. In such cases we ought to avoid the mistake of fashioning our fully institutionalized organization of decision space according to mechanistic patterns, limiting decision making to the top echelons of the decision hierarchy. A cybernetic type of organizational principle will be preferable in this case.

The emergence of *pluralistic structure in developed economies* introduces new complexities into the tactics of manipulation of decision space. The influence exercised by the scientific and public opinion communities and by various civic organizations on the selection of solutions for major development problems exemplifies the interference of pluralistic structure in a straightforward politico-administrative process. Almost by definition, pluralistic structure is averse and allergic to central control, which would have to be political control.

From the point of view of the decision-making process, pluralistic structure has its positive as well as its negative aspects. The obvious positive aspect is the introduction into problem solving of greater variety and often of a higher level of abstraction. The major negative aspect lies in the disturbance of the decision-making process by the introduction of independent structures that do not lend themselves to integration.

Effective operation in a pluralistic socioeconomic system requires stressing the positive aspect to improve the quality of the decision process and minimizing the negative aspects which tend to paralyze the process. This might be effected by confining the influence of indirectly involved hierarchies upon the evaluative phase related to the selection of the most desirable among the alternative feasible metalanguage solutions, and by strictly excluding these hierarchies from the operative phases of the decision process and all object-language subprocesses, which would continue to be handled by the directly involved politico-administrative decision hierarchy.

AN EXAMPLE OF PLANNING THE MANIPULATION OF DECISION SPACE

The essence of manipulative planning of decision space can best be demonstrated in a relatively simple phase space, such as that of *community water supplies*. The example selected will deal with the introduction of group water-supply schemes in areas in which individual projects have prevailed for many years. This group of problems is now coming into the limelight in most developed countries; the proposed application of manipulative tactics of decision space could greatly ease the difficulties and resistances being encountered.

We shall assume that our example refers to a relatively densely populated mainly industrial area containing numerous small and large communities, each served by an independent waterworks. The individual waterworks will be assumed to have been developed according to policies laid down by local political authorities, and in most cases they will also be owned and operated by such authorities. They thus represent pure object-language solutions of such local authorities. Such a locally conceived and implemented development could continue until serious discrepancies between resources and demand geometries start to develop in some of the communities. However, the accelerated development of the economy of the region will sooner or later call for an acceleration of water-supply services. Some communities might, even at that stage, dispose of sufficient resources to continue to base the expanded supply upon independent community works; others might encounter serious difficulties and arrive at the conclusion that their problems can be solved only by the establishment of a group water-supply program. Their efforts to propagate a group solution will be met by resistance from the former type of communities and by indifference from communities which, although disposing at present of sufficient resources, anticipate scarcities in the far future.

It will furthermore be assumed here that the metalanguage analysis of water-supply development of the region has established the economic advantage of the group water-supply solution for the regional economy as a whole. However, from the point of view of individual communities, the economic advantage of a group water-supply scheme will vary from community to community. For communities having control over adequate resources, the economic advantage of the group solution might be marginal to negative, while for communities lacking adequate resources, a regional scheme might in fact constitute the only feasible solution. We shall further assume that the government is not invested with the necessary legal powers to enforce the formation of a group solution and that, therefore, such a solution would be conditional upon an agreement being reached between the principal communities of the region.

To increase the chances of such an agreement, the decision space of the individual communities, envisaged as continuing to analyze and decide in their own object language (i.e., exclusively from the point of view of each individual community economy), will have to be modified. This modification, taking into account that resistance against group solutions will not be exclusively economical, while it would somewhat decrease the economic attractiveness of the group solution for its protagonists, would increase its attractiveness for the opposing group of communities until it would become (in their own object-language terms) attractive to them. Barring legislative solutions imposed from above, such modification of the decision space could take the following two basic forms:

1. Creating incentives to encourage those opposing or indifferent to the group solution to adopt it, e.g., easing their share of the financial burden of owning and operating a group facility and debiting the communities that are dependent on the group solution with the difference, or receiving state or government financial aid (if available) for this purpose

2. Creating disincentives to discourage the continued adoption of independent community schemes, e.g., using existing legislation to enforce allocation of existing water resources among all communities of the region, granting a less favorable fiscal status to independent projects, or making participation of attractive public funding in the financing of projects dependent on compliance with metalanguage type of criteria

The modification of decision space to be achieved by such incentives and disincentives ought to be carried to a point where each community, through object-language analysis of the modified decision space, would select the group solution. The group solution that will result from such a pluralistic decision process will not represent the optimum solution from the point of view of the regional economy, since the artificial modification of decision space at specific nodes will tend to distort decision making there. But it will be the best group solution that can be achieved, barring mandatory legislative decisions.

Finally, we ought to bear in mind that once a group solution is adopted and a regional water authority created, the authority will represent a new element in the power balance of the region, one which will exert its growing influence in the direction of institutionalization of group solutions. Thus when the subsequent development phase comes up for discussion, decision space will be fundamentally different from what it was before the establishment of the authority and there can be much greater reliance upon mandatory legislative tools. Therefore in the initial phases of negotiating group solutions, the main emphasis should be upon establishing the authority, rather than upon fully spelling out future commitments of communities, etc.

CONCLUSIONS

Every resources development operation can be represented by the decision streams that have to be generated in various parts and levels of the socioeconomic system in order to implement the operation. Thus, decision streams constitute an all-important link in the chain of events that starts with selecting objectives and general planning and ends with commissioning of projects; the operation will be as good as the decision stream it elicits. The quality of the decision streams will in turn depend mainly on the quality of the relevant decision hierarchy or hierarchies.

Unfortunately, decision hierarchies, like most other institutional frameworks, comply with the requirements of an irrelevant past rather than with those of a dynamic present and an anticipated future. Furthermore, institutional adaptation to new conditions and requirements will be extremely slow and will encounter great inertial resistances. Therefore, institutional structure, and the quality of the decision streams related to it, will rarely suit the requirements of major development projects, especially in the less developed countries where discrepancies between present and future, and between present and past, are greatest.

In order to make the priming of the development process less dependent on the extremely sluggish transformation of institutional frameworks, and at the same time inject into the development process some comprehensive thinking representative of a more advanced stage of institutional organization, existing (or moderately modified) decision processes should be utilized and their course and direction should be influenced by modifying the decision environment of each individual decision maker so as to ensure a voluntary shift toward more comprehensive thinking. The individual decision maker, while continuing to apply his old decision ideologies and criteria, ought to be induced by the incentives and disincentives injected into his decision environment by the higher level of the decision hierarchy to make decisions reasonably like those which would have been arrived at if the whole decision hierarchy were organized according to the requirements of the overall development program. These incentives and disincentives constitute the reconciliation streams which ought to be injected into the existing decision process to correct for its inappropriate structure and to achieve reasonably adequate decision streams without having from the outset to basically modify the decision hierarchy.

14

THE PLANNING SPACE OF COMMUNITY WATER SUPPLIES

Ceux qui s'appliquent trop aux petites choses deviennent ordinairement incapable des grandes.[1]

LA ROCHEFOUCAULD (*Maximes*)

LOCAL VS. REGIONAL WATER-SUPPLY SYSTEMS

The administrative boundaries of most towns are delineated long before their water-supply problems become pressing enough to warrant major engineering works, and, consequently, the planning space of a community water-supply system, in most cases, is determined by the administrative boundaries of the municipal area.

Existing institutional municipal structure thus favors the case-by-case approach. The planning model of a water-supply system, intended to serve a single city, comprises, on the one hand, the demand stream of the community and, on the other hand, the economically closest available water resources that are, or can be brought, under the control of the community. In this context, the planner aims at minimizing the costs involved in upgrading resources available to the community in a way that will meet the requirements of the community. The time horizon in this approach is selected in a rather arbitrary manner.

Under this approach, in which the planning space is a priori confined to a single community, no attempt is made to investigate water demand and resources beyond the community boundaries, unless a specific request is made by one of the outlying communities. The single-community solution is an acceptable approach as long as there are ample resources to meet demand, as long as no major discrepancy develops between resources and demand geometries, and as long as the pollution of resources does not reach prohibitive limits.

However, as major quantitative or qualitative "tensions" between demand and resources geometries begin to develop, the case-by-case approach becomes less and less adequate and, in extreme cases, breaks down completely. Moreover, the authorities are generally slow to realize that a breakdown of the case-by-case approach is imminent, and, consequently, existing institutions

[1] Those who stick too much to small things normally become incapable of great things.

generally begin to consider the necessity of transcending institutional boundaries only when the situation has already become critical.

It is in response to such an increase in tensions that true regional solutions have been adopted in a number of countries over the last twenty or thirty years. In fact, the regional, or comprehensive, approach (in contrast to the case-by-case approach) is steadily gaining ground and has led, in some cases, to the initiation of a dialogue between neighboring regional authorities, with the aim of exploring the possibilities of further integration of existing regional systems and the adoption of even wider planning spaces. Adoption of this approach may eventually lead to overall national planning.

It is against this background that the following comments on the definition of appropriate boundaries for water-supply and waste-removal systems have been conceived.

BASIC PLANNING APPROACHES

Analysis of the planning process indicates that two basic approaches are prevalent in the planning of community water-supply systems; these are as follows:

The Institutional Approach This approach identifies the boundaries of planning space with those of the institutional space; it considers only those potential resources which are associated with such a space and only those waste streams directly affecting the aforementioned resources. The institutional approach thus results in case-by-case solutions, delimited, in the time dimension, by arbitrary time horizons.

The Field Approach This approach treats demand, resources, and waste streams as variables in a theoretically unlimited multidimensional phase space, within which, for pragmatic reasons, we define, from time to time, appropriate planning spaces.

These two approaches are, of course, theoretically related, the first approach being a pragmatic approximation of the second one for the special case in which demand and resources geometries are so compatible that the adoption of the more general "field approach" would yield no significant gain.

THE PHASE SPACE

The phase space of water-resources planning is defined, in addition to the two dimensions of the plane, by the dimensions of elevation (representing potential energy), time, flows of resources, demand, and waste discharge, as well as by a number of quality dimensions; these quality dimensions may, again, be subdivided into the two somewhat interconnected main groups of chemical and biological quality. A number of institutional dimensions are also to be considered, in addition to the "physical" dimensions; these consist of the institutional structure at the municipal level and at the level of the political decision process which controls the allocation of financial and other resources. From the point of view of the water-resource planner, the values of the demand and waste-discharge variables are, within a certain confidence range, given to estimation, though they lie beyond his control; these variables thus constitute his planning environment. Resources dimensions, on the other hand, though stochastic in nature, are subject to the management control of the planner; institutional dimensions usually have an in-between status.

The values of the uncontrollable variables of phase space change continuously and cumulatively; locations of demand and waste-discharge concentrations, which may originally have been dispersed, will show a tendency to spread and merge; demand will increase as a consequence of population growth and as a result of the rise in per capita consumption. Waste flows will increase in volume and load and create an actual or potential threat to the quality of water resources.

The institutional dimension also changes and expands, though generally at a much slower rate. As a consequence of this lagging behind of the rate of adaptation of institutional structure, "tensions" build up between the two complexes; corrective action to "relieve" these tensions—by making institutional structure more compatible with the requirements of the actual resources-demand geometry—may then become necessary.

To simplify this exposition, the institutional and political dimensions will at *first be omitted* from our phase space. In the resulting space free of institutional "friction," the engineering interventions into resources geometry, aimed at meeting demand, are controlled exclusively by the optimization requirements of upgrading water resources in geometry, flow, and quality characteristics. Since, as a rule, quantitative growth and change in the distribution patterns of demand are controlled by factors lying outside the planner's control, and are not significantly influenced or constrained by the existing resources geometry, the two systems (demand and resources) have a tendency to "grow apart." As a consequence, the cost, at constant prices, of upgrading resources to requirements of demand will show a tendency to increase with time. Similar considerations apply to waste removal.

The question of political feasibility will reappear wherever engineering interventions connected with such upgrading operations transcend existing institutional boundaries. In such cases, institutional dimensions will have to be reintroduced for a second iteration of our analysis.

Allowance must also be made for uncertainties which arise either from the stochastic nature of phenomena related to resources (such as climatic variations) or from the possibility that future trends (e.g., of the demand geometry) are not fully predictable.

In planning upgrading interventions, we must consider the present state of the phase space, as well as its future states, as modified by changes occurring in the uncontrollable variables and by sequences of planned engineering intervention in the controllable ones. The success of every decision taken at any point of time will depend, to a great extent, on the appositeness of our assumption as to what the future decision environment will be like. In a rapidly changing phase space, we should beware of assuming that future decisions will be taken from our present perspective. We should instead attempt to predict, to the utmost of our ability, how the already existing discernible change trends are going to influence the point of view, perspective, and technological outlook of future decision makers and attempt to guess what decisions they are likely to arrive at within the greatly modified phase space. As we move from the present to the future, uncertainty as to the actual unfolding of phase space will increase, as a matter of course, and, hence, our chances of correctly predicting the future decision environment and the decisions of future decision makers will diminish accordingly. Such a dynamically conceived "decision space" generates—as a consequence of the great uncertainty regarding its future unfolding and the implications for present decisions of this uncertainty—a large number of possible alternative solutions for upgrading resources geometry to the requirements of the demand geometry.

It is more difficult to make selections from such a proliferation of variety of alternative outcomes than from a statically conceived decision space. It is, nevertheless, a much more apposite procedure and offers a better chance of minimizing investment risks and needs for extra safety margins than any decision based on a statically oriented decision space.

In other words, the proposed phase space ensures that the decision process can operate within the "requisite variety," whereas the case-by-case approach, owing to its limited static and oversimplified phase space and its neglect of uncertainty, results in an inadequate variety of the decision space.

DETERMINATION OF PLANNING SPACE

The first step of the planner embarking on an analysis of community water-supply problems conceived within a comprehensive dynamic planning phase space will be to define the boundaries of the planning space. Theoretically, our planning space could include the whole of the accessible phase space, but, for practical reasons, a narrower definition is called for. The main reasons for the adoption of this narrower definition are as follows:

The Physical Decay Function The influence of peripheral areas upon the central areas diminishes with the increase of the planning space; eventually this influence loses all significance.

The Economic Decay Function The importance of future interventions decreases in accordance with the time that is expected to elapse before these interventions are made.

Institutional Limitation As the scope of the planning space increases, its boundaries will have to cross existing institutional boundaries; institutional and political resistance against such encroachments will tend to grow at a pace that eventually makes further expansion politically unfeasible.

Uncertainty Uncertainty of parameter estimates increases as a result of the expansion of the time horizon, thus reducing the usefulness of our predictions and projections.

Cost Limitation The cost of integration increases, as a rule, with the increasing size of the planning phase; this cost increase will, of course, be reflected in the evaluation of alternative sequences of interventions for the various boundary definitions. However, to reduce the cost of analysis, it may be worthwhile, as a foregone conclusion, to exclude from the investigation any expansion of the planning space that will involve excessive integration costs.

If engineering interventions could be designed in a way that would result in a continuous smooth time-supply curve hugging the time-demand curve, and if the effects of current interventions on future resource upgrading could be neglected, we would be able to expand our planning space gradually in response to the increases in demand. However, since, in most cases, neither of these assumptions holds, we have to postulate for our practical planning tasks a planning space whose boundaries, on the one hand, are assumed to remain unchanged for a specific period of time, while, on the other hand, they are assumed to be sufficiently extended so as to comprise all the significant effects of immediate decision on future ones. When, with the "maturation" of our planning space, we reach the stage at which increasing demand necessitates consideration of additional resources, it will become necessary to make an appropriate expansion of the planning space.

The intensity of incompatibilities between demand and resource geometries will differ at specific times for different parts of the phase space. In some parts, these incompatibilities will not be of major significance and the engineering interventions required to bridge them not very costly; in others, the trouble spots of our space, incompatibilities will be acute and the engineering intervention required both complex and costly.

In areas where resources and demand geometries are largely compatible, solutions drawn up under the case-by-case approach may not basically differ from those devised under the more comprehensive approach. However, it can be assumed that incompatibilities between geometries will increase with the "maturation" of the phase space, and, hence, as time passes, it will become essential to endorse a generously conceived definition of the planning space; this becomes especially necessary if we wish to influence future decisions. We have, in fact, to be in a position to anticipate future decisions, and it is obvious that any prediction as to the future must be conducted within the expanded planning space that, it is assumed, will prevail in the future.

In engineering terms, the expansion of the planning space requires that we continuously integrate resources and demand complexes into ever-expanding systems. Foreseeing and making appropriate allowance in present decisions for the anticipated increase in incompatibility between resource and demand geometries and for the increasing necessity of integration will lead to a more economic plan than would be obtained by providing for such integration only when the actual need for it becomes acute.

Considerations relevant to waste removal will, *mutatis mutandis,* be analogous to those of water resources and demand.

THE RELATION OF SUPPLY TO DEMAND

So far, we have made the assumption that the water-supply planner has to consider the demand for potable water as an exogenous variable. This is not strictly true, since water demand has considerable price and income elasticities; elasticity values, however, vary from one country to another, as also from one city to another.[2]

For a specific demand area, anticipated income growth is predictable within a relatively narrow range; thus, projected demand will vary, basically, with the price of water. Whatever the mechanism of price fixing—according to either purely microeconomic or national economic policy considerations (as an example of the latter, we may cite the high prices levied for water in scarcity areas as an incentive to reducing water consumption)—the price structure for water, once established, will determine the demand level for metered water.

We have assumed in the above that the cost of water (at constant prices) will not rise abruptly as a consequence of having to resort to a new and costly supply resource. However, in cases where, according to the anticipated development of the geometry of demand and resources, we predict the need to set up in the near future major costly works involving indivisible investment, and which entail higher water costs, we might consider the possibility of delaying these investments aimed at meeting the demand, for example, by an appropriate increase in water rates as a measure for controlling the increase in demand.[3]

SEQUENCES OF INTERVENTION

Having once established the boundaries of the planning space and having determined the functions of demand and resources, we can now proceed to the definition of alternative engineering interventions for "upgrading" resources geometry to the requirements of demand geometry.

The more extensive the planning space, the greater the number of demand and resources concentrations it will contain, and since interventions can be represented by "interconnections" between the "centers of gravity" of these two groups of concentrations, the variety of potential engineering interventions will increase more rapidly than the planning area; however, it is obvious that only some of the theoretically conceivable interconnections will be technically or economically acceptable. Furthermore, since the cost of interconnection, or integration, in an expanding planning space increases at a

[2] Joe E. Bain, Richard E. Caves, and Julius Margolis, in *The Northern California Water Industry* (The Johns Hopkins Press, Baltimore, 1966), quote price elasticities varying between -1.1 to -0.40 and income elasticities varying between $+0.28$ and $+0.58$.

[3] This point has been made by Hirshleifer, de Haven, and Milliman in *Water Supply,* The University of Chicago Press, Chicago, 1960.

much slower rate than the number of possible alternative interconnections, we may assume that the economies offered by the proliferation of variety—implied in the expansion of planning space and the wider choice of alternative solutions—will, in many cases, offset the increase in cost due to integration.

This proliferation of variety is not limited to the number of possible interconnections of demand and resources centers; it should include the possible sequential order of implementation of such interconnections, the capacities of the several terminal and interconnecting installations, possible partial or full switchovers (e.g., change of direction of flow), and intertemporal storage functions to enable postponement of costly indivisible facilities. All these combinations of interventions increase our "response variety" beyond the number of simple interconnections and, thus, improve our chances of arriving at a more efficient solution. The greater the incompatibilities, whether present or anticipated, between resource and demand geometries, the more important this proliferation of variety becomes.

The proliferation of variety created by the expansion of the planning space will, of course, increase the amount of analytical work required; however, once demand functions and basic alternative interventions are defined and basic unit costs established, the subsequent analytical work can be greatly simplified by use of a computer. The program and most of the inputs can then be reused in the future and reviewed at subsequent decision points, after appropriate modifications have been made to allow for the additional information obtained in the interim period.

SOME SPECIFIC ADVANTAGES OF AN EXTENDED PLANNING SPACE

A number of the specific advantages obtained by extending the planning space are reviewed in the following; these include reduction of sensitivity of solutions to uncertainty, economy of scale, reduction of idle sunk cost related to indivisibility and lumpiness of investment, better shock absorption, greater decision liquidity, and better financial image.

Uncertainty and sensitivity of solutions to uncertainty The smaller the planning space, the greater the probability of encountering extreme variations of uncontrollable variables, the greater the uncertainty as to the quantifiability of such variations, and the larger the extra safety margins which have to be allowed for in such extremes. These considerations apply both to variables which, from the water-supply planner's point of view, are uncontrollable and to design parameter estimates which are determined at the designer's discretion.

Extremes in climatic variations, and the extremes in resources availability linked with these climatic variations, can be classified under this first group; the larger the resources area we consider, the greater the chances for compensation for variations within the area, and the less pronounced the extreme variations which must be allowed for. Similar considerations apply to uncertainties relating to the location of major industries or to local irregularities in population growth, since, in the latter case, local growth figures as a consequence of population mobility are difficult to predict, whereas aggregate figures involve much less uncertainty. Hence, integration of individual demand concentrations into a larger system reduces the range of probable demand variations and, therefore, also reduces the margins of safety which must be allowed for to cope with such variations.

Similar advantages stemming from integration are encountered in relation to engineering design parameters: uncertainties in flow estimates (these parameters include average flow, to define maximum dependable supply; the extent of flow variations, to determine regulation requirements; and maximum flow, to decide upon spillway capacities) all decrease with the increase in area and require smaller safety margins. Analogous considerations apply to provisions for outages.

However, the full importance of the expansion of the planning space and its impact upon overall project economics can be realized only when we visualize the aggregation and compounding of extra safety margins implied in the case-by-case approach. This approach implies that every community has to incorporate in the design of its facilities its own individual safety margins to meet every potential uncertainty—at the high values required in relatively small supply and resources areas. Thus, uncertainties of population growth are compounded with uncertainties related to the growth of per capita consumption, with uncertainties due to our inability to predict local industrial development, and with uncertainties related to daily and seasonal fluctuations of demand. Uncertainties related to the resources inventory require additional safety margins; uncertainties as to dependable flow, it will be readily understood, require a larger inventory; uncertainties as to maximum flow call for appropriate margins in dam spillway capacities, and uncertainties as to plant dependability call for the provision of adequate standby capacity. Finally, the economy of scale characteristic of some types of facilities makes it attractive to install large units and thereby take advantage of economy of scale, involving, however, maintenance of idle capacity over a considerable period. Moreover, most of these uncertainties have to be allowed for as occurring simultaneously. In short, their compounded cost will often constitute a substantial portion of the project cost. The cost of these extra safety margins is recurrent in each of the individual community projects.

Integration thus tends to reduce the cost of compounded safety margins in two different ways:

1. By reducing the amplitude of variations as a consequence of the expansion of the planning space.
2. By reducing the necessity of repeating these allowances for every individual community. One large dam, for example, with one safety margin built into the one spillway will suffice in an integrated scheme, whereas two or more dams might be required under the case-by-case approach. Similarly, less standby capacity for outages will be required in an integrated scheme. Numerous other examples could be cited.

Furthermore, the safety margins that have to be provided for in an integated scheme need not constitute a sunk cost with low probability of being utilized in the near future. This is due to the fact that application of the phased construction approach (this approach is given more easily to adoption in an integrated scheme) makes it possible to temporarily redistribute to adjoining demand centers any prebuilt supply capacity provided as a safety margin in one area for anticipated future contingencies.

Finally, the very fact that, in a phased integrated scheme, project units are constructed only to the extent that the rise in aggregate capacity warrants expansion makes it possible to delay for considerable periods the final planning and design decisions relating to facilities proposed for construction in the later phases of the program. This delay enables us to collect additional data and thus to reduce the range of uncertainty and to lower the related cost of safety margins accordingly.

Economies of scale Integration provides opportunities for economies of scale. The economics of interlinking resources and demand concentrations is governed by two counteracting factors, namely, by cost increases due to greater conveyance distances, on the one hand, and by economy of scale, on the other hand, the latter varying with the type of facility. Economy of scale will be greatest in dams, still considerable in conveyance and distribution facilities, and less important but, nevertheless, significant in treatment and energy-conversion facilities. The optimal combined value of these two factors will be decisive in determining planning space boundaries.

Indivisibility and lumpiness of investment The more indivisible the investment in a water-supply facility, the more attractive will integration become. Building indivisible large-capacity installations implies prebuilt capacity which will be taken up only over a long period of time. Repeating such prebuilding decisions for a large number of individual nonintegrated water systems will inordinately increase the aggregate unutilized capital sunk into such prebuilt capacity and the resultant financial burden of community water supplies.

Integration of a number of individual works involving major lumpy investments into one large supply system makes it possible to phase the construction of facilities, in compliance with the development of the overall aggregate demand, through temporary allocation of spare prebuilt capacity to areas of shortage within the system. As the available spare capacity nears full utilization, the facility next in priority is constructed, again offering to the overall system a spare capacity that can satisfy demand growth throughout the system for a certain period. Hence, in an integrated system of this type, there should never by any significant volume of unutilized prebuilt capacity; in other words, its plant use factor will be extremely high, and hence the cost involved in owning spare capacity minimized.

Expressed in cybernetic terms, confining the planning space in a way that results in "proliferation" of spare capacity means that we create a variety of supply without providing a complementary response "variety" in "absorbing" such spare capacity. Such a variety discrepancy constitutes an ineffective solution. On the other hand, expansion of planning space and the resultant increase in the number of alternative potential "supply absorbers" are equivalent to a corresponding proliferation of response variety. The better "variety fit" of an expanded planning space, in most cases, results in more attractive solutions than the case-by-case approach.

We should beware, when comparing these two extreme variants of the planning space (i.e., the case-by-case versus integrated solutions), of the fallacy of comparing unit costs calculated for full plant loads, since such comparisons may be misleading. Waterworks are mostly capital-intensive investments; the fixed part of the unit cost is, therefore, very high for the lower ranges of plant use factors characteristic of the protracted gestation periods of individual nonintegrated systems. Although, as a consequence of adopting a larger planning space, we add the cost of integration to that of individual facilities, integration, through the temporary redistribution of the locally available spare capacities it affords, still reduces the length of the gestation period to such an extent that the saving achieved will often be found to outweigh its cost.

Better shock absorption Every supply system, from time to time, faces unprecedented or unpredictable amplitudes in climatic or demand fluctuations or encounters other contingencies that have not been allowed for in planning. Ability to maintain satisfactory service under such shock conditions depends, to a great extent, on the inherent "requisite variety" of the system to respond to contingencies, i.e., on the number of potential lines of action open to us to meet such contingencies.

Since expansion of the planning space is equivalent to increasing (much more than proportionally) the number of possible lines of action, the probability of locating a satisfactory sequence within this potential range is considerably increased. Thus, a large integrated system has a better chance of being able to absorb shocks and maintain satisfactory service under extreme conditions than a corresponding number of small individual community supply systems.

Greater decision liquidity The desirability of obtaining "decision liquidity" arises out of the uncertainty inherent in predicting the future; since we cannot safely predict the future, we should strive to reduce current decision commitments.

The establishment of individual community schemes, by necessarily compounding indivisibilities and extra safety margins, increases the number of early commitments of funds in sunk investments and, thus, constricts our future freedom of action, i.e., our decision liquidity.

In contrast to this approach, a phased integrated program, conceived within a wide planning space, reduces the volume of aggregate commitments, especially during the early phases of the program which are characterized by the greatest extent of uncertainty; the phased integrated approach, hence, considerably increases our decision liquidity.

Better image related to financing The disadvantages of the case-by-case approach also find expression in the financial image of community supply systems. Uncertainties, extra safety margins, and prebuilt capacity are, as a matter of course, reflected in the revenue and in the overall financial image of individual small-sized schemes. The diseconomy of small-scale operations, the nonavailability (or excessive cost) of adequately trained manpower, the lower quality of institutional infrastructure, as well as other incidental factors, all contribute to the creation of a less attractive image for schemes devised under the case-by-case approach.

On the other hand, programs based on a large planning space generally possess a much more attractive financial image, since their initial sunk investments per service unit are lower and their chances of securing trained personnel and implementing adequate organizational structure are better. The higher financial rating of the larger communities also tends to compensate for the less satisfactory financial standing of smaller communities incorporated in a regional scheme, whereas separate projects for the latter type of communities would have only a slender chance of securing credits.

THE POLITICO-INSTITUTIONAL DIMENSION

The above analysis has been conceived within a planning space from which the politico-institutional dimension has been abstracted. In the following, the impact of this dimension upon the definition of the planning space will be outlined.

Planning the development of a community water-supply system implies an attempt to forecast its future behavior, boundary conditions, and adaptation to environmental requirements. Institutions, on the other hand, look backward; they are fossilized forms of responses to requirements of the past, and, consequently, they have a severely limited growth potential. The higher the growth rate of demand and the longer the institutional history, the greater the discrepancy which develops between dynamically adaptive planning and slowly evolving institutions. As a rule, the stronger institutions, realizing the necessity of accelerated integration into ever larger planning spaces, will not oppose integration outright, as long as they anticipate the "absorption" of the other, weaker institutions. Consequently, the strongest resistance to integration often originates from the weaker institutions, which fear to lose their identity. The chances for rational interinstitutional agreement are slim, unless the situation becomes truly critical.

To facilitate this integration, without waiting for "adaptation by crisis," we must, as explained earlier, abandon the "object languages" of individual institutions and adopt the "metalanguage" of the appropriately expanded planning space (as expounded in Chapters 6 and 13). Translated into concrete terms, this can be done by adopting general legislation which grants the relevant central or national (or state or regional) authority the necessary power to initiate the fusing of local utilities into larger units. Even where such legal powers have been promulgated, the outcome of integrating efforts initiated by central authorities often leads to a disappointing compromise between the requisite extent of integration and the centrifugal tendencies of existing institutions. Although such compromise may be far from an optimum solution, it will, nevertheless, constitute a step in the right direction and as such might, in time, help to catalyze further integration.

Legislative powers required for initiating integration are not easily adopted: a nationwide, long-term study, juxtaposing water-resources inventories and their anticipated deterioration (accelerated by the lack of an integrated pollution-control policy) with demand and anticipated demand growth will be required to demonstrate that major discrepancies between supply and demand geometries will occur, and also to indicate when they are likely to occur. The likelihood of the required legislation being adopted will depend on the realization of the fact that without legislation and its catalyzing effect in expanding the planning space, demand in major supply areas will not be met. Even where the need is recognized, the various groups of vested interests existing within legislative bodies will attempt to whittle down the scope of legislation by insisting on excessive checks and controls.

In short, planning the institutional infrastructure represents an essential part of planning for integration and should be considered as an instrumental objective in its own right.

EXPANSION OF THE PLANNING SPACE IN UNDERDEVELOPED COUNTRIES

In the developed countries, integration of individual community supplies into larger supply systems will increase efficiency of investment, shorten gestation periods, reduce risks and extra safety margins, and improve the quality of service. However, integration in mature economies is rarely a precondition for providing financing for water-supply service, since most community supply systems are able to raise the required funds and implement their plans without having recourse to integrated programs.

In the underdeveloped countries, however, the capital available for the community water-supply sector is strictly limited and is sufficient to provide, within the foreseeable future, only part of the water-supply services considered as vital. Optimization of the use of money, i.e., providing, within the prevailing capital constraint, the maximum possible extent of service, is therefore much more important in these countries; funds sunk into the prebuilt capacity of individual nonintegrated installations with large extra-safety margins and long gestation periods will, without providing any appreciable benefit to the communities for which these funds have been invested, deprive the nonserved communities of a greatly needed supply. It is thus the nonserved communities that will benefit most from a rational definition of the water-supply planning space.

Furthermore, developing countries, much more so than developed countries, are plaged by uncertainty in all planning dimensions. Minimizing the cost involved in planning under conditions of uncertainty, through the expansion of planning space boundaries, is, therefore, of special importance in the developing countries.

Finally, human and institutional resources, under conditions of underdevelopment, are limited in volume and training; there will be few, if any, sufficiently trained professionals with the experience required to manage costly water-supply systems; organization will be poor and the decision process slow. The acute scarcity in technological and managerial talent is thus an additional reason for extending the planning space since it economizes trained human resources.

Underdeveloped countries often have an important advantage over the developed countries when the institutional aspects of integration are considered. Institutional resistance against integration is often less pronounced and less influential, owing to the fact that institutional patterns related to water supplies are relatively new and consequently these have not had sufficient time to entrench and build up support for their perpetuation. Furthermore, the central authorities also wield greater power, with the result that local authorities will not generally be in a position to contest decisions made at the central level, decisions usually made without even so much as consulting the local authorities.

CONCLUSIONS

The preceding attempt at a rational definition of the boundaries of the planning space of community water supplies has brought out the following two basic facts:

1. That the phase space of community water supplies in rapidly expanding economies is too complex for a "static" approach of fixed "prefabricated" decision rules and recipes.
2. That the time is over for an unquestioning "taken for granted" identification of the boundaries of the planning space for community water supplies with administrative or even with geographical (hydrological) boundaries.

Determination of rational boundaries in a specific demand and resources context requires that analysis be conducted in a phase space comprising all relevant dimensions. The final determination of boundaries will often have to be made according to the outcomes of an analysis performed for a number of alternative boundary definitions.

This analysis might in some cases result in the retention of the old administrative boundaries. In most, it will indicate the numerous economic and operational advantages presented by an expanded planning space. Rational definition of boundaries, considered important in any type of economy, will be of paramount importance in the underdeveloped countries.

15

A PRAGMATIC APPROACH TO NATIONAL COMMUNITY WATER-SUPPLY PROGRAMS FOR DEVELOPING COUNTRIES

If a thing is worth doing, it is worth doing badly.
CHESTERTON

The subject of this chapter is national water-supply programs, municipal and rural; the planning context is that of developing countries; the point of view is that of the senior official of the ministry responsible for drawing up national water-supply programs within the overall economic development program.

Funds allocated in developing countries for overall water-supply programs generally fail to cover all legitimate needs of the sector. Hence, one must assume sectorial capital scarcity for the proposed planning period, and probably for the next few planning periods as well.

The problems posed under these conditions can be listed as follows:

1. To define demand (requirements) and supply functions for water

2. To resolve demand-supply relationships and to express them in the form of a project list

3. To rank potential projects or project phases

4. To select the best sequence of projects that can be implemented within the limits of the sectorial capital allocation

Water supply assumes the following forms:

1. Water as an infrastructural element of economic activity, e.g., in industrial manufacturing and maintenance of general services

2. Water as a social amenity for those portions of the population which cannot be charged directly for its use, such as communities served by public standpipes (i.e., service by street outlets)

3. Water as a commodity offered to the public through house connections

It should be remembered that water demand will depend mainly on the price of water, facilitation of its use, and per capita incomes. Two of these factors, namely, price and facilitation of use, can be manipulated by the water-supply authority, and hence the per capita requirement is, in fact, a partially controllable variable.

Here we shall introduce two terms that will be used in the following: adequate service level and the unit of adequate service. "Adequate service level" is the service level that corresponds to, but does not exceed, socioeconomic objectives; with reference to domestic services, "unit of adequate service" refers to a unit of domestic consumers served by metered or unmetered house or street connections at adequate service levels; this unit will be used to express the utility of the domestic supply sector. Political, social, or other preferences may be allowed for by the application of coefficients to the above basic utility units.

The utility of water in its infrastructural function, i.e., mainly water allocated to industry, hardly shares a common denominator with its utility in domestic supplies. In industrial use, volumetric measurement still seems to be the best measure of utility of water, though this could possibly be multiplied by a coefficient to express the relative importance to the economy of the industries to be supplied. Generally, most infrastructural requirements, because of their stimulating effect upon the economy, will rank high.

The ranking and selection procedure here proposed attempts to maximize the number of adequate service units (discounted for time preference) that can be created by a specific capital allocation in community water supplies or, to put it differently, to maximize "cost effectiveness" of sectorial capital allocation. In addition, a method will be outlined for expressing in economic terms the cost to the nation of superimposing indirect and sociopolitical criteria upon direct efficiency criteria.

ALLOCATION OF CAPITAL TO THE WATER-SUPPLY SECTOR

Any similarity that in an ex post facto analysis might be found to exist between the sectorial programmer's original request for funds for a specific planning period and the actual capital allocated is, as a rule, purely coincidental. The overall economic planner and the political decision maker to whom he reports are often faced with requests for investment funds that grossly exceed anticipated public incomes. In his attempts at rationalizing the allocation of the limited resources, the planner will be faced by the following typical difficulties and constraints:

1. Pressure of time, which in most cases appears to be a built-in phenomenon.

2. The difficulty of establishing trade-off functions to express the relative economic, social, and political utility to the nation of such incommensurables as production, infrastructure, education, social welfare, and defense. Developments undertaken for reasons of national charisma are even more difficult to evaluate.

3. Lack of trust in the reasons given by sectorial planners for backing up their projects.
4. Suspicion that some of the most vital projects, those likely to prove the most effective, are not included for lack of political backers.
5. Overriding political pressures and counterpressures.

Attempts to influence allocation to the water-supply sector by producing complex pseudoquantitative calculations of the utility to the nation of water-supply projects will rarely be warranted, since most political decision makers will prefer to apply decision-making patterns adopted in past planning periods. These decision patterns tend to consist of a set of rationalizations taking one of the following forms:

1. The "as-before" argument: the political authority contends that there is no good reason why the share in budgetary allocations of water-supply projects should be greater in the current fiscal period than that in previous budgets.
2. The "prestige" argument: national self-respect calls for elimination of substandard community water-supply conditions within X planning periods of, say, five years (four and five are fashionable figures); adoption of this course involves predetermined five-year capital outlays.
3. The "productivity" argument: since we are poor, production should be given top priority—to the regrettable, but unavoidable, neglect of welfare issues. According to this doctrine, water supply for industrial and similar uses takes precedence over all other uses, while water as a welfare function is considered only to the extent that it is related, more or less directly, to production. Since development for production is, in the main, located in or near major towns, and since the loss of income per working day in the towns is much higher than in the village, the productivity approach implies that major towns be given overriding priority over smaller communities.
4. The "cash-and-carry" argument: water is provided only to the extent that the consumers can pay for it. Under this argument, those who cannot pay for water must wait until they earn enough to be able to do so. This approach again leads to concentrating water-supply project investments in major towns.
5. The "political" argument: this may extend anywhere from the contention that town X lies in Y's constituency or in that of the minister or of the president, etc., to the argument that improving the water supply in the capital city, or in some other particular district, may have a decisive influence on the outcome of the forthcoming election, thus qualifying these towns for preferential treatment.
6. The "let's do it once and for all" approach: if for one of the above or similar reasons it has been decided to carry out a water-supply project in a specific town, then it should be "done once and for all" so as to meet water requirements for the foreseeable future.

This list, though it contains most of the current arguments, does not claim to be exhaustive. Some of these rationalizations are also implicit in the conditions, requirements, and procedures for the granting of loans by some funding agencies.

To develop a rationale for capital allocation to the water-supply sector, we must begin with primary social value judgments. Do we live in order to produce? If so, the production function should be the governing one and the productivity argument would hold. Or do we produce in order to live? In which case we must also consider social needs. The choice between these intentionally contrasted alternatives or any desired intermediate point between them constitutes a value judgment and does not lend itself to economic analysis.

The position taken here is that our choice should be closer to the second approach, the welfare approach, and that the creation of facilities for preserving and improving life and health should have priority over expanding those production complexes which are not essential for supplying the bare necessities of life. Making this choice, however, only begs the question. It can be claimed that even if we adopt a pure welfare approach, initial emphasis on expanding production to the neglect of social welfare may be preferable in the long run, since increasing public income through emphasis on production ultimately makes possible expanded welfare services. In most real-life decision situations, the production-welfare dichotomy will defy quantification and our actual choices will be guided by value judgments and emotional hunches rather than by economics. If we adopt the welfare approach, water-supply projects will, in most cases, rank high, once the more obvious life- and health-preserving measures are implemented.

THE OBJECTIVES OF WATER-SUPPLY PLANNING

To the planner of national water-supply programs, the above considerations with regard to capital allocations will seem remote, since in most cases he will have little if any influence on decision making related to sectorial allocation of capital. As a rule, he will simply be informed of the allocations determined by the political decision process and be requested to draw up a program within the limits of such allocations. The problem of the planner is then to select from the list of alternative suboptimized projects the "best" sequence that can be implemented within the given capital ration.

In order to draw up a list of suboptimized projects for ranking, the planner must select boundaries in time and in physical space for the analysis of the individual subsystems entering his project list.

As for the time horizon of analysis, the customary four- to six-year time span for national economic planning will obviously not be long enough for an economic analysis of the heavy capital investments usually involved in water-supply projects whose useful physical lives last twenty to fifty years or more. Under discounting conditions prevailing in developing countries, a time horizon of twenty to twenty-five years will usually be sufficient for most water-supply projects.

As to the physical boundaries of individual projects, it is difficult to outline general rules. The project may be limited to a single town, or it may extend over a whole basin; under certain conditions it might encompass a number of basins. In some projects the definition of boundaries will be obvious; in others, difficult.

Once the planning space is chosen, we can turn to program objectives and project suboptimization.

PROGRAM OBJECTIVES

In general terms, our overall program objective will be to provide—within the prevailing capital constraints and those assumed for subsequent planning periods—adequate service to a maximum number of people with due regard to time preference (expressed by a discounting procedure). This objective, of course, implies the following assumptions:

1. That the utility (value) of domestic water is not measured by quantity but by the number of people served at predetermined levels. Thus, if a supply of 1 cubic meter per day in a 200 liter per capita per day demand environment provides 5 units of adequate service, the same quantity, supplied through public standpipes at a per capita daily rate of say 20 liters, will have a utility of 50 units of adequate service.

2. That any quantity in excess of adequate service requirements has nil utility as long as it remains surplus.

3. That time preference for utility units can be expressed by a discounting procedure.

4. That water requirements and investments anticipated for subsequent planning periods ought to affect decisions to be made under the current program.

"Adequate service level" here will mean the minimum quantities of water that have to be supplied to the various user categories in order to meet the standards adopted for these categories in accordance with economic considerations and our social-value judgments. Adequate service levels will be achieved by the manipulation of those factors which control the demand levels of the various user categories, for example, water rates. Since our basic assumption is that the capital allocated to the water-supply sector is too small to allow meeting in the near future all water-supply needs of the nation, our aim ought to be to confine supplies made available to those communities which have been selected for the current program to volumes that ought to be as close to the adequate supply level as can be reconciled with economy of scale. In other words, the supply at adequate service levels to the whole nation should, within economic reason, be given priority over the increase of the supply to some communities above that level.

Considerations governing the definition of adequate service levels will differ from user category to user category; for some categories, these considerations will be purely economic; for others, they will be rooted in social-value judgments. A review of the considerations applicable to the various consumer groups is given in the following.

Adequate service levels as related to industrial use, which we assume to be completely metered, may be defined in purely economic terms: a service level that establishes itself after water rates have been fixed which represent actual costs, calculated at the same interest rates used in evaluating other investments. This procedure ensures water demand levels compatible with economic optimization.

Similar considerations apply to metered house connections—domestic, public, and commercial. Domestic demand will be influenced mainly by two variables: price of water and per capita income. In the U.S.A., price elasticity of demand appears to vary between −0.4 and −1.0, and income elasticity between 0.3 and 0.5.[1] No reliable figures are available for developing countries. A prima facie case can be made for establishing domestic rates at the actual cost levels to the economy. However, since pricing is one of the most effective tools for influencing demand levels, we ought not to confine our analysis to short-term economic considerations. There appears to be no valid argument against setting higher water rates if a special need exists to keep consumption low, with a view to postponing high-cost expansion programs.

As regards nonmetered domestic, public, and commercial consumer connections, use rates will depend mainly on housing standards, water-use habits, and type of plumbing; the level that in the course of time establishes itself will be the adequate service level of this group of water users. Since this level is usually high, metering ought to be introduced to the extent that it is economically justifiable.

In community supplies based on public standpipes, conveyance distance to homes, which depends on standpipe spacing and location, is the main controlling influence on demand. Demand levels in areas of new installations can be influenced by varying standpipe spacing, according to economic and/or welfare considerations. By economic considerations we mean here the ability of the inhabitants to pay for water through municipal or other taxation. Welfare considerations postulate a level of consumption compatible, at least, with minimum sanitary requirements.

There exists no valid reason why the distribution of the financial burden of water supply ought to be based *exclusively* on purely economic criteria, while socially oriented criteria are preferred in distributing the burden related to other fields of public service, such as defense and basic education. A greater emphasis on social criteria might well be indicated for community water supplies operating at low per capita levels. Such an emphasis implies that every community, while paying according to its means, will still be served in accordance with minimum health standards.

In estimating adequate service levels, we should also bear in mind that the uncontrollable variables which influence these levels change with time. This applies especially to per capita income: higher incomes bring about an increase in domestic per capita demand. Higher incomes also increase the payment ability (or rather taxability) of the sector drawing water from public standpipes; thus, closer spacing of standpipes to facilitate use may become justified.

[1] Joe F. Bain, Richard E. Caves, and Julius Margolis, *The Northern California Water Industry*, The Johns Hopkins Press, Baltimore, 1966.

SUBOPTIMIZATION OF PROJECTS

Having dealt with desirable planning horizons, planning boundaries, and adequate service levels, we can now approach the question of suboptimization of individual projects. The aim of the suboptimization procedure is to determine the most desirable water-supply solution for a specific project area. Depending on the space-time geometry of water resources and demand, the project area might be a single town or a whole region. The geometric context of water and demand may be clear cut and the decision obvious; where contexts are not clear, it becomes necessary to establish alternative project layouts for tentative alternative planning spaces to be followed by the ranking of these alternatives.

After one or a number of alternative planning spaces have been set up, alternative projects, or effective, self-contained sequences of phases of projects, can be drawn up to meet the requirements of the planning space at adequate service levels; all these project alternatives will comply with the basic requirement that supply at any point of time will be larger than or equal to the respective demand. If the alternative project layouts fulfill this basic condition, if they have the same ultimate capacity and useful life, and if we assume that the utility of any supply capacity that exceeds demand is nil, then all project alternatives will have the same utility and their ranking could be based on their discounted cost streams. The project, or project sequence, to be selected would be the one with the lowest discounted cost stream.

It is, of course, impossible even to attempt to outline the typical layouts encountered in drawing up alternative water-supply projects or project sequences; a few general comments may nevertheless be useful. A number of groups of basic elements can be singled out in every project: headworks consisting of interception and storage facilities, conduits to adapt supply geometry to demand requirements, energy converters for adding or withdrawing energy from the system, holdover facilities to regulate flow by storing surpluses against periods of deficiency, treatment works for upgrading water quality to supply specifications, terminal works for redistribution and regulation of flow and energy levels according to local demand requirements. Each installation can, in turn, be constructed for long-term needs or broken down into phases, each phase meeting the needs of a shorter period. The various self-contained combinations of partial and full-capacity installations based on a specific source would, in a general case, have to be compared with similar layouts for alternative sources. It is sometimes necessary to combine phases of several projects, a phase of one project being followed by a phase of another.

Our basic problem of choice stems from the discrete nature of our engineering intervention as opposed to the continuous development of demand. We are thus forced to respond to the smooth and continuous rise in demand by a stepped supply-response curve. Each supply step will, during its gestation period, have a plant-use factor below one; the existence of unused capacity, constituting idle sunk capital, will increase water costs above those calculated for the fully exploited works (plant-use factor = 1.0). On the other hand, the larger the step, the greater the economy of scale; economy of scale will vary, in turn, with the type of installation and the absolute sizes involved.

In a waterworks, the optimum capacity of the individual installation will, as a rule, not be equal for all project installations: the reservoir, with a typically great economy of scale, might be constructed to satisfy, say, an anticipated twenty- to thirty-year demand growth; the conduit and pumping station, with an intermediate economy of scale for, say, a ten-year demand growth; the treatment plants and distribution storage, with still lower economy of scale, say, for only a five- to seven-year period.

Planning considerations in real-life cases are often more complex, since we are frequently faced with a multiple-source situation where each source may again be developed in a more or less phased manner. In principle, basic planning considerations will be similar to those outlined above. However, a large number of combinations and permutations will have to be compared and ranked; the order within the sequence of various waterworks phases will also have an influence on outcomes. We may thus emerge with a considerable number of sequences of project phases, all complying with the basic requirement of meeting the demand curve over a planning period.

Cost and income curves will, of course, be extended to cover the physical (or accounting) life of installations. The sequence chosen will again be that which results in a minimum present worth of the cost stream, allowing for the difference in quantities of water produced by the various alternative sequences after the planning period, and allowing for their respective costs.

RANKING OF PROJECTS WITHIN A NATIONAL PROGRAM

A universal yardstick of benefits must be established in order to rank individual water-supply projects for various communities according to their investment efficiency. Assuming that all alternative projects comply with their respective demand requirements and assuming that they have been suboptimized, we know that their relative economic efficiency would then depend on the cost per unit of benefit achieved, where cost and benefit are calculated by discounting the two streams.

As regards domestic water, the benefit unit suggested for ranking is the service year per man achieved by a project assumed to be operating at adequate service levels, as defined above. In other words, we would consider the utility of 25 liters per capita per day supplied from a standpipe to a slum dweller equal to that of 300 to 500 liters per capita per day supplied to the owner of a luxury home. The discounting rate to be applied would, as a rule, be lower than that prevalent for financial transactions, since financial discount rates comprise other elements beside time preference (e.g., the impact of anticipated inflation, risk).

If, on the other hand, the sectorial planner judges capital scarcity in the water-supply sector to be relatively greater than in other sectors (as a consequence of what he regards as an "unbalanced" sectorial allocation), his sectorial discount rates ought to be raised above prevailing (corrected) levels to allow for the higher time preference of the water-supply sector.

This ranking approach meets serious difficulties where infrastructural functions of water (mainly industrial use functions) play a major role. Unfortunately, the approaches open to us when we come to incorporate industrial water supplies into our ranking procedure are both arbitrary:

1. We may decide that industrial development has overriding priority.
2. We may decide on a trade-off rate between the value of expected additional industrial production to be achieved due to the water-supply project and the utility of the proposed community supply.

In reality this difficulty is not as formidable as it appears in this abstract presentation, since industries are usually concentrated near or in major towns which in any case (for reasons stated below) receive higher priority ranking.

The proposed egalitarian ranking procedure for community water supplies will, as a rule, be unacceptable to the political decision makers. It will therefore be necessary to adapt it to the explicit and implicit prevailing scales of utility. The political level might, for instance, claim that a service year per man in a major town with important industries and many vital services has a higher economic value than the same unit in a remote village. The income per man and per day in the town will average two to four times higher than in the village, and therefore the loss of a working day caused by waterborne diseases would be much heavier in the town. A similar reasoning with application of a much higher coefficient could be applied to areas housing executives or other persons important to the economy.

Higher priority to large communities might also be justified for reasons of public health: health hazards related to unsatisfactory water supply might be greater in large communities than in a corresponding number of smaller ones. Furthermore, high-standard and readily available water-supply services in major towns may have a kind of "forward-linking" effect upon the economy, stimulating the establishment of industries, tourism, etc. To express the higher utility of service years per man in towns, and for specific user categories within a town, a coefficient could be applied expressing the political decision maker's judgment of utilities.

A list of projects ranked according to the costs of service units (whose utility would be modified by the application of appropriate coefficients) would express what the political decision maker can regard as a desirable combination of social and economic thinking. It will often be necessary to modify the choice further in order to accommodate peremptory political demands for inclusion of specific areas. Under such circumstances we should determine the coefficient by which the benefit units of the community backed by the political level must be multiplied if the project is to be retained in the program; should the coefficient be, say, 2.0, the political decision maker will have to consider whether he prefers to forego two service units in another community for each service unit supplied to the community he is backing.

From the point of view of the logistics of data and project engineering, the proposed ranking procedure implies the gathering of basic engineering and economic facts about projects for all communities before deciding upon the communities to be included in the forthcoming program. This may sound like a formidable demand to make upon the programmer in a developing country; in fact, this demand must be relaxed in order to make national ranking feasible under the real-life conditions prevailing in many countries. A most important relaxation which would not involve sacrificing too much accuracy would be to list minor and medium-sized projects in groups according to the type of source available, its distance from the community, and the type of community. The more obvious criteria for subdivision into groups would be: local availability of groundwater, deep or shallow; local availability of river water, perennial or seasonal; conveyance distance for areas without local water resources; and small or medium-sized communities. For every such group, one or two typical sample projects could be planned in sufficient detail to establish the basic engineering economic data that are required for the ranking process. In the ranking process proper, cost and benefit units (obtained from sample projects) are multiplied by the number of communities in each such group, corrected for the number of inhabitants actually served in each community.

With this relaxation, the planning process could be subdivided into the following basic operations:

1. Drawing up estimates of water demand and of the sources available to supply this demand; subdividing small and medium-sized communities into typical water-supply groups; collecting basic data for major demand concentrations (major communities) and typical demand groups
2. Drawing up alternative projects or sequences of project phases for each demand group or major community, and suboptimizing to determine the best typical or individual solutions
3. Modifying the relative utility of projects by applying socioeconomic utility coefficients to service streams generated by alternative projects
4. Comparing individual projects and project phases for specific communities and sample projects for typical water-supply groups for their cost effectiveness, i.e., for the discounted cost per discounted service unit (modified according to 3), over the assumed useful life of projects
5. Ranking projects (and project phases) according to their cost effectiveness and cutting off list at capital allocation.
6. Modifying programs to allow for political utility coefficients
7. Defining modified programs

In our attempt to rank community water supplies in developing countries, we shall, as a consequence of the scarcity of technically trained human resources, often be faced by the lack of project studies. In such cases, development will be hand-to-mouth and ranking on a national basis might have to be postponed. However, a rough evaluative procedure ought still to be adopted which would be based on sample projects and sample estimates of cost effectiveness for typical resources and demand constellations. Cost criteria per service unit levels could then be set up for the planning period; socioeconomic and political utility coefficients could again be applied. Costs per service unit calculated for specific projects could then be compared with cost criteria. The introduction of such an approximative procedure might also induce the water-supply authorities to review the overall availability of plans and set up procedures to increase the number of available project studies (by streamlining planning procedures, increasing personnel, and commissioning work to outside groups) so as gradually to make possible a more rigorous evaluation procedure.

CONCLUSIONS

In the course of establishing a ranking procedure for national water-supply programs, we have introduced so many qualifications and subjective judgments as to make the value of the procedure questionable. However, with a subject as complex as water, this is unavoidable; water fulfills numerous functions of unequal utilities in human society, and the same basic functions have different utilities in different localities. We have therefore attempted to focus value judgments on issues on which the average decision maker can form a scale of order of utilities. While such a procedure cannot obviate subjective value judgments, it does transpose the issues involved into terms allowing the decision maker to arrive at his value decision in full awareness of the consequences involved.

This chapter has omitted such important and relevant issues as uncertainty, legal and institutional problems, and organizational structure. These are treated elsewhere in the book. Our aim here has not been sophistication of evaluation, but rather the following four main objectives:

1. To assist the planner of community water supplies in developing countries to free himself from the mental blocks originating in procedures valid in richer countries, where capital scarcity in the water-supply sector is, for all practical purposes, nonexistent.

2. To establish methodological trends specifically designed to fit economic and political conditions of developing economies in which capital constraints prevail almost universally.

3. To contribute toward a higher cost effectiveness of the allocation of the limited funds available for the development of community water-supply projects—by minimizing idle investments and allocating available funds according to some rational ranking procedure.

4. To outline a strategy for creating a more effective public and political image of national community water-supply programs by stressing the overall long-term aims and the contribution of the current program toward their fulfillment. Comprehensive development programs will have a better chance to attract political attention and the interest of the major funding agencies than the project-by-project applications.

16

ORGANIZATIONAL ASPECTS OF WATER-RESOURCES DEVELOPMENT

The Golden Rule is that there are no Golden Rules.

G. B. SHAW

ORGANIZATIONAL PHILOSOPHY ADOPTED

McLuhan's "the medium is the message" succinctly expresses a widely held concept on the formative influence of communication media on communication content. The same general principle has yet to be applied to organizational forms and contents. Development plans and programs are "messages" of development organizations; their qualities reflect the organizations that produce them. Indeed, if we seek family similarities between programs and organizations, we can trace a counterpart to every organizational flaw and seam in corresponding faults in the conceptual structure of the plan. In fact, one can safely diagnose from a flaw in the program to a flaw in the organization. It would therefore be unrealistic to expect orderly program conceptions and implementation from a chaotic organization. Adaptation of organizational structure to program requirement is part and parcel of program conception.

Recognition of the basic interrelationship and interaction between organizational form and content leads to an important corollary conclusion: since both organizational forms and organizational structural requirements of development programs vary substantially from society to society, no generally valid organizational rules will exist.

This conclusion is the point of departure of the present chapter, in which no attempt will be made to outline specific organizational recipes and solutions. Emphasis will be upon the interrelationship of organizational form and content, i.e., the types of organizational solutions indicated for certain types of development problems. Compatibility between the decision process that underlies development and the decision hierarchy required for its implementation will emerge as the most important requirement of organizational synthesis.

DETERMINING FACTORS OF ORGANIZATION

Organizational requirements will depend on the following four main factors:

1. The content of organizational activity, i.e., functional objectives of the organization
2. The extent of interventions that the organization has to apply to the socioeconomic system in order to reach its functional objectives
3. Geographic and economic scale
4. Ruling political philosophy, social models, and the organizational style they imply

Organizational thinking in developing countries has been deficient on all four points. In selecting the functional objectives of an organization, the mistake is often made of confining development planning and related organizational frameworks to one of the intermediate instrumental objectives (such as irrigation) of a production complex (such as agriculture) without formalizing the necessary coordinative interlocking with the organizations responsible for the complementary aspects of the production process. When determining the extent of interventions by the organization into spontaneous socioeconomic processes, only the most obvious hardware elements are included. Scale is either neglected or overemphasized in analogy to the country which has served as the organizational model. Finally, the social models underlying prevailing political philosophies may often have a distorting influence on organizational style: they may force the organizational planner into either too authoritative and centralistic or too decentralized and uncoordinated organizational frameworks. Rethinking organizational planning principles is therefore a necessity if organizations are to be established that are capable of performing their intended functions.

Organizational planning will be understood here to mean the formalization of structural relationships of the various levels of the decision, communication, and control processes related to a specific functional objective. Our concern here will be with organizational planning related to the development and management of water and its economic uses.

Conceptually speaking, organization ought to be considered as one of the tools of the development process. Its effectiveness ought to be judged by the extent to which it facilitates achievement of the organization's functional objectives. Optimization of organizational structure ought thus to be considered as part of the optimization of the overall development process and not as an independent aspect to be judged by independent criteria.

However, in actual planning of organizational frameworks, we may often be forced to consider the planning of organizational structure as an afterthought, after having optimized the development complex without considering organization. Where we have to resort to such a procedure, it will be only because of the state of the art of organizational planning and not because organization is a separate aspect of planning.

If organizational planning is understood as an integral part of development planning, it ought to adapt to changes in development thinking and in the functional objectives of the organization. Organization planning will thus cease to be a once and for all decision taken in the early days of development, and will become a continuous process of adaptation.

More specifically, when considering organizational planning of water-resources development, we must keep in mind that water fulfills a number of different functions in the socioeconomic system, with subsequent difference in organizational requirements. In irrigated agriculture, water represents a basic means of production; in industrial uses, water usually is a minor production input; in community water supplies, water is part of the basic infrastructural services that are a precondition for life and economic activity. While it may be feasible to isolate, in short-term development and organizational planning, the water-resources system for industrial and community water supplies from the sectors they are intended to serve, without significantly affecting the quality of solutions, such isolation in the case of irrigation uses of water will lead to poor planning and poor organization.

THE "RATIONAL" APPROACH TO ORGANIZATIONAL PLANNING

The approach to organizational planning outlined in the following represents an attempt to base organizational structure on the requirements of development programs. In contrast to the "classical" approach to organization, which relies mainly on generally valid a priori formal organizational principles, a pragmatic approach is proposed which consists in the consecutive application of a set of criteria related to the compatibility of organizational patterns with the requirements of the development program.[1] Compatibility criteria may be subdivided into four main groups:

1. Structural compatibility of the organization with the structural requirements implied in the program.
2. Functional compatibility of the organization with the requirements of the development program, i.e., the existence of capabilities for performing all program operations.
3. Compatibility with institutional status quo ante. We never start from scratch; even when founding a completely new organization we will have to operate it within an existing politico-administrative hierarchy and with models and organizational styles that are acceptable in our culture. Thus, when creating an organizational structure for a new type of program, we must make allowance for the organizational status quo. Should we neglect this, our efforts are liable to bog down even before the new structure becomes operative.
4. Compatibility with organizational theory and practice. A functionally conceived organization will have to be checked for its organizational feasibility (span of command, adequateness of control, etc.).

We shall now proceed to apply this abstract conceptual framework to organizational structure for national water-resource planning in developing economies.

[1] See also D. R. Daniel, "Reorganization for Results," *Harvard Business Review*, November–December, 1966.

STRUCTURAL COMPATIBILITY

The group of criteria related to structural compatibility between the organizational system and the program system involves analysis in three main directions:

1. Compatibility of boundaries between the two systems
2. Compatibility of hierarchical structure between the two systems
3. Compatibility of subsystem emphasis between the two systems

These three directions of analysis are elaborated in the following.

Compatibility of boundaries The boundaries between the water-resources subsystem and the rest of the economy should be determined so as to include the six main inputs essential for agricultural production within the direct or coordinative control of one organization. Three of these inputs are material: major capital investments, supporting capital investments, and current production inputs; three are nonmaterial transformation inputs: the inputs required to improve know-how and techniques, to modify psychological space, and to restructure institutional space. Exclusive control over any one of these inputs by an outside agency, not bearing direct responsibility for the main program objectives, will lead to excess growth (hypertrophy) of some elements of the program and to subnormal growth (hypotrophy) of others. In the context of water-resources development related to irrigation this will cause more damage than in other development contexts, because a kind of negative feedback process usually develops which tends to strengthen the more vigorous and weaken the less vigorous arms. Usually, the major capital-investment spheres will be overextended while most other essential input fields will suffer subnormal growth or even stagnancy. The net effect of so unbalanced a water program will be that scarce resources will be absorbed with little prospect of fruition, leading, as in a vicious circle, to more unproductive investments.

In the more *developed* economies the comprehensive approach may be of less importance. However, even in these economies demarcation of organizational boundaries should ensure some type of *overall unified control* over *all* forms of *water resources* and *all* types of *water use*. This is desirable because of the complementary nature of surface water and groundwater and of water use for irrigation and for urban and rural water supply. Much better results can be obtained from integrated management programs for water-resource utilization than from the sum total of separate programs. There is little chance of achieving integration without an organizational structure maintaining unified control.

In the vast majority of *developing* countries, existing boundary definition between the water resources and related sectors does not comply with the criterion of boundary compatibility. Organizational boundaries cut through major nerve paths serving the water-resources subsystem serving irrigation and thereby disrupt the connection of the subsystem with the rest of the system of which it forms a part. If full integration of the respective subsystems should prove to be politically unfeasible, a higher level coordinative body with the appropriate authority should be set up to do the metathinking for the disjointed part of the system and provide the required coordinative planning.

Compatibility of hierarchical structure The extent of integration and coordination necessary in a water-resources development program will depend mainly on the geometric configuration of resources and demand concentration and their anticipated change. In one country (or region) this configuration might point toward the necessity of national (or regional) planning from the outset, while in other countries such integrative thinking could be postponed or not be required at all. Where changes are anticipated in resources and demand configurations, decentralized planning ought to be supplemented by generalized but gradually expanding regional or national planning. The extent of integration required by the planning context will be one of the decisive factors in determining the structure of the corresponding organizational hierarchy.

First to be considered in this connection are the number of hierarchic levels and their respective functions; the desirable number of levels will depend on the necessary extent of integration, the organizational configuration of the relevant political hierarchy, and scale. When defining the functions and interrelationships of the various organizational levels, we shall have to reconcile requirements of integration with the need to decentralize problem solving and decision making according to the dictates of scale.

In complex and diffuse development tasks, the decision-making processes should be located as close as possible to the environments in which they operate. Overemphasis of localized decision processes, without supplementation by higher level integration, might, however, lead to ineffective solutions and in time to anarchy. Decentralized decision making, guided and oriented by higher level integration, will ensure the necessary flexibility and receptivity to feedbacks from the environment.

The arguments for keeping decision processes at the higher levels stress the emergence of a wider overall conception of problems and solutions, i.e., higher levels of abstraction in planning, better coordination of subsystems, and more efficient allocation of available resources (by minimizing autarkic tendencies of subsystems). On the other hand, the disadvantages of locating too many decision processes at these higher levels lie in greater rigidity and lesser adaptability to the actual planning environment and in lesser responsiveness to feedback from this environment.

The extent to which decision streams emanating from the higher levels have to be spelled out for use by the lower levels will depend mainly on the latter's capacity to transpose and expand these decision messages from the more abstract "strategic code" (the desired "natural" mode of upper levels) into the more concrete "tactical codes" of the lower levels, and into still more concrete instruction codes for the use of still lower levels. Each level of the hierarchic structure should be able to think and encode at least at the level of abstraction appropriate to it. In developing countries, due to the limited professional qualifications of lower level personnel and often also to reluctance of higher level personnel to delegate responsibility, it might be necessary to enunciate top-level decision streams in greater detail than would be needed in more mature countries. Under such conditions the hierarchy will tend to become overcentralized.

The ascending hierarchic levels of the decision process ought to operate at ascending degrees of abstraction: the higher the level of the organization, the more inclusive and abstract the process of analysis; the lower the level, the more concrete the analysis. The necessity in the early phases of development to transfer part of the lower level analysis and decision to higher levels carries with it some dangers: it is likely to lead to the reinforcement of the tendency, already inherent in the top-level echelons of developing countries, of emphasizing analysis at the lower degrees of abstraction to the neglect of the higher degrees of abstraction needed to solve the essential strategic problems.

Decision streams stemming from inadequate abstraction will result in random choices rather than in planned selection; they will be incomplete and, therefore, ineffective as regards production outcomes; they will take the form of uncoordinated decision spurts rather than purposeful, controlled interlocked chains of action.

Compatibility of subsystem emphasis Fierce competition between various programs for scarce human and material resources will be encountered in emerging economies. Such competition will also be met with between the various phases of the same program, e.g., data collection, data evaluation, overall long-term planning, short-term planning. Hence, the success of a program will greatly depend on careful balancing of the competitive claims for resources and on adoption of allocation patterns determined by short-term and long-term returns.

Under the prevailing type of organization for water-resource programs, the responsibility for creating the various inputs will be located in a number of independent agencies. These agencies compete for limited resources without being in a position to judge true priorities or to reconcile conflicting claims according to objective payoff functions. More aggressive units of a subprogram will grab more than their share, thereby moving ahead faster than other subprogram units. Holding positions of strength when resources are again allocated, they will attract the best professional manpower, thereby impoverishing the stock of human resources of other units or agencies that most need them. The proposed hierarchic structure of the decision-making process with its strong power center at the top of the program organization can provide a coordinating and regulative mechanism. In addition to allocating locally available resources, it would define critical deficiencies in human resources, draw up stopgap resource-creating programs, or as an interim measure, import these resources.

Transformation of the preexisting fragmentized organizational structure into the comprehensive hierarchy-type structure advocated here will, in the earlier development phases, often be the most critically needed operation. Such a major task will require at least a few high-level professional leaders capable of abstraction and possessing leadership and managerial skills. Often too few such professionals will be available to catalyze the commencement of the organization's transformation process, and some might have to be imported. Induced catalyzation of the organizational transformation will encourage the emergence of leadership elements from within the nation. Under the guidance of the catalyst, such elements would within a reasonable time acquire the techniques, basic attitudes, and response patterns needed for further catalyzation.

FUNCTIONAL COMPATIBILITY

As repeatedly pointed out, inadequate capacity of development organizations is the most widespread and probably the most damaging disability of developing countries. Achievement of functional compatibility might therefore be difficult and protracted.

Some of the development tasks related to water (e.g., irrigated agriculture) are of a highly comprehensive and complex nature and require an adequate number of personnel trained in a considerable number of disciplines. Furthermore, the disciplines involved cannot operate on separate paths but must evolve the necessary *interdisciplinary metathinking* cooperation and coordination.

Finally, at various phases of development some activity will prove *critical,* both because relevant matters had been neglected in the past and because its turn had come in the development sequence. To perform these critical operations in time, steps will have to be taken to develop and shift the necessary capacities.

The first test of functional compatibility will be the capacity of the development organization to prepare an outline development program which would define the principle functions which have to be performed by the organization. Few development organizations in developing countries will pass this first test.

Induction of development orientation is a difficult and gradual process that must be pursued for a considerable period of time before we can expect orientation to become self-sustained. Furthermore, the greatest difficulties and resistances are likely to be encountered in the first phases of development. To be able to undertake successful planning development, the senior personnel have to be turned into highly motivated and persevering professionals capable of long-range vision—a far cry from role occupants encountered in most development agencies in emerging countries.

In the light of the above, organizational planners in developing countries must be wary of overstressing structural aspects of organization, while neglecting capability aspects. A "perfect" organizational structure manned by inadequate personnel will rapidly degenerate into operational anarchy.

COMPATIBILITY WITH ORGANIZATIONAL STATUS QUO

The organizational structure the planner is faced with when initiating water-resources development and management programs is more often than not a "geological" accumulation of past organizational compromises. The organizational status quo can be analyzed from the point of view of its "macrostructure" and from the "micro" point of view of organizational style.

Institutional macrostructure Regarding institutional macrostructure, three principal paths can be followed to adapt existing organizational structure to the requirements of a new water-resource program:

1. Changing existing basic structure at one stroke, i.e., by law, by edict
2. Gradually improving organizational structure by effecting a series of consecutive structural changes designed to fit into a preconceived long-term organizational plan
3. Bypassing the existing structure and creating new ad hoc authorities structured to control all essential parts of the program or parts thereof

No hard and fast rule determines which approach is best for each specific case, but one can attempt to define the conditions under which each approach is applicable.

Approach One In actual organization history, this approach has rarely been adopted, although it would most expeditiously bring us close to the desired organization. However, implementing this approach depends on the political decision-maker's authority and his determination to wield the power required to effect major structural changes in existing organizations. The danger inherent in this approach lies in adopting new external organizational forms (say, the external trappings of a comprehensive development authority) without attempting to fill them with the proper comprehensive content and authority.

Approach Two This approach, possibly combined with approach 3, will under the prevailing political conditions generally constitute the rule. It will have serious implications on early program phases, since it implies postponement, for political reasons, of essential organizational reforms. The number of ministries involved in water-resource development utilization and agriculture will generally be governed by "political arithmetic," and political arithmetic has a tendency to proliferate ministries. Such proliferation will result in fragmentation of the authority related to the agricultural production process. The only way to provide the necessary coordinative thinking is by creating a coordinating agency, one headed by a minister of cabinet rank with authority and power to enforce coordination and supported by adequate staff. This formal solution has sometimes been chosen without vesting the coordinating authority with adequate powers.

Approach Three This approach suffers from the inherent and dangerous temptation of multiplying authorities without reducing the authority of existing bodies. Such an organizational jungle, once it has struck roots, is difficult to control and to prune. Malignant development or organizational proliferation can be avoided only by firm action rooted in long-term organizational programs. However, such a combination of organizational insight with determination and power to act will in most real-life situations prove rather utopian. New ad hoc project authorities organized by this approach ought gradually to change their organizational allegiance and assume the role of irrigation districts conceived within a national coordinating framework.

Nevertheless, under certain political-institutional conditions the establishment of an independent authority might be the only available alternative toward achieving a comprehensive development approach, initiating a transformation process, and eventually creating a spontaneous growth process. Despite apparent lack of structural elegance and its incompatibility with organizational requirements of the later development phases, this solution should be kept in the armory of the organizational planner. The need for it is supported by the observation that ineffective central agencies may, in some countries, exist side by side with dynamic ad hoc authorities.

Institutional style Turning to organizational style, a taxonomy will have to be devised that will again be based upon the three basic social models, the mechanistic, the laissez faire, and the cybernetic. Earlier analysis of these models will be supplemented here by probing their organizational implications.

The Mechanistic Model Sustaining the mechanistic model will lead to a centralistic, authoritarian, and in extreme cases, dogmatic style of leadership and organization. Since the tacit assumption is that good decisions are made at the top of the hierarchy, communication will be predominantly from top to bottom. Feedback in the reverse direction, to the extent that it disproves validity of top-level decisions, will be discouraged. Thus, policies once established at the top will tend to become "test proof" and will persist whether they are successful or not. In extreme cases, this will lead to a schizoid attitude in which projections of personal delusions are substituted for analysis of reality.

Barring its more extreme forms, centralistic leadership style makes possible overall integration and coordination, greater leadership incisiveness and directiveness, and better reconciliation of national with regional and local considerations. Its disadvantages are rigidity of the decision system, lack of adaptiveness, and danger of degenerating into more extreme psychotic styles.

The Laissez Faire Model The tacit assumption behind sustaining the laissez faire model is that organizational and administrative processes are self-regulatory, an assumption which might hold for certain processes and socioeconomic contexts but not for others. Following the laissez faire model, leadership style will be decentralized, regionalized, and overly democratic, and national coordination will be slighted. Since in developing countries many processes are most certainly not self-regulatory, failure to take appropriate and timely measures might lead to runaway conditions and the necessity to introduce emergency measures under duress. In extreme cases the laissez faire model might lead to a "manic-depressive" pattern of regulation by crisis. The main advantages of leadership style fashioned by this model are the close connection of the decision process with feedback from the grass-roots level, extreme flexibility, and high degree of delegation. The disadvantages stem mainly from the lack of an effective mechanism for reconciling the requirements of the part with those of the whole and from the lack of authoritative high-level guidance and control.

The Cybernetic Model This model strikes an "organic" balance between the extremes represented by the other two models. It is based on two-way communication between top and bottom of the hierarchy. It can develop the advantages of the other models without their disadvantages. In our opinion the cybernetic model is the one most likely to achieve effective organization for water-resources development.

Leadership style and managerial philosophy, no less than organizational structure, affect the success of a program. The best structure in the world will be of no avail if manned by a civil service that has been conditioned over decades to the make-believe game of "pen pushing" and quenching initiative in subordinates. The type of organization here advocated envisages a professional leadership capable of thinking at a sufficiently high level of abstraction. This leadership must possess vision, imagination, insight, drive, and perseverance, or at least the potential to develop these traits under the influence of a catalyst. Where the desired leadership qualities cannot be developed on a sufficiently large scale in the central functional agencies, it may be necessary to confine comprehensive planning and implementation to more limited development nuclei. Properly organized according to the requirements of the program, these nuclei could be provided with the necessary human resources and adequate catalysts. They could also be used as informal schools for retraining and recatalyzing existing professional personnel according to production-oriented doctrines. Thus, within a relatively short period, cadres would become available for further spreading of the new approach. Feedback from successful implementation of such water-resources development nuclei would, in due time, have its effect upon the central functional agencies and, finally, upon the sectorial political decision makers. It might in time conquer the administration from the bottom level upward, since notwithstanding the apparent unpredictability of the political sphere, nothing succeeds there like success.

COMPATIBILITY WITH ORGANIZATIONAL THEORY AND PRACTICE

This subject will not be discussed at length, since there is no basic difference between organization theory and practice as applied to water-resource development and as applied to other disciplines. A review of the organizational structure conducted in accordance with organization theory and practice is certain to result in improvements of structural details. However, a cautionary comment might be in place. National water-resource planning, as understood here, is a highly political subject, and the work must perforce be conducted in a political space. Actual organizational choices might more often than not have to depart from the strictly "Euclidean" geometry of classical organization theory, since the political space of national water-resource planning follows an extremely "non-Euclidean" type of organization geometry.

HEURISTIC GUIDELINES FOR ORGANIZATIONAL PLANNING

As pointed out at the beginning of this chapter, rigid organizational rules and prefabricated patterns are but of limited validity. Nonetheless, heuristic guidelines derived from general structural features of the development process may prove useful; a few such guidelines follow.

Guideline one Supplement object-language decision groups at the nth level of an organizational heirarchy by metalanguage groups for integration at the $(n + 1)$th level, at least to the limit of the requirements of the sectorial plan. In more specific terms, this guideline would read: diffuse formal decision processes related to a production process ought to be supplemented by formal or informal metaplanning groups at the appropriate level.

Guideline two Invest every part of the decision hierarchy with the authority required at the several levels, and define the necessary control by higher levels.

Guideline three By organizational means, separate long-term from short-term, high-level from lower level planning. Otherwise, short-term planning will drive out long-term planning by the operation of a Gresham type of law.

Guideline four Avoid direct interference of metaplanning in object-language planning. Assuming that each type of planning has its separate organizational level, such interference will be resented by the object-language level. The task of the metalanguage level is to devise the overall framework for object-language work, not to replace it.

Guideline five The higher the requisite level of analysis, the more will difficulties be encountered in inducing a metaplanning process. The reasons are obvious: the higher the operational level, the more abstract the framework of thinking and the more numerous the institutions, interests, and people involved. On the other hand, the higher the level of thinking, the greater the potential impact upon the development process.

Guideline six Alain's saying "continue and commence" may serve as guideline 6. If you need a better organization, do not smash the old one, but induce it to perform at higher levels.

17

RATE STRUCTURE VIEWED AS A DEVELOPMENT TOOL

The every-day language reeks with philosophies. . . . It shatters at every touch of advancing knowledge. At its heart lies paradox.

ARTHUR F. BENTLEY

Il se peut bien . . . que les principes qui règlent l'administration des finances publiques soient un peu trop métaphysiques . . . que nous oublions toujours que l'homme a devant lui des choses, et non point des papiers et de l'argent.[1]

ALAIN (*Propos*)

ECONOMIC EVALUATION AND RATE DETERMINATION

This chapter reviews the principles of rate determination for services supplied by utility-type projects from the ex post point of view of the department or agency looking for the "correct" way of distributing the burden incurred by owning and operating the project, as contrasted with the ex ante point of view of the decision maker evaluating its socioeconomic feasibility.

Before proceeding to the subject proper, it should be made clear that these two points of view are governed by different criteria. The ex ante point of view focuses on evaluation of the socioeconomic desirability of allocating actual resources (economic factors) to construct new production facilities; such evaluation is a decision problem related to the allocation of national resources. The principal problem of ex post rate determination, on the other hand, relates to distributive patterns of financial "burdens"—transfer payments and financial accounting. The thesis here expounded assumes a clear distinction between these two basic points of view.

[1] It might well be . . . that the principles that control public financial administration tend to be a bit too metaphysical . . . that we are wont to forget that man is faced by things and not by paper and money.

RATE PARADOXES

Since both developed and developing countries are subject to continuous socioeconomic changes, rate determination has to be carried out in a rapidly changing phase space. No wonder that rate determination is beset by a number of serious difficulties, all stemming from a common problem, that of the selection of ground rules for determining rates for a specific project operating under specific socioeconomic conditions. The question might arise, should the depreciation rate adopted for rate calculations of a government-financed project be calculated according to repayment requirements or be sufficiently high for financing of physical replacement? Should the interest for rate calculations be that charged in the loan contract or be the marginal interest rate of the economy? Should rates in the gestation period of a project reflect the higher unit cost during this period, or should the initial cost margins be charged to capital costs? These are but a few of the serious and challenging questions that could be asked; unfortunately, there are no univalent definitive answers to any of them. A number of alternative answers are possible, and they all appear to represent "correct solutions." This indeterminacy certainly cannot be accidental. It points to a wavering between two incompatible sets of criteria: one implied in the question and a different one in the answer.

Similar considerations apply to cost allocation of multipurpose projects; different approaches lead to different solutions. The problem is again to establish the "correct" approach.

Restated in general terms, the basic problem of rate analysis is to establish a set of internally consistent ground rules for posing meaningful questions and arriving at meaningful answers in relation to cost allocation and rate determination of utility-type projects. The applicability of such ground rules will be confined to the ex post point of view of the rate analyst and ought not to extend to the ex ante point of view of preconstruction project feasibility evaluation. It would be futile to attempt to devise ground rules applicable to both basic points of view. This would lead only to ambivalence or multivalence of answers and to emergence of the paradox originating from a switch in points of view during the analytical operation.

DIAGNOSTIC ANALOGY

The emergence of paradoxes in rate analysis recalls similar phenomena in linguistic contexts: if we attempt to describe, in the object language of our universe of discourse, events occurring at its boundaries, we encounter paradoxes which originate from the vacillation of definitions as seen from inside and outside the above boundaries. The village barber who shaves all the men in the village except those who prefer to shave themselves is the prototype of paradox proliferators: if he does not shave himself, he is conflicting with the first conditions; if he does, with the second. The poor barber would have to remain in his quandary, if linguistic philosophers had not, some time ago, taught him a new trick to avoid paradoxes: the definition of boundaries between two (or more) universes of discourse ought not to be couched in the object language of one of them, but in the metalanguage encompassing both.

The problem of the rate analyst is analogous to that of the village barber, and a metalanguage approach is equally required in our present context. Shift in point of view between question and answer accounts for the paradox behind boundary vacillation in rate philosophy. How, then, is one to avoid boundary vacillation?

ETIOLOGY AND DIAGNOSIS

Rate problems may be viewed from two platforms:

1. The backward-looking platform, oriented toward the source of financing and the liabilities and constraints inherent in that source
2. The forward-looking platform, oriented toward the purpose and objective of investments and the policies they imply

Rate analysis may be conducted according to one of two basic approaches:

1. The accounting approach, transposing "costs" into the "microeconomic" terms of firm economics, thus operating solely with accounting concepts
2. The planning approach, operating with the "macroeconomic" terms of the national economy, thus with "real" resources

The *microeconomic* approach is compatible with the *source-oriented* platform, and their combined application in rate analysis will therefore lead to single-valued solutions. Such a combination of platform and approach would apply to rate determination of privately owned utilities financed by funds raised in the capital market.

The *macroeconomic* approach is compatible with the *objective-oriented* platform. An analysis on these lines will again avoid paradoxes—as long as we do not admit an incompatible doctrine through an ideological backdoor.

Combining the "micro" approach with the objective-oriented platform or the "macro" approach with the source-oriented platform would be to combine incompatible universes of discourse. This would lead to paradoxes—unless a metalanguage analysis were undertaken, prior to the rate analysis proper, to reconcile internal discrepancies.

Changing approaches and platforms in the course of analysis leads to *paradoxes*. It is not difficult to explain the mental mechanism underlying these paradoxes: we are unwittingly transferring a methodology valid in structurally "pure" contexts to structurally mixed ones. Since our economic-accounting training rooted in structurally "pure" contexts of private firms has accustomed us to think in microeconomic and source-oriented terms, we fail to make the necessary adjustment for a "mixed" context such as public utilities financed, say, from both public and commercial sources. As long as we confine approaches relevant to structurally "pure" situations to structurally pure contexts, we shall not get into trouble. If, for example, we use orthodox accounting procedures in privately financed utilities, our analysis will remain free of paradoxes. In such a context there are no macroconsiderations, and a source-oriented analysis will constitute an economically meaningful analysis of the enterprise's finances. The same would be true for a situation that is completely "public." When the old Pharaohs built their large irrigation works, they had to consider only "macro" aspects, and they could remain exclusively objective oriented. They took the resources which they needed without incurring any "repayment" commitments, and their resources allocation was governed solely by the aim of creating and maintaining a vital public service. No paradoxes in this situation, either.

Stated more abstractly, the operational rules demonstrated so far define the *structural compatibility criterion:* the *ground rules* to be used in setting up a body of rates ought to comply both with the *requirements laid down by financing the program from a specific type of source* and with those *stemming from program objectives.* Where these requirements clash, a *metalanguage* platform is needed to *reconcile* them.

Adoption of the structural-compatibility criterion does away with a priori ground rules, with exclusively "correct" rate-fixing policies. Every category of program, according to source of financing and objectives, will call for a specific set of ground rules for rate determination. In short, we insist upon a structuralist, rather than a formalist, approach to rate determination.

THERAPY

The criterion of structural compatibility leads directly to the basic ground rules that must be complied with in order to avoid paradoxes. Rate analysis should comply with one of the following two *operational rules:*

1. It ought to be conducted wholly within *one* universe of discourse, i.e., either combining a "micro" platform with a source-oriented approach or a "macro" platform with an objective-oriented approach.
2. If the *two* universes of discourse have to be combined in rate analysis, the analysis has to be preceded by a *metalanguage* analysis aimed at reconciling the discrepancies between the two incompatible universes of discourse.

Having defined the basic structural axioms of rate determination, we can now look more closely at the two basic approaches to rate analysis (source orientation and objective orientation) and their applications.

SOURCES OF FINANCING

Funding may be public or private, and sources of financing in both cases may be local savings or foreign loans.

Government funding from internal sources Funds for government financing of development projects derived from internal sources will originate from either some kind of forced saving (taxes) or voluntary saving (e.g., sale of government bonds). Such saving implies renunciation of current consumption; macroeconomically speaking, such a sacrifice does not, and in fact cannot, represent a commitment involving a sacrifice of future consumption. To the extent that funds for investment are raised by taxation, such forced savings need have no effect whatsoever on aggregate consumption in the future, though they might affect future patterns of taxation, for one part of the population might have to be taxed to repay the loan due to an overlapping, but not identical, part of the population. Such a transfer of commitments from the present to the future does not, however, constitute a change of "real" consumption-saving ratios or in allocation patterns of "real" economic factors, but is merely a system of transfer of obligations.

Seen from the point of view of the source of financing, funding by forced saving does not commit the government to any repayment ground rules, either to the present generation or to future generations. Any such "repayment" raised from the present generation would be equivalent to duplicating the burden imposed upon it by the project investment. Imposing such a repayment burden upon the next generation cannot lighten the real burden imposed in the past upon the present generation, and would of course have to be invested in facilities benefiting the next generation.

When saving is voluntary (e.g., purchase of government bonds), provision will usually have to be made, from the point of view of the source of financing, for raising from project users (of the present and possibly also of the next generation) the funds needed to service the bonds. Amounts and schedules of such funds need not be larger than the stipulated repayment conditions of the bonds. As already mentioned, these payments are, macroeconomically speaking, current savings that will be utilized for current investments. Since the professed purpose of water charges for repayment of voluntary savings is servicing of bonds, water charges need not follow inflationary movements—except where bond-repayment conditions stipulate linkage to some relatively stable yardstick.

Within the above limitations, the government is free to devise a repayment policy (capital and interest) that is compatible with the overall objectives of the project.

Government funding from foreign sources Insofar as the funds for a project are raised abroad, the generation benefiting from the project will receive benefits without having actually saved.

This "anomaly" of getting something for nothing will in time have to be "normalized" by imposing upon the economy a saving stream big enough to service the foreign debt and thus replace foreign by local saving. This repayment stream will constitute a true current saving over the repayment period of the foreign loan, during which period the money to be repaid to foreign loan agencies will have to be earned by net current exports which will, of course, reduce current consumption.

Again, repayment amounts and schedules ought to be governed by the terms of repayment of the foreign loan. If this loan is repayable in foreign "hard" currency, repayment amounts expressed in local currency will have to be continuously adapted in accordance with the prevailing rate of exchange.

There would be no rationale in allowing for inflationary shrinkage of the foreign currency of the loan agreement; the influence of such inflationary shrinkage is normally allowed for in the interest rates charged by the foreign loaning agency.

Public funding from foreign sources will rarely be the sole source of financing for major development projects. As a rule, funding will be made up from both local and foreign sources. Therefore, repayment amounts and schedules will be fixed according to a combination of the patterns outlined above.

Private financing from local sources Two modes of private financing have to be considered here:

1. Some form of loan made by private lending agencies to a public-utility type of project. Here the considerations outlined for voluntary saving under Government Funding from Internal Sources will apply. Again, macroeconomically speaking, the saving involved implies no real burden contracted for the future.

2. Direct investment, in the form of stock, by private investors or financial agencies in utility-type undertakings. For such investments the term "repayment" ceases to be meaningful. Within constraints imposed by statutory regulatory authorities, the utility will attempt to maximize the return on shareholders' investments. It will at the same time accumulate a depreciation fund that will, when added to the accumulated interest and to the residual value of investments after write-off, maintain in real terms[2] the value of original investments. The ground rules for determining return and depreciation are usually laid down by the regulatory authorities.

Private financing from foreign sources Considerations outlined under Government Funding from Internal Sources and Government Funding from Foreign Sources will apply, *mutatis mutandis.*

THE INFLUENCE OF PROJECT OBJECTIVES ON RATE POLICIES

Definition of rate policy To establish a rate policy, we shall have to consider:

1. Source orientation, i.e., considerations related to sources of financing and the implications and commitments stemming from them

2. Objective orientation, i.e., considerations related to our desire to use rate structure as one of the tools for achieving overall project objectives

To the extent that the two aspects are *compatible,* i.e., that the rate determined according to 2 is greater than or equal to the rate according to 1, the higher rate determined according to 2 will be adopted. This might be the case, for instance, where water scarcity motivates the use of water rate as an instrument to limit water use.

Where the two aspects clash, i.e., the rate determined according to 1 is higher than that determined according to 2, a metalanguage resolution of the

[2] Real values may be conserved by reinvesting the fund.

dichotomy, involving give and take in relation to both aspects, will have to be attempted.

The criterion for such metalanguage resolution can be defined as follows: the selected rate structure should create for all parties concerned (i.e., utility users, government, national and foreign leading agencies, and investors) a decision space conducive to the greatest possible fulfillment of overall project objectives, while at the same time ensuring the continuation of an adequate rate of investments by the relevant categories of investors, and without affecting the operational efficiency of the project beyond what might be justifiable on socioeconomic grounds.

We propose to call "rate policy" the ground rules for determining utility service rates by combining the aspects of financing sources and the commitments they involve with the aspects of project and overall socioeconomic objectives, using the above criterion to reconcile the two aspects. We can now describe the influence upon rate policy of the commonly encountered project objectives.

Production and service objectives Projects are manifestly undertaken to achieve some production or service objective. In developing countries we have to add to this group of primary objectives a second group of intangible, but certainly not secondary, objectives which we have called "development capacity." Since the project is undertaken in order to realize these two groups of objectives, and since rate structure is a powerful tool to accelerate or decelerate the rate of progress toward their consummation, it would be illogical not to utilize the leverage of rate structure for this purpose.

The problem is that the use of such leverage implies deviation from investment ground rules applied to most other investments; such deviations might cause a distortion of the decision patterns of the individual utility user, leading to a lowered efficiency of water uses. In irrigation, for instance, water rates will have a decisive influence on the extremely diffuse individual decision patterns related to such factors as efficiency of use and selection of production complexes. If the introduction of a "distorted" water rate seriously unbalances these decision patterns, the economic wisdom of introducing such "doctoring" becomes extremely questionable. On the other hand, some such distortions might be temporarily or permanently justifiable because of their inherent positive effects, e.g., acceleration of production and capacity generation. Other sectors of the economy openly and unashamedly use such distortions with a similar motivation.

In short, the extent to which acceleration in growth of production and development capacity ought to be taken into account in rate policies is certainly a complex issue. Each case will have to be decided and periodically reviewed according to prevailing socioeconomic conditions. (See Rate Policies for Irrigation Projects for further discussion of this problem.)

Income-redistribution objectives Utility rates can also be used to achieve income redistribution that might be politically difficult to effect by other means. Such redistribution might aim at changing relative income distribution between regions (e.g., higher burden to regions of accelerated growth, lower burdens to retarded areas) and between sectors (e.g., higher burden on high-income sectors). As to the redistribution effects between regions, the very mechanism of internal public funding through mandatory saving will be instrumental in achieving some income-redistribution effects; the more advanced regions will contribute the lion's share of such savings. Voluntary saving will operate in a similar fashion. Redistribution effects between more and less prosperous sectors of the economy would be similar to the interregional effects just outlined.

As to shifting in time of burden related to project financing, the only case in which a burden related to investments made by the present generation can be imposed upon the next generation is that of long-term funding from foreign financial sources. If such funding requires that part of the foreign-currency debt be repaid by the next generation, the latter will have to save the respective foreign-currency amounts through exports.

The problem of whom to charge for the cost of prebuilding supply capacity also has a bearing upon intergeneration shift of burdens. In order to benefit from economies of scale, some irrigation and community water-supply projects require bulky initial investments. During the lengthy maturation period of such projects, this prebuilt capacity will raise the fixed-cost part of the unit cost of water considerably above the corresponding cost at capacity operation. This high unit cost will coincide with relatively low production and return characteristic of pioneering phases of programs and with relatively low per capita income of water users.

Business accounting procedures would burden the present generation, which has made the decisive contribution (in real terms) for the funding of the project, with the high unit cost of low-capacity operation. This additional burden would come at a time when the present generation can least afford it, while most of the benefits of prebuilding would accrue to the next generation. Application of the orthodox accounting procedure would thus result in an extremely lopsided allocation of burden between the present and the next generation.

To the extent that foreign financing significantly participates in the funding of the project, the inflationary loss of value of money will act in the same direction: while scarcely easing the repayment burden (in real terms) of the present generation, it may significantly decrease the burden of the next generation.

Resources-conservation aspects To the extent that a resource is scarce, or is anticipated to become so in the near future, resources conservation might become the overriding objective of rate policy. The resources scarcity that will be reviewed first is a Ricardian type, that is, a resources environment in which unit costs rise significantly with increasing utilization.

According to orthodox accounting procedures, the users of each consecutive plant would be charged with unit cost corresponding to the cost of owning and operating each individual plant. This procedure will, of course, result in unequal and increasing rates within the same general supply area. Two or more installations having different unit costs will often have to operate jointly within the same area. In such cases the orthodox solution might be a weighted average rate. Neither of these two methods complies with the economic requirement that preexisting demand be adjusted to the anticipated unit cost of the proposed next installation before the latter may be regarded as economically justified. The adjustment could, of course, be made by raising rates for all existing services some time before the deadline date for the next installations.

As the cost of new services continues to increase, and the gradient of the supply curve becomes steeper, a point will be reached when the manipulation of the demand side by fiscal measures might no longer be sufficient. At this point we might have to review the very resources base of production complexes. Application techniques of water would have to be reviewed and their compatibility with anticipated high water costs evaluated. The higher, in absolute terms, the unit cost of water, and the larger its share in the total production cost, the more important will such rethinking of the resources base become, and the greater will be the necessity to secure its adaptation to anticipated water costs. Rethinking and remodeling application techniques and resources base will make it possible to present to water users a meaningful package specifying application techniques correlated with specific unit costs of water (see also Chapter 32).

The above approach, based on purely economic considerations, would be justified as long as these considerations could be expected to initiate in the utility user the decisions leading to the desired production objectives. We would have to assume that the utility management and water user operate in an identical decision space and use the same decision criteria. This will often not be the case. The user of the utility service might arrive at the conclusion that because of risks, marketing uncertainties, the opaqueness of future behavior of government bureaucracies, etc., production would cease to be attractive for the producer at water costs determined according to the above considerations. This might especially apply to the early phases of project gestation, when productivities may be expected to be low and difficult to predict, and when the effectiveness of the new resources basis has not yet been sufficiently demonstrated. In such a case, a rate policy would have to be adopted that would reconcile these two points of view; we shall return to this subject in the next section.

Considerations similar to those outlined for natural-resources scarcities would, in countries with foreign-currency problems, apply to projects involving highly import-intensive investments or operational costs.

The common feature of rate objectives for projects in which resources scarcities prevail is the introduction of a braking policy upon demand with a timing that will ensure that demand braking becomes effective before the next investment decision becomes due.

Integration objectives We have already emphasized the attractiveness, with the maturation of planning space, of expanding planning boundaries by integrating a number of formerly independent planning spaces into a more comprehensive system. Such integration will not be equally attractive for the various potential participants and might even prove disadvantageous to some. Selection of an appropriate differential rate structure favoring the disadvantaged might be one of the ways of making integration more palatable to its opponents (see Chapter 14).

Operational objectives If the ground rules used by a utility for rate determination are different from those generally applied to similar investments in the same economy, the price mechanism and the allocation patterns of resources stemming from the utility are being interfered with. If not carefully watched and countered through appropriate corrective measures (to the extent that this is feasible), distortions of rate will lead to a parallel distortion in utilization patterns.

The level of water rates will thus have an important influence on the makeup of the resources base into which water enters as one of the elements. To a certain extent, investment in water can be replaced by investment and measures aimed at water saving. It will be the relation of the value of water saved to the amount of money spent in water-saving measures that will determine to what extent the individual water user will implement such investments and measures. As long as charges for water and the costs of water-saving measures are calculated according to the same ground rules, decisions taken will lead to economical solutions and resources allocation. If water rates are determined according to a preferential set of rules, the scope of water-saving investments and measures adopted by water users will be depressed below the economical level, and vice versa.

When considering such operational objectives, we must remember that within a certain range of rate levels operational objectives will clash with the main project objective, i.e., accelerating production and capacity growth. "Metalanguage" rate policies will have to determine the appropriate level of reconciliation for every project phase.

Financial image To the extent that projects depend on the capital market for part of their funding, rate policies will be predominantly influenced by the requirements of this market. Most international funding agencies have spelled out their requirements as to ground rules for rate determination, but even such fully elaborated ground rules still leave some leeway for limited application of objective-oriented rate policies. However, as long as international funding agencies do not adopt a more flexible and permissive attitude toward rate policies, the "rate-image" requirements will have the controlling influence.

The adoption of financial image as a controlling factor in rate determination represents the extreme case where source orientation governs rate policy.

This is a good point at which to turn to the various approaches to reconciliation of source and objective orientation, i.e., to rate policies.

SOURCE-CONTROLLED AND OBJECTIVE-CONTROLLED RATE POLICIES

Controlling orientation As pointed out earlier, the principal cause for confusion in rate determination is the vacillation between source and objective orientation within the same operation of rate determination. Some types of investment are by their very nature almost exclusively source oriented; rate policies for them will be clear cut and exclusively governed by orthodox accounting rules. No metalanguage reconciliation with objective orientation will be necessary. In other types of investment objective, orientation will play an important and sometimes a controlling role; however, even in these types of investments some allowance will still have to be made for source orientation. For the reconciliation of conflicting orientations in the latter type of investment, a metalanguage rate policy will have to be adopted.

Before we consider the criteria that ought to govern such reconciliatory rate policies, it will be useful to review a typical case of each of the two basic types of investment.

Source orientation The typical and most important case of source orientation is, of course, an investment by a business corporation. The sources of financing will be the capital market and retained profits, and it will be the first type of source that will exercise a controlling influence on financial and accounting policies.

To create or retain a favorable financial image with the capital market, the corporation will have to include among its objectives an attractive return upon investments in the form of a dividend stream, maintenance of the true value of investments through accumulation of a depreciation fund large enough to finance the replacement of the depreciated part of the investment or its equivalent, and the creation of capital gains through increasing material and technological assets.

These corporation objectives will fully determine accounting ground rules: rates of return will have to be sufficient to create the required dividend stream, as well as to leave an adequate surplus for financing expansion of capital and technological assets; depreciation rates ought to be at least large enough to finance replacements.

Objective orientation Public investment projects represent the other extreme pole; they will rely for their financing mainly on government funding, supplemented in some cases by financing facilities of the international funding agencies (especially, but not exclusively, in the developing countries). In other cases, financing will be provided by various public institutions (regional, municipal, etc.) and by raising money through bond issues in the capital market (mainly in the developed countries).

Every type of financing will exert a specific influence on rate policies. Public sources of financing (government and local authorities) will tend to be more permissive from the point of view of an objective-oriented rate policy.

International funding agencies will hold an intermediate place. Private funding sources will exert a pull toward higher source orientation, but, since loan conditions will be expressed in nominal values and stipulate a fixed rate of interest, this type of source orientation will be much more flexible and permissive than that of stock-type investments in business corporations. In publicly financed projects, objective orientation will thus be the determining factor in rate policy, and it might become the controlling one in such projects in developing countries.

A public investment of the utility type (e.g., a community water-supply works or an irrigation project) once constructed will principally aim at making its services available on the widest possible scale and with minimum delay, while improving applicative and operational efficiencies. This would represent its objective orientation. Its source orientation might stem from the servicing conditions of the government loan, from the necessity to cover operational costs, from the desire to create an attractive financial image in order to attract international funding, and from the necessity to finance extensions from project incomes. The various components of objective orientation might prove incompatible, and some components of the objective orientation are certain to clash with some of the source orientations. The ideal case would be to have considerable leeway for a reconciliatory rate policy; this could best be achieved by a flexible type of repayment commitment, at least for the government share in financing, but preferably also for the share of the international funding agency.

Whatever repayment commitments are imposed upon a publicly financed utility, three principles will hold for this type of investment.

1. Seen macroeconomically, amortization payment would represent a participation of project beneficiaries in the financing of current investments in all sectors of the economy. Repayment ought to be considered as an amortization of a loan expressed in nominal values and not as an installment toward the accumulation of a depreciation fund for replacement expressed in real values. Replacement can be financed only from real savings at the time such replacements are due. There is a tendency to adopt amortization periods equal to technical lifetimes. From the point of view expressed here, there appears to be no logical connection between the two; however, this approach has the pragmatic advantage of specifying long amortization periods for major investments, which as a rule have long technical lives.

2. Similar considerations apply to interest rates. There is no a priori reason why a public investment should pay interest at a rate higher than that charged by lending agencies (government or international). The contrary would be more to the point: the government ought to agree to a flexible approach to the interest rate and leave it to the rate analyst to propose for every specific case an appropriate interest rate, possibly one allowing interest concessions during the maturation period (see the next section). The adoption of an approach diametrically opposed to the above recommendation would imply the introduction of a repayment schedule that provides for accumulation of a replacement fund at real values, and for interest charges made at prevailing rates, which of course comprise an inflationary component. Such a procedure would represent a duplication of the inflationary allowance.

3. As far as the next generation is concerned, the approach selected here would leave it in a much better position than that of the present generation. The next generation would "inherit" from the present generation a depreciated project value corresponding to, say, half the original investment value (assuming a technical lifetime of about two generations), and it would, at the same time, inherit other installations financed from repayment funds collected from the present generation beneficiaries of the project.

The introduction into project financing of very special funding conditions, such as outright grants, or cushioned supersoft loans, e.g., loans from some bilateral and international agencies (such as the International Development Agency) does not justify any change in approach. We ought to consider these special conditions as a boon from heaven, greatly increasing the flexibility of our rate policy and making it possible to follow objective orientation with less jeopardy from sources considerations than in ordinary loans. Therefore, it would be wrong to shy away from this freedom of action and reimpose some artificial accounting constraint, e.g., the condition that the project ought to fully "repay" the grant to the treasury.

Repetition of a cautionary comment made at the beginning of this chapter may be in place here. We are discussing considerations related to determination of water rates of completed projects and not criteria to be used when deciding whether a project ought to be constructed or not.

RATE POLICIES FOR IRRIGATION PROJECTS

The point of departure of rate analysis, as understood here, is that the construction of a project and the creation of its social and institutional infrastructure have been decided upon independently of the rate analysis. Such a decision will be based on the comparison of the direct and indirect socioeconomic benefits of the project with its socioeconomic cost and the payment ability of project users with the actual financial commitments incurred by its funding.

The task of the rate analyst is here understood to consist of forging the rate structure, within the constraints of source commitments, into a powerful tool for the rapid and efficient achievement of project objectives.

This conception of rate analysis deviates greatly from the classical approach which aims at a rate structure that would ensure an automatic and theoretically perfect resources allocation and which applies to the type of investments considered here accounting ground rules compatible with those of other contemporary investments. The justification for our approach lies mainly in two considerations:

1. Application of the orthodox approach during the protracted gestation period of production-oriented irrigation projects would constitute a formidable obstacle on the way to consummating objectives, and would thus be self-defeating.

2. As a consequence of the desirability or necessity of intersectorial, interregional, or similar kinds of income redistribution, actual allocation of economic resources will in any case have to deviate from the theoretical, classical pattern.

The tool approach to rate structure implies a continuous, dynamic, sequential type of "retooling process" in harmony with gradual consummation of project targets and intermediate objectives. Though the details of this process will vary from project to project, three distinct characteristic phases of project maturation and corresponding retooling approaches may be distinguished:

1. The transformation phase: breaking away, in strategic aspects of the project, from preexisting traditional equilibria and moving toward higher level equilibria. In this phase, in which we have to overcome the superimposed inertial momentum of developers and developees, the leverage of the rate tool is essential.
2. The consolidation phase: spreading of the transformation process over the whole project area and gradual consolidation ("refreezing") at higher level equilibria. At this phase, the leverage of the rate tool, though gradually diminishing, is still essential.
3. The expansion phase: completion of the consolidation process and gradual introduction of more advanced technologies, inputs, and management procedures. In this last phase of project maturation, we ought to initiate, within existing source constraints, a rate structure governed by a well-balanced and internally compatible mix of relevant project objectives.

Project objectives generally fall into one of two discordant groups.

1. The group that tends to depress rate levels, comprising production, income redistribution (favoring lower income population strata), and integrative objectives
2. The group that tends to raise rate levels, comprising resources conservation, operational (use efficiency) and financial-image objectives

The process of retooling will generally be guided by the following basic rules:

1. In the early phases of gestation (transformation) the first group of objectives will govern, while the second group and source orientation remain mostly dormant.
2. In the intermediate phase (consolidation) the second group of objectives will be introduced and reconciled with the first group; also, the first constraints related to source orientation will be imposed.
3. In the last phase of development (expansion) the correct balance between the objectives of both groups and source orientation will be struck.

From the viewpoint expressed here, the above procedure represents the ideal unfolding of the rate-analysis process; it presupposes extreme flexibility (in magnitude and timing) in introducing source constraints. In reality, source constraints will often be too rigid from the very start to allow the rate analyst to veer from the orthodox attitude.

The proposed process of rate analysis involves two types of quantification problems:

1. Reconciliation of the selected mix of objective orientation and source orientation
2. Internal reconciliation of the two objective-orientation groups

As to the first problem, we need to define the extent to which source orientation, spelled out by loan conditions, is beyond the analyst's control, and the extent to which it can at least partially be modified by arguments based on objective orientation. The first type of source orientation has to be treated as a constraint; as to the second, the analyst must convince the funding source to agree to stepping up source orientation gradually, on the lines described above.

As to reconciliation of the two objective-orientation groups, the two major goals demanding higher rates are increased efficiency in water application and water-resources conservation. Water-use efficiency will not loom very large in the initial phase of project gestation, when water utilization is still at a low level; at this phase it will be important to prime transformation and water use. As utilization increases, efficiency will become more important; as utilization approaches plant capacity, the conservation argument might become a controlling one. Thus, the two major rate-raising arguments gather weight as the project matures, production increases, and payment capability rises. In the final "steady-state" phase, the balance between the production type of rate-lowering argument and the efficiency and conservation argument ought to be struck at a level at which the water user has sufficient incentives to adopt commercially available and economically sound water-saving measures. Should this rate prove excessive from the production point of view, a lower water rate combined with special incentives (e.g., special loan conditions to help finance water-conservation measures) might be adopted.

POLITICAL ASPECTS OF RATE STRUCTURE

The rate structures of many countries where irrigation is important are more "production oriented" than are those recommended here. The reason that permissive attitudes toward water charges are widespread is obvious: water rates in most countries are a sensitive political issue.

Since political factors often determine rate policies, the political feasibility of a rate structure must be considered in rate analysis. In the early phase of development, the political factor might have to be treated like a constraint; however, as prosperity rises in the project area, the political decision hierarchy might come to accept a more rational rate fixing. At that stage, politicians might prefer a rational analytical approach to rate determination, allowing for political susceptibilities, over one which is exclusively governed by crude political expedience.

Finally, it might be claimed that adoption of a rising rate, though logical on paper, might meet with insurmountable psychological and political resistance. If a low-rate structure has been introduced as a permanent measure, such resistance might well arise. But if the principle of a rising rate is made clear from the outset, resistance can be considerably lessened.

RATE-POLICY CONSIDERATIONS APPLYING TO COMMUNITY WATER SUPPLIES

The following considerations on rate policies applying to community water supplies have been drawn up with special reference to developing countries. They presuppose that a substantial number of citizens receive no piped water, that the capital allocated for constructing new services is rationed at annual rates, and that a long period will elapse before all communities are served.

Rate considerations for community water supplies will vary greatly from those for irrigation works. This is true for four main reasons:

1. Community water supplies are usually owned and operated by municipal or local authorities or by specially established utilities and not by government. Therefore, the macroeconomic type of arguments that were meaningful in the case of irrigation works will have to be replaced by utility or municipality economics. Since such decentralized management has overwhelming operational advantages, the tendency to decentralization and to the establishment of independent water authorities should be encouraged.
2. Government financing will be supplemented by financing from municipal taxation, local bond issues, and loans from national and international banks. Therefore source orientation might be a stronger controlling factor than in the case of irrigation projects. The need to create and maintain a sound financial image will also act in the same direction.
3. The need to keep per capita consumption at reasonable levels and to avoid waste of water may become paramount earlier than is the case with irrigation works.
4. In the case of community water supplies, "rational" rate levels are not prima facie politically objectionable. Even if they are politically unfeasible, the introduction of such levels will induce less resistance than is the case with irrigation works. Municipal water rates are in fact generally much closer to costs as calculated by orthodox accounting than is the case with water rates for irrigation works.

The basic objective orientation of water-supply works in countries with capital rationing is to ensure maximization of the discounted streams of people served at what (in Chapter 15) has been defined as adequate service levels. This maximization presupposes both planned manipulation of demand and avoidance of waste.

Source orientation in community water-supply works will be much more influential than in irrigation works, because nongovernment capital sources are of greater importance and because basic objectives are less affected by higher water rates. In certain cases higher water-rate levels may have a favorable influence on objective achievement, since high efficiency of use will generally operate in the same direction as source orientation.

A third factor influencing rate structure in the direction of source orientation is the need to accumulate funds from current income to finance at least part of the continuous investment in extensions, improvements, and modifications of the water system.

From the point of view of rate analysis, we can distinguish three types of customers:

1. Unmetered services without direct water charge, in which demand can be manipulated by the extent of facilitation of water use. Here we can observe a correlation between facilitation and demand. Street pipes are an example of this type of service.

2. Unmetered services with a flat water charge, in which we have no tool to influence demand, and in which demand will therefore consolidate at use levels that will depend on water-use habits.

3. Metered services with a charge varying with actual use, where demand can, within limits, be manipulated through rate structure.

While we have no direct means of influencing the demand of group 2, except by exhortation, we can and should influence the demand of groups 1 and 3 until all citizens are served by piped systems. Facilitating levels (e.g., distance of street pipes) can be modified and rate structures altered to bring about adequate use levels, leaving unused water for quarters not yet served. Some time before aggregate use approaches capacity, category 2 uses should be converted into category 3 uses through the introduction of metering, and thus become modifiable through rate structure.

If the waterworks supplies the whole community and still has a considerable spare capacity, the latter might be used:

1. To cater for population growth.

2. To cater for the increase of the number of class 2 and class 3 users with their much higher per capita consumption as compared with class 1 users.

3. To cater for industrial demand.

4. To raise use levels of adequate use. This might occur automatically through a gradual increase in demand of classes 2 and 3 users and might be induced in class 1 users by increasing facilitation of use (e.g., reducing spacing of street pipes). Such a rise of use levels is justified insofar as the community does not require major additional investments before the less favored communities reach the adopted minimum level of "adequate use."

The rate levels for directly chargeable water-supply services (categories 2 and 3) will, as already mentioned, be governed by a source of financing orientation. This will be more evident in waterworks organized as independent authorities and bearing full responsibility for raising their own funds for expansion than in works organized as part of the overall municipal services and whose finances are inextricably entangled with municipal finances. This consideration will also hold if government or government-sponsored financing is a major contributing factor.

In spite of its necessarily greater source orientation, with all that this involves, the independent organizational structure of a community (or group) water supply has so many advantages that it ought to be adopted wherever possible. An independent authority will be less subject to political pressures and to politically motivated nomination and turnover of senior personnel; weakness in its financial position will be more difficult to conceal and cover up; efficiency or lack of efficiency will become measurable and comparable and, in time, improvable. It will therefore be a better solution in the long run even from the point of view of the objective-biased rate analyst.

The control which source orientation exercises on accounting procedures and rates depends on capital structure. Where financing is derived mainly from government, state, and municipal sources, easier repayment schedules and (usually artificially) low interest rates will prevail. In an inflationary environment, great flexibility in determining the fixed rate portion of water charges is left to the rate analyst as between nominally valued financial commitments and collection for a replacement fund based on real values. This flexibility might be used to implement at least the most pressing requirements stemming from objective orientation. However, it might be equally valid to use such inflationary gains to increase the share of self-financing in future extensions, thereby freeing public funds for financing waterworks in other communities.

To the extent that local banks participate in the financing, the interest rate will generally be high and will allow for inflationary devaluation. In such cases the capital charge of the water rate ought to be determined by the loan's repayment requirements.

Collection for services difficult to charge directly (category 1, e.g., street pipes) poses a problem encountered by many water-supply schemes in developing countries. Some type of local taxation, possibly imposed as a percentage on an existing tax, might be the solution. To ensure local participation in financing improvement of services (such as decreasing the spacing of street pipes), such improvement ought to be conditional upon increased taxation, even if the added income does not cover the extra expenditure. In any case, whatever "flexibility" source orientation leaves to the rate analyst will, at least in the early phases, be used mostly to subsidize such services. As the question of sewerage is solved and income rises, street pipes might gradually be converted into house connections and some type of direct charge introduced.

CONCLUSIONS

Rate analysis and the resulting rate structure are powerful tools. Judiciously used within the constraints imposed by sources of financing, they can help to accelerate achievement of project and program objectives. Rate structure, therefore, should not be considered the automatic product of orthodox accounting procedures taken over from private investments financed by the capital market.

Some project objectives (such as production, income redistribution, and integration orientation) tend to lower rates; others (such as use efficiency, resources conservation, and financial image orientation) tend to raise them to levels close to those which would result from orthodox accounting procedures.

The importance of the rate tool in achieving project objectives will depend on the scope and depth of the transformation that must be produced. Thus, irrigation and agricultural development projects, whose success depends on a basic transformation in most socioeconomic dimensions, will be much more dependent on the rate tool than will, for example, community water-supply projects.

The potency of the rate tool will greatly depend on the constraints that sources of financing impose upon accounting procedures and upon the resulting flexibility left to the rate analyst for implementing a balanced mix of project objectives. Government, state, and municipal financing will as a rule leave more flexibility, while banks and similar funding agencies will leave less; however, some major international and multinational funding agencies have become more permissive with regard to projects whose success greatly depends on rate tools. Fortunately, agricultural and irrigation projects are classed within this category, and their supplemental local financing is, as a rule, derived from government financing. Thus, there is a good chance that a higher flexibility will be available where it is most needed.

The rate-decreasing and rate-increasing objectives have to be reconciled, and this reconciliation will have to be modified as the project matures. Furthermore, objective orientation will have to be reconciled with constraints stemming from sources of financing. When performing these reconciliations, the rate analyst should take into account the present and anticipated maturation of the project and the relation of the project to the sector as a whole.

18
LOGISTIC PROGRAMMING

God gives nuts to those who have no teeth.
BRAZILIAN PROVERB

The universe of discourse within which development planning is here conceived is based on three aggregates:

1. The natural-resources vector, comprising the developee and his socio-economic and natural-resources environment.
2. The development-resources vector, comprising the developer (i.e., the human-resources constituent) and the inventory of resources at his disposal.
3. The "product" of the above two vectors, i.e., the process of development properly speaking, representing the application of the development-resources vector upon the natural-resources vector. Where the planning space extends over an entire sector, the product represents a sectorial program; where it extends over a specific area, a project.

The present chapter focuses upon analysis of the development-resources vector, which is broken down into constituents. General procedures are outlined to establish program requirements for these constituents and their scheduling and to identify development-resources bottlenecks and define programs to overcome them. Since in developing countries the human-resources constituent of the development-resources vector will usually be deficient in quantity and quality, part of the development-resources inventory may have to be diverted from direct application to the improvement of the human-resources constituent.

Logistic analysis can thus be defined as simulation of the evolvement and deployment of the development-resources vector according to the requirements of a program or project. Logistic programming based on such an analysis is a definition of the movement in space and time of the constituents of the development-resources vector to the natural-resources vector, with a view to upgrading production and decision environments, and to the development-resources vector, with a view to upgrading the latter's human-resources constituent.

A logistic analysis may show that a specific program may be logistically feasible without having to siphon off significant quantities of development resources back to the development-resources vector. Or it may indicate that a program will become logistically feasible only with such siphoning. Finally, it may prove a program to be logistically unfeasible, in which case it would have to be reshaped to reduce demand upon critically short resources. When the initial resources inventory together with resources created (or improved) by siphoning back become sufficient, the program becomes logistically feasible.

DEFINITIONS

To establish a logistic terminology that is compatible with the development terminology used so far, we shall have to designate for every development term its logistic counterpart. The development terms we shall use are, in descending order of generalization, program, project, operation, intervention; their proposed logistic counterparts are aggregate development-resources vector or inventory, project inventory, resources bundle, resources strand.

A *project inventory* is that part of the development-resources vector which is needed for the implementation of a specific project. A *resources bundle* is a set of related resources needed to implement an operation, i.e., a relatively independent part of a project. All activities connected with investigating, planning, and constructing a groundwater supply system feeding an agricultural-settlement irrigation project would constitute an operation; the relevant development resources, a resources bundle.

The implementation of an operation involves a number of interventions, which, in turn, involve the deployment of resources strands. Drilling a well, for example, would be an intervention forming part of the groundwater development operation. Physical and human resources involved in erecting, operating, and dismantling the drilling rig and appurtenant equipment would represent the resources strand related to the above intervention.

LOGISTIC PROGRAMS

A logistic program is the transposition of a logical network of project (or program) activities into logistic terms, i.e., into the deployment of development resources. To effect this transposition, the basic constituents of the logical network will have to be spelled out, down to the level of interventions, and the relevant transposition coefficients that relate the intervention to the resources strand involved will have to be applied. The term *resources-outcome ratio* is used for this transposition ratio.

The value of the resources-outcome ratio for a specific intervention and resources strand is not the same for all societies and regions and, within a society, for all development phases. Its value depends on past experience in applying the relevant resources, on spontaneous current learning, and on the extent to which development resources have to be siphoned back into the development-resources vector.

Differences in specific resources-outcome ratios between developed and underdeveloped countries are extremely high, a fact which leads to two basic conclusions:

1. We must beware of using resources-outcome ratios of developed countries in logistic programming for underdeveloped countries.

2. Progress in underdeveloped countries greatly depends on systematically speeding up improvement of strategic resources-outcome ratios.

In actual programming, our point of departure will be resources-outcome ratios derived from past performance. If the relevant data are not available, for the first round of application we shall have to operate with resources-outcome ratios derived from operations in similar socioeconomic contexts. However, since information based on such analogies will not be very reliable, more dependable ratios should be obtained from local pilot operations before embarking upon large-scale undertakings.

In logistic scheduling for long-term programs, allowance ought to be made for the gradual improvement of resources-outcome ratios through operations undertaken with that purpose in mind and through the effects of spontaneous learning. We ought to be mindful of spillover effects that tend to spread improvements from one resource application to others. After all, the resources taxonomy that we used in the analysis of upgrading human resources, with its implied atomization of the human mind, is an artificial construct to make systematic analysis and quantitative planning of such upgrading operations possible. Psychological phenomena are not, in reality, atomistic. As long as we deal with a short time horizon, the error implied in an atomistic taxonomy will be negligible; if we plan for longer time periods, resources-outcome ratios related to human resources ought to be periodically revised.

Development resources can be traced back to either capital resources or human resources. Upgrading either requires the deployment of both in varying proportions. We might, for instance, wish to improve capital-resources availability by improving our development image and credit standing with the international funding agencies; to achieve this, we might have to upgrade the human-resources constituent, and through it, planning, designing, and implementation capacity and organization. This "second-degree" transformation leading to the desired improvement of the image of the development agency will require both capital and human resources, which would have to be diverted from direct "first-degree" applications. The same reasoning applies if our most essential immediate aim is improvement of the human-resources constituent of the development-resources vector.

The application of resources-outcome ratios to the logical network will enable us to set up the *logistic network* of the project or program. In the logistic network, the resources to be deployed at every node of the network (i.e., at every intervention) as well as their sequence in time will be identified. Such a first program will often show extreme unevenness in the need for various resources; such an irregular buildup and fade-out might prove either unfeasible or extremely difficult. A more practical sequence of deployment of resources will therefore have to be worked out, one which will allow a more even deployment of resources without a significant sacrifice in overall timing.

Logistic programming as thus far described would have to be extended to all important fields of the development process: data collection, planning, design, supervision (in the engineering, agrotechnic, economic, financial, training, and institutional dimensions), contracting, operation and maintenance after completion, and finally, operating the relevant institutions. All logistic flows will also be translated into financial flows.

Comparing the program of logistic (including capital) requirements with the logistic inventory will indicate if, where, and when development-resources shortages (in quantity and/or quality) may be anticipated. Such shortages may be serious enough to make a project logistically unfeasible; or they may require siphoning resources from direct uses for upgrading of the development-resources inventory; or, finally, they may be overcome by rescheduling. Logistic programming is complete only when it has somehow achieved compatibility between resources requirement and inventory.

CONCLUSIONS

Study of development practice in the less developed countries reveals that, except for short-term financial scheduling, logistic programming has been greatly neglected. Major undertakings are launched without full analysis of the availability of essential resources. If the relevant resources can be purchased, leased, or hired abroad, resources deficiencies may be made good by "imports"; however, operations that depend on resources that cannot be "imported" will be greatly jeopardized if their resources requirements are not properly programmed and the deficiencies found are not corrected by appropriate corrective operations. The difficulties of logistic scheduling are frequently by-passed by conveniently omitting all program elements that require an upgrading of the human-resources constituent of the development-resources vector, even if the truncated program will result in a great reduction of objective achievement. Achievement of conspicuous portions of the project (which without the complementary aspects are virtually meaningless) serves to divert attention from the futility of the basic planning approach.

Equally disturbing is the failure to develop mechanisms that would gradually correct such imbalances in the development process. On the contrary, the lopsided development process tends to solidify into extremely skewed institutional patterns, which in turn increase the imbalance.

Detailed and realistic logistic programming must be considered a vital and integral part of the planning process.

19 THE INVENTORYING PROCESS

That man can interrogate as well as observe nature was a lesson slowly learned in evolution.

OSLER

THE INVENTORYING PROCESS: DEFINITION, NATURE, AND LIMITATIONS

Inventorying of resources comprises the collecting, generating, and processing of information on resources and their interaction. Resources information refers either to the natural-resources vector, e.g., the farmer, soils, water, and agroclimate in their natural state, or to the development-resources vector, i.e., the resources at the disposal of the development agency. Resources inventorying is an extremely diversified operation in developed countries. In the context of underdevelopment, it will be still more complex, while the capacity to master the inventorying process will be limited in scope and inferior in quality. Hence, the need will be to focus the inventorying process upon the most important information on the resources most relevant to the development process. Such focusing, however, presupposes the existence of a reasoned development program which provides the necessary rationale. The preparation of a development program is dependent on a resources inventory —which brings us back to our starting point.

The way out of this vicious circle is through an iterative, sequential approach: planning proper will have to be preceded by a very general inventory survey to determine the overall potential, orientation, and boundaries of development. This survey will make it possible to generalize an outline for long-term development, which in turn will help define the type and depth of resources information required for a concrete development program.

The inventorying process aims at achieving informational feasibility for a specific program, i.e., at attaining the relevant information thresholds and, to the extent possible, higher information levels. To minimize resources outlay, the inventorying process should be oriented toward specific programs. This normative statement needs one qualification: the lead time of the inventorying process will often be considerably longer than that of the program planning period; in such cases, program orientation of the inventorying process ought to refer to two or more programs rather than to the current one only.

Theoretically, the diversity and depth of information that can be gathered or generated by the inventorying process are infinite. Because of the overall limitation in resources availability and because of diminishing returns, we ought to set concrete limits to the process.

Information, the end product of inventorying, can be considered as one of the *inputs of development;* theoretically, we ought therefore to apply the same economic criteria to information generation that we apply to other inputs; in practice, this will hardly be possible because of the difficulty of establishing marginal input-output ratios for informational types of input. These quantification difficulties notwithstanding, we ought always to keep in mind that the inventorying process competes for resources with the development process proper and that allocation to inventorying at the margin should result in "marginal returns" to the development process comparable to those attainable by investing these resources in the development process proper. Compliance with this economic constraint implies limiting the inventorying process to the most relevant resources complexes and, within these complexes, to their most significant aspects.

The type and depth of inventorying that must be applied to reach informational feasibility for a project or program will depend on the hypothesis or model that we adopt to "explain" the functional interrelationship between the resources variables. To establish a meaningful inventorying program we need workable hypotheses on the behavior of the development-resources vector and on mechanisms underlying resources-outcome ratios.

The scope and depth of inventorying will also depend on the relative abundance (as between present and future requirements) of the resource to be inventoried. If a resource is practically unlimited, the inventorying process related to it could be confined to establishing this fact. The greater the proven or anticipated scarcity, the greater the scope and depth of inventorying ought to be.

The exploration of the role of water resources in development undertaken here has amply proved that effective development of water resources depends on concurrent transformation in most dimensions of the socioeconomic space. The inventorying process connected with a production-oriented water-resources development must, therefore, comprise data collection related to all these dimensions. Our exploration has also demonstrated the dynamic nature of the transformation processes involved; inventorying, in allowing for this dynamism, will have to treat resources as ever-changing, interacting processes or events.

The multidimensional and dynamic nature of the phase space of water-resources development forces us to abandon the traditional *static* concepts of resources inventories which result in lists of permanent resources packages with specific input-output characteristics. We ought to adopt instead the dynamic conception of inventorying as a collection of pointer readings of interacting and changing resources events. If such events do not occur spontaneously, we might have to induce "sample events" to generate the necessary data. The processes of inventorying, of planning the development transformations, and of planning management and operation cease to be discrete and independent. Inventory packages cease to have input-output ratios that can be determined apart from the respective development and management patterns. We are instead investigating behavior and responses of a specific natural-resources system submitted to simulated alternative development and management patterns, and we are determining alternative outcomes and their deployment, in time.

We have so far used the terms collection, generation, and processing. Collection refers to the "passive" accumulation of parametric data, such as pedological data on soils and water-resources information. Generation implies "active" information gathering and refers to the application of sample resources packages originating from the development-resources vector upon sample configurations of the natural-resources vector—in situations where no opportunities exist to gather such information from ongoing operations and where therefore special pilot operations have to be devised, or added to current projects, in order to create such opportunities. Processing refers to the transposition of raw informational data into terms that can be used by the project or program planner.

The interpretational yield of a certain volume of "raw" data will greatly depend on the appositeness of the data and on the effectiveness of the processing applied to it. Since the informational feasibility of an operation will mainly depend on this interpretational yield, sophistication in data processing will be needed most in the early phases when the volume of raw data is most limited.

Scope, depth, and quality of the inventorying process ought to be governed by the following factors:

1. Extent of scarcity of the resource as compared with program requirements
2. Availability of human resources (and justification of their allocation to the inventorying process), their training, organization, and need for achievement
3. Maturity of available technology for exploration, inventorying, etc.
4. Availability (and justification of allocation) of capital resources
5. General economic considerations, and the technology and economics of the production processes into which water enters as an input
6. Flexibility in the composition of the resources base into which water enters as an input
7. Legal-institutional factors, existing rights, etc.

TAXONOMY

Depending on the point of view of the classifier and the purpose of classification, a number of taxonomic principles could be applied to the resources system involved in water-resources development. The point of view taken here is a purely operational one: development consists in deploying the development-resources vector for upgrading the natural-resources vector in order to achieve the development objectives. The natural-resources vector consists of the natural-resource complex, sunk capital, human resources directly involved in the production process, and related services and institutional resources.

The development-resources vector has a similarly diversified makeup; it comprises the mobilization of current production inputs, investment of capital resources, and deployment of human-resources inputs for transforming the human resources directly involved in the production process.

The resources taxonomy that seems best suited to the operational needs of water-resources development is a division into five resources groups which, though they interact, can be considered separately.

1. The natural-resources system, comprising mainly water, soils, and agroclimate
2. Capital resources—available for the development process
3. Current crop production inputs that are required to sustain the production process at a certain level of productivity
4. Human resources, comprising the developee, the developer, and the developer of the developer
5. Institutional resources, both those existing at the outset of the development process and those which will have to be added during the process

Group 1 is wholly contained in the natural-resources vector; groups 2 and 3 are contained in the development-resources vector; groups 4 and 5 are contained in both vectors.

The remainder of this chapter deals with the inventorying process for the first four groups of resources. Group 5 does not lend itself easily to inventorying proper and is therefore not included in this chapter. It is treated in some detail in Chapters 16 and 20 to 24.

NATURAL-RESOURCES SYSTEM

Water resources Throughout the ages, thinkers have used flowing water as a metaphor for change. Heraclitus, the first propounder of a dynamic universe, used the river metaphor in one of his most striking passages: "You cannot step twice into the same river, for fresh waters are ever flowing in upon you." The inventorying approach prevailing in many water-resources development authorities contrasts sharply with this traditional dynamic "image" of water. As a rule the inventorying approach will be statically oriented as far as groundwater or its interrelation with surface-water flows is concerned. It will stress steady states and associated safe yields, while neglecting stock levels, transients, and quality deterioration.

Adoption of a dynamic and comprehensive inventorying approach would first require selecting a model expressing the dynamic nature of functional relationships of the variables entering into the resources equation.

The specification for data collection would be a direct outcome of such a model. Since the adoption of such a model would, in turn, presuppose a basic insight into the resource mechanism, we shall again have to adopt here the iterative sequential procedure in order to "prime" the inventorying process. The *priming* would be initiated by a general inspection of the geology, climate, pedology, and ecology of the region and of past records relating to water resources. At this phase, we ought to avoid committing ourselves to any model or flow mechanism. In the subsequent *scanning* phase we would attempt to fit data collected during the preceding phase into a limited number of potentially feasible *models,* and to determine which alternative models ought (by the collection of appropriate data) to be investigated and what indications would prove or disprove every specific model. In some cases, a hierarchy of alternatives and subalternatives of models might be required to cover all reasonable assumptions on flow mechanisms; in such cases, the greatest emphasis should be placed on collecting data related to the operationally most important dichotomies.

Assignment of priority to the type of information essential for the forthcoming major decision should not blind us to the fact that we must schedule concurrently the collection of information related to later decisions. Scheduling should ensure the availability of this information at the respective decision dates—allowing for the lead time necessary for its collection.

Where information is scarce and development needs are urgent, the time and effort required for reaching the information threshold for the forthcoming development decision (and corresponding times and efforts to reach subsequent decisions) might be the decisive criterion for giving priority to the development of one or another water resource. The time and effort involved in reaching a specific information threshold for a specific decision will depend on the specific "information yield" per unit of time and effort that is characteristic for the relevant resource; this information yield will be called "information import." For instance, in seeking the best alternative sequence for developing the water resources of a basin comprising both groundwater and surface-water phases, close attention should be paid to the differences of information import of the two phases of resources.

Surface flow is made up of two parts, whose share in the total flow will vary from basin to basin, and in the same basin, from season to season and from year to year. Part of the flow usually consists of the direct response of the basin to recent highly variable precipitation, with only a limited amount of smoothing out of precipitation variations; the remaining part (which becomes important in periods of dry-weather flow) consists of the basin's "delayed" and greatly smoothed-out response to climatic events of a more prolonged nature; this latter part is fed from snow melt, bank storage, springs, and groundwater outflows. Readings of surface flow will therefore show great seasonal and interannual variations, and the "information import" of discrete observation of surface flow will be extremely small.

In this connection we have to remember that the decision thresholds for the initial investments related to surface flow are, with the exception of relatively small run-of-the-river diversions on perennial rivers, extremely high; that these initial investments represent a large portion of overall investments; and that decisions related to these investments must be made before we initiate development. If we intend to rely on unregulated run-of-the-river diversions, the minimum flow has to be known before the decision can be taken to use the river source for a specific purpose. Long observation periods are required to establish minimum dry-weather flow (of a specified frequency), and analogies with other basins will not be too reliable. Close quantification of average flow will be required in situations in which requirements are of the same order of magnitude as average annual flows. Determination of average flows requires long observation periods. Finally, maximum flows have to be determined in order to avoid excessive safety-allowance margins in spillway construction.

Thus, the major decisions related to the development of surface water in areas where flow information is insufficient or nonexistent will have to be made when information is at its lowest ebb. Such decisions, involving major investments, will greatly limit future decision liquidity. The economics involved in this type of decision are also extremely sensitive to errors of assumptions.

In contrast to observations on surface flow, those related to groundwater represent a highly smoothed-out and accumulative response of the groundwater formations to climatic events of an extended past. Flow variations in groundwater formations will therefore have relatively small amplitudes.

Furthermore, in groundwater formations large stocks of water could if necessary be drawn upon for considerable periods of time (see Part 3). In a groundwater formation, a single set of observations obtainable within a few days represents an accumulation of information reaching back for a considerable period and averaged by the groundwater formation. The information import of such observations is therefore considerably greater than that of comparable observations on surface flow.

Furthermore, information thresholds for decisions related to the early phases of groundwater development (mainly because of the extreme subdivisibility of investments) are extremely low. The combination of high information import and low thresholds makes groundwater (where available) the ideal source with which to initiate development.

The initial decision to start the use of groundwater in a specific area requires but little information. It can be based on general hydrogeological information supplemented by inexpensive geophysical evidence and on test results from a limited number of wells. Such information can be assembled quickly; initial exploitation decisions based on it will involve little investment and will leave practically unlimited decision liquidity for the future. Data derived from initial exploitation and from more detailed geohydrological investigation will make it possible to expand development gradually. A rigorous quantitative model will be required only as we approach full exploitation, by which time accumulated information should suffice for setting up such a model. Sensitivity of economic outcomes of decisions related to groundwater to errors in assumptions is extremely low in the early and intermediate phases, in that future utilization can still be cut down (or increased) without significant loss of investments. Sensitivity is not excessive, even in the later development phases, since major buffer stocks usually make a higher interim utilization possible.

Sophisticated mathematical models coupled with the use of computers have, it is true, stretched the information import of surface flow; the same consideration, however, applies also to groundwater. Because of this basic difference in information import, and because of the related longer lead times of surface-water inventorying, great emphasis ought to be placed on inventorying groundwater resources in the early development phases wherever sizable groundwater bodies are indicated.

Emphasis on groundwater ought not to blind us to the fact that surface and underground flows are but two phases of the total basin's flow and that intervention into one phase will, in time, affect the other. When sufficient information becomes available, we ought therefore to attempt to *optimize the combined use of both phases.* In the early phases we ought at least to remember the basic fact that the two phases are interdependent and interacting.

A combined and properly ordered and scheduled groundwater–surface water system will compound the advantages of both sources and will result in a low initial information threshold which will be retained until the very last phases of development. The economics of such a combination will also have extremely low sensitivity to errors in assumptions.

Land resources The specific aspects of soil classification and land use are of course beyond the scope of this book. What nevertheless needs emphasis in this context is that, once basic soil-classification and land-use data are available, the physical aspects of the natural-resources vector, i.e., soil, irrigation water, shallow groundwater, and climate, have to be treated as one interconnected system and not as separate issues that can be analyzed separately and for which separate solutions can be established. Treating these issues separately will result in ineffective and expensive solutions and may even lead to a complete breakdown of the system; the abandonment of large tracts of land in Pakistan, as a consequence of salinization, is an example of such a breakdown. The success of the remedial action based on a conceptual reintegration of the irrigation-drainage complexes proves that the crisis was due to lack of comprehensiveness in the original solution. Long-term management, extending to qualitative equilibria in the groundwater, will require a further expansion of comprehensiveness.

Where long-term experience is lacking, prediction of short-term and long-term equilibria of the soil-water-climate-crop system and of its transients and steady states will necessarily have to be tentative. Caution, flexibility, and the conscious adoption of a sequential decision process will minimize risks.

Climate Climatic factors, for the most part inaccessible to human intervention, will be treated as stochastic events, with some qualifications as to the future. Manipulation of climatic factors is in sight and will become more important as our knowledge of the relevant mechanisms increases. Successes so far achieved in cloud seeding, in evaporation reduction, and in increasing water yield from uncultivated areas, though still modest, are nevertheless promising.

The climatic factors taxonomy chosen for inventorying operations related to agricultural development planning ought to be operational and iterative—operational because we must confine ourselves to the factors most relevant to our planning purpose; iterative because we must make our major choices (such as irrigated or rain-fed farming) first and only afterward resort, on the basis of additional significant climatic inventory factors, to selection of crops, cultivation methods, etc.

The following principles of taxonomy suggested in Volume II of the Report of the President's Science Advisory Commission on the World Food Problem,[1] possibly modified or amplified according to the requirements of the program, might serve for the first general round of inventorying:

Temperature and available moisture are the two principal climatic factors that determine the agricultural and food production characteristics of the nearly 8 billion acres of arable land of the world. They determine either singly or in combination the number of months of the year during which food crops can be grown with reasonable certainty at acceptable levels of production. When temperature and moisture conditions are adequate for vegetative growth throughout the year, the ecological requirements for maximum food production are available. If low temperature or moisture deficit or both prevent or render plant growth very hazardous in an area, say for 4 months each year, the area would be classified as an 8-month agroclimatic region and designated as 8 M if the constraint is caused by moisture deficit or 8 T if low temperature is the limiting factor during the remaining four months.

CAPITAL RESOURCES

Our basic point of view is that of the sectorial planner who must make the best use of a sectorial allocation which is assumed to have been determined by an overall budgetary planning group. Thus, from the sectorial planner's viewpoint, capital resources at first sight represent an exogenous factor. This view will certainly be valid for the earlier years of a development program; if the sectorial planner takes a wider and more dynamic view of the capital-resources inventorying, it need not remain valid for the later years. It is to this, usually neglected, aspect of inventorying capital resources that this section will be devoted.

The capital resources for financing a sectorial development program may be subdivided, according to the origin of funds, into three categories:

1. Forced saving, i.e., funds raised by government internally through taxation, customs levies, etc., and allocated to the capital budget

[1] "The World Food Problem," *A Report of the President's Science Advisory Committee,* The White House, Washington, D.C., May, 1967, vol. II, p. 421.

2. Voluntary saving, i.e., funds saved by the individual or the corporation and invested either in his own means of production or, through banks, shares, etc., in other undertakings

3. Foreign capital raised bilaterally or through a regional or international funding agency

The kind of decisions taken at these three sources of capital regarding allocation to a sectorial program will largely depend on the image that the sector has built up through past performance as measured by achievement criteria which vary from agency to agency. A dynamic approach to inventorying capital resources would therefore consider decisions related to capital allocation receptive in some degree to achievement feedbacks from the programs. Achievement criteria applied by the agencies or groups controlling capital resources ought therefore to be included among the yardsticks applied for comparing alternative programs. In order to improve our financing image, and thereby increase capital resources for the later part of the forthcoming program or for subsequent programs, we might very well select a program which would improve the "external" image yet be less satisfying in terms of "internal" achievement criteria. In such cases, the benefits accruing in the course of the program from better availability of financial resources would have to compensate for the immediate loss in terms of the internal criteria. In other words, capital allocation should be considered a variable to be introduced into the development model before selecting the most satisfying alternative. Since each one of the three basic capital-resources categories might have different achievement criteria, different degrees of responsiveness to achievement feedbacks, and different ranges of potentially mobilizable capital, the three categories might have to be introduced into the model alternatively or in combination. Such inclusion of the dynamic aspects of capital resources in the analysis will rarely, if ever, lend itself to rigorous evaluation; this, however, should not deter us from considering them.

CURRENT PRODUCTION INPUTS

This resource category comprises all those resources which have to be mobilized currently in order to maintain a specific level of productivity in the agricultural production process. It might include, among others, improved seeds, fertilizers, plant-protection chemicals, soil conditioners, plastic coverings. These resources are either imported, in which case their availability is subject to limitations in the availability of foreign currency, or manufactured, partially or wholly, locally, in which case agricultural sectorial planning is interlinked with that of the relevant industrial sector.

Incorporation of current inputs into the production process presupposes the availability of an extensive infrastructural system, which is, in turn, dependent on the availability of the respective capital, human, and institutional resources. In the case of fertilizer inputs, this infrastructural system might, for instance, include intermediate storage, mixing, and distribution facilities. Making inputs available without the supporting infrastructure would seriously slow down their acceptance and reduce their effectiveness. Our program inventories ought, therefore, to include the resources required to set up the relevant supporting infrastructure in addition to the production inputs proper.

HUMAN RESOURCES

Taxonomy The basic operationally oriented taxonomy of human resources refers to their roles in the development process and distinguishes between developee and developer. Developees are the people who, together with the natural-resources complex and the institutional complex, constitute the natural-resources vector. Developers are the people who, operating within the framework of the relevant institutions, constitute that part of the development-resources vector whose task it is to upgrade the natural-resources vector.

From the point of view of the sectorial planner, the quantitative aspects of developee resources are an almost completely exogenous variable whose parametric values depend on demographic, general macroeconomic, and political factors. In the short run, the influence of alternative programs upon this inventory dimension will be minor; in the long run, however, this influence might become significant.

The principal items in the inventorying process of human resources of the developee type are basic demographic data (population, age structure, growth rates, migration), traditional social structure and its rigidity, literacy, and educational levels, responsiveness to incentives and to changes in production environment, and anticipated resistance complexes to change and innovation. Since developees are the most important part of the production complex, ways and means to improve their quality are usually mentioned in general development reports among the preconditions for effective development. However, the logistic side of upgrading the developee resource is usually lost sight of in the transposition of overall development programs into specific development projects and operations.

Regarding the developer resource, the inventorying process is rarely, if ever, applied systematically even at the general planning level. Most development programs assume that the developer resource is available, in sufficient quantity and of satisfactory quality, and that it is only the cash flows that need planning and programming. Consequently, upgrading of the developer resource is rarely elaborated in operational detail in specific projects. In contrast to this "official" attitude to the developer resource, most field workers agree that the inadequacy (both in numbers and quality) of the developer's resource is one of the two most important reasons for unsatisfactory progress, the other being inadequacies and instability of the political environment and decision process. This section will therefore focus on the developer resource.

Four aspects of inadequacy of the developer's resource For the purpose of setting up an inventory, we ought to study the developer's resource from four aspects:

1. Quantity, i.e., the number of available professionals and subprofessionals
2. Formal training, i.e., availability of training in the relevant techniques
3. Professional decision making, i.e., capacity (based on past on-the-job training) to make satisfactory decisions in the relevant professional fields
4. The motivational complex, i.e., need for achievement, perseverance, esprit de corps

Observation of the development process as practiced in the Third World since the Second World War indicates that the development-resources vector in general and its human-resources constituent especially are among the controlling aspects of the rate of growth. Apart from the political process, the measure of adequacy of the developer's resource, as expressed by the average levels related to the above four aspects, would constitute a reasonably characteristic yardstick to express the status and potential of a sector's development.

In countries that are in their initial development phases, the developer's resource will be found grossly inadequate in all four aspects. In countries with a short development history, inadequacies in numbers and formal training will be much less pronounced, the crippling inadequacies will be confined mainly to professional decision making and motivation. In countries approaching "takeoff," numbers and professional training might have reached satisfactory levels (in some cases even surpluses of professional manpower might have developed), professional decision making might have greatly improved (inadequacies being confined mainly to problem areas involving high-level abstraction), leaving only metaplanning and the motivational complex as unsatisfactory areas.

The initial inventorying process of the developer's resource ought to extend to all four aspects of the resource; the same applies of course to inventorying program requirements. The difference between program requirements and the initial inventory will indicate the deficit in numbers and quality. Since expansion and improvement of the developer's resource have a long lead time, human-resources aspects should be treated with a time horizon of, say, two development programs or more. Aspects 1 (numbers) and 2 (formal training) can be improved by setting up or expanding permanent or temporary formal training facilities and, if necessary, establishing incentives to use them. Aspect 3 will depend on the availability or the creation of successful projects with which to develop professional decision-making capacity and reinforce motivation. Aspects 3 and, especially, 4 are highly dependent on the availability of professional leadership elements to catalyze the relevant processes. Availability of professional leaders to serve as catalysts for the improvement of the last two aspects of the developer's resource ought therefore to be included as a fifth and extremely important aspect of the inventorying process. Since the operational facets of upgrading the developer's resource are covered in Chapters 3 and 24, we can now turn to the vexing question of allocation of the extremely scarce developer's resource to the numerous activities comprised in the development process.

Allocation of the developer's resources Human resources of the development-resources vector must be allocated among the following main areas of activities:

1. Collection and generation of information
2. Metaplanning covering both the interministerial and the intraministerial aspects of the program
3. Project planning and design and management of project implementation (the latter to include control of project implementation)
4. Operation, management, and maintenance of completed installations
5. Upgrading human resources in the development-resources vector

Farming out services to local or foreign private organizations might be an interim substitute for allocating local personnel to some of the activity areas, mainly area 3; cooperation with outside groups might help to bridge over initial personnel deficiencies in areas 2 and 5; the assistance of foreign specialists in areas 1 and 4, however, will be confined to establishing procedures and providing training.

An effective development process requires an appropriate number of professionals and subprofessionals in all five areas of activity. A serious deficiency (in quantity or quality) in any area will seriously jeopardize the whole sectorial development effort. Allocation as actually practiced is usually rather unbalanced, overemphasizing technical aspect 3 for which substitution happens to be easiest, insufficiently emphasizing data collection and operation and maintenance aspects 1 and 4, and practically neglecting metaplanning and personnel formation aspects 2 and 5. The reasons for this regrettable imbalance in allocation of human resources can be easily traced: the technical aspect (3), conspicuous and involved with funds, is the main line of interest of the political process, chances for promotion (dependent upon this process) are thus highest for professionals employed in this area; this aspect is also considered the most satisfying professionally, and it offers the greatest material opportunities. Data collection is usually considered a professional dead end removed from the main stream of the political and development process. Metaplanning is passed over because of failure to realize its significance and because of the lack of relevant training and methodology. The same applies to personnel formation. It is impossible to evade operation and maintenance activities, but these activities, for reasons similar to those quoted for data collection, are also starved for good personnel.

Improving the manpower balance among the main areas of activity is essential for improving the capacity and effectiveness of the development complex; the chances of success for such reallocation depend on our capacity to refashion the image of the neglected areas of activity, thereby inducing better professionals to choose them for their careers.

Collection and generation of information This area of activity does not attract talent even in developed countries; in underdeveloped countries it is looked down upon. The reason for the poor image of this activity area is its insufficient identification in the mind of the professional with the development effort: the better sort of professional who looks for motivation mainly in the professional aspects of his work feels that joining a data-collection group isolates him from the principal development effort. This feeling is strengthened in cases where the data-collection group is organizationally separated from the main development group, i.e., the group handling metaplanning and project planning. An operationally illogical organizational affiliation severs the vital tie between data collection and the respective development process. Data collection ceases to be based on operational hypotheses related to actual development requirements, loses its relevance, fails to produce the essential data, and instead proliferates information of secondary importance. This loss of focus on the relevant issues, in addition to greatly reducing the utility of the data-collection group, badly damages its image and thereby reduces its attractiveness for career selection.

Increasing the organizational distance between the development and the data-collection operations is often motivated by the desire to pool data-collection operations of similar nature and thereby more effectively use scarce professional resources.

However, loss of direct contact with development often proves costlier than gain of efficiency resulting from pooling—especially in underdeveloped countries. The image of data collection and generation can be improved by restructuring the operation itself and by integrating it within the development process as follows:

Data collection and generation are best placed within the respective development organization or close to it. The hypothesis underlying the data-collection program ought to be firmly rooted in the development program. The data-collection program ought to define specific information targets for specific development periods, these targets being related to the several information thresholds and requirements of the development program. When drawing up such targets, we should keep in mind that timely fragmentary information is preferable to exhaustive information after the decision. Procedures and criteria for data processing and for incorporating processed data into the development process ought to be established. Furthermore, a schedule ought to be drawn up to review periodically the relevance of the hypothesis underlying data collection and its related procedures.

To ensure the best use of the resources allocated to data collection and processing, we ought to aim at consistency between the various aspects of data collection. Information gathering ought not to be confined to "passive" data collection from existing operations, but ought also to comprise "active" data generation from experimental setups, pilot projects, etc., especially in relation to social and psychological factors. To supplement the "information import" of data resulting from direct (active and passive) data collection, we ought to develop correlations and analogies between related data series, e.g., complementation of direct flow records by synthetic records based on the rainfall-runoff relationship or on data from comparable basins.

Metaplanning This development operation requires the highest personal and professional qualifications: creativity and synthesis combined with logic and analysis; capability of high-level abstraction combined with a highly developed sense of reality; on the professional side, a fair knowledge of the disciplines involved (or at least of the most relevant variables and their interconnections) and a capacity to integrate them. Furthermore, methodologies, criteria, and routines have not yet been formalized and, except for general approaches and strategies, are probably not directly transferable from country to country.

No wonder, therefore, that metaplanning is an extremely neglected activity and one for which it is most difficult to develop personnel. Metaplanning personnel can apparently be developed only by job training within successful metaplanning operations, and metaplanning in turn requires specifically trained personnel that is not available.

Under such circumstances, metaplanning can be initiated by setting up a joint planning group consisting of trained foreign experts led by a generalist of high integrating capacity, and a national counterpart of personnel earmarked for the proposed metaplanning group. Initially, the foreign group might have to accept the professional responsibility and leadership. Gradually, one or more leaders will emerge from the national group and take control of the operation. (This subject is more fully covered in Chapters 3, 6, and 24.)

Project planning, design, and control of implementation To support the desirable rate of development, a fair amount of contracting of project-related services will have to be resorted to in the early phases of development. Where local professional firms are available, contracting might represent an acceptable permanent solution for most aspects of project-related services, leaving some specific aspects of management and control of implementation for direct handling by the staff of the development agency. Joint ventures between local and highly experienced foreign groups might be the solution for larger and more complex schemes or for projects requiring a high degree of specialization. Where competent local firms do not exist, project groups will have to be built up gradually within the development agencies. Such project groups could be initially deployed for smaller and simpler projects and in time be entrusted (possibly with some foreign support) with more ambitious ones.

Project aspects connected with transforming the sociopsychological and institutional dimensions of developees occupy a special position. Activities here must start during the early phases of development and must continue long after formal completion into the operation and maintenance period. Subcontracting these transformation operations is hardly feasible. As a consequence of the length of the transformation period, the number of such personnel required will sharply increase with time.

Operation, management, and maintenance Problems related to this type of activity are similar to those of personnel charged with transformation operations. Operation and maintenance will require ever-increasing numbers of permanent personnel. Recruitment of operation and maintenance personnel will also be confined mainly to the national manpower pool; the role of foreign manpower will as a rule be limited to assistance in establishing methods, procedures, controls, and criteria, except perhaps in the case of very large installations for which foreign shadow managers might be required for a limited initial period.

Upgrading the human-resources constituent Here we again face the basic quandary of development: how much of our resources should we allocate directly to development and how much to upgrading and increasing the human constituent of the development-resources vector. In countries still in their earliest development phases, the basic emphasis will be on increasing the number of professionals and subprofessionals; in countries that have made some progress, the question of upgrading existing human resources will also loom large. In the latter countries, manpower with formal professional qualifications is often in ample supply, but is frequently inexperienced in professional decision making and low in motivation. Upgrading operations here will have high priority and ought to be allocated sufficient resources. Upgrading targets ought to be carefully analyzed and broken down into specific operations and provisions for which intermediate targets ought to be defined and scheduled. Achievement control procedures, similar to those used for engineering operations, ought to be established to make proper follow-up possible.

20
SECTORIAL PLANNING IN TRADITIONAL AGRICULTURE

Many are stubborn in pursuit of the path they have chosen, few in pursuit of the goal.
NIETZSCHE

DIAGNOSIS

Development in the postwar years Agricultural development in the Third World during the past quarter of a century has been extremely disappointing. By the mid-sixties, the per capita agricultural product of many Third World countries barely rose above prewar levels; in many Latin-American and African countries it actually fell below these levels.[1] Poor as they are, aggregate growth-rate figures do not fully reflect the development picture: we must also consider distribution of production within a country and differences in product growth between the relatively advanced areas (or producer groups) and the retarded ones.

To the extent that data are available for Third World countries, the evidence indicates that the growth of the subsector of traditional farming has been considerably slower than the aggregate growth of the agricultural sector.

Flaws in development planning for traditional agriculture This inadequate growth, as well as its unsatisfactory distribution, may be attributed to low rates of investment and to poor project-implementation procedures. But these causes in themselves do not fully explain the disappointing agricultural growth rates of practically all Third World countries. Moreover, growth in the agricultural sector has been unsatisfactory even in countries where relatively high sectorial investment levels have been maintained for years and where project implementation has been reasonably satisfactory.

In order to explain the agricultural sector's unsatisfactory response to investment, we must postulate a structural defect in development thinking which in most countries is superimposed upon inadequate investment levels and implementation procedures. In Third World countries it is not sufficient to

[1] *The State of Food and Agriculture,* 1965, F.A.O., Rome, 1965.

raise investment levels, alter the composition of investments, and improve the quality of project implementation in order to initiate in the agricultural sector sustained growth processes essential for overall national development. To become fully effective, the underlying development thinking, planning approaches, and success criteria need to change.

The impossibility of converting, at a single stroke, an underdeveloped agricultural society into a modern, predominantly industrial one is now generally recognized. Such conversion is by necessity a gradual process, requiring that the maturing agricultural economy pass through consecutive intermediate stages. In each stage, aggregate agricultural production will continue to grow, though its relative contribution to the economy will gradually decline. In this context it should be realized that we are dealing with economies in their early development stages, economies in which the primacy of agriculture will still prevail and in which overall economic growth will largely depend on the maintenance of sustained and adequate growth rates in the agricultural sector. However, achievement of such growth rates in this sector may be the most complex and difficult of all the development tasks.

The nonagricultural sectors of emergent economies are rudimentary or nonexistent, and related institutional frameworks are embryonic. Innovation will therefore largely depend on disseminating imported and easily transferable know-how among a limited number of semiqualified to qualified local professionals. In the agricultural sector of these emergent economies, on the other hand, traditional production processes have operated for generations with inadequate inputs and within inadequate institutional frameworks. Innovation here cannot be confined to importing new production techniques. It must remove deeply ingrained obsolete response patterns and obsolete institutional structures, and it must reach the mass of often illiterate producers at the grass-roots level. More specifically, past development thinking reveals the following four basic inadequacies:

1. Fragmentary, arbitrary, and inconsistent nature of the planning process
2. Inflexibility and inappositeness of evaluation criteria
3. Institutional petrification and self-reinforcing mechanisms resulting from inappropriate yardsticks and criteria
4. Lack of insight, bias, and instability of the political decision process in relation to resources allocation

This chapter outlines distortions of the development process attributable to the first three factors, referring to the fourth only insofar as the political process can be indirectly influenced (in the required direction) by improved planning approaches and criteria. The basic thesis is that development failures are often due to incompatibilities in structure and complexity between planning and implementation methodologies and the socioeconomic space for which they are designed. That planning methodologies with similar incompatibilities have succeeded in mature economies does not, in our opinion, alter our thesis, since emergent economies require a much more complex development effort.

Piecemeal and systematic planning Planning approaches in developing countries vary along a continuum whose extreme poles are piecemeal planning and systematic planning. In piecemeal planning, the planner does not aspire to incorporate into his analysis all the relevant dimensions of his sectorial socioeconomic system or to weigh the merits of all the possible operations that could be applied to improve performance. His goal is much more modest: he will be satisfied to prove that some input—capital investment will be the usual choice—will lead to a short-term production benefit and that the relation of this benefit to the resources employed to achieve it complies with specific performance criteria.

The logic employed in this approach is faulty on the following two counts:

The Fallacy of Performance Analogy Let us suppose that a group of inputs, say, A, B, C, . . . , J have to be deployed in order to bring the desired state Q into being. In a mature economy, application of input A, within the existing socioeconomic structure, suffices to generate by spontaneous response of that structure inputs B, C, . . . , J; it is similarly inferred that in the emergent economies, provision of this input A to a radically different socioeconomic structure will also suffice to generate inputs B, C, . . . , J and to bring about the desired state Q.

The Fragmentary Nature of Performance Measurement The fact that a fragmentary aspect of project performance complies with a rather arbitrarily selected performance criterion—one usually related to a single dimension (generally, a criterion measuring short-term economic performance) of our multidimensional space—is taken as sufficient proof of the project's superiority and as sufficient justification for allocating extremely limited resources to such a project.

In the more elaborate version of the piecemeal approach, the sectorial investment program, alternative groupings of projects—aggregating the total sectorial capital allocation—are subjected to the same type of criteria. More often than not, the sum total of actually available plans will not exceed the sectorial capital allocation; in such cases ranking, properly speaking, will not be possible, and feasibility analysis will have to be limited to checking the compatibility of the performance of projects included in the program with the adopted performance criterion.

In contrast to the piecemeal approach, the systematic planning approach is based on an analysis of the complete set of interventions capable of improving the two basic aspects of the socioeconomic system, i.e., production and structure:

1. Improving the production aspect emphasizes interventions undertaken with a view to improving those outcomes which, in the short run, can be achieved by better utilization of the existing socioeconomic system. The type of interventions involved consists in the application of input mixes to a statically conceived socioeconomic structure with a view to improving production within this structure.

2. Improving the structural aspect emphasizes interventions undertaken with a view to improving those structural features on which the achievement of a more effective production process is dependent. The type of intervention involved is more dynamic in its nature and consists in the application of input mixes aimed primarily at modifying structure.

In reality, every input mix will, as a matter of course, have both static and dynamic effects; different mixes, however, will differ in the extent to which they affect the static or dynamic aspects of the system.

After comparing the benefits (expressed in short-run static production terms and long-run dynamic structural ones) of the alternative sets of inputs that can be deployed within prevailing resources constraints, the planner then selects the set that will result in the highest expected objective achievement (expressed in short-run and long-run benefits). The basic reasoning behind this systematic, comprehensive approach is that optimization of the benefits attainable for a given resources aggregate can be achieved only through comparison of the effectiveness of an exhaustive set of interventions both upon short-term production and long-term structural aspects of the socioeconomic system.

A shift from piecemeal to systematic planning is a necessary, though not a sufficient, condition for a satisfactory development program.

A sectorial program would have to pass two additional tests before it can be pronounced satisfactory: the test of convergence and the test of intersectorial adaptation. The purpose of the test of convergence is to check whether the selected program and continuing programs which will be similarly selected in the forthcoming planning periods do, in fact, lead to our long-term goals.

Program selection is, to a great extent, determined by the targets which we have set, by the constraints (relating to capital, talent, and the political decision process) which we have assumed to prevail, and by the interaction across the interface between the sectorial system and other sectors of the economy which we have posited. These three types of assumption will set limits to the possible performance of the sectorial system.

A program selected might represent a truly optimized utilization of available resources, while its outcomes might be so limited in their scope as to be insignificant from the point of view of national development. Such a program would comply with the requirements of an optimized program selection procedure, without, however, passing the test of convergence of development activity upon the nation's long-term goals. To improve convergence, we would have to go back to the basic assumptions of optimization, i.e., to goal setting (and trade-offs between goals), constraints, and intersectorial interaction, and modify these assumptions in the required direction. With these redefined assumptions, we would have to iterate the process of program selection.

The purpose of the test of intersectorial adaptation is to establish whether the services, decisions, and policies which the selected program will require from the other sectors of the economy or from the various branches of government will, in fact, become available, at times and at rates specified in the program. It might, for example, be found that the transportation sector will not be able to cope with the proposed increased flow of commodities created by an agricultural sectorial development program or that the economic incentives stipulated in the program are incompatible with government's economic thinking. To resolve these discrepancies between the selected sector and other sectors and between the sector and government, some metasectorial reconciliation would have to be undertaken which, in turn, might involve downgrading of the originally selected program and therefore reduction in its objective achievement.

Since both the test of convergence and the test of intersectorial adaptation transcend the subject matter of this book, no attempt will be made to spell out the complexities involved in these two additional tests. However, we shall have some additional comments of a general nature to make on this subject in the last chapter.

Support from the political decision process in the adoption and subsequent implementation of a comprehensive development plan is a complementary condition for success. This support will be most needed—and, generally, most difficult to marshall—in the first decisive phase of development, when great momentum is required to move the socioeconomic process related to traditional agriculture from its stable equilibrium. The comprehensive planning approach must allow for these difficulties, introducing modifications into the substance, phasing, and semantics employed so as to increase the political feasibility of the program.

The planning approach and productivity The decisive influence on agricultural productivity of comprehensive development planning is best illustrated by a comparison of productivities of countries (such as the first seven in the accompanying table) which have stressed expansion of area under irrigation (at the expense of other essential production inputs) with productivities of countries (such as Taiwan and Japan) which have adopted the balanced comprehensive input approach.

The table, quoted in Theodore Schulz's *Economic Crises in World Agriculture,* gives data on the agricultural productivity of nine Asian countries.

The difference between the first seven and the last two countries in the table is most certainly also due to a combination of factors; yet to explain a 1:8 to 1:4 yield gap we have to resort to the assumption that underlying differences in planning approaches have played a decisive role. The fact that recent changes in development methodology in parts of India, the Philippines, and Pakistan (such as the introduction, on a massive scale, of "miracle" rice varieties combined with adequate fertilizer application) have led to spectacular results only serves to bear out this assumption.

Evaluation procedures The piecemeal planning approach could not have retained its controlling position in development thinking if it had not been systematically reinforced over the years by evaluation procedures that tend to consolidate the negative implications of the approach rather than correct

FARM SIZE, PRODUCTION PER ACRE, AND PRODUCTION PER CAPITA OF THE RURAL SECTOR OF NINE ASIAN COUNTRIES

COUNTRY	*AVERAGE SIZE OF FARMS (ACRES)*	*PRODUCTION PER ACRE (DOLLARS)*	*AGRICULTURAL PRODUCTION PER CAPITA OF RURAL SECTOR (DOLLARS)*
Thailand	9.5	42	45
Phillippines	8.8	74	72
Burma	7.6	49	79
Cambodia	5.6	48	47
India	5.4	33	39
Pakistan	4.2	55	54
Indonesia	3.3	60	38
Taiwan	3.1	279	114
Japan	2.1	274	102

Source: Lester R. Brown, *An Economic Analysis of Far Eastern Agriculture,* Foreign Agriculture Economic Report no. 2, U.S. Department of Agriculture, November, 1961.

them. This refers both to the evaluation criteria adopted by the political process in underdeveloped countries and to those stipulated by the principal funding agencies.

The basic achievement criterion adopted by the political decision process is volume of activity; the basic reasoning applied is: activity leads to development, development to production; therefore, the more activity, the more production. Economic performance criteria, e.g., benefit cost and rates of internal return, to the extent that they are applied, represent lip service to formal loan requirements of funding agencies.

Unbiased analysis of the criteria and the evaluation procedures actually employed by many development agencies in emerging economies would undoubtedly reveal that the true purpose of evaluation is to make the adopted planning approaches immune from criticism, i.e., to make them test-proof, rather than—as a naïve observer might have assumed—to weigh the relative merits of various approaches for achieving specific predetermined objectives.

To achieve this feat of "test-proofing," a criterion is dragged into the evaluation which, although not directly relevant to the manifest development objectives, still possesses some positive connotations. For example, the scope of investment may be used as a yardstick of development achievement. An unsubstantiated afterthought may be added to the effect that such investment, through the operation of unspecified processes, will initiate additional production.

The danger of adopting criteria which do not reflect the real achievement of objectives is twofold: we fail to realize that we are off the right course and are strengthened in continuing on the wrong course, for even a badly conceived project evaluated by the adopted criteria will appear to be a step in the right direction.

The institutional implications of applying irrelevant criteria are especially damaging. In judging the merits of competing agencies, application of irrelevant criteria could, for instance, lead to the conclusion that the agency which develops a forte for capital investment is the successful one. This agency is then allocated increasing volumes of capital and consequently continues to gain prestige and status, again and again attracting scarce capital and human resources, thereby further accentuating the imbalance of resource allocation. At the same time, the performance of those agencies responsible, according to the formal organization chart, for generating the complementary inputs needed to bring the investment portion of the project to its full fruition falls behind that of their investment counterparts. These agencies fall behind because of the greater complexity of their task, their greater dependence on coordination, and the absence of conspicuous features by which to measure short-term performance. They will be viewed as less able to use their budgetary allocations and consequently will get smaller capital allocations, will lose status and image, and will fail to attract motivated and trained personnel.

Evaluation procedures of funding agencies for investment projects usually apply to specific projects, and attention is generally focused on investment aspects and economic feasibility. Complementary aspects may also be reviewed, but proof of logistic and institutional feasibility is not always insisted upon.

In order to ensure that the scarce resources of developing countries are used to initiate the most rapid growth feasible, the systematic planning approach should, among other things, adopt criteria and evaluation procedures which are compatible with this approach; such criteria and procedures should be designed with the object of creating a self-reinforcing feedback in the right direction, a feedback that would reinforce growth stimulation and restrain expenditures which are not directly growth oriented. These criteria should be applied both to capacity factors, i.e., those relating to long-run structural improvements, and to direct short-run improvement of production.

Evaluation procedures, if they are to fit the complexity of the phase space of traditional agriculture, must be interdisciplinary and dynamic; they must specify all the inputs and interventions required, their sequence and phasing, their expected outcomes and interaction, and the anticipated logistic bottlenecks and ways to overcome them. In other words, *structural transformation operations,* in spite of their incomparably greater complexity and lesser predictability, *must be given the same detailed and systematic treatment as is given to engineering operations.* The assumption that the major weaknesses of underdeveloped economies are structural, that these weaknesses extend over most of the socioeconomic system, and that elimination of these weaknesses is essential for overcoming underdevelopment leads us to the conclusion that evaluation of alternative programs must encompass the structural effects of these programs, as well as their direct production effects.

Since it is postulated that the basic transformation—on which the generation of sustained growth processes is conditional—does not evolve spontaneously in underdeveloped countries, complete development programs must fully specify the nature and scope of the transformations needed and the interventions required to achieve them. Evaluation criteria will have to be developed to assess the effectiveness of these interventions in achieving the necessary transformation objectives. Operative procedures should be developed for formulating such criteria and for ranking programs accordingly.

The formulation of such evaluation criteria will gradually change the development process in the following ways:

1. It will lead to a more rational selection of programs.
2. By comparing and evaluating all the relevant input-output ratios of the alternative resources packages, it will lead to the identification of those interventions which have the highest relevance to attainment of specified objectives. This will lead to a greater emphasis of the nonmaterial development dimensions.
3. Through such change of emphasis, it will generate a negative feedback stream which will, in the short run, bring about a better allocation of resources among the agencies responsible for the various aspects of development.
4. As a consequence of the above, it will, in the long run, initiate a positive circle of causation that will lead to better adaptation of organization and planning to the true needs of a country.
5. This process will, in turn, leave its imprint upon the political structure.
6. The structural changes referred to in 3, 4, and 5 will lead to improvement of planning.

Outline of a new approach The weaknesses of prevailing planning, evaluation, and selection approaches are now generally recognized; there also exists a concensus on the type of reorientation that will have to be applied in order to overcome these weaknesses. Gunnar Myrdal in his *Asian Drama*[2] has put strong emphasis on this reorientation, which he refers to as the "institutional approach." Many academic and executive groups have reached similar conclusions, and the following recent statement may be regarded as representative: "The planning, authorization, and operation of irrigation projects should reflect the necessity for providing not only water but all the inputs and processes that are required if the high costs of irrigation projects are to be optimized in increasing agricultural productivity."[3]

This change of climate in development thinking has also found partial expression in a number of informal modifications to funding requirements lately introduced by the major development financing agencies. However, this change in thinking has not yet been applied on a significant scale to project planning executed by or on behalf of developing countries, except perhaps for

[2] Gunnar Myrdal, *Asian Drama*, Pantheon Books, a division of Random House, New York, 1968.

[3] "The World Food Problem," *A Report of the President's Science Advisory Committee*, The White House, Washington, D.C., May 1967, vol. I, p. 28.

projects related to the introduction of the new wheat, corn, and rice varieties (see page 272).

The present chapter represents an attempt to outline a methodology for comprehensive planning and evaluation. It is hoped that the methodology described is conceived at a sufficiently high level of abstraction to cover all important aspects of the problem and their interconnection and yet that it is sufficiently realistic to allow for the lack of information, institutional infirmities, and other weaknesses of planning and implementation agencies actually found in developing countries.

THE SECTORIAL DEVELOPMENT PROCESS

The planner of the agricultural sector in a developing country operates under two basic handicaps:

1. Inadequacy of the development-resources vector, i.e., of the tools of operation with which the development task is carried out
2. Inadequacy of the natural-resources vector, i.e., of the object of development

The term development-resources vector is broadly synonymous with development agencies and the resources they can muster. The term natural-resources vector comprises the individual farmer and the natural agro-resources with which he operates. (Both these terms are defined in greater detail in the next section.) In underdeveloped countries the natural-resources vector is extremely sluggish in generating spontaneous improvements in the production environment and in responding to improvements provided by the development-resources vector.

The task of the development planner with reference to the natural-resources and development-resources vectors is both static and dynamic. The static aspect in relation to the development-resources vector consists in allocating existing capacity to specific development tasks; the dynamic aspect consists in defining and locating the critical weaknesses of the vector and diverting part of the vector resources to operations and projects to overcome them. Similar considerations apply to the natural-resources vector. Here the static aspect of development is related to improving the production environments and current inputs to be used by the existing producer; the dynamic aspect relates to transformation of the producer and his institutions.

The *static* aspect of development will depend mainly on the availability of *capital* resources, with human resources playing a secondary role; deficiencies in human resources can here be largely remedied by importing personnel. The *dynamic* aspects of development, on the other hand, involve mainly the deployment of *human* resources, with capital resources playing a secondary role. The role of imported human resources will be limited to catalyzing new attitudes and responses.

When planning his interventions, the planner will, of course, bear in mind the diversity in development levels that often exists within the same sector. In extreme cases, agriculture within the same country may vary all the way from a fully matured to a traditional underdeveloped sector. In such situations, the application of a comparable input package to the mature and the underdeveloped subsectors will, because of the great differences in adequacy of response, result in very different production outcomes.

Growth in underdeveloped economies will greatly depend on dynamic transformation; this is even more true in the case of developed economies. Such transformation will in turn hinge on the availability and quality of human resources within the framework of the development-resources vector.

Wherever underdevelopment prevails, the human-resources part of the development-resources inventory will be critically short. This basic fact must therefore be allowed for in the preliminary phases of planning, i.e., in establishing main planning strategies. It should induce the planner to look out especially for projects which, while resulting in the best outcomes per unit of critically short human resources applied, still make efficient use of the other less critical but still extremely scarce resources such as capital.

PROGRAMS, PROJECTS, AND DEVELOPMENT INPUTS

A project is a self-sustained viable set of interrelated discrete interventions initiated by the development-resources vector with a view to achieving specific targets, mainly related to specific production complexes, but possibly also having important spillover effects to other parts of the socioeconomic system.

An intervention, in turn, is the deployment of a set of interrelated and mutually supporting resources inputs aimed at achieving one of the partial tasks that enter into the project target.

Project targets can be classified as belonging to one or to a combination of the following three categories:

1. To increase *production* and improve income *distribution* by relying mainly on the existing natural-resources and development-resources vectors. Some transformation of these vectors will, of course, take place in any case, but it will be a by-product of the development process.
2. To *transform* and upgrade the *natural-resources vector;* this target is usually combined with the improvement of the production and income-distribution target mentioned under 1.
3. To *transform* the *development-resources vector;* this target is usually part of a program comprising also target categories 1 and 2.

A program is an interrelated set of projects selected with a view to achieving, within the framework of broad national objectives, and subject to prevailing political, institutional, and resources constraints, direct economic and social benefits and indirect transformation benefits.

The inventory of the development-resources vector is the complete set of inputs at the disposal of the development agency for incorporation in the program. Inputs may be increased in volume and quality by special input-generating and upgrading projects and as a result of the learning function inherent in the development process; the development-resources inventory has, therefore, to be conceived on dynamic lines.

The institutional framework (including its respective role occupants) within which development programs are initiated, approved, planned, and implemented and the inventory of development resources available for development are here referred to as the development-resources vector.

The term natural-resources vector is introduced to signify the following:

1. The individual producer, i.e., the farmer, his social conditioning, belief system, experience

2. His physical production environment, i.e., soil, climate, water, and the permanent facilities connected with soil and water application and conservation such as irrigation, drainage, erosion control, and land-preparation facilities

3. The production complexes, i.e., the crops grown, the current production inputs and operations applied, and the methods, tools, and equipment used for such input applications

4. The local (village, county, and regional) institutions supporting the farmer in his economic activities

We can now redefine a program as the detailed spelling out of a purposeful deployment by the development-resources vector, in self-sustained but interrelated packages termed projects, with a view to improving both output and growth capacity of the natural-resources vector, while simultaneously upgrading the development-resources vector.

The deployment of the development-resources vector upon the natural-resources vector has two principal aspects:

1. Investment, i.e., incorporation of inputs into the natural-resources vector to improve the physical production environment, the human resources operating within it, and their supporting institutions. Investment in physical facilities enriches the variety of the response environment; similarly, investment in human and institutional resources enriches the response variety of the producer to the improved response environment; concurrent improvement of response environment and response capacity will lead to improved production complexes.

2. Current provision of improved production inputs represents a complementary operation to investment and comprises all those inputs which have to be provided in order to sustain an effective production complex. These inputs will again be partly material (e.g., fertilizers, seeds, and pesticides) and partly nonmaterial (e.g., techniques, skills, and incentives). Ultimately, most current production inputs will again lead to permanent investment (to produce these inputs) and current production inputs of the second degree (raw materials and services necessary to produce these inputs).

The parallel deployment of the inventory of development resources within the development-resources vector will lead to a similar subdivision:

1. Investment type of resources used to effect a permanent improvement in the quantity and quality of human resources and their institutional structure

2. Current inputs to make possible the planning process proper—here represented by information and communication

The development-resources inventory available to the planner can be subdivided into two basic categories: capital and human resources. Capital resources are derived mostly from the national economy at large or from foreign economies which, directly or indirectly (e.g., through international agencies), are willing to lend or give money to economically underprivileged countries. Part of the capital resources will, however, originate with the farmer; the farmer's share in capital resources may be assumed to increase with economic maturation. The human resources are at the disposal of the planner and are intended to operate upon both vectors.

The three basic categories of project targets mentioned above (see page 277) correspond to three types of "investment" of human inputs:

1. Investment in the permanent physical features of the natural-resources vector, i.e., data collection, planning, engineering, agronomy, and related disciplines; construction of engineering works related to the improvement of soil resources and of availability of water; contract supervision and management; and operation and maintenance.
2. Investment in the transformation of human resources and institutions of the natural-resources vector. "First-degree" human resources acting directly on the farmer and his institutions (to be referred to as "first-degree transformation inputs") are here required.
3. Investment in the transformation and amplification of the development-resources vector. For this operation, "second-degree" human resources, i.e., trainers of trainers, will be required ("second-degree transformation inputs"). A limited volume of "third-degree" resources, which will be called the "catalyst," will have to supplement first- and second-degree resources to provide the necessary overall orientation, induce the emergence of necessary local leadership elements, strengthen motivation and perseverance, and generally induce a stronger achievement orientation.

GOAL SETTING

Goal setting is a complex and puzzling phenomenon that will be mainly influenced by the following three interconnected factors:

1. The time horizon which we adopt
2. The relative emphasis on production and capacity aspects
3. Political bias for a specific economic sector, region, or producer group

The longer the time horizon that we choose to adopt, the more readily will the paramount importance of transformation be conceived, and the more emphasis will there be on long-term (i.e., mainly capacity) aspects of development. A dynamically conceived development program realizing the significance of transformation of existing capacity ought therefore to select long-time horizons. On the other hand, as we move into the future, uncertainty as to changes of political attitudes, technological innovation, intersectorial influences, cumulative errors in assumptions, etc., will increase disproportionally. We have therefore to confine planning to a manageable stretch of the time dimension. As development unfolds, and as we approach the initially selected time boundary, we should renew our analysis for the remaining stretch of time against the background of an extended time horizon, thereby reducing the unavoidable distortion of analysis for the period close to the original horizon ("rolling" time horizon).

The longest period of goal setting for which we can make a meaningful analysis in this era of rapid technological and sociopolitical change appears to be a sequence of three to four planning periods, i.e., fifteen to twenty years. Such a time span is sufficiently long to make possible the analysis of long-term trends and changes, and yet not long enough to introduce an excessive number of conjectural elements. The goal-setting complex applying to such a time span will be referred to as the "national development aims."

Already at this first, generalized phase of goal setting, we are faced by the basic semantic difficulty that dogs us throughout our analysis of goal setting. The limitations of language and the related limitations in our reasoning constrain us to use a two-valued logic, although we well realize that such a polarizing, dialectic classification is an artificial mutilation of the many-valued development process. The two poles of our long-term goal setting are content and structure, or more specifically production and capacity. Production represents here the short-run outcome of development conceived within a static framework; capacity, the long-run outcome of a gradual transformation process, leading to potential increases of future production.

If we could reliably correlate every intervention with its respective production and capacity effect, and if we had sufficient parametric information on the time series of future production that would result from every specific change of capacity, we could express capacity in terms of future production. Such information, however, will rarely be available in the early phases when we have to put greatest emphasis upon capacity development. Thus, the dualism introduced by the production-capacity dichotomy is a consequence of our ignorance rather than of a basic structural dichotomy.

In actual development, every concrete intervention affects both content and structure, production and capacity; the proportion of the two basic effects, however, varies from intervention to intervention, project to project, program to program, and society to society.

In nonauthoritarian political regimes it is rarely possible to arrive at detailed and concrete development programs on the basis of a generalized study of a fifteen- to twenty-year period. It might not even be desirable to do so, since the full implications of adopting a specific long-term line of action might not be clearly predictable in the early stages of analysis. By adopting too rigid a long-term strategy before evaluating its results as measured in a concrete medium-term program, a dogmatic attitude might develop, one which could readily entrench itself.

Long-term strategies of the type described here have been adopted by the communistic countries in their early development phases. Once adopted, they have tended to become inflexible, contributing to dogmatism in development thinking.

Long-term analysis best serves its purpose when used to produce a general and flexible strategy to orient concrete development planning for program periods of, say, four to six years. The main purpose of such strategies would be to serve as a "true north" to test the "compass bearing" of medium-term programs, i.e., their convergence upon the national development aims.

In focusing upon a specific medium-term program, we have to transpose generalized national development aims into more specific medium-term program objectives. The basic dichotomy remains the same: allocation of resources between short-term product and long-run capacity. However, in a medium-term program the dichotomy exists at a more concrete level: what portion of the development resources ought to be allocated to the human constituents of the natural-resources and the development-resources vectors and what portion to the physical constituents of the natural-resources vector. Allocation to the former will be inherently more capacity oriented, allocation to the latter more production oriented. Different programs will result in different shares to production and capacity in both vectors.

In terms of resources allocation to the *development*-resources vector, the dichotomy is whether to generate projects rapidly by commissioning plans from outside organizations (production emphasis) or to execute all or most planning work within the agency and thereby improve the agency's capacity (capacity emphasis).

The product-capacity dichotomy with reference to allocation to the *natural*-resources vector will find its expression mainly in different shares of resources allocation to different producer groups: it may emphasize either producer groups with relatively developed capacity (production orientation) or producer groups with lagging capacity (capacity orientation). Emphasis upon different regions is in many cases equivalent to emphasis upon specific producer groups.

More specifically, the production-oriented "economic" emphasis might be represented by stressing short-term aggregate production and improvement of the balance of trade by import substitution and expansion of exports. The capacity-oriented "social" emphasis will stress a wider distribution of new means of production and employment and, as a result of both, a wider distribution of added income.

Since the structurally less developed producer groups happen also to be the socially underprivileged, the product-capacity dichotomy of development aims can be transposed into a dichotomy of emphasis on social orientation. Emphasis may be upon increasing the aggregate product by allocating development resources to the (high-capacity) socially privileged producers or, alternatively, stressing resources allocation to the (low-capacity) socially underprivileged producers. The first alternative is "economically" and the second "socially" oriented. However, when switching from the relatively short-term point of view of analysis of a single program to the long-term view of analysis of a program sequence, this dichotomization will lose most of its bite.

If sufficient resources are channeled their way, the low-capacity producer groups will eventually, through subsequent structural changes, increase their capacity and become high producers.

The changes in the distribution of means of production and income resulting from allocation emphasis upon low-capacity producer groups will also change the demand profile of the economy: since additional income will accrue to the lower level income groups, the higher income elasticity of the demand at lower income levels for the cheaper agricultural products and simpler industrial products and services will favor expanding production of these commodities. Resources allocation in agriculture favoring wider distribution of the added income, by adding momentum to the growth of the demand for agricultural products, will generate a secondary development incentive whose ramifications will be far reaching. They will affect the balance of trade, employment, marginal propensity to save, and, finally, the political and institutional structure of the nation.

The dichotomy between "economic" and "social" orientations proves ultimately to be a short-sighted oversimplification. It stems from attempting to measure long-term effects by short-term yardsticks that are not sufficiently sensitive to register the initially low amplitudes of long-term changes. Nevertheless, the economic-social orientation dichotomy still has its usefulness in underlining the anticipated differences in short-term economic effects of alternative programs. The aggregate of short-term and long-term economic effects of alternative programs representing different emphasis upon economic and social criteria will depend on numerous factors and will usually not be fully quantifiable. It will not be possible to quantify the indirect political and institutional repercussions which might represent the most important effects of a specific emphasis. Thus, greater stress on so-called social criteria ought not to be interpreted as implying lower economic effectiveness as expressed in present worth of future production streams.

Because of the extreme diversity of economic, social, and political factors in the various developing economies, it is impossible to specify a generally valid ratio between resources allocation oriented toward production and capacity, respectively. However, underdevelopment implies structural similarities which lead to common constraints, and these in turn suggest widely applicable typical strategies and tactics:

1. In economies with a negative trade balance, foreign currency might be the critical input for financing development. In such cases improvement of the trade balance will usually be given priority over other objectives. Often this will imply emphasis on production, and especially on production which does not depend on major investments in foreign currency.

2. Production and capacity orientation make different demands on capital and human resources. Production orientation will generally be more capital intensive, while capacity orientation, involving more transformation in the human and institutional dimensions, will be more intensive in the use of trained human resources. In most countries of the Third World, availability of appropriately trained human resources of the first, second, and third degrees, rather than economic considerations, will control the logistic feasibility of emphasis on capacity.

3. The influence upon saving of varying emphasis in allocating resources to production or capacity has not yet been fully investigated. It may be conjectured that greater emphasis on production will often tend to increase the incomes of middle and higher income groups who are characterized by a relatively high propensity to save, thus generating relatively high saving, but it would usually also increase the wages of landless agricultural laborers who generally have a low propensity to save. Emphasis on capacity aspects, though increasing incomes predominantly in the lower income groups, would still create opportunities for the small farmer to invest his savings attractively in his own production complexes. It might therefore result in a higher propensity to save than would be attributed to the income level of the farmer. However, this type of small-scale savings might prove difficult to measure.

4. Emphasis on capacity invariably carries political implications. Underdeveloped countries are characterized by an extremely skewed distribution of income which is reflected by a similarly skewed distribution of political power. Gradual democratization of the political process and the advance of socially oriented thinking in some of the authoritarian regimes will militate against this economic and political skew. This change of attitude might in the beginning find its expression merely in political rhetoric, but it will gradually gather momentum, even in a completely authoritarian political regime (e.g., a military dictatorship). Improving the distribution of new income will act toward reducing both the economic and the political skew. In the long run, no nation can resign itself to leaving a considerable portion of the population (in some cases the majority) permanently on the margin of the market economy. Cybernetically speaking, this would be equivalent to letting a significant part of a main system operate as an almost closed subsystem, without being subject to major impulses from the former and without being able to emit significant impulses into it. Unless remedied, the gap between the main and the subsystem will rapidly widen, and the subsystem might reach a runaway condition that might result in a most destructive impact upon the main system. Gradual integration of the subsystem into the whole and the establishment of mutual regulative loops between the subsystem and the main system might represent the most "economical" way of avoiding a complete system breakdown.

5. Even after having decided on the allocation between production and capacity orientation, another major dichotomy has to be resolved which partially cuts through our production-capacity dichotomy. Should we direct most of our limited resources to massive investment in improving the permanent features of a narrow sector of the production environment (e.g., the construction of major irrigation facilities), or should we give precedence to a selected set of inputs that would ensure the maximum return on a broad sector of the development front? In more concrete terms, the dichotomy in dry climates might read: should we spend our resources predominantly on expanding the irrigated area or on increasing yields of areas already provided with irrigation facilities? Transposed into humid climates, the dichotomy might be expansion of cultivated areas as against increasing productivity of areas already under cultivation.

The answer to these questions for every individual case will, of course, depend on a concrete quantitative analysis. In many underdeveloped countries, considerations of a *logistic* type will play a decisive role: investments focusing on intensification of existing irrigation and dry farming will often require a larger proportion of trained human resources from the development-resources vector than comparable investments in expansion of irrigation and cultivated areas. Where human resources are the limiting factor, the scope of intensification might therefore be strictly limited by logistic considerations.

Speaking generally, and on a program rather than on a project scale, it appears that emphasis will in the future have to shift from expansion to intensification. The President's Science Advisory Committee Report on "The World Food Problem" stresses that under most conditions irrigation is an expensive means of improving the physical production environment.[4]

The report further estimates that during the period 1965–1985, a total worldwide investment of 20 billion dollars would be required to construct the manufacturing facilities for providing the current production inputs necessary to double the Third World's food production. Fertilizers alone would require investment of 17 billion dollars, the remaining principal items being seeds, pesticides, and farm machinery. The annual cost to farmers of these improved inputs will amount, by 1985, to approximately 14 billion dollars.

In comparison to these high, but certainly attainable, figures, the report quotes an estimated low investment in new irrigation (applicable only to very large projects and under very favorable conditions) of $300 per acre ($750 per hectare). At present about 400 million acres are under irrigation, about 80 percent of which are in the developing countries. Thus, allocation of 20 billion dollars (the investment required for constructing facilities to produce the complementary inputs for doubling Third World food production during the 1965–1985 period) would not be sufficient to increase irrigation significantly in the developing nations. Annual cost of investments in irrigation would, of course, be relatively much lower than that for equal investment in input producing industries.[5]

When comparing these figures, we also have to bear in mind the following facts:

1. Investments in manufacturing facilities for complementary inputs could to a great extent be financed by private capital from the developed countries; investments in irrigation will have to be provided mainly by state funds from both the developed and the underdeveloped nations.

2. Complementary inputs facilities have very short lead times and, once established, can build up production to full capacity within a few years at most; irrigation facilities, on the other hand, have notoriously long lead times and gestation periods.

[4] "The World Food Problem," The White House, Washington, D.C., 1967, vol. II, p. 408.
[5] *Ibid.*, chaps. 6 and 7.

3. The large-scale acceptance of complementary inputs is, in any case, a precondition for an economical irrigation project.

To the extent that it is agroclimatically possible, therefore, introduction of current production inputs ought to precede that of costly irrigation.

PROGRAM TARGETS

Program targets are the quantified transposition of program objectives within medium-term contexts; target achievement is measured by the yardsticks selected for program objectives. Targets will thus be related to production aspects, such as increase of aggregate product, improvement of distribution of newly created incomes, improvement of the balance of trade, and to capacity aspects, such as transformation effects, human resources of the first, second, and third degree, information, and demonstration loops.

Optimization of a program will require the selection of trade-offs expressing the relative utilities of the various targets. In most cases, it will be difficult, perhaps impossible, to determine trade-offs in abstract terms at the outset of the planning process. Although operation with alternative trade-offs will complicate the planning process, this difficulty should be accepted. A planning process operating with alternative trade-off ratios will delay the decision on trade-offs until alternative outcomes, related to alternative trade-off ratios, can be presented in terms meaningful to the political decision maker. Selecting from a number of alternatives of a specific program implies, of course, adopting the corresponding trade-off ratios. Such selection, however, is made at a point of the planning process where the decision maker can compare concrete outcomes in politically meaningful terms, rather than ratios between abstract objectives.

According to the planning approach outlined above, only general objectives, related to predicted internal and external demand for sectorial products, ought to be laid down as guidelines at the outset of program planning. The determination of specific and concrete targets, as well as more detailed elaboration of demand forecast, ought to be left to the later stages of program planning.

The comparative achievements of alternative sets of projects can best be presented in an objective space with as many dimensions as the program has objectives. In this multidimensional space every program will be represented by a point signifying the several objective achievements of the program. The envelope line (for a two-dimensional space) or surface (for a three-dimensional one) that would be formed by programs of high performance will represent the "frontier." The programs below this frontier need not be considered in the comparison, since their objective achievement is lower than that of the respective program on the frontier. Thus, the program that in a two-dimensional target achievement space has the highest achievement of objective B (represented on the Y axis) for a certain range of achievement of objective A (represented on the X axis) would be the frontier program for this range of A. Such preselection would leave a limited number of alternative programs for a narrower choice. This choice will of course be governed by explicit or implicit trade-off ratios between objectives and by logistic, informational, and institutional constraints.

The actual choice may still further be narrowed down by a more detailed scrutiny of the frontier. Staying with a two-dimensional objective space, the frontier curve will in certain ranges show relatively large gains in objective A at low loss in objective B and, vice versa in the opposite range, small gains of objective A will require a great sacrifice in objective B. For obvious reasons these extreme parts of the frontier curve may be excluded from further analysis. This will limit actual options to be submitted to the political decision maker to a relatively limited part of the frontier curve on which trade-off ratios between objectives vary within a significant range.

The projects that will enter into a sectorial program of agricultural development can be subdivided into two main groups, according to the controlling orientation: those aimed at the natural-resources vector and those aimed at the development-resources vector.

The first group, again, will include:

1. Projects that aim mostly at improving the physical production environment, i.e., irrigation, drainage, soil conservation and preparation, without specific provisions for improving the response patterns of the developee and his institutions to the new production environment, i.e., by relying mainly on spontaneous "learning"
2. Projects that will provide, in addition to the above, complementary production and transformation inputs and thus basically transform the physical and human aspects of the production complex
3. Projects that will provide predominantly complementary inputs (current production and transformation inputs) to areas where such inputs can effectively and economically raise productivity without having to provide major capital-intensive improvements to the physical production environments or to areas where such improvements have been fully or partially provided by earlier programs

The second project category aimed at expanding and improving the development-resources vector will include projects related to manpower resources required for purely professional planning tasks, to those connected with direct transformation of the production vector (transformation inputs of the first degree), and to those connected with amplification of transformation capacity (transformation inputs of the second degree).

LIMITATIONS OF PROGRAM SYNTHESIS

To ensure the selected program's best use of available resources, the project population introduced into the evaluation procedure must include the most attractive projects. This entails defining by a scanning procedure an exhaustive list of projects and preselecting those which prima facie appear most attractive and thereby merit more thorough study and evaluation. This again will necessitate defining all building blocks of potential projects, i.e., all the potential interventions that could, now or in the future, be applied to the natural-resources and development-resources vectors. It is proposed to call the totality of these potential interventions, their possible combinations and outcomes, the field of potential development, or for short, "development field."

Except for extremely limited development contexts, it will be impossible to define fully the development field of a developing nation. This feat will also not be easy, perhaps not even possible, in the developed world. An exhaustive definition of the development field encounters the following difficulties:

1. Lacunae in our knowledge of the physical aspects of the natural-resources vector and of the response of crops to existing or improved production environments
2. Lacunae in our knowledge of the human and institutional constituents of the natural-resources vector and their potential transformation
3. Lacunae in our knowledge of the human, institutional, and political constituents of the development-resources vector and their anticipated response (at present and in the future) to transformation inputs of the second and third degrees
4. The influence of timing and sequence of most transformations operations upon outcomes and the resulting additional proliferation of variety
5. Difficulties in predicting long-term trends of technological development and, connected with these difficulties, uncertainty as to future resources-outcome ratios and, generally, to the composition of the resources base of the production complexes relevant to our planning
6. Limitations in the quantity and quality of the manpower that is, or ought to be, available for the planning of sectorial programs, and limitations in the leadership necessary to provide integration

In many underdeveloped countries the "population" of eligible projects for which a reasonable amount of backing-up information is available (say, at the level of "feasibility reports") is smaller than could be accommodated within the sectorial capital allocation. In such (not infrequent) situations every project that complies with the generally slack funding requirements of the country or agency is executed.

It will be difficult to remedy this situation rapidly: expanding and improving the planning and decision capacity of the development-resources vector in a developing country is a notoriously slow process. Nor will the commissioning of planning services always solve the problem, since they require a strong and sophisticated backing-up force. The appropriate solution therefore appears to be a planning process which, while adapted to the structural weaknesses and limitations of the development-resources vector, promises a reasonably close approximation to an optimized program. In such a planning process, the main emphasis would be on generating a reasonably exhaustive "basket" of eligible projects rather than on refining evaluation procedures. For it will usually be more important to have marshaled most of the eligible choices than to apply sophisticated selection procedures to a very limited and arbitrarily assembled project population.

NECESSITY OF SCANNING

Since we cannot fully circumscribe a development field, we shall have to reduce the scope of synthesis by introducing a variety absorber which, while reducing the scope of analytical operations, will not appreciably degrade the quality of selection. The arbitrary selection of projects which is generally in use at present in setting up sectorial investment programs does, of course, imply variety absorption; however, the absorption principle applied is an arbitrary one. If we want to maintain a reasonably good "catch" of attractive potential projects, we should introduce a variety-absorption principle that will constitute a valid type of *preselection*. Such a preselection principle introduced into our scanning process would have to ensure that only the more attractive alternatives "pass the mesh" of preselection and be available for further evaluation. Attractiveness in this context will, of course, be related to the degree of achievement of program objectives.

The scanning process will consist of a number of passes, each characterized by the application to the development field of a screening operation of different "mesh configurations"; at this initial phase the development field will still be conceived in generalized and abstract terms. Each scanning pass will lead to the discarding of specific parts of the development field, which it is proposed to call "domains," and the preselection of other domains, which it is proposed to call "preferential domains," which comply sufficiently with program objectives to make projects within these domains prima facie potentially eligible for inclusion in the project population.

The basic difference between the prevailing planning approach and the procedure proposed here is one of variety generation and of orientation of variety absorption. The planner using the conventional approach, although vaguely sensing the vastness of the planning field and the size of the potential project population, makes no effort to define a significant part of this population. He might realize that the principle governing the preselection of projects to be included in the evaluation "basket" ought to be closely related to program objectives, but the preselection principle which he actually applies is arbitrary. Any project that for one reason or another catches the planner's attention or to which his attention is drawn by politicians and that passes the locally accepted "feasibility hurdle" is considered to be eligible and is included in the evaluation basket. The rest of the potential project population is dismissed.

Psychologically or sociologically speaking, the principles governing preselection will not really be arbitrary, but will express the planner's or the political decision maker's basic bias. The planner's basic bias will more often than not be a "tool bias," i.e., he will tend to preselect interventions that are related to his professional tools. The most important interventions in underdeveloped countries, however, happen to be those related to interdisciplinary transformation. These require a complex set of interdisciplinary tools rarely to be found in the stock-in-trade of the planner in developing countries. The chances are, therefore, that the evaluation basket will not contain the most important and (in terms of achieving the program objectives) the most attractive projects. Even a casual sample inspection of sectorial investment programs in developing countries bears this out. This biased and simplistic preselection will greatly reduce the variety of alternatives open for evaluation, thus radically reducing the chances of optimized resources allocation.

The preselection procedure proposed here seeks

1. To increase the variety of selection by increasing the population of eligible projects. This is achieved by applying to the planning field a systematic scanning approach.
2. To absorb irrelevant variety by applying a specifically oriented and flexible variety absorber in the form of a screening principle rooted in program objectives. This variety absorption will lead to the definition of the "preferential domain." The preferential domain represents a reduction of the potential project population which will not result in a significant loss of relevant variety.

THE SCANNING PROCEDURE

The proposed scanning procedure is a tentative probing of the anticipated resources-outcome ratios of potential interventions upon the development-resources and natural-resources vectors. A listing of such potential interventions and of their approximate resources-outcome ratios will define the development field in a generalized and preliminary way. The inputs of interventions will comprise all resources, capital and human, *presently* or *potentially* available for development. The outcomes will be expressed in terms of the economic and social targets (and in some cases in terms of intermediate targets) of the program.

The development field whose structure we attempt to explore by the proposed scanning procedure can be conceived as four interacting complexes of formative (i.e., variety-generating) variables: the input complex, the input destination complex, the input focusing complex, and the outcome complex. The scanning procedure consists in generating all logically meaningful permutations of these complexes, i.e., all combinations of application of the input complex, oriented by the input focusing complex, to all relevant input destinations, and in determining the respective outcome complexes. The development field consists in the totality of these permutations. The scanning process thus represents a probing of all possible interactions of the development-resources and natural-resources vectors, with a view to defining the development field or the preferential domain.

The input complex comprises all development inputs, actual or potential, that are contained in the development-resources vector and their combination into input packages. Isolated inputs will only in rare cases represent a desirable input package; in the great majority of cases, packages will include a number of inputs.

Input packages can, in turn, be subdivided into a number of groups:

1. Packages consisting predominantly of capital-investment types of inputs—at present the most popular type of package

2. Packages of type 1 but tempered by a modest admixture of complementary inputs (mainly current production and "first-degree" human-resources inputs)

3. Packages of balanced mixture of capital and complementary inputs

4. Packages consisting predominantly of complementary inputs

5. Packages consisting predominantly of second- and third-degree types of human resources (obviously applicable only to the development-resources vector)

The input destination complex represents the totality of destinations—geographical, functional, social—to which the input complex may be allocated. The primary subdivision of this complex is of course the development-resources and the natural-resources vectors.

Resources are channeled to the development-resources vector to improve capabilities related to planning and managing projects and providing transformation inputs to restructure the human and institutional aspects of the natural-resources vector.

Prebuilding the capacity of the development-resources vector beyond the immediate needs of the current development program, in order to avoid anticipated bottlenecks in the subsequent program, will represent a variant of the same allocation policy. Pilot-type projects, undertaken mainly to generate information and methodologies and to provide training and indoctrination opportunities, would also fall into this category.

Within the second main subdivision of the destination complex, i.e., the natural-resources vector, we have three further subdivisions of destination: ecological regions, economic regions, and producer groups:

1. Ecological regions can be classified according to main soil categories and agroclimates and availability of water resources. Water resources may in turn be subclassified according to availability of surface water and groundwater resources and according to the order of magnitude of costs involved in upgrading water resources to the requirements of the use for which they are intended. Lumpiness of investment might also be a useful subclassifying principle.

2. Economic regions can be classified according to type and availability of markets, transportation facilities and their costs, the general socioeconomic level of development, and availability of prior investments. Investments made during previous planning periods and that have not yet reached full fruition constitute a natural attraction for additional investment as long as they do not involve throwing good money after bad. Such prior investments will therefore represent potential destinations for additional resources inputs.

3. Producer groups ought to be operational and related to the development context. Since we are exploring input-output ratios, the most meaningful classifying principle of producer groups will be the scope and quality of their response to potential input packages. On one end of the scale we have the modern *commercial farmer* adequately responding to an input package of the first or second group (i.e., predominantly capital inputs) by spontaneously providing, directly or through agencies which he creates, the necessary

complementary inputs. On the other end of the scale we have the *traditional subsistence farmer* depending on public intervention to provide input packages of the third to fourth group (i.e., with emphasis upon current production and human-resources inputs of the first degree).

The input focusing complex represents an additional mode of variety related to the input destination complex. In every ecological or economic region or for every producer group we must still explore alternative types of focusing approaches, e.g., whether to apply inputs to rain-fed farming or to irrigation farming, to a diversified crop pattern, or to selected strategic crops.

The outcome complex represents our best estimate of the response of input destination complexes to input packages, applied with a specific input focusing approach. Responses or outcomes will be expressed in terms of program objectives. Unless the relevant authorities have in advance selected specific trade-off ratios between objectives, multiple objective yardsticks will be used.

The most difficult problem in defining the outcome complex is the determination of resources-outcome or input-output ratios. Resources-outcome assumptions from existing project documentation (related to past, present, and future projects) will provide a certain amount of information whose dependability is uncertain. As a rule, little if any follow-up information will be available on actual performance of existing projects or projects under development to confirm the validity of such planning assumptions. Furthermore, project information will usually be confined to a relatively limited number of domains of the development field. Assumptions on anticipated resources-outcome ratios for the uncharted part of the development field will therefore be tentative and will have to be based on analogies with other projects and countries and on theoretical considerations.

SCREENING OPERATIONS

Many of the domains of the development field will, for logical or substantial reasons, be easily identifiable as prima facie unattractive or unfeasible; others will be considered unattractive from the point of view of program objectives; the rest will be considered as eligible for further evaluation.

The purpose of screening operations is to separate the last group of domains from the former two. The screening criterion will be the anticipated degree of achievement of program objectives. Since there will usually be more than one objective, simple ordering of the domains will be impossible. Here again we can resort to the technique of establishing the "frontier" within our two- to multi-objective space and introduce for final evaluation and selection only the domains at the frontier. Projects at the frontier are, of course, projects which—in a two-objective space—have, for every value of the first objective, the highest achievement in the other objective. The objective space in this context will be formed by representing, for each alternative input application, the outcome per unit of input, the former measured by yardsticks representing program objectives.

Political priority, or the political necessity of an equitable allocation of resources to the various regions or producer groups of a country, will represent another type of screening criterion. The adoption of allocation patterns rooted in political priorities need not preempt the issue of project selection: what is usually specified is the demand that a specific or minimal development effort be directed to a certain area or producer group. It is often falsely claimed that a specific project has an overwhelming political priority, while actual political priority refers to a favored region or group of people. Political-priority stipulation thus constitutes only a constraint as to the destination complex. It usually does not imply a constraint as to the type of project to be adopted. Political priority would thus represent a constraint on the screening operation related to the destination complex, leaving the remaining screening complexes undetermined and therefore open to the screening process.

The proposed combined scanning-screening procedure will result in a relatively large number of alternative input applications or domains and subdomains of the development field. Since the aim of this variety generation is not to swell the project basket available for evaluation, but to ensure that the domains and subdomains entering the basket do in fact include the most attractive projects, we ought to try to define, at as early a stage as possible, those domains which appear to have the most attractive resources-outcome ratios, i.e., the "preferential domains". If the main emphasis is on a single objective, we shall be looking for domains with the highest achievement in the favored objective. Definition of preferential domains will be especially important in the early phases of development, when information is scanty, professionals are untrained and insufficient in number, and planning experience is rudimentary.

DEFINITION OF PROJECTS

The combined scanning-screening procedure will result in the definition of the preferential domains. In other words, it will underline the most favorable application of input packages upon alternative destination and focus complexes. The preferential domain will consist in a comprehensive list of generalized and abstract resources input-outcome ratios that are not necessarily intended for direct evaluation as such, but rather for use as *project-generating principles.*

Some of the projects that have been planned and evaluated prior to the adoption of the proposed scanning-screening procedure will be found to fit into one or another preferential domain. Others might not fall into this category.

The most important outcome, however, will be the realization that complete domains or subdomains shown to be eminently eligible have in fact not been represented at all in the original project basket, or have not been represented in a sufficient number of applications. Often it will prove impossible to generate the "unborn" projects in time for evaluation. In such cases, lack of project definition ought not to be considered a sufficient reason for excluding preferential domains from the evaluation basket or including them with inadequate representation. If specific project studies on the attractive domains are not available, such domains ought to be represented in the project population in a generalized form. The latter would contain parametric information (mainly data on input-output ratios) derived from samples of similar available project plans or existing operative projects from similar planning contexts. In analogy to a "synthetic" hydrograph, it is proposed to call such generalized projects synthetic projects. The extent of elaboration that can be incorporated into the definition of synthetic projects will vary according to the size of the sample of actual (blueprinted or operative) projects available as a source for parametric information and the quality of this information. The incorporation of synthetic projects guarantees to the evaluation basket a sufficient representation of projects belonging to the preferential domains.

If the project basket includes major projects involving lumpy (i.e., unsubdivisible) investments, we ought to consider whether the projects might not be better subdivided according to their constituents to the extent that the latter represent self-contained viable subprojects. Alternatively (sometimes also concurrently), we ought also to investigate whether it would make sense to adopt phasing for major projects, dividing the whole or significant parts of the project into two or more phases, each representing a partial capacity. In cases in which a division according to one or the other (or both) principle of subdivision makes sense, the respective portions of the project should be separately introduced into the basket and the extent of their complementariness or mutual exclusiveness specified. This procedure will ensure that we avoid (1) the "lumping fallacy," i.e., the lumping together of less attractive and more attractive elements into a mix which, though acceptable, has less utility than would have a combination of selected attractive project elements; (2) the "scale fallacy," i.e., that we be impressed by scale, losing sight of the loss implied in overlong maturation.

DEFINITION OF PROGRAMS

The project basket, a set of concrete projects (or self-sustained project portions) and synthetic projects, constitutes the basis for the generation of programs. In every program the initial aggregate resources input will have to be smaller than the available resources inventory or equal to it. Every project, concrete or synthetic, will be characterized, on the one hand, by the input package (material and nonmaterial) involved and, on the other hand, by its objective achievement. The generation, during the program period, of the most essential information and resources inputs for the subsequent program ought also to be considered one of the objectives of the current program.

Alternative programs will differ by

1. Achievement levels measured in terms of program objectives
2. The extent of "prebuilding" production facilities and growth capacity in the natural-resources vector achieved in the current program period that will

yield full fruition in subsequent periods, possibly only after the incorporation of additional input packages

3. The extent of improvements in the development-resources vector

A mathematical model and computerization will usually be required for systematizing definition of alternative programs. Programs will again be represented as points in an objective space, with as many dimensions as there are objectives. Inspection of this space will result in the definition of the frontier set of programs.

The selection of the most satisfactory program from the frontier set of programs is, of course, a matter of value judgment of the political decision process. The definition of a frontier set of programs will enable the decision maker to focus his evaluative efforts upon the programs represented by the frontier set and to weigh their respective merits by comparing trade-offs between objectives that every selection implies. When comparing the merits of the alternative programs represented in the frontier set, we ought to allow for differences in growth capacities.

However, before arriving at a final choice from among the programs in the frontier set, the constraints stemming from scarcity of information and from the politico-institutional framework ought to be considered. To the extent that analysis of these constraints significantly modifies the definitions of programs in the frontier set, iteration of the evaluation procedure allowing for such modifications will have to be undertaken. The following sections deal with these constraints.

AVAILABILITY OF INFORMATION AND UNCERTAINTY

The data used in the inventorying, scanning, screening, and definition of preferential domains and in programs will be unhomogeneous in quality and of unequal dependability. Part of the data on the resources-outcome ratios related to man and crops will have been gathered from existing full-scale project applications, part from pilot or demonstration type projects, and part from analogies with similar development contexts. Data on natural resources will vary from data derived from long-term observations to data derived from generalized analogies.

While the use of such unhomogeneous data might be defendable for a screening analysis undertaken with a view to defining the preferential domains of the development field, more stringent specifications for information will have to be laid down for applicative uses. We shall therefore have to scrutinize the projects, concrete or synthetic, entering into the frontier set of programs as to their "information feasibility," i.e., as to the adequateness of available information. We can distinguish three main ranges of information feasibilty (see also Chapter 11):

1. A project is unfeasible, i.e., available information or essential parts thereof do not reach the relevant information thresholds.
2. A project is feasible, but information on the important project issues,

though above the relevant thresholds, is still significantly below the respective levels of the optimal information requirement

3. A project has adequate information on all important issues, i.e., information on these issues is close to, equal to, or above the optimal information requirement.

Inclusion of projects which fall within the first category will have to be postponed until appropriate information can be generated. Special types of intervention specifically aimed at generation of the necessary information, or interventions generating this information as a by-product, will have to be defined and included in the project basket so that the relevant projects will become eligible for implementation in the later part of the present or in the subsequent program.

Projects (concrete and synthetic ones) falling within the second category will have to be subjected to a sensitivity type of analysis defining the range of outcomes if we assume data to vary within the anticipated range. The type of provision necessary for each range of outcomes (allowance of safety margins, downscaling, etc.) will have to be allowed for in the project definitions. Here, again, special information-generating interventions could be defined in order to raise information levels.

Projects falling within the third category will need no modification.

After (1) analyzing the project in the basket as to information feasibility, (2) specifying the admittance requirements in terms of information for the first category of projects, (3) determining the modifications required as a result of the unsatisfactory information level for projects of the second category, and (4) including in the basket a sufficient number of projects aimed at generation of information, we can resort (if modifications are significant) to an iteration of program definition which will result in a new frontier set. The projects included in this revised frontier set of programs will all be feasible from the point of view of information availability.

The subdivision of the program definition into two runs is here suggested intentionally. If we performed the operation in one run, we would automatically discard extremely attractive projects not supported by sufficient information and therefore requiring an information-generation effort that might extend beyond the current program period. The proposed iteration will highlight such projects or project groups and their information lacunae and lead to the definition of an information-generation program aimed at overcoming information limitations.

POLITICAL AND INSTITUTIONAL ASPECTS OF SECTORIAL PROGRAMS

The politico-institutional constraint Sectorial programs drawn up according to the procedure described in the preceding sections have been conceived in a "technocratic," i.e., apolitical, space. Such programs, nevertheless, need not represent a purely "objective" optimum in utility for the society as a whole, assuming we can define an objective optimum. The definition of aims and objectives, and particularly the weights attributed to them *implicitly* in the presentation of results to political decision makers, imply a bias for specific producer groups, regions, parties, etc.

When restoring the politico-institutional dimension into our planning space to establish the political feasibility of the program, the political bias introduced into program evaluation will be of a much more explicit nature. In a sectorial program the question of political feasibility will arise in a much more acute form than in a ministerial investment program made up of individual and disconnected projects. The reasons for this are as follows:

Political Compatibility Sectorial programs have to state development objectives explicitly and, at least implicitly, weights attributed to objectives; they thus openly manifest their political orientation. Individual projects can be motivated by generalized and politically innocuous aims, such as increasing agricultural production through the construction of irrigation facilities. Compatibility between the goal-setting complex of a sectorial program and that of the political decision process will therefore be a question of paramount importance.

Macroorganizational Compatibility Sectorial programs are conceived at a much higher conceptual level than that at which the politico-administrative hierarchy operates. The latter level is determined by the macroorganizational structure of the politico-administrative decision process (i.e., the division into ministries and departments) and by channels of communication and coordination. In contrast to sectorial programs, the project-by-project approach does not make "metaplanning" claims upon the political decision process that exceed its operative capacity.

Microorganizational Compatibility A discrepancy will be found to exist between the personality traits and group attitudes and responses required for the conception and implementation of a true sectorial program and those actually present. The operational capacity of an organization will be governed by attitudes and responses of its role occupants rather than by the formal organizational layout. These attitudes and responses will generally be incompatible with the requirements of sectorial programs; this discrepancy between available and necessary capacity may well represent the controlling institutional weakness of most programs.

A good program requires for its conception and implementation at least a reasonable degree of compatibility of the above three kinds. In underdeveloped countries, the degree of compatibility will almost by definition be extremely low. The way out of this impasse might consist in mutual adaptation of the program to the structure and quality of existing institutions and of the latter to the institutional requirements of the program. In the early phases of development, the first type of adaptation will prevail; gradually, program implementation will, subtly but consistently, improve institutions; in subsequent programs, the reshaping of institutions might be the controlling form.

In any case, this mutual-adaptation process between programs and institutions is too important to be left to chance. Its continually changing modes ought to be planned and implemented as integral parts of the program.

MUTUAL ADAPTATION BETWEEN PROGRAMS AND INSTITUTIONS

Political Compatibility In political processes we can distinguish two levels: the manifest, nominal, rhetorical level and the latent, actual, operative level. The manifest level is the direct "logical" outcome of the professed political philosophy, the application of political ideology to basic problems of society; it is analogous to the formal structure of organizations. The latent level represents the Realpolitik, the actual motivational complexes of political groups and individuals; this level is rooted in the real power structure of society; it is analogous to the informal structure of organizations.

The basic incompatibility between a program and the political process usually stems from the fact that programs, while fashioned according to the manifest political ideology, have to be approved and implemented by the political decision process, which is governed by the latent type of political motivation. The national charter, the law of the country, for instance, might proclaim redistribution of land and the provision of the appurtenant means of production to be the paramount aim of agricultural development; at the same time, the actual political decision process might systematically sabotage every attempt at actually implementing land reform.

The basic strategy for priming a sectorial development program handicapped by great political incompatibility is to modify the initial phases of the program so as to reduce discrepancies between the program and the political process, while generating sufficient feedback toward the latter to further reduce such discrepancies and the necessity for adaptation of the program to the requirements of Realpolitik. In other words, the problem is to establish a bridgehead in the territory of Realpolitik for the development philosophy represented by the sectorial program and, once this bridgehead is established, to concentrate upon widening and deepening it in order to create the necessary leverage for later action on a wider base.

The tactical approach described by Hirshman[6] of having politically unattractive or problematic projects "ride on the back" of a politically desirable one would be an application of the above strategy. Once the politically unattractive project has been smuggled in, a new vested-interest group will be formed by individuals involved in its implementation, by its beneficiaries, and by its political backers; this new vested-interest group will constitute a new force acting on behalf of the unattractive project in subsequent political decisions. Unfortunately, the recommended approach of "compromise" is often spurned by the technocratic level of the administration, and political incom-

[6] Albert O. Hirschman, *Development Projects Observed,* The Brookings Institution, Washington, 1967.

patibility is often taken as an excuse for doing nothing. Such perfectionism is, of course, the least defensible approach: nothing will come of nothing.

The detailed modalities of the application of the proposed strategy will, of course, depend on the specific factors encountered in every case. However, a generalized checklist of steps to be taken might prove useful.

The first step ought to be the conscious adoption of a basic positive attitude to action even under the most unfavorable political conditions. This should be followed by a thorough analysis of the governing Realpolitik, its actual latent achievement criteria, areas of great resistance, and areas of low resistance that might be suitable for the establishment of "bridgeheads."

The second step would be to modify the program to avoid, in the early phases, operations in relation to which we anticipate great political resistance, or if such operations are unavoidable, to downgrade them in a way that will significantly reduce resistance.

The third step would be to introduce for the measurement of project achievement the yardsticks of Realpolitik and to ensure that the program has a sufficient volume of achievement as measured by such yardsticks. We should make proper allowance for the short time span of the political process and plan that politically important achievements become operative as early as possible.

The fourth and last step would be to design the institutional and decision process of the program so as both to minimize the damaging interference of the political process and to maximize the upward loop, i.e., the feedback from the program to the political process.

Macroorganizational Compatibility As we have repeatedly pointed out, the structure of the organization is reflected in the structure of the program it produces. Structural adequacy of the organization and structural compatibility between programs and organizations are therefore a precondition for adequate programming. Unfortunately, true sectorial programs require a high level of abstraction, which in turn presupposes an effective decision hierarchy. Since such hierarchies do not exist in developing countries, a structural incompatibility is created between program and organization. We are thus faced with one of the typical vicious circles of underdevelopment: to create satisfactory growth we require an appropriately comprehensive planning approach, involving high-level conceptual thinking; the existing decision hierarchies are not able to operate at high levels of abstraction and therefore fail to initiate a comprehensive sectorial approach. To move into positive causation, we must somehow prime a comprehensive planning approach. The detailed modalities of such a priming operation will depend on local organization, power structure, and personalities; however, priming operations will share the following structural similarities (see also Chapter 6).

Metaplanning group Unless supplemented by interministerial metaplanning, planning at ministerial levels cannot result in a comprehensive sectorial program, where the operations involved in such a program are the responsibility of more than one ministry. The danger of metaplanning is that the existing body politic will consider it foreign and will not accept it. To minimize such rejection symptoms, we ought to confine the scope and depth of metaplanning to the minimum interministerial framework of the sectorial program necessary to ensure the requisite interministerial cooperation. Planning operations that can be executed within ministerial levels ought to be left to the ministerial organization.

Organizational location of the metaplanning group The metaplanning group ought to be organizationally located at a point of the hierarchy that will ensure the best control of the interministerial aspects of sectorial programs, while keeping rejection symptoms at a minimum. Logical points would be the Chief Executive's Office, the Bureau of Budget, the Ministry of Finance, and the Ministry of Development. Where one of the ministries directly concerned in a major way with a sectorial program has a sufficiently controlling position in the power hierarchy, it might represent a possible choice. Wherever we choose to locate the metaplanning group organizationally, participation in metaplanning of the ministries concerned ought to be maximized by specifying their delegation of high-level representatives to the planning committee that will review the program and pass it on for approval to the Cabinet or the Chief Executive.

If the metaplanning group is attached to the Chief Executive or to a ministry that does not have direct sectorial responsibility, special efforts ought to be made to obtain the support of the strongest "sectorial" ministry. The latter ought to be so involved as to become in time the sponsor of the program.

Once the sectorial program has reached a firm course, attempts should be made to gradually upgrade the organizational framework according to plan requirements. This will reduce the amount of coordination required and the constraining effect of inadequate organization on subsequent programs.

A special difficulty will be encountered in connection with the legal, institutional framework. This framework will as a rule lag behind the already backward organizational framework and be even more change resistant. Here, again, the strategy of priming improvement will consist in mutual adaptation between program and framework. In the early phases the emphasis will be on the downgrading of the program, leaving the upgrading of the framework for the later phases.

Organizational weakness This aspect is covered elsewhere (see Chapter 16).

INTERCONNECTION WITH OTHER SECTORS OF THE ECONOMY AND WITH FUTURE PROGRAMS

The isolation of the agricultural sector from the rest of the economy and the introduction of a medium-term time horizon that are implied in sectorial planning are, of course, artificial. At some point of the analysis, the sectorial planner will have to focus his attention on the "interface" between the *agricultural and the industrial and service sectors,* and between the *present and subsequent programs,* and attempt coordination of interrelated activities on both sides of the interface. Since these interface aspects will be treated in the concluding chapter, we can confine our comments here to some of the more obvious interface problems of the "backward-linkage" and of the "forward-linkage" type.

Backward linkage refers mostly to production inputs and related services that will have to be produced by the nonagricultural sectors for use by the agricultural sector. The distribution, intermediate stocking, and selling of these inputs and the setting up of the necessary financing facilities will require close intersectorial collaboration between the relevant industries and the agricultural sector and will call for joint elaboration of a detailed plan and program.

Forward linkage in this context refers mostly to sorting, packaging, processing, canning, and similar industrial "upgrading" processes of agricultural raw materials. Here, too, coordinative joint planning and programming on both sides of the interface will be required.

21

THE TWO APPROACHES TO DEVELOPMENT POLES

He gave it for his opinion, that whoever could make two ears of corn or two blades of grass grow upon a spot of ground where only one grew before, would deserve better of mankind, and do a more essential service to his country than the whole race of politicians put together.

JONATHAN SWIFT (*Gulliver's Travels*)

NECESSITY AND DEFINITION OF DEVELOPMENT POLES

The conception of development poles is a direct outcome of our diagnosis of the structural inadequacies of underdevelopment set out in earlier chapters. To recapitulate the essential points: the principal agent responsible for the delay of growth in response to capital investment in the Third World is inadequate "growth capacity," a complex function comprising mainly the human, institutional, and technological resources of a socioeconomic system; acceleration of growth is conditional mainly upon the development of growth capacity which, in turn, is dependent on planned deployment of "transformation inputs," i.e., trained human resources capable of remedying the crippling structural weaknesses; acute logistic constraints in most underdeveloped countries prevail for such transformation inputs; these inputs must be deployed at an intensity that is above specific critical thresholds.

The above diagnosis leads to the further conclusion that the available transformation inputs ought to be focused in sufficient intensity upon *poles of development.* This can be done in two ways:

1. Setting up geographical poles in the form of "comprehensive regional projects" by concentrating available scarce transformation inputs and capital in a number of regions. The suboptimization principle underlying this approach calls for incorporating the scarce transformation inputs in a number of input packages and applying these packages to a limited number of regions in order to achieve accelerated local growth.

2. Setting up functional poles, i.e., deploying available scarce transformation inputs in selected production complexes on the broadest possible front, subject to the constraint that resources intensity must be above the critical threshold; this approach will result in "strategic crop–critical input" type of projects. The underlying suboptimization here consists of using the critically short transformation input in order to reinforce the growth capacity of the production complexes with the highest direct share of the sectorial product.

In the present chapter, we shall attempt to define the roles of these two approaches in the take-off phase of underdeveloped economies.

COMPREHENSIVE REGIONAL PROJECTS

This approach concentrates professional and subprofessional manpower in selected areas, in order to restructure the production process. Concurrently, it provides appropriate training facilities within this controlled environment that are isolated from the surrounding ill-structured production systems. Since the subject of training will be decision and action ideology, only on-the-job training will prove effective; a development project is the only possible framework for such on-the-job training. However, professional retraining by itself will be insufficient for producing and maintaining a sustained growth process; attitudes to work will have to be completely reshaped. For this "transformation process of the transformation inputs," leadership elements will have to be enlisted to act as catalyzing agents for creating basically new response patterns on the part of professionals and subprofessionals.

The sociological aspects of the proposed training process will be treated in Chapter 24. Here we shall confine ourselves to a few general comments.

The objective of comprehensive regional projects is a dual one:

1. To implement a transformation in a specific region and there achieve an increase in production

2. To develop personnel capable of performing all duties connected with the transformation of the human-institutional factors in development processes and information related to it

When viewing the development of a specific region, the first objective is, of course, the controlling one; however, in the wider context of national development, the second objective, though only an instrumental one, is more important. In the second context a regional project is primarily a training facility for developing personnel beyond the requirements of the region proper, a proving ground for methodologies and input packages, and a source for generating information.

The number of professionals and subprofessionals needed to overcome the initial inertia momentum against change, Kurt Lewin's "unfreezing process,"[1] will be relatively large; reducing it to manageable scope might require limiting the initial front of attack to portions of the selected development areas. As change processes are initiated and start to strike roots, the intensity of inter-

[1] Kurt Lewin, "Frontiers in Group Dynamics," in *Field Theory in Social Science*, Harper Torchbooks, Harper & Row, Publishers, Incorporated, New York, 1964, especially pp. 228–229.

vention can be gradually reduced. Part of the manpower trained on the project can be used to prime the "transformation" in the remaining portions of the selected areas and, in time, also can be used to initiate "colonization" of a second group of development areas. Similar considerations apply to professionals acting as catalyzing agents. Thus a sustained growth process can be created.

A comprehensive regional project will include operations similar to those described in Chapter 20, dealing with comprehensive sectorial planning. In applying such operations within a comprehensive regional scheme, the planner will attempt to define input packages which, when superimposed upon the existing natural-resources vector, will help bring about the desired type of change. This input package might, depending on prevailing conditions, consist of the following:

1. Catalyzation of transformation of development personnel: catalyzation of change of motivation and action ideology among the subprofessional and professional development personnel, and training them for improved decision making. Transformation and training inputs might have to be supplemented in the early phases by supervision and control.
2. Dissemination of information on production techniques and production planning—i.e., agricultural extension services—including adaptational investigations aimed at optimizing agricultural input packages (seeds, fertilizers, plant-protection chemicals, cultivation approaches) under local ecological conditions.
3. Providing manpower to initiate, control, and/or manage the institutional network involved in the agricultural production process; procurement, storing, and distribution of current production inputs; production and other credits; processing; marketing; mechanical cultivation equipment that is beyond the reach of individual farmers; and operation and maintenance of water-supply facilities.
4. On-farm agroengineering measures, e.g., field irrigation, leveling, drainage.
5. Planning and implementation of investments in regional water-supply and drainage facilities, including soil classification, land-use planning, farm economics, project economics, relation to sectorial economics.
6. Inputs required to adapt the administrative-institutional framework to project requirements.

Although the main emphasis of the comprehensive regional approach lies in defining and providing a "complete input package," i.e., one introducing all the missing elements into the existing production process ("downward loop"), regional projects should also radiate information and transformation impact well beyond the boundaries for which they were originally designed. In other words, regional planners ought to pay attention to the "sideway loop" of their project. They also should attempt to influence the development thinking of top-level decision makers ("upward loop"). To achieve a *sideway-loop* effect, some of the more effective and conspicuous operations of a comprehensive regional plan, which do not involve major financial, technical, or organizational difficulties, might be adopted by a neighboring region, there initiating a development process only slightly dependent on public intervention; it might then spread to still other regions. In time, this special feature might be taken up by the higher decision levels of the hierarchy and turned into a national program of polarized development efforts of the second type, that of functional poles, to be described below.

If a comprehensive regional development program is implemented in stages, such a *demonstration effect* will also operate within the region itself, radiating from the areas initially included in the early phases of the project to areas not yet incorporated; by reducing initial inertial resistance to change, such internal demonstration effects will considerably facilitate subsequent full-scale operation. The demonstration effect might, in the later phases, make possible reduction of the human-resources input of the project. Demonstration effects are valuable instrumental objectives of comprehensive regional projects, and measures to achieve such effects should therefore be specifically provided for in project planning. Such measures might, for example, include farmers' meetings in demonstration areas; short training courses for selected farmers; setting up model farms managed by the most intelligent farmers (after a minimum amount of training); provision, with a minimum of specific applicatory advice, of selected inputs (e.g., seeds, fertilizers, plant-protection chemicals) ahead of others.

The spreading of regional tube-well schemes in Pakistan, aimed at combining drainage and irrigation, is a good example of the demonstration effect. Originally started through government action in a few regions, these schemes rapidly initiated similar spontaneous operations in other regions.

The comprehensive *regional project* provides the development region farmer with specifically designed concentrated packages of inputs necessary to increase his production efficiency, initially to the levels of intermediate agriculture and subsequently to those of modern agriculture. This approach increases regional production rapidly and effectively, but it suffers from one basic disadvantage: because of the logistic limitations of human and institutional resources so typical for underdeveloped countries, it takes a long time before its impact is felt nationally. The *functional focusing* of development logistics has a much greater potential for accelerating production nationally. We now turn to this approach.

THE FUNCTIONAL FOCUS: STRATEGIC CROP–CRITICAL INPUT APPROACH

The aim of the functional-focus approach The point of departure of the functional-focus approach is that the agricultural sector in an underdeveloped economy has to be developed under the constraints of both capital and human-resources limitations; in most instances the latter is the controlling factor.

Development planning under such limitations attempts to maximize streams of benefits that can be generated by available material and nonmaterial resources. Because of lack of data and appropriate methodologies, a rigorous analytical approach to the solution of this optimization problem is rarely possible. The suboptimization proposed here aims at maximizing objective achievement that can be obtained with the available stock of the critically short resource (typically transformation inputs), assuming that no other resource (e.g., capital) will, in turn, become critical through suboptimization. The proposed suboptimization has a good chance of achieving results reasonably close to those obtainable from rigorous optimization if the latter were feasible.

The two planning objectives of the functional-focus approach Functional focusing has two basic objectives:

1. Short-term objectives: obtaining immediate production effects with the existing resources inventory
2. Long-term objectives: expanding the resources inventory according to the sector's long-term requirements

Although they are but two facets of a single process, for the sake of simplifying demonstration, we shall treat the two objectives separately.

Short-term planning objectives In planning for the short-term objectives of functional focuses, we should start by investigating the principal production complexes comprising the sectorial production, by investigating the present and anticipated shares of these complexes in the sectorial product. For each production complex we need to know the availability and quality of resources needed and the resources-outcome ratios. Status quo conditions will serve as a reference system for evaluating ways to incorporate alternative inputs in order to improve production: direct inputs, designed for channeling through the existing production framework, and transformation inputs, designed for improving this framework. Such an input evaluation will operate with input packages rather than with individual inputs; it should, however, not be limited to defining packages with optimal proportions of inputs, but should include evaluation of packages in which the proportions of the respective critical inputs are lower than optimal. This analysis will result in the definition of alternative input packages and their anticipated production effect.

The above survey of alternative input packages for upgrading the sectorial production process ought to be supplemented by a survey of the logistics involved. The logistic requirements of a functional "attack" on a national scale should be worked out and compared with the inventory of available resources and that of resources accruing from program activities. The existing resources inventory and its short-term accretions will define the possible scope of activities.

Program selection will result from comparing input requirements of programs promising good production increases with the inventory of available inputs. The critical items in the inventory will be first-degree and second-degree[2] human resources, and these will constitute the active constraint upon

[2] See in Chapter 20 the discussion on programs, projects, and development inputs.

the program's scope. Because of this limitation in the original inventory and in the anticipated inventory accretions, the proportioning of the critical resources within the input package need not, in the beginning, be the theoretically optimal one that would prevail did such limitations not exist. In order to stretch our front of functional attack to the limit imposed by logistics, we might reduce the proportion of scarce human resources in the input package below the optimum and sometimes perhaps until a level is reached where the return on inputs is still attractive enough to make the farmer select the package. An incentive pricing policy for the controlling material input in the package (e.g., fertilizers) might help to extend the development front for a specific stock of critical transformation inputs.

The effect of a functional-focus program transcends the development areas proper: ripples of demonstration effects (sideway loops) and upward effects are created; such demonstration effects may create considerable pressures on the already overextended logistic front. These demonstration effects must be allowed for in long-term planning.

Long-term planning aspects While short-term planning attempts to increase productivity by optimizing use of existing input inventories, long-term planning aims at increasing the inventory of development inputs in accordance with overall sectorial requirements. Even a preliminary evaluation will demonstrate the principal logistic constraints of the sector. These constraints may be human resources needed to improve the resources-outcome ratio of the production process (first-degree resources, or transformation inputs) or human resources needed to upgrade the quality of transformation inputs (second-degree resources); they may be current agricultural inputs, their production, control, and distribution; finally, they may be current industrial inputs (such as fertilizers). An ever-present major weakness is the lack of adaptive field investigations to firm up experience gained in other countries on the optimal makeup of input packages for various crops and various ecological regions. Such investigations are needed for the transfer of foreign experience to local conditions. The basic task of long-term planning is to estimate anticipated requirements in the above types of inputs and to plan their systematic generation.

Regarding human-resources inputs, initial stress will be on training or importing second-degree input, i.e., trainers of transformation inputs. As soon as second-degree inputs are available, training programs can start. These training programs for transformation inputs are intended to comprise, at all levels of work, as large a number of extension personnel as possible, from extension foremen to senior agronomists. To achieve such a broad coverage, the training curriculum should be limited to issues directly relevant to the functional inputs and strategic crops selected for the current program.

An important alternative source for trained human resources can be found in "mature" comprehensive regional programs. These programs, as well as operating functional ones, can be used to provide on-the-job training and to indoctrinate personnel. The more intelligent and experienced trainees could be used as second-degree inputs, while the others could be assigned responsible positions in field projects.

Large-scale production of current agricultural inputs, i.e., seeds, will have to be preceded by adaptive field investigations. Seeds selected because of similar ecological environment in foreign countries will be checked for viability and productivity under local conditions and modified if necessary. These adaptive investigations will be executed with alternative designs of fertilizers and plant-protection chemicals and, where relevant, with alternative cultivation methods. The results of the first rounds of adaptive research should be accepted as the basis for the initial phase. While this phase is being carried out, research on improvement can continue. The control of seed quality, distributive organization, etc., will all need special care and institutionalized solutions.

It is with the last category of inputs, i.e., fertilizers and pesticides, that we leave the boundaries of the agricultural sectorial system and encroach upon the industrial sector. Here intersectorial coordination is necessary at an early stage. Production and implementation of industrial inputs can be subdivided into a number of operations: production of base materials, blending, packaging, distribution, storage, sales, credits, specific application know-how. The whole gamut of operations is required to achieve satisfactory results; however, not all the operations will, as a rule, be handled by the same organization. Furthermore, different operations will have different break-even points between imports and local manufacture. Private "initiative" might be best qualified to handle some of the operations (e.g., production, blending, packaging, distribution, storage, wholesale sales); cooperatives, others (procurement by village, local storage, sales to individual farmers, credit); and finally, government, still others (extension service, price control of agroproducts and inputs, quality control of inputs, adaptive research).

Until local demand for an industrial input approaches the break-even point between import and local manufacture for that input, imports may be used; industrial facilities for local manufacture will be scheduled to become operative close to the time when this break-even point is reached; distributive operations and adaptive research, on the other hand, will have to begin during the importing phase of the operation. If the utility of foreign currency is higher than expressed in official exchange rates, appropriate modification will be required in determining the break-even point.

Production and associated distributive operations, on the one hand, and demand for them, on the other, ought to be planned together rather than by relying on mutual adaptation to unbalances. Such coordinative planning will give the supporting industrial sector vitally needed growth data related to the anticipated growth rate of demand and the time it will take demand to reach the break-even point between import and local manufacture. This information will facilitate rational development planning of manufacturing facilities and related complementary services; such planning is bound to shorten gestation periods of manufacturing plants, prevent demand surpluses that cannot be met, provide timely indication of necessary imports, etc.

Integrated intersectorial coordinative planning of the industrial inputs of functional-focus programs will also solve one of the main difficulties so far encountered in similar programs: the absence or inadequacy of the complex infrastructure that has to be interposed between the production process proper and field uses, i.e., blending, packaging, distribution, intermediate storage, sales, credit, specific extension work, adaptive research. This infrastructure will have to be established before setting up the production process proper, operating in its early phases with imports. It will be in the creation of this infrastructure that most of the transformation inputs will be needed. This input-oriented infrastructure will be found to be interconnected at a number of points with the infrastructure of the agricultural production process; these two organizational systems ought, therefore, to be planned as complementary features of a single production complex.

Should the crops require industrial processing, facilities for processing will have to be included in the functional-focus program; these facilities will pose problems similar to those encountered with current production inputs. To solve these problems, similar organizational solutions will be needed; both private and cooperative organizations, or a combination of both, may be used.

Since this is one of the infrequent points where our analysis encroaches upon a nonagricultural sector, let us comment here briefly on the difficulties likely to arise from the necessity of cooperation between two sectors. Since the planning of industrial facilities must be integrated with the supporting agricultural sector, and since planners of these two sectors will normally report to different political decision makers, a coordinative organ between the sectors will have to be created. The composition of this organ must ensure that even though each sector's delegate speaks the object language of his sector, the organ's outside members (possibly delegated from the president's office or from the ministry of economic planning) can resolve the intersectorial differences by a metalanguage analysis. To minimize sectorial resistance, the task of this coordinative organ should limit the scope of analyses and decisions that have to be conducted in the metalanguage to a minimum, leaving all object-language analyses and decisions to the respective ministries.

At this point it may also be useful to review briefly the interconnection between a functional sectorial program and the service and policy sectors of government. Since the aim of functional sectorial programs is, of course, the production of crops for the market, and since markets may be located at some distance from producing areas, the need to coordinate transportation facilities with agricultural production will arise. The rate of provision of such facilities and the anticipated cost of transportation will influence the timing, scope, and type of agricultural development. The construction of a new road may also change the whole economic geometry of an area and lead to important forward-linkage effects. Such forward-linkage effects could, of course, be greatly reinforced by the concurrent implementation of a functionally focused agricultural program.

Similar considerations will apply to fiscal, financial, and economic policies relating to the agricultural sector. Such policies may have been set up by government at various times with a view to regulating intersectorial distribution of burdens, terms of trade, and income redistribution and to providing incentives in specific directions. These policies, however, will often be found wrongly conceived to start with or to have outlived their usefulness.

The introduction of a major functionally oriented agricultural development program will call for the rethinking of the whole system of fiscal, financial, and economic policies and for their remodeling to suit the requirements of such a sectorial program.

The above admittedly rough and fragmentary comments do not purport to cover in any sufficient measure the subject of interconnection between sectorial and overall economic planning and are intended only to stress the complexity of the subject. This subject was touched upon in Chapter 20 and will also be mentioned in the concluding chapter.

Some heuristic guidelines for functional-focus projects

1. *Dangers to Avoid* Functional-focus projects ought to beware of two fundamental dangers that beset projects of this type:

   a. The danger of subliminal spreading, i.e., of using input packages which are below the critical mass and which do not therefore control sufficient power to unseat initial inertial resistance

   b. The danger of loss of continuity, caused by the withdrawal of political support for the program

   To avoid the first danger we ought to focus our initial input packages on a limited front, expanding our operations only as additional human resources become available or spontaneous processes emerge which make withdrawal of part of the project forces possible. To avoid the second danger we ought to plan to increase the effectiveness of the upward loop, most safely effected by the ability to announce impressive early successes. Many of the following heuristics have been devised with this objective in mind.

2. *Selection of Production Complex* First priority should be given to production complexes (i.e., crop, ecology, production inputs, and technology) that contribute a large share to the aggregate sectorial product. Such a selection will comply with the basic overriding strategy mentioned before: maximizing the production return on the critically scarce resource. This heuristic is valid only if yields of the relevant crops, as compared with some standard achievable yield levels, are low; otherwise we should choose that crop for which the application of available inputs promises to maximize added production value.

3. *The Role of Complexity* The basic heuristic requirement of maximizing outcomes of critically scarce resources will require another supplementary comment to heuristic 2. Since the amount of human resources (here assumed to be the controlling scarcity) that have to be applied to a production complex will also depend on the extent of refractoriness encountered in the solution of the related agrotechnical, logistic, and marketing problems, we ought initially (i.e., as long as human resources remain scarce) to give preference to complexes lacking complications.

4. *The Role of Socioeconomic Planning Objectives* In some economies (especially agricultural economies at the "take-off" stage) the most important socioeconomic objective might not be the aggregate product but distribution of new production facilities and added income and employment connected with it or improvement of the balance of payment. In such cases priority for initial selection of the production complex should be governed by such overriding objectives—subject to qualifications mentioned before.
5. *Role of Forward and Backward Linkages* The role of such linkages should be given its proper weight, especially if the growth in the "interlinked" sector has an independent high political and/or economic priority.
6. *Role of Resistance from Institutions and Vested Interests* Since institutional resistance is most difficult to overcome, a "path of least institutional resistance" ought to be chosen for initial interventions; resistance barriers should be attempted only when the program has accumulated sufficient political and economic momentum. The same would apply to major vested interests with heavy political backing.
7. *Regard to Future Growth Rates* Providing the logistic and organizational requirements for the subsequent program period ought to constitute one of the most important tasks of the current development program. The planning and scheduling of this task should fully allow for the "response lag" involved in the creation of the relevant inputs. One, and possibly not the least important, "prebuilding" effort in the current program is to create initial demonstration effects in areas or crops that will be taken up and reinforced in the subsequent program. This leads us to the eighth heuristic, related to secondary loops.
8. *Regard to Secondary Loops* Our program should plan for actively reinforcing spillover effects in adjoining areas. The motivation for this emphasis transcends that mentioned under 7 and is rooted in the desire to strengthen the effect of the program upon the higher levels of the decision hierarchy. One way to achieve such an effect is to create secondary reinforcing communication streams from the adjoining benefited areas to these high levels, so as to strengthen the political backing of the present project and of future similar ones. The importance of the upward loop increases as we reach some of the "bridges" that we preferred not to cross in the initial stages, i.e., when we have to face resistance from institutions and power groups to the later phases of the program.
9. *The Role of Adaptive Research* The early establishment of demonstration nuclei (priming projects) in areas intended for subsequent full-scale coverage can be combined with field research which works out the details of the necessary adaptation to local conditions of production processes transferred from other regions or countries. Such adaptive experiments require a considerable lead time and should therefore be undertaken well ahead of full-scale operations.

RESPECTIVE ROLES OF REGIONAL AND FUNCTIONAL FOCUS PROJECTS

The two types of focusing have many common and some divergent features. The common features all stem from the joint basic instrumental objective, i.e., to transcend direct production outcomes and to initiate "upgrading" of the socioeconomic infrastructure of the production process, thus creating "growth capacity" which in turn ultimately increases production. This common basic objective also determines the other common features of the two focusing approaches: the careful logical and logistic planning of all types of operation, including the more elusive ones; emphasis on planned spillover and demonstration effect; emphasis on the "upward loop"; the establishment of complementary and supporting projects to create scarce human-resources inputs; emphasis on the necessity of detailed planning of the production process, down to its very "grass-roots" level.

The differences between the two approaches are as important as their similarities. The regional focus attempts to create, within its limited regional radius, changes and development ripples that are mutually supporting and that add up to a powerful localized but all-inclusive development thrust. The aggregate production effect of this type of program will therefore be highly intensive but limited in its scope. The relative "closure" of the institutional framework and its relative isolation from the rest of the economy create an environment that is especially favorable to the motivation and training of the human resources of the development agency. The functional focus places the main emphasis on achieving, on a national scale, the greatest possible production impact that logistic resource limitation will make possible; since the front of attack will be much wider, it might be possible even in the initial phase to reach a significant portion of the sectorial economy. However, the criterion of "critical mass" will severely limit the number of production complexes that can be comprised in a specific action program, as well as the scope of operations for each selected production complex. Mainly because of its lack of "closure" (as a consequence of its close interconnection with the whole agricultural sector and certain aspects of the industrial and service sectors), the functional-focus type of program does not create conditions favorable for the development of human resources.

From the point of view of total economy, the functional focus, at least in the early stages, represents the more efficient use of critical resources. Most of the resources ought, therefore, to be allocated to this approach. Regional focusing might still be necessary as a complementary policy to provide the optimal setting for the formation of senior personnel, for adaptive applicative research, etc. Regional focusing would also be indicated in areas where past major investments in upgrading water and land resources have not led to significant increases in productivity. Under such conditions the return on complementary operations might be great enough to warrant giving priority to regionally rather than functionally oriented projects.

In conclusion it may be said that a combined policy, including some regional foci but allocating the larger portion of the critical resources to functional foci, constitutes the best overall solution. The regional foci would be undertaken to areas that, owing to prior investments or special conditions (e.g., proximity to major markets), may be expected to yield exceptionally good returns per unit of critical resources; regional foci would also serve as centers for adaptive research aimed at optimizing the compositions of input packages for specific regions and crops and for measurement of resources-outcome ratios. Regional foci would also provide the setting for developing senior professional decision makers for all types of sectorial programs.

If, for one of the above reasons, it has been decided to set up a regional project, such a project could also be used as a center for priming a functionally oriented program. To achieve the latter objective, special care ought to be taken to intensify spillover effects and initiate demonstration effects in areas that are within a reasonable radius of the project but beyond project boundaries. These demonstration operations ought to be functionally oriented and planned to form the priming phase for functionally oriented projects to be undertaken subsequently in the general area surrounding the regional project. The objective is to reinforce the development ripples initiated by the regional project. Thus, demonstrating effects radiating from a regional project could prepare the ground for more extensive functionally oriented projects and concurrently serve as their center of training and adaptive research.

22

TYPICAL MILESTONES OF THE DEVELOPMENT OF THE AGRICULTURAL SECTOR

... je les (les hommes) vois paresseux devant une fin raisonnable .... C'est pourquoi il y a tant d'oeuvres devant nous que nous jugeons bonnes et que nous ne faisons point.[1]

ALAIN (*Propos*)

UNFORMED AND PREFORMED DEVELOPMENT INSTITUTIONS

Even a cursory review of the case histories of development projects in emerging countries reveals milestones characteristic of specific development phases. Actual development trajectories pass close to these milestones. Their existence in spite of extreme variety in resources geometry, sociopolitical space, and growth capacity of various countries points toward common structural features which "bend" the trajectories close to these milestones. Their description may provide some kind of bench mark for the orientation of development planners.

Typical bench marks cannot, of course, be used to set up a development program; there is no substitute for pùrposeful planning based on specific material and sociopolitical conditions. Nevertheless, the use of bench marks enables us to check whether we are traveling in the right direction, and if not to change direction in order to get on course.

The present chapter describes such bench marks for two typical sets of conditions, two characteristic points on a continuous scale of resources development:

1. A planning space with no significant past development history in the relevant resources sector

2. A planning space with a significant past development history

The first case is characterized by a lack of predetermined paths of least

[1] I find them (people) dilatory when confronted with a reasonable goal .... Therefore we are faced by many tasks which we judge useful but never accompish.

resistance and institutionalization, on the one hand, and the low capacity of the development authorities, on the other hand. The second case has the advantage of a development capacity performed to a certain extent by past operations and formalized in development routines and institutions. It will, however, suffer from lack of relevance of preformed paths of least resistance created during the early days of development. It is difficult in the first case to find the right path because of limitations in information experience and scanning capacity. In the second case, difficulties stem from systematic bias accumulated during a mostly misdirected development history.

The above two positions on the development scale are but transition phases to a position on the scale marking a mature economy. Their joint location on the less mature end of the development scale accounts for some of their similarities, the distance between their positions on the scale for the differences between them.

The joint characteristics are limitation of angle of view and limitation of development capacity. The angle-of-view limitation manifests itself in inability to see the overall resources and demand pattern of the sectors and to comprehend all relevant dimensions of phase space. Programs drawn up under such limitations suffer from the arbitrariness of the composition of their project population which does not stand up to the test of exhaustiveness. Limitations of capacity result from quantitative, qualitative, and structural deficiencies of human resources. For obvious reasons these limitations are more crippling in the first category of conditions.

The differences between the two positions on the development scale stem, of course, from differences in their past development history and its imprint on human resources and institutions. Where no significant past development history exists, there will be little bias, few institutional barriers, few preformed paths of least resistance—in short, relatively greater freedom of choice, but freedom counterbalanced by relatively low operative capacity.

In countries with a significant development history, biases will have been developed and formalized in irrelevant success criteria; institutions will have been entrenched, vested interests created, paths of least resistance formalized. All these tend to create hypertrophies of specific aspects of development—usually capital investment in the politically strong departments—and hypotrophies of others—usually the nonmaterial dimensions in the politically weak ones. Such skewed development severely limits freedom of choice in relation to future development planning; yet it does lead to a strengthening of the development capacity of the human resources of the favored departments.

It is difficult to decide which of the two cases is the easier to plan for: the *tabula rasa* situation of case 1 with few prejudices but extreme limitations of resources, or the "running concern" atmosphere of case 2 where progress made on a wrong development path is painstakingly measured by irrelevant criteria. One thing, however, is certain: if we wish to induce improvement of planning, the two cases need different approaches. The recommended approaches are outlined below.

CASE ONE: UNFORMED DEVELOPMENT INSTITUTIONS

The basic problem encountered in areas with little or no development experience is lack of development tools and information. Development tools and information can be created only within a successful development process which, in turn, requires tools and information. To overcome this hen-and-egg dichotomy, we must introduce a priming process characterized by three basic features:

1. It will have to comprise a "catalyst."
2. It will have to emphasize initially generation of tools and information rather than production of commodities.
3. It will have to establish the external framework which, in the prevailing context, is most conducive to the generation of tools and information.

The catalyst will be needed in order to initiate organization of the planning space, to provide the necessary basic orientation, and to assist in the generation of new motivation and indoctrination. The catalyst can be introduced from other sectors of the economy or borrowed from other countries.

The creation of development tools refers to tools for the transformation of the whole institutional framework at the production level. The type of transformation implied here is not limited to production techniques but refers principally to the responses of man to stimuli and incentives.

To ensure propitious conditions for the emergence of transformation of human resources, pilot projects might have to be established. In such projects, controlled conditions are created which provide both an atmosphere conducive (in the presence of catalysts) to the necessary transformations and the isolation from the less propitious general atmosphere necessary to protect incipient transformation until it becomes "refrozen" (to use Kurt Lewin's suggestive term). Pilot projects perform duties similar to those of nurseries in a plantation project (see also Chapter 21).

Also of importance are the mobilization and maintenance of political support. The greatest possible identification of the political hierarchy with the development program ought to be ensured from the beginning and maintained throughout the critical development period. To make a priming program politically attractive it would have to be spelled out as the first step of a more ambitious development program, the outcomes of which would be sufficiently important to become meaningful to larger groups of the population. Maintaining political identification with the proposed priming program will require avoidance, at this stage, of sensitive political issues related to powerful vested-interest groups—at least as long as the impetus of the program is not strong enough to justify such a luxury. This constraint will imply limitations of initial priming activities to aspects and areas politically least controversial. With the growth of the development program, new vested interests related to program objectives will emerge; with the emergence of such support, areas of application can be expanded and the easier of the sensitive problems tackled.

Albert Hirschman[2] has described how change can be "smuggled in via side effects"; the side effects of development involved here are the creation of new vested-interest groups related to the program and interested in its continuation and expansion and the gradual modification of the development concepts of the political hierarchy.

It is, of course, impossible to design a generally applicable blueprint for a successful pilot project for case 1 situations. (The basic structural features and the potential building blocks for such blueprints are described in various parts of this book.) Every specific set of conditions calls for a specific program solution. Though details and tactical approach might differ from case to case, structural similarity in the basic planning situation implies similarities in basic planning strategies.

In the following, we shall delineate some typical phases of development programs of land and water resources for countries with scant development histories in this sector. A desirable program sequence falls into three characteristic phases:

Phase one: better use of existing basic means of production, mainly by the addition of current production inputs and intangible inputs—human, structural, and institutional—with relatively little emphasis on capital investment

Phase two: improvement of the existing basic means of production with a balanced emphasis on both capital investment and input improvement

Phase three: creation of new means of production

From the point of view of marginal analysis, these three phases should be implemented chronologically. However, there will, and there probably should, be much overlapping or intermingling of phases. Phase 1 will generally contain some elements of phase 2 or even initial steps relating to phase 3. This dilution of a program based on purely economic analysis by elements unwarranted according to such analysis is nevertheless justified: we must allow in each phase for the need to lay the structural and institutional foundations for the coming phase, and we must keep in mind political and psychological desiderata.

Some characteristic features of the three typical phases of development programs are described in the following.

Phase one This phase is concerned with improved use of existing basic means of production combined with the provision of improved production inputs. The basic means of production in emergent economies are generally inefficiently used and inadequately backed up by inferior production inputs, and a relatively small current outlay and capital investment are sufficient to bring about a significant increase in efficiency. Hence, this aspect of growth will be the obvious initial choice from the point of view of marginal analysis.

The difficulties that crop up in the first phase lie mainly in the fields of human and institutional resources. The measures we take are an initial frontal

[2] Albert O. Hirschman, *Development Projects Observed,* The Brookings Institution, Washington, 1967, p. 168.

attack upon a firmly entrenched but stagnant subsistance economy. Patience and perseverance will be required if a breach is to be made in the front. Apprehensive of such effort, many planners despair and choose the easy way by seeking a glamorous "hardware package." However, without at least a partial breakthrough on the front there is no hope of achieving sustained growth in any later phase. On the other hand, overenthusiastic, large-scale adoption of first-phase measures not based on realistic appraisal of the development-resources inventory are not less dangerous than hardware escapism: our forces would be so thinly spread over a vast front of resistance that their impact would remain subliminal and resistance against change would only be strengthened.

Breaches in the stagnation front are not the only effect of the proposed procedure. The gradual change brought about in motivation and structure of both the developer and the developee will also indirectly affect the political hierarchy and thereby create the necessary social, institutional, and structural preinvestment atmosphere for phases 2 and 3, both of which involve large-scale capital investment that would remain only partially utilized or wholly idle without preparatory structural transformation. The very emergence of such new structural and institutional foundations gives the development group the necessary self-confidence to plan further massive growth-oriented interventions reaching into phases 2 and 3. It engenders trust on the part of national and international financial institutions, encouraging them to support such programs.

The phase 1 "attack" is the most important part of our development campaign; to a considerable extent the success or failure of the whole campaign depends on the outcome of this initial thrust. Neither the human resources required for success nor the strength of the forces of resistance against change should be underestimated.

Programs eligible for the first phase of the project generally include improvement of cultivation and irrigation methods, crop and seed selection, plant-protection chemicals and fertilizer application, livestock improvement, provision of semi-industrial home facilities, improvement of land tenure and fragmentation, and improvement of potable water supplies. Implementation of such measures, simple as it looks on paper, involves the creation of major structural and institutional capacity, and it is this aspect which constitutes the most difficult task of the phase 1 program. The necessary dilution with phase 2 and 3 elements will have to be built into phase 1 programs so as to ensure continuity of the development process beyond phase 1. In this context, each phase constitutes also an infrastructural preinvestment program for the subsequent phase.

Phase two The basic means of production actually in use in emergent economies are rarely developed to their full capacity. Phase 2 aims at raising utilization of basic resources to full capacity levels. The structural and institutional involvement, though less pervasive than in phase 1, will still be commanding. Stepping up and improving the conservation and utilization of water resources in partial use will often represent the central investment features of this phase. These features will include: increasing water-resources yield by conservation measures, construction of effective conveyance structures, improvement of existing irrigation methods and introduction of new methods, increasing seasonal and overall availability by storage and other manipulative measures, adding new facilities to increase withdrawal and conveyance capacity of the water resources to their sustainable yields.

In the agricultural sector, phase 2 measures might include: measures relating to crop planning, increase of the cropping area and introduction of new crops, seed improvement suited to local soil and climatic conditions, initiation of more basic methods for improved cultivation, more rational use of fertilizers and irrigation water, establishment of production incentives, cooperative organization for storage, transport, and marketing of produce and for credit procurement, provision of supporting industrial facilities utilizing agricultural products.

Some phase 2 aspects will have already been initiated in phase 1, and the impetus there obtained can be utilized in the subsequent larger phase 2 application; most aspects of phase 1 will be carried over to phase 2, and those of phase 2 into phase 3.

Phase three The third phase, the project phase in the orthodox sense of the word, is usually the exclusive concern of planners. It is generally the capital-intensive, less subdivisible, and therefore more lumpy phase, lower in marginal benefits, and more dependent for these benefits on a developed socio-institutional infrastructure that can be created only in the earlier phases discussed above. Benefit from phase 3 investment will greatly depend on the extent to which structural and institutional preconditions have been created by prior implementation of phases 1 and 2. The third or project phase needs no defenders: for the technocrat, it is the phase for which he has been trained; for the politician, this most spectacular phase of development is the one that has the greatest political appeal.

Choosing a program mix From their beginning, programs should be made up of elements of all three phases. Development should be initiated with a program embodying mainly constituents of phase 1, followed by elements of phase 2, and including aspects of phase 3 only to the extent that they are necessary to build up the potential of the development group for the later phases of the program. Subsequent programs should be based mainly on phase 2 features, but in addition to some carry-over and continuation of phase 1 features they should also include a much larger proportion of phase 3 features. The later stages will be composed mainly of constituents of phase 3.

CASE TWO: PREFORMED DEVELOPMENT INSTITUTIONS

As already mentioned, our freedom of action in case 2 will be more limited than in case 1. Possibly the most striking manifestation of the limitation in our freedom of action is the modification brought about in planning space and in institutional framework by lack of balance in past development programs. Certain aspects of development might have been given special emphasis. Institutions entrusted with these aspects will have had a chance to develop and grow (usually at the cost of other, possibly even more important ones), and positive feedbacks will have emerged that will further strengthen strong and further weaken weak institutions. Information collection will have emphasized these favored aspects. Finally, the political hierarchy will gradually identify itself with the hypertrophied aspects of development which it helped to create.

Distortions encountered in case 2 situations and measures to correct them will bear certain structural similarities and will therefore be easier to define than in the less structured case 1 situations.

The hypertrophied aspect of development in developing countries will usually be the physical engineering one. Originally this aspect might have been given priority because of the easy transferability of engineering know-how and the possibility to purchase it. Design, construction, and commissioning of facilities can be bought from other countries and organizations. The physical aspects also do not require the creation of highly specific information that would have to be generated by pilot projects, such as data on responses of crops to local ecology, of development institutions to programs, and of the producer to incentives and other changes in his decision environment.

Faced by such a case 2 situation, the planner ought to initiate three types of operations in relation to existing programs:

1. Design programs for the provision of those complementary investments and inputs required in order to bring prior investments to full fruition. Investments referred to here will usually be of the agroengineering type (field drainage, field irrigation, leveling, tools and equipment); complementary inputs will comprise production inputs, know-how, incentives, and the human resources required to improve or set up the necessary institutions.
2. Complement the resources aspect of the planning space by including in it all relevant resources and their potential manipulation. In an irrigation project this might, for instance, take the form of introducing into the resources inventory groundwater as well as surface water and integrated management measures comprising both types of water resources on a basin-wide basis.
3. Expand the planning space to include, for instance, adjoining basins and integrate utilization of their water resources with those of the original basin.

Regarding new projects, the planner ought to anticipate what scarcities might jeopardize development in the forthcoming planning period. Most of the nonmaterial complementary inputs will be among the scarce resources. The planner ought therefore to design special projects to accelerate generation of the scarce inputs. Similarly, he ought to propose pilot operations to generate the information relating to the use of inputs.

Complementary investment and input programs Analysis of investment in irrigation projects in developing countries with a significant development history typically uncovers projects whose principal physical features (diversion, storage, conveyance, and distribution facilities) have been completed, yet which are not fully productive, for these projects still lack complementary investments (e.g., the agroengineering aspects of on-farm development, such as leveling, irrigation and drainage, tools), complementary transformations (e.g., modification of response patterns of the producer, institutional infrastructure), and complementary inputs of adequate quality (e.g., seeds, fertilizers, and plant-protection chemicals).

The obvious rational approach would be to compare the return on such complementary investments and inputs with the return on basic plus complementary investments and inputs in proposed new projects and select the alternative with the highest return. However, in most situations the division of work and the balance of power between the relevant departments create formidable obstacles against adopting such a rational approach. The responsibility for the basic investments, on the one hand, and for the complementary investments and inputs, on the other hand, will often be located in different ministries. In the absence of integrative metaplanning, each ministry will attempt to maximize the operational level within its own scope of responsibility, without regard to the necessary complementary activities of other ministries. Each ministry will also promptly identify maximization of its own operational level with optimization of the overall operation. In many cases, ministries responsible for different facets of the same program will compete aggressively for the same scarce resources, instead of agreeing upon an investment pattern that would optimize overall fruition.

Complementary investments and inputs for existing projects generally merit priority over new large-scale projects for two basic reasons: firstly, because they yield a higher return (except where the original investment was based on radically wrong assumptions) and, secondly, because they are in any case necessary for all new projects.

Awareness of the unsatisfactory return on past investments will not necessarily lead to the correct diagnosis, much less to the correct therapy. Attitudes and procedures will have become so fossilized as to be unamenable to change by reasoning. Some special combination of circumstances will be required to effect the necessary change. The demonstration effect of a successful project, one which for special reasons was implemented on multidimensional lines, might constitute such a turning point toward a deeper development approach. Exploratory attempts by the strongest ministry, at coordinative metaplanning, might also lead toward the adoption of a more comprehensive approach. Finally, orientation of development thinking can be changed through pressures applied by funding agencies.

Fruition of projects will be obstructed not only by lack of complementary facilities and inputs but also by equally forbidding legal and institutional barriers, often rooted in powerful vested interest. These barriers will usually be the most difficult to breach. Land tenure is the most important example of such a barrier. Barriers which trace their source to purely administrative deficiencies are more easily removed. Overcomplex procedures for obtaining production credits are an example of this second category of barriers.

Comprehensive basin programs Water-resources development will often proceed for years and decades in direct response to current requirements. In such cases no attempt will have been made to fully evaluate the various resources and the anticipated demand of a basin and to establish a long-term optimized plan for upgrading resources according to demand. Piecemeal decision making might continue until the basin reaches its limit of utilization inherent in prevailing use patterns. The development path chosen will usually be rather arbitrary, determined by piecemeal decisions of the local development institutions or the engineering groups entrusted with the development. Selection of the source for initial development and the management pattern to be applied in its utilization will often follow the most conventional but not necessarily the most desirable line. Once a pattern of development is selected, the chances are that it will be retained until its ultimate limitations are reached.

When these limitations are reached, one of the following circumstances or a combination of them will occur:

1. At prevailing management patterns, the total available flow of the resource will not be sufficient to meet anticipated needs.
2. Flow variations might prove greater than anticipated, necessitating more regulative facilities than can be economically constructed.
3. A number of demands might compete for the same supply, with no authority available to arbitrate.

The planner, finding himself in such a fix, will realize that past decision patterns are inadequate, and he will become amenable to a change in planning approach, i.e., adoption of a comprehensive basin program.

The comprehensive basin approach could begin by analyzing the resources geometry—in space, time, and the other relevant dimensions of water quantity and quality—and the demand geometry. Such an analysis would indicate the optimal roles of the available resources in providing a supply satisfying the requirements of the several water uses involved. In such a comprehensive plan, every source would be assigned its role in the firming up and in the other regulative operations necessary to overcome flow variations. Every use would in turn be analyzed for extent of consumptive use, suitability of waste or return flows for reuse, and sensitivity to mineral and biological water pollution.

Adoption for a "mature" basin of the comprehensive resources-development approach could have important implications for water-development planning in general. Once the usefulness of the comprehensive approach is proved in a mature basin, it will also become the logical choice for new development projects. Greater emphasis upon the role of groundwater will often be one of the important features of a comprehensive development policy. In mature basins, groundwater will provide a vitally needed firming up supply and regulative facility. In early phases of development, groundwater will frequently (for reasons given in various parts of this book) be the most suitable source for priming the development process. Occasionally the pilot role of groundwater proves so important as to warrant higher priority to development of basins where groundwater, along with surface water, is available in quantities sufficient for the initial priming phase.

Interbasin integration Unless the planning platform and the level of metaplanning are continuously raised, projects will sooner or later reach the capacity limitation of the planning space originally selected. Their water-resources management within the previous planning boundaries might have to be supplemented by an interbasin plan, i.e., by extending the boundaries of planning space to include one or more additional basins.

Seen from a long-term point of view, expansion of the planning space in response to the emergence of resources scarcity therapies represents the introduction of metaplanning on a limited scale. Such partial metaplanning will gradually raise the planning point of view until the regional plans fit and merge into a national planning mosaic.

Generation of critically short resources A fourth typical remedial approach (more fully covered elsewhere in this book) needs mention here for the sake of completeness: the generation of critically short inputs or other remedial measures for overcoming development bottlenecks. These short inputs will, as a rule, be the training, motivation, and organization of the human resources required for the diversified tasks inherent in comprehensive development. Complementary aspects of these short inputs relate to the legal-institutional framework.

23 TRANSFORMATION AT THE VILLAGE LEVEL

Les hommes se hâtent de ressembler au portrait que vous vous faites d'eux.[1]

ALAIN (*Propos*)

THE EMPATHIC APPROACH

The farmer's supposedly irrational economic behavior and paradoxical responses have been explained by a number of ingenious theories. However, the farmer's apparent response inconsistency primarily reflects the analyst's own lack of imagination.

Two basic approaches, the naïve and the empathic, hypothesize about human behavior within different cultures. Farmers in subsistence economies live in cultures that greatly differ from those of the analysts, local or foreign. The naïve approach implies projection of the psychological space and response patterns of the observer. The observer using the empathic approach attempts to keep his analysis free from the preset patterns rooted in his own psychological space. On the basis of actual field observations, he attempts to construct a psychological space that is relevant to the society he is studying. Since the naïve approach introduces attitudes and criteria alien to the psychological space being studied, hypotheses based on this approach fail to find regularities of response and generally have low predictive value. Theories claiming that the farmer responds irrationally to incentives belong to this category.

The present chapter outlines the basic framework of the transformation of the village-level agricultural production process in terms of the empathic approach.

THE FARMER'S EXTERNAL AND INTERNAL ENVIRONMENTS

Theodore Schultz has repeatedly refuted the myth of the low efficiency of the traditional farmer. Given the quality of his inputs, his institutional framework,

[1] People quickly come to resemble the image you make of them.

and the state of art available to him, the farmer makes a reasonably good use of his means of production. Provided with improved inputs, relevant techniques, and incentives, the traditional farmer responds much as would the farmer in developed countries. This claim is proved by recent development history (e.g., West Africa during and after the Second World War and recent developments in India and Pakistan).

The low production efficiency of traditional agriculture is the combined result of an inadequate production environment and an inadequate socio-psychological space. *Inadequacies in the production environment* can be traced to material factors (low quality of basic resources, i.e., land and water, and of inputs and tools), informational factors (inadequate agrotechniques, lack of marketing data, insufficient knowledge of crop responses), and institutional factors (institutions for procurement of inputs, for marketing, for extending credits, for supplying information, and for the whole land tenure–water rights complex). *Inadequacies in the farmer's psychological space* can be traced to socially conditioned, though individually acquired, personality traits such as low achievement needs and resistance to innovation. The farmer's conservatism is reinforced by his low risk-taking propensity. His reserves are as a rule extremely tenuous or nonexisting. Investments and risks in his traditional agrotechniques are well known to him; they constitute the lowest possible risk he is bound to take to assure a crop. New techniques involve additional outlays financed by loans generally obtained under unfavorable conditions—a serious risk. Because of his lack of reserves, the farmer as decision maker is biased toward low risk taking and will generally reject innovations that involve risks.

To obtain a prompt response on a wide production front, we shall have to transform the farmer's psychological space in line with the improvements effected in his production environment. It is not sufficient to increase the variety of the environment if the farmer's *response variety* remains limited; transformation of the psychological space ought to bring the farmer's response variety to a level consistent with an achieved or intended improvement of the production environment.

The division into production environment and psychological space is of course a simplification introduced for analytical purposes. In reality, the two interact, every major change in the production environment altering the farmer's psychological space, and vice versa.

THE TRADITIONAL FARMER'S PRODUCTION ENVIRONMENT

Material factors We need not dwell upon the more conspicuous deficiencies in the traditional farmer's basic production environment, i.e., his small plot, short water supply, and frequently poor soil. The development planner has generally focused on these deficiencies, which a reasonably proficient conventional planning capacity (national or foreign) can adequately redress. Improvement of the basic production environment usually involves relatively heavy, and sometimes indivisible, investments. Financing difficulties will often be eased by the assistance of international financing agencies, and planning and implementation difficulties by foreign consulting and contracting firms. Thus, considerable progress in upgrading the basic production environment of the traditional farmer may be achieved without major transformations of development agencies or of the farmer and his production process, hence the relatively advanced status of this type of operation in many developing countries.

The low quality or insufficient rate of application of current production inputs, i.e., seeds, fertilizers, pest and weed controls, and soil conditioners, is possibly the most crippling deficiency of the farmer's production environment. The desirability of providing adequate production inputs seems as obvious as that of upgrading basic production facilities. However, since provision of improved production inputs involves a new institutional framework, successful consummation of this type of operation is much less widespread. The great success recently achieved by the large-scale campaigns in East Asia for the provision of improved production inputs may help to introduce similar campaigns in other parts of the world.

Since emphasis will usually be on improving the output of existing labor rather than replacing it by capital-intensive mechanical equipment, the stress on improving tools and equipment will fall on introducing relatively simple and inexpensive tools to replace ineffective traditional ones.

Informational factors The most important informational deficiency in the traditional farmer's production environment is of course his obsolete agrotechnique. Theodore Schultz might be right in his claim that traditional agrotechniques are relatively well adapted to the low quality of some production inputs or the complete lack of others. However, once the new or improved production inputs are introduced, their successful application will depend on the dissemination of the relevant new agrotechniques. Similar considerations will, of course, apply to information related to introduction of new crops.

Information on market opportunities and prices (especially for new crops) will also be extremely inadequate in traditional agriculture. The creation of new channels of information on these subjects will therefore be an essential part of improvement of the farmer's production environment.

Institutional factors Traditional institutional structure will as a rule be limited to the village level and will cover only a few specific aspects of mutual help—all adapted to traditional inputs and agrotechniques. Introduction of new or improved production inputs will be conditional upon establishing some new type of institutional framework for procuring and distributing these inputs, for extending seasonal credits to finance purchase inputs, for disseminating specific information on their application, and often also for marketing crops. Similar considerations will apply to introduction of new crops, where emphasis will be mainly on information and marketing.

Land tenure and water rights Land tenure and sometimes also water-rights complexes are among the most formidable obstacles to upgrading the traditional farmer's production environment. Prevailing crop-division rules and insecurity of tenure will act as powerful disincentives against investment in the land and in crops. Often the landlord will also control marketing channels, and the farmer will (probably rightly) assume that increase in crop yields will lower prices paid to him.

THE TRADITIONAL FARMER'S PSYCHOLOGICAL SPACE

The most striking feature of the psychological space of the traditional farmer is the stable equilibrium that governs his behavior. This equilibrium is a direct result of the extreme limitations in the range of opportunities inherent in the traditional production environment and in the traditional response patterns available to the farmer. Because of this double limitation, the traditional farmer's production behavior will appear to be highly routinized.

The individual farmer is extremely self-sufficient. Rejecting outside interference, especially if sponsored by government, the farmer will doubt both the disinterestedness and the proficiency of outside intervention and will suspect the honesty of those implementing such intervention. Farmers in a Middle Eastern country, to cite one striking case, offered bribes to the extension agents carrying out a livestock inoculation campaign so as to have their cattle excluded from the campaign.

We have already mentioned that the traditional farmer, because of lack of reserves, has an aversion to risk taking, especially to such risks that might endanger his economic survival. Unfortunately, he will classify many important innovation measures in this category. Finally, we need to keep in mind that the traditional farmer's patterns of reasoning will differ from those of the transformation agent.

ALTERNATIVE THERAPEUTIC APPROACHES

Transformation of the traditional farmer's psychological space is obviously a complex, slow operation and one that has to be applied on an enormous scale: in developing countries 40 to 80 percent of the economically active population are traditional farmers. The task can hardly compete for glamor with the more spectacular aspects of upgrading the physical production environment. No wonder that the attempt is sometimes made to evade the Herculean task of transformation by "dissolving" it—to use Stafford Beer's apt term. Dissolving the problem of transformation implies bypassing the traditional small farmer and his decision and production problems and initiating a new decision and production process implemented by local or foreign entrepreneurs employing farm labor and gradually absorbing some of the traditional farmers. Foreign agricultural entrepreneurs may be assumed to possess the know-how and capabilities necessary for setting up and operating a reasonably effective agricultural production venture. In many cases this would at least partially be true also of local entrepreneurs. Even where some publicly initiated support might be necessary to guide local agricultural entrepreneurs, such guidance will be incomparably easier to furnish to a limited number of entrepreneurs than to the multitudes of traditional small holders in the agricultural sector of a developing nation. Where agricultural development is handled by entrepreneurs, the government will, as a rule, be called upon to provide only the basic development of the production environment, e.g., irrigation facilities; in some cases such major investments might be undertaken (wholly or in part) by entrepreneurs. Procurement and distribution of inputs, marketing, financing, etc., may all be left to private initiative.

An entrepreneurial agricultural undertaking is of course profit oriented. Since, for political reasons, the minimum wage level of agricultural labor is liable to rise more rapidly than the income of the often underemployed marginal small holder, replacement of labor by mechanization will become attractive sooner for the entrepreneur than for the small holder. As a matter of course, mechanization also presupposes a minimum scale which will be met by the entrepreneur but not by the small holder. Furthermore, entrepreneurs will favor mechanization because it diminishes their organizational and social problems. Thus mechanization and displacement of labor will gain ground rapidly in entrepreneurial operations. If the latter are carried out on a large enough scale, massive displacement of agricultural labor will result. This displacement will not be compensated for by the development of additional absorptive capacity in the nonagricultural sectors, and the results will be increased unemployment and premature migration to urban communities.

In underdeveloped countries, the industrial base is relatively small and partly made up of capital-intensive and labor-extensive undertakings. The service sector is often overstaffed. Because of the differences in the growth base, the growth in absolute terms of employment opportunities in the industrial sector is relatively low, and the absolute number of workers in the agricultural sector will therefore continue to increase for one to two generations, even though their percentage share in overall employment will continually decrease. The entrepreneurial solution, while locally increasing production efficiencies and volumes, tends to reduce agricultural employment; simultaneously, the size of the labor force in agriculture will, as a result of population increase, continue to rise. Thus the basic structural problems of agricultural countries are intensified rather than solved. Confining the development of agricultural production capacity and of new sectorial income to a narrow sector of the working population will also adversely influence effective demand for both agricultural products and services and for the simpler industrial commodities. Because of the relatively high income elasticity of agricultural demand in the low-income strata of the population, the stimulating effect of a better income distribution will be especially pronounced in the area of agricultural demand.

Lastly, confining production growth to a limited number of entrepreneurs without concurrent absorption of redundant manpower in nonagricultural sectors will lead to a dramatic polarization of a self-perpetuating dual-economy situation with all its implied social tensions and conflicts.

Bypassing the traditional small farmer and the difficult task of transformation might in specific situations effectively accelerate agricultural production. This approach has been successful in short-range economic terms both with local entrepreneurs (e.g., the Pacific Northwest in Mexico) and with foreign entrepreneurs (e.g., sugar-cane plantations in Peru's coastal plain). Although bypassing transformation might in some countries be justified for urgent economic reasons, programs based on evading transformation cannot solve the fundamental structural problem of agricultural underdevelopment, i.e., how to increase the effectiveness of the agricultural production process, thereby raising the income of the agricultural sector, without dislodging more people from agriculture than the nonagricultural sectors can absorb. This problem can be solved only by upgrading the production environment and transforming the psychological space of the farmer on a truly nationwide scale.

TRANSFORMATION AT THE VILLAGE LEVEL

Transformation at the village level is a painstaking and complex process whose dimensions are psychological (the psychological space of the farmer), institutional (institutions from village to regional levels), and informational (generation and dissemination of applicative know-how). To be effective, the transformation campaign would have to be carried out simultaneously in all three dimensions to ensure that progress in each is supported by progress in the others. Planning and conducting such a transformation campaign require management talent, a scarce commodity in Third World countries. Nevertheless, there is no way around transformation if our paramount aim is to develop the nation rather than boost production by a dual-economy system.

The proposed grass-roots approach might also have another important side effect: institutions, services, and processing industries built up from the bottom upward will require physical facilities which will tend to be located relatively close to crop areas. Thus, a more harmonious geographic distribution of primary, secondary, and tertiary activities related to the agricultural sector will be achieved. Such a distribution of facilities will divert a considerable percentage of village migrants to small and medium-sized service and industrial centers distributed throughout the countryside. If undertaken systematically and on large enough scale, this distributive effect might significantly alleviate the danger of explosive growth of population in a limited number of large urban communities.[2]

The first and most agonizing difficulty facing the planner of transformation will of course be availability of resources. To make a nationally significant impact, transformation must be conducted on a large scale: hundreds of thousands or even millions of decision makers must be reached. This calls for training, organizing, and deploying a great number of people in the very specific tasks involved in transformation. In developing countries, personnel trained in the appropriate disciplines will almost never be available in sufficient numbers. Our first dilemma will therefore be how to divide available

[2] See also Barbara Ward's survey, "The Poor World's Cities," *The Economist*, 233:6589, Dec. 6, 1969, especially pp. 67–70.

human and capital resources *between direct application* to the production level (i.e., their use as direct or first-degree transformation inputs) and the *training* of additional human resources (or second-degree inputs), i.e., to expand the basis of the transformation process by training trainers.

Our second dilemma will be related to the *geographic distribution* of the first-degree transformation inputs: should we concentrate them to achieve effectiveness in depth over limited geographic areas, or should we spread them to gain partial effects over wider areas? There exists no ready-made solution to these two dilemmas. To obtain the solution for a specific context, the planner must apply an optimization procedure to the long-term use of available resources. Solutions typical for the early development phases will emphasize application of resources on a broad front to achieve selected high-return transformations rather than concentration of resources aiming at a full gamut of transformations on a limited front. When selecting the first type of policy, the planner will have to be wary of subliminal resources applications.

The third dilemma facing the planner will be the decision between *publicly* initiated and controlled *intervention* and reliance on *spontaneous* transformation processes. Since scarcity in human and capital resources in Third World countries will continue for a long time, we ought to aim at utilizing, catalyzing, and supporting spontaneous processes to the greatest possible extent. This can be achieved by an "internal-induction" type of learning effect (for instance, less transformation effort will be required to introduce modern techniques for the second crop than for the first) within the group to which transformation inputs have been channeled. It may also be achieved by intentionally setting up the transformation operation so as to maximize "external induction," i.e., the emergence of a widespread demonstration effect. Well-planned transformation projects might combine both effects.

Maintaining *compatibility of progress* in the various dimensions of transformation throughout the transformation process is an aspect of transformation planning that needs special attention. This is absolutely essential to maintain viability of the transients of the system under transformation. Since the transformation operations in the various dimensions will be undertaken by different sections of the development organization with diverse degrees of efficiency and needs for achievement, central coordination will have to prevent rapid progress in one dimension without appropriate progress in the complementary dimensions. Such coordinative control may necessitate curbing the ambitions of the more capable sections of the organization. If production of new crops, for instance, outpaces provision of packaging, storing, transporting, and marketing facilities and institutions, a great deal of the economic effect of the production increase would be lost; such failure in coordination might have a shattering psychological effect on the farmer. Should coordinated growth rates of production and supporting institutions prove unfeasible, a compromise might have to be made by giving priority to such crops for which the lag of new supporting institutions would be least damaging, continuing such emphasis until institution building catches up.

Since *availability of human resources* for institution building might be one of the bottlenecks of transformation, the allocation of this limiting resource ought to be weighed carefully: introduction of crops that would yield attractive economic results at the price of excessive allocation of critical resources for complementary institution building might have to be set aside temporarily in favor of economically less attractive crops requiring smaller allocation of critically scarce resources.

For the same reason, transformation operations should be set up so as to encourage the "induction" of transformation and the formation, at the village level, of locally based auxiliary forces that could support and speed up further transformation. To achieve this end, the basic orientation adopted for transformation ought to be catalyzation of change, making it more acceptable rather than imposing it. Once change is initiated, public intervention ought to consist of supervising, advising, and guiding rather than of conducting operations.

The details of the transformation operation proper are beyond the scope of this book and the professional competence of the author. Therefore, we shall here confine our discussion to a few basic comments.

1. When establishing the format and style of communication with the farmer, the transformation agent—the professional or subprofessional whose task it is to set up and implement transformation—ought to make allowance for the difference in cultural conditioning between the farmer and himself. The farmer's reasoning will probably be less verbalized and less quantified than the agent's.

2. The agent ought to remember that the status conferred by his training will not necessarily be sufficient to convince the farmer of the wisdom of his practical advice. To obtain the farmer's confidence in his practical proficiency, the transformation agent should discuss with him his most pressing practical problems in the most down-to-earth manner, quoting actual experience and results achieved. Such a discussion ought to be conducted as an exchange of experience rather than as teaching sessions.

3. Generous use should be made of visual aids (slides, films, posters), stressing not only demonstration techniques but also results achieved. Films and slides made in village environments are preferable to those from agricultural research centers.

4. One of the first and perhaps most crucial tasks after establishing first contacts in village meetings will be to identify within the farmer's group individuals of relatively high need achievement and propensity for innovation. These personality traits as well as social status ought to be decisive in selecting farmers for the first innovation thrust.

5. Participation in innovation campaigns should be voluntary; the agent's tasks are to create the necessary incentives, remove the risks that most alarm farmers, communicate to participants the necessary techniques, and make certain that the qualifications of the majority of those joining in the first campaign conform with those outlined above.

6. A precondition for the campaign's success will be provision of the necessary input in the right quantity and quality at the right time, at prices that will create sufficient incentives to apply such inputs, and at conditions of financing that will minimize hardships and risks. The task of the initial campaign is to "unfreeze" traditional response patterns and demonstrate new ones and not to supply inputs to a few farmers at economically justifiable conditions. Therefore, opposition to supply inputs for the initial thrust below current self costs does not seem justified.

7. During the growing season, the demonstration plots ought to be periodically supervised and the necessary guidance provided.

8. Provision ought to be made to record inputs provided and to measure yield achieved in demonstration plots and in comparable untreated reference plots.

9. Proper use ought to be made in the second campaign of results achieved during the first campaign. The second campaign should need less "padding" to ensure response and a lesser participation of transformation agents (per farmer), since demonstration would have taken full effect; in addition, first-campaign farmers might be enlisted to assist (for a remuneration) in the second campaign.

10. At this stage, cooperative cells might be initiated at the village level. The purpose of these cells will be to gradually take over those tasks which the farmer cannot undertake by himself and to link the village with the county-level cooperative and other organizations. Village cooperatives might, for instance, handle distribution of production inputs, distribution of seasonal production credits, some marketing functions.

11. The participation of village cooperatives in the wider county-level organizations ought to be reinforced. This will enable the development group to gradually hand over responsibilities to farmer's organizations.

Finally, some comments on creating incentives to convince the farmer to innovate. Incentives are a difficult policy area and must be weighed within the context of the economy as a whole. Incentives represent part of the interface of our sectorial system with the national socioeconomic system. Incentives might be limited to particular measures such as lowering prices of specific inputs, or they might be conceived on a broader basis. The first type of incentive might be justified in many cases in order to compensate the farmer for local industry's low efficiency as compared with world-market standards. Since farm products will often be sold at world-market prices, such an intersectorial corrective would certainly be indicated in the early phases of transformation. The accelerated growth rate of input uses resulting from such incentives might in turn make possible larger plants, in which economy of scale might lower production costs of inputs.

Since incentives are to a certain extent interconnected and interchangeable, they ought not to be considered in isolation but as a composite policy. Incentives may include measures to minimize the farmers' risks (e.g., minimum price, crop insurance), measures to reduce the farmers' production costs (e.g., setting lower prices for production inputs), and fiscal measures (e.g., tax concessions or direct subsidies). In a developing country, where the great majority of the economically active population live from agriculture, and the product of the secondary and tertiary sectors is relatively small, only a limited extent of incentives will prove to be financially feasible.

24
TRANSFORMATION OF THE DEVELOPMENT AUTHORITY

Wenn wir die Menschen behandeln, als waeren sie, was sie sein sollten, so bringen wir sie dahin, wohin sie zu bringen sind.[1]

GOETHE

THE DECISIVE ROLE OF THE DEVELOPMENT AGENCY

The subject of this chapter is the upgrading of the development authority and its role occupants according to the requirements of development programs. The quality of the development authority alone, of course, does not fully determine the rate of agricultural development; the political decision process, the natural-resources and the development-resources vectors all bear upon the success of development programs. However, experience indicates that the most important single determining factor is the *quality of the development authority*. It is well known that developing countries, though deficient in most or all of the determining factors, can provide examples of highly successful operations. When analyzed, such examples reveal that in every case a specially gifted and motivated individual succeeded in establishing an effective development authority, an island of adequate organizational structure, within the deficient organizational environment of his country. Islands of effective organization develop more readily in the industrial and service sectors. These sectors lend themselves to a relatively high degree of isolation from the rest of the socioeconomic system, and within them both organization size and necessary front of change are relatively limited. There have been instances where an individual or a small group of individuals has succeeded in creating islands of organized growth even within a stagnating agricultural sector. All such success stories share one common feature—a relatively effective and motivated organization which, through some mechanism or other, retains its quality despite a deficient environment.

Since development is conceived, formalized, and implemented by develop-

[1] If we treat people as if they were what they ought to be, we shall head them to where they ought to be headed.

ment authorities, the discovery that development success depends on the quality of development authorities is hardly original; it is, nevertheless, a fact that is rarely acted upon. If rate and quality of development depend mainly on the quality of the development authority, upgrading of the latter ought to rank high among the targets (admittedly instrumental) of development programs and ought to be emphasized in the evaluation procedure.

Recognizing the importance of motivation and the performance level of development authorities, both national and international agencies have organized formal training programs to teach specific subjects or skills. Upon returning to his job, a trainee of such a program will certainly know more about the subject taught, but his basic attitudes and responses will remain unchanged. Moreover, he will still have to operate within a group and within a hierarchy of people whose basic attitudes are similarly inadequate. Improvement of development authorities, especially those responsible for agricultural transformation in developing countries, requires a broad re-formation conception which extends to basic attitudes and responses, action ideology, and professional decision making.

Basic attitudes of individuals and groups cannot be changed by formal teaching and training of individuals; such change requires fundamental reconditioning and retraining within a "well-conditioned" group, preferably one operating in a field and a socioeconomic environment close to those in which the authority will be expected to function. In developing countries, such well-conditioned groups will be conspicuous by their absence. Here we can trace our first vicious circle: developers in developing countries need upgrading; upgrading development presupposes adequate developers' groups to serve as training or transformation agents and environments; the absence of adequate training groups results in the perseverance of inadequate performance levels.

The attributes and capacities of developers that are most relevant to the development process are:

1. Need achievement, in our specific case, internalization of goal-setting complexes related to national objectives and to personal status
2. Adequate time span
3. Capacity to organize planning space
4. Capacity and readiness to make correct professional decisions

The attributes cited above (1 and 2) are the outcome of lifelong conditioning within family, school, and other social groups; deeply rooted in the personality structure, they are extremely resistant to change. The capacities cited above (3 and 4) are the outcome of professional training and conditioning in the use of professional concepts, models, and strategies.

For obvious reasons we cannot adopt Moses' solution to the problem of achieving basic transformation, namely, a forty-year sojourn in the desert awaiting the emergence of a new and, hopefully, better generation. That individuals and groups can change their attitudes under certain conditions has been proved by numerous specific successes in developing countries, as well as by some of the more radical political movements on both the left and the right. Some basic considerations that ought to govern our approach to the transformation of development authority officers (with special emphasis on water resources and agriculture) are outlined below.

PROBLEMS ENCOUNTERED IN THE TRANSFORMATION OF DEVELOPMENT AGENCIES

The sociopsychological space As we have pointed out, transforming developers implies changing their most firmly entrenched basic attitudes and response patterns. It will therefore not suffice to view the developers' specific professional problem-solving patterns in terms of their compatibility with program requirements, pointing out incompatibilities and "correct" responses. We shall have to probe the "internal logic" underlying prevailing response patterns, that is, define the sociopsychological space within which the developer operates and which, together with his largely preformed personality structure, determines these patterns.

Once we enter the developer's sociopsychological space, we are able to gain insight into what the biologist Jacob von Uexkill calls the *Bedeutung* (significance) of the various *Bedeutungstraeger* (carriers of significance) of the developer's *Umwelt und Innenwelt* (environment and internal space). We may then develop an operative *Bedeutungslehre* (science of signification) which will teach us how to modify the developer's sociopsychological space in order to transform his response pattern in the desired direction.

Limitations in the analysis of the sociopsychological space What we have termed the sociopsychological space is an extremely ill-defined and ill-structured type of phenomenon. It does not lend itself to rigorous definition of its variables and their interrelationships. The hypotheses which we shall have to use will be more metaphorical than logicomathematical. Although these difficulties do not lessen the importance for development planning of changing the sociopsychological space of the developer, they do determine our operational approach to the problem. We shall have to renounce the analytical and, to a great extent, even the experimental laboratory approach, resigning ourselves to a pragmatic combination of reasoning and trial and error, feeling our way toward a solution. Such a pragmatic approach—playing it by ear rather than using standard rules and checklists—will have to be entrusted to experienced practitioners in this field. Kurt Lewin's topological psychological models are an extremely useful tool in this context, and the following discussion leans heavily upon his concepts and terminology.[2]

The focus of remedial action Our next problem is the focus of remedial action: should we focus our retraining, reconditioning, and reindoctrination effort (a complex called transformation) toward a selected few, or should we apply it to a group, e.g., a planning team? Experience teaches that permanent

[2] See, for instance, Kurt Lewin, *Social Conflict,* Harper and Row, New York, 1948.

change of basic attitudes will depend on modification of a group. If we confine transformation efforts to individuals, they will be exposed during and after retraining to the negative attitudes of the "nonconverted" members of the group; such exposure will cause a serious erosion of newly acquired response patterns before they have had time to strike roots.

Nature of transformation process: catalyzation vs. imposition The subjects of the proposed transformation process are grown-up and mature individuals. If transformation is to change their sociopsychological space, changes effected will have to be internalized. This can be achieved only by change being freely opted for by individuals and groups, and gradually assimilated into their psychological makeup. The process of transformation will therefore have to be one of opting for rather than of imposing change. Since change cannot be assumed to evolve spontaneously at the desired rate, a catalyst will have to be introduced into the group to prime and accelerate change processes and to supplement available capacity insofar and for as long as is necessary. The emphasis in the catalyst's task will be upon formative rather than upon direct performance aspects. However, a certain scope of successful performance is a precondition for catalyzing change: the catalyst will therefore have to strike a balance between emphasis upon direct performance and emphasis upon the catalyzing aspects of his task.

The development process as framework for transformation The transformation process comprises modification of basic attitudes (e.g., need achievement) and improvement of professional decision skills. Neither can be effectively taught in formal courses or in simulations of case histories. Both require on-the-job training, which can be executed only within the framework of a well-managed development project. Only in such a context can we hope to comply with the following basic requirements of transformation of development groups:

1. "Closure" of a group created by common purpose or "goal concensus"[3]
2. Strengthening of the need for achievement
3. Emergence of leadership elements and organizational structure
4. Development of decision-making skills by current decisions made in real-life situations under the supervision of a highly trained operator
5. Providing "protection" from an "unimproved" environment during the gestation period of the transformation process, the group in training being "isolated" from the rest of the development authority

The formal task of the catalyst within a project group will be to draw up the program of operation, to design the initial organizational structure, to provide the necessary metathinking, guidance, and control, to help overcome unforeseen difficulties, and to provide professional support if and where necessary. His no less important informal task will be to help group members

[3] See Anthony Downs, *Bureaucratic Structure and Decision Making*, The Rand Corporation, Santa Monica, Calif., 1966.

organize the psychological space involved in problem solving, to catalyze the emergence of attitude changes, and to identify and support emerging leadership elements.

Intergroup relationship involving an upgraded group In order to be effective, the catalyzing operation will have to be applied with a certain minimal "critical mass" of catalyzing agents. To ensure this critical mass in spite of limited availability of "catalysts," and in order to facilitate the formation of methodology and accumulation of information, catalyzation initially will have to be confined to a specific project or program within the agricultural sector. Upgraded development groups will therefore have to face "nonconverted" groups from the same sector and other sectors, groups which supply services to the project or upon whose decisions some aspects of the project depend. These nonconverted groups will represent constraints (partly modifiable) upon the freedom of action of the "upgraded" group. To minimize the range of these constraints, the project selected as framework for upgrading operations ought to depend as little as possible upon services and decisions of other groups. Insofar as this is not possible, we ought to resort to one or a combination of the following operational modes:

1. Reducing such dependence, and increasing the authority of the selected project group by giving it a special status
2. Allowing for the constraint implied in the dependence
3. Bypassing the constraint
4. "Eroding" the constraint

THE TOPOLOGICAL MODEL OF THE DEVELOPERS' GROUP

Using for the following demonstration a simplified version of Kurt Lewin's topological approach and some of his terminology,[4] we can envisage the sociopsychological space of a typical professional member of a development agency planning group as follows:

The space is characterized by two poles: the developers' group at one end and a goal at the opposite end. From the developers' group issues the goal-seeking complex, characterized by a force vector changing over time. Between the developers' group and the goal lie obstacles, passive barriers or active counterforces, blocking the progress of the goal-seeking complex. The obstacles that the developers' group will strike first are usually those related to the sector or originating within it. Beyond the intrasectorial obstacles the developer faces others originating outside the sector.

Transposed into these terms, development planning as seen from the planner's point of view, i.e., from inside his psychological space, consists in his structuring his sociopsychological space sufficiently so as to enable him to identify a path through the complex topology of the development represented in his sociopsychological space.

[4] See also Kurt Lewin, *A Dynamic Theory of Personality,* McGraw-Hill Book Company, New York, 1935.

The psychological makeup of the planner in developing countries is characterized by two basic kinds of deficiencies:

1. Deficiencies in basic personality attitudes as expressed by weakness of motivation, lack of perseverance, and instability of the goal-seeking complex
2. Deficiencies in professional skill as expressed by lack of insight into the structure of obstacles and by limitations in capacity to structure psychological space

The development planner, striving after the development goal, will soon be faced by the opaqueness of the obstacles (intrasectorial and intersectorial) ahead of him. Limitations in his structuring capacity usually prevent him from finding a clear path through or around the obstacles. He will feel trapped by them, as did Ibsen's Peer Gynt when faced by the shapeless but all-engulfing "Great Crooked One." His goal-seeking complex being limited in strength and preseverance, the planner will not long persist in seeking a true path toward the goal; sooner or later he will escape into a world of pseudoresponses, either descending along what Lewin calls the "reality-irreality axis" to make-believe, or withdrawing into "encystment" and the negativistic attitude toward society and achievement connected with it. Both types of pseudoresponses are familiar phenomena. The make-believe world of development programs, which, upon inspection, proves to be lists of project names or arbitrary collections of half-digested project ideas, is the most common example of the first type of escape; the despair and cynicism of the intellectual elite of many developing countries are examples of the second type.

THE TRANSFORMATION PROCESS

Since the two basic deficiencies (i.e., in personal attributes and in professional skills) of the planner in developing countries are interrelated, they must be attacked simultaneously. A remedial program must encompass measures for transforming both. Experience accumulated in this field has rarely been adequately documented and subjected to systematic analysis. Therefore, the time may not yet have arrived for a full-scale exposition of approaches to transforming the psychological space of planners in developing countries. Some general comments may, nevertheless, be helpful.

The deficiency in personality attributes most important for development planning is the weakness of the goal-seeking complex resulting from the low need achievement characteristic of developing societies. Need achievement is a sociopsychological orientation whose content, direction, and strength are formed by family and other social groups before the individual reaches intellectual and emotional maturity. Later professional education and conditioning will not, as a rule, basically modify earlier attitudes. Since most development operations are performed by teams made up of individuals who have been preformed on similar lines, socially conditioned basic attitudes will tend to be reinforced within the work context. Promotion criteria that have no relevance to achievement will also tend to keep need achievement low. A group composed of individuals with low need achievement would typically exhaust its efforts in intraorganizational strife and pseudoactivities. To raise a group from this ultrastable equilibrium, its group dynamics will have to be radically changed by the introduction of an outside force, the catalyst.

A description of the operations involved in transforming personality attributes and group dynamics is beyond the scope of this book. These operations would include analyzing existing differentiation between individuals as regards need achievement, identification and support of potential leadership elements, establishing short-term attainable targets to focus the goal-seeking complex, establishing achievement-oriented promotion and reward criteria—in short, gradual creation of an achievement-oriented organizational structure within the group. To the extent that such structure emerges, the goal horizon and performance requirements could be raised and the group induced to operate at the next higher level.

Transformation related to *professional skills* might start with reducing the opaqueness of obstacles. Under the guidance of the catalyst, the group will learn to analyze obstacles, their extension and depth, and to locate gaps in obstacles or roundabout ways to bypass them; in short, they will learn to structure their psychological space. They will identify variable (resistances) and invariable (constraints) portions of obstacles. Gaps and loopholes of constraints, once identified, may serve as bench marks for defining feasible project paths. By defining such paths through and around obstacles, the planner's psychological space will cease to be dominated by seemingly impregnable barriers.

The planner can then be taught to transpose the several interventions into *logistic terms.* Logistic programming would lead to the design of the organizational structure required for channeling and controlling the application of logistic streams.

The continuous process of transforming personal attitudes and professional skills can be conveniently subdivided into three phases, characterized by Kurt Lewin[5] as: unfreezing existing equilibrium, establishing new equilibrium, and refreezing the latter.

THE THREE PHASES OF TRANSFORMATION

Unfreezing phase The unfreezing phase consists in gradually displacing old personal and professional attitudes by priming a sequence of personal and professional response changes that are related to more advanced attitudes. In this phase, old attitudes remain active and coexist with new ones which, though rationally approved by the individual, are still not truly adopted and internalized.

Mature individuals resent direct attempts to change their basic attitudes. We shall therefore have to achieve the necessary transformation indirectly, as

[5] Kurt Lewin, *Field Theory in Social Science,* Harper Torchbooks, Harper & Row, Publishers, Incorporated, New York, 1964, pp. 188–237.

a "by-product" of an improved professional operation. The transforming agent, the catalyst, by helping the group to structure its sociopsychological space in relation to specific development tasks, to X-ray obstacles, and to define development paths, will initiate a more goal-oriented stream of activities, one that will gradually reinforce need achievement and structural differentiation within the group. Such a stream will erode old associations of goal aspiration with frustration and establish new ones of aspiration with achievement. It will reverse the dissociation of self-seeking and self-transcending tendencies and create a link between the two. It will help dormant leadership capacity to assert itself.

When planning his "catalytic" interventions into group activities, the catalyst will have to base his proposed program of operation on a meta-analysis of the group's actual and potential roles in the development process. He would then have to select an operations sequence which, while ensuring a reasonable goal achievement, would provide training in the relevant professional problem-solving and decision-making skills and would also provide for internal restructuring and the emergence of a new group dynamics.

Establishment of new equilibrium This phase and its subsequent internalization are characterized by a gradual consolidation, as a consequence of a continued generation of responses initiated by the catalyst, of new attitudes and response patterns in group members. In this phase, changes in attitudes and professional skills will find expression in the group's organizational tone and structure and in the emergence of operational routines. Group dynamics will become a significant driving force, and self-seeking and self-transcending tendencies will be brought still closer.

The refreezing phase The refreezing phase is characterized by the setting of changed attitudes and skills into new organizational structures and routines with built-in self-reinforcing mechanisms. At this stage, the new group identity will have been fully established and the group will be ready to embark upon an expansion program which might take the form of introducing additional aspects of the development process, "colonizing" new areas according to acquired patterns, or finally, expanding the scope and horizon of planning. The group will have become sufficiently strong to withstand resistance and even attack from outside.

SUMMARY

Development agencies play a decisive role in the development process. The attitudes and skills of professional role occupants in these agencies are therefore determining factors. In emerging countries, neither attitudes nor skills comply with the requirements of development. To prime a process of positive causation, development groups have to be studied from the "inside" and the weaknesses of their sociopsychological space established. Transformation operations will then have to be initiated which, while affording reasonable goal achievement, will provide ample opportunity to induce changes in basic personal attitudes and professional skills; organizational differentiation and raising of the tone of group dynamics should also be encouraged. The transformation will have to be conceived and guided by an outside agent, but his role ought to be limited to providing the necessary initial insight and metaplanning and to serving as catalyst of the transformation process.

THREE
WATER-RESOURCES MANAGEMENT

25

THE SUBSPACE OF RESOURCES GEOMETRY AND ITS RELATION TO THE PLANNING SPACE

. . . the means and instruments of handling water become increasingly complex, the concern with tracing environmental impacts more acute, the adjustments to human preferences increasingly sensitive and the demand for citizen participation heavier. The emphasis shifts from construction to scientific probing, and from long-term commitment to short-term flexibility.

GILBERT F. WHITE
Strategies of American Water Management

JUSTIFICATION OF THE USE OF SUBSPACES

The emphasis so far has been on reorientation from an oversimplified, static, single-discipline, narrow-angle type of development thinking to a complex, dynamic, multidiscipline, wide-angle one. The first part of this book outlined the nature of the necessary reorientation. By applying this reoriented thinking to a number of development issues, we attempted in the second part to define the nature of the resulting phase space and to indicate some approaches to its analysis. Hopefully we have demonstrated the importance of adopting a phase space that is sufficiently comprehensive to embrace all essential dimensions of development phenomena and that is structurally compatible with them.

However, this expansion in complexity, scope, and depth forces us to introduce dimensions that, at least at the present state of the art, lend themselves only to low-level quantification. The dimensions most refractory to quantification happen to be the ones most essential in launching the growth process. If functional relationships in all the dimensions of our phase space were equally unamenable to quantification, we would have to resign ourselves to a groping kind of analysis largely dependent upon trial and error. Fortunately, within our overall phase space, there exist subspaces that lend themselves to a reasonably high-level quantification and whose interaction with the overall space is not too complex. The very existence of quantifiable subspaces points toward the usefulness of isolating such subspaces, for analytical purposes, from the overall phase space, while simultaneously representing their interconnection with the overall space by appropriate boundary conditions. If properly selected, analyses of such subspaces will result in quasi optima that are reasonably close to the results obtainable through an analysis performed on the full phase space.

The proposed procedure may be described by the term "reductionism," i.e., reduction of the number of dimensions of the phase space within which we conceive phenomena in order to fit the conceptual framework of a specialized discipline. This procedure, at first sight, might appear to conflict with the "dimensionalism" adopted so far.[1] The conflict, however, is only an apparent one: the reductionism proposed here is not structural but heuristic. We do not propose to discard the other dimensions but to isolate the more quantifiable ones purely for the purpose of more rigorous partial analysis. In provisionally, as it were, focusing attention on a subspace, we do not cease to realize its setting in the more comprehensive space. Such focus does not impoverish our phase space.

This type of reductionism might, in fact, constitute a generally justifiable approach to specialization. Such specialization would be based on reductionism from the top downward, as it were, as contrasted with specialization based on reductionism stemming from an inherently narrow angle of view. The former type represents a provisional and intentional narrowing down of analysis adopted for purely heuristic purposes, one which conserves, through the identification of boundary conditions, the interconnection with the main space. In contrast, the latter represents a naïve and permanent attitude, firmly conditioned through specialized formal training, divorced from the variety proliferation of actual phenomena, and precluding later reanalysis within a wider and richer framework.

The interconnection between the overall planning space and the selected subspace may be ensured in three ways:

1. Introduction into the subspace of the significant variable that connects the overall planning space, with the selected subspace (in the present context usually demand for water) as an exogenous variable.

2. Selection of an instrumental objective of the overall planning space to serve as the objective of the subspace.

3. An iterative process of adaptation of the subspace to the requirements of the main space: results obtained from an analysis of the subspace might, when reintroduced into the analysis of the overall planning space, necessitate a modification of the original "boundary conditions" for the subspace (as defined under 1 and 2). If the modified values differ significantly from the original ones, the analysis of the subspace might have to be iterated with the new values.

Looking at the proposed reductionism from a cybernetic point of view,

[1] Terms taken from Prof. Victor E. Frankl's paper "Nothing But," given at the interdisciplinary conference at Alpach, Austria, 1968. See *Encounter* XXXIII:5, November, 1969, pp. 51–61.

one could easily trace the structural principle of a cybernetic hierarchy, here applied to the taxonomy of scientific specialization. At the top level, we would have the complex, multidimensional phase space that we have attempted to define in Parts 1 and 2; at the next level, the less complex but still multidimensional phase space which will now be outlined in Part 3; still lower down, the specific scientific disciplines which supply our basic analytical tools. In this hierarchic taxonomy, the cybernetic principle of orientation of each hierarchic level of specialization by the next higher level is represented by the definition of the subspace boundary conditions by the overall phase space; the cybernetic principle of feedback is represented by the adaptation procedure outlined above.

THE RESOURCES-GEOMETRY SUBSPACE

The subspace to be treated now is that of resources geometry. The term resources geometry has been selected because it is this aspect of the overall phase space which comprises its principal endogenous variables. Demand, though it enters into the analysis of the resources space, is introduced into resources geometry as an exogenous variable, one which expresses, as it were, the "pull" of the rest of the planning space upon the subspace of resources geometry. Since the dimensions used in resources geometry comprise both quantitative and qualitative functions of water resources, the term water-resources geometry will be interpreted to comprise the pollution aspect.

At this point we can confine ourselves to an operational definition of the term "resources geometry." Resources geometry (as applied to water resources) is an analytical representation of resources and demand and of the interventions necessary to modify the resources vector to demand requirements (specified in quantitative, qualitative, and temporal terms), while fulfilling the subspace objectives taken over from the overall planning space. Resources pollution, a corollary of water consumption, is expressed in changes of the qualitative dimensions of the resources vector. Resources geometry uses the dimensions of space, time, quality (mineral and biological), and costs of the development-resources packages utilized in the interventions.

The selection of the proposed resources subspace seems to be justified for the following reasons:

1. Because of the nature of its variables and the relatively more developed analytical tools available for these variables, the resources subspace lends itself to a higher level quantification than does the overall planning space. It will thus be possible to define within this subspace relatively rigorous quasi optima. Less complex and less remote from our ordinary universe of discourse, the resources subspace also offers better insight into the responses of resources to human interventions.
2. The distortion implied by discarding part of the dimensions of the overall planning space may be reduced by a process of iteration.
3. The ultimate object of our analysis is to ensure as good a definition of the potential development field as is practicable and a selection procedure that

will result in the greatest possible objective achievement. In the phase space encountered in development work, the great number of dimensions represented imply numerous degrees of freedom and numerous alternative interventions. This excessive variety renders analysis difficult and increases its cost. Reduction of the number of dimensions, by provisionally discarding the less well-structured ones, will greatly reduce degrees of freedom and contract variety to manageable levels.

4. The segregation of a resources space from overall phase space harmonizes with the structure of the politico-administrative decision process in most countries. Usually, various agencies have been designated to handle the various dimensions of planning space. Each of the institutions involved has authority and capacity to operate only in relation to partial aspects of planning space; this applies to the gathering and generation of data, to planning as well as to implementation of programs. Splitting up our overall phase space in accordance with institutional structure might thus prove to be an operational necessity. It need not be too damaging as long as the subspace analysis is supplemented by a metaanalysis of the overall planning space.

5. Using the resources space is justified so long as such use is part of the overall planning process and not a substitute for it.

DEVELOPMENT OBJECTIVES IN THE RESOURCES SUBSPACE

To ensure the greatest possible compatibility between the analysis of overall phase space and that of subspace, we shall have to take over from the overall phase space the development-resources vector and water demand. Furthermore, we shall have to derive from the objectives of the planning space the objective of the resources subspace.

The demand taken over from the overall planning space into the resources subspace will be provisional. The demand for water will *inter alia* depend on the water price—which in turn will be an outcome of the analysis of the resources subspace. If the results of a first analysis of the subspace indicate a cost of water which significantly differs from original assumptions (and we assume price to be related to cost of water), a second iteration of the analysis of the resources subspace, based on an appropriately revised demand, will have to be undertaken.

The dependence of the resources subspace upon the overall planning space will not be very great in the case of community and industrial water uses. In such uses, water, as a rule, represents an insignificant portion of living or production costs, and within the anticipated price range demand will not be greatly influenced by minor cost variations (except in "wet" industries); furthermore, in this type of use major changes in use technologies are not anticipated. Therefore, objectives of the subspace will generally consist in minimizing, over the planning period, the present worth of cost streams involved in upgrading resources according to demand requirements, allowance being made for the value of spare capacity at the time horizon of the planning period.

Irrigation demand will depend on price more than will nonagricultural demand, and in addition, price ceilings will become effective above which no demand will develop. Where the availability of water, as compared with demand anticipated over the planning period, does not pose any problems, the objective of the resources-subspace analysis will again be to minimize present worth of upgrading resources to demand specifications; however, in this case we shall have to introduce the constraint that the marginal cost of upgrading ought not to exceed marginal benefits achieved, or specific ceilings.

Where limited availability of water is anticipated not too long after the planning period ends, the planning horizon ought to be extended accordingly. Where the availability of water is limited (within the planning period) as compared with demand, the development objective will be to maximize the amount of water that will result from upgrading resources, but to do so within the constraint of a ceiling for the marginal cost.

If both agricultural and nonagricultural uses occur within the same planning space, nonagricultural uses will be added to agricultural ones and the analysis then undertaken according to one of the two approaches proposed for agricultural uses—the choice between them being determined by availability of water.

THE TARGET STATUS OF THE SYSTEM

The derivation of objectives for the resources subspace outlined so far implies a simplification that will rarely be found acceptable, i.e., indifference as to the use potential of the resources system beyond the selected planning horizon. The usual underlying assumption of planning the use of resources renewed by nature is basically conservationist: resources are to be used so as to ensure their continued use without significant qualitative deterioration. If we adopt this doctrine, we cannot remain indifferent to the status of the resources system at the end of the planning period, since this status will determine the future use potential. To comply with this requirement, we shall therefore have to add to the definition of the objective of the resources subsystem a definition of the desired status of the water-resources vector at the time horizon of planning. It is proposed to call this status the target status. Seen from the ex ante point of view of the subsequent planning period, the target status represents the "present worth" of potential future uses.

Since definition of the target status will be guided by water requirements and specifications of the next and subsequent generations, and since much uncertainty will prevail regarding such future uses, attempts at rational definition of the target status will be beset by numerous difficulties. Quantitative and qualitative water requirements of production processes, especially those of agriculture with its characteristically high consumptive use, greatly depend on production technologies, and these are undergoing rapid change whose effects are virtually unpredictable. Prediction of long-term water requirements becomes even more complex when we introduce pollution variables and attempt to specify qualitative aspects. As we shall demonstrate in the following chapters, almost all water uses involve some qualitative deterioration. This deterioration is often slow and thus need not worry us overmuch in the immediate future. The outlook, however, changes decisively when we consider water quality as a secular problem; seen from a truly long-term point of view, slow mineral accumulation might at some future date exceed the tolerance ceiling of a specific use.

Every qualitative deterioration involves some reduction in the utility of water and therefore some reduction of its value. Such reduction may not lend itself to easy quantification, especially if the deterioration level is still some distance from tolerance ceilings of our use, but we must make allowance for its existence. We have to envisage the damaging effect of quality deterioration as following some type of continuous function, in which tolerance ceilings express critical levels. This functional relationship between quality deterioration and the resulting disutility is, however, still very little explored. What is worse, it is very difficult in practice to isolate this relationship from other environmental factors and from the influence of production techniques. Nevertheless, we are justified in assuming that our knowledge of the functional relationship between water quality and the production function into which water enters as an input will eventually increase, enabling us to improve quantification of this important relationship. As long as such quantification is lacking, we shall have to make do with tolerance ceilings as planning constraints.

The extent of our ignorance of the influence of water quality on utility becomes even more manifest when we try to predict quality requirements of the next generation. To predict water requirements (in quantity and quality) of the next generation we need to know:

1. The future mix of production complexes
2. The future role of water in the resources base of the various production complexes, and the extent to which other resources can be substituted for water
3. The functional relationship between water quality and production in future production processes
4. The future development of quality "upgrading" techniques and of techniques to desalt seawater

Unfortunately, our ignorance extends to all these aspects, and as a consequence of the unpredictability of long-term technological development, there is little chance that we shall be much wiser in the near future. Furthermore, water requirement of the future will depend on more general factors such as on the overall rate of economic development, on specific sectorial development rates, and on politico-administrative conditions.

Confronted by so many facets of uncertainty, the planner will have to adopt a conservative and conservationist approach in defining the target status. Lacking firm proof to the contrary, the planner should assume that future quality requirements will resemble those in the current program. This does not imply limiting ourselves only to such uses that will result from a target status identical in quantity and quality with the status-quo-ante system;

in that case we would have to accept a drastic curtailment of water uses, which would exclude, among others, many groundwater uses. Assuming that future generations would continue to adhere to it, such an untenable policy would lead us to discard permanently the use of a most substantial part of our water resources. Every water use implies a change in flow patterns and levels, and most water uses also involve some deterioration of quality. Thus we shall rarely be in a position to specify a target system that is identical (from the point of view of future water uses) with the status-quo-ante system, even though anticipated deterioration will often be very gradual.

If we are justified in assuming that the technology of upgrading qualitative factors will continue to gather momentum, slow qualitative deterioration of water resources need not disturb us too much so long as we can safely predict (1) that when such deterioration reaches tolerance ceilings (today's, since we do not know tomorrow's) means will exist to restore quality to acceptable levels and (2) that such means will be economically feasible by the time they are needed.

Since such techniques have already been developed beyond the laboratory or pilot-plant phase, the availability of technology is reassuring. Our real difficulty will be to predict long-term economics of quality upgrading. Upgrading economics will depend, on the one hand, on the anticipated gradual drop in costs of upgrading processes and, on the other hand, on the anticipated future role of water in production processes and the anticipated efficiency of these processes in terms of outputs per unit input of water. Although at present it might prove impossible to quantify the future course of these two factors, we can nevertheless make a significant statement on future trends. Since qualitative upgrading processes are still in their infancy, we may assume, in analogy to what we can learn from development histories of other technologies, that unit costs will continue for some time to decline along a relatively steep curve, which will gradually tend to flatten out.

The gradient of this curve will vary from process to process, and only detailed study of potential improvements of the constituent parts of each process will show what to expect. We may also assume that the outputs produced per unit input of water will continue to rise in the more important (mainly agricultural) water-using production complexes as a consequence of the anticipated rise in production efficiency.

These considerations justify us in modifying our original conservationist postulate for defining the target status for planning water-resources management measures. We can now say that the target status should reflect conservation of the quantitative potential of the status quo sysem and confine economically unavoidable cumulative qualitative deterioration to rates that will remain within accepted tolerances until such a time as appropriate upgrading measures become available at economically justifiable costs. As to economically avoidable deterioration (e.g., substitutions of alternative sources developed at higher immediate costs for recharging sewage to groundwater formations) the decision will depend on outcomes of a specific economic analysis.

MINING OF RESOURCES

The above comments and recommendations will not apply to one-time stocks that are not renewed or that are renewed at a rate that is insignificant as compared with the rate of utilization. For such nonrenewable resources the concept of target status loses its meaning. Here our exclusive consideration ought to be to manage resources so as to maximize objective achievement.

Nonrenewable resources are either a kind of one-time premium that becomes available during the process of moving from a status quo system to a target status, or they are resources that have accumulated in underground storage in the past and are not replenished or that are replenished at an insignificant rate. The first type of resource will be treated as a one-time boon that is utilized in conjunction with the renewable resource. Only the second type of resource will require reformulation of management policy. To utilize a resource of this nature, we shall have to treat it as a minable mineral; if, however, we erroneously transfer conservation ideologies to this type of resource, we shall have to wholly avoid its use. The latter approach does not make sense, since an unusable resource potential does not constitute a true potential and therefore for all practical purposes does not exist.

A case could possibly be made out for keeping such stocks as a reserve for the needs of future generations or for some unspecified contingencies, and conceivably there might be situations where such an attitude would be justified. In the majority of cases, however, the opposite attitude, i.e., use of the resource by the present generation, will be the more meaningful one. Utilization of such one-time stocks will create new economic assets that might make it economically feasible either to replace in the future the then exhausted supply by the import of water (natural or man-made) or, alternatively, to adopt a change in the resources base that would substitute other inputs for water or at least significantly reduce water requirements. The longer such a substitution can be delayed, the better the chances of commanding the choice of selecting better alternative substitutes. If mining of water, for example, is undertaken to make possible some industrial enterprise, the utilization period over which the supply ought to be spread should equal the physical lifetime of the plant. However, a case might be made out either for a shorter time span (reliance on innovation) or for a longer one (assuming that after the "retirement" of the first plant, another economic activity possibly making less demanding claims on the water stocks might be introduced). In any case, the very fact that an economic project is based on water mining will require the extension of our planning horizon (at least for indicative planning) beyond the resource's anticipated exhaustion point.

TARGET STATUS VS. INDEFINITE PLANNING HORIZON

The need to define a target status to act as a constraint on planning water-resources management policies could be obviated by extending planning to an indefinite future. This might be preferable in a system (1) that does not manifest peculiarities characteristic for its initial development period, (2) in which the intended water uses will not change drastically and in which the value of water remains fairly constant, and (3) about which our knowledge is adequate. Water-resources development in developing countries will rarely comply with any of these three requirements: peculiarities that characterize the early phases of development usually do exist, and they are highly significant both in relation to water availability and its relative value; use technologies and the role of water in the resources base of production complexes, it may be assumed, will change dramatically over the next decade or two; and, finally, in the early phases of development, our knowledge of the system is incomplete. Therefore, subdivision of the time dimension of planning into manageable planning periods and replacement of the continuity in time by the introduction of a target status seem well justified.

26
RESOURCES GEOMETRY: A CONCEPTUAL MODEL

Because the entire hydrological system is so directly interconnected, we must be able to measure the effect of the actions we take on specific parts of the overall system. Unfortunately, although we know a great deal about certain of the critical elements of the system, we are quite ignorant in other crucially important areas . . . . So it is that years after an action is taken, effects occur that were not foreseen and that are often more important than the advantages offered by the development itself.

ABEL WOLMAN
A Report to the National Academy of Sciences

THE DIMENSIONS, VARIABLES, AND OPTIMIZATION PROCEDURES OF RESOURCES GEOMETRY

The dimensions of water-resources geometry are the familiar dimensions of space time, the dimension of economic value, and the three hydraulic dimensions of flow, chemical quality, and biological quality.

Resources geometry operates with four basic interconnected vectors: resources, demand, pollution, and upgrading (intervention).

The resources vector varies in the dimensions of resources geometry. These variations are assumed to be the result of stochastic (climatic) factors, and their specific values for specific points of time are, of course, not known. If we assume that the future probabilistic distribution of these factors will resemble that of the past, we shall be able to derive the former from the latter within a range of uncertainty whose spread will depend on the time period for which data are available and on the quantity and quality of our data.

The demand vector, in resources geometry, will in principle be considered exogenous, depending on economic, social, and political dimensions that are not represented in the resources-geometry phase space. To the extent that the cost of upgrading alternative eligible interventions is assumed to vary within a relative limited range, and to the extent that this range is known in advance, demand may be introduced as two time series defining the range of the demand forecast. Where this assumption does not apply, and where the price elasticity of demand is high, a functional relationship (possibly changing in time) between demand and cost of upgrading will have to be introduced, implying the demand vector's functional dependence on the intervention vector.

The intervention or upgrading vector, representing the "work" required to adapt the resources vector to requirements of the demand vector, will ultimately be transposed into economic terms. Whereas the resources and demand functions must be conceived as smooth and continuous curves, the upgrading, as a consequence of the lumpiness (or unattractiveness of subdivision) of many engineering features, will be represented by a stepped curve.

The pollution vector is a direct and largely unavoidable outcome of water uses resulting from the demand vector. At a certain cost, part of the pollution may be diverted out of the system and part may be upgraded before reaching the resources vector; part may reach resources and thereby increase the direct cost of their upgrading. Moreover, pollution may affect the general environment and engender claims upon the resources system. Costs related to pollution will have to be added to the direct cost of resources upgrading.

The basic operational policy of resources geometry is to optimize application of the intervention vector upon the resources vector so as to comply with the requirements of both the demand vector and the system's target state. The optimization to be employed will depend on development objectives or criteria: the objective in a community water-supply system, for instance, might be to minimize the upgrading cost. Since upgrading is a stepped function, every discrete upgrading decision will involve a certain amount of "overshooting" above immediate needs. If the step involved is especially large, the regret at delaying its implementation for a particular period, with the consequent failure to comply with demand requirements, might, upon examination, prove to be smaller than the cost related to implementing the large step. In such cases we should postpone implementing such a step until incremental regret exceeds the additional costs involved.

The above description of operational policies evades the probabilistic nature of the resources vector. Insofar as our analysis is confined to long-term policies, we may operate with averages. However, in defining short-term and medium-term operational decision sequences, we must introduce probabilistic distributions and allow for the extreme amplitude of variations which are characteristic of such shorter periods. As long as resources safely exceed demand requirements, even for a dry cycle of extremely low probability, the probabilistic nature of the resources vector, even though it might influence outcomes somewhat, will not be a controlling factor.

In systems in which resources may, in dry cycles, fall short of demand requirements, we shall have to define in advance the minimal probability of precipitation for which we shall provide in order to comply fully with those requirements; we shall also need to determine the extent of compliance in the range beyond such a probability threshold. Here again the limit of full compliance ought to be set by comparing costs of marginal additional compliance beyond a specific probability with marginal regret of noncompliance. Later in this chapter there will be discussion on probabilistic management policies.

A number of solutions (consisting of alternative intervention vectors) will exist to upgrade the resources vector to the requirements of the demand vector. To ensure that the solution (i.e., project or program) selected is in fact an optimum, we shall again have to apply a planning process that will ensure requisite variety. In other words we shall have to generate, in the context of our new resources-geometry space, a "field" of potential development that comprises all possible solutions. We shall thereby guarantee that the chosen solution is the outcome of a review of an exhaustive "project population" (see Chapter 20 for a more detailed description of the procedure).

Since an intervention represents a connection between a specific resource and a specific demand, and since connections (some of which, we may concede, might prove meaningless) will increase at a much higher rate than the number of resource and demand complexes introduced into our geometry, expanding the scope of resources geometry will by itself increase variety and better chances for an optimal objective achievement. Another degree of freedom, and an additional source of increasing variety, lies in varying capacity, type, and location of interventions. A further degree of freedom may be achieved by varying the timing and order of interventions.

Our analysis will grow in complexity in that the resources vector can be described only by probabilistic distribution and because of uncertainties in our estimates of demand, pollution, and costs, which will be definable only within a relatively broad range.

The intervention vector designed to overcome the "resistance" between the resources and demand vectors will comprise three types of operations:

1. Operations aimed at upgrading the resources vector in its several dimensions (location, potential energy, time, chemical and biological qualities) to requirements of the demand vector.

2. Operations aimed at crossing institutional obstacles; these operations may require modifications in operations specified under 1; if such obstacles prove impregnable, they will block upgrading interventions and will have to be introduced into planning as constraints.

3. Operations aimed at creating information to reach information thresholds, but also, preferably, additional information to improve the quality of decisions.

From the point of view of long-term planning we have to conceive major projects and programs as a sequence of interventions related to specific resources and specific demands, often involving specific pollution. Optimization procedures aimed at maximizing some objective achievement ought to be applied to such a sequence of interventions rather than to an individual intervention. A sequence designed to meet requirements up to a specific time horizon would, according to the scope of operations, constitute a project or program. As long as we do not, within the foreseeable future, anticipate the resources vector to fall short of the demand vector, the optimization procedure will consist in devising the "path of least resistance" between the resources vector and that part of the demand vector which is contained within the time horizon of planning. When defining this path of least resistance, we must keep in mind, on the one hand, the pollution stream resulting from water use and, on the other hand, the chosen target state. If we anticipate water-resources shortages, the relevant considerations (outlined in Chapter 32) will have to be allowed for in setting policy goals.

When comparing alternative projects or programs, we should also give proper weight to the degree of dependability of water supplies. Thus, a program comprising a number of sources feeding into a demand area through a number of conduits would normally offer greater dependability than an appropriately larger single-conduit system fed from one source. Were the conduit of the latter to break down, supply would cease until repairs could be made. Breakdown of a single conduit in a multiconduit system would not cut off supply. Availability can also be expressed in probabilistic terms, its probability being complementary to probability of breakdowns involving partial or complete disruption of supply. Probability of breakdowns will depend on construction standards (and investment levels ensuring them), operation and maintenance standards, type of installations (some being more prone to breakdowns than others), and external natural and human factors (storms, seismicity, and sabotage). Since in some types of projects (e.g., community water-supply systems) high availability is of extreme importance, differences in availability should be fully considered when evaluating alternative programs. Where feasible, the damage caused by full or partial outages should be calculated and used in comparisons. A less rigorous way to introduce the differences of availability into comparisons would be to specify the maximum tolerable probability of occurrence and of duration of total or partial system outages and treat this requirement as a constraint with which all alternatives must comply to become eligible.

THE CONVENTIONAL VS. THE RESOURCES-GEOMETRY APPROACH

The difference between the conventional and the resources-geometry approach is one not of detail, but of basic principle.

The point of departure of the conventional approach is a specific need or demand which is expected to arise over a specific time period. Only those parts of the resources geometry (in space and time) which, from the ex ante point of view, appear to be directly relevant to this specific demand are included in the analysis. The influence on decision making of the parts of the resources geometry that lie beyond the directly relevant boundaries is ignored. In "philosophical" terms, the conventional planner's attitude is that of reluctant generalization; he limits conceptualization to narrow confines of space and time and neglects interconnections with other relevant parts of resources geometry.

While resources geometry agrees with the conventional approach in confining problem solving to a planning space of manageable size, it selects the boundaries of planning by a process of conceptualization that descends from the general to the particular. Once boundaries of planning are selected, the interaction across such boundaries (in space and time) is allowed for. This method takes pains to incorporate in resources, demand, and pollution vectors all the elements of major relevance to the problem at hand.

The concepts employed in the conventional and the resources-geometry approaches likewise differ greatly. The conventional approach prefers static concepts such as "safe yield" of a resource and operates with initial and final (usually steady) states. The resources-geometry approach operates with dynamic concepts such as upgrading sequences applied to a supply to meet demand requirements and emphasizes transients between the initial and the target state at the time horizon.

Furthermore, and most important, the resources-geometry approach introduces into current system planning the future of the system extending beyond the time horizon by the concept of "target status," which constitutes, as it were, the desired "discounted" future potential operations of the system.

ADAPTATION OF MANAGEMENT POLICIES TO THE STOCHASTIC NATURE OF THE RESOURCES VECTOR

In a fully developed and fully utilized system, management policy will limit itself to defining optimal operational rules. In a physically undeveloped system, management policy will be incorporated in the planning process for developing the system. In actuality, most systems fall somewhere between these extremes. For purposes of analysis the differences between the various systems lie in the measure of freedom they allow the planner. A fully developed system with a resources geometry greatly modified by past interventions will leave the planner far less freedom than will a system most of whose options remain open. In the latter case we are in a position to define a system, its boundaries and target state, as well as to agree on development objectives; this, however, does not necessarily imply that we are in a position to produce a workable management policy. Analysis may in some cases indicate that no management policy exists which can achieve the desired objectives (e.g., meeting a specific demand below ceiling marginal cost). The "object language" of the system will not lead to a solution if the system's definition and development objectives prove incompatible. In the latter instance we shall have to apply a "metalanguage" to analyze the original system, its constraints, development objectives and the factors from the more comprehensive phase space that have determined objectives. By the use of this metalanguage a compatible set of objectives, target states, and boundary conditions will be defined. The analysis of the newly defined system will result in a viable management policy. Similar considerations and procedures will apply if a management policy proves politically unfeasible upon introduction of the political dimensions.

The success of a management policy will depend on the system's range of predictability, availability of compensatory responses to wrong decisions, and the amplitude of variations of its variables.

Predictability of a water-resources system will depend on two types of uncertainties as to specific values of resources functions at a specific time: uncertainty due to the stochastic nature of the functions (e.g., climate); uncertainty stemming from the state of the art and the quantity and quality of available information (e.g., response of crop to water). Even if this taxonomy in time proves untenable on theoretical grounds, it still has an important short-term operational advantage. The first type of uncertainty in the present context refers to the prediction of climatic factors and their influence upon the hydrological cycle; such uncertainty cannot be dissolved by any amount of data, at least not until we succeed in developing a scientific method for forecasting climatic cycles. The second type of uncertainty, though it too probably cannot be dissolved, can be reduced by accumulating relevant data and improving the forecasting hypothesis. The first type of uncertainty implies the impossibility of predicting, even within a wide range, specific values of the resources functions for specific time periods. All we shall be able to predict with reasonable confidence is the probability distribution of these values. The second type of uncertainty will also introduce ranges of values instead of single values; for this type of uncertainty, however, the range of variation in short-term prediction of specific values of functions will often be reasonably narrow, though widening for a more remote time horizon.

The range of response to compensate for wrong predictions for specific values of functions will depend on the system's specific structural features and degree of isolation from other systems which could, if needed, supplement system requirements, sometimes at a cost higher than that of water developed in the main system. The range of response will also greatly depend on what might be termed the utilization factor of the water potential (i.e., the portion of the total water potential actually utilized) and on the feasibility and justification (political and economical) of reducing supply during extremely adverse climatic cycles.

The more isolated a system, the more restricted its range of response. The higher the potential utilization factor, the greater the discrepancy between anticipated extreme short-term and medium-term climatic variations and our capacity to remedy them by interventions related to the relatively small volume that remains to be developed and can be mobilized for such interventions. The more rigid the demand specifications and the greater their divorce from the current status of stock and supply, the less will be the policy planner's flexibility in using demand reduction as part of his management policy under adverse conditions and the greater will be his dependence on remedial action.

Short-term and medium-term management policies will also be greatly influenced by the maximum variation for which available regulative storage is sufficient for regulating available runoff in a dry cycle so as to facilitate supply at the design capacity. If existing storage facilities cannot cope with climatic variations of relatively high occurrence probabilities, then major deviation from the design level of supply will have to be accepted when climate is extremely unfavorable. Storage is, of course, connected with cost, and in addition, its maximum extent will often be limited by geographical and geological factors.

Because of the stochastic nature of the resources functions and the uncertainty regarding future demand, water-resources management policies will generally be *probabilistic* rather than deterministic.

Climatic and interrelated hydrological variations of extreme amplitudes will usually have very low probabilities. Solutions for such probabilities might therefore prove uneconomical, and management policy might prefer to provide only for a reasonable range of probabilities. The extent of this range will depend on the damage expected by deficiencies of supply, the amplitudes of variations, and the cost of providing for such variations.

The limit up to which we intend to provide solutions need not be absolute but may be contingent: the planner may, for instance, stipulate that his design solution ought to hold good for a probability range down to, say, 0.1 probability. At the same time, however, he may outline the corrective measures for the contingency range, i.e., for probabilities below the specified design range and down to a much lower specific probability of, say, 0.03. He may even go so far as to provide a third contingent step: solutions for the catastrophy range (i.e., conditions below the latter probability and down to any desired still lower limit of probability).

A management policy on probabilistic lines will thus take the form of a decision tree, with the "design solution" as the main trunk, the "contingent solution" the first branching off, and the catastrophy solution a further branching off from the latter. It will often prove desirable to confine system development to the design range and to delay action indicated for the contingent or catastrophy ranges. Action can be taken once the system approaches a state that will allow the necessary lead time to implement corrective measures before the system can reach its low-probability contingent status. Should climatic conditions improve before corrective measures have been fully implemented, they may be discontinued at a logical point. On the other hand, should conditions continue toward the catastrophy range, we may again decide to take the action indicated by the second branching off of the decision tree.

The advantage of this type of sequential decision process is that it confines actual intervention into the system to such action as is dictated, at any point of time, by the expectancy that controlling conditions may deteriorate. Since every such intervention will of course involve costs that are liable to rise unproportionally if we wish to provide for the excessive amplitudes associated with very low probabilities, the probabilistic response approach will tend to minimize the expected value of the cost.

Thus, from the ex ante point of view, the probability of a succession of, say, three low-rainfall years, defining the contingent range, may be, say, 0.1. If the system, however, has passed through two dry years, the probability at that point for another dry year that would bring the system into the contingent range will be much higher (say, 0.25) than the ex ante probability for three consecutive dry years. The policy planner, who at the outset might not have felt like providing for a probability below 0.1, will now feel obliged to recommend action for one of 0.25. Similar considerations will apply when approaching the catastrophy range.

When setting the above three ranges for the decision tree—the design range, the contingency range, and the catastrophy range—the planner might try a number of boundary definitions and calculate for each the expected value of costs at the margin and compare it with that of benefits foregone if the boundary is marginally selected more restrictively. At the selected design range boundary, expected marginal costs of provisions to ensure the selected design supply will be equal to those of expected marginal benefits.

It will often prove impossible to provide, at justifiable costs, corrective action for the contingency, or the catastrophy range, within the set of criteria and constraints laid down for the design range in relation to demand requirements as to quantity, quality ceilings, and the nature of the target system. Part of these requirements and constraints might have to be relaxed for the contingency range, and additional relaxations might have to be accepted for the catastrophy range. Some types of relaxation will prove reversible but may require adoption of a "decision-tree" policy, like that outlined above for the "low" contingency range, to be put into effect when the system approaches the "high" contingency range (i.e., a number of exceptionally humid years) in order to make good the "overdraft" in the dry cycle by increasing the scope of water conservation in extremely humid cycles. Temporary lowering of groundwater levels below design levels (say, below levels that, in the long run, would induce seawater encroachment into coastal aquifers) might, for instance, fall into this category.

HEURISTICS FOR A PROBABILISTIC MANAGEMENT POLICY

It will not always be easy to define in advance a probabilistic management strategy based on a number of probability ranges and the several subpolicies that ought to become effective once we approach the boundary between two ranges. In many cases our information about probability distribution of the resources functions will be too limited for a rigorous analysis. This limitation will certainly apply to developing countries, especially to their earlier project phases. Even where our information on the probabilistic distribution of the resources functions does meet analysis requirements, we might find it difficult to define marginal losses caused by marginal water deficiencies. Where information does not suffice for a quantified probabilistic analysis, the adoption of the proposed sequential decision procedure will still result in reasonably efficient decision patterns. Furthermore, a few pragmatic heuristics may assist the policy planner in designing a decision-tree type of action program, even if he is not yet in a position to spell out a fully quantified action program based on a rigorous analysis. A few such heuristics are described in the following.

1. Within the design range, the policy planner ought not to resort to the last safety margins which might be contained in the most permissive version of the target status (such as temporary "overdrafts" to be made good under more propitious climatic conditions) and in a conservative definition of quality ceilings. For he might be called upon to use these margins in the contingency and catastrophy ranges, or in case demand grows more rapidly than he had assumed, before he has had time or funds to make the necessary provisions. In other words, as long as the system operates within the design range, the planner ought to avoid any action that precludes measures related to the contingency and catastrophy ranges.

2. Provisions beyond the design range might have to be made for both sides of the range, i.e., for extremely humid cycles as well. Since such humid cycles will usually occur too seldom to warrant providing for their full exploitation from the outset, we ought to explore the possibility of initially providing for their partial exploitation through relatively low investments, delaying the decision to implement more cost-intensive complementary measures until warranted.

3. Although action related to the contingency and catastrophy ranges may be delayed until the system approaches these ranges, the sequence of operations involved and the lead times required to implement them ought to be carefully worked out. Lead times ought to be established both for physical measures and for legislative or politico-economic measures. These lead times will be used for defining "red lines," i.e., a status of the system at which operations related to the contingency and catastrophy ranges should begin. Adherence to such red lines will ensure that if the climatic cycle continues unfavorably, the relevant facilities will be operational when the range boundary is reached.

4. As the system approaches such boundaries, or even a short time after it has crossed them, we may prefer to initiate some short-term and relatively inexpensive palliative or partial measures to "buy time" before having to decide on more costly full-scale emergency actions. We might, for instance, choose to implement a modest reduction of consumption. Such a solution might suffice for an interim during which climatic conditions might sufficiently improve to make the more costly and possibly politically more delicate full-scale emergency actions unnecessary.

5. Entrance of the system into the contingency and catastrophy ranges need not be confined exclusively to climatic causes. Physical breakdowns in the system might lead to the same type of problems. Two major differences exist, however, between climatic causes and physical breakdowns: (*a*) breakdowns come upon us suddenly and without notice, while climatically related contingencies occur gradually and usually leave us the necessary lead time for remedial action; (*b*) breakdowns may affect a much larger portion of the supply than even the most extreme climatic variations. On the other hand, the duration of breakdowns is as a rule incomparably shorter than that of climatically caused shortages. Both emergencies are of course of a stochastic nature. Provisions for breakdowns will be similar to those for extreme climatic ranges. Comparison of the cost of providing for an emergency of a specific probability with that of the damage caused by such an emergency may provide a guideline for decisions related to provision of standby capacity. The damage caused by breakdowns will usually be less than that due to extreme climatic variations (affecting the same portion of the system capacity) because breakdowns last less time.

LONG-TERM AND SHORT-TERM POLICIES

A comment might be in place here on the relation of relatively long-term policies stemming from the resources-geometry approach to the political decision process. An optimized long-term policy for the management of water resources will represent the best way of handling the resources system in a space without political "friction." When reintroducing this friction into current decision making, we shall have to have a second look at the proposed optimized management policy. Such a reappraisal might convince us to modify the policy according to the following principles:

1. Rejecting politically prompted compromise which involves irreversible degrading of the resource or degrading that is reversible only at high costs
2. Judicious phasing of implementation of management policies so as to minimize political resistance in the initial phases and avoid encroaching into politically sensitive issues, while keeping open as many options as possible for the future
3. Initiating operations aimed at reducing political resistance to subsequent policy steps.

27

BASIC PATTERNS OF WATER-RESOURCES MANAGEMENT POLICIES

In the view of man as the cooperator, man the harmonizer, construction is only one means of coming to terms with an environment he never fully explores and that is constantly changing under his hand.

GILBERT WHITE

STATIC AND DYNAMIC YIELD CONCEPTS

Two opposing conceptions of management, the static and the dynamic, may be applied in managing a water-resources system.

The static management concept operates with steady states: the initial steady state defining the resource system at the outset of the utilization, and the ultimate steady state describing the system in its planned "final" state when it supplies the desired "safe yield." Transients are recognized, but their utilization potential is not put to proper use. The safe yield is generally expressed as a percentage of the average recharge.

Although the simplification implied in the static concept may do for a first approximate evaluation of a resources potential, it will not enable us to evaluate the optimal role which a resources system may play within a specific development context. Water resources are "flowing" systems upon which every intervention (or absence of intervention) has an impact which in some measure modifies the future behavior and utilization potential of the systems.

The dynamic management concept consists in devising alternative sequences of intervention and selecting the sequence that will optimize objective achievement.

If our knowledge of resources, demand, and pollution were perfect and our professional resources unlimited, analysis should extend over an indefinite period. Since they are not perfect, a time horizon will have to be introduced and a "target state" of the system defined to represent the boundary conditions of the resources system at the horizon.

According to this conception, a water-resources system ought not to be characterized by its "perennial safe yield" but by the extent to which it is capable, temporarily or perennially, of complying with the requirements of a demand geometry. In such a dynamic system, evaluation will extend not only to intervention and its expected benefits but also to inaction and its related regrets.

Because of the incomparably greater sluggishness of groundwater movement as compared with surface-water movement, the difference between the static and dynamic conceptions of water-resources management will be much more significant in systems in which groundwater occupies an important place.

The importance of operating with dynamic concepts in systems featuring major *groundwater* resources becomes self-evident once we extend our analysis to qualitative features. Comprehensive analysis will show that most "steady states" of flow of groundwater systems do in fact result in disequilibria of quality. These disequilibria are normally neglected because of the extreme sluggishness of the process itself due to various dilution retention and delay mechanisms. However, if we wish to predict long-term effects of a management policy, the slow cumulative process of qualitative deterioration cannot be neglected.

The dynamic approach to water-resources management is especially important for developing countries where availability of water in the early phases of development might be a precondition to transformation of the socioeconomic system. Early availability of local groundwater resources—the development of which does not require the major and indivisible investments implied in surface stream utilization—may therefore have an importance that greatly transcends its anticipated direct economic effect. Adoption of the dynamic concept will also enable the planner to initiate exploitation with a smaller stock of information than would be possible with the static approach. Application of the dynamic development approach need not conflict with water-conservation doctrines.

The closer a water-resources system approaches the "target state," the less significant will the difference be between the static and the dynamic management approach. In such cases little room would be left for utilization of transient states. However, even where we have actually reached the target state, the dynamic management approach might occasionally have important advantages. The more flexible utilization patterns which it implies would result in a more adaptive system, one which would enable the planner to absorb greater amplitudes of variation than would be possible with the static approach.

This introductory statement to management policy will conclude with an attempt to define "yield" according to the dynamic conception. The yield of a water-resources system is defined to be a measure of the extent to which the system can be upgraded according to the requirements of demand geometry, without conflicting with the stipulations of the target state at the time horizon of planning.

DEMONSTRATION OF THE DYNAMIC MANAGEMENT CONCEPT

To demonstrate the dynamic water-resources management concept, a situation will be selected in which its advantages are especially conspicuous, i.e., a coastal groundwater formation.

To define such a formation's original "steady state" in relation to the planned "target state," we shall introduce the following variables:

R = annual recharge to the formation.
S = one-time stock located between the original groundwater level and that corresponding to the target state and stock available between the original interface separating salt and fresh water and the anticipated interface at the target state. In actual fact, owing to dispersion effects at the interface, the latter stock might not all be of usable quality. Change in stock will be ΔS.
I = interception of groundwater for actual exploitation
ΔI = return flow to the formation
F = outflow to base level lost from formation

The original steady state will be defined by the equation: $F + \Delta S = R$.

Over a longer period of time, ΔS will tend to balance out, and the equation will then read: $F = R$.

Once intervention starts, part of the natural recharge will be intercepted at some point between the recharge and the outflow; the equation will then become

$$F + I - \Delta I + \Delta S = R$$

In this equation, R, the recharge, is a stochastic variable, I is an independent variable, and F, ΔI, and ΔS are dependent variables. A management policy aiming at maximizing water utilization consists in proposing a withdrawal pattern in space and time that will keep the outflow F close to an economically justifiable minimum. The most rapid and therefore the most effective way to reduce outflow F is to locate interception in space and time so as to ensure reduction of groundwater levels near the coast and thereby control outflows to the sea. Locating interception wells in a strip adjoining the seashore[1] would thus constitute the most radical policy to ensure maximum "yield" of the resource within the planning period.

This policy might, however, involve construction of wells in locations that are at some distance from areas of concentration of demand and that would therefore necessitate further investments to adapt location and possibly also potential energy of resources to demand requirements. Such additional investments might or might not be economically justifiable.

At the opposite end of the scale we might have a policy specifying location, in space and time, of the water interception line (chain of wells) in

[1] The strip would have to be located somewhat inland of the toe of the fresh water–salt water interface in its anticipated farthest inland position.

accordance with the demand geometry. The latter policy would involve a minimum cost of adaptation of location (and possibly also of potential energy), but, on the other hand, it might involve continuing high levels of groundwater close to the coast for a lengthy period with the consequence of large outflow losses to the sea.

The two alternative policies outlined above would thus represent the two extreme ends of the scale of possible policies: the first would define timing and location of withdrawals so as to minimize losses from the formation (and thereby maximize the total volume available for use over the planning period) to an economically justifiable extent; the second would minimize cost to meet demand requirements, while accepting losses to base flow and reduction of the overall volume available for exploitation over the planning period. Both approaches may lead to the same target state and thus to the same use potential beyond the time horizon (if the planning period is sufficiently long); however, they may differ greatly in the yield over the planning period. The first policy will cost more and yield more, while the second will cost less but also yield less.

It is impossible in a specific context to determine the point on the scale of policies that will lead to maximum objective achievement without full analysis of all relevant factors. Rapid growth of demand, low cost of adapting to a specific demand geometry of a water-interception pattern designed according to the first type of policy, high utility of water, and anticipated high cost of development of alternative water resources—all these favor an approach fashioned according to the first type of policy. Opposite conditions favor an approach close to the second type. In-between conditions favor a policy based on a balanced compromise. To realize fully the basic difference between the two polar policies, it may be useful to trace their implications (neglecting, at this stage, the complex problems related to the control of sea-water encroachment).

The first policy aims at minimizing losses to the system by intercepting the major portion of the outflow to base level, even if such intervention involves pumping the strip close to base level beyond current demand needs and conveying the intercepted surplus water inland and upstream for underground storage, if such a procedure is feasible.

Assuming an average climate throughout the period of analysis and (for the sake of simplicity of demonstration) interception that from the outset equals average recharge ($I = R$), and assuming (again for the sake of simplicity of demonstration) that $F = 0$ and $\Delta I = 0$, the first year's operation will diminish the one-time stock S by ΔS and

$$-\Delta S = I$$

However, the current recharge R will renew the stock by the same amount, i.e., $\Delta S = R$, and thus groundwater levels, interface location, and one-time stock will at the end of the first year be where they were at the beginning of the year.

If we use the same rate of withdrawal combined with the second type of policy (assuming withdrawals concentrated on a line parallel to the coast and at a considerable distance from it), the formation during the first year will lose two volumes of water:

1. The outflow to base level which will be slightly smaller than the recharge volume R
2. The withdrawal which has been assumed to be also equal to R

On the other hand, the formation will be enriched by the natural recharge R. Thus, by the end of the first year the one-time stock S will be reduced by $-\Delta S \backsim R$, and, as a consequence, groundwater levels and interface will start moving down and up and inland, respectively. By the end of the year, driving groundwater levels will be slightly below their original superelevation above sea level.

During the second year the first type of approach will leave the system basically unchanged. The second type of policy, however, would again result in a dual loss to the formation consisting of the withdrawal value ($I = R$) and the outflow to base level (now somewhat reduced as a consequence of lowered driving groundwater levels) partly compensated for by a recharge R.

In the third year (and in every following year) the first type of policy would again leave the system stock unchanged. The second type of policy would continue to incur the dual loss of interception and the outflow to base level which, however, would decrease with time as the one-time stock is depleted and driving groundwater levels drop.

This schematic simplified example demonstrates the great difference in water yields between the two policies. The first policy in the example would at the time horizon have an intact one-time stock, implying a greatly expanded utilization potential beyond the time horizon. The second would be confined in uses beyond the horizon to an appropriate percentage of the basic recharge rate, without having yielded any more water during the planning period. Whether the additional cost involved in adopting the first policy is in fact justified will depend on the specific context.

If we are dealing with a new development in a coastal area similar to that described in the above example, and if the location of demand areas (in the case that available water is sufficient to develop only part of the area) may be freely adapted to water-resources management requirements, *ceteris paribus*, we should locate demand so as to maximize interception of flow to base level, i.e., at least a substantial part of it should be located in a strip that is parallel and relatively close to the coast. Such a position of the demand would minimize loss to base levels. If the location of demand is determined by external factors, we would have to evaluate the extent to which emphasis on interception of flow to base level might still be justified. If other codetermining factors exist in addition to water conservation (e.g., location of high-class soils), we would have to outline a number of alternative patterns of management and compare their costs and benefits.

In actual planning situations, demand will neither be concentrated along a single line nor, as a rule, be constant throughout the planning period. The first policy will be indicated where it is important to exploit the formation beyond recharge levels for long periods, especially in cases where a more expensive and less subdivisible supply will become available for later development (to stop the "overdraft" from the formation and the inland movement of the salt water–fresh water interface when the one-time stock is depleted). The second policy will lend itself to similar use patterns, but the time during which such overutilization may be continued before exhausting the one-time stock and incurring salt-water encroachment will be substantially shorter.

THE THREE ALTERNATIVE BASIC DOCTRINES OF MANAGEMENT POLICIES

The adoption of the dynamic management concept leads to three basic alternative long-term management policies:

1. The equilibrium policy aimed at attaining, after transient stages, a target state that is in stable equilibrium, subject only to short-term fluctuations
2. The quasi equilibrium policy aimed at attaining, after transients, a target state that requires continuous corrective intervention to keep the system in a quasi equilibrium and to avoid "run-away" conditions
3. The nonequilibrium policy reconciled to a nonequilibrium final state (i.e., relinquishing the aim of ending up with an equilibrium or quasi equilibrium), while ensuring for a specific period our ability to utilize the resource under such conditions

The above-mentioned equilibrium conditions refer to both quantitative (i.e., flow) equilibria and qualitative (i.e., mineral and biological) equilibria. Quantitative and qualitative processes are generally interdependent and develop in the same direction, though their rate of development may differ greatly. Qualitative processes are usually much more sluggish than quantitative ones. If we confine our attention to the more conspicuous quantitative aspects of a groundwater system and ignore its less pronounced long-term qualitative ones, we might falsely conclude that it is operating under a stable equilibrium policy. In reality, the qualitative aspects of the system would be developing slowly but cumulatively according to quasi-equilibrium or even nonequilibrium patterns.

To establish a management policy of water resources, we shall therefore have to first decide which of the three policy doctrines (assuming that all three are possible in the given resources situation) to select for the quantitative aspects and then determine what type of management doctrine this decision implies for qualitative aspects. We might of course also start by selecting a policy for the qualitative dimensions of the system and then deduce the corresponding quantitative management implications. Because of our greater ignorance of long-term qualitative processes, this latter procedure will be difficult and will therefore rarely be chosen.

The great difference between the "response lags" of quantitative and qualitative aspects to management interventions into groundwater formations stems from the difference in the participating portion of the stock of formation water.

As far as quantitative aspects are concerned, the "active" stock of water is confined to that part of the stock which is above the "target gradient," the groundwater gradient to which we desire to bring the system at the time horizon. In a sizable formation, the depth of water below the target gradient may be many times (say, one half to one and a half orders of magnitude) larger than that above the gradient. From the point of view of quantitative management the predominant portion of the water stock in the formation will thus represent "dead storage." Furthermore, we have to keep in mind that part of the storage capacity (and part of the related stock of water) above the target gradient is required to regulate fluctuation of groundwater due to interannual and seasonal climatic variations.

Qualitative management, on the other hand, can depend on the whole stock of formation water; it will thus have at its disposal an incomparably larger amplitude of response, or alternatively a much longer period of time until a specific amplitude of response is reached. If we confine ourselves to problems of chemical (as opposed to biological) water quality, a specific annual interception of groundwater for use within the same drainage area will result in a reduction of the discharge of minerals to base levels and in a salinity buildup within the formation. The introduction of minerals into the drainage area, in connection with agricultural or industrial production processes, will lead to additional mineral accumulation. In the theoretical case of a homogeneous formation, and assuming perfect drainage of residual wastes to the formation, the mineral buildup will in time spread throughout the whole physical stock of formation water. Because of the resulting great dilution, the average annual rise in dissolved solids will usually be very slow. Furthermore, various delaying and absorptive mechanisms will often operate to further slow down responses.

In relation to quantitative management of water resources, the dead storage below the target gradient need not be absolutely inoperative. If, as a consequence of a lengthy drought period, groundwater levels have dropped to the target gradient, it might still be feasible—if the drought continues—under certain conditions and for limited periods of time to draw water from the stock below the gradient, without necessarily prejudicing future uses at previously prevailing rates of use. What is required is that we later restore the "overdraft" to storage. Alternatively, we might continue to draw water from dead storage until a new lower target gradient is reached, one which could be maintained only by perpetual intervention. The latter alternative implies a switch from a stable equilibrium to a quasi-equilibrium policy. Groundwater is so flexible a resource that even such "negative storage" (i.e., stocks below target gradient) may prove extremely useful in time of need.

In actual planning of qualitative management measures, we rarely find a truly homogeneous formation; aquicludes (impermeable formations) or partially permeable formations will often subdivide the formation and obstruct dilution.

Thus only part of the formation water might in fact participate in the dilution, unless specific (and often costly) measures are taken to ensure full dilution.

THE CONSERVATION ISSUE

In medium-term planning terms, the selection of a long-term management policy will be equivalent to defining the target state of the water-resources system. Both will depend on our attitude on the water-conservation issue, that is, on the state in which we feel we ought to leave the resources system to the next generation. We have repeatedly referred to this question in other chapters, but it might be useful to restate the main lines of the argument.

Conservation, of course, needs to be applied only to renewable water resources, since utilization of water resources that are not renewed, or that are renewed at an insignificant rate, cannot be reconciled with their conservation. But even if we deal with renewable resources, we ought to beware of falling into a fundamentalist and basically negative conservationist attitude. Such an attitude, if carried to its logical conclusions, would lead to an extreme impoverishment of the water-resources inventory that would benefit nobody. For if applied to the next generation in relation to the next but one, it would also preclude the proper use of the inventory by the next generation.

Chandler Morse of Cornell University has aptly put the case of a rational conservation policy in his paper "National Sources of Economic Growth: The Quality Problem" read at the 1961 Meeting of the Western Resources Conference.[2] He has exposed the conventional conservationist viewpoint usually implied in the engineering approach to resources conservation as a static simplification, unwarranted in a dynamic society of expanding technology. He has shown that a "changing resources spectrum" will change the "resources base" of production and that it is therefore not economically, or even morally, justified to insist on quantitative conservation of a resource with a view to achieving a continuous and constant sustained yield of the resource. He does not deny the existence of a moral obligation to future generations in relation to resources use; rather, he maintains that these "obligations must be framed and discharged in the most sensible manner available to us." His thesis is that this could be achieved by maintaining what he terms "social welfare output": "social welfare output means the gross output of society valued in non-economic as well as in economic terms, full provision being made for the replacement of wasting assets, for research . . . . Thus, we may and should act on the assumption that future generations will welcome, or at least will have no legitimate cause to complain if they receive an unimpaired per capita stock of social wealth." Owing to the variability of the resources base, the share of different resources in the stock transmitted to future generations will also change. Morse concludes that "regardless of what happens along the way, the

[2] Chandler Morse, "National Sources of Economic Growth: The Quality Problem," *Western Resources Conference—1961 on Land and Water: Planning for Economic Growth,* University of Colorado Press, 1962, pp. 9–27.

aim must be to avoid a final loss of social welfare . . . . Policy should be framed in the positive terms of optimal resource use, not in negative terms of optimal conservation."

TIME PREFERENCE FOR WATER

Selection of a water-resources management policy and the approach we take to water conservation will to no small degree be determined by the time preference for water related to specific water uses. This time preference is dependent on the anticipated utility of water in every specific context and time. It should determine the "discount rate" that would be applied to express the relation of expected future to certain present utility of water.

Unlike money, which within a specific time and in a specific context is usually assumed to have constant utility, the utility of water will greatly depend on the overall development context. In some cases, the "absorptive capacity" for water beyond a specific level of use will, within a specific resources base and at a specific point of time, be extremely limited. Availability of water beyond such a demand limit will be of no use, and since water is here assumed to have no alternative uses, its utility beyond the above limit would be very low to nil. In such a case, time preference for water above that limit would cease to be meaningful. There will be other cases where no such limitations of absorptive capacity exist. Here earlier availability of water would be desirable, and time preference will certainly be meaningful.

There exist cases where the utility of water greatly transcends its direct economic effect. A predevelopment operation preceding major investment in irrigation facilities would be a relevant example. Here the whole socioeconomic system supporting agricultural production is transformed in conjunction with the application of water. Such predevelopment of the productive capacity will from the outset ensure a high economic return to subsequent investments. Furthermore, the predevelopment of demand effected through the temporary use of a local water source might greatly shorten the time required to reach a high plant use factor for later larger and more expensive water installations. In such cases utility of water would certainly transcend its direct short-term economic benefits, and this high utility ought to be adequately expressed in an appropriately set time preference and discount rate.

Where the development of the source in question also has the secondary role of "buying time," the utility of water might also be much higher than its direct economic impact. Buying time might be all-important where the information available for the development of the water resource that is next in turn for development is not sufficient for making the relevant major decisions, and where considerable time might be required to collect such information. It might be still more important where the development of the resource that is next in turn is dependent on a technology that is still in its early (and rapidly improving) phase of development. In both these cases, but especially in the latter, predevelopment of demand and the related acceleration in reaching high plant use are also important considerations.

28
QUALITATIVE ASPECTS OF WATER-RESOURCES MANAGEMENT

No one is willing to admit that national defense, general welfare, recreation, stream pollution, etc., are not yet convertible into quantitative economic terms of dollars and cents although they are obviously of tremendous importance to society.

ABEL WOLMAN

TYPES AND SOURCES OF QUALITY PROBLEMS ENCOUNTERED IN WATER-RESOURCES MANAGEMENT

Of the two basic types of pollution of water, biological and chemical (mineral), the former is the "softer" type from the point of view of water-resources management. It lends itself to satisfactory manipulation at costs that, even at the present state of the art, are tolerable for most systems. Mineral pollution, on the other hand, must be considered as a "hard" type of pollution. The methods available at present to remove most types of objectionable mineral pollution from water not only are expensive but are often above economic ceilings justifiable for most water uses.

The sources of pollution of surface runoff can, as a rule, be easily traced; those of groundwater are often much more difficult to identify. *Emphasis here will be on pollution of groundwater, and especially on mineral pollution.*

Biological pollution of groundwater is usually traceable to human, animal, and plant wastes and to economic activities of man.

Mineral pollution stems from a greater variety of sources, principal among which are:

1. Meteorological, i.e., minerals collected by raindrops during the hydrological cycle.
2. Water imported into the basin: any minerals contained in imported water will (unless discharged outside the basin, barred from recharge process, or retained during the infiltration process) ultimately reach formation water.

3. Disintegration of human, animal, and industrial wastes.
4. Accretion of minerals from rocks and soils during surface and underground flow of water.

The waste-disposal regime adopted will greatly affect mineral accumulation. A regime oriented toward minimizing mineral pollution, on the one hand, might identify sources of major pollution and discharge them outside the basin. Since it will often be difficult or uneconomical to isolate sources of major pollution from other less polluted sources, the discharge of pollutants might involve a significant loss of water. A regime oriented mainly toward water conservation, on the other hand, might reclaim most waste waters for reuse, thereby accelerating the buildup of pollutants in formation.

Quantitative management of water resources has qualitative implications which must be considered together with quantitative factors. Taking the simplest case of management, i.e., utilization of part of the recharge of a groundwater formation within the basin (without concurrently providing for the discharge of use-related waste water out of the basin), withdrawal from the formation will lower groundwater levels, thereby decreasing outflow of water to base levels and, consequently, decreasing discharge of minerals. Salinities of formation water will rise until a new salinity equilibrium is reached in which the salt discharge at the reduced outflow will, at the higher salinity equilibrium, again equal the original salt input plus any salts added in the process of water use.

OBJECTIVES OF QUALITATIVE MANAGEMENT OF WATER RESOURCES

Qualitative management distinguishes four principal water uses: biological (drinking water for man and animal), domestic and commercial, industrial, and agricultural (mainly irrigation).

We may assume that tolerances to mineral pollution and the disutility of such pollution will, within operational limits, vary according to a smooth curve. Unfortunately, our knowledge of such functional relationships as those between pollution on the one hand and disutility on the other is still extremely fragmentary; therefore, we are often forced to adopt ceilings (usually incorporating generous margins of safety) in lieu of these relationships.

Quality objectives of biological uses of water are usually expressed in ceilings (or floors and ceilings). Most of these ceilings are based on satisfactory experience rather than on extensive statistical or experimental work. Since this is an area where rigorous information is difficult to obtain, we shall probably, at least for some time, have to go on using these ceilings (and/or floors) as qualitative constraints of water-resources management for potable supplies. Since practically no water-supply system separates potable uses from other domestic and from commercial uses, we shall as a rule have to adopt the same constraints for the two latter uses that we specify for potable uses.

Some domestic and commercial uses of water entail additional qualitative aspects. Hardness and related soap consumption have, in this age of detergents, become less important controlling aspects but retain some importance in connection with deterioration of water-using facilities and gadgets. The same applies to corrosivity of water. Both aspects can largely be controlled through corrosion-resistant materials or protective measures. Costs and benefits of management measures related to domestic and commercial uses lend themselves to quantification and economic justification. Qualitative aspects of industrial uses of water are similarly quantifiable.

Our ignorance about the functional relationship expressing the dependence of production upon mineral pollution principally affects agricultural uses. Although rigorous data are here obtainable with time, the range of applicability of specific data is still rather limited because of the low transferability of data obtained in one set of ecological conditions to other apparently similar sets. Therefore, we must resort too often to ceilings. Since irrigation involves very large volumes of water, it will be in this sector that the adoption of ceiling constraints, instead of a production-pollution functional relationship, will involve the greatest departure from the optimal path.

Since every type of water use implies a specific set of ceilings (or functional relationships between pollution and disutility), we might be tempted to use separate systems for each type of use. Such separate systems would prove extremely costly and inflexible, and therefore we normally combine a number of uses into one system. Potable domestic and commercial uses are almost universally combined; often some or all industrial uses draw their supply from the same system. In some cases irrigation uses are also fed from a community industrial type of water supply. In cases of combined uses, the most sensitive use will determine the pollution ceiling for a specific mineral.

POLLUTION GEOMETRY

Water use and water-resources pollution are interdependent, interacting processes. The patterns evolving in space, time, quantity, and quality earlier described for water-resources utilization reappear in pollution streams. The same type of maturation patterns evolving in the time dimension will be found: on the one hand, polarization of pollution due to agglomeration of population (more typical for the developing world) and the greater per capita waste production (more typical for the developed world); on the other hand, dispersion of pollution as economic activities spread. The fact that river courses, lakes, and springs have, in addition to their utility as sources of exploitable water, intrinsic value as part of our general habitat and environment will also, and in increasing measure, affect qualitative management policies.

This obvious interrelationship and interaction between the quantitative and qualitative aspects of water resources demands that exploitation of water and manipulation of wastes be regarded as one single system. The same integrative aim of course applies to where major uses and waste discharges occur within a single water-resources system.

Although the exploitation in waste-disposal interrelationship is well recognized, the integrative approach is not too often adopted in actual planning. As a matter of fact, institutional fragmentation of water-resources development and waste-disposal agencies often operate against such an integrative approach. The incompatibility between institutional structure and the requirements of resources (and pollution) management, discussed earlier in connection with community water supplies (see Chapter 15), can also be observed in connection with the integration of water supply and waste disposal.

Comprehensive analysis of the quantitative and qualitative aspects of a water-resources system will be an optimization problem with two decision variables: exploitable water (its quantity and quality) and preservation of the environment. The former will lend itself to a reasonable degree of quantification, the latter will sometimes resist rigorous quantitative analysis. It will be still more difficult to define a common (say monetary) yardstick to express respective utilities and trade-off ratio between objectives. Here again the problem should be transposed into terms that fit the value scales of the decision maker. In the present case this implies establishing a number of alternative management patterns, all of which comply with the demand requirements (quantitative and qualitative) of water but result in different levels of environmental qualities and involve different cost levels. The decision maker then decides how much environmental preservation he wants to "buy."

To the extent that such decisions prejudice future environment-preservation measures, conservationist problems will arise. If decisions do not lead to irreversible deterioration (or deterioration reversible only at disproportionally high costs) of the environment (or water resource), the decision should be dictated by the value judgments of the present. If irreversible deterioration is involved, the plan ought to be reshaped to ensure future generations the necessary freedom of action to preserve or restore high quality levels of the environment (or resource).

Optimizing or satisfying the system would thus consist in minimizing costs to comply with quantitative and qualitative requirements, while maintaining the selected level of environmental quality and reserving the possibility of future quality improvement.

Switching from system optimization to institutional implications, we again find the familiar patterns outlined in Chapter 15 for community water-supply development: institutional structure lags behind developments of the resources-demand geometry. Originally, what might be termed the "biological" solution is adopted: wastes are removed from the immediate habitat of the individual. When pollution disposal becomes the responsibility of the community, the approach does not basically change: the emphasis shifts to disposal of pollution from the immediate communal habitat. Joint action in a resources system will usually stem from a crisis in a major part of the system or in the system as a whole. Again, we have adaptation by crisis.

SEPARATION OF RESOURCES AND POLLUTION STREAMS

The most extreme approach to pollution control is represented by the separation of resources and pollution streams. Such a separation would in fact break down the comprehensive resources-pollution system into two separate subsystems—resources and pollution—which might have to be planned and optimized in conjunction with one another, but which would leave the greatest freedom of operation within each system, once the overall layout is adopted.

Such a separation of streams may be effected in one of two ways (or by a combination of these two ways):

1. Collection of pollution streams (or at least of their most objectionable component parts) and their diversion and disposal beyond the utilized portion of the resources system (or the portion proposed for future utilization)
2. Collection of the clean water resources (or of major portions thereof) at points where the resource has not yet been significantly affected by pollution and where pollution is not anticipated in the future, and their diversion from the natural hydrological system into a man-made system, leaving the former to serve as a channel of waste disposal

The advantages of such complete separation would in every specific case have to be weighed against such disadvantages as:

1. Cost of collecting pollution or resources streams
2. Cost of conveying the above streams and cost of disposal
3. Unavoidable loss of water involved in both approaches

In some cases, separation might initially prove economically unfeasible. But as the region "matures," its pollution problems increasing as well as its "payment ability," separation not only becomes economically feasible but may constitute the sole possible solution. In such cases, phasing of separation might be indicated. Phasing would at the outset of the program provide the most affected areas with partial separation, so planned as to admit later integration into an overall streams-separation plan.

BASIC QUALITATIVE MANAGEMENT POLICIES

Pollution streams are not always manifest and easily detected; they may pass unnoticed for years or decades. Slow cumulative pollution processes prove the most insidious in their effect and the most difficult to cope with. To avoid neglecting the slow cumulative pollution streams, we ought to make an exhaustive analysis of the interconnection between the pollution and the hydrological systems. If, for instance, we withdraw water for downstream use from an upstream portion of an underground formation, or if we export water for use outside the hydrological basin, such water uses will not affect upstream qualitative equilibria. In the former case, the mineral discharge, carried at the original equilibrium by the water (M_{orig}), will now de divided between the continuing flow (M_{cont}) within the system (or upstream part of the system) and the diverted part (M_{div}), but will not be diminished in aggregate. Thus, the original qualitative equilibrium $M_{\text{orig}} = M_{\text{cont}} + M_{\text{div}}$ will continue indefinitely.

If, however, some of the activity for which the intercepted water is used is conducted in a place that is hydrologically connected with the resource, and if the water use is predominantly consumptive, two new factors will be introduced:

1. The minerals contained in the water used in the interconnected part, or at least part of them (ΔM_1), will ultimately reach the resource and will, to some extent, mix with the stock of water stored in the formation ($S =$ part of stock participating in the mixing), thereby increasing the mineral concentration of water in the basin by $\Delta M_1/S$.

2. The activity for which the water is used may introduce some additional minerals into the system, and the portion that will ultimately reach the formation (ΔM_2) will cause a further salinity increase in formation water $\Delta M_2/S$.

Increase of salt concentration in the formation, represented by $(\Delta M_1 + \Delta M_2)/S$, will continue until the resulting salinity is sufficient to maintain an equilibrium between the discharge of minerals, at the remaining flow rate, and the total current salt input.

Thus, every interception executed for predominantly consumptive water uses at a place that is hydrologically connected with the water resource will alter the qualitative as well as the quantitative equilibrium. If such interception approaches average outflow (or inflow plus return flow) levels, outflow from the basin would practically cease and the basin would be transformed into a closed basin; since no (or very little) water, and consequently only a small amount of minerals, would be discharged out of the basin, minerals would accumulate within the formation water. In such a case, a qualitative nonequilibrium would result, even though a quantitative equilibrium might be maintained indefinitely. By applying a perpetual remedial intervention, such a nonequilibrium could of course be turned into a quasi equilibrium. This example indicates that quantitative and qualitative transients and equilibria or disequilibria need not be in phase; in fact, in the great majority of cases they will be out of phase; qualitative transients and equilibria will lag considerably behind quantitative ones.

So far we have neglected the complexities introduced into qualitative transients through the travel of pollution agents contained in water through interjacent media before actually reaching a groundwater formation. During this travel period two important types of mechanism come into play:

1. Breaking down of complex organic components by biological action
2. Operation of some chemicophysical retention and/or delay mechanism, the nature, strength, and effectiveness of which are still little known

When the pollution agents do in fact reach participating formation water, dilution will of course become effective and, as a consequence, the rise in the salinity of formation water very slow.

In addition to these natural delay mechanisms, the planner of water-resources management policies has at his disposal a number of manipulative measures to slow down or delay salinity buildups. Pollution tends to travel downstream; to reduce a downstream buildup of pollution, the planner can either change the direction of the travel of pollution (e.g., by diversion of some important concentrations of upstream pollution out of the basin, or by reducing their pollution load) or change the timing or phasing of its appearance downstream (e.g., by storing it, underground, at such places and depth that it will reappear downstream much later, and in much diluted form).

Delaying the impact of a major pollution burden (and here we have mineral rather than biological pollution in mind) may be justified for a number of reasons:

1. The present quality situation may be critical as a consequence of specific and passing conditions (such as an unfavorable climatic cycle); phasing the appearance of the additional pollution burden until the peak of the temporary salinity buildup has passed would avoid dangerous peak superimpositions.

2. It might be planned to import high-quality water from outside the basin at a later date; phasing a pollution burden so that its reappearance coincides with the availability of the new high-quality water would greatly soften the impact of pollution when it finally strikes the protected part of the system.

3. It may be assumed that the cost of applying corrective measures such as extractive desalting processes (e.g., electrodialysis or reverse osmosis) will decrease with time; "buying time" might therefore have the dual effect of postponing major investments and greatly increasing the chances of a later lower cost operation.

29
TYPICAL APPLICATIONS OF THE THREE BASIC MANAGEMENT POLICIES

Also I believe we need to do a great deal more work in developing skills in synthesis—that is, the bringing together of diverse elements harmoniously into complex systems. We need to develop carefully the people who have some initial abilities in that direction and then strengthen and improve their skills.

PHILIP SPORN

The present chapter deals with a few selected examples of applications of the three basic water-resources management policies, i.e., the stable equilibrium, the quasi equilibrium, and the nonequilibrium policies. In line with the general orientation adopted, we shall confine ourselves to basic underlying policy without attempting exhaustive quantitative analysis.

THE STABLE EQUILIBRIUM

The stable-equilibrium policy is implied in the conventional management pattern of groundwater resources based on sustained safe yield concepts. Such a policy provides for exploitation of the groundwater resources at a rate equaling the mean recharge (natural and artificial) minus the amount of outflow (if any) necessary to prevent encroachment of substandard water from outside the basin (e.g., sea water in coastal areas).

However, even this simplest of all management rules calls for caution in its application: when applying the safe yield management policy, we usually focus on quantitative equilibria, tacitly (and often erroneously) assuming that qualitative equilibria will be achieved in line with them. If, for instance, we assume a case in which exploitation equals the mean recharge, and if the economic activity related to the use of water is carried out within the basin and residual wastes (return water from irrigation, waste water) discharge into the underlying formation, stable equilibrium use of water will result in a qualitative disequilibrium, i.e., a gradual buildup of mineral pollution within the formation.

As pointed out in Chapter 28, this mineral buildup can be traced to two main sources: the minerals contained in the water applied (highly concentrated in the residual return water from irrigation) and the minerals incident to the economic activity for which the water was used (e.g., fertilizer and plant-protection chemicals in agriculture). Since we have assumed that, at the stable equilibrium, exploitation has caused a discontinuation of the discharge of groundwater to base level, minerals from the above two sources will tend to accumulate in the formation and cause a gradual salinity buildup in the formation water. As this mineral pollution will be distributed throughout the formation water (assuming a homogeneous aquifer without aquiclude intercalations), and as the stock stored in the formation is usually large in comparison with the annual withdrawal and the annual pollution contribution, mineralization will be sluggish and therefore may for a long time be overlooked.

To ensure a stable qualitative equilibrium under the assumption that exploitation equals mean recharge, we would have to stipulate that the economic activity related to water use be conducted outside the basin or that wastes involved in such economic activity within the basin be diverted and discharged outside the basin.

Even if we assume that a minor portion of the recharge will continue to flow to base levels, minerals will still accumulate in the formation. However, in the latter case mineral accumulation will be somewhat slower than in the case of no outflow, since the residual outflow will continue to discharge minerals out of the basin. The salinity buildup will also not be perpetual but will approach a salinity ceiling: the mineral content of water will rise until salinities are reached at which the flow to base levels will discharge out of the basin an amount of minerals that is equal to the mineral input.

In the above simplistic description of qualitative disequilibria related to quantitative equilibria, we have assumed that minerals involved in the economic activities related to the use of water do in fact reach the formation without any major delay or exchange en route. Observations indicate that in actual fact delays and possibly also adsorption and exchanges do occur, the extent and nature of which have not yet been adequately explored. The time that will elapse until mineral pollution of water reaches the tolerance level of the most sensitive use for which the water is intended will depend mainly on (1) the composition of the pollutant, (2) the volume of the diluting water stock, (3) the retentive and "exchange" power of the "barriers" between water application and the formation, and (4) the portion of minerals discharged outside the basin.

The qualitative disequilibrium induced in groundwater formation by implementing a quantitative equilibrium management policy may of course be changed into a quasi equilibrium (or induced equilibrium) condition, if we decide to apply remedial measures in order to maintain certain qualitative standards in the formation. We shall come back to this question in the section devoted to quasi equilibria.

Stable equilibrium policies need not and, in our opinion, ought not be confined to a static interpretation. They lend themselves to a broader, more dynamic interpretation: stocks of water which lend themselves to a one-time exploitation will, as a rule, be found between the original levels of groundwater formation and those related to the final steady state; the same applies to the stock between the original interface between seawater and fresh water in coastal areas and the interface related to the steady state at equilibrium utilization. If utilized within the framework of a dynamically conceived stable-equilibrium management policy, such stocks will represent a most valuable supplementation of exploitation levels based on static sustained safe yield. The utilization of such quantitative transients need not induce a significant qualitative deterioration. When setting up management policies for formations possessing important transient stocks of water, it ought to be kept in mind that if utilization is limited to safe yield levels the transient stocks will flow to base level and, in the case of coastal formations, be forever lost to the sea.

An interesting and useful application of the dynamic interpretation of the stable-equilibrium policy is the manipulation of the flow of springs. Spring discharge is controlled by storage levels of the groundwater formation sustaining the spring. These levels (and the spring flow controlled by them) are usually highest in the rainy season or during humid cycles when the demand for water is lowest; they are lowest in the late summer or in dry cycles when demand is at its peak. Availability of spring water therefore does not match requirements and depends on vagaries of climate; management measures will seek to upgrade availability by making it fit the requirement schedule. This upgrading of flow availability may be effected by lowering the groundwater level controlling the spring flow to an elevation at which the flow is under control. The lowering will be produced by pumping from wells, thereby intercepting groundwater feeding the spring.

The drop from original to ultimate levels may extend over a considerable period of time, and the quantity of water stored between these two levels will, as a one-time stock, again become available for mining during the transition period.

The upgrading of the flow parameter of springs will sometimes result in a concurrent upgrading of the qualitative parameters: some springs pick up minerals as they flow through mineralized formations, and the water becomes brackish. Wells can be so located as to ensure interception of the flow before it comes in contact with the mineralized formations. An operation of this nature will result in upgrading both flow and qualitative parameters.

THE QUASI (OR INDUCED) EQUILIBRIUM

The quasi-equilibrium policy is most often encountered in long-term plans for managing the *qualitative* aspects of water resources. It is seldom adopted exclusively, but is usually part of a diversified approach embodying stable-equilibrium and nonequilibrium patterns as component parts. A groundwater utilization project intercepting the whole formation flow for utilization in an area overlying the basin and draining into it will, for example, constitute a qualitative nonequilibrium policy, although it might take a considerable period of time for the consequences to be noticed and a still longer period for them to seriously jeopardize use. Introduction, at a later period, of increasing quantities of imported high-quality water would represent a remedial measure which would turn the nonequilibrium into a quasi-equilibrium policy.

Lowering of qualitative levels can be halted and the resource held at a chosen qualitative level by one of four methods of intervention, or by a combination of them:

1. Artificial abstraction of minerals and discharge of concentrated brine out of the basin
2. Recharging groundwater with high-quality imported water to reduce the formation water salinity by dilution
3. Dilution within the engineering system of pumped groundwater of high mineral content with high-quality water
4. Selective diversion of highly mineralized water out of the basin

These methods are dealt with in the following:

Artificial abstraction In order to reach qualitative equilibrium by artificial abstraction of the minerals and subsequent discharge of the concentrated brine, it will be necessary to abstract at a rate that, together with the continued discharge to base level at the acceptable salinity, would equal the average salinity input. Suitable processes to achieve this kidney effect are electrodialysis and reverse osmosis. In the present state of technology, these processes are still generally too expensive for large-scale application, but these or similar processes are already economically feasible for specific uses and may in time prove more widely applicable.

Underground recharge with imported high-quality water In a formation of continuous mineral accumulation, importing a fixed quantity of high-quality (i.e., low-salinity) water into the formation cannot restore equilibrium permanently. To create a quasi-equilibrium condition at a salinity level that would comply with use specifications, such imports would have to be continuously stepped up.

Let us assume that importing high-quality water into a formation used at sustained yield levels is justifiable only on a dual-benefit basis, i.e., if the imported water is required both to supplement the supply that can be made available from the formation and to maintain the quality of formation water. Let us, furthermore, assume that the pumping of formation water (at sustained yield levels) is continued without resorting to imports until the salinity buildup in the formation water reaches use tolerances. To avoid further salinity buildup, we now would have to initiate the import of low-salinity water and increase this at a rate that would depend on the current salt input. If the rate of increase of imports dictated by such quality management considerations is equal to that controlled by quantitative management consideration, we shall be able to maintain a qualitative quasi equilibrium even if we posit that imports can be justified only on a dual-benefit basis. If the volume of imports dictated by quality considerations is larger than that controlled by quantitative management, the difference between the two would have only the quality (and not the quantity) benefit; in the opposite case, the difference would have only quantity and no quality benefits.

Dilution before use This method does not attempt to interfere with the normal processes of mineralization of the formation water, and the mineral content is allowed to increase. The dilution to required salinity levels is achieved by mixing the pumped formation water, after its transfer into the engineering system, with imported low-salinity water. This method must ensure the distribution and supply of the diluting water to all areas of groundwater use or to main distribution points. Because it demands setting up a second separate distribution system, this approach will usually prove relatively expensive, unless dilution can be confined to a very limited number of points favorably located in relation to the source of imported water.

Finally, we ought to remember that the salinity buildup of the formation water must be kept within relatively modest limits if the dilution approach is to remain economically feasible.

Diversion of highly mineralized water This is a palliative measure which by itself will seldom solve the quality problems of a closed or quasi-closed basin. It usually consists in collecting the highly mineralized industrial wastes and agricultural drainage water and discharging them out of the basin. Combined with one of the three other approaches, it will reduce their scope or allow delay in their application.

Combination of measures Usually a combination of two or more of the above approaches, implemented simultaneously or consecutively, will be adopted to manage the qualitative parameters of a basin. Owing to the sluggishness of the processes involved and the built-in delaying mechanisms, the incorporation of transients into a dynamic management plan will be even more important than in the case of quantitative parameters.

Transcending basin boundaries When the exhaustion of local resources forces us to look for additional resources outside narrow hydrological boundaries and adopt wider regional or national management systems, the salt balance need no longer be planned for a hydrological basin as a closed unit, but may be considered in the framework of the wider management system. This wider approach will open new avenues for the manipulation of quality balances. The use of a formation afflicted with mineralization problems both as an underground storage reservoir for imported low-salinity water and as a mixing basin can solve its salinity problems, without necessarily causing a crippling deterioration of the quality of the stored water. While flowing through the formation, the imported water will mix with the formation's indigenous water to an extent that can be predetermined by proper planning of withdrawal operations in the dimensions of space and time and in recharge rate. The combined use of a mineralized formation as underground storage reservoir for imported low-salinity water and as mixing basin may solve the salinity problem of a formation by making use of the dilution potential of the re-exported water temporarily stored there.

Selective salinity levels Quality management may also set different levels of quality equilibria for water uses with different mineral tolerances. The higher salinity water may be selectively allocated to less salt-sensitive uses, such as municipal and some industrial or high-tolerance agricultural uses; or, preferably, it may be used to maintain the unavoidable discharge of the formation to base levels. Quality differentiation may also be practiced in the time dimension. Where summer irrigation is the most salt-sensitive use, the basic salinity of the formation may be kept at a level considerably above that permissible for irrigation; at such salinity, the water would be used directly, or via storage, for municipal and industrial uses. The winter flow of the dilutant could be stored, possibly underground, and reused together with its summer flow for intensive dilution of the formation water during the dry season, predominantly for irrigation; dilution could again be selectively varied for various water uses, according to the salt tolerance of the prevailing principal crops.

Transcending boundaries of a hydrological system Numerous combinations of the above approaches may be worked out within the management framework concerned with the quantitative and qualitative aspects of a hydrological system. As long as no major disequilibrium problems appear, analysis within the above framework may prove sufficient. However, where such disequilibria or serious quality problems are anticipated, and if we still desire an optimized management solution, we may have to expand the system definition to include additional aspects of the relevant production complex. In such cases we may, for instance, have to include in our system the removal of wastes from irrigation (i.e., drainage), cultivation methods, the biological material, or additional variables and draw up a system of management in which we could vary those dimensions as well as the quantitative and qualitative hydrological variables. Obviously crop response to various salinity levels will depend on soil type and on the kind of drainage measures applied to removal of wastes. Crops, and even various types of the same crop, have different salinity tolerances, and cultivation methods and agroinputs influence these tolerances. Where maintenance of quality levels below conventional ceilings would require major investments and operational costs, an overall optimization including the above aspects will become imperative. Such an optimization might indicate intensified drainage for a certain crop at a higher salinity ceiling, rather than maintenance of a lower ceiling. Alternatively, or in addition, a relatively unimportant change in crop patterns might allow higher salinity ceilings.

As qualitative problems become more serious, we shall have to resort to more elaborate models, which will, in turn, require more elaborate data. The generation, collection, processing, and supplementation of such data ought to be included in the earlier development phases where qualitative problems are still tolerable. Since assemblage of such data takes time, lack of provisions to ensure their availability may leave us in a critical position when finally faced with acute quality problems.

THE NONEQUILIBRIUM

The most obvious example of the nonequilibrium decision pattern is the "mining" of a stock of water, i.e., exploitation at a rate that will remain permanently above recharge rates. Such mining will be continued until the resource is exhausted, groundwater levels drop to depths from which pumping becomes uneconomic or unfeasible, the danger arises of substandard water infiltration from adjoining basins or from the sea, or other undesirable changes occur. The instinctive aversion of conventional analysis to the mining approach probably stems from fundamentalist *water-conservation doctrines.*

The traditional conservationist ethic, however, cannot contend with an analysis based on the principle, discussed earlier, of maintenance of the stock of social wealth. Mining water could be the precondition for developing a region and for creating production and production capacity that will in time warrant importing into the region more expensive water from the outside and in extreme cases even desalted seawater. A region developed by mined water constitutes a more valuable stock of wealth to be transmitted to future generations than an untouched resource in an undeveloped environment, even if expensive imported water will, ultimately, have to be substituted for mining or further use discontinued by substituting alternative economic activities that are less dependent on water and which have become feasible only as a consequence of prior use of mined water. "Buying time" by mining postpones the heavy investment of importing or even desalting water. Interim technological developments may allow cheaper processes and considerable savings in setting up the ultimate solution. Mining groundwater can also be phased according to the growing requirements of the economy, while importing water is much less subdivisible—a fact that is especially important in the early low-demand development phases. When imports become unavoidable, demand will have been fully developed by using mined water and the maturation period for the expensive and lumpy import project will have been considerably reduced.

Where mining is carried out within a closed basin or within one that management patterns will transform into a closed basin, the slow qualitative deterioration of the water by mineral accumulation or by inflow of substandard water may in time constitute a problem. Where conditions are unfavorable, qualitative ceilings may be the controlling management consideration and it may become necessary to control the extent of the mining even before the stock is exhausted. In such cases, the mined water may, as an interim measure, be diluted by import of low-salinity water.

ROLE OF GROUNDWATER AND SURFACE WATER IN THE MANAGEMENT OF A BASIN

The present section will analyze the roles of underground and surface water in developing and managing a basin's water resources. We shall assume here the more general case of a basin that possesses both underground and surface-water phases in relatively significant volumes. There are basins with no significant underground resources (e.g., river basins in impermeable base rocks) or with no significant surface flows (e.g., basins in highly permeable soils or rocks); however, in such basins no alternatives, and therefore no competing options, exist. We can therefore confine our analysis here to the more general and more complex case in which a decision has to be taken on priority of development of the two phases of the water resource.

Before we enter the subject proper, a cautionary remark might be in order. Surface and underground water are not separate and independent resources. The terms underground phase and surface-water phase, rather than the term resources, are intentionally employed to emphasize a single resource that appears in two interdependent phases. Interventions into surface flow (where the river contributes to groundwater formation) will influence groundwater flows, and, vice versa, interventions into groundwater flows (where groundwater formations interact with the river) will influence surface-water flows. In the lower reaches of basins, some part of the groundwater may discharge directly to a base level outside the basin (say, into the sea or a lake); in other cases, the boundaries of the underground basin may not coincide with those of the surface basin. In the latter two cases, that part of the groundwater located within the basin which does not drain into the surface-water basin may, of course, be utilized without greatly affecting surface-water resources. Otherwise, utilization of one phase will in time preclude full utilization of the other. "In time" must be emphasized, since owing to the size of the water stock stored in the formation and the sluggishness in underground flow processes, the mutual interaction may become substantial only after a lengthy period. In other words, even in basins where from the long-term viewpoint it is certain that surface water and groundwater are but two phases of the same resource and that utilization of one of the two phases will in time affect the other phase, even in such basins, the transients available on a one-time basis may prove an important and desirable supplemental resource.

In analyzing those decision patterns of planners in the developing countries which are related to the priority given to surface-water or groundwater resources, we find that most planners favor surface water. Even in regions where available geologic evidence points to the existence of sizable and attractive groundwater formation, groundwater is often not even investigated as an alternative, surface water being resorted to as a foregone conclusion. In probing for the reasons for this unwarranted disparagement, one is usually given a set of specious arguments which prove to be rationalizations of a deep unavowed bias.

Arguments against groundwater utilization The usual objections to the development of groundwater can be summarized under four headings:

1. Groundwater exploitation is expensive, especially if significant pumping heads are involved.
2. Planning of groundwater development is conditional upon the availability of long-term data, and such data are usually nonexistent.
3. The evaluation of such data depends on highly trained personnel which are not available in developing countries.
4. The quantitative and qualitative responses of a groundwater formation to a chosen exploitation pattern are difficult to predict.

So much for groundwater development. Similar arguments, urged with even greater emphasis, are raised with respect to underground storage.

In short, most water planners in developing countries consider the priority given in some other countries to groundwater development and underground storage as something akin to a fad invented by hydrological eggheads to confuse the hydraulic and civil engineering professions. Such a poor image of groundwater must have some deeper reasons than the flimsy arguments given by these planners. One is tempted to apply amateur depth psychology to trace the reasons for the poor image of groundwater.

Examination of opponent views To start with, let us look more closely at the list of arguments given above. The first argument—the cost of groundwater development—is usually coupled with some arbitrary ceiling for economically justifiable pumping lifts. The same planners will often unflinchingly recommend large-scale, costly river diversions which may require fifteen or twenty years of maturation, and which when properly analyzed would result in water costs well above those of groundwater. The second argument—making groundwater development dependent on long-term data—is as much of an optical illusion as the first one: groundwater levels and gradients, the flow dependent on these, and other aquifer parameters constitute a long-term cumulative record of the groundwater runoff, whereas river flows in most cases represent no more than short-term responses to short-term climatic fluctuations. The information (and here we come to the third and fourth arguments) that one can derive from groundwater records extending only over a few years can be far superior to and more dependable than that yielded by an equivalent surface-water record.

Evaluation of such groundwater records by modern hydrological procedures supported by analog and digital computers is not more complex, but can often be a great deal more solid, than attempting to extend existing surface flow data by analogy.

None of the customary arguments against the wider use of groundwater stand up to close examination. On the other hand, groundwater development and storage have the great advantages, especially important for developing countries, of relatively low capital investment, high subdivisibility of investment, great flexibility, and built-in margins for error.

The reason for the unpopularity of groundwater must therefore lie elsewhere and deeper. In our judgment, it lies in the difference between the problem-solving processes applied to surface water and groundwater. Surface water is a resource exposed to view, flow measurements are direct, and the problems posed are solved by the construction of solid civil engineering and hydraulic structures. Groundwater is a hidden resource that lends itself only to indirect evaluation and is more highly dependent on a problem-solving response based on resources manipulation and management rather than on straightforward engineering.

In short, problem solving as applied to groundwater requires a higher level of abstraction than that applied to surface water; it requires the substitution of dynamically conceived resources systems, manipulated by hydrological management measures, for the statically oriented hydraulic engineering approach to surface-water problems.

The above digressions into the "depth psychology" of engineering are not meant to imply automatic preference for groundwater (where available); the relative merits of underground water and surface water can be evaluated only by specific comparison of the respective costs of upgrading alternative sequences of the two phases of water resources according to the requirements of the demand vector. It may, nevertheless, be useful to review in an abstract and nonspecific manner the most important aspects to consider in determining choice of priority.

Location Extension of surface resources is linear, that of groundwater plane; furthermore, upgrading the flow and availability variables of surface water might necessitate construction of regulative facilities which could reduce availability of part or all the surface water to a point location. Regarding location, springs of course fall into the category of surface water. Where groundwater formations underlie demand areas, upgrading location will therefore require little investment in groundwater and much more in surface water. This aspect will be of special importance in projects in which the absorptive capacity for water is dependent on the gradual transformation of the production capacity of an agricultural population spread over the whole supply area.

Flow and Availability Surface-water resources often show relatively low flow minima (equal sometimes to no flow) during the season of maximum demand. Groundwater flow characteristics are much more smoothed out. Spring flows occupy an intermediate position, varying according to climate and geohydrological context but often resembling surface-water flows more than groundwater flows. Upgrading surface-water flow availability will require construction of dams to create regulative reservoirs. Spring flow may be upgraded in a similar way, or (where feasible) by transforming spring flow into underground flow (see the first section of this chapter). Underground water as a rule does not need structural intervention for upgrading flow characteristics and availability; simple, inexpensive management patterns will normally suffice to achieve the required regulation and availability. Closely connected with the question of flow regulation is the feasibility (economic and/or engineering) of including flows of medium to low frequencies within regulative patterns. With surface water, economic considerations will keep the justifiable regulation ceiling to relatively low limits. Because of the low costs of implementing respective management patterns, groundwater regulation may warrant much higher ceilings.

Annual and Seasonal Variability Variability, both annual and seasonal, and extreme highs and lows will be much more pronounced in surface water than in groundwater. This will imply larger unavoidable spills in surface-water resources, or alternatively much higher cost of regulation. In the case of groundwater systems the availability of a buffer stock, coupled with the sluggishness of hydrological responses, will in addition provide an important shock absorber that will enable the system to respond satisfactorily even under extremely unfavorable (and perhaps unprecedented) climatic cycles.

Energy Groundwater will require upgrading of its potential energy in the majority of cases, although there are important cases in which the available energy potential is sufficient for intended uses and cases where there is a residue of surplus energy. In many cases the potential energy of surface-water resources may be adequate, and in numerous other cases it may leave surplus energy which will represent a supplementary (sometimes controlling) benefit of the project. In some cases the potential energy of part or of all the water of a surface resource also needs upgrading.

Energy upgrading of groundwater resources is an efficient process requiring relatively low capital investment but necessitating a relatively high operational expenditure.

Biological and Physical Quality In many regions, groundwater does not pose major biological or physical quality problems. River water will much more often be encumbered by such problems, seasonally or permanently. Man-made pollution will also tend to deteriorate surface-water resources much more rapidly than groundwater resources.

Upgrading of the biological or physical quality of groundwater will therefore generally pose no major problems or no problems at all. With surface water, some water uses (community or industrial water supplies) may require construction of capital-intensive treatment facilities from the outset.

Mineral Quality No general statement can be made regarding mineral quality, but more often than not surface-water resources will be less liable to pick up mineral loads than will underground water. Since upgrading of mineral quality is moderately to extremely expensive, heavy and refractory mineral pollution that would seriously interfere with uses may lead to the rejection of such a resource, at least until the cost of the relevant upgrading procedures is greatly reduced through technological development.

Impact on Drainage Problems Where drainage problems exist or are induced as a consequence of irrigation, groundwater utilization (where it causes lowering of the phreatic water level inducing the drainage problems) may improve drainage conditions or even solve the problem, whereas application of surface water might aggravate the condition. In the former case, however, we would have to watch the formation's mineral equilibrium, which in time could prove a controlling factor.

Informational Aspects We have repeatedly stressed that information thresolds and information requirements of groundwater resources are usually lower —sometimes decisively so—than those of surface water and that information yields obtainable within a specific time are higher. This aspect tends to favor groundwater in cases where information is scanty or nonexistent.

Lumpiness of Investments in Upgrading Investments in surface resources requiring major regulative and/or conveyance structures tend to be extremely lumpy and therefore undivisible and burdened by long lead times. Because of the very high economy of scale of such facilities, phasing will rarely be justified. Upgrading of groundwater resources, on the other hand, is extremely subdivisible with much less (in some cases insignificant) economy of scale. This difference in lumpiness will be especially important where the growth of the absorptive capacity of water uses will depend on a gradual transformation process and where water supplied ahead of actual needs would therefore have no utility.

This difference in lumpiness of investment may sometimes have an additional important implication: the major capital investments characteristic for development of surface-water resources will require major decisions, and such decisions will involve considerable lead times for the relevant decision processes. In contrast, initiation of groundwater exploitation will involve little initial investment and will have much shorter lead times of decision making.

Legal-Institutional Aspects Since in development history the exploitation of surface-water resources has preceded large-scale underground water utilization (a relatively recent development), the legal-institutional framework of surface-water resources is usually already in existence when the water-resources management planner enters the field. This historically evolved framework usually constitutes a major constraint upon the planner's freedom of action. On the other hand, groundwater legislation is often rudimentary or nonoperative, and the planner can therefore act with fewer constraints. Once the most desirable management patterns are defined, the planner can propose an appropriate institutional-legislative framework for their implementation and control.

Combined groundwater–surface-water programs The advantages of groundwater in the development of Third World agriculture, notwithstanding, there will still be numerous cases where the existence of a demand (or an anticipated speedy build-up of such a demand), considerations of economy of scale, etc., will indicate the *desirability of giving priority to surface water.* However, even in such cases, and still more so in cases where the advantages of groundwater and surface water seem balanced, the possible contributory role of groundwater as a complementary source of a surface-water project ought to be investigated before relegating groundwater to the role of a second-rate resource to be resorted to only at a later unspecified period.

In general, the desirability of selecting groundwater as a first-priority development will depend on two considerations: the extent to which groundwater in every specific case proves, upon analysis, to possess advantages with respect to the above ten principal upgrading aspects and the importance attributed to each of these aspects.

The rigorous solution will be to set up a number of alternative sequences of development operations which meet the requirement of demand and in which different sequences of priorities and roles are allotted to surface water and groundwater and their combined uses and then to select the alternative with the highest objective achievement. Such a procedure will ensure for the resulting optimal management sequence the greatest possible utilization of the advantages of both types of resources and the most suitable appropriate timing for the several phases of their utilization.

A comprehensive water-resources analysis of this type would be justified not only for basins which are in their early development phases but also for basins in which the one or the other resources phase is in partial or full use, or where both are fully utilized but where an analysis on the above lines might indicate ways and means to increase yields and maintain quality.

Although it is impossible to outline a generally valid development sequence, one can sketch a typical sequence that may apply in areas in which both phases of resources are significantly represented and in which groundwater appears to be the logical priority selection on most accounts.

Operations would start with the gradual upgrading of groundwater resources to the requirements of demand. Interception of discharges out of the basin might be started concurrently or at some intermediate point, its timing and extent depending on its cost as compared with that of the relevant surface-water substitute. Groundwater utilization could be carried beyond static sustained yield levels and could include one-time stocks. Introduction of the surface-water phase might start with the diversion of the perennial part of the flow, groundwater capacity (both that developed within sustained yield limits and that related to one-time stocks) being switched (and thereby upgraded) to supply peak demand and/or to supplement low-flow periods. Recharge of surface water into underground storage could (where feasible) come next. Supplementation of regulation by surface storage could complete the operation. An appropriate qualitative management pattern would constitute a complementary part of the development policy.

The above generalized and highly simplified sequence of the development of a basin, in which both phases of water resources are represented, includes an upgrading technique that warrants a closer look: the *transformation,* where geologically and hydrologically feasible, of part of the surface phase of water resources into the underground phase. In situations in which the underground-water phase will, on most accounts, seem the preferable priority choice, such a transformation in relation to the demand geometry may be an important "upgrading" process. An upgrading operation of this type will greatly improve location, availability, variability, biological and physical quality, informational aspects, subdivisibility, and legal-institutional aspects. It may decrease somewhat the potential energy of the system, but this aspect will often not be a controlling one. Qualitatively, transforming the surface phase into the underground phase will provide additional qualitative management flexibility.

Underground storage The upgrading we have in mind is of course effected by *underground storage*. Its feasibility and size will be primarily determined by geological and hydrological considerations. In a combined system utilizing both phases of water resources, part or all of the above underground storage effects may be achieved either by physical recharging of surface water into the underground formation or by what may be termed "indirect regulation." Indirect regulation operates by combining underground and surface supplies into an aggregate system with a capacity that exceeds maximum demand requirements. In periods of drought, deficiencies in surface flow are made up by pumping from the groundwater formation, whereas surface flow will be resorted to in periods of high flow.

Upgrading by underground storage may be especially important and attractive in relation to resources that on one or a number of accounts diverge significantly from demand requirements, e.g., sewage reclamation (low biological quality), intermittent flood flow (low availability, low physical and biological quality).

There is one overriding limitation to underground storage: the rate of recharge is subject to the percolation capacity of the recharge facilities and to the conveyance capacity of structures leading to them. A properly designed regulative system may therefore have to *combine surface and underground storage sites*. Surface storage will serve as a shock absorber between the sometimes highly flashlike flow of the resource and the limited absorptive capacity of recharge installations; it will also perform part or all of the seasonal regulation. Underground storage will in some instances serve as cyclic storage, and in others as combined cyclic and seasonal storage. It will furthermore have a seasonal regulative function, which will often consist in deregulating the relatively regular flow of a major conduit according to the time schedule of demand.

This division of regulative functions between *surface* and *underground storage* indicates the desirable relative general location of the two types of storage. Where geologically feasible, surface storage might best be located near the general area of the principal water resources; underground storage, near the area of demand. Where a resource has to be not only regulated for its flow but also upgraded in its other parameters, some underground storage may also have to be provided near the source.

The conveyance link between source and demand areas will thus also serve as the connection between major surface and underground storage facilities. This interconnection will make it possible to operate storage both directly and indirectly, provided that such a management pattern has the necessary legal and institutional backing.

This type of integrated system has a considerable amount of built-in flexibility, and it can take a fair share of qualitative and quantitative shocks without serious deterioration of the service. As such shocks are usually local or at most regional in nature, their effects can be spread through integration over a much larger area, where they will often remain subliminal over considerable periods of time. Even if major unpredictable variations strike the system, the flexibility of underground storage will act as a major shock absorber.

This integration may include the main surface and underground storage facilities of one or a number of water-resources basins, whether groundwater or surface water. If necessary, the boundaries between adjoining groundwater basins can be moved by changing the original flow direction through proper planning of the spacing and timing of pumping; in such cases the formation will serve as a conduit. Integration will also include qualitative aspects. Although few economically feasible methods exist as yet to reduce significantly the overall amount of minerals accumulating within a basin, partial redistribution of the mineral "burden" between resources and resources stocks can be effected, thus diluting resources of marginal quality to acceptable salinity levels. It will sometimes also be possible, within certain limits, to plan the storage of objectionable minerals along the time axis, i.e., to postpone their impact until additional remedial measures become feasible.

The *dispersion* and related phenomena of water of a certain quality flowing through a formation containing water of a different quality have until recently not been properly studied, although they are often of decisive importance in managing the qualitative aspects of water resources. Only recently have experimental and analytical investigations been initiated (an important pilot project under the auspices of the U.N. Special Fund[1] has been completed in Israel) that allow us to predict these mixing phenomena with some confidence and to plan their manipulation in space and time.

Summarizing our review of the roles of surface and underground storage, underground storage can claim the following inherent advantages:

1. Available storage space is usually large, and its development does not involve any major investments.

2. The levels representing full and empty storage are not as sharply defined as in surface storage; an underground storage reservoir drawn down to the planned minimum level can, under extreme conditions, be temporarily overdrawn, and a full reservoir will not immediately overflow. Where springs whose flow has ceased due to previous management measures begin flowing again as a consequence of a high storage level, the flow surplus can be recycled elsewhere into temporary underground storage.

[1] United Nations Development Programme, *Underground Water Storage Study: Israel. Final Report,* Rome, 1969. (FAO/SF:39/ISR-9.)

3. Underground storage represents a powerful tool of manipulating (usually upgrading) the quality of water.

4. Investment in underground storage space can be phased as needed; no major lumpy investments are required; therefore, maturation cost will be negligible.

5. In a properly managed system, water losses from underground storage will generally be much lower than those from surface reservoirs.

Difficulties naturally arise in the use of underground storage: the recharge operation may prove tricky, and the long-term behavior of formations through which the water percolates is not always fully predictable. If wells are used for recharging, the purity of water must be high to avoid clogging. Even in spreading operations, the quality of water must be carefully watched.

Fortunately, far-reaching regulative effects can be achieved by the implementation of indirect storage without resort to physical recharge operations proper. In indirect storage, the storage effect is achieved by proper manipulation of the surface water–groundwater relationship or the relationship between two or more groundwater basins. In such a management plan, the respective share of groundwater and surface water (the latter either from direct flow or from surface storage) in the current consumption will vary in response to fluctuations of surface flow.

MANAGEMENT OF COASTAL BASINS

The management of coastal basins is of special interest because it is in such basins that qualitative problems due to salt-water encroachment first occur and first come to the planner's attention. Furthermore, in coastal areas, a well set up management plan will not only ensure the maintenance of appropriate quality standards but will also offer the uses of important one-time stocks of water. Management of coastal basins comprises, of course, both surface water and groundwater. In this section, however, we shall confine ourselves to management policy related to coastal groundwater formations.

Every utilization of a coastal groundwater formation will ultimately lower the groundwater levels near the coast which control the location and the rate of movement of the *interface* between salt and fresh water. Every utilization pattern will thus in some way cause a movement of this interface. This movement and the final location of the interface at the equilibrium state will decisively influence long-term utilization of a coastal formation.

A coastal formation possesses considerable one-time stocks of water located between original and target-state groundwater levels and original and target-state interface. The latter stock will often be of much greater importance than the former.

The extent to which these two one-time stocks may be utilized will depend on the geometric pattern of pumping wells (in relation to the present and anticipated location of the interface) and their rate and timing of pumping. Proper planning and programming of this geometry will ensure the maximum utilization of the one-time stock. Since this one-time stock will often be very substantial, withdrawals beyond the sustained yield levels may be continued for considerable periods of time without prejudicing the ultimate target state of the system. Once the one-time stock is used up, we would of course have to reduce withdrawals to rates corresponding to the predetermined steady-state levels. To do so without reducing supplies, we will have to introduce an alternative source, either a surface source within the same basin or imported water.

Varying the transient and steady-state locations of the interface will increase planning flexibility during the transient period. Accepting a deeper inland encroachment of the interface, on the one hand, will increase the one-time stock available for utilization; however, such a regime will exclude the zone between the coastline and the ultimate location of the interface toe from permanent utilization by conventional wells. Specifying a more limited steady-state encroachment of the interface, on the other hand, will reduce the one-time stock available for utilization, but simultaneously it will also reduce the width of the zone in which conventional wells will ultimately salt up. If recharging of surface water underground is considered at any stage, location of the recharge areas and of the steady-state interface will have to be coordinated.

To keep the interface at the final steady state in the predetermined location with reference to the coastline, we shall have to maintain a specific controlling superelevation of formation water near the coast. This superelevation will imply a specific outflow of water to the sea. From the point of view of quantitative management, the sole purpose of this superelevation is to maintain the steady-state location of the interface near the coast. Thus, there can be no objection to intercepting this outflow before it actually reaches the shoreline. A pilot operation for such interception was successfully implemented in Israel in the late fifties and early sixties, and full-scale installations have since been constructed there. The latter have proved an effective means of reducing the controlling outflow necessary to maintain a specific steady-state interface location and, generally, of controlling the salt water–fresh water interface.[2] The interception cannot be complete; part of the outflow must continue to the sea to avoid pollution through upcoming salt water of the coastal intercepting wells located above the interface. Where geologically feasible and economically justified, the construction of such an intercepting chain of wells provides the management planner with a most welcome and effective means of control over the outflow from underground formations.

As already mentioned, the space and time pattern of withdrawals in a coastal formation will determine the rate of movement of the interface and of the groundwater elevation, and consequently also of the extent of utilization of the one-time stock. To optimize the utilization of a coastal formation (and of its one-time stock), we should initiate management planning at the earliest possible date and design installations according to the dictates of the management plan.

[2] United Nations Development Programme, *Experimental Coastal Groundwater Collectors: Israel. Final Report,* Rome, 1968. (FAO/SF:43/ISR-3.)

This seems the right point at which to mention, if only cursorily, some related water-resources management problems. Management of groundwater formations draining into sweet-water *lakes* bears some resemblance to management of coastal formations, but offers a greater measure of management flexibility. Lowering of water levels, resulting from withdrawing water from the lake, will of course increase groundwater gradients and thereby the flow of groundwater into the lake. Gradually, groundwater levels will drop and equilibrium will be established at a new, lower level. The stock between the original and the new groundwater level will represent a one-time stock available for utilization. The gain in evaporation effected by decreasing the water area of the lake will represent an additional permanent source. Such a lowering of groundwater levels, when it finally reaches the watershed line, may occasionally even change drainage boundaries between underground basins. Combining various withdrawal patterns of underground water with various withdrawal rates from the lake will provide us with a great variety of management patterns. Analysis of these alternative patterns will indicate the most satisfactory management policy.

Where lake water is too mineralized for direct use, lake levels may be manipulated by intercepting groundwater before it reaches the lake and thereby decreasing inflow into the lake. Otherwise, problems encountered will be similar to those met in managing coastal formations.

The quality problems created by the several management patterns described in this section are dealt with in the first three sections of this chapter.

INTERMITTENT RUNOFF

The parameters of intermittent runoff do not, as a rule, meet the demand requirements; runoff location is usually unfavorable in relation to areas of demand; its timing is unseasonable, and its flow fluctuations are extreme; its annual volume is not dependable, and its physical and sanitary quality is unsatisfactory for some types of uses. The water is generally of low mineral content, though even this asset is not fully exploited if not utilized within a broader framework which includes water of high mineral content.

The upgrading of intermittent runoff through underground recharging instead of surface storage, or as a complementary measure to surface storage, has much to offer. Although some surface storage will be required for retention of the greatly variable flows and their preregulation to flow levels that can be handled by the proposed recharge facilities, surface storage may usually be confined to a relatively modest impoundment with some reserve for silting up. The principal storage basin, i.e., the storage for seasonal and cyclical regulation, will be underground. This procedure will result in the following upgrading effects:

1. Space Parameter The water would often be stored closer to areas of demand.

2. Quantitative Parameter Storage cannot by itself increase the average quantity of water; it can, however, by seasonal and cyclic regulation ensure that a specific average quantity will be available under predictable climatic cycles.

3. The Flow-rate Parameter Through underground storage, the source becomes available at call and at a rate adaptable to demand requirements.

4. Biological-quality Parameter The process of recharging and storage by underground detention constitutes a most effective treatment; this process, possibly combined with disinfection, may, under most geological conditions, prove sufficient to keep the water potable.

5. Mineral-quality Parameter This single positive parameter of intermittent runoff can be turned into a more effective asset by underground storage, since in storage it will mix with the formation water. The dilution of runoff water with possibly more mineralized formation water may constitute a most important side benefit of storage.

Underground recharge with water from intermittent runoff thus will effect an upgrading of a "lower rank" resource to a "higher rank" resource. However, recharging is a complex operation requiring regular observation of the quality of the water and of the infiltration capacity of the recharging medium. For this and other reasons, upgrading will often be expensive and resorted to only after more advantageous resources have been developed.

RECLAMATION OF WASTE WATER

Similar considerations will apply to the upgrading of waste water. Ranking waste water according to the same scale will show that whereas space and quantitative flow parameters are more favorable than for intermittent runoff, the qualitative parameters, both mineral and biological, are more problematic. Here again upgrading may be based on recharging and storage underground. Waste water requires considerable biological treatment before recharging; the water recharged and ultimately withdrawn from underground storage will usually be more mineralized than the original water and may still contain objectionable pollutants. Nevertheless, this form of waste-water conservation may in some tight water-resources situations prove relatively favorable: it solves the question of sewage disposal, grants seasonal storage, bridges over sudden quality fluctuations, furnishes one of the best available methods of qualitative upgrading, and, provided that it is integrated into an overall management scheme, it may supply satisfactory water. Proper siting of recharge and withdrawal areas in space as well as in time will allow for a considerable period of grace until quality problems become acute. If and when such problems ultimately appear, they may be solved within the overall management plan by dilution, selective use, intensification of initial treatment and after-treatment, etc. Qualitative problems can sometimes be considerably reduced by installing separate sewage systems to convey the toxic or highly mineralized wastes from industrial areas or by confining waste reclamation to residential areas and light industries, while objectionable industrial wastes continue to be discharged out of the basin. Where reclaimed sewage represents a substantial portion of the water inventory, qualitative considerations may prove to be the limiting factor.

CONCLUSION

Our cursory survey of typical applications of management measures has taken us a long way from the conventional approach. Departing from the static sustained yield methodology for which every water source is a separate entity, we have surveyed important aspects of a dynamic, comprehensive system approach.

The system is so complex that, in order to describe it here, we have had to break the phenomena down into specific aspects and describe each aspect by single-discipline semantics, reconstructing the coordinating links by pointing out connections to other aspects and disciplines.

The complexity of the system does not imply in every case the need from the outset for an analysis of high complexity. Early development may start at a lower range of complexity; however, the sooner we succeed in foreseeing the later, more complex, stages and the sooner we make proper provisions for them, the less will be the ultimate loss in resources and production.

FOUR
CASE HISTORIES AND SPECIAL PROBLEMS

30 COMPREHENSIVE WATER-RESOURCES DEVELOPMENT CASE HISTORY: ISRAEL

and everything shall live whither the river cometh
EZEKIEL 47:9

The distribution and availability of water have, since biblical times, had a decisive influence on the political, economic, and cultural development of Israel. Ingenious responses were evolved for solving the problems created by the scarcity and relative inaccessibility of water resources; but these responses, though adequate at their time, cannot guide the planner in the solving of Israel's present problems. Solutions adopted in recent years in the development of Israel's water resources have been based on modern engineering approaches.

INITIATION OF LONG-TERM PLANNING

The development of water resources in Israel, prior to the country's attainment of independence, was of a local and piecemeal nature: the overriding objective, at that stage, was the initiation of a process of resettlement by Jewish farmers on randomly distributed tracts of land that could be procured under the then prevailing extremely restrictive legislation. Under those conditions, it was not feasible to attempt a clear evaluation of national resources or a definition of growth and production targets.

The approach to development changed abruptly with the establishment of the State of Israel in 1948: intensive activity was initiated in the inventorying of resources, the definition of growth objectives, the formulation of the methodology of development planning, and the determination of planning strategies. In fact, the development of water resources, of resettlement, and of agricultural production were the first sectors of the Israeli economy for which long-term plans were drawn up and implemented.

The necessity for comprehensive long-term planning in Israel's irrigation development was recognized from the outset, since it was realized that this development would have to be confined by a number of scarcity factors: scarcity of water and land resources, scarcity of capital, scarcity of time, scarcity of data, and scarcity of the basic facilities of development. Only a broadly conceived plan extending over a long period and allowing for all these scarcity factors, as well as for current and anticipated needs of the economy, could furnish an effective solution. A first draft plan for the development of water resources was adopted in 1950; the planning and revising process has been energetically continued ever since, incorporating ever closer integration of resources, agriculture, and resettlement.

PLANNING LIMITATIONS

The most serious and most lasting scarcity factor was the scarcity of water. The earliest results of the inventorying process already indicated that the supply of water in Israel was neither abundant nor very dependable and that the quality of the water was not always satisfactory—with further predictable gradual deterioration as a consequence of intensive utilization. Proof was not lacking of the unfavorable distribution of the water resources in relation to the location and elevation of centers of demand (a shortcoming resulting in an overwhelming negative balance of potential energy).

Capital shortage was most acute in the early years of development, when a small and poor economy was attempting to pull itself up by its own bootstraps, i.e., creating the fundamental infrastructure of a modern economy and the most urgently needed means of production, while having to absorb an inpecunious and initially unproductive immigration at an annual rate of some 20 percent of the total existing population. *Time* was critically scarce, mainly because many of the immigrants were waiting in the new villages for the basic means of production (amongst them, first and foremost, water) so as to join in the productive process and achieve rehabilitation as human beings. Time was not less critical from the viewpoint of production of the food and fibers needed to feed and clothe Israel's rapidly growing population, to which the bare necessities of life were being doled out under a system of wartime rationing. The basic facilities for development were scarce to nonexistent: industrial capacity to supply at least part of the commodities needed for investment and production, contracting firms for many types of civil engineering works, the very organization of the development authorities—all were weak or altogether absent. The creation of these basic facilities therefore became a part of the development process.

DEVELOPMENT POLICY

A heuristic type of water-development policy making allowance for all these dimensions of scarcity, and taking into account the welfare approach underlying Israel's political thinking, was elaborated and, with time, more and more systematized. The basic tenet of this policy is that, in order to ensure the maximum benefit to the nation, the plan for the development of the country's limited water resources is to be based on a management approach ensuring (within economic reason) a maximum water conservation and on carefully considered water allocations. In the field of engineering heuristics for the design of waterworks, the policy found its expression in the adoption of approaches that provided for minimizing (within economic reason) losses involved in storage, conveyance, and distribution; providing for adequate capacity for flow regulation to cope with the rather severe climatic fluctuations experienced in the eastern Mediterranean area; and adopting a high degree of system integration, in order to facilitate efficient management patterns aiming at lower overall system losses.

TECHNIQUES AND APPROACHES ADOPTED

In choosing the techniques of water application, such *irrigation installations* were preferred as would facilitate control of the amounts applied, minimize conveyance losses, and be economical in the use of labor. Since available application technologies were found to be implicitly based on low-cost water, an extensive research and development program was initiated with a view to evolving economical application approaches adapted to Israel's high water costs, including the investment of capital in substitution for water.

In the field of *comprehensive planning,* the approach that was adopted provided for a relatively even distribution among potential areas of demand of the basic means of production (and first among them, water). This was coupled with concurrent provision of production inputs and nonmaterial inputs, relating to know-how and skills; the retraining of farmers and the restructuring of organizations, with a view to ensuring a rapid absorption of new production capacity; and the early inception of the self-sustained growth of agricultural production and of related economic activities.

In the field of *water-resources management,* the approach adopted was based on a dynamic and comprehensive conception of the water-resources inventory and management patterns. The best use was sought of one-time stocks of groundwater available in various formations; operating patterns were evolved for the combined and coordinated utilization of surface and underground storage, with a view to achieving such overall availability and dependability of the water resources as could be justified by economic considerations.

In the sphere of *legislative* and institutional management, water laws and regulations were drawn up and promulgated and procedural patterns adopted that would fit the statutory needs of the development plan and of the optimal water-management system.

PRIORITY CRITERIA APPLIED TO PROJECTS

The above approach was translated into a number of medium-term development programs. These programs were based on the following priority criteria applied to the projects chosen for implementation:

1. Minimum investment per unit of water supplied

2. Low technological complexity of the project
3. Ability to subdivide the investment into stages
4. Low sensitivity of the project to variations in data
5. Sufficient flexibility of the project to maintain future decisions liquidity
6. Maximum spread of production inputs

In more specific terms, the programs proceeded from local groundwater projects, through groundwater projects extending over county-size areas, to regional projects embodying groundwater, springs, storm runoff, and reclaimed wastes. The main objective of these regional projects was to spread, within a certain region, surpluses of water that were available at any location or time in such a manner as best to meet the needs in that region.

GRADUAL INTEGRATION OF PROJECTS

In order to minimize the risk of misinvestments, at a time when data were still inadequate and of low dependability, the concept of "project generations" was adopted. This concept implied that the layout of each group of projects undertaken within the first medium-term program (first-generation projects) was conceived in a way that would permit interconnecting these project groups with projects proposed for subsequent programs (second- and third-generation programs). Such interconnection made it possible to supplement supply shortages or to absorb surpluses that developed owing to wrong assumptions in the original planning.

Thus, a *hierarchical layout pattern of projects* was gradually evolved, with a built-in dynamic self-corrective mechanism controlled by data feedback, where each project generation integrated the projects of the preceding generation and was, in turn, recombined into larger project units by the subsequent project generation. Since groundwater, which is a resource of great inherent adaptability, played a decisive role at this stage, the application of the project-generation concept resulted in maximum flexibility of the system. The adoption of this concept made it possible to apply, without incurring any unreasonable risks, relatively high utilization rates of local resources, at a time when development was almost wholly dependent on local resources as a consequence of scarcity of capital, time, and data. Any capacity that, by later estimates, proved to constitute an overdraft on resources was first directly utilized on a base-load basis, until the one-time stock of groundwater stored in the formation was exhausted, and was then only used to carry peak loads in the subsequent project generation or in the one following it.

COORDINATION BETWEEN INVESTMENTS AND TRANSFORMATION

Israel's achievements in resettlement, irrigated agriculture, and water supply were largely based on these development strategies and criteria. Between 1948 and 1966, the utilization of the country's proven water resources rose from 17 percent (representing mainly the use of shallow local groundwater formations) to almost 90 percent (including the utilization of Israel's only two rivers, the Yarqon and the Jordan). During the same period, the irrigated area expanded from 70,000 acres to over 400,000 acres; agricultural production, predominantly derived from irrigated agriculture, increased (at constant prices) sevenfold. This high rate of growth was maintained despite the fact that more than one half of Israel's farmers had taken up agriculture only in the last fifteen years, most of them with no previous farming experience and with an educational and motivational background comparable to that of underdeveloped countries.

The high rate of agricultural productivity and the extremely high overall plant factor of water-project capacity that were achieved in spite of the lack of experience of the new farmers were due mainly to the close coordination between water-resources development and the provision of complementary inputs—material, human, and organizational. Through this coordination, development funds were switched, according to feedback indications, from one sector of the development front (say, water) that may have progressed ahead of the other sectors to lagging sectors (say, agroinvestments). Thus, a straight and continuous development front was maintained throughout, which resulted in an early achievement of satisfactory productivity rates and in a continuous and almost full utilization of capital investments.

COMPOSITION OF THE NATIONAL WATER SYSTEM

The physical system that has evolved from this approach is a fully integrated national water grid that, on the one hand, interconnects the country's major water resources and regulative storage facilities and, on the other hand, caters to practically all the major water needs of the country.

Only the desert areas in the southernmost part of Israel are not effectively connected to the national grid and are served instead by regional projects.

The major water resources directly or indirectly interconnected by the national grid have a total average annual yield of about 1,400 million cubic meters and include:

1. The Upper Jordan and its tributaries at the northernmost extremity of the grid, including the Sea of Galilee and the Beit Shean spring area (37 percent)
2. The groundwater formations of the Galilee Mountains in Northern Israel and of the Valley of Esdraelon, subintegrated into the regional Qishon-Esdraelon system, which also comprises spring flows, storm runoff, and reclaimed waste water from the Greater Haifa Area (9 percent)
3. The groundwater system of the coastal aquifers (a western shallow one, of unconsolidated formations, and an eastern deeper one, of limestone formations) receiving also recharge from the waste water of many coastal towns and villages—subintegrated into a number of regional systems (29.5 percent)
4. The Yarqon River, subintegrated into a regional Yarqon project system extending from Tel Aviv to the Negev (14 percent)
5. The storm runoff in the major coastal intermittent streams, mainly stored in the coastal unconsolidated aquifer (5.5 percent)

6. The reclaimed waste water (again stored underground) from the Tel Aviv Metropolitan Area, numbering over one million inhabitants, subintegrated into the Greater Tel Aviv waste-water reclamation project (5 percent)

THE SYSTEM'S REGULATIVE ELEMENTS

Regulation of cyclical and seasonal fluctuations is achieved by two main storage facilities. The Sea of Galilee, in the north, provides seasonal storage for the Jordan River. The groundwater formations in the coastal area, owing to their great storage capacity, serve as the main cyclical holdover storage of the national system and as the deregulative storage bumper between the discharge of the Jordan conduit (determined by resources management requirements) and the seasonally changing demand. The total storage capacity needed to fully regulate climatic fluctuations and achieve maximum yields is more than 4,000 million cubic meters; economically justified capacity will be considerably below this figure.

Interregional transfer and conveyance from the northern storage in the Sea of Galilee to the southern storage in the groundwater formations are effected by a conduit system consisting of canals, tunnels, and pressure pipes, which have a design mean capacity of about 10 cubic meters per second but are capable of carrying, should extreme climatic conditions demand, up to 20 cubic meters per second.

The regulation of the potential energy of the system which, in balance, is highly negative (since the main areas of demand lie well above the elevation of the main water resources) is effected by two main pumping stations on the Jordan System in the north, with an installed capacity of over 100,000 horsepowers, and a number of booster stations along the conduit system.

MANIPULATION OF SUPPLY

Israel's water grid is operated according to heuristic rules evolved from system simulation under meteorological cycles based on statistic expansion of past climatic history. Regulation of all the water resources does not call for the physical connection of all local resources to the national grid; many regulative functions can be accomplished by nationally conceived management patterns.

In humid years, surface water is used to the maximum possible extent, and the exploitation of groundwater formations that are interconnected with the grid is low; the demand ordinarily dependent on these formations is covered instead by the increased use of surface water, while the exploitation of isolated formations is continued; recharge of surplus surface water into groundwater formations supplements direct uses. Reduction of groundwater use and concurrently conducted recharge operations will, in such years, increase the underground storage and cause a rise in groundwater levels. In dry cycles, on the other hand, when surface flows are scarce, groundwater utilization in most formations would have to be stepped up to substitute for surface-water deficiencies, and thus the groundwater accumulated during previous humid periods would be drawn upon.

Switching, according to climatic fluctuations, from surface water to groundwater, recharging for storage, and withdrawing water stored in the formation require, of course, a pumping capacity from underground formations that exceeds the perennial yield. In the present specific case, such capacity had already been created in the earlier phases of the project (in the mid-fifties) for the exploitation of the one-time stocks of water stored in the aquifer.

A system of this nature is highly flexible and is capable of absorbing extreme climatic shocks, without having to reduce the supply or adopt rationing. In fact, in dry cycles, the system is able to provide amounts in excess of the average supplies, so as to allow for the greater irrigation demand in dry years. The system can, furthermore, redistribute among the various uses such burdens as may arise from inadequate quality of the water (say, high mineral content in agricultural uses), in keeping with the sensitivity of these uses to those qualitative inadequacies. It can also readjust itself smoothly to errors in inventory estimates of local resources. Finally, by mobilizing, in one way or another, part of the large quantities of groundwater accumulated in the formations over geological periods, the system can markedly defer the impact of quantitative scarcities and qualitative inadequacies of water resources.

By applying such a comprehensive system approach to Israel's water-supply thinking, it has become possible to manipulate and control a supply of about 1,400 million cubic meters of water through the use of the aforementioned interconnecting conduit.

OPERATIONAL POLICIES

Some of the problems connected with the operation of this complex system had to be researched and investigated before the system could be completed. The most outstanding example is the study of the problems connected with the manipulation of the major underground storage facilities. Basic research and demonstration-scale work had to be carried out, for example, for the quantitative evaluation of the mixing and movement of water of a specific quality introduced into a formation containing water of a different quality.[1] Control of groundwater outflows near the coast had to be researched and means devised (and applied on a demonstration scale) to minimize such outflows while avoiding salt-water encroachment.[2]

Anticipated cumulative qualitative changes which will occur when some of Israel's main groundwater formations are transformed into practically closed basins had to be studied. Such a transformation will be effected by almost completely cutting off the outflow of a coastal formation to the sea. The isolation of the formation from its drainage base will step up the accumulation of

[1] See also United Nations Development Programme, *Underground Water Storage Study: Israel. Final Report,* Rome, 1969. (FAO/SF:39/ISR-9.)

[2] *Ibid., Experimental Coastal Groundwater Collectors: Israel. Final Report,* Rome, 1968. (FAO/SF:43/ISR-3.)

minerals resulting from the hydrological cycle, from the consumptive use of imported water, from the use of chemicals in agriculture, or from recycling municipal and industrial wastes. Long-term management patterns will have to be devised to neutralize such changes by the employment of appropriate facilities likely to become available (or, if already available in a relatively primitive form, that might become economically acceptable) by the time such undesirable changes in the quality of the water are expected to become critical. Finally, the mathematical models for simulation and elaboration of heuristic operational rules had to be elaborated and improved as data accumulated and the mechanisms operating on the system were better understood.

PRESENT SITUATION AND FUTURE PROSPECTS

The point of departure of Israel's present planning is the prospect that by the early seventies practically all the country's potential water resources (including reclaimed wastes) will be in use. Any further economic development will therefore have to depend on intensifying still further the yield of the natural-resources system, on a transfer of water in actual use from lower value to higher value products, on increasing the efficiency of utilization of water, on the introduction of man-made water, or on a combination of these approaches.

An analysis of the constraints inherent in the natural-resources system, of anticipated demand developments, of prevailing sociopolitical constraints, and of final development objectives arising from the social-welfare ideology accepted by the majority of the nation has indeed led to the adoption of a combination of all the enumerated lines of action. Appropriate proposals based on this approach have been incorporated in the elaboration of Israel's long-term water development plan for the fifteen-year period of 1965 to 1980. The final section of this chapter will deal with the criteria underlying this plan.

THE LONG-TERM WATER DEVELOPMENT PLAN, 1965–1980

One may assume that limitations in natural water resources will, in the seventies, no longer constitute an absolute (Malthusian) barrier to growth; the development of man-made fresh water will have become technologically feasible, albeit still at relatively high costs. Supplementing natural water by man-made supplies will, however, steeply increase the cost of marginal quantities of water and thereby, to a marked extent, the average water costs; the limitations imposed by the lack of further accessible natural resources will thus be of an economic (or Ricardian) nature. When the proportion of costly man-made fresh water to cheaper natural water becomes substantial, the economic efficiency of prevailing water-application techniques will have to be reevaluated and the present uses of water for low-value production will have to be reconsidered. To put it in a more general form, the system space of planning will have to be expanded from the limited contexts of new water and demand streams to include both introduction of new water-application techniques and reallocation of existing water uses.

To achieve this higher level system approach, the area of analysis for the fifteen-year plan was expanded to include the following manipulative patterns:

1. Selection of management patterns for the natural water resources and the overall water grid that will result in optimal water yields and qualities
2. Engineering intervention into the natural water cycle that will, within economic limits, improve the yields and quality of the natural water resources
3. Shifting of water allocations in keeping with anticipated rising water costs
4. Adjusting and changing water-application technology, so as to adapt it to anticipated higher costs of man-made water

CHOICE OF MANAGEMENT PATTERNS FOR WATER RESOURCES

The first group of manipulative management patterns enumerated above resulted in the following ground rules of planning.

To improve the yield, quality, and dependability of the system, the few still undeveloped water resources are to be developed within the framework of the national system and the utilization of resources in actual use stepped up. The "upgrading" process of natural water resources that has been included in earlier programs is to be completed by the transformation of most of the remaining surface-water resources (inherently wanting in regularity, dependability, and biological quality) into groundwater resources of higher quality, unconditionally available at call. The part of the municipal waste water that is not yet utilized will be incorporated into the system also, mostly through underground storage. Thus, the process of upgrading will result in more than 75 percent of the total water resources being kept in underground storage, as against the original proportion of 48 percent.

Management patterns of the national water grid cannot be confined to quantitative manipulation but also must extend to manipulation of qualitative parameters. The high utilization percentage of the country's water resources, the concentration of major agricultural and nonagricultural activities in the coastal area, and the relatively high mineral accretions in the natural hydrological cycle will, in time, raise the mineral content of the groundwater in the coastal plain. This mineral accumulation can, to a certain extent, be slowed down by proper control and the application of manipulative measures, but it will ultimately have to be countered by special mineral-extracting or diluting measures involving the desalting of brackish and sea water—a practice which will anyway become necessary in order to expand the volume of supply.

Concurrently with these developments, such marginal natural resources will be reinvestigated as have been considered in the past too costly to exploit, but which have since become economically justifiable owing to the rising cost of water in outstanding alternative projects and the improved efficiency of production processes utilizing water. The possibility of squeezing out of the system, at costs that may now have become economically justifiable, limited marginal quantities of water through fuller integration, generally improved manipulative patterns, and the selective use of substandard waters for nonsensitive applications falls within the same category.

INTERVENTION INTO THE NATURAL WATER CYCLE

The second group of manipulative management patterns has as its main objective to increase the water harvest and improve the water quality by intervention into the natural hydrological cycle. Cloud seeding has so far proved to be the most successful experimental operation in this group: sizable increases of rainfall have been statistically proved at satisfactory significance levels. Manipulation of the vegetative cover with the objective of increasing runoff in uncultivated areas where the rainfall is between 300 and 600 millimeters per year has also proved to be effective and is planned to be expanded on a substantial scale. Evaporation suppression, mainly from open water surfaces, may possibly become economically justifiable in the not-too-distant future. Finally, soil treatment to increase surface runoff may also have a sizable contribution to make in improving the yield from the hydrological cycle.

SHIFTING OF WATER ALLOCATIONS

The third group of operations, aimed at adapting the allocations of water to anticipated rising costs, will become in the next decade one of the principal means of releasing water for essential new economic uses. Manipulative approaches to achieve these releases of water will, according to the requirement of every case, vary from direct administrative measures to such steps as the creation of economic incentives; the emphasis will be on the latter approach.

In *municipal* supplies, universal metering, combined with disincentive block rates, has proved to be an effective means of reducing per capita consumption to economically justifiable levels.

In the *industrial* sector, a water rate reflecting real costs to the economy may by itself be sufficient to introduce patterns of thrifty water use. The application of such water rates in industry may have to be combined with an adequate control over releases of toxic or highly mineralized industrial wastes into the sewerage system, where reclamation and reuse are intended.

Agricultural uses, in which water constitutes a significant production input, will probably prove to be the most recalcitrant to reallocation dictated by purely economic considerations, since it may prove politically difficult to raise the water rates for agricultural uses to anything approaching actual costs. Stringent allocation of water to the farmer has, however, proved to constitute a considerable economic incentive to raising efficiency in the use of water; this measure will, in all probability, become still more effective in the future, when the farmer will have to seek increased production and income from a practically unchanged water allocation. Statistics for the last few years prove the effectiveness of this policy: there has already been a most significant shift of water use from low-value to high-value crops. This shift can be assumed to continue, with the exception of areas where, for agroecological reasons, the freedom of crop choice is limited.

Another aspect of the same approach would be the *change of the resource base,* i.e., the substitution of other, relatively cheaper inputs for costly water. In municipal and industrial uses this substitution will, over time, become effective, once the rates charged approach marginal water costs and the pertinent technologies are made known to users. In agriculture, allocations to the farmer will, in the long run, have similar effects; but if the process is to be speeded up, additional, special incentives will have to be introduced.

The ultimate purpose of all the above measures will be to accelerate the shift of water use until a point is reached where, at least theoretically, the lowest existing use level would justify the development of additional water at the anticipated higher cost. In actual fact, the economic system cannot be expected to operate without some political and institutional "friction," and some lower value use "islands" can be expected to remain in existence over considerable periods of time.

ADJUSTMENTS TO USE OF MAN-MADE WATER

The fourth group of manipulative measures is connected with the introduction of high-cost man-made fresh water by desalting seawater or brackish water. The introduction of these resources will result in an abrupt jump of the marginal cost levels of water. This cost jump ought to lead to a reconsideration of water-application technologies in all uses, and especially in agriculture. Prevailing application techniques in irrigation that are based on low-cost water will no longer remain satisfactory at the anticipated high costs of man-made fresh water. These production complexes should, therefore, be reconsidered and new ones researched and developed that fit the new cost levels. These production complexes should, as far as possible, be developed ahead of the introduction of major quantities of man-made fresh water (see also Chapter 32).

CONCLUSION

The scarcity of Israel's water resources and their qualitative deficiences do not constitute any longer an absolute limitation to the development of the country's economy. This scarcity will, however, necessitate in time the introduction, on an ever-increasing scale, of reclaimed and man-made fresh water at considerably higher costs than previously met.

In order to adjust the use of water to such higher cost levels, the system analysis, which in the past put the main emphasis on measures of water-resources management, will have to be expanded to cover additional aspects. The new system space will have to include, in addition to the natural resources (including their quantity and quality and the physical installations required to manage and control them), the whole hydrological cycle and ways for its modification, the allocation of water, the application of techniques, and the institutional implications relating to such an expansion of the system space.

If such a broad system approach is adopted and consistently implemented, Israel's limited water resources need not stand in the way of an accelerated development of the nonagricultural sectors of the economy; even for agricultural uses they may leave considerable leeway for future expansion.

31

SOME COMPOSITE CASE HISTORIES OF COMMUNITY WATER-SUPPLY DEVELOPMENT

The professional must continue to provide the evidence for the illumination of choices, for the clarification of alternatives, and for the evolution of more satisfactory criteria of evaluation. Decision makers, in spite of many supposed lapses, do ultimately succumb to logic and to impressive argument. The search for utopia, however, is likely to be endless.

ABEL WOLMAN

Faulty development thinking in the field of community water supply often stems from adoption of system boundaries that are irrelevant to the intended optimization. System boundaries adopted by the politico-administrative hierarchy for definition of projects and for decision making on priority of resources allocation are usually those of existing politico-administrative units, such as boundaries of municipal areas. In contrast to this approach, development thinking oriented toward the achievement of predetermined objectives looks for boundary definition of planning that will yield the highest objective achievement for a specific resources-geometry context (see also Chapter 14). The planning objectives that the planner will seek to optimize will vary from economy to economy: in the less developed countries, they might consist in maximizing the number of people served within predetermined budgetary constraints; in the more developed countries, in minimizing costs to comply with a specific demand for services (see also Chapter 15).

From the point of view of cost effectiveness, the politico-administrative boundary definition for community water-supply planning systems is arbitrary. Because of lack of relevance to planning objectives, such boundary definition will severely limit the variety of available solutions and, therefore, also the efficiency of the selected solution. Because of the crippling reduction in variety and cost effectiveness of solutions inherent in adopting administrative boundaries, the planner ought to avoid such boundary definitions. He should do so even where he anticipates major politico-institutional resistance to ultimate adoption of rational boundaries. In such cases, political constraints might necessitate some downgrading of the earlier phases of the solution; however, such partial downgrading of a project, originally conceived within the framework of an appropriately defined system, will usually admit of some corrective readjustment in the later phases.

Faulty definition of system boundaries of planning will lead to a piecemeal planning approach resulting in inefficient investments. Where the administrative boundaries are adopted for the definition of water-supply systems, planning of individual waterworks for the various municipal areas will be assigned to various consulting engineering firms. The latter, by their very terms of reference, will be prevented from adopting an integrative approach.

This chapter will attempt to demonstrate that systems with boundary definitions rooted in resources-geometry concepts are superior in cost effectiveness to systems with politico-administrative or other irrelevant boundary definitions. Three case histories, conceived at three rising levels of generalization, will be used for this demonstration. While not representing any actual set of conditions and solutions, these case histories do give a composite image of actual ones.

The first case history, representing the lowest level of generalization, will demonstrate the advantages of defining the system boundaries of community water-supply planning so as to comprise a whole hydrological basin or significant part thereof. The second case history will illustrate the need, under certain conditions, to look beyond the basin concept and to adopt a wider definition of the management system. The third case history, representing the highest level of generalization, will demonstrate the role of national planning in establishing priorities of development.

We shall show in each case the type of institutional framework required by systems based on resources-geometry concepts and the extent to which prevailing institutional structure needs to be modified to fit requirements of a broader systems approach.

CASE HISTORY ONE: THE HYDROLOGICAL VS. THE ADMINISTRATIVE MANAGEMENT UNIT

Description of prevailing conditions A number of major, medium, and minor towns, as well as numerous villages, are distributed over a relatively narrow river basin. Geologically, the basin consists of basement formations that are notoriously poor in groundwater. The annual yield of the river is ample, but in the season of high demand the flow is insufficient or the river runs dry. The climate is either tropical or semiarid. Few of the major towns and none of the medium size or smaller towns or villages have a water-supply system, and the few systems that exist are completely inadequate. Our problem is how to provide adequate water supplies to the communities of the basin with minimum cost and delay.

Prevailing management approach As the water-supply situation becomes more acute, internal pressures build up; requests for water-supply projects are forwarded to the government, each request backed by political pressure. The responsible ministry has a certain capital budget at its disposal for water-supply development and will prepare a politically ranked list of individual community water-supply projects, cut off at the budget limit.

Among the communities selected for water-supply development during the budgetary period, one or two might be located within the basin of our case history. A consultant will be asked to design the project, and subsequently implementation will start. In the following budgetary planning period, another community in the basin might be selected for water-supply development, engineering commissioned, and a separate project constructed. Over the years a considerable number of individual schemes will be constructed, each with separate dry-season storage structures, treatment works, pumping stations, conveyance system, storage tanks, etc. A few minor communities may sometimes decide to pool resources and construct a regional system.

Planning data are completely inadequate: flow data are nonexistent or short-term and unreliable. Consequently, practically nothing definite is known of minimum flow, length of the dry season, maximum flood flow, long-term average flow. Further, the local demand forecast cannot be firm, since the extent of urbanization, industrialization, and modern-type housing is much less predictable for a specific community than for a whole basin.

Implications of prevailing approach The main storage structures, such as dams and spillways, are the most expensive single cost item, accounting for 30 to 50 percent of the total cost; a treatment plant and pumping station account for say, 15 to 20 percent of the total cost; the remainder is divided between such items as conveyance and distribution pipe and tanks.

A closer analysis of the cost of storage facilities shows that increasing storage capacity within the relevant range results in only a slight rise in total cost; the cost of the cutoff barrier does not depend on dam height, and foundation costs increase only slowly with the height of a dam; the increase of the cost of the body of the dam is, likewise, not proportional to the respective increase in storage volume. The cost of the spillway, possibly 25 to 35 percent of the total cost of the dam or more, will hardly change with the size of the reservoir. We see, therefore, that as the size of the reservoir increases, the parallel increase of cost will, within the relevant range, be slight to moderate. The cost of treatment and pumping facilities depends to a greater degree on the increase in capacity; but here too there will be a considerable economy of scale. Similar considerations apply to conveyance facilities.

Separate waterworks for individual communities, each based on an individual storage structure, must under the conditions described allow for ample safety margins in planning and design in order to compensate for possible erroneous assumptions in hydrological data, demand forecast, etc. Since the range of uncertainty is wide, the safety margin will have to be considerable. Furthermore, each project must provide standby units to ensure supply, in case of failure of an operating unit. Each plant and station will require a separate connection to the available power system, or separate prime movers. Finally, projects will compete for scarce trained and skilled manpower to design and supervise construction of works and later on to operate and maintain them; the standard of operation and maintenance will often be unsatisfactory due to the scarcity of skilled manpower.

Proposed change of management boundary It is clear that the prevailing approach entails a number of economic and engineering disadvantages, the principal ones being the high initial cost and the lumpiness of investment of storage facilities. The expansion of the size of the management unit will therefore be an obvious way to avoid the repetition of this high and lumpy investment for every major community or group of smaller communities. The recommended management unit will here be identical with the hydrological basin. One dam and spillway will be built on the upstream reach of the river; it will be of sufficient size to regulate the flow of the river so as to satisfy all possible demand along its entire course during the dry-weather season for a period of, say, ten to fifteen years. The water stored behind the dam in the wet season will be released in the dry season in order to sustain a flow that is sufficient for water-supply needs throughout the year; thus, none of the municipal or regional projects would need any additional storage facilities. Regarding the other facilities, i.e., pumping stations, treatment plants, and pipes, separate systems could be constructed for every town, or, preferably, a number of communities could combine into one regional scheme. The extent to which it would be economical to pool a number of communities under such a regional scheme would depend on the comparative cost of fewer and larger pumping and treatment facilities as against that of longer conveyance pipes. When making such comparative studies, the unavoidable lowering of operation and maintenance standards that will result from proliferation of plants should be allowed for.

The proposed expansion of the management unit to include the whole hydrological basin has the following major advantages:

1. The cost (per capita) of the most expensive single cost item—that of storage facilities—will be considerably lower.
2. Safety margins related to storage functions must be allowed for only once, thus reducing overall costs.
3. Once the river flow is regulated, the cost of individual waterworks based on this regulated flow not only will be significantly lower, but will be less lumpy, more phaseable, and, therefore, more flexible, and will involve less risk of misinvestment.
4. To the extent that communities agree to combine their efforts into a regional scheme fed from the regulated river, the cost of the safety margin and standby services will be reduced, the quality of operation and maintenance improved, and the reliability of the service increased.

Institutional aspects The proposed management solution need not involve any major organizational or institutional difficulties or friction: the task of regulating the river flow could be part of the duties of a central or regional government, while the individual water projects that obtain their water from the regulated river may, after construction, be handed over to the municipality or group of communities. No new institutional setup would be required for major cities; smaller communities might in any case have had to pool their resources.

CASE HISTORY TWO: MANAGEMENT BASIN VS. HYDROLOGICAL BASIN

Description of prevailing conditions Case history 2 concerns a densely populated and cultivated coastal region comprising a large number of communities of all sizes. A number of rivers drain the area to the coast; the major rivers have adequate dry-weather flow, whereas most of the other rivers do not flow at all during the dry season. Water-supply systems exist only in the major communities but have become inadequate due to the rapid process of urbanization and industrialization. An optimum way is sought as soon as possible to provide the maximum number of people with an adequate water-supply service —within the limits of a predetermined budget. No groundwater is available. Data are as inadequate as in case history 1 and for the same reasons.

The conventional solutions Each municipality or group of communities will stake out its claims to a specified, though usually exaggerated, quantity of water from the nearest river, as well as its claims for the largest possible chunk of the budget. Each project will start with costly and lumpy investments in storage structures. Each project will incorporate safety margins and provide facilities capable of generating an adequate supply for the next fifteen to twenty-five years. Each project will have to provide for a power connection or prime mover, for standby capacity of treatment and pumping facilities. Since each project will be able to grab only part of the required money, construction will be protracted. This approach will result in high per capita capital investment, very long lead times, and maturation periods with a large percentage of sunk capital remaining idle, or expressed differently, less people will be served for the available budget, and those served will have to pay more for the service.

Analysis The criterion for an improved solution would be the maximization of the number of service units (adequate water-supply service per man and year, without differentiating the per capita demand) for a given budget, the time preference being expressed by a discounting procedure of the service units; concurrently, due allowance has to be made for the potential contribution of the proposed facilities to future service (see also Chapter 15).

The proposed solution An overall general plan is drawn up for the whole region which should provide for all its needs for a period of, say, fifteen to twenty years. This overall plan will be based on a number of river intakes, some with and some without storage structures. A conduit system will connect the intakes to the communities. This plan is subdivided into phases, each sufficient to provide service for, say, a five-year period. In consecutive phases, the source for a town might change; the flow in the conduits might change in direction and quantity. Intakes, storage structures, treatment and pumping plants, conduits and distribution facilities are provided only to the extent necessary for the immediate phase; capacities are increased as demand growth warrants the development of new resources which will be fed into intermediate points of the conveyance system.

In such a system every dollar outlay is spent for immediate service; there is little idle capital, and the number of people served will be at a maximum, without, however, resorting to temporary investment; investment in safety margins of every description is minimized; data are accumulated for the later phases; the whole region is opened up for industrialization from the point of view of water supply. The facilities requiring the big lumpy investment characterized by great economy of size, e.g., dams and other headworks, are constructed full scale, but only those are included in every phase which are required to supply the planned service during the forthcoming phase. Discrepancies developing between actual and estimated demand will matter little in such a regional approach, since correction one way or the other can be made in the next phase. This approach also has considerable advantages from the funding point of view: firstly, because the regional solution has a much higher economic justification than have a limited number of local ones with their necessarily more restricted benefit range; and, secondly, because more communities, industries, and individuals will participate in repaying the loan.

Institutional aspects The approach advocated here will require, in addition to the adoption of a regional plan, the establishment of a regional authority or of a limited number of cooperating authorities. Concerted and well-planned action is a necessity. The question of participation in investment and operating costs will not be an easy one, since the basis for cost allocation may change with time. A simplified approach, using a per capita or quantitative basis, might be a good shortcut to avoid protracted squabbles.

CASE HISTORY THREE: REGIONAL VS. NATIONAL MANAGEMENT BASIN

Description of prevailing conditions Case history 3 refers to arid or semiarid countries or regions in which water is scarce or is anticipated to become scarce in the foreseeable future. Under such conditions long-term planning of water-resources management and development takes on a new importance.

The basic problem New dimensions of scarcity, e.g., water scarcity, if added to those of the first two case histories (capital, human resources, data scarcities), compel us to reconsider our approach. The use of the scarce resource, i.e., water, under such conditions, can be optimized only if we continue to expand management unit boundaries, beyond the region, until they comprise the whole country, considerable portions of it, or (in extreme cases) a number of countries.

Suboptimization of regional autarkic units will lead to inefficient use of the scarce resource. Detailed planning on a national scale and, still more, implementation on such a scale will, however, not be feasible owing to lack of time, human resources, data, and capital. A realistic approach under such conditions will be to define the main features of the plan on a national scale (where the scarcity is national) and to use such a national analysis as a guideline for the elaboration of more detailed regional analyses. This approach will facilitate intensive development from the outset, without, however, creating irreversible facts contrary to the overall plan and likely to jeopardize its future realization.

Generation of projects follows generation: the earliest generation at a local level, subsequent generations on regional and interregional levels, the final generation on a national level. The projects would, however, all be planned so as to fit ultimately into one overall national pattern, like pieces in a jigsaw puzzle. The integrating features that will, to a lesser or greater extent, be built into all project generations will be partly physical and partly operational; they will refer to integration in space as well as in time, in quantity as well as in quality.

The planner will use a dynamic process approach in inventorying, planning, and scheduling and will utilize transients of the system to the fullest possible extent; he will operate with direct and indirect, positive as well as negative storage (i.e., withdrawals below lowest design level). He will propose a phased legislative and institutional framework that is mandatory for the implementation of the program in its several stages. This program will not only extend to development aspects but will also include exploitation. The latter, too, will be planned on a national scale and be based on optimization procedures.

All of this may seem like a very tall order, especially in the framework of a developing economy. We should certainly beware of being overambitious; on the other hand, particularly in developing economies, we cannot afford to deviate too far from the optimum use of scarce resources without endangering growth.

32
PROBLEMS OF ARID COUNTRIES

The time was ripe for some new thinking on this topic, some thinking which would not be constrained by the orthodox boundaries of a university syllabus.

STAFFORD BEER

A WATER-RESOURCES PLANNING MODEL FOR ARID COUNTRIES

Within the present context, *aridity* refers to water-resources conditions that seriously limit survival or economic growth. In operative terms, a country will be considered arid if and when the quantity or quality of water is the controlling planning variable.

Due to the development of water-extraction and conservation techniques over the last century, water-supply limitations have in many countries ceased to be absolute and have become economic. There do, however, exist extensive inland areas where even today we can devise no solutions to alleviate natural water scarcity.

The aridity situations which will be treated in this chapter pertain to countries which have developed and used most or all of their natural water resources for developing their economy and which therefore will depend on new ways of water-resources management for future economic growth. The State of Israel now finds itself in this situation, and the comments that follow are based on an analysis of Israel's water-resources management policies proposed for the next decade or two.

When first faced with the problem of aridity, the planner suddenly discovers that the conventional problem-solving devices bequeathed him by his professional training are relevant to humid areas only. Hydrological and management concepts, water engineering, techniques of water application and of water quality control—all originated in countries which possessed adequate water supply when these professional tools were developed. If adapted to the requirements of arid countries, modified versions of the specific concepts and approaches developed in humid climates might provide palliative solutions. However, where we must solve major water problems under conditions of aridity, a completely new approach is required. This approach must be based on a planning model sufficiently comprehensive to comprise all aspects of water conservation, extraction, and application. The optimization of such a comprehensive model will hold the key to management planning of water resources in arid countries.

Conventional problem solving in the field of water resources assumes demand for water to be an exogenous variable. According to this approach, the aim of water-resources development and management is to harness water resources with a view to complying with the requirements of such a demand. In situations of aridity, this problem-solving path will be blocked: available resources will not be sufficient to comply with the requirements of an exogenous demand. Under such conditions, we ought to discontinue separate object-language solutions for supply and demand of water and set up a model by which they can be considered and solved simultaneously by metalanguage analysis.

A water-resources management model that fits the requirements of arid countries ought to comprise six complexes:

1. The water-supply function conceived within the framework of the natural hydrological cycle

2. Possible modification of the hydrological cycle by human intervention

3. The composition of the resources base of production complexes and services into which water enters as a substantial input

4. Man-made water

5. Resources pollution

6. Political and institutional implications

Increasing the quantity of water by applying measures related to complexes 1, 2, and 4 and improving its quality by applying measures related to complex 5 will have to compete with measures related to the modification of the resources base (complex 3), while complex 6 (politico-institutional) will usually be treated as a constraint. The optimum solution will select the lowest cost combination of water-resources management measures and modifications of the resources base that will make it possible to maintain the desired and economically justifiable scope of production of commodities and services.

THE WATER-SUPPLY FUNCTION WITHIN THE FRAMEWORK OF THE NATURAL HYDROLOGICAL CYCLE

Properly speaking, the water-supply function of our model falls within the speciality of water-resources engineering. Conditions of aridity introduce two main points of emphasis:

1. Management of water resources must be so designed as to ensure the most satisfying yield deployment in the dimensions of time and space—subject to the constraint that marginal cost not exceed predetermined cost ceilings.

2. Engineering features should be designed to achieve maximum conservation, again subject to the constraint that marginal costs of the water conserved not exceed predetermined cost ceilings.

To comply with these planning requirements, we need intimate knowledge of the hydrological cycle and its fluctuations. An economic analysis encompassing the commodities or services made possible by the incremental use of water will determine the cost ceilings for various water applications at various times.

Within the framework of the comprehensive model, such management and conservation measures will have to compete with alternative measures related to the remaining five complexes.

THE HYDROLOGICAL CYCLE AND ITS POSSIBLE MODIFICATION BY HUMAN INTERVENTION

The natural hydrological cycle may be modified in two ways:

1. Once precipitation has occurred, we may attempt to increase conservation of runoff.
2. We may attempt to increase precipitation.

Regarding runoff conservation, a number of approaches have been tried on an experimental, pilot, or demonstration scale. Results achieved so far are not very conclusive. As long as more accessible resources exist, this type of conservation will not be competitive. However, when we have to resort to the more problematic resources, some of the unconventional conservation approaches may warrant detailed analysis.

Among the conservation approaches tried out during the last decade, reduction of evaporation is worth mentioning. The evaporation barrier used in large-scale experiments was a monomolecular film, though other barriers have been tried on a laboratory scale. The difficulties barring the way to an economically feasible process of evaporation reduction are numerous: difficulties in maintaining the film effective under wind and wave conditions encountered in large open water areas; heating up of the water body as a consequence of evaporation reduction, leading to a subsequent increase of evaporation and a reduction of the net quantity saved; finally, difficulties in the evaluation of results.

Another aspect of unconventional water conservation is the increase of runoff. It has been proved in a number of areas (Arizona, Israel) that trees and shrub vegetation consume more rainfall than does a grass cover. Where ecologically, geologically, and hydrologically feasible, and where justified from the point of view of overall environmental management, shrub vegetation, for instance, could be replaced by a grass cover in order to increase the underground recharge; grass might also provide an economically more attractive vegetative cover. Increasing surface runoff by chemical treatment of the surface soil is a similar approach which, however, has as yet been little explored.

The most important manipulative approach for modification of the hydrological cycle is *weather modification,* especially by means of cloud seeding. The experimental history of the latter over the past fifteen years has been both extensive and uneven. The science of weather modification remains in its infancy, lacking even the basic facts of rain formation from clouds. Cloud seeding is but in its alchemistic phase, consisting of numerous repeated trial-and-error efforts. Indeed, it is easier to prove the existence of gold in the alchemist's crucible than that of a rainfall increase in the records of a statistical experiment. Present evidence, however, indicates that *increases can be achieved under certain climatic conditions.* Since the possible benefits are very high and the experimentation cost is relatively very low, it will usually be worthwhile to attempt cloud seeding wherever climatic conditions are favorable. Such experiments may extend our basic understanding of cloud physics as well as provide applicative data. Nevertheless, even if we can muster convincing statistical proof of an aggregate rainfall increase over an area, it will not be easy to transpose these results into specific runoff terms that could be used for the design of water-conservation engineering facilities.

THE RESOURCES BASE

In arid countries that possess a sizable agricultural sector, *irrigated agriculture* will be the most important production process related to water, and we shall therefore confine our comments on manipulation of the resources base to irrigated agriculture.

The makeup of the resources base of irrigated agriculture has not substantially changed since the invention of irrigation thousands of years ago. Over the last 100 years there has been little incentive for any major innovation to improve efficiency in the use of this most "priceless" (in both senses of the word) of all commodities, water. The provision of irrigation water since ancient times has been considered a state responsibility, and the direct charges made for water have usually not been high enough to encourage innovation. This custom of undercharging for water has continued to this very day, and few regions charge the farmer for the real cost of water. In some extremely arid areas, people have in the course of time been faced with absolute limitation in their water supply (e.g., the eastern Mediterranean area, and especially the Northern Negev of Israel), and in such cases they developed extreme ingenuity to make the best possible use of their water resources.

However, because of the incomparably larger scale, the innovation required in a modern arid-area economy will be more far-reaching than that introduced in arid areas in historic times. It will have to extend to the whole resources base of the agricultural production process: the soil in which crops are grown, the biological material (seeds), water (natural precipitation and irrigation), fertilizer mix, plant protection, soil conditioning, and cultivation method. Modification of some of these inputs will influence water requirements (per ton of crop yield), so will variation in the time pattern of water application. With improved understanding of the functional relationships between the relevant input volumes and qualities and the water requirement per ton of crop and of the influence of applicative patterns of water, we shall be able to set up a model to help optimize—for every cost level of development of new water or of improving water quality—the makeup of the resources base. Until that time we must resign ourselves to experimenting with specific relationships that appear promising and to using attractive results for palliative improvements of the resources base.

The first type of improvement to be studied will be irrigation techniques and related applicative patterns of water. Some solutions are available for the engineering aspects of this complex problem, and these could be rapidly applied on a large scale. One improvement, for example, would be homogeneity of supply, i.e., ensuring that every part of an irrigated plot receives only as much water as we propose to apply. If, for instance, we use sprinkling irrigation and apply a long sprinkling line, the pressure upstream would be controlled by the minimum residual pressure that we have to maintain at the farthest downstream end of the line; this will provide surplus pressure upstream and in the central section and (assuming the use of identical nozzles) consequent overirrigation there. Pressure-maintaining devices could avoid such waste. Similarly, we could take the guesswork out of irrigation spacing (in time) and irrigate in response to local moisture-content measurements. Minimizing losses of the distribution system would fall into the same category of measures. Such measures and similar engineering solutions can considerably increase efficiency of water use.

However, it will be from a modification of space and time patterns of application of water that we may expect the most important improvement. The whole relationship of the sequence and intensity of application of water to resulting crop yield and crop quality is still little known; we know still less about the relationship of crop yields to the spatial distribution of irrigation water in relation to plant rows. The introduction of trickling irrigation has put at the disposal of the irrigation researcher a practical tool for experimenting with such microregulation of both the spatial and time distribution of irrigation water. The little that we know from results achieved so far suggests that systematic application of such regulative patterns may become an extremely promising approach for improving the ratio of tons of water to tons of crop.

A different though interrelated approach to improve water-application effectiveness would be reduction of evaporation from irrigated areas. This could be effected by introducing an evaporation-reducing barrier (e.g., a film). An alternative way would be to reduce evaporation losses per ton of crops, for instance, by increasing the intensity of crop growing per unit of area (such as in hydrophonics). Both approaches point toward the necessity of increasing our control over environmental factors.

A different, and probably also promising, approach would be genetic modification of the biological material with a view to developing seeds that would lead to a better water-crop relationship. Most of the successful genetic developments of the last ten to fifteen years have sought to optimize other ratios, such as response to fertilizer. Emphasis in genetic work on reducing seasonal water requirements will undoubtedly lead to a significant improvement; however, since relatively little work has been done in this direction, it would be idle to speculate as to how important such an improvement might become.

Yet another area of improvement of the resources base, again one that has been little studied, is manipulation of the quantity and quality of the other inputs in the resources base in order to reduce, directly or indirectly, the water requirement (i.e., through the agency of the soil, the biological material, or other inputs).

Whether still more far-reaching modification of the agricultural-production process, such as the growing of plant tissue, will in the distant future become technically and economically feasible, thus revolutionizing the agricultural-resources base, is a moot point.

Our enthusiasm for the technological potentialities of modifying the resources base of the agricultural-production process should not blind us to the fact that most of the above modifications will tend to be *capital intensive.* They will result in overall production costs higher than those of countries which possess sufficient water supplies and which therefore need not modify their resources bases to the same extent. As the cost of water increases with growing utilization of the resources potential, one or the other modification of the resources base will become eligible; such a modification, though more economical than a corresponding expansion of water-supply facilities, might still raise production costs. To compensate for such a rise in cost, we shall have to develop special advantages, which might not be achievable to the same extent in more conventional agriculture, such as higher quality, homogeneity of quality, availability out of season. Since the modification of the resources base involves increasing environmental control, which in turn increases our control of important biological factors, such special advantages should not prove impossible to achieve. The rising cost of production will also in time tend to change the composition of crops grown: low-value crops and easily importable crops will be gradually displaced by high-value crops (mainly export cash crops) and crops for internal consumption that are difficult to import.

Finally, we ought to keep in mind that major modifications of the resources base of irrigated agriculture will affect the decision patterns of a great number of small producers. Far-reaching changes in agricultural policies, e.g., changes in attitudes to charges for water, creation of incentives for adopting innovations, will be required in order to modify the decision space of producers. The necessary impact on the latter will have to be achieved through the action of the price mechanism and by the creation of specific incentives and disincentives, rather than by direct administrative action. Such changes of economic policies and of related administrative measures will require considerable efforts to transform the political decision process and to restructure the relevant institutions.

It is true that we are still extremely ignorant of many of the technological aspects of resources-base modification; however, even today a case could be made out for a partial innovation program in countries with acute aridity problems. No major innovation program has as yet been initiated in arid regions. The main reason for the delay may be sought in distortions of the price mechanism and in lack of institutional adaptation. The restructuring of economic policies and institutional frameworks implicit in such a program might well prove the most difficult aspect of manipulating the resources base under conditions of aridity.

MAN-MADE WATER

From the point of view of the analysis of our comprehensive model, man-made water will be treated like natural water except that:

1. When available, its supply may, for all practical purposes, be physically unlimited.
2. In most cases its cost in the near and possibly not-so-near future will be high.

Since a special chapter is devoted to this subject (Chapter 33) we shall confine our comments here to the qualitative implications of incorporating man-made water into a water-supply system. As pointed out in Chapter 33, the benefit of adding desalted (and therefore low-salinity) water may be a triple one. Such addition may:

1. Directly increase the volume of supply
2. Make possible, through dilution, the incorporation of brackish water, and thereby indirectly increase the volume of supply
3. Provide a dilutant to improve the quality of existing supplies

The reduction of the salinity of natural waters achieved through dilution could likewise be achieved by the "kidney effect" of salt-extracting methods such as electrodialysis and reverse osmosis. As a water system in an arid country "matures," quality problems tend to build up and in time necessitate either dilution or salt extraction. Reclamation and reuse of domestic and industrial wastes will contribute to mineralization and will necessitate earlier introduction of dilution or kidney effects.

POLLUTION

Ecologically speaking, man is an aquatic animal once removed. Although he no longer lives in water, he lives close to water, and a great part of the pollutants which he discharges into his environment ultimately reaches and pollutes his water supply. Other things being equal, the more mature the economy, the greater the pollution problems, and the higher the rate of pollution buildup.

Some of the most ubiquitous and refractory sources of pollution originate in the agricultural-production process. To illustrate basic considerations of pollution control within a comprehensive management model, we shall comment on these sources of pollution in this section. Some of these sources involve pollutants that are difficult to handle, while others employ pollutants that disintegrate with or without human intervention. The first type may be called "hard" (in analogy with hard detergents), the second "soft."

It will often be found that two types of chemicals are available to fulfill a certain requirement in the agricultural-production process: one may be hard, and possibly slightly less expensive or more effective, the other soft, and possibly more expensive and/or less effective. If the selection is left to the individual producer, he will of course select the less expensive hard chemical, even if the ultimate correction of the pollution caused by the use of this chemical will greatly exceed the saving made by selecting the hard instead of the soft chemical. This selection is not surprising, since the chemicals are paid for from the income of the farmer, while the cost of pollution control is borne by an anonymous state authority.

To avoid selections that are unfavorable to the economy as a whole, we must introduce metathinking both on optimizing the selection and on ways to induce the individual producer to adopt the optimal selection.

Unfortunately, the technical aspects of pollution travel, selective retention, and delay are still very incompletely understood.

Generally speaking, pollution may be manipulated at source (e.g., by selection of a soft pollutant) by disposal of wastes or extraction of pollutants before they reach the resource (e.g., sewage treatment and disposal of residual wastes), by dilution, by a "kidney effect," and by retention in selected areas or for a specific period of time. All these alternative measures have to be better understood before we can incorporate pollution control into our comprehensive model and submit it, as part of the model analysis, to a quantified evaluation (see also Chapter 28).

POLITICAL-INSTITUTIONAL IMPLICATIONS

In diffusely distributed decision processes (such as those related to water uses) awareness of the need to abandon customary decision patterns will not by itself lead to adoption of new, more integrative decision models. The new decision models, conceived at a metalevel, might require from the individual decision maker responses that strike him as contrary to his own short-term interests; prevailing policies, incentives, disincentives, and institutional frameworks might also favor old and obstruct new decision models.

It will therefore not suffice to spell out the technological aspects of a new decision model and to disseminate the relevant technology. To ensure actual adoption of a new decision model, we shall also have to refashion the whole decision space of the individual decision maker. This refashioning can be achieved by a combination of mandatory rules—aimed at staking out the decision range of the individual decision maker through legally enforced constraints dictated by public welfare—and policies aimed at providing incentives (and disincentives) that would make a decision complying with the public interest worthwhile for the individual decision maker. The extent of emphasis on administrative and incentive measures will of course depend on the prevailing political philosophy and administrative style.

The modifications of the political framework related to the change of the resources base of agriculture may prove especially difficult to implement. This resources base has been handed down through millennia with relatively little change. Its conservation has been ensured by a firmly established legal and institutional framework and by various policies, principal among which are distortions of water prices.

Major changes in the agricultural resources base will therefore require a complete refashioning of prevailing policies and institutions. Distortions in the price of water will have to be corrected either by establishing a realistic water rate or, should that prove impossible, by combining a higher water rate and a system of incentive policies related to prices of new inputs and investments. Such a combination would encourage the individual decision maker to switch to the new resources base. The most straightforward way to change prevailing decision patterns would be to place the greatest possible reliance on the price mechanism, tempered during the initial demonstration period by incentive policies to overcome inertial forces. However, such a direct policy will rarely be politically feasible, and therefore in most cases a set of policies might have to be adopted that would rely more on creating new incentives than on abolishing the prevailing price distortion.

The most immediate obstacle preventing or delaying adoption of a new resources-base policy in agriculture might be the difficulty in achieving the integrative metathinking that the identification of a new resources base involves. The very organizational structure of the politico-administrative hierarchy, with its fragmentation into divisions, subdivisions, and sub-subdivisions, each responsible for a specific and specialized aspect of the resources base, militates against such metathinking. Left to itself, the guidance provided by such a fragmented decision process would lead the production process to a crisis from which the prevailing planning and decision processes would see no way out. Only at this point would the need for a metalanguage solution arise.

To avoid the wastefulness of "regulation by crisis," a metasolution involving a gradual but cumulative change of the resources base ought to be undertaken by an administrative group vested with the necessary qualifications and authority. This solution ought to comprise both the technological and the politico-institutional aspects of the change involved.

Finally, allowance ought to be made for the lengthy lead time that the process of obtaining agreement on policy and institutional aspects might claim. Action toward such agreement might therefore need to be taken long before the purely operational aspects are to be implemented.

CONCLUSIONS

History has recorded cases of civilizations faced with water scarcity; the simple adaptive pattern usually adopted is neatly expressed in e. e. cumming's pungent lines "there's a hell of a good universe next door; let's go." Nowadays this type of solution will rarely be available. Where it is not, we shall have to look for solutions based on a metareview of the whole complex of water conservation, exploitation, application, policy, and institutional structure. Such a metareview may lead to a very different type of agriculture and to a very different type of crop mix; it may require that we discard our customary problem-solving tools for attacking separately each of the six complexes of water conservation and application (outlined in this chapter). We shall have to substitute an integrative model encompassing all six complexes, look for the manipulative combination of these complexes that will result in the most satisfying solution, and then determine if the solution is economically feasible. Finally, we shall have to identify the policy changes and the institutional framework that will lead to the adoption of the solution by the individual water users.

33

A DESALTING PLANT AS A PART OF A WATER-SUPPLY SYSTEM

Après la certitude préliminaire, le doute créateur.[1]

ALAIN (*Propos*)

We are rapidly approaching an era in which virtually unlimited quantities of water suitable for use in all spheres of human activity can be made available by the desalting of seawater. The problem of water resources will then turn primarily into an investigation of the economic feasibility of desalting water, and the magnitude of the use of desalted water will depend on the relation of the benefits achieved to the costs incurred. Desalting is at present a highly capital-intensive investment involving extremely high operative cost. General use of desalted water will therefore become economically feasible only under special conditions, in accordance with our ability to boost the benefits obtained from the application of such water and/or to reduce the costs involved in its production.

APPROACHES TO INCREASE DESALTING BENEFITS

Selection of the right product The selection of the right product will be considered separately for municipal, industrial, and agricultural sectors.

Municipal Use Municipal use of desalted water will be highest in the scale of priority. Only part of the water supplied to municipal networks is consumed and unrecoverable. Considerable quantities ejected as wastes may be recovered for reuse, and safe potable water may be obtained by the use of up-to-date reclamation practices such as recharging the wastes underground after complete treatment, possibly including removal of some mineral nutrients. The salt content of desalted water being negligible, the salinity content of these reclaimed waste waters will, in all probability, not be prohibitive even after a number of use-reclamation cycles, especially if the reclaimed water is itself diluted. The use of virtually salt-free desalted water will thus make it

[1] After the preliminary certitude, the creative doubt.

possible to apply *very intensive recycling* to community water supplies. Reclamation of used desalted water will generally prove worthwhile despite the additional cost of reclamation facilities.

Industrial Use The cost of water is generally a very minor element in the production costs of numerous manufacturing industries, and will remain so even with desalted water. Although high-cost water may be a considerable burden on some "wet" low-cost commodity industries, such as pulp, it will rarely determine the economic viability of a "dry" industry. The ratio of consumptive to nonconsumptive use in industry will also be important, for here also numerous reclamation cycles may be carried out, especially where water is used for cooling on a cycling basis. The use of practically salt-free desalted water will again make it possible to greatly increase the number of reclamation cycles, thus significantly reducing the consumptive use of water. However, difficulties may arise in reclamation due to the toxicity and refractory nature of some industrial waste streams. Some industrial water uses may have a high salt tolerance, admitting use of very brackish water or even seawater. Such selective water uses will reduce the requirements of high-quality water.

Agricultural Use Water is one of the more costly inputs of agricultural production in arid and semiarid zones, even where it is available from untreated natural sources; consequently, at prevailing cost levels, the application of desalted water for agricultural use is most questionable. The cost of the water input, based on predictable desalting costs for the early seventies, will far outweigh that of all other inputs and may even be higher than the value of the end product. A special combination of circumstances resulting in a unique, specific advantage of location or off-season and multibenefit application, together with the development of a highly efficient organization for production and marketing, will be required to make desalted seawater economically feasible for agricultural production in the near future.

Choice of application and production technology Water the world over is considered a cheap expendable commodity, and as a result the production technology of water application is geared to conceptions of low-cost water. The maintenance of subsidized low water rates, even after production costs of water have risen considerably, has reinforced this low-cost technological approach which is the approach presently taught in universities and almost universally applied by engineers. The application of desalted water, many times more expensive than the natural water, necessitates complete reconsideration of the conventional application technology. This would seem obvious; yet mental blocks militate against any basic change, tempting us to adopt the most incongruous combinations of high-cost water and low-cost application technology. A new technology, based on high-cost water, must therefore be adopted if the use of desalted water is to be economically feasible.

Community water-supply systems should incorporate all the techniques so far developed in the field of water conservation and waste reduction, such as metering, disincentive rate structure, leak suppression, piping and plumbing devices to conserve water, new methods of sewage handling (e.g., vacuum conveyance).

In industry, selective use of low-quality water and air cooling should be introduced wherever possible and preference given to dry over wet processes.

The impact of the change of application technology will be greatest in agriculture. The integration of outdated irrigation practices with the use of desalted water is neither intelligent nor commendable. Only scientific methods of cultivation and irrigation, optimized for the anticipated water costs, can bring the application of desalted water in agriculture nearer to the point of economic feasibility. Agricultural technology must be based, first and foremost, on a rational application of water, together with use of selected seed, highly intensive cultivation, and optimum application of fertilizers to increase crop yield and quality. Measures should also be taken to optimize the maturation season and marketing services.

The appropriate technologies for optimizing the benefits of desalted water to make its use feasible in agriculture are not yet available. A number of techniques have recently been developed, but major research and development remain to be carried out in order to adapt agricultural practices to conditions of high-cost water. This work must be conducted concurrently with research on desalting processes, and it must be conducted on a considerable scale if desalted water is to be brought within the economic reach of the water-needy nations. This aspect was treated in more detail in Chapter 32.

Plurality of benefits Water may be applied in situations from which more than one benefit may result. The benefits that may be derived from the use of desalted water may be subsumed under five headings:

1. Direct use—supplementing natural waters
2. Dilutant use—diluting natural waters with desalted water to improve their mineral quality
3. Integrated use—integrating a desalting plant into an existing natural water system
4. By-product use—exploiting the by-products of the desalting process
5. Indirect benefit—the catalyst effect brought about by supplying additional water to an undeveloped region

These benefits will be dealt with in greater detail in the following paragraphs.

Direct Use The benefits that may be obtained from the direct use of desalted water have already been enumerated, but it is necessary to add here some pertinent comments on the evaluation of direct production benefits. The evaluation of the benefits of desalting, like that of any other investment, is plagued by the uncertainty of the future behavior of the market. This uncertainty may, however, have more serious consequences for agricultural production based on desalted water than for other production processes, because of the high level of investment required for desalting and its long-term nature. Furthermore, agricultural and industrial products sustained by desalted water will have to compete with foreign products sustained by natural water sources or by more up-to-date and efficient desalting plants.

Dilutant Use The use of desalted water as a dilutant for slightly saline waters may be considered at present as its most important secondary benefit.

The high salinity contents of some natural waters may be ascribed to one or a number of factors:

1. Natural processes taking place at equilibrium conditions, i.e., natural salinity of groundwaters and surface waters
2. Disturbance by man of natural equilibria, i.e., change of groundwater flow gradients
3. Recycling of reclaimed waters, i.e., sewage waters
4. Gradual salt accumulation in closed or quasi-closed groundwater formations, i.e., "salinity creep"

The desalting of seawater and the salt-extraction processes suitable for brackish waters, such as electrodialysis or reverse osmosis, may be applied to improve water quality, although other more attractive water-management measures are often available. Where the latter measures are either unavailable or uneconomic, the application of desalting processes by salt extraction or dilution may be the only course, if such substandard natural resources are to be exploited. In such cases, the development of the substandard natural resource and that of the supporting desalting process should be considered as one investment package. This will result in a combined water yield whose cost will equal the weighted average of the costs of the two processes.

The pros and cons of these two basic desalting approaches (i.e., desalting of seawater and lowering the salinity of brackish water) as applied to our four categories of salinity conditions cannot be analyzed here in detail; we shall mention here only the main factors on which the selection of one or the other, or a combination of both, will depend. These are as follows:

1. Local hydrological conditions
2. Relative costs of the alternative desalting processes
3. Possibility of alternative, selective, direct use of the substandard waters
4. Comparative cost of brine disposal
5. Quantity and location of the additional high-quality waters needed
6. Extent of integration into the water system
7. Institutional authority available for integration

At present, a fully quantified evaluation of the benefits resulting from the improvement of the mineral quality of water for agricultural use is seldom possible. Such evaluation can be made only if the function relating the salinity content to the value of the crop yield is known. This function is influenced by soil texture and structure, soil drainage, cultivation methods and fertilizer application, irrigation requirements and methods, the amount of natural rainfall, as well as other factors; this function is at present known only for a limited number of crops grown under highly specific local conditions.

Integrated Use We shall confine ourselves to listing a few of the more important advantages of integrating a desalting plant or plants into an existing water-supply system:

1. The conveyance capacity of the system can be significantly improved by locating the desalting plants so as to feed directly into strategic points of the system.

2. Seasonal and short-term cyclical flow variability in the system will be decreased.

3. Long-term cyclical dependability of the yield will be increased by incorporating a desalting plant which will operate independently of climatic cyclical variations.

These advantages, although real, are difficult to evaluate quantitatively.

By-product Use The possibilities of utilizing desalting process by-products are as yet little known. Utilization of by-products may be combined with pretreatment of seawater; the concentrated brine discharged from the plant may also be utilized for further processing. Where the by-products of desalting are exploited by industry, it may be justifiable to attribute a value to such by-products and debit part of the costs to the desalting operation.

Indirect Benefit The supply of additional quantities of water to water-deficient areas or the introduction of water into an area which prior to desalting may have had no natural sources of water may bring about a far-reaching catalytic effect on all sectors of the economy as well as bringing in its wake important social changes. Most of these effects are difficult to evaluate quantitatively.

Maximum loading of plant The methods of desalting anticipated for the early seventies will be capital intensive to a very high degree. The investment that can be allocated to the "water portion" of a dual-purpose plant may be as high as $1.00 per gallon per day (1970 prices), and annual fixed capital charges at a 10 percent rate may be well above half of the total annual cost at full load. The plant-use factor and its development over the lifetime of the project will therefore have a decisive influence on the economics of a desalting plant: the nearer the plant will operate to full load conditions on a daily, seasonal, and long-term basis, the more economic the plant.

In a single-purpose plant, once the full capacity of the plant is called for, no difficulties will arise from daily and seasonal fluctuations of demand, since the product water can (within economic reason) be stored in surface or underground storage during off-peak hours or seasons. In a dual-purpose plant, the requirements of the water system must, in addition, be coordinated with those of the electric grid. Difficulties will arise mainly during the maturation period of the desalting plant during which the full plant capacity is not yet required.

Operation at low load during the maturation period of a single-purpose plant will add a heavy and possibly unbearable burden to desalting. Hence, measures must be taken to ensure that the plant will operate fully from the date of its commissioning until its retirement; demand manipulation may provide a satisfactory solution to this requirement. As an example of this, part of the demand to be satisfied by the proposed desalting plant may be developed a few years ahead of the commissioning of the desalting plant. Demand buildup may take the form of "prefinancing" the water needs of the economy through a properly planned and controlled "overdraft" from existing groundwater resources. This prefinancing can be carried on to a point where the installments for "repayment" of the "debt," together with the demand created, will approach the rated capacity of the plant. A less attractive alternative would consist in using part of the unused capacity of the plant to create a water stock to be kept in storage for future use; drawing upon the stored water at a later date would make it possible to postpone for some time the investment required for the construction of a subsequent desalting plant.

The first approach has the double advantage of generating benefits before the plant is actually commissioned and of allowing full-capacity operation from start-up to retirement. Thus the burden of interest to the national economy during construction, as well as the cost of maturation, can be greatly reduced. An attractive spacing in time of investment may be achieved by applying a similar procedure when a subsequent plant becomes necessary.

The program adopted in planning desalting plants should embody all or a majority of the approaches outlined above. The adoption of only one approach will generally not be sufficient to make the plant economically feasible at present-day costs.

MEASURES TO REDUCE COSTS

Plant cost All persons (except born pessimists), and especially those associated with engineering, tend to underestimate the overall product costs of new processes. This underestimation springs from two sources:

1. Underestimating the annual cost of a plant
2. Equating annual cost of the processing plant proper with total production cost

The first error is much exploited in sales tactics. Reputable firms will often furnish estimates of investments involved in desalting plants without taking into account water intake, conveyance or brine-disposal structures, site preparation, plant or administration buildings, laboratory, communication, or transport facilities—in short all the major items essential for the operation of the plant. Running-in costs and allowances for modifications which may prove necessary in an untried process are also often omitted from such estimates. These complementary investments will add considerably to the original figures.

The second source of underestimating total production costs stems from equating production costs with annual costs of the desalting plant proper. This error stems basically from equating the ownership cost and the costs of plant operation at full load with the real overall costs. The former do not take into account other costs such as below-capacity operation during the early lifetime of the plant, i.e., maturation costs, maintenance of a standby service for outages, provision for supplies for periods of maximum demand, and last but not least, the cost of conveyance, pumping, and regulation of supplies in accordance with demand. These secondary costs add considerably to the actual operational expenses of a desalting plant. However, the need for some of these provisions may not arise, or their cost may be reduced by integrating the desalting plant into a regional or national water system. Some of the advantages of integration will now be outlined.

Savings through integration

Maturation Costs The importance of the full loading of a desalting plant for plant economics has already been mentioned; neglect of this factor may greatly increase real costs.

When integrating a desalting plant, and especially a dual-benefit one, into a water system, the plant will be put on base load and some of the existing natural resources may be switched to production (through storage) for future needs. In the case of groundwater, pumping may be reduced and groundwater levels allowed to rise. This "indirect" storage may be used later, when the plant can no longer meet demand, to supplement the plant's supply.

Still more advantageous would be the use of the stored water stock and formation water proper ahead of the commissioning of the desalted plant. Such use would create a "negative storage" that could be compensated for by reducing the amount of groundwater pumping during the desalting plant's maturation period.

The extent to which such manipulative measures would be justified will of course have to be determined by economic analysis.

Peaking Costs Nonintegrated plants should be able to supply the peak quantities of water called for during short periods of the year, unless supply restrictions can be introduced for such periods. Peak loads will lower plant-use factors and therefore increase the unit cost of water. Desalting plants integrated within a water system will not be required to supply peak loads which may be obtained, at incomparably lower costs, from conventional groundwater or other sources.

Cost of Standby Capacity Water-supply systems should be equipped with a standby unit equal in capacity to the largest equipment unit that will require shutdown periods for maintenance or may involve incapacitation due to outages. Desalting plants cannot be considered in the near future as highly dependable pieces of equipment, and adequate standby capacity must therefore be provided. The provision of such standby capacity in an independent desalting system, or the provision of storage capacity to provide a standby supply in case of breakdowns, will add considerably to production costs. In an integrated system, standby capacity may be provided by conventional and relatively cheap alternative sources.

Choice of Location The location of water-conservation facilities is usually dictated by the resources geometry[2]; desalting plants, on the other hand, leave us more flexibility of location. We will often be in a position to locate the plant at the most beneficial points with regard to the demand requirements of an existing water system, and particularly in certain areas where the system, owing to unforeseen development, may have become strained. Thus the addition of a desalting plant or plants at a judiciously selected location may reduce investments for modification and extension of the existing conveyance system that otherwise would have become necessary. We should, therefore, weigh the advantages of subdividing a desalting plant capacity with a view to feed into the system at a number of vital points as against the diseconomy inherent in reducing the scale of the plant.

Damping Effect on Resources Fluctuations A desalting plant is the only water resource completely independent of the vagaries of climate. Its constant yield will have a relative damping effect on the seasonal and cyclical fluctuations of natural resources. This is especially important in arid and semiarid climates, where fluctuations are more extreme, and in areas for which long-term data are not available and the extent of variation is not fully known. Hence, the integration of a large-scale desalting plant within a water system will lower relative regulatory requirements.

THE ECONOMIC JUSTIFICATION OF DESALTING

Marginal analysis of existing water allocation We have so far expounded the marginal analysis of new uses of water and their benefits, assuming complete lack of transferability of water from present uses. However, such a simplifying assumption and the incomplete analysis based on it do not yield the true value of desalted water to the national economy. A complete analysis should consider all existing uses of water in the agricultural as well as in the nonagricultural sectors, together with the proposed new uses, allowing for the possibility of transferring water from less profitable to more profitable uses.

In reality, the mobility of water resources will depend on a number of

[2] This does not strictly apply to a fully managed system with major groundwater resources.

political, social, legal, institutional, and economic factors and will differ from society to society. Resistance to transfer is not static and immutable, but is to some extent amenable to change. Where dramatic stress on resources develops—and no country would at present consider construction of a large-scale desalting plant without such stress—resistance to transfer will soften and some reallocation of resources will be effected in the right direction. Nonetheless, a considerable hard core of resistance will remain.

Let us, for the sake of simplicity, start with the assumption that our political universe is "frictionless" and that water can be freely transferred from one use to another without cost to the economy. When all natural resources have been utilized and before we resort to desalting, we should investigate the economic feasibility of applying desalted water to the existing use that carries the marginally lowest benefit to the economy. Desalting should be adopted only insofar as use of expensive water is justifiable for that marginally lowest use. Should such use of desalted water be unjustifiable—and this will normally be the case—desalting should be delayed and water switched from the lowest benefit use to the next higher application. A similar analysis, and subsequent reallocation procedure, should be applied when the first reallocated amount of water becomes exhausted. The procedure will be repeated until what then constitutes the lowest marginal use justifies the use of expensive desalted water. Only at this point would desalting be theoretically justifiable.

Our analysis thus far has employed static parameters of benefit, water cost, etc. This is unwarranted for the analysis of processes extending over long periods of time. To avoid the distortion of such simplification, benefits and cost must be introduced as variables. Efficiency in the use of water and with it the value of benefits per unit of water will markedly increase in time; the forces of the market will exert a pull on low-value uses, tending to effect a spontaneous gradual reallocation of water resources to higher value uses.

Moving from our model to real-life conditions we must determine:

1. The economic and social cost to the economy in suspending the allocation of water for a particular use
2. The cost of effecting the physical transfer from the original to the new application

The transfer will be economically justified if the value of benefits foregone as a result of the transfer and the cost of effecting the transfer are lower per unit of water than the cost of desalted water and lower than the benefit of the newly proposed use.

We must also determine the social, political, legal, and institutional resistance to such a reallocation of water resources. Transfer of uses which will arouse considerable resistance might have to be excluded from the marginal analysis, leaving islands of economically incompatible low use; market forces or softened resistance to mobility may in time erode part or all of these islands.

A similar analysis should be applied to water quality, mainly mineral quality. Again the mobility question as regards allocation of saline waters arises; in this context, mobility implies exchange of water of lower salinity content for water of higher salinity content for crops that are not particularly salt sensitive. Resistance to reallocation of the "salt burden" for agrotechnical reasons will generally be greater than resistance to attempts at shifting water to a different use. The cost of the installations required for the selective allocation of saline waters may also be relatively high. The procedures and approaches described for quantitative mobility, *mutatis mutandis,* apply also to qualitative mobility. Where desalting is undertaken as a multibenefit proposition which includes the quality improvement of natural resources among its benefits, marginal analysis must encompass both aspects of mobility.

Resource expansion and efficiency of use One last simplification must now be resolved. We have thus far considered the recoverable part of the natural-water resources and the "duty" of water to be constant. Changes in these factors, although very slow, cannot be neglected.

Resources utilization is to some extent amenable to change. Water systems can be designed for minimum loss, and resources which have been left untouched or only partially developed in the past because of their relatively high development costs may become attractive when comparing their anticipated cost with that of desalted water. All existing projects and known project opportunities should be examined for the possibility of squeezing out additional yield at costs below those of desalted water. Regional and interregional integration of water systems and regional and interregional management plans will often measurably increase a system's water yield. Reclamation of marginal resources, waste water, etc., may also play an important role.

INSTITUTIONAL AND ORGANIZATIONAL CONSIDERATIONS

The remodeling of institutional structure is particularly important [illegible] the introduction of large-scale desalting, for as has already been explained, the benefits of desalting can best be maximized by integrating the desalting plant into a national, regional, or area water system. The narrower the scope of the system, the greater the diseconomy of singling out an autarkic area from a wider supply context. Feasibility of coordination will depend on an adequate institutional and legal framework.

Attempts should be made to coordinate the water system partially or fully even before resorting to large-scale desalting, for such coordination is certain to save water. The introduction of desalting into an unsuitable institutional framework is liable to increase the real cost of such water to the economy and to give rise to considerable difficulties in cost allocation, distribution of the desalting cost burden, and dues collection. Aspects of the institutional structure bearing directly on desalting should be remodeled; the acute or anticipated water shortage that precedes a decision to adopt large-scale desalting will ease such an attempt.

Operation of dual-purpose (power-water) plants requires coordination between the two partners, i.e., the power and water authorities. The interests of the power and water authorities must be reconciled in the planning and evaluation stages in order to achieve the best solution from the point of view of the national economy. Later on, problems of cost allocation, operational problems, maintenance problems, base load penalty, etc., will require resolution. Generally, owing to the size of the operation and its financial scope, neither utility will be prepared to entrust the other with the entire responsibility. On the other hand, separate management of the water and power sectors of the desalting plant is difficult, or even impracticable. Actual organizational experience in connection with dual-purpose plants being extremely limited, it is difficult at this stage to prescribe much more than the establishment of a joint organization to represent both utilities.

SOME ECONOMIC CONSIDERATIONS RELATED TO DESALTING PLANTS

Plant economics seeks to determine how the service decided upon in the overall economic analysis may be obtained at minimum cost, while maintaining reasonable reliability throughout the lifetime of the project. The study of plant economics is based on various data provided by the overall economic analysis, such as the annual cost of capital, size of demand and its anticipated growth rate, location of demand, quality specifications for the product water, and availability of energy. In accordance with the data, the general plant parameters, such as plant capacity, type of process, energy form, number of benefits, siting, fuel supply, integration into water and power system, may be determined. Plant economics attempts to determine which set of general plant parameters will result in a minimum unit cost of water. After the determination of the general plant parameters, the secondary parameters, specific to every process, can be optimized; occasionally, an iteration may be found necessary.

General plant parameters

Plant Capacity The plant capacity will depend on three factors:

Demand The demand at the anticipated date of commissioning may refer to one, two, or more benefits, e.g., volume of water, quality improvement together with additional quantity. Water demand will be made up of current demand growth, the substitution of new water for overdraft on groundwater, and diluting requirements.

Economy of scale Econony of scale will have an important influence on selection of plant capacity.

Time span A decisive factor in determining plant capacity is the time span over which the proposed plant is intended to meet unsatisfied demand and demand growth. Consideration should first be given to the lead time between decision and start-up of the subsequent plant, since it will be most desirable to wait until sufficient operating data from the proposed plant have been collected before designing new ones. In large single-purpose plants, lead time will be three to four years, whereas in a large dual-purpose plant, at least five years will probably be required.

Three other factors which should be considered are:

1. Comparison of the economy of a larger plant against its higher maturation costs.
2. Comparison of the economy of scale against anticipated technological improvement.
3. In dual-purpose plants, the time span must be determined separately for power and water and the two values reconciled.

Water Quality and Type of Plant The quality of water obtained from desalting processes will usually be adequate for single-benefit use. However, where water is to provide two benefits, extremely low salinity may be an important asset. Some desalting processes, e.g., distillation, produce high-quality water without significant additional cost; other processes, such as salt extracting and perhaps freezing, entail considerable additional costs to produce low-salinity water. The water-quality requirement is therefore an important criterion in selecting the desalting process.

Energy Supply and Cost The type and cost of the available energy have an important bearing upon the selection of the desalting process. Two types of energy are generally required for desalting processes:

1. Electrical energy for driving pumps, compressors, and other auxiliaries
2. Heat for raising the temperature of the water as part of the desalting process

The unit costs of these two forms of energy differ considerably, and comparison of energy requirements of two processes utilizing different proportions of these two forms of energy is of little value. The correct procedure would be to compare the aggregate cost of energy of alternative processes. Cost calculations should be based on incremental costs; thus, waste heat—i.e., heat that without desalting would run to waste—incurs no real cost, and the use for desalting of exhaust steam of a power plant incurs only such cost as would be represented by the value of its energy content for alternative power production.

Siting Comments on siting will be confined to a dual-purpose plant for desalting seawater and for power generation. The optimum location of a dual-purpose plant will mainly depend on the five factors listed below in the order of their importance.

Area of concentration of water demand and demand growth The location of the center of gravity of the water demand (including its anticipated growth during the time span of the plant) will probably be the most important factor in the general location of a dual-purpose plant, conveyance of water being many times more expensive than that of electricity. The layout of the existing and proposed water grid and the location of storage and distribution facilities will be decisive factors in the detailed siting.

Area of concentration of dilution demand in a dual-benefit plant The location of the center of gravity of the demand and demand growth for dilution purposes in dual-benefit plants should be considered next in importance. Dilution demand should not be analyzed in bulk but rather on a marginal basis for every region or area. Only such demands should be included for which the marginal benefits achieved justify marginal costs incurred in supplying the dilutant to the area.

Area of concentration of electric power demand and demand growth In view of the great difference between the costs of water and power conveyance, the location of the center of gravity of electric power demand will not decisively influence the location of a dual-purpose plant. Correlation between the location of water and power demand, however, will often be satisfactory.

Location of fuel supply Fossil fuel, if imported, will not significantly influence site choice, since the desalting plant will in any case have to be on the coast and the plant will generally be equipped with submarine unloading facilities. However, if the plant is to utilize local fuel, the site of the plant and the location of fuel-supply lines may be important factors. Obviously, this factor will be absent in the case of nuclear power plants.

Population concentrations In siting the plant, consideration must be given to available sites, with special emphasis on locating the plant at an appropriate distance from densely populated areas. The need for hazard zoning of nuclear plants or prevention of air pollution of fossil-fueled plants makes such distancing imperative.

Selection of Process We do not intend to delve here into thermodynamic or other technological criteria, but rather to enumerate some of the factors that govern the selection of a desalting process which will operate reliably throughout its life span. These factors are as follows:

1. The experience in design, manufacturing, operation, and availability compiled from data on successful existing plants
2. The size of existing successful plants related to the size of the proposed plant; anticipated difficulties, elements of uncertainty, lead time of upscaling, and anticipated economy of scale
3. Investments and annual costs—at anticipated interest rate and the extent of uncertainty relating to costs
4. The quality of product water, especially in the case of dual-benefit plants with dilution as the second benefit, and its relation to water costs
5. Incremental cost to the economy of available waste energy and of additional energy required for the process
6. Site requirements and availability
7. Requirement and availability of highly skilled personnel, repair facilities, etc.

FIVE
CONCLUSIONS AND OUTLOOK

34
CONCLUSIONS AND OUTLOOK

The truth remains that today nothing stands in the way to the attainment of universal freedom and abundance but mental tangles, egocentric preoccupations, obsessions, misconceived phrases, bad habits of thought, subconscious fears and dreads and plain dishonesty in people's minds—and especially in the minds of those in key positions. The universal freedom and abundance dangles within reach of us and is not achieved, and we, who are citizens of the Future, wander about in the present scene like passengers on a ship overdue, in plain sight of a port which only some disorder in the chart-room prevents us from entering.

H. G. WELLS

THE CYBERNETIC-HIERARCHIC PRINCIPAL OF CONCEPTUALIZATION

The resources aggregate required to lift the Third World from its status of near stagnation or slow growth and to initiate satisfactory and sustained growth is formidable. The resources made available for development over the last two decades were far from adequate. However, even when this limitation is taken into account, results are far from satisfactory.

Our basic thesis is that the disappointing results of Third World development efforts are due mainly to structural inadequacies, faulty planning methodology, and irrelevant evaluation procedures. The raising of investment levels will not of itself lead to self-sustained growth. To achieve such growth we must above all concentrate on the structural, planning, and evaluation inadequacies of developing countries, and we must fashion programs to correct these inadequacies.

Inadequacies of development thinking may be subsumed under seven main categories, all of which are present in varying proportions in most agricultural-development case histories.

1. Structural incompatibility between development planning and the political decision process: the wider the scope, the deeper the grasp, and the longer the time span of planning, the more comprehensive, integrative, and continuous will it become, and the more will it clash with the political decision process and its disjunctive, short-breathed, unstable bureaucratic framework with its limited capacity for abstraction. If planning aims too low and adapts itself to the political decision process, it will remain extremely ineffective; if, on the other hand, it ignores the political process, it will in turn be ignored.

2. The incompatibility of goal-setting tendencies: incompatibilities between manifest goal setting, which finds its expression in political double-talk, and latent goal setting rooted in the actual power structure of a country; between short-term production orientation derived from development thinking in mature economies and the long-term capacity orientation mandatory in developing countries.

3. Failure to realize the paramount importance of transformation for the development of Third World countries, and failure to realize the complex and interdisciplinary nature of the transformation process.

4. Failure to define a reasonably exhaustive set of alternative projects (development field) or to define the types of projects that would prima facie have a good chance of proving effective (preferential domain) and to concentrate efforts on such projects. Inadequacies in defining project population and weaknesses in the selection process proper radically reduce the chances of selecting a satisfactory program.

5. Failure to realize the interconnection and interaction among most socioeconomic processes when limiting analysis to a reductionist approach to analysis, i.e., when confining planning at one time to one sector, region, project, crop. Reductionist analysis will often have to be adopted, *faute de mieux,* for heuristic purposes. To compensate for the error involved in such an analysis, we ought to reconcile its results with the requirements of the larger context (e.g., intersectorial adaptation, if planning is confined to a sectorial scope).

6. Failure to grasp the need for testing a program's convergence with the nation's long-term goals and for redefining resources allocation patterns, trade-offs between objective yardsticks, constraints, etc., if the program does not converge.

7. Failure to plan the implementation process by making due allowance for logistic bottlenecks, bureaucratic constraints, weaknesses, etc.

We have attempted to outline the basic principles of a planning approach to avoid these seven basic inadequacies of development thinking as applied to agriculture, irrigation, and community water supply. The guiding principle of this planning approach is that of the cybernetic-hierarchic system of development planning. According to this principle, development planning is conceived as a hierarchy of analyses of subsystems and sub-subsystems. The boundaries, flows across interface, objectives, and constraints for every subsystem are defined by the next higher level of the hierarchy. If such definition is not forthcoming, the subsystem planner, using the metalanguage of the level above his subsystem, undertakes a substitute analysis of the relation between the subsystem and the next higher level.

Once boundaries, flows across interfaces, objectives, and constraints are defined, the planner may focus his attention on defining the development field and/or the preferential domains related to his subsystem and on formulating an objective selection process for choosing the most satisficing program. After selecting the latter, the planner would have to revert to the overall socioeconomic system and to a continuously conceived development process. To establish the relation of his subsystem analysis to the overall system, the planner will have to apply a test of intersectorial compatibility that will lead to a process of intersectorial reconciliation. To establish the relation of medium-term programs to the continuous development process, the planner will have to apply the test of convergence by comparing the program's objective achievements and their projection over three to four additional planning periods with the nation's long-term goals. Should the results of these two tests indicate the need for major changes in basic assumptions, the analysis of the subsystem would have to be repeated.

The principal advantage of the cybernetic-hierarchic principle of analysis is that planning may be conducted at intermediate (e.g., sectorial, subsectorial, or regional) levels of the socioeconomic system, while still leading to a satisficing selection of projects at the selected level and concurrently ensuring adaptation to the total system and to long-term development trends. In other words, although it leans heavily on simplified partial analyses, the cybernetic-hierarchic approach incorporates a self-corrective mechanism that will compensate for the simplifications introduced and that will in time lead to a higher level of integration.

The proposed planning approach will assist the planner in avoiding or overcoming the principal weaknesses of prevailing development planning. By selecting the leverage point of planning at the highest politically feasible level, we may avoid structural incompatibility between the system selected for analysis and the political decision process. By minimizing initial emphasis on politically sensitive issues and by tempering capacity and social orientation with production and economic orientation, we can ensure political feasibility. By confining planning to a sector, a subsector, or a region and by setting a time horizon, we make possible an analysis in depth that can be conducted in a multidimensional space. This pragmatic limitation of the planning space also makes it possible to define the development field and its preferential domains and to ensure a satisfactory program selection. Reintegration of the results of subsystem analysis into the overall planning of the socioeconomic system will ensure that heuristic reductionism will not result in significant distortion.

THE SELECTION OF A SYSTEM

The systems we have dealt with are subsystems or sub-subsystems of the socioeconomic system. Such a system may be described by four defining complexes:

1. Boundaries delimiting the subsystem selected from the whole from which it has been segregated.
2. Objectives to be achieved by the subsystem and flows occurring across the

interface between the subsystem and the socioeconomic system. These objectives and flows will have to be derived by meta-analysis of the subsystem as part of the whole.

3. Facilitation of the subsystem's objective achievement and constraints upon it originating from other subsystems.

4. Induction function, expressing the capacity to improve resources-outcome ratios within the subsystem.

Boundary definition The scope of the system selected for development planning will be determined mainly by the requirements of political feasibility. If proposed planning boundaries involve crossing politico-administrative boundaries, we are certain to face problems of structural incompatibility which might ruin our whole effort.

Once the subsystem boundaries are defined, we shall have to supply a mapping principle to describe the significant features of the subsystem. The type of mapping principle that will best describe the composition of a system will depend on the purpose of analysis. Since the main purpose of planning within our present context is to define the type of public intervention into resources allocation to agricultural development needed to increase productivity and production, the mapping principle we have selected is based on two vectors: the natural-resources vector, representing the medium to which public interventions are applied, and the development-resources vector, representing the components of public intervention.

As long as these two vectors are within the control of the same politico-administrative unit, we shall encounter no problem in defining system boundaries for analysis. The system will comprise the totality of the natural-resources vector on which we wish to operate and the totality of the relevant development-resources vector.

A problem will arise if the development-resources vector involved in upgrading the natural-resources vector of a system is itself controlled by more than one politico-administrative unit (such as a ministry). Planning here requires including the totality of the development-resources vector; political feasibility dictates limiting planning to that part of the vector controlled by the political unit responsible for the natural-resources vector on which we operate. Because of the intersectorial connection and dependence of practically all development activities, such incompatibility between planning and political requirements will occur in every major development task. However, for some tasks intersectorial dependence may be of a secondary nature, while for others it will be very basic. In the former case, limiting analysis according to political requirements with later interministerial and intersectorial adaptation will not introduce significant loss of rigor. In the latter case, conducting separate analyses in conformance with the boundaries of political organization, and later introducing interministerial and intersectorial adaptation to reconcile the separate analyses with the requirements of the planning task in hand, will imply considerable loss of rigor.

In such cases we ought to implement the principle of cybernetic-hierarchic conceptualization. The analysis of the subsystems defined by political expedience (conducted in the object languages of these subsystems) ought to be preceded by a metaanalysis of the relevant overall system (conducted in the metalanguage of that system).

To keep clear of the danger of political incompatibility, we ought to preserve the subsystems intact and leave subsystem analysis proper to the relevant political units. The metaanalysis ought to concern itself only with the interrelationships between the subsystems, the common goal-setting complex (and, if possible, its subsectorial components), the overall system optimization, the allocation of resources to subsystems following from the optimization—in short, the terms of reference and range of solutions for the detailed subsystem analyses. With the terms of reference arrived at by the metaanalysis of the system, the detailed analyses of the subsystems will result in solutions which hardly differ from those obtainable by full analysis of the system.

Objectives and flows across the interface From the point of view of the system under concrete planning analysis, objectives are external derivatives of a metaanalysis extending over the relevant portions or the whole of the socioeconomic system. On a long-term basis, however, goal setting will be significantly influenced by past objective achievement and thus dependent on system performance: objective fulfillment on a large enough scale will create new social forces and new vested interests which will in turn modify and influence goal setting.

Among flows across the system interface, the most important is capital allocation. From the point of view of concrete subsystem analysis, capital allocation will be an exogenous factor determined by a macroeconomic type of metaanalysis, by simple reconciliation procedures of budgetary requests from the various political units (ministries), by the influence of political fashion, or by the interministerial power balance. From the long-term point of view we shall again find that subsystem performance will influence capital flow from national, foreign, or international sources.

Facilitation and constraints Facilitation and its negative counterpart, constraints, designate the positive and negative influences, respectively, of other systems upon the performance of the system under analysis. When we renounce overall national planning and adopt planning for sectorial, subsectorial, or even lower levels of the socioeconomic system, we resign ourselves to operating with the quasi optima of the respective lower level subsystems, relying on intersectorial adaptation to reconcile lower level programs with higher level requirements.

Facilitation aspects may have varying degrees of importance. Some may be so important that a postanalysis reconciliation may not be sufficient. In such cases a metaanalysis encompassing the original subsystem and the selected facilitation aspect from another system may have to be conducted prior to the sectorial analysis (see under Boundary Definition). For example, the transportation of agricultural commodities might be a facilitation aspect of paramount importance in some development context. In such a context transportation facilities may be so decisive as to turn whole domains of the development field (which had proved unattractive within the framework of a sectorial analysis) into prime preferential domains. Tentative metaanalysis extending over the agricultural sector and interrelated problems of transportation controlled by the transportation sector would establish the revised natural-resources vector. This revised vector could then be the basis for a sectorial study and especially for a definition of the preferential domains.

The opening up of undeveloped regions for agricultural colonization through the construction of a new road illustrates modification of a domain's status by facilitation originating from a different sector.

In other cases, intersectorial adaptation may be sufficient to effect reconciliation of sectorial programs. Every sectorial system could be planned separately, with boundary conditions of each sectorial system defining the initial assumptions regarding the support which the sector would receive from or extend to other sectors. From the results obtained, the actual intersectorial support required could be defined and the results from the individual sectorial studies reconciled. Where necessary, the analysis could be iterated with the new values for intersectorial support.

Intersectorial support for the agricultural sector will be highly diversified. It will include physical support of the forward-linkage type, such as sorting, packaging, transportation, storage, refrigeration, and processing facilities; it will include physical support of the backward-linkage type, such as production and distribution of seeds, fertilizers, plant-protection chemicals; it will comprise general infrastructural features, such as education, power supply, health services; finally, it will include policy features requiring coordination with the ministries of economic planning and finance related to such production incentives as minimum prices, production subsidies, tax reliefs, price support of inputs or disincentives such as levies, selective taxation.

Induction Improvement of growth capacity through transformation of both the natural-resources vector and the development-resources vector is the basic precondition for a sustained growth process in the Third World. Both types of transformation depend mainly on the deployment of trained human resources and to a lesser extent on capital allocation.

Even a cursory analysis of the contexts of underdevelopment will show that upgrading the capacity of available human resources and expanding this all-important constituent of the development-resources vector ought to be awarded high priority. It is this vector constituent which will play a decisive role in upgrading the human and institutional components of the natural-resources vector. In most cases logistic and organizational limitations will constrain capacity expansion in the development-resources vector rather than availability of funds.

Since trained human resources will be the limiting resources aspect, we shall have to devise ways to maximize the impact of available resources in achieving:

1. Induction of growth of capacity and quality within the development-resources vector

2. Induction of growth of capacity and quality within the natural-resources vector

Since both the first and the second objectives have been dealt with (mainly in Chapters 23 and 24, respectively), we shall confine our comments here to a special aspect relating to the second objective. In order to maximize the impact of a limited volume of human resources of the transformation-input type, we should set up our program so as to create sizable demonstration effects and thereby spread growth orientation. Resources to produce the transformation of Third World agriculture will remain inadequate for a long time; also, the resources-outcome ratio will initially be very unfavorable. To improve the chances of initiating on a massive scale sustained and expanding growth with the mobilizable resources, we shall have to improve the resources-outcome ratio of transformation in addition to expanding the volume and quality of the development-resources vector. In other words, we shall have to induce growth orientation by demonstration effects from one type of operation to another, from one farmer to another, and from one village to another. To a certain extent such an "induction" process of growth orientation is also feasible within the framework of the development-resources vector.

A PLANNING MODEL FOR AGRICULTURAL DEVELOPMENT IN THE THIRD WORLD

The range of planning models applied in the Eastern and Western worlds can be defined by three bench-mark models: the mechanistic, the classical, and the cybernetic.

Protagonists of the mechanistic model posit that there can be no reliance upon intermediate-level self-regulative mechanisms and that the socioeconomic system (and its development processes) ought therefore to be governed by a national (or regional) normative program that spells out instructions down to the lowest level of the hierarchy. The mechanistic model assumes that the development process, down to the grass-roots responses of the individual decision makers, is predictable and deterministic. As a result of its inherent bias, the model discards decision potentials at the intermediate and lower levels of the decision-making hierarchy where decision processes would be open to feedback from the environment. While programs based on this model represent a powerful tool for rapid dissemination and implementation of policies conceived at the top level of the political hierarchy, they nevertheless lack the necessary flexibility to allow for the stochastic nature of environmental factors and human responses which are so important in inducing and maintaining growth in agriculture.

The planning procedure of the mechanistically oriented planner provides for a detailed spelling out of material- and human-resources inputs at all levels of the operational hierarchy. All operations and suboperations are fully programmed, but no provision is made for variations in environmental factors or in human responses. The action ideology rooted in the mechanistic model has been aptly described by the French philosopher Alain in one of his famous *Propos:*

Ces hommes à idées, que je voudrais nommer idéalistes, étaient persuadés qu'une entreprise où tout était prévu devait réussir; les effets les ont étonnés sans les instruire. Ils ont su très bien reconnaître qu'il manquait quelque chose à leur beau projet; et en conséquence ils ont mis sur pied quelque nouveau projet auquel, cette fois, il ne manquait rien; en effet il n'y manquait rien de ce que l'intelligence peut prévoir. Mais l'évènement réel, tel que le monde nous le propose, est fait d'une poussière de détails que nul ne peut prévoir.[1]

The difficulty encountered in the past of effectively processing the enormous amount of details involved in such programs has been considerably eased by the use of digital computers. The computer has most probably strengthened the mechanistically oriented planner in his approach, but it has not significantly alleviated the basic structural discrepancy between sectorial phenomena and the conceptual grid used to represent them. Since the mechanistic model presupposes that the individual decision maker at the production level responds "automatically" according to the requirements of the program, the latter curiously lacks any psychological or social dimension.

The classical model is the antonym of the mechanistic one. It assumes the prevalence, at all levels of the socioeconomic system, of self-regulative mechanisms which, through the operation of individual self-interest motivation, maintain a kind of socioeconomic homeostasis. Orthodox protagonists of this model reject all forms of public intervention. In developing countries this brand of unadulterated laissez faire ideology will be rare. Third World adherents of the classical model will adopt a mixed ideology, holding that, where justifiable, public intervention be confined to upgrading the physical engineering aspects of the production environment. They falsely assume the same self-regulating mechanisms which purportedly exist in developed countries.

The development planner operating with the classical model, somewhat diluted by the mechanical one, will therefore limit his program to its heavy engineering aspects and the latter's direct economic implications, and he will adopt a passive laissez faire attitude to all other essential program elements —tacitly assuming that the farmer and his institutions will adequately adapt to the changed physical environment.

The cybernetic model assumes the prevalence in the socioeconomic system of structural patterns similar to those encountered in a biological system.

[1] These people with set ideas, whom I propose to call idealists, were convinced that an enterprise in which everything had been foreseen had to succeed; results surprised them without teaching them anything. They readily realized that something was lacking in their fine schemes; and they therefore devised some new project in which, this time, nothing was missing; nothing was missing, in fact, that human foresight could provide. But real events, those that face us in real life situations, are made up of a myriad of details that nobody can fully predict.

The system is assumed to initiate change and to respond to change through the operation of a hierarchy of self-regulating processes in which the acceptable range of response or variation at every level is determined by control mechanisms emanating at the next higher level. This "normal" pattern is assumed to be operative as long as an innovation remains within the response range of the system at its several levels. If innovations are introduced that transcend this range, existing self-regulative mechanisms would have to be reinforced and their response range increased and/or new regulative mechanisms interpolated at the appropriate levels.

The cybernetically oriented program will fall somewhere between those which are mechanistically and those which are classically oriented. While not spelling out in advance, at the top level of the hierarchy, all the ramifications of development, as is so characteristic of the mechanistic model, it would also not confine itself to hardware aspects, as is characteristic of the "diluted" classical model. It would include interventions into all those dimensions of development for which existing response mechanisms at the grass-roots and intermediate levels are inadequate. Such interventions would emphasize operations aimed at improving existing response mechanisms and strengthening their respective control mechanisms. New organizational entities would be interpolated only when the potential of the above upgrading operations is exhausted.

The development history of agriculture during the last fifty years, especially that of the Third World, reveals that the mechanistic and classical models have been extensively applied, whereas the cybernetic model has been used only in a few notable instances, including Japan, Taiwan, and Israel. The further that development planning has moved from the cybernetic toward either the mechanistic or the classical model, the less successful has been the outcome. Where the planner has leaned toward the mechanistic model, extreme rigidity of the decision process and limited access to feedback information have impeded rapid growth. Agricultural development in the Third World is apparently too extensive, too fragmented, and too complex to be fully predictable or programmable; it cannot be fully imposed from the top downward. Where the planner has been guided by the classical model, his failure to catalyze new responses and initiate new control and regulative mechanisms has left the farmer with old response patterns applied to new production environments created by costly engineering works. This lack of adaptation led to a sad lag of fruition behind investments. Apparently the structural pattern underlying the cybernetic model possesses the closest similarities to that of the agricultural sector in Third World countries.

Given this experience and the paramount importance of speeding up agricultural development in the Third World, the time has come for an improved synthesis of planning methodology. The synthesis adopted in this book is based on four fundamental interrelated postulates:

1. *Variety Compatibility* Third World countries require a planning methodology which ensures the best conceivable use of their meager resources. To

maximize the achievement of development objectives we have to ensure the necessary variety in scanning potential development operations, in defining project populations, and in selecting optimal programs.

2. Structural Compatibility Since it is here assumed that the socioeconomic structure of developing countries is best represented by the cybernetic model, development planning of the agricultural sector ought to be based on this model.

3. Dimensional Compatibility The planning space of Third World agriculture ought to extend into all those dimensions of the socioeconomic system where major transformations through public intervention are needed to ensure fruition of projects.

4. Political Compatibility Every program involves the initiation and implementation of specific decision sequences. The latter in turn depend on the existence of an effective political decision process. Introducing the political dimension into our planning space raises the question of compatibility of the existing political decision process with the requirements of the program. Compatibility will have to be achieved by mutual adaptation.

Compliance with these four postulates will lead to optimum resources utilization. In all those countries in which the orientation of the political decision process and the magnitude of the resources inventory admit of convergence, a program's compliance with the four postulates will also lead to its compliance with the all-encompassing criterion of convergence. Where the preconditions for converging development do not exist, we will be forced to conclude that retaining the "object language" demarcated by prevailing conditions effectively blocks a converging solution.

Adoption of a "metalanguage position" which transcends prevailing political and resources constraints will indicate the changes in the political decision process, or in the resources inventory, or in both that are required to make convergence feasible. Even in those countries in which "object-language" planning does not yield converging solutions, a planning methodology based on the four postulates is recommended since it will lead to optimal use of resources. Furthermore, during the process of development an opportunity might arise to break out of the confines of object language and to introduce a metalanguage solution.

The improved planning synthesis that is built on the above four postulates is not limited to development programs on a nationwide scope; it is equally applicable to regional development programs and even to individual projects. Loss of generality through limitation in planning scope will, of course, reduce efficiency: the narrower the boundaries of planning, the more autarkic the solution, and the greater the loss involved in a quasi optimization as compared, say, with a nationwide sectorial optimization. Nevertheless, once the scope of planning has been set, the application of a planning methodology based on the four postulates cited above will ensure the best possible use of resources.

The postulate of variety compatibility is perhaps the most neglected of the four. Emphasis upon requisite variety has in other areas of human effort been termed the "morphological approach" (as developed by Fritz Zwicky of the California Institute of Technology and others). The basic tenet of variety compatibility is that we cannot approach requisite variety in our development decisions and optimize use of resources unless we first define all potential uses, their costs and benefits, the total universe of discourse of development planning—what we call the "field of potential development." Only by spelling out the latter will we achieve the requisite variety for selecting the optimum approach.

Structural compatibility is a precondition for a correct diagnosis and a workable therapy. Decision patterns encountered in traditional agriculture are scattered over a great part of the working population; the individual decision maker is isolated from sources of relevant information, and little mutual induction will exist. Since traditional decision patterns have developed within obsolete production contexts, the decision maker faced by improved production contexts will not show adequate response variety, i.e., he will either use his obsolete response patterns or be blocked in his responses. The cybernetic structural model implies a development approach bent on improving, expanding, and supplementing existing decision and regulative processes rather than on imposing new ones.

Decision processes will be improved by extension-type operations aimed at upgrading the psychological space of the individual decision maker and by creating incentives for the farmer to select certain responses while reducing the risk involved in his selections. While decision processes are being improved, institutions will have to be formed to provide the relevant inputs, services, and facilities.

The importance of dimensional compatibility stems from the need to transform the socioeconomic system in development programs of Third World countries. In mature countries, publicly financed development is usually confined to improving the engineering features of the production environment. Existing socioeconomic mechanisms are relied on to adapt to the new production environment and to lead to an improved production process. Development agencies or departments thus focus their activities on the engineering elements of development, which they are generally eminently qualified to plan and implement.

Third World development involves, above all, basic transformation of socioeconomic processes at all levels of the system. Development agencies, however, tend to be fashioned according to patterns of developed countries and thus cannot conceive, plan, and implement the essential transformations of the socioeconomic system. To compensate for this deficiency, the development process in the Third World must comprise two different levels of activity concurrently: development of capacity in the development agencies in all those dimensions related to transformation and broad deployment of these capacities to achieve the necessary basic transformation of the socioeconomic system.

Since fruition of the capital-intensive engineering side of development is conditional upon a socioeconomic system that can appropriately respond to improved production environments, priority ought to be given to transformation in the psychological, social, and institutional dimensions before embarking upon the bulkier and costlier portions of heavy engineering projects. Such scheduling will minimize the loss involved in idling or underutilization of expensive project facilities.

The postulate of political compatibility is perhaps the most refractory to analysis and planning. Every program will involve a certain hierarchy of decision processes. This hierarchy will rarely, if ever, be compatible with the politico-administrative hierarchy encountered at the outset of the program. To achieve political compatibility we would have to compare the two hierarchies and devise such mutual adaptation as would ensure political acceptance without incurring a crippling downgrading of the program. To minimize resistance against such adaptation, supplementation rather than basic modification of institutional structure and coordination rather than interference should be aimed at.

Having outlined the postulates of a planning methodology for agricultural development in the Third World, we can recapitulate the main features of the planning process that comply with them and that are set forth in Part 2.

THE PLANNING PROCESS

Goal setting The alpha and omega of planning is goal setting: defining long-term aims and from them deriving medium-term objectives and quantified short-term targets. In most developing countries it will prove impossible to confine oneself to a single aim and objective, and two or three groups of objectives that are not reducible to a common denominator will have to be introduced.

The most common groups of objectives encountered in development planning are increase in aggregate sectorial (regional or project) product and distribution effects of the new income created by the proposed investments. Balance-of-trade improvement will also often be an important objective. For every objective we shall have to lay down yardsticks and measurement methods.

Goal setting depends predominantly on political value judgments and ought therefore to be the prerogative of the political decision maker. The same applies to the selection of trade-offs between the various objective yardsticks. However, it will rarely prove feasible to agree at the outset with the political decision maker on abstract trade-off ratios. Where ground rules defining trade-offs between objective yardsticks cannot be agreed upon in advance, the planner will have to operate with dual or multiple objectives. The outcomes of every eligible project will be expressed by two or more objective yardsticks. Programs, i.e., sets of projects that comply with the inventory constraints (initial capital and human resources), will again have their outcomes defined by the same yardsticks. The political decision maker will then be able to select between programs on the basis of their absolute levels of objective achievement. Every such selection implies an indirect selection of trade-offs between objective yardsticks.

Selection of trade-offs decisively influences the extent of "convergence" of our operation. Once our long-term goals are set and the resources inventory is defined, there exists only a limited range of trade-offs that will lead to the transformation of the status quo system into the long-term target system. This optimal development range of trade-offs will limit the freedom of choice of a specific trade-off ratio between objective yardsticks for a medium-term development program. Because of the complexity of the problem, the state of the art, and the lack of data, the planner is not and may not for a long time be in a position to define this range safely. A further difficulty arises from the frequently encountered incompatibility between long-term goals and directly or indirectly selected trade-off ratios: goals tend to be more "welfare oriented" and trade-offs underlying current decisions more "vested interests oriented."

Neither the political decision maker nor the planner possesses absolute compass bearings and knows exactly where true "north" lies; yet the planner, being less involved in short-term political issues, will usually be a better judge of the right direction. It will therefore be his task to see that trade-offs selected by the political decision maker do not lead us too far from the convergence upon long-term development goals and that any past deviations be gradually offset by later selections of compensating trade-off ratios.

The two development vectors The two basic development vectors are the natural-resources vector and the development-resources vector. The natural-resources vector comprises all factors that enter the status-quo-ante agricultural production process, i.e., mainly land, water, human and institutional resources, and production techniques. The development-resources vector comprises all resources (capital and human) that are at the disposal of development agencies. Since the definition of the field of potential development comprises potential applications of all existing and future development resources, the development-resources vector used in the definition of the field ought not to be quantified. The inventory of the development-resources vector would thus consist of a listing of resources types and the anticipated resources-outcome ratios for every specific application of a resource or resource bundle upon a specific natural-resources complex. In this ratio, resources will be measured in volumes of material and human resources, outcomes in objective achievements.

Development in the narrow sense is the aggregate result of applying specific resources bundles in the development-resources vector to specific complexes in the natural-resources vector. In the wider sense, development also includes the results of applying selected bundles of the development-resources vector to other bundles (mainly human resources) within the same vector, in order to upgrade the effectiveness of their subsequent direct deployment upon the natural-resources vector.

By including in the natural-resources vector all those facets which need transformation, and in the development-resources vector all those resources which are needed to effect such transformation, compliance with the dimensional compatibility postulate will be achieved.

Using the existing decision hierarchy and self-regulative processes properly, improving the existing structure, and interpolating complementary structures rather than imposing new ones will ensure compliance with the postulate of structural compatibility.

Definition of the field of potential development The field of potential development is defined by the set of all possible applications of relevant parts of the development-resources vector upon one another and upon relevant parts of the natural-resources vector.

Development operations as defined here will comprise changes of the physical production environment (e.g., improvements of water availability through irrigation, land reclamation), improvement of production inputs (seeds, fertilizers, plant-protection chemicals, soil conditioners), improvement of the basic producer's response variety (through incentives and risk attenuation), improvement of the institutional space, improvement of the inventory of transformation inputs, improvement of intersectorial terms of trade. Operations may be applied jointly or separately; however, some resources bundles will be found to be highly complementary.

In most cases it will be impossible to spell out the whole field of potential development. Yet it should nonetheless be attempted in order to determine (by scanning procedures) which combinations of specific parts of the natural-resources vector with specific parts of the development-resources vector promise to give highly attractive objective achievements. Further scanning and planning efforts could then be channeled primarily to such "preferential domains" of anticipated high-objective achievements. Where time, money, and personnel suffice, we shall be in a position to spell out projects for such preferential domains in specific terms; otherwise, project groups (i.e., application of typical development-resources bundles to typical natural-resources complexes) would have to be defined only in "synthetic terms," i.e., by listing anticipated resources outlays and objective achievements. Such synthetic project groups ought to be represented in the field of potential development in accordance with their greatest possible occurrence in the overall project population.

Using the field of development, representing an exhaustive inventory of all potential development operations as the basis for selecting programs will lead to compliance with the postulate of variety compatibility.

Selection of a program Programs representing sets of projects that can be implemented with available resources within a specific period of time will be selected from the field of potential development.

Some of the projects represented in the field will be specific projects with specific resources-outcome ratios; others will be generalized layouts of typical project situations in preferential domains accompanied by estimates of their resources-outcome ratios. Since we assume that outcomes ought to be measured by more than one objective yardstick, we shall not be able to define a unique absolute optimum; instead we shall have to operate with the "frontier set" of programs, the set of optimal programs for specific trade-off ratios. This frontier set, together with the respective objective achievements, will be submitted to the political decision maker for his selection; the planner at this point would guide the political decision maker as to which programs (and what implied trade-off ratios) will lead to convergence and which will not.

When approaching the time to start planning for the subsequent program period, we shall again be able to use the original definition of the field of potential development as modified by additional information.

Test for informational feasibility Planning and implementation of the projects included in the optimum program presuppose a minimum amount of information on the composition of both vectors. Projects for which information does not reach such threshold values will have to be delayed. If they appear attractive, their failure to pass the informational feasibility test will indicate that the program ought to include special operations to collect or generate the missing information.

Test for political feasibility Political feasibility may refer to two aspects of planning:

1. Preferences given to specific regions or producer groups for purely political reasons
2. Political compatibility as described under A Planning Model for Agricultural Development in the Third World

Regarding the first aspect, preferences for regions or producer groups may be introduced into the selection procedure as planning constraints. The second aspect of political feasibility refers to mutual adaptation between the decision flow stemming from program requirements and the structure of the decision hierarchy (see the section above). Adoption of procedures aimed at such adaptation will lead to compliance with the political-compatibility postulate.

Tests for economic and financial feasibility. The procedure outlined ensures for the selected program the highest possible objective achievement. However, this does not guarantee that all projects in the program will pass the conventional economic and financial tests that the funding agencies or the planner might require in order to compare investments incurred and benefits achieved in the agricultural sector with those in the industrial and services sectors. The planning procedure will therefore have to include such conventional economic and financial evaluation of projects.

The above full-fledged planning process is warranted even where information is meager or where, for some reason, most of the choices are foregone conclusions. The proposed planning procedure will define preferential domains, i.e., where to look for good projects and how to generate them. The estimates of the expected resources-outcome ratios of projects in the preferential domains will be found to be excellent yardsticks for evaluating the comparative effectiveness of actual projects.

The above procedure is also applicable to a narrower scope than sectorial planning as well as to a wider one. Regarding the first type of application, *mutatis mutandis,* the procedure can be applied to individual or regional groups of projects. In such cases the natural-resources vector would be confined to the respective project area (or areas) and the project selection would be made with due regard to the relevant development-resources vector, i.e., the resources allocated to the project (or project group). The selection will result in a quasi optimization of the use of allocated resources. Regarding applications at a wider scope than the national sectorial scope, interstate regional applications or resources allocation applications by international funding agencies can be conceived, although they will be more difficult both to conceive and to implement than national sectorial analyses.

THE REINTEGRATION OF THE SYSTEM

One would assume that the basic purpose of planning is to ensure that we are going where we want to by the best path and that our results converge upon our development goals, in short, that we have a reasonable chance of reaching our goals within a predetermined period of time. The astonishing thing is that only a minority of development programs in the Third World pass this simple "test of convergence."

Does this mean that we are moving in the wrong direction? Not necessarily. Most projects, at least on paper, will show an attractive increase of production and a reasonable rate of return on investments for the project area covered. What is wrong is the contraction of the angle of view, the narrowness of the basis of optimization.

In the resources-scarce Third World, nothing less will do than a nationwide sectorial plan to use available resources so as to combine generation of short-term production effects with long-term capacity effects.

In the seventies, justification of a national agricultural development program in the Third World should require more than proof of reasonable rates of return. No major program ought to be accepted unless it passes the test of convergence. To apply this test would involve simulating a long-term projection of the approach adopted in the program under investigation, based on a rough estimate of the anticipated resources streams. Resulting outcomes could then be compared with development goals to determine whether the recommended approach in fact converges upon these goals within a predetermined lead time (say, one to two generations, but varying in each instance).

Curiously, the test of convergence applied to an adopted program will sometimes show, mainly as a result of the population explosion, a widening gap between goals and performance. The protagonists of such a program might point to both an increase of product and a conventionally acceptable rate of return, thereby justifying their program. Such reasoning might pass in a mature economy, but the crippling resources scarcities in underdeveloped countries force us to reject the merely "feasible" in favor of the best solution. Any allocation of resources to projects that have proved only feasible diverts sorely needed resources from truly "converging" projects, an unjustifiable deviation from the main road of development.

In system terms, the juxtaposition of the feasibility and the convergence approaches is equivalent to short-term optimization of arbitrarily defined subsystems or sub-subsystems as compared with long-term optimization of the socioeconomic sectorial system as a whole. As long as we focus on arbitrarily selected specific individual subsystems we seriously limit the variety (in cybernetic terms) of possible solutions. Lack of the requisite "variety" binds us to solutions which differ greatly from the "overall optimum." Widening our angle of view to include the sector as a whole and all resources available for its development and deploying the latter within the sector on a long-term basis increase the variety of potential solutions and, therefore, the chances for optimal use of development resources.

Testing programs for long-term convergence provides a compass bearing to check the orientation of program and project planning, but does not take the place of such planning. Once long-term goals and overall strategies are determined by sectorial scanning and selection based on the test of convergence, we still have to fix medium-term objectives and targets and elaborate the programs and projects to achieve them.

The validity of the convergence approach is so self-evident that one wonders why the opposite approach is almost universally prevalent. The explanation may be sought in the historic connection of development thinking as applied to the Third World with development thinking evolved in mature economies. In the latter, the conventional evaluation procedure to prove feasibility has so far performed reasonably well, thus seemingly justifying its transplantation to developing countries. However, even with regard to the developed countries, it is doubtful whether the narrow-angle view will produce valid solutions for the pressing problems facing them in the seventies and eighties.

When conducting a convergence test we are of course transcending the boundaries of the sectorial (or regional) system and those of a short-term time horizon. The convergence test thus constitutes an attempt to compensate for the simplifications and distortions introduced into our analysis by isolating a sectorial system from the rest of the socioeconomic system and by setting up a definite (and usually only medium-term) time horizon.

If the convergence test shows lack or insufficiency of convergence, either we must assume that the resources allocated, or the constraints imposed, or the restrictiveness of the planning system, or, finally, the selected trade-off ratios between objectives have to be blamed, or we must conclude that within the assumed overall framework the long-term goal setting is too ambitious and cannot be achieved. We must make the necessary revisions in every case and arrive at a redefined system and goal complex that, when analyzed, will have a reasonable chance of convergence.

In many Third World countries, convergence will be found lacking in one most vital aspect of agriculture development, namely, distribution of employment. Third World agriculture employs more people than any other sector, usually between one half and two thirds of the population. The secondary sector (i.e., mainly industry) still has a very narrow base and an unfavorable investment-employment ratio; therefore, even a high industrial growth rate will result in extremely low absolute absorption of labor in industry.

The service sector is usually overstaffed and has therefore an extremely low marginal productivity.

Agricultural development will therefore have to keep that part of the agricultural population gainfully employed in agricultural production that cannot be employed more gainfully in the nonagricultural sectors. In typical development contexts this will imply that the number of people employed in agriculture (in absolute figures) will not decline. Rather, the number will continue to grow for a considerable period of time at a rate slightly above half of the population growth rate in less-developed, and somewhat below for the more-developed, countries. To keep this growing labor force employed, we must specify as one of the principal orienting principles of development the widest possible distribution of new sectorial investment and the related widest possible spreading of new income and employment. We shall, furthermore, have to accord to this principle a high priority, even if such priority results in some loss of overall productivity. Failure to provide the necessary planning orientation will result in great numbers of unemployed flocking to the larger towns where neither employment nor decent living conditions can be provided. This imbalance in the labor force will create sociopolitical pressures which under prevailing Third World conditions will lead to counterpressures and to a continuous escalation of political unrest. Such social and political unrest may damage the nation more than will the limited reduction in production that may, in some cases, result from a wider distribution of agricultural investments.

Lack of convergence attributable to focusing investment on a too narrow basis need not always be caused by preference for a specific more efficient producer group or region. In many cases it will be caused by overemphasis of a specific capital-intensive resource destination and neglect of alternative less capital-intensive ones. Overemphasis of investment in irrigation, which is characterized by high capital requirements, is the most common instance of contracting the distribution base of investment by overemphasizing one specific resource destination. Irrigation has to be relegated to its proper role, which is that of an instrumental objective that must compete with other instrumental objectives (such as improved inputs, agrotechniques, drainage) for scarce resources.

Convergence associated with the distribution of employment is but one example of a set of problems related to the selection of trade-offs between objective yardsticks. We have taken the attitude that the "explicit" or "implicit" selection of trade-offs is related to political values and thus is properly the domain of political decision makers, the task of the planner being confined to pointing out the loss in achievement of the less-favored objective, by preferring a specific objective. Introduction of the convergence test considerably expands the planner's responsibilities: he will have to identify long-term goal complexes, compare programs selected on the basis of alternative trade-offs for their long-term convergence, determine which trade-off ratio leads to the best convergence, and decide how much convergence would be lost if other trade-offs are adopted in the forthcoming program. Should the political decision maker decide upon a nonconverging trade-off ratio, he implicitly commits himself to a radical change in trade-offs in future programs if, at a later date, he sincerely intends to bend the development trajectory toward better convergence.

Introduction of the convergence concept greatly limits the political decision maker's freedom of choice. Convergence is an acid test for manifest political goals: if the political decision maker selects a program with either no or bad convergence toward manifest political long-term goals, he has demonstrated, at least in the eyes of the planning group, his lack of sincerity and the true nature of his latent goals. To the extent that convergence touches upon politically sensitive areas, and it usually does, discussion of its implications will therefore require a great deal of political insight and tact.

The kind of compromise that the political leader, with the proclaimed intention of minimizing resistance, will suggest in discussions on trade-offs will be acquiescence with low convergence in the forthcoming program and compensation for the loss of convergence resulting from such a decision by selection of a more radical trade-off in subsequent programs. When considering such compromises, the planner should point out that because of growing social expectations the trade-offs to be adopted five years hence to ensure convergence might in any case have to be more radical than those proposed for the forthcoming program. A compromise would be justified only if we entertain a justified hope that the anticipated decision environment for the next programs would favor trade-offs capable of radically righting the development trajectory.

An overrestrictive definition of the planning space will be a further frequent cause for lack of convergence. If two closely interconnected subsystems are optimized separately, outcomes may not converge even if we attempt to reconcile incompatibilities. The way out would be either redefinition of a new planning space comprising both subsystems or, at least, relatively detailed metaanalysis setting the terms of reference and limits of solutions for the separate subsystem analysis. The problem of intersectorial facilitation may in some cases play a similar role and require a parallel modification of procedures (see the section on Facilitation and Constraints).

Insufficient resources allocation to the sector will be the most frequent cause of lack of convergence. The intersectorial allocation pattern resulting in an insufficient allocation to agriculture might have been the result of an intersectorial comparison of short-term returns on investments in which traditional agriculture did not fare well. Here the agricultural sectorial planner ought to point out to the relevant political authority that a significant part of investments in his sector is capacity oriented and that economic results from such capacity upgrading could be expected to become effective only over a somewhat longer period of time. He ought also to stress the great economic and political importance of a wide base of employment and income distribution, whose intersectorial impact, although difficult to quantify rigorously, is certain to materialize.

It is hoped that greater emphasis on capacity orientation on the part of international and regional funding institutions will support the sectorial planner in his efforts to ensure a better convergence of programs.

The scarcity of appropriately trained and motivated human resources in the development-resources vector has been repeatedly mentioned; strategies to mitigate the consequences of this constraint have been touched upon in the section on Induction.

Possibly the most refractory reason for lack of convergence is the political constraints imposed upon the optimization of the sectorial system. These constraints may be so restrictive and may so reduce the variety of solutions remaining for selection that the chosen program will result in resources-outcome ratios so unfavorable as to preclude convergence. If, for instance, constraints refer to improvement of land tenure, and if the alternative is intensive irrigated agriculture on mini-fundia, the program—though economically feasible in the conventional sense—may not converge because of the high capital intensity implied in that type of development and because of the excessive requirements in transformation inputs. It will be in situations in which lack of convergence stems from political constraints that resistance to applying the test of convergence and to acting in accordance with its outcomes will be greatest.

Finally, the most obvious reason for lack of convergence is overambitious goal setting. The gap between the desirable and the possible may be reduced by corrective action at both ends: we can make the desirable more possible by gradually improving the program's image with funding agencies. Concurrently, we may also have to equate the desirable with the possible by reducing our goals so as to least affect national welfare and growth capacity.

INDEX